ROBERT MCCORMICK ADAMS

DATE DUE

SERIES: IDEAS, DEBATES AND PERSPECTIVES

Cotsen Institute of Archaeology
Ideas, Debates and Perspectives

SETTLEMENT AND SOCIETY

ESSAYS DEDICATED TO ROBERT MCCORMICK ADAMS

EDITED BY
ELIZABETH C. STONE

COTSEN INSTITUTE OF ARCHAEOLOGY
UNIVERSITY OF CALIFORNIA, LOS ANGELES
AND
THE ORIENTAL INSTITUTE OF
THE UNIVERSITY OF CHICAGO
2007

THE COTSEN INSTITUTE OF ARCHAEOLOGY at UCLA is a research unit at the University of California, Los Angeles that promotes the comprehensive and interdisciplinary study of the human past. Established in 1973, the Cotsen Institute is a unique resource that provides an opportunity for faculty, staff, graduate students, research associates, volunteers and the general public to gather together in their explorations of ancient human societies.

Former President and CEO of Neutrogena Corporation Lloyd E. Cotsen has been associated with UCLA for more than 30 years as a volunteer and donor and maintains a special interest in archaeology. Lloyd E. Cotsen has been an advisor and supporter of the Institute since 1980. In 1999, The UCLA Institute of Archaeology changed its name to the Cotsen Institute of Archaeology at UCLA to honor the longtime support of Lloyd E. Cotsen.

Cotsen Institute Publications specializes in producing high-quality data monographs in several different series, including Monumenta Archaeologica, Monographs, and Perspectives in California Archaeology, as well as innovative ideas in the Cotsen Advanced Seminar Series and the Ideas, Debates and Perspectives Series. Through the generosity of Lloyd E. Cotsen, our publications are subsidized, producing superb volumes at an affordable price.

This book is set in 10-point Janson Text, with titles in 18-point Slimbach.
Edited and produced by Leyba Associates
Cover design by William Morosi
Index by Robert and Cynthia Swanson

Library of Congress Cataloging-in-Publication Data
Settlement and society : essays dedicated to Robert McCormick Adams
/ edited by Elizabeth C. Stone.
p. cm. -- (Ideas, debates and perspectives ; 3)
Includes bibliographical references and index.
ISBN 978-1-931745-33-8 (cloth : alk. paper) --
ISBN 978-1-931745-32-1 (pbk. : alk. paper);
Oriental Institute: ISBN 1-885923-47-3 (cloth : alk. paper) --
ISBN 1-885923-48-1- (pbk. : alk. paper)
1. Archaeology--Middle East--History. 2. Middle East--Antiquities.
I. Stone, Elizabeth Caecilia, 1949- . II. Adams, Robert McCormick,
1926- .
DS56.S43 2006
939'.4--dc22   2006028966

CONTENTS

FIGURES AND TABLES

Figures

Tables

CONTRIBUTORS

Guillermo Algaze	University of California, San Diego
Elizabeth Carter	University of California, Los Angeles
George L. Cowgill	Arizona State University
Frank Hole	Yale University
Mohammed Afzal Khan	Lahore Fort Museum
Nicholas Kouchoukos	Forest one Inc.
Hans J. Nissen	Berlin University
Rana Özbal	Bogaziçi University
Gregory L. Possehl	University of Pennsylvania
Jennifer R. Pournelle	Lead Technologies, Inc.
Mitchell S. Rothman	Widener University
Joseph Schuldenrein	Geoarchaeology Research Associates
Gil J. Stein	University of Chicago
Piotr Steinkeller	Harvard University
Elizabeth C. Stone	Stony Brook University
Donald Whitcomb	University of Chicago
Tony Wilkinson	Durham University
Irene J. Winter	Harvard University
Henry Wright	University of Michigan; Santa Fe Institute
Rita Wright	New York University
Aslıhan Yener	University of Chicago
Paul Zimansky	Stony Brook University

INTRODUCTION

ELIZABETH C. STONE

This collection of essays by Robert McC. Adams's students and colleagues is offered as a tribute to the breadth and depth of his research and as an appreciation of the influence he has had on all of us. We are better scholars thanks to his ability to cut to the heart of matters in a world of social complexity. There is no need to provide a description of Bob's life and work here, as this has already been done by Yoffee (1997b) and to a certain extent by Wright (2001b), but a discussion of how his biography unites the contributions to this volume is certainly in order. Adams's scholarship covers a very broad area, ranging from the minutiae of Mesopotamian ecology (Adams 1965: 3–29; 1978) to broad theories on subjects as varied as frontiers, trade, and civilizational collapse. His work also melds and synthesizes epigraphic and archaeological data (Adams 1974a; 1974b; 1988). Adams never allows himself to get lost in the trivial details that so often obfuscate key findings in the published works of both archaeologists and Assyriologists. We have encouraged the contributors to this festschrift to follow Adams's example and attempt to provide "big picture" views on a wide range of topics.

Adams is probably best known for his pioneering use of archaeological survey as a means of understanding the rise of urbanism and complex society in southern Mesopotamia (Adams 1965; 1981; 1972a; Adams and Nissen 1972). Today, archaeological survey forms a basic and critical part of our endeavors; indeed there is even a branch of archaeology known as "landscape archaeology," which is itself sufficiently established for a schism to have developed among its practitioners (Wilkinson 2003; Ashmore and Knapp, eds. 1999). When Adams first began his field research, apart from the pioneering work of Gordon Willey in the Viru Valley (1953) and Thorkild Jacobsen's observation that ancient canals and sites were easily viewed in the

Iraqi desert, archaeology involved digging holes. Ultimately Adams's work in Iraq has had as great an impact on the field as Willey's work in Peru. Whereas the Viru Valley project provided a broader perspective on the archaeological sequence of the area, its conclusions were resolutely culture historical. Adams's work in the Diyala was quite different in his focus on understanding the how and why behind patterns that he saw in the data.

This perspective can also be seen in his comparative approach to the development of complex society, initiated in his dissertation and later published as part of the Henry Morgan Lecture Series (Adams 1966). At the time, Adams's approach to the development of complex societies was associated by many with the then-emerging "New Archaeology" movement, but the ideas of this early phase of his career are still taught, I suspect, in all undergraduate courses on the emergence of social complexity. Unlike other contributors of the "big ideas" to this field—for example, Service (1962), Fried (1967), Carneiro (1970), and Wittfogel (1957)—Adams has never seen a single factor or a single trajectory of development as the explanation of the emergence of cultural complexity around the world. Thus, although we now know much more of the details of the process in both Mesopotamia and Mesoamerica than we did in the 1960s, *The Origins of Urban Society* was sufficiently nuanced in its approach that its basic ideas continue to ring true, unlike many other works published at that time.

Adams has also attacked a number of topics of general anthropological interest by invoking data from the ancient Near East. These include investigating Lattimore's (1940; 1962) ideas about the significance of frontiers (Adams 1974b), refuting Polanyi's (1957a) ideas of marketless trading (Adams 1974a), offering an extensive investigation of the role of technology (1996), and, most recently, examining the issue of "agency" (Adams 2005). Each of these topics has been picked up by at least one of the contributors to this volume.

ECOLOGY

Bob Adams is perhaps best known for his surveys of southern Mesopotamia and Iran and the principles that lay behind this work. His approach was thoroughly ecological, but unlike the fashion of the times, which too often invoked the environment as a prime mover, Adams saw it more as a backdrop, having the ability to constrain or enable changes in society, but not to cause them. This approach runs as a leitmotif through this volume. Where some, such as Schuldenrein et al., Pournelle, and Kouchoukos and Wilkinson, bring more tools to bear on landscape assessments than were available when Adams was conducting his fieldwork, they join him in understanding that modern environments represent a palimpsest—and one created by both anthropogenic and natural forces at that. This subtle interplay between changes wrought by humans, usually but not always inadvertently, and the larger natural forces with which they had to contend, forms a clear subtext through much of this book. Although Adams has always stressed the uncertainties of Mesopotamian agriculture, Algaze builds on the wetter world that Pournelle posits for the early Uruk to argue that southern Mesopotamia was a veritable "Garden of Eden," endowed with the routes of communication and the economic resources necessary to build a great civilization.

Beyond Mesopotamia, Carter and Zimansky examine ecological boundaries that could be used, in Carter's phrase, to "resist empire." Possehl sees the Indus penetration into the Gujarat as representing not just the expansion of complex society, but the adaptation of that way of life as it incorporates indigenous groups practicing quite different lifestyles.

Related to this is Adams's insistence on the importance of the interaction of groups practicing different lifestyles, even if some parts of the society, such as pastoral nomads and marsh dwellers, are poorly represented in both the textual and archaeological records. Pournelle's contribution emphasizes this point, as she argues that we have placed too much emphasis on irrigation agriculture as a factor in the rise of complex society in Mesopotamia, and not given enough to the economic potential of wetlands, which were widespread during Uruk times. Winter brings these elements into her discussion of the idea of "abundance" as reflected in both Mesopotamian literature and art. This abundance is not limited to the products of irrigation agriculture; indeed, sheep, cattle, reeds, and fish are also prominent in both the written and visual media.

Zimansky and Carter stress the key role played by the adoption of nomadic or transhumant lifestyles as a way of avoiding incorporation into empire. The surveys conducted by Matthews in Paphlagonia (R. Matthews, Pollard, and Ramage 1998) and Hole in the Khorramabad Valley give indirect evidence of this strategy in the paucity of archaeological sites dating to the periods when these areas were homes to the Kaska and Elamites and thorns in the sides of the Hittite, Babylonian, and Assyrian Empires.

Another part of Adams's approach was the judicious use of ethnographic analogy as a means of understanding past societies. This is reflected in the work of Pournelle, who has delved into records of marsh dwellers to understand how early Mesopotamian settlement may have developed. Possehl turns to descriptions of pastoral nomads from both the Near East and India to explore how interactions between indigenous hunter-gatherers and pastoralists might have affected the Indus experience in the Gujarat. I have used analogy with late Medieval Islamic cities to understand how the ancient

Mesopotamian city might have functioned, and suggested modern tribal *mudhifs* as analogies to ancient palace throne rooms.

All of us, I think, appreciate the subtlety of Adams's approaches. He never used ecology—or indeed anything else—as the sole explanation for the past, but always understood that it served as a critical backdrop, one that limited options and made some paths easier to follow than others. I hope that we too have been able to maintain so careful a balance.

MULTIPLE LINES OF EVIDENCE

Adams always uses all possible sources in his work, whether he controls the primary literature or not. Thus, he has incorporated the work of Arab geographers, Assyriologists, and soil scientists in his analyses, to name but a few specialties. In an early project, he worked with the Assyriologist (and instigator of archaeological surveys in Iraq) Thorkild Jacobsen to bring together environmental, archaeological, and textual data on agricultural regimes in Iraq (Jacobsen and Adams 1958). In my most recent conversation with him, Bob indicated his intention of spending the summer of 2005 figuring out how sheep were reared in early Mesopotamia, for which he would depend heavily on the written record. This emphasis on using all lines of evidence reverberates throughout this volume.

Henry Wright presents an optimistic view of our ability to identify agents in preliterate Mesopotamia. He discusses excavated data, arguing that modern methods, be they detailed examination of human remains, micromorphology, or the like, will allow us to develop hypotheses about individual agency in prehistoric times that can be tested with some certainty. Both Steinkeller and I use a mélange of textual and archaeological data to come to a more general understanding of Mesopotamian settlement patterns, Steinkeller focusing on the rural hinterland and I on the urban core. What is striking, though, is that from very different perspectives (although both heavily influenced by Adams) we come to the same conclusion—that there is considerable continuity of structures and institutions between the rural and urban sectors. Winter also brings archaeological and textual sources together in looking at art and literature to illuminate Mesopotamian attitudes toward their immediate environment.

An important element within archaeology is the synergy between survey and excavation. Too often dirt archaeologists have seen survey as useful only to identify sites for excavation. Nissen turns this approach on its head, showing how the "urban implosion" visible in the Early Dynastic I Uruk survey data led to a reevaluation of what before had been thought of as a "degenerate" period because of the simplicity of the cylinder seals in use at the time.

Whitcomb argues that Adams's surveys, which focused heavily on the later, Islamic periods (especially *Land Behind Baghdad)*, also played a role in changing Islamic archaeology. More than is the case with ancient Iraq, the archaeology of Islamic periods has often narrowed its focus to the discovery and analysis of objects of great beauty, especially from Samarra. Although to this day Islamic archaeology is mostly taught more as art than as archaeology, the fact that there are Islamic archaeologists at work today on broader social and cultural issues is no small part of Adams's legacy.

It is not only that Adams uses diverse lines of evidence in his work; he has also taken on some of the major theoretical approaches that have come in and out of fashion. In so doing, he never embraces any theory uncritically, but rather tests it for logic and compares its predictions with hard data. Where such ideas were simplistic, he would ruthlessly expose their flaws. This approach to theory is well reflected in the essays of this volume, although the rigor of his evaluations is a hard standard to meet. Algaze uses theories developed by urban economists and geographers to posit a causal chain that led inextricably to the development of complex society in southern Mesopotamia and not in the north, which otherwise had an equally early floruit. Rothman assesses a broad range of anthropological approaches in his discussion of the development of administrative tools in the fourth millennium, and Wright invokes new ideas about agency and sets out to find actors in the archaeological record. Zimansky revisits Lattimore's ideas of frontiers, finding them to fit well the Hittite-Kaska boundary, while Nissen follows Christaller in his evaluation of another kind of boundary, that between areas directly and indirectly administered by the central city. Although Adams would probably have been less sanguine on the usefulness of some of these approaches, it is a credit to him that in every instance the contributions to this volume present a subtle approach to these ideas.

In stressing that all members of society, then as now, play significant roles, Adams looks beyond cities to the countryside. Besides the relationship between city and hinterland in Mesopotamia by both Steinkeller and myself, there is Schuldenrein et al.'s focus on the city and its rural underpinnings. The countryside lies at the heart of the work of Kouchoukos and Wilkinson, Nissen and Pournelle. Hole's contribution is entirely rural—the Khorramabad Plain doesn't even have cities in it. Cowgill's offering, while devoted to Teotihuacan, notes the relationship between this large city and the area around it, especially in terms of resource exploitation.

Adams eschews a top-down approach to society and examines the interaction between elites and non-elites wherever possible. This is another strand that winds through this volume. Rothman looks at how the practice of sealing, once a general activity at Tepe Gawra, becomes more exclusive over time. At

Alalakh, Yener does not so much see a shift from centralized to decentralized manufacturing, but rather metallurgy in both spheres, aimed at different audiences. I examine the relationship between large, well-appointed houses and small, poorer ones over time and space, and compare large settlements to small in southern Mesopotamia, while Steinkeller looks at the size and associated features of various kinds of small sites in the Umma countryside. For Algaze, the explosion of complexity in Mesopotamia in the fourth millennium was made possible in part by the ability of the new elites to channel dependent labor toward the production of goods, many of them for export.

These many examples of looking at our material from multiple viewpoints, of bringing together information or ideas from different fields, or of seeking those ancient players who are easy to find in the written and archaeological data together with those less visible are all part of Bob Adams's legacy.

SOCIAL SCIENCE AND HUMANISTIC APPROACHES

Although firmly grounded in anthropological, social science approaches and even the "New Archaeology," Adams is unusual, especially within his generation, for having a strong respect for more humanistic approaches to ancient Mesopotamia. This is again reflected in this volume, which includes contributions from Assyriologists and art historians, and archaeologists trained in both Near Eastern studies and Anthropology departments. Adams has a strong sense of history; he is both interested in longer trajectories—patterns of boom and bust, for example—and in periods of more revolutionary change. Long before it became trendy, he stressed the importance of shared ideology as part of the glue that held Mesopotamia together. This lack of dogmatism is another element that I see running through this volume.

The issue of the effect of past histories on later events is seen most clearly in the contributions of Carter, Zimansky, and Yener. Carter argues that it was the very adaptation of the Elamites to resist incorporation into the Babylonian and Assyrian spheres that made it almost inevitable that they would become a key part of the larger Persian Empire. Yener sees the beginning of the Iron Age not so much as forced by tin shortages caused by the collapse of the Bronze Age empires, but rather as part of a great spate of metallurgical experimentation made possible only when the dead hand of these polities was lifted. Zimansky sees the Kaska more as a people who came into existence *because* the Hittite Empire was on their doorstep than as a group of foreign invaders. In all three instances, changing political configurations spurred the peoples in question to adapt their societies to new circumstances.

History also plays an important role in Algaze's model of Mesopotamian expansion. He sees a process of increasing waves of "import substitution" wherein Mesopotamia found ways to manufacture items it had once had to import and thus ramped up its economic power. This is paralleled, in many ways, by the increasing use of seals for administration outlined by Rothman. Another approach is taken by Stein and Özbal, who identify key differences within the superficially similar ʿUbaid and Uruk expansions. Although some of the archaeological markers of these two developments—Mesopotamian ceramics found far from their points of origin—are identical, Stein and Özbal argue convincingly that they represent two quite different phenomena, one based on emulation and the other on colonization.

Emulation, of course, implies a shared ideology more than political domination, which is another area where Adams stood firm as others looked only for more materialist factors of causation. The importance of ideology, both as a force and as a symptom, is made clear in many of these papers. Kouchoukos and Wilkinson come from somewhat different places within landscape archaeology—Wilkinson more avowedly processual in approach and Kouchoukos more influenced by the postprocessual movement. With Adams's example before them, they have given us an article, free of polemic, in which there is space for both approaches: ecology and ideology together shaping society and society's imprint on the larger environment.

Where Winter sees the expression of the fruitfulness of the land—the very opposite of Adams's view of the landscape as fraught with peril—as part of the ideological justification for rule, Wright sees the elaborate burial of a leader at Arslantepe as a way of expressing a saga of competition, ethnic tension, and conquest. Stein and Özbal show that in the ʿUbaid period, Mesopotamian styles were used over a broad geographic area in public spaces, suggesting the existence of a common cult or system of beliefs, but without implying any political unity.

That the ʿUbaid might be more of a cult than a conquest brings to mind the New World phenomena of the Chavín. It was comparisons between the Old and New Worlds that first made Adams a household name. The papers on geographic areas other than Mesopotamia reflect Adams's breadth of interests in this regard. Two papers discuss the enigmatic Indus civilization. Both Schuldenrein et al. and Possehl look at the Indus from an Adamsian perspective, Schuldenrein et al. focusing closely on the environmental parameters, and Possehl stressing interactions among farmers, pastoralists, hunter-gatherers, and urbanites. Cowgill, however, sets himself a different task, simply to present a digest of what we know about one of the best-understood Mesoamerican cities, Teotihuacan. Although clearly different in organization in every way, there are striking similarities between Teotihuacan and its Mesopotamian counterparts—such aspects as the role and position of temples, the structure of the residential districts, and the importance and localizing of craft activities. These similarities show that the comparisons that Bob drew between Mesopotamia and Mesoamerica some four decades ago (1966) still stand, even if many of the details have been modified through new research.

Adams's most recent book was on the role of technology in society (1996) and was not addressed to archaeologists; indeed, when he was working on it he would claim to be in a quite different field. As such, perhaps it has had less impact on the papers gathered here, although both Yener's and Algaze's contributions pick up on some of his key themes—especially that the combination of appropriate social mechanisms and technological break-thoughs lead to real change.

In spite of the diversity of the topics discussed in this volume, and indeed within the broad range of issues that Adams himself has tackled, there are important consistencies in both his and our work that reflect his basic principles. These involve rigorous fieldwork, careful consideration of both data and theory, and an eye for the big picture. None of us lives up to these ideals, but our experiences as his students and colleagues mean we keep them in sight.

Landscape Archaeology in Mesopotamia: Past, Present, and Future*

Nicholas Kouchoukos and Tony Wilkinson

Abstract

We trace here the ways that recent developments in landscape archaeology have built upon the foundations laid by Robert McCormick Adams. Overall, Adams appears to have influenced the development of the field along four broad lines: first, an improved understanding of the ways in which the Mesopotamian landscape has been transformed through time; second, refined methods of interpreting spatial patterns; third, an increased awareness of the role of landscapes in the shaping of human action; and fourth the increased attention paid to patterns of exchange and population dynamics within the landscape. The paper ends with a plea for archaeologists to include more landscape archaeology into the interpretation of long-term and large-scale social processes. Adams blazed this trail, and to omit this vital source of information and interpretation would weaken the development of Mesopotamian archaeology.

* An earlier version of this paper was prepared for and presented at the symposium "Theoretical Foundations in the Dust: The Past and Future of Mesopotamian Archaeology" at the 2001 meeting of the American Anthropological Association. We thank the organizers, Gil Stein and Guillermo Algaze, for their invitation and the discussants, Robert McC. Adams and Henry Wright, for their comments and criticisms. We also thank Robert McC. Adams, Abbas Alizadeh, McGuire Gibson, Frank Hole, Robert Schacht, Robert Wenke, and Henry Wright for access to notes, references, and collections from their surveys of the Susiana and Mesopotamian plains.

INTRODUCTION

The roots of something called *landscape archaeology* in the Near East might properly be located in the explorations of such seminal figures as Layard (1894), Schmidt (1940), M. Oppenheim (1899–1900), de Morgan (1894), and Poidebard (1934), whose descriptions and identifications of peoples and places established the categories, conventions, and, to a certain extent, the agenda of much subsequent archaeological, ethnographic, and historical research. But it is fair and probably unnecessary to point out that in the Near East, landscape archaeology's transition from reconnaissance to science was largely wrought by Robert McCormick Adams and his students at The University of Chicago. To the historical topography that preceded him, Adams brought the anthropologist's compulsion to abstract the general from the particular, the geographer's talent for seeing process in spatial patterns, and the modern archaeologist's conviction that the past has much to tell us about our present and possible futures.

From this convergence of sensibilities and interests emerged what many would agree has been Robert Adams's central contribution to the archaeology of the ancient Near East, namely, the construction of detailed settlement records for crucial regions of lower Mesopotamia (Figure 1) and, equally important, the articulation of key problems addressed and raised by this work. And, given the traditional centrality of lower Mesopotamia and its cities in narratives of social and political evolution, it goes almost without saying that Adams's scholarship has framed conceptually and empirically much of the historical and archaeological research conducted in Mesopotamia in the four decades since his publications first began to appear. Rather than attempt a full review of Adams's contribution to the field or, more boldly, some sort of a critical evaluation, we take this opportunity to trace broadly the ways in which researchers engaged in "landscape archaeology" have built upon Adams's founding investigations and insights and what—in the Near East, at least—this slippery term has come to mean.

At the risk of being overly schematic, we note that major advances in the field of landscape archaeology have followed four general lines, which have crossed and reinforced each other in important ways. Briefly, these advances are:

1. Improved understanding of the intersecting geomorphic, climatic, and cultural processes through which physical landscapes are created and transformed

2. Refined methods and theories for recognizing and interpreting spatial patterning in the archaeological landscape record at a range of scales

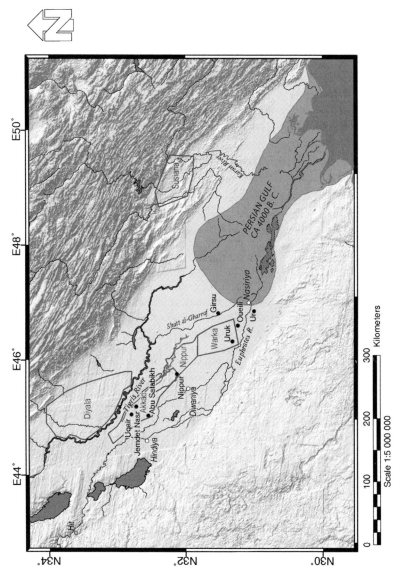

Figure 1. Regions of southern Iraq and southwest Iran surveyed by Robert McC. Adams.

3. Growing appreciation for landscapes as enduring material and symbolic forms, which shape, constrain, and enable various forms of human action

4. Increasing attention to spatially extended processes such as long-distance exchange, colonization, and diaspora and their effects on the construction of local landscapes

In what follows, we clarify and expand on these assertions, providing examples of each and considering their implications for future research.

MODELING LANDSCAPE PROCESS

The seemingly flat and featureless alluvial plains of lower Mesopotamia and southwest Iran mask a very complex processual environment and an equally complex and convoluted archaeological record. In order to untangle this record, it is necessary first to take account of the interacting physical and cultural processes that have obscured, transformed, or destroyed archaeological features in particular regions, filtering and distorting the observations on which reconstruction of past social organization and change depends. Thus, as a first step in unpacking ancient landscapes, one must recognize the linked physical and cultural processes that have obscured sites and other landscape features or have exposed them by deflation. In addition to physical transformations, cultural factors entail the progressive loss of landscape features through attrition or the recycling of building materials. When these processes have been characterized adequately enough to support estimates of landscape loss and recovery, emergent patterns can then be interpreted according to various organizing principles, which may be ecological, economic, and/or social in nature.

We suspect that few would argue with this characterization of landscape processes and patterns. Where things get tricky, however, is when social and economic processes themselves feed back into physical transformations of the landscape record, such as when the construction of dams and canals alters sedimentary regimes or forest clearance changes microclimatic conditions (Figure 2). Interactions of this sort present a very complex problem in which one despairs of ever dissociating natural from cultural processes. Nevertheless, landscape archaeologists have made considerable strides in modeling the operation and evolution of what we might call *cultural landscapes*—groups of related processes and practices, such as irrigation techniques or fluvial history, that transform both the physical environment and cultural landscapes.

A simple example of how these insights can be put into practice comes from the Susiana plain in southwest Iran, a region first intensively surveyed

Figure 2. A schematic model of landscape formation.

by Robert Adams in the winter of 1960–61 (Adams 1962) and then, largely under the guidance of Henry Wright, scoured by some ten further survey projects over the next eighteen years. In all, more than 1300 sites spanning the prehistoric to the Early Islamic periods have been recorded, roughly 260 of which date to the sixth–fifth millennia BC (Figure 3). A quick glance at a map shows that the spatial distribution of these sites is radically discontinuous: large areas of apparently inhabitable and productive land are almost completely void of settlement.

While this distribution may preserve some cultural information, it is largely attributable to the action of the three major watercourses that cross the plain. Controlled by tectonic uplift of the Zagros Mountains to the east and fluctuations in sea level and sediment load, these rivers have, since the mid-Holocene, moved gradually westward across the Susiana plain and have incised it deeply—burying and eroding hundred of sites in the process. Some idea of the pattern and magnitude of this destruction can be gained from analysis of geomorphic maps produced in preparation for the construction of irrigation systems in the 1960s (Veenenbos 1958). These show that the vast majority of prehistoric sites in alluvial areas occur only on the oldest river terraces, which make up less than one-third of the total area of the plain. The very few sites located on younger terraces and flood plains have narrowly escaped erosion or deep burial and hence represent only a small fraction of the original number of sites in these areas. It is possible, therefore, to arrive at a crude estimate of the original number of prehistoric sites on the plain by multiplying the total area of later alluvial landforms by the density of sites recorded on the old terraces. The resulting figures show that at least 140 sites have been destroyed, and this, shockingly, is more than half the number recorded by surveys.

In a similar manner, the floodplain of the Euphrates Valley in the area of the Tabqa Dam (Syria) has been virtually entirely removed by erosion over the last few millennia, taking with it all archaeological sites except those located on small relict patches of old floodplain. This sustained fluvial activity has effectively wiped out the record of early ceramic and Chalcolithic occupation, the absence of which is otherwise difficult to explain (Wilkinson 1999: 561–562).

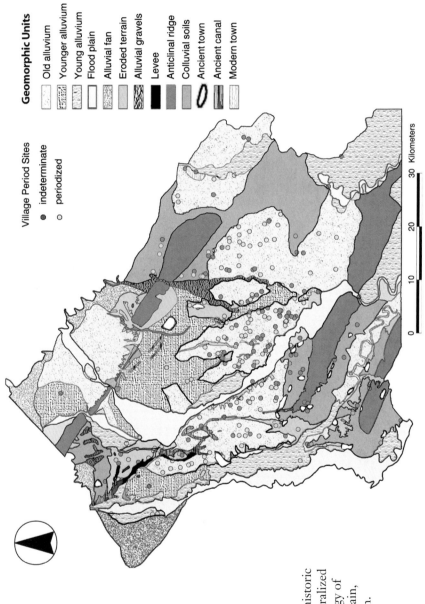

Figure 3.
Surveyed prehistoric sites and generalized geomorphology of the Susiana plain, southwest Iran.

These examples show how one taphonomic field may be modeled, but, as we argue above, the next step is to show how it operates in connection with other physical and cultural processes. On the Susiana plain, for example, the distribution of sites on the old terraces—where preservation is nominally very good—has still been modified extensively by many thousands of years of canal building, farming, and settlement growth. And these processes have fed back into physical processes in important ways. One needs only to point out that the Shaur River, on which the city of Susa is now located, is actually a "feral" canal once dug out of the old bed of the Kharkheh River to show how intricately entwined nature and culture can become. Put simply, the problem is that people are always transforming—sometimes subtly, sometimes radically—the basic conditions of their existence.

The complex interaction of physical and cultural processes is especially clear (and hence critical to model) in lower Mesopotamia, where it is possible to find sites of the same date pedestaled above plain level, flush with the ground surface, or buried beneath sediments. Here, such variation is in part a result of patterns of sedimentation that are usually tied to the history of irrigation (Figure 4). Where settlement and cultivation prevail, irrigation results in a steady aggradation of the land surface as a result of the incremental deposition of fine sediments within channels and on levee slopes, canals, and fields (Figure 4: case A). On the other hand, should irrigation cease, either as a result of a channel

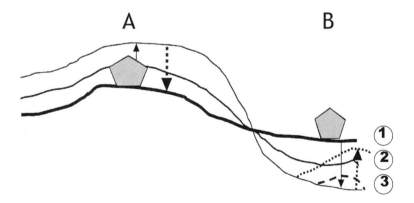

Figure 4. Potential erosional and sedimentary cycles in lower Mesopotamia. 1 indicates an initial ground surface with sites represented by pentagons. Surface 2 represents a phase of aggradation derived from a channel system (A). 3 indicates the final stage of aggradation along channel A, counteracted by associated deflation in the nearby desert away from the locus of channel aggradation. The end result of these processes is the burial of sites along channels and their exhumation in areas dominated by deflation (from Wilkinson 2003 fig. 5.5).

shift or because human desertion has nullified the need for irrigation, then sedimentation is curtailed, the protective ground cover of palm trees and cultivated plants disappears, and the land turns into an arid alluvial desert. With this switch, the geomorphological environment changes to one of degradation in which former sedimentary deposits are blown away, frequently to fuel the growth of sand dunes that then migrate downwind out of the area (Figure 4: case B; Brandt 1990). Such deflation results in the degradation of the ground surface; this can be seen where early sites remain on low pedestals above the ground surface.

A good example of the operation of these opposed processes comes from the Abu Salabikh/Nippur region of the central Mesopotamian plain (Figure 5). Here the main ʿUbaid/Uruk land surface is obscured by what appears to be a mainly post–Early Dynasty irrigation levee (B in Figure 5). A broad northwest–southeast band of plain, which has been scoured by sand-transporting winds (A), not only shows evidence of relict meanders but also archaeological sites, sand dunes, and relict canals (C). Forming a broad tract to the west and south-

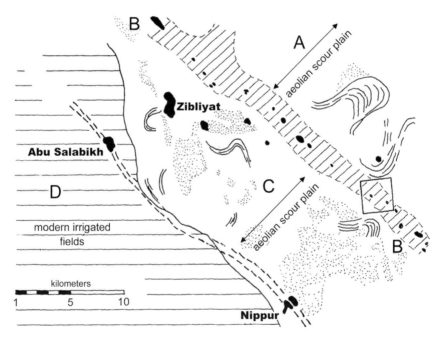

Figure 5. Geomorphic and taphonomic map of the Abu Salabikh and Nippur regions, Iraq, showing the distinction between areas of long-term aggradation within the irrigated zone D, areas in which deflation predominates (zones A and C), and a linear zone of aggradation and archaeological sites along a major levee system (B) (from Wilkinson 2003: fig. 5.6).

west is the zone of modern cultivation which includes irrigated fields and canals as well as a number of archaeological sites that have been buried (D). Of these, two sites date to the Uruk period and are therefore contemporary with several sites in the meandering area (Wilkinson 1990). This example illustrates how in a complex alluvial landscape a land surface of a given date may be close to the modern surface in one locality (A), be deeply buried (as along the levee, B), near the surface or pedestaled (as at C), and buried (as at D). More importantly, it shows the extent to which cultural practices such as irrigation, constrained by terrain and climate but controlled by their larger socioeconomic context, can transform the physical landscape and in the process set new parameters for their operation. As such, continued characterization of cultural landscapes and their interactions will remain an essential component of landscape archaeology.

THE FRACTAL LANDSCAPE

By mapping the physical structure of large areas and documenting through archaeological and textual sources their organization under the territorial empires of the Neo-Babylonian and later periods, Robert Adams made a major contribution to the interpretation of macro-scale patterns in ancient landscapes (Adams 1965). A great deal of research has followed Adams's lead but has, in general, focused on the recognition and interpretation of patterns in progressively smaller areas of terrain. This work has shown that, as one moves from the macro to the micro, the landscape record becomes ever more complex, taking on an essentially fractal character. We present here a series of three examples that illustrate the descent from macro to micro and the kinds of landscape patterns that archaeologists have discovered embedded within larger patterns.

At the macro scale (Figure 6), we compare at the same scale two coherent (but by no means closed) regional systems that have been articulated through the delineation of settlements linked by canals and ancient routes. The first, on the left, is a Bronze Age "city-state" in the Iraqi North Jazirah, and the second, on the right, is a Sasanian imperial district in the Diyala region, west of Baghdad. The striking difference in system scale can be partially attributed to the differences in the agricultural potential and economic infrastructure (see Algaze 2001a) of the two regions—a contrast frequently drawn between the rain-fed north and the irrigated south (for instance, Weiss 1983). But this difference must equally relate to a difference in the operational reach of the two polities. In the Sasanian case, although the general organization of the Diyala/Nahrawan system depended on the hydrology and geomorphology of the Tigris region, it would have been impossible to construct a system of such scale unless the political economy of the region extended over a sufficient area to allow for large-scale earthworks to be built. What we wish to show with this example is the variation in macro-scale structures that can be recognized in the landscape record and the kinds of interpretive possibilities they pose.

Descending to the meso-scale (Figure 7), we illustrate a relict, low sinuosity Euphrates channel to the south of Nippur with a forked distributary channel leading water off to the north. The channel and distributary canal system, both distinguishable from surrounding cultivated areas by their pale colored levees, compare rather well with a hypothetical agricultural cell for third millennium BC lower Mesopotamia sketched by Nicholas Postgate (1992: fig. 9.1) from textual sources.

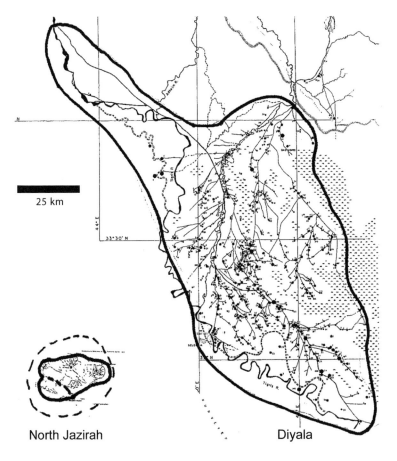

North Jazirah   **Diyala**

Figure 6. Comparative structure and scale of Bronze Age and Sasanian settlement systems in the Iraqi North Jazirah and on the Diyala Plain, respectively.

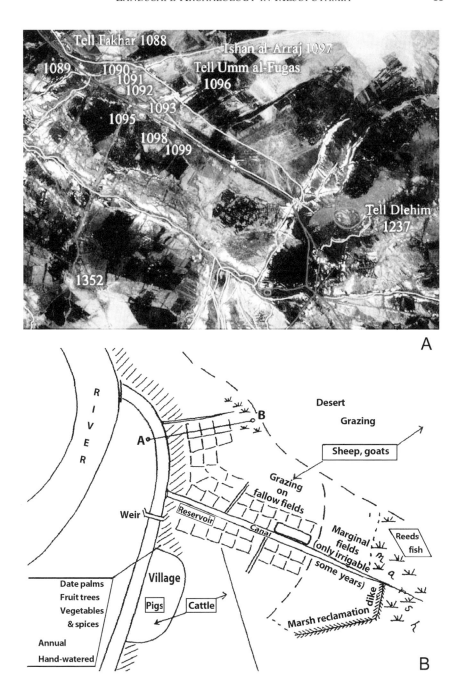

Figure 7. Archaeological (A) and textual (B) reconstruction of Bronze Age irrigation systems in lower Mesopotamia. CORONA satellite photograph courtesy of the US Geological Survey (processed by C. Hritz). (B) After Postgate 1992: fig 9.1.

At the micro-scale (Figure 8), the intensive surface collection of 1 square kilometer of desert southeast of Mashkan Shapir (Abu Duwari) emphasizes the fractal nature of many Mesopotamian landscapes: structure emerges at all scales of analysis. In this case, the darkest hues of the contour plot represent the highest recorded densities of pottery sherds littering the

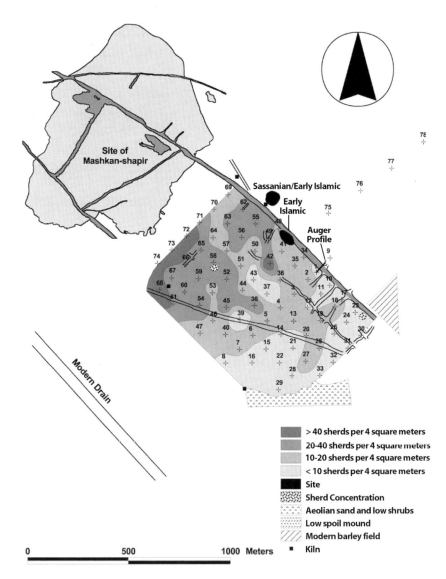

Figure 8. Offsite sherd scatters to the south of Abu Duwari (Mashkan Shapir: from Wilkinson in Stone and Zimansky 2004: fig. 347).

surface between the soil marks of a rectilinear network of small canals fed by the main west-northwest–east-southeast canal that flowed through the center of Mashkan Shapir. (Both the rectilinear canal system and the sherd scatters appear to be of Parthian to Islamic date; the age of the oblique east–west canal soil mark is yet unknown.) Given its association with irrigated fields, this scatter most plausibly indicates the use in antiquity of organic and nitrogen-rich sediments spread from nearby settlements as fertilizer. This case, together with the two previous examples, illustrates how, through analogy, coherent systems of relations can be recognized and interpreted at an ever-widening range of spatial scales.

THE SYMBOLIC LANDSCAPE

As the postprocessual critique of archaeological method and theory has crept out of Europe and into its peripheries, there has been a significant shift in the ways in which Near Eastern archaeologists have understood and deployed the concept of landscape. What was once a neutral (and conveniently vague) way to refer to and assert tacitly the coherence of archaeological and geographic features observed at various spatial scales is now used by many scholars as a way of deconstructing the very assumption of coherence. Landscapes, we are told, are not the patterns we tease out of our survey data, our maps, and aerial photographs, nor are they the deeper patterns that our imperfect methods inevitably miss. On the contrary, landscapes are the network of concepts, knowledge, and strategies that people use to move through and to make a living in the world. Put most strongly, the postprocessual position holds that the coherence of the world does not lie in the world itself but in social projections of order upon it. These projections, which consist of buildings, charts, paths, names, fields, borders, and myriad other material and symbolic forms, are both constrained by the material world and also frame the cultural practices and processes that continually reshape it (again, see Figure 2).

The implications of this conceptual shift for traditional landscape archaeology are at once troubling and exciting. On the one hand, it is clear that the cultural processes that shape and transform the physical world do not leave unambiguous material traces and therefore that total facts about past societies will not simply jump out from our maps of sherd densities and canal traces. On the other hand, a re-theorized concept of landscape does promise a landscape archaeology that is more tightly integrated with other lines of archaeological inquiry and thus has greater scope and explanatory power. The value of the postprocessual critique, we argue, is that it has encouraged landscape archaeologists to reach beyond their own data sets toward theories of social process to guide them in the collection and interpretation of landscape data.

One very straightforward example of such an analysis comes from the later prehistory of the Susiana plain. Here, in preliminary analyses of site survey data, both Frank Hole (1987a) and Abbas Alizadeh (1992) noticed a gradual shift in late fifth millennium settlement from the eastern to the western half of the plain and an aggregation of populations at Susa on its western edge. Taking inspiration from a suggestion by Henry Wright and Greg Johnson (1975) that one impetus to population centralization in this region during the later Uruk period may have been raiding by transhumant pastoralists inhabiting the Zagros foothills to the east, both Hole and Alizadeh invoked "pastoralist pressure" in their explanations.

More recently, a revised periodization scheme for the prehistoric periods on the Susiana plain (Kouchoukos 1998: chap. 3) has documented this population shift in greater detail (Figure 9). The picture is indeed one of widespread abandonment of sites in the eastern part of the plain between the Susiana D and Susa A periods, and a corresponding founding of sites in the west. In a recent synthesis, Alizadeh (in press) has used these survey data together with archaeological and faunal evidence from sites in Khuzistan, Luristan, and Fars to make a strong case for the emergence of specialized nomadic pastoralism in western Iran and the parallel development of new social relationships and new modes of human–environment interaction. This example illustrates both how the interpretation of landscape data must take into account archaeologically 'invisible' factors such as the actions of nomads within a social field, but how, conversely, landscape data can orient and become an integral part of archaeological explanations.

A second example of the ways in which a reconceptualization of landscape can push our thinking in new directions comes from the Warka region in the fourth millennium BC. Here surveys by Robert Adams and over a century of archaeological investigation have documented a rapid increase in populations during the fourth millennium BC and an aggregation of populations into large settlements of many thousands of people. Along with this growth, we find in the archaeological and textual record much evidence of institutional forms projected on the landscape. We learn that the institution of the temple played a significant role in the organization of property, of agricultural labor, of herding systems, and of food preparation and processing and hence must have had a profound effect on the material structuring of the landscape. What is most curious about these developments, however, is that they appear to have taken place at a time when drastic changes in the environment and human ecology were taking place. We have good evidence both for decreases in the strength of the summer Asian monsoon, which shifted the seasonality of precipitation, and for the stabilization of sea levels, which led to the recession of the Persian

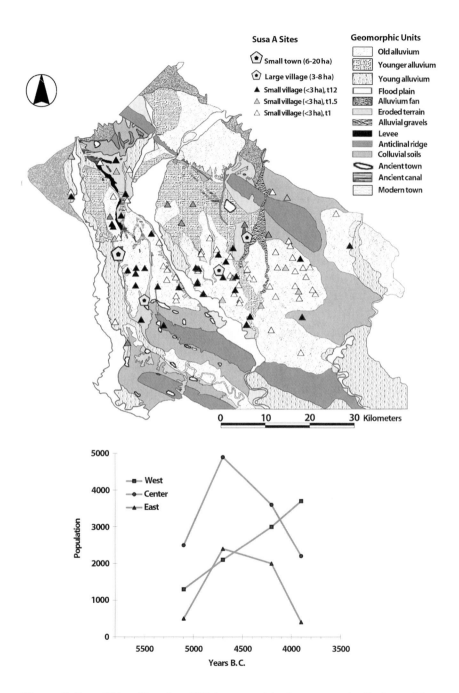

Figure 9. Late fifth millennium BC demographic changes on the Susiana plain, southwest Iran. White triangles on the map indicate sites abandoned during the Susa A period; black triangles indicate sites founded during this period.

Gulf away from Uruk and destabilized river regimes (Kouchoukos 1998: chap. 5). Under less centralized conditions and indeed in many prevailing, overly mechanistic models of human–environment relationships, these changes would certainly have caused crisis and collapse. But in the Uruk case, it appears that the social response to these changes was coordinated, quite successfully, within the discursive frame of the temple and other institutions that mediated human–environment interactions in complex, essentially unpredictable ways. What this example shows us clearly, then, is that understanding landscape changes and corresponding social changes requires that we pay careful attention to the symbolic as well as the material structure of the landscape.

THE GLOBAL AND THE LOCAL

The last trend in landscape archaeology that we would like to point out has emerged in part from the critique of the landscape concept but also follows from contemporary debates about the nature of transregional economic and political processes and their coordinated effects on different and distant societies. Over the last three decades, ambitious efforts by many scholars have sought to understand theoretically and to ground empirically questions concerning how long-distance trade in the past was organized, how it created spatially and temporally extended relationships of production and consumption, and how these new relationships intersected with and transformed local social relationships. In reviewing recent syntheses of these topics, notably those by Algaze (1993a), G. Stein (1999a), and Rothman (ed., 2001), what is striking is the limited extent to which evidence from landscape archaeology has been incorporated into arguments about the development and consequences of long-distance exchange systems. While reference is commonly made to settlement patterns, or to the variegated nature of localized settlement growth and decline (Algaze 1999; Wilkinson 2000), these are rarely taken as anything more than an index of socioeconomic hierarchy. This need not be the case, however, and rather than criticize these readings of the landscape record, we would like to illustrate with a final example how the theorization of transregional process can inspire new approaches to the analysis of survey data.

As noted in our last example, the fourth millennium BC in lower Mesopotamia was a period of spectacular urban growth. Much recent scholarship on long-distance trade and early imperialism has focused on evidence for the expansion of the Uruk economy out of the heartland and into adjacent regions. Although much remains to be clarified about the nature of these developments, most scholars have assumed that they had a significant effect on social relationships in these regions, and we might expect these effects to be clear in the landscape record. And, indeed, when one compares the trajectory of developments in the region around Uruk to those in adjacent regions of Nippur, Susiana, and the North Jazirah, such an effect is clear and striking: while the magnitude of settled populations in the Uruk heartland (Warka) grow steadily, those in the three adjacent regions decline monotonically (Figure 10). The demographic curves presented here result from the reanalysis of gross settlement trends employing the algorithm of Dewar (1991). In the case of the North Jazirah, this reanalysis demonstrates a local fourth millennium BC decline in population following an earlier peak. In other words, more

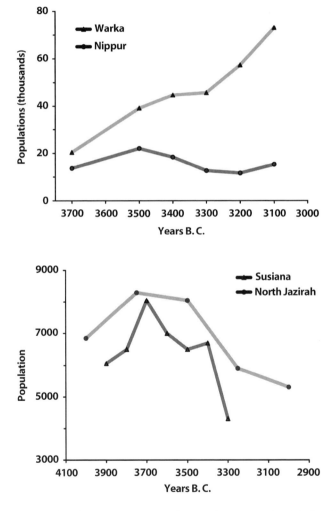

Figure 10. Fourth millennium BC population changes in the Warka, Nippur, Susian, and North Jazirah survey regions calculated by method of Dewar 1991. See Kouchoukos 1998: 233–249 for details.

rigorous analysis of existing data allows for more demographic configurations to emerge.

One possible explanation for these contrasting demographic trajectories, as Kouchoukos (1998: chap. 6) has argued, is an increase in nomadic pastoralism in the Uruk periphery in response first to a growing demand at Uruk for woolen cloth, a key element of the increasingly centralized political economy, and then to the consequent emergence of cloth as a transregional form of value. Whether this explanation holds water or not is immaterial to our point here, which is simply that regional landscape and settlement processes can be articulated over great distances. The implications of this are that explanations of local landscape records must take global factors into consideration, and, conversely, theorizations of transregional processes can be guided by patterns seen in the comparative analysis of landscape records from different regions.

CONCLUSIONS

In conclusion, we have tried to demonstrate through our various examples that landscape archaeology in Mesopotamia stands now at a very productive convergence of theories and methods drawn from geomorphology, a revitalized geography, contemporary ecological anthropology, the postprocessual critique of landscape, and tempered world systems models of local and global interaction. We have charted what we find to be several very productive directions the field has taken and point out that these together promise sure progress in disentangling the complex dialectical processes of human–environment interaction and ultimately an improved understanding of the spatial dimensions of Mesopotamian social worlds. We close by pointing out that this project should be of interest not only to Near Eastern archaeologists, but to other scholars interested more generally in the relationship between landscape and society but who do not have access to the stratified landscapes of the archaeological record, on which, as Bob Adams has shown us, our understanding of this relationship crucially depends.

ARCHAEOLOGICAL SURVEYS AND MESOPOTAMIAN HISTORY

HANS J. NISSEN

ABSTRACT

The phase conventionally designated Early Dynastic I in early Mesopotamian history had long been characterized as chaotic or a phase of decline, based on the art historical evaluation of objects of art, primarily cylinder seals. It was only through the results of archaeological surface surveys of parts of the lower Mesopotamian plain that this period could be shown to have been a particularly inventive and formative stage in the early development of Mesopotamia.

Today, systematic archaeological surface reconnaissance work is established as a fully developed and accepted research tool in archaeology in general and in Near Eastern archaeology in particular. It is widely recognized as a means of taking stock of the archaeological heritage of an entire region, and has served to make inventories to provide guidelines for rescue operations on archaeological sites before their inundation by the many new water reservoir projects (Hole 1995). While such survey work often is seen as a tool in the process of selecting the site or sites that supposedly would yield the best answers to the research aims of the archaeologist, such surveys also provide overall information on past settlement systems. Two approaches can be identified here. One studies the settlement patterns of a region and their changes over time, leading to various insights on, for instance, changing land utilization or population development; or the surface of a settlement may yield information on changing settlement sizes over time (for instance, Finkbeiner 1991). The second approach focuses on the dynamics of the relationship between centers and their hinterlands.

Surface survey thus provides important sources of information for the study of any past civilization, whether literary or not, and indeed, surveys over the past several decades have contributed to our knowledge of the early history of various regions of the Near East to an extent that cannot be over-estimated. However, survey data plays an especially important role in literate areas like ancient Babylonia because it provides data that complements our written sources. While the written record has enabled us to develop a good understanding of the political, social, economic, and cultural history of much of Babylonian civilization, our understanding of the origins of these develop-ments is largely missing from the written record. The texts speak of kings, their realms, their acquisitions, and conquests (and defeats) but do not tell us how many people were involved (except when bragging about the number of killed enemies) nor the size of settlements both within Babylonia or in the areas they conquered. In addition, since the texts were primarily written in highly urbanized Babylonia, only rarely do they provide information about life in the countryside and the important role of rural settlements and popu-lation in Babylonian society.

Of course, survey data cannot answer all of these questions or fill all of the gaps in the written record, but the results of such surveys carried out over the last three decades have been shown to contribute invaluable information to the study of Babylonian history. This is due both to our ability to compare the results of textual studies and the archaeological data, and to the superb preservation of the archaeological record in southern Mesopotamia (Adams and Nissen 1972; Adams 1981).

Of the many examples where survey work can offer important contribu-tions to the study of ancient Near Eastern history, or even change our view completely, two cases will be singled out for discussion in this paper: the nature of Early Dynastic I, and the issue of the relationship between cities and their hinterlands.

EARLY DYNASTIC I

In our present terminology, the Early Dynastic I period (ED I), dated roughly between 3000 and 2800 BC, is the time immediately following the Jemdet Nasr period. While today the ED I is a well-defined chronological and cul-tural entity, this has not always been the case. Although the term *Early Dynas-tic* was coined as early as the 1920s by Henri Frankfort (1924) and developed through the discoveries resulting from the Diyala excavations during the 1930s (published in due course as a series of Oriental Institute publications), the earliest period, ED I, remained remarkably ill defined. Although the Diy-ala excavations uncovered substantial architecture associated with a distinct pottery assemblage, the ED I phase did not receive adequate attention. This was the result both of the excessive reliance on art objects for defining chronological sequences at that time, and on the almost complete lack of evidence from Babylonia proper. For example, in spite of the extensive archaeological explorations at Uruk—the source of the only reliable sequence for the early periods in the 1920s and 1930s—neither the Early Dynastic period nor its subdivisions were defined there. At Uruk at that time, there was considerable archaeological evidence for what was then called Archaic Level VI–IV, and also for the Archaic Level III, later equated with the Jemdet Nasr, but next to nothing had been uncovered for what was known as Archaic Level I. As the uppermost phase encountered below the so-called historical levels—that is, the context of Urnammu's ziqqurrat—Archaic Level I was supposed to bridge the gap between the time of the Archaic Level III and the time of the Third Dynasty of Ur (the end of the third millennium). To be sure, this long span of time was subdivided into seven phases on the basis of major and minor alterations on the Eanna terrace, but since none of these stages was associated with finds other than architecture, they did not lend themselves to comparison (Lenzen 1941), particularly not with the results of the Diyala excavations.

In the assessment of the early development of Babylonia, the two leading archaeologists of that time, Henri Frankfort and Anton Moortgat, came from an art historical tradition which placed primary emphasis on stylistic development of art objects, especially cylinder seals. From the point of view of today, it is clear that this particular approach was doomed to failure in its assessment of the EDI period, since the study of the seals from this period led to two fallacious conclusions. Frankfort had numerous ED I seals from well-stratified levels in the Diyala sites to work with, but they tended to be geometric or abstracted to a high degree ("Brocade Style"). For him, "these seals differ fundamentally from those of the preceding period," and they do not "rise much above the low level to which glyptic art had sunk in the preceding period" (Frankfort 1939a: 39), reason enough to state that the first ED period was "a transitional age of short duration" (Frankfort 1939a: 42).

Moortgat, on the other hand, had been using stylistic change rather than stratigraphic context for his chronology. Establishing a chronological order of cylinder seals based exclusively on art historical considerations had proven to yield good results for the slightly later periods. Using the seals from the Royal Cemetery of Ur and those from Fara, Moortgat had been able to establish a reliable sequence from the time of the Akkadian Dynasty well back into the "pre-Sargonic" period. The new material from Uruk and Jemdet Nasr was different, however, and could not be shown to be straightforward predecessors of that sequence. Both thematically and stylistically, these seals seemed to differ quite a bit from the seals of the later tradition. He was thus unable to single out seals that ought to close this gap from the collection of undated and mostly unprovenienced seals at his disposal. Thus, the inevitable conclusion was that major changes had occurred between the Uruk and Jemdet Nasr periods. This, it was thought, was demonstrated by the seals, which exhibited a shift from the plastic, figurative designs of the Uruk period to the abstract, schematic patterns of Jemdet Nasr seals. Moortgat (1940) interpreted this change as a deterioration and found no evidence for a recovery until his Mesilim stage (roughly contemporaneous with ED II). As a consequence of this approach, Moortgat placed the ED I seals into this "transitional period," which gave him "the feeling of a total dissolution of the old values of the Jemdet Nasr period," and calls this period "one of the most violent fermenting periods of Near Eastern history" (Moortgat 1940: 9). Although the hundreds of seal impressions recovered from Fara had been known for some time (Heinrich 1931), Moortgat's approach prevented him from recognizing anything earlier than his Mesilim style within this corpus. Moortgat's conclusion, therefore, was that the Jemdet Nasr was followed by a "period of internal and external transition when at first all achievements of the preceding time seem to get lost, before they live on in different disguise and consolidated order" (Moortgat 1940: 9). A few years later, he speaks more pronouncedly of "a chaotic transitional phase," claiming that the Mesilim phase represents a completely new cultural inventory "as against the Uruk IV and Djemdet Nasr phases" (Moortgat 1950: 229).

A more appropriate assessment of the ED I phase should have already been possible at that time. Frankfort's 1930s excavations in the Diyala region, primarily in Tell Asmar and Khafaje, had been the first to uncover a continuous series of layers that spanned the time between the Royal Cemetery of Ur and Jemdet Nasr. The major changes in the layout of the building phases uncovered in these excavations led to the subdivision of the Early Dynastic period into three subphases. Within that sequence, a substantial part was assigned to the first of these, or Early Dynastic I, which was understood to follow immediately after the Jemdet Nasr levels. Judging from the architecture, these remains by no means gave the impression of a mere transitional period; instead ED I turned out to be an important stage in its own right. In spite of such clear evidence, Frankfort was too much of an art historian to dismiss the evidence of the cylinder seals as his primary source of information on the chronology and interpretation of this period. While he did not share Moortgat's designation of this time as "chaotic," Frankfort agreed (1954: 18) that this was a transitional period and spoke of a "deterioration of the arts."

Both authorities continued to propagate this view into the 1950s (Moortgat 1950; Frankfort 1954: 18), a view shared both by Edith Porada in her catalog of the Pierpont Morgan collection published in 1948 and by Adam Falkenstein in the Fischer World-History published in 1965. Porada attributed these changes to "foreign influences" (Porada 1948: 8) and Falkenstein to the "influx of Semitic-speaking groups" (Falkenstein 1965: 56).

This assessment of the period as transitional was generally accepted in the 1960s and early 1970s, while at the same time all authors agreed that there was strong evidence for continuity. Evidently there was a discrepancy between the evaluation of the artistic development seen as evidencing deterioration, and the data for continuous development provided by the Diyala sites. At that time, however, the emphasis was still on art historical reasoning, and archaeologists were not ready to abandon this approach and to use architecture and pottery as the main sources of evidence for social continuity or discontinuity and to leave the question of artistic interpretation open.

A reevaluation began with the discovery of some new pottery groups in Uruk and the search for some comparanda in an attempt to date them more precisely (Nissen 1970). The main corpus of pottery on hand for comparative purposes was the monumental work on the Diyala pottery with its precise allocation of pottery types to specific architectural levels (Delougaz 1952). Given the previous neglect of pottery at Uruk, it came as a surprise that the pottery from the Uruk squares K/L XII almost exactly matched that from the Early Dynastic I levels of the Diyala sites, for the first time presenting proof for extensive material of that period at Uruk (Nissen 1970).

The actual breakthrough, however, came with the preparation for the planned surface survey of the hinterland of Uruk, which Adams and Lenzen had agreed upon. One of the main aims would be to date the settlement sites according to the pottery sherds found on the surface. A detailed analysis of the chronology of pottery types was therefore vital if we were to achieve as exact a dating as possible. We had to define the ceramic "index fossils" which had been in use for only a short time and could therefore provide a more precise dating of the particular settlement on which they were found. Here again, the Diyala pottery publication proved to provide the best and most complete sequence. Moreover, it offered a most valuable set of forms to be used for the purpose of the survey, as quite a number of types were found exclusively in Early Dynastic I levels (Delougaz 1952: 135–141). Since these were not exotic items but part of the normal pottery assemblage, it seemed highly likely that they would be present on the surface of any settlement inhabited during Early Dynastic I.

Following the process described in Adams's work in the Diyala (Adams 1965: 121–122) and refined for the Uruk survey (Adams and Nissen 1972: 97–104), a set of ceramic indicators could be established that would allow the compilation of maps, each containing only the settlements dating to a particular period that had been recognized in the course of the survey. It was in the process of comparing these maps in order to understand changing settlement patterns that the most conclusive evidence for the necessity of a reevaluation of the ED I period was found.

Comparing the maps for the Late Uruk, Jemdet Nasr, ED I, and later ED phases, a clear trend became clear: a significant but steady decline in the number of settlements over time. Meanwhile, the average size of settlements increased. Thus, when comparing the aggregate settled areas—that is, a calculation of the areas of all settlements inhabited during one particular period—the trend went in the opposite direction. Thus, the aggregate settled area increased from 440 hectares to 950 hectares between Uruk and Early Dynastic I, while the number of settlements decreased from 100 to 70. Of course, these figures must be taken with a grain of salt, given the inherent insecurities in both the dating process and the determination of the settled areas. Nevertheless, the differences are striking, and this trend remains valid even when all questionable sites are removed (see Pollock 2001). Both the trend toward increased settled area and that of decreased number of sites continue through the later part of the Early Dynastic period.

These data are more than enough to show the importance of the Early Dynastic I period and found their counterpart in the results of a preliminary (unsystematic) inspection of the surface of the city area of Uruk itself undertaken as a sideline between 1964 and 1967. The more recent systematic survey of the city conducted under the direction of Uwe Finkbeiner (1991) has confirmed this impression, indicating that Uruk grew to its largest extent in Early Dynastic I, not only encompassing the area within the city wall but extending beyond it (Pongratz-Leisten 1991). We should also note that it is likely that this very city wall was built during Early Dynastic I (Haller 1936; Nissen 1972).

By now, it is generally accepted that the Early Dynastic I period is one of the most important and formative phases of Babylonian history (Kuhrt 1995; Nissen 1988; 1998; Pollock 1999). For example, it appears that this period corresponds to the beginning of large-scale irrigation with the aid of long canals, the feature that, from then on, becomes one of the salient characteristics of the Babylonian civilization. Again, this critical insight resulted from survey work of the kind pioneered by Bob Adams.

THE QUESTION OF THE NATURE OF CENTER– HINTERLAND RELATIONS IN EARLY BABYLONIA

The descriptions of Herodotus, the decipherment of cuneiform, and the large excavations in Mesopotamia of the nineteenth century all provided information that the large plain of southern Mesopotamia housed great old cities like Babylon, Nineveh, and Ur. Since the 1920s, the excavations at Uruk have demonstrated that this fully urban culture dated back to the fourth millennium BC and indicate the enormous longevity of this urban culture. Indeed, there is every reason to believe that it is in southern Mesopotamia where the kind of organization we call a *city* first originated. Or, to use the title of one of Adams's main works (1981), Babylonia was not only the heartland but also the homeland of cities.

This evaluation is based on the textual evidence preserved on thousands of clay tablets. The economic and juridical texts found their place either within an urban society or within a network of several urban centers; this is also true for the less numerous, so-called historical texts such as the royal inscriptions or lists of rulers. Indeed, we find evidence for the importance that the Babylonians placed on cities in the so-called Sumerian Kinglist, composed in the beginning of the second millennium BC, which uses cities and not larger entities as the organizing principle for the numerous rulers and dynasties it described, in the process making clear that they saw cities as the centers of power. The same picture emerges from the literary texts where the protagonists each derive from and represent a particular city. The only allusion to non-urban contexts is made when reference is to the antithesis to urban life—that is, to nonsedentary groups, referred to generally in negative, derogative terms, as in the treatment of the figure of Enkidu in the Gilgamesh epic.

While this attitude of hostility to nonsedentary populations may be understandable inasmuch as the normal peaceful coexistence—even economic interdependence—between the cities and these groups could become hostile at times of economic disturbance, it is difficult to understand why sedentary life outside the cities is never mentioned. Since the sheer size of Babylonian urban centers means that they never could have been self-supporting, we have to assume that part of their sustenance must have been provided by those living in their hinterlands. Furthermore, it has been argued convincingly that Babylonia did not have a market economy but worked on the principle of redistribution, so we have to assume that the city and its surrounding lands were part of a tightly organized network. There must have existed, therefore, a systemic reason why these relations were never included in the written record.

Whatever the answer, the fact remains that we cannot expect any help from written documents and must therefore look to other sources. Fortunately, this is an area that is covered by the regional archaeological surveys which provide the necessary data on location, size, and date of settlements in a given area. It also happens that the survey of the Uruk area used above also provides exactly the kind of evidence we are looking for.

Above, I referred to the settlement distribution maps of the hinterland of Uruk only in general terms; here, by contrast, attention will be given to the details of that distribution. Again, the focus will be on the periods between the Late Uruk and later Early Dynastic, or roughly between 3400 and 2400 BC. And again, reference is made to the trend, discussed in more detail above, of a decrease in the number of settlements co-occurring with an increasing average site size

A closer look, however, shows that this trend does not affect the entire region, but only areas at some distance from Uruk, and not its immediate hinterland. This precision is made possible because the two areas are separated by a 3- to 4-kilometer-wide belt devoid of any settlements, encircling Uruk at a distance of 13 to15 kilometers from the city. This can best be seen on the map for ED I where the increasing size of the remaining settlements is most visible (Figure 11); but this belt is present on the other maps as well.

For a possible explanation, we may refer to a proposal of Christaller's on the nature of relations between settlement distributions and the primary means of cohesion between the settlements with a system (Christaller 1933; 1966). For him, the main forces were either economic or political, each resulting in clear locational differences. In particular, he postulated that voids existed between settlement systems if the basic relations within the systems and between the systems were political or administrative rather than economic. Anyone living in such a border area would run the risk of having their affiliation questioned, and thus would be safer either moving into the area of control, or moving out of reach. This model therefore suggests that this unoccupied belt on the ED I map marked the border between direct and indirect control by the center and furthermore suggests that the main relationship between Uruk and its hinterland was a political/administrative one.

This comes as a surprise because the textual sources would have suggested another kind of primary tie. Recognizing the fact that so many of our texts dating from the end of the fourth millennium talk about food resources and about securing them and, as mentioned earlier, since it is clear that cities the size of Uruk can hardly be expected to have been self-sufficient, there can be no doubt that much of Uruk's food must have been supplied by rural producers. From this it would seem logical, without other sources of information, to assume relations of an economic nature to have been the main bond between Uruk and its countryside.

Nevertheless, it does make sense to see political/administrative relationships as more powerful than these economic ties. It would be idyllic to assume that the abstract bonds within a settlement system would have been the trading of excess food supplies from the countryside for services provided by the center—without any tensions. On the contrary, if we recognize the nature of Babylonian irrigation agriculture, with its sharp yearly fluctuations of available water, one can easily see occasions when rural settlements may not have been able to adequately supply the city, even as the city's survival depended on a more regular supply of food. It is therefore inevitable that on such occasions the center would have used its superior power to fulfill its needs. While there is no limit to the distance regulating forces could cover once on a raid, constant control needs communication paths; half the daily marching distance seems to be adequate to delimit the area of close control. This is, of course, almost exactly the 13- to 15-kilometer distance around Uruk which the application of Christaller's theories would suggest to have been the limit of the area of direct control.

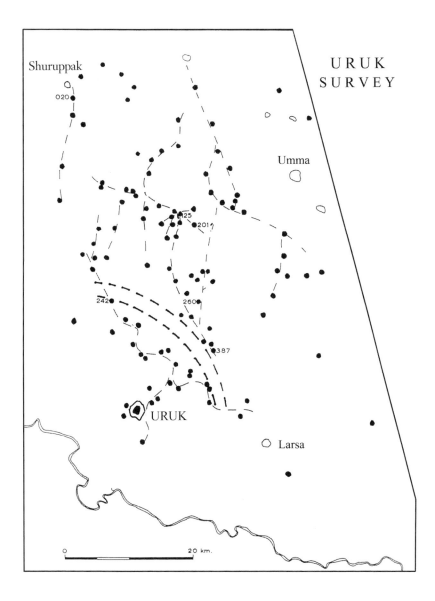

Figure 11. Warka Survey: Settlements of the Early Dynastic I period with reference to the belt separating the areas of direct and indirect control.

The suggestion, then, is that the relationship between Uruk and its hinterland—and this probably applies to the other Babylonian cities as well—was primarily a political/administrative one that itself governed the economic ties.

Considering the inherent weakness of survey data, this may sound like stretching the evidence but, if nothing else, it makes us aware that the unvoiced assumption of primarily economic relations between the center and periphery needs to be questioned. It is still regrettable how little we know about the details and the organization of the interchange between centers and their hinterlands, but at least the results of archaeological surface surveys help us ask new questions.

As mentioned earlier, to have introduced, propagated, and refined these methods is one of the lasting achievements of Bob Adams. Others may be proud of having added new material to our picture by excavating smaller or larger sites, but it is very rare that a scholar can be attributed with having altered an entire field of study by adding a new dimension to research.

KLM TO CORONA:
A BIRD'S-EYE VIEW OF
CULTURAL ECOLOGY AND EARLY
MESOPOTAMIAN URBANIZATION*

JENNIFER R. POURNELLE

ABSTRACT

A hallmark of nineteenth-century beliefs about non-urban landscapes was that marshes are inherently diseased, sodden wastelands, and that the appropriate effort of good government was to transform them into cultivated agricultural land. This emphasis on the importance of transforming "waste" marshes for "useful" agricultural endeavor was especially operative during the formative period of Mesopotamian archaeology. Through the mid-twentieth century, it was embedded in research paradigms that viewed the birth of Mesopotamian civilization as inherently tied to drying of primordial lands, accompanied by state (or temple, or household) administration of irrigated plow agriculture.

* I am grateful to Robert McC. Adams, Guillermo Algaze, Helmut Becker, Helmut Brückner, Elizabeth Carter, Robert Englund, Jörg Fassbinder, McGuire Gibson, Jennifer Hyundal, Nicholas Kouchoukos, Joan Oates, Margarete van Ess, and Tony Wilkinson for substantive comments on earlier versions of this paper. Errors and omissions naturally remain my own. Mr. Richard Pattee generously converted the site indices from Adams 1972a and 1981, and Wright 1981b to electronic database format. Drs. Leta Hunt and Lynn Swartz-Dodd, University of Southern California, developed imagery digitization protocols. I am especially indebted to Mr. R. Neil Munro for his considerable assistance in locating geomorphologic materials. All images were processed using ENVI™, manufactured by Research Systems International (RSI), now ITT Industries, who granted steep educational discounts for their software

During the final quarter of the twentieth century, Robert McC. Adams insisted that any characterization of Mesopotamian civil complexity must include due consideration of both cities and their surrounding rural- ized zones. He used KLM aerial photographs collected during the late 1950s to address problems of both geographic and temporal scale in map- ping and contextualizing data collected during archaeological survey con- ducted through the 1970s. Adams's definitive 1981 study, entitled Heartland of Cities, quite literally placed rural settlements on the map of urban genesis and decline. In it, he envisioned a complex urban hinterland, comprising grain agriculture, livestock husbandry, and marshland exploi- tation.

However, geopolitics and war meant that access to the detailed KLM air photos was never guaranteed, and this work halted. During the early 1990s, Adams and others successfully lobbied for public access to high-reso- lution declassified satellite photographs, code-named CORONA. Relying on Adams's CORONA legacy, this paper revises that map, by showing that the urbanizing/ruralizing heartland was, at its core and urban incept, a del- taic heartland. It outlines with greater precision than was available to mid- twentieth century theorists the paleogeography of the lower Mesopotamian alluvium during the formative Chalcolithic and Early Bronze Age periods. It emphasizes the essential nature of wetlands in supporting and shaping the complex social institutions that underlay urbanization in southern Mesopotamia. It concludes that marshy deposits underlay or surrounded the earliest occupation layers of all early urban sites, suggesting that these set- tlements were subject to (or bordered) seasonal inundation.

We cannot wrest the origins of alluvial Mesopotamian cities from an irrigated version of the modern landscape. The predecessors of early allu- vial Mesopotamian cities were not beads strung along the filaments of rivers and canals. They are better imagined as islands embedded in a marshy plain, situated on the borders and in the heart of vast deltaic marshlands. Many desiccated waterways are ancient transport routes through those wetlands, not relict irrigation canals. The stability of those early urban centers was largely contingent upon the vicissitudes of human interaction with those wetlands during deltaic progradation. The pre- dominance of reeds, reed bundles, and reed structures in the earliest pro- toliterate texts point to their major role in fourth-millennium tributary economies. It may well yet be shown that a lasting importance of marsh- grown reeds was not only as a commodity per se, but in the way the demands of their production structured the underpinnings of urban-cen- tered labor control.

INTRODUCTION

In a United Nations report based on NASA analyses of LANDSAT satellite images, Hassan Partow documented the demise of the vast marshlands of southeastern Iraq. That demise was the end result of a half-century of systematic flood control, damming, and drainage aimed at asserting centralized political authority and expanding agricultural export production (Cotha Consulting Engineers 1959; Iraq 1956; Koucher 1999; Macfayden 1938; National Aeronautics and Space Administration 2000: 2001; Partow 2001). The LANDSAT multispectral system, released to public access in the early 1970s, was itself produced in response to demands for an accessible aid to landform analysis that could be used in service to regional development schemes. Within the public arena, LANDSAT launched hopes that satellite imagery, when compared with traditional aerial photography, would both expand coverage and lower costs.

But imagery of this kind was barely imaginable to archaeologists and public planners when, in the 1950s, the Iraqi government contracted for a series of engineering studies aimed at harnessing the water and power of the Tigris and Euphrates Rivers. Among its aims, the Iraqi monarchy then in power intended to implement ambitious schemes first proposed by British engineer Sir William Wilcox a half-century earlier. These proposed to systematically drain marshes, lower the saline water table, and rationalize irrigation systems in order to reclaim waste land for high-profit agricultural production.

Thus, both the demise of the marshlands and their documentation were, in a sense, a terminal outcome of nineteenth-century beliefs that marshes are inherently diseased, sodden wastelands, and that the appropriate effort of good government was to transform them into cultivated agricultural land. This emphasis on the importance of transforming "waste" marshes for "useful" agricultural endeavor was especially operative during the formative period of Mesopotamian archaeology. Through the mid-twentieth century, it was embedded in research paradigms that viewed the birth of Mesopotamian civilization as inherently tied to sufficient drying of primordial lands to allow irrigated plow agriculture (for example, Nissen 1988). This was true despite the many clues pointing to the importance of other resources to Mesopotamian culture, such as the remains of burned and unburned fish recovered from Eridu, Ur, Uruk, Tello, and Tell Asmar (van Buren 1948: 102).

Robert McC. Adams was among the first to seriously challenge this paradigm. The Iraqi Crown had contracted KLM Dutch Airlines to conduct systematic aerial photographic mapping of the alluvial areas of Iraq. The Mesopotamian plain was rendered in a series of high-quality photographic mosaics intended to aid geomorphological studies. Adams insisted that any characterization of Mesopotamian civil complexity must include due consideration of both cities and their surrounding ruralized zones. He used the KLM aerial photographs as an interpretive tool for mapping and contextualizing data collected through archaeological survey. He envisioned a complex hinterland, comprising grain agriculture, livestock husbandry, and marshland exploitation. He examined not just the deep past, but its continuous transformation until the onset of the modern age and its drainage efforts, marked by the construction of a massive flood-control barrage at al-Hindiyah at the turn of the twentieth century (Adams and Nissen 1972; Adams 1981).

LANDSAT imagery would never have sufficient ground resolution to identify the fine detail of small site locations and associated ground features that had made Adams's ambitious study possible. However, access to the more detailed KLM photos was never guaranteed, dependent as it was on the variable goodwill of Iraqi officials. During the early 1990s, even as the final drainage installations were emptying Lake Hammar of water, Adams and others successfully lobbied for declassification of, preservation of, and public access to a hoped-for replacement from the United States military sector: satellite photographs, code-named CORONA. Not only were these images of much higher resolution than other imagery commercially available at that time, but they dated to the late 1960s and early 1970s, before modern development and war had transformed earlier landscapes.

Adams did not, of course, invent the use of aerial photography in archaeology or even in the lower Mesopotamian alluvium. Hall, Woolley, and others used British Air Services to scout locations and photograph individual sites as early as 1918. But it was Adams who understood and used the power of aerial mapping to address problems of scale: both geographic scale (in considering a vast region) and temporal scale (in considering the palimpsest of human activity over this terrain). He was also the first to use photography toward a systematic rooting of Mesopotamian societies within their natural environment. This approach—the use of overhead imagery to link regional-scale studies with ground-based point data to produce comprehensive studies—is a powerful one and, for the newest generation of scholarship, one for which Adams's prescience has secured immeasurable opportunity.

Bracketing the half-century from the mid-1950s to the present, the KLM and CORONA bird's-eye views of lower Mesopotamia have twice provided a unique framework within which to reinterpret the cultural ecology underpinning urbanizing landscape transformations (and allow for direct relation of many data sets and scales of analysis). Adams's definitive 1981 study, entitled *Heartland of Cities*, quite literally placed rural settlements on the map of urban genesis and decline.

Relying on Adams's CORONA legacy, I seek to rewrite that map, by showing that the urbanizing/ruralizing heartland was, at its core and urban incept, a deltaic heartland. This work takes a viewpoint at a regional scale inaccessible through single-site excavation. It reconstructs with greater precision than was available to mid-twentieth century theorists the paleogeography of the lower Mesopotamian alluvium during the formative Chalcolithic and Early Bronze Age periods (Pournelle 2003a; 2003b). It emphasizes the essential nature, not merely of water but of wetlands, in supporting and shaping the complex social institutions that underlay urbanization in southern Mesopotamia. I review available ground evidence in light of fundamental geomorphology that is only visible from above the earth. I conclude that marshy deposits underlay or surrounded the earliest occupation layers of all early urban sites, suggesting that these settlements were subject to (or bordered) seasonal inundation. I argue that desiccated waterways cannot be uniformly interpreted as relict irrigation canals; many were more likely transport routes through vast wetlands. We should not conceive of alluvial urban precursors as beads strung along the filaments of rivers and canals. They are better imagined as islands embedded in a marshy plain. The stability of those early urban centers was contingent upon many things, but not the least of these were the vicissitudes of human interaction with the wetlands characteristic of deltaic progradation.

* * *

In a recent article, Guillermo Algaze posits that "geography, environment, and trade can be seen as the most important factors helping shape the initial nature of social complexity in the Mesopotamian alluvium" (Algaze 2001a: 213–214) in that "the unique ecology and geography of the alluvial lowlands . . . gave Mesopotamian societies important advantages in agricultural productivity and subsistence resilience not possessed by contemporary polities on their periphery" (Algaze 2001a: 199), spurring a "synergistic cauldron" that created "high levels of social and economic differentiation, promoted unprecedented population agglomerations and selected for the creation of new forms of social organization and technologies of social control" (Algaze 2001a: 204–205). In this process, first internal, then "inherently asymmetrical external trade" led to import substitution (Algaze 2001a: 199, 208), with concomitant innovations in information management and manufacturing technologies (Algaze 2001a: 207 and passim), at a pace unmatched outside the alluvium (Algaze 2001a: 213, 214, 217).[1] Algaze's work was spurred on by findings of the Mesopotamian Alluvium Project, a CORONA satellite photographic analysis lab run at UC San Diego[2] by myself and Robert McC. Adams between 1998 and 2002 (Pournelle 2001; 2003a; 2003b). Central to Algaze's hypothetical model is a fundamental reconception of the ecology of the southern alluvium during the formative period in question. This radical reconception can be characterized by two words: Tigris marshes.

During historical periods of the later third and second millennia BC, the climatic regime of the southern Mesopotamian alluvium had dried to something approximating its present state, with urban pearls strung along riparian filaments. Direct travel experience spurred by reliance on historical texts led scholars to assume that the alluvial past of Mesopotamia was characterized by a largely flat, uniform, desertic-steppic plain, devoid of the meanest resource save silt and shrub, transited by its two great rivers, the Tigris and the Euphrates (for example, Nissen 1988: 2). But mounting climatic and geomorphological evidence requires a reconsideration of the southern Mesopotamian terrain during the fifth and fourth millennia BC, and thus of the social developments arising from it. At the point of Uruk's dramatic expansion, the rivers-through-the-desert image simply does not adequately characterize reality on the ground as we now understand it (Sanlaville 1989; 1996; Geyer and Sanlaville 1996; Lambeck 1996; Kouchoukos 1998; Aqrawi 1997; 2001, Margarete van Ess, Helmut Brückner, and Jörg Fassbinder, personal communication 2002). In short, we cannot wrest the origins of alluvial Mesopotamian cities from an irrigated version of the modern landscape. They grew instead from their 'Ubaid predecessors, located on the borders and in the heart of vast deltaic marshlands. These wetlands were in part derived from Euphrates overflow, supplemented by rainfall, but the greatest portion of their annual recharge was the result of Tigris discharge. They served as a massive sponge, absorbing water during flood sea-

---

[1] The argument, made by Algaze, for precocious urbanization (in terms of scale and complexity) in the southern alluvium may or may not be subject to modification on the basis of ongoing excavations at Tell Brak. Algaze and Wilkinson note that the estimates of site size for Brak at the Middle Uruk assume that the totality of the intervening area between the main mound and the ring of satellites surrounding it was occupied (Algaze 2001a: 27). Wilkinson argues that much of this space was in fact dedicated to builders' clay pits (Emberling et al. 1999: 16–17, 25; Wilkinson 2000: 227.

[2] Funded by The Smithsonian Institution, The National Geographic Society, and the University of California, San Diego, Department of Anthropology. I am especially grateful to the National Science Foundation, the University of California Institute on Global Conflict and Cooperation, and the American Schools of Oriental Research for support of my work.

sons and releasing it to soil moisture and groundwater during the remainder of the year.

Results of geomorphological investigations that relate mid-Holocene Nile Delta paleogeology to fifth-millennium BC site locations (Butzer 2001; van den Brink 1989; 1993) provide a point of departure for interpreting declassified CORONA photography of the southern Mesopotamian alluvium. As an archival data set, this imagery is especially useful now, since the region in question is likely to remain closed to coring operations for the foreseeable future. Landform analysis shows that in alluvial Iraq (roughly south of the 32nd parallel), archaeologically visible early villages were concentrated on river levees at locations bordering swamps and marshes during the Neolithic 'Ubaid 0 periods (6500–900 BC). Many of these early sites continued to be occupied into the Chalcolithic 'Ubaid 4 (4900–350 BC), accounting for half of the sites known in the Warka and Eridu survey areas for that period. Of the newly founded sites, as in the Nile Delta, all but one were situated on exposed surfaces of Pleistocene "turtlebacks" that once overlooked anastomosing distributaries subject to seasonal flooding. These turtlebacks were formed during the Pleistocene, when meandering rivers cut through the alluvium, leaving former surfaces exposed above the newly formed floodplain. The channels between these exposures infilled during subsequent Holocene alluvial aggradation, leaving weathered humps of the older surface protruding slightly above the newer alluvial plain—like a floating turtle's back, protruding above calm water. The Nile data cited above suggest that innumerable smaller, scattered sites may be buried beneath the Holocene deposits, leaving visible only the larger sites, situated on the once-elevated turtlebacks. These archaeologically typical 'Ubaid towns presaged an explosion of new (or newly visible) sites founded during the Early Uruk period, when virtually all identifiable turtlebacks became inhabited (Figure 12).

Placing excavation data within this overarching geomorphological context suggests that a significant component of the resource basis for precocious, large deltaic towns (such as Eridu) was derived from surrounding marshland. Mesopotamian urban civilization could and did flourish only following Chalcolithic specialization and integration of not two, but three productive economies: agricultural/horticultural, pastoral/husbanding, and littoral. By productive economy, I mean a sophisticated organization and level of extraction above and beyond opportunistic hunting/fishing/gathering within riparian, lacustrine, marshland, estuarine, and coastal environments. These activities became sanctified and administered in their own right. They were not merely adjunct, supplemental, or subordinate to agropastoral production.

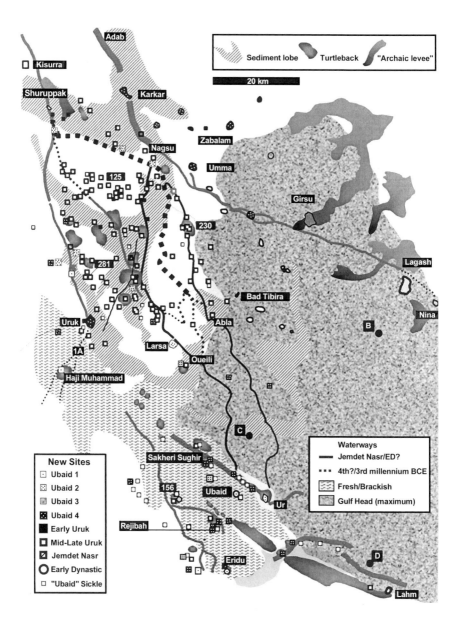

Figure 12. Archaeological sites and relict waterways mentioned in the text, with the approximate extent of the Persian Gulf ca. 3200 BC. Borings show at (B), a transition from fresh marsh to brackish marine conditions, ʿUbaid 1–4; at (C) and (D), brackish marine ʿUbaid 1 Middle Uruk, followed by brackish marsh Late Uruk III and salt panne thereafter.

As for the Mesopotamian heartland, until the latter quarter of the twentieth century, similar arguments regarding the evolution of complex societies in Egypt posited "a swampy Nile delta hostile to all settlement" (Rizkana and Seeher 1987: 21). Challenging this view are careful faunal analyses at deltaic (Maadi, Buto, and Merimde) and lacustrine sites (Brewer 1989: 28; Boessneck, von den Dreish, and Ziegler 1989; Eiwanger 1984). Comparison of these studies to the Mesopotamian case suggests that broad processes were in play; a "third pillar" must be added to the agro-pastoral dyad thought to underpin urban origins. We must reconsider the role of littoral propinquity (in the broad sense including all borderlands between land and water, freshwater and saltwater, and grassland and marsh), not in originating agriculture, but in establishing the territorial precursors to later, enduring social institutions.

THE MESOPOTAMIAN HEARTLAND REVISITED

Four factors are important in assessing the extent and character of surface water and vegetation in the archaic Mesopotamian southern alluvium: (1) Tigris-Euphrates discharge, (2) seasonal rainfall, (3) marine penetration, and (4) river distributary form. The timing, rate, and volume of Tigris and Euphrates water discharge is determined primarily by the quantity and seasonality of precipitation and melting snow packs at their respective Zagros/Taurus headwaters. These are in turn affected by climatic oscillation of the Mediterranean storm track (Mann and Bradley 1998). The amount, extent, and seasonality of rainfall on and east of the alluvium are affected by northwest–southeast displacements of the summer Indian monsoon (el-Moslimany 1994). The extent of saline penetration and related tidal flushing[3] is related to the location and timing of marine transgressions and regressions at the head of the Persian (Arabian) Gulf, as influenced by tectonic uplift, sediment compaction rates, and global sea level variation. Major Tigris and Euphrates distributaries build inner deltas with associated marshlands. Paleoclimatological and sedimentological work regarding the first three

---

[3] Diurnal tides twice daily push Gulf waters up the Shatt al-Arab estuary, raising mean sea levels in shipping lanes by up to 2 meters. This tidal action also checks freshwater outflow, similarly raising estuarine freshwater levels ahead of the tidal surge. Palm groves situated in low-lying ground along the Shatt are thus irrigated and drained twice daily by this tidal action, with no need for human intervention beyond occasional clearing of drainage ditches between the stands (Wirth 1962: 150–51, fig. 34). The regions subject to tidal flushing, ideal for date palm gardening, were thus directly influenced by variations in mean sea level and Gulf head progradation.

factors aids interpretation of new evidence derived from satellite photographs.

The degree and extent of inundation, as well as local groundwater levels and soil and water salinity, are obvious considerations critical to the location of specific communities. Taken as a whole, the alluvium is so flat that even small changes in precipitation and sea level markedly affect these. Nevertheless, conclusions regarding the effect of such geologic events on the habitability of the southern alluvium have been driven largely by the embedded notion that the earliest large, permanent settlements were a result of "colonization" under conditions newly, uniquely, or primarily favorable to agro-pastoral production. As argued by Potts, this position becomes increasingly untenable (Potts 1997: 47–55). Joan Oates's early views regarding the attractions of a rich hunting and fishing potential in southernmost Mesopotamia (Oates 1960) would seem, over recent decades, to have been borne out in a number of Middle Eastern locales. Paleobotanical evidence suggests that, in general, the early to middle Holocene (seventh to fourth millennia BC) was considerably wetter than at present, and that, especially during the late fifth millennium, the alluvium may even have experienced summer rains (el-Moslimany 1994; Hole 1998b; Miller 1998; Zarins 1990: 49–50). Even well outside the alluvium, the close association of large, sedentary sites to wetlands has been noted (Agcabay et al. 2001; Bar-Yoseph 1986; Helbaek 1972: 39; Hole 1998b: 45; D. Oates and Oates 1977: 116–117; Oates 1972: 124–127, pl. 23).

Seeking to understand the origins and development of civilizations in the alluvial lowlands of the Tigris, Euphrates, and Diyala Rivers, Adams, Nissen, Wright, and Gibson conducted broad-scale regional settlement surveys that located, recorded, and dated (based on pottery seriation) thousands of archaeological sites. Then, by means of passive association with archaeological sites located along their courses, Adams dated relict watercourses that intricately lace the region (Adams 1965; 1981; Adams and Nissen 1972; H. T. Wright 1981b; Gibson 1972). From the beginnings of settled towns to the present day, the surveyors were thereby able to provide a broad view of long-term settlement patterns and demographic changes in the Mesopotamian lowlands.

Prior to these studies, it had been generally thought that heavy alluvial deposits over the lower Mesopotamian alluvium would have made it impossible for surveyors to find deeply buried sites. However, the surface surveys showed that this was not necessarily the case. Wind erosion periodically re-exposes long-buried artifacts which, when systematically collected, dated, mapped, and plotted with reference to ancient canal traces, indicated settlement cycling over a period of five millennia (Wilkinson 2003: 71–99, especially fig. 5.5). Thus, the corpus of archaeological survey data for Mesopotamia, although incomplete, succeeded in adding a corrective rural and nonliterate dimension to the predominantly urban, literate, elite focus of excavations and excavated historical texts. On the other hand, the texts lent interpretive dimension to the archaeological data.

Adams's work is especially well known for its clarification of how human engineering interacted with the natural environment. He laid out through deep time the changing strategies Mesopotamian societies used to adapt to shifting hydrology, identifying successive anthropogenic transformations of that environment. He argued that environmental pressures in the region selected for urbanization as an adaptation to social and environmental contingency (Adams 1981).

Overview, Viewed Over

A significant conclusion of Adams's study was that the present-day courses of the Tigris and Euphrates Rivers are, geologically speaking, of recent and anthropogenic origin. He argued that the late mid-Holocene rivers ran down a narrow corridor demarcated by ancient cities strung along now-relict watercourses through the lower alluvium. Following Jacobsen's attempt to reconstruct the main watercourses of ancient southern Mesopotamia from textual sources (Jacobsen 1958), Adams attempted to overcome the inherently speculative problem of attempting to attach precise geographical localities to watercourses attested in early historic itineraries. He undertook to identify actual waterways using extensive ground survey and the KLM air photography, and documented thousands of now-deserted canals in association with these sites. He also hypothesized linear connections between them. The accumulation, argued Adams, of silt carried and deposited by these irrigation activities gradually aggraded the central steppe through which the progressively canalized rivers and canal offtakes ran, ultimately forcing the "wild" rivers respectively westward and eastward (Adams 1981). Once abandoned, aeolian deflation of levees formed dune fields that then scoured their way across the plain. In many cases, this left archaeological features pedestaled above the deflated surface.

Meandering through the Upper Alluvium

While individual channels such as those studied and mapped by Adams from the KLM air photos are suited to localized study supported by ground-based geomorphological assessment, orbital scanners are better suited to detection and analysis of paleochannels at a regional scale. This is especially true for the analysis of adjustments to discharge, sediment load, drainage diversions, and cataclysmic flooding (Baker 1986: 259). Thus, although the original air photos are no longer available,[4] declassification of late 1960s and early 1970s-era satellite photographs enabled me to expand on his original work. Comprehensive mapping of the multiple relict courses of the Tigris and Euphrates, from Samarra in the north to ancient Ur in the south, shows entire, connected systems associated with sites of varying periods. This helps to clarify channel dating and subsequent anthropogenic geomorphology in a way impossible through the analysis of individual localities (Pournelle 2001; 2003a; 2003b; 2004b).

Changes in river regimes related to regional tectonic movements are of particular interest to this study. As the surface slope of alluvial channels levels off en route to the sea, the riverbeds undergo threshold changes, from braided, to meandering, to straight, with the latter in some cases assuming multichannel, anastomosed patterns (Baker 1986: 257–59, figs. 4 and 5 citing Schumm and Khan 1972). River meanders leave fossil traces up to several kilometers in width, characterized by more or less parallel, curvilinear ridges on their crests (Gasche and Tanret 1998: 5–7). Their contours can be preserved for millennia, due in part to their durable function in shaping subsequent agricultural systems as they delineate systems of irrigation dikes and levees that hold recessional silt and demarcate field and crop boundaries. The breadth and periodicity of relict meanders were determined by channel size, sediment load, bank resistance, and volume and flow rate of water discharge (Verhoeven 1998; Baker 1986; Adams 1981: 8). This aids identification of system components and comparison with modern systems (Pournelle 2003a: figs. 19, 21; Pournelle 2003b: fig. 6).

Down the upper Mesopotamian alluvium, meandering systems are visible within the relatively narrow belts of their archaic floodplains. Between Samarra and Adab, Adams posited interconnecting watercourses among hundreds of Late Uruk sites. Others posited riparian connections between 'Ubaid and Early Uruk towns such as Ras Al-Amiya and 'Uqair (Stronach 1961; Adams 1981; Adams and Nissen 1972; Wilkinson 1990b). Careful analysis of imagery and remotely sensed elevation data shows the seemingly interconnected meanders and levees of this zone to be a palimpsest dating primarily to

---

[4] Three accessible copies of the KLM mosaics are known to have existed. One, held by Hunting Surveys Ltd. and its successors, and utilized for its numerous development contracts in Iraq, was discarded by company librarians in 1989. Multiple frames of this set, along with related geomorphologic assessments, were salvaged and are currently held privately. A partial second set, held for field reference at the Deutches Archälogisches Institut excavation house at Warka, is now presumably held by the Iraqi government. The whereabouts of the original set, made available to Adams for field use by the Director General of Antiquities in the 1960s and 1970s, is unknown.

the Pleistocene, on the one hand, and to the late third/mid-second millennium BC, on the other. Late ʿUbaid through Uruk sites seem instead to have been situated within the aggrading floodplain of anastomosing channels (see Pournelle 2003b: 145–155). This situation certainly allowed for exploitation of littoral biomass (food, construction materials), intensification of intersite boat traffic, and (related to this) exploitation of bitumen seeps for waterproofing. Only after the fourth millennium BC, following the progradation of the Mesopotamian delta, did this Tigris/Euphrates admixture become canalized and subject to the more or less continuous human intervention that has so profoundly affected the hydrologic evolution of lower Mesopotamia.

Studies of toponyms in third- and second-millennium BC cuneiform texts recording shipping and travel itineraries along stretches of the major watercourses largely confirm this view (Nissen 1985; Steinkeller 2001). E. C. Stone (2002b) critiques details of Steinkeller's (2001) argument, but broadly agrees that the watercourse serving Umma and Zabalam was a distributary branch of the Tigris. Areas to the west and south of Uruk *were* significantly augmented by delivery from the Euphrates into fluvial catchments now defined by present-day Euphrates flood zones, the Eridu Basin, and the western portion of Lake Hammar. While details of these interconnecting channels are still being worked out, dated, and confirmed, it is now clear that the later primacy of cities such as Isin, Kish, and Babylon postdate this state of affairs. Progressive channel successions (under conditions of climatic drying and seasonalization) resulted in the view of ancient Mesopotamian cities as pearls strung through the desert, as well as the eventual separation of the Tigris and Euphrates systems. Geomorphological reconstruction of major fluvial systems from Samarra south to Eridu (Northedge, Wilkinson, and Falkner 1989; Gasche and Tanret 1998; Wilkinson 1990a; Adams 1981; E. C. Stone 2002b) paint a revolutionary picture of the Tigris's overall contribution to alluvial settlement and irrigation during the subsequent third and second millennia BC.

Deltaic Changes

In the Tigris-Euphrates alluvium south of Adab, where average surface elevation drops barely 2 meters per 100 kilometers (Cotha Consulting Engineers 1959: fig. 4.1), few relict meanders are visible. Instead, from roughly the 32nd parallel southward to the high desert lands skirting the south rim of the Eridu depression, surface morphology is strewn with relict landforms characteristic of a delta. Orbital imagery is of prime importance to the study of these landforms, as it allows entire deltas to be examined in the context of their surroundings (Coleman, Roberts, and Huh 1986: 317).

Considerable effort has been expended in clarifying alluvial processes and main channel formation during the early historical periods from the third to first millennia BC (Wilkinson 1990b; Gasche, Herman, and Tanret, 1998; E. C. Stone 2002b). South and east of a line between Shuruppak and Jidr, an area where watercourses are from the earliest historical times epigraphically well attested, much of the ground was covered by standing water, drifting dunes, and accumulated alluvial silt. Current understanding of regional climate cycles and mid-Holocene marine transgressions makes clear the need to account in antiquity not only for altered coastlines, but for marsh, estuary, and deltaic conditions such as those now[5] obtaining along, south, and east of the modern Shatt al-Gharraf, the lower Tigris and Euphrates, the Shatt al-Arab, and the delta mouth on the Persian Gulf (Sanlaville 1996; Geyer and Sanlaville 1996; Kouchoukos 1998; Aqrawi 1997).

Within the lower alluvium, two zones of geomorphologic action may be distinguished. The first is the outer delta, where rivers dump their sediment loads into the sea. Northwestward lies the inner delta (the primary focus of this study), a flood-prone region of channel and marsh formation (Wirth 1962). The joint Tigris-Euphrates outer delta, constrained in its outflow westward by the Wadi Batin fluvial cone, and eastward by the Karkheh-Karun Deltas emanating from the Susa plateau, is characterized by a littoral zone transitioning from (1) freshwater marshes at the Tigris-Euphrates confluence at Qurna, through (2) brackish channels south of Basra and the Karun confluence at Mhuhammera, to (3) permanent salt marshes at the Persian Gulf head. North of Basra, annual floodwaters mingled, spread, and slowed as they met the strong action of tidal flushing. Here lies a domain where permanent and seasonal lakes and marshes prevailed until massive agricultural reclamation programs completed in 2001 drained the joint Tigris-Euphrates outflow directly into Gulf waters (National Aeronautics and Space Administration 2000; 2001; Partow 2001; Kouchoukos 1998; Sanlaville 1996).

The mid-Holocene marine transgression, pushing gradually northward through the deltaic cones during the sixth to fourth millennia BC and subsequently receding, at its maximum pushed the brackish estuary zone inland and further slowed outflow already constrained by the Wadi Batin and Karun-Karkheh Deltas (Potts 1997: 31–42, 47–55; Kouchoukos 1998: 216–231; Sanlaville 1989; 1996; el-Moslimany 1994; Lambeck 1996; Aqrawi 1997; 2001; Pournelle 2003a: 107–129; 2004a). Thus, conditions similar to those obtaining in twentieth-century Tigris-Euphrates marshlands would at that time have been

---

[5] By 2001, these marshlands ceased to exist (Partow 2001), However, repetition of the phrase "until the close of the past decade," while accurate, is needlessly tedious. Unless otherwise noted, throughout I adopt the convention of a historical present as of 1968–1969, the year documented by the CORONA photographs.

extended along then-extant river distributaries north and west of the present-day Shatt al-Gharraf, into the Warka (Uruk) and Eridu survey areas (Geyer and Sanlaville 1996; Sanlaville 1996; Aqrawi 1997) (Figure 12). The CORONA photographs, imaged before massive irrigation, drainage, and water diversion projects brought an end to millennia-old marsh formation processes, allow us to compare the geomorphology of active Lower Tigris-Euphrates delta, marsh, and alluvium formation with that of the now-desertic Chalcolithic urban heartland. Relict landscapes are photographically revealed especially clearly following the May Euphrates floods that saturate soils, replenish groundwater, and temporarily cover tracts of what is now desert with sheets of water that ultimately drain through a series of seasonal lakes into the Shatt al-Arab. In the Warka and Eridu survey areas, the more comprehensive photographic record may be referenced to the limited, but not insubstantial archaeological record. Ground evidence includes artifacts, botanical and faunal remains, stratigraphic profiles, and other geomorphologic data where it has been recorded.

Levees, "Bird's" Feet, and Dune Deposits

Three relict features help to chart and date the relict fluvial system in its entirety. Over time, flood deposits along riparian distributaries build massive levees. Examination of the putative Chalcolithic alluvial zone in the now-arid Warka survey area revealed a 5-kilometer-wide levee system, extending south–southeast from meander traces recorded by Adams near Warka Survey (WS) site 175, to a series of distributaries dissipating into relict marshland from site WS 427 to WS 447. The width of these eroded natural levees indicates a past discharge capacity equivalent to that of the modern-day Tigris south of Amara (Pournelle 2003a: figs. 20–22; 2003b: fig. 4). Chains of sites situated along and on top of such levees can indicate the dates for the system. Sites located on top of flood season discharge splays, where dramatic annual flooding would make permanent habitation exceedingly hazardous and unlikely, can serve as termini post quem for active inundation from the breach, aiding in dating the system of which they form a part (Pournelle 2003a: fig. 25; 2003b: fig. 5).

Active sediment deposition as rivers abruptly slow on encountering slack water results in the multiple, bifurcating channels of a "bird's-foot" delta, with newly forming sediment deposits creating webs between the toes, such as those surrounding Warka and present-day Amara (Pournelle 2003a: fig. 26; 2003b: fig. 7). In arid coastal climates, alluvial sediments also form similar depositional lobes between dune channels and behind dune dams (Wells 2001). During floods, active channels may scour and rescour, mixing sedimentary layers. The complicated stratigraphy of such structures may be more clearly revealed in overview than by individual core samples (Figure 13).

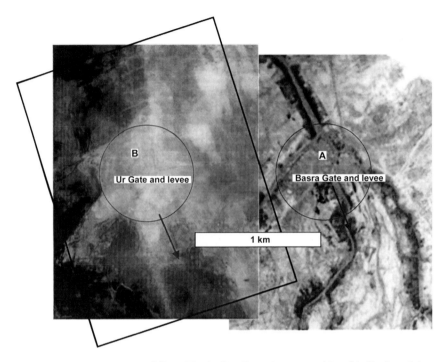

Figure 13. (A) Amara, straddling Tigris distributaries arrayed in a bird's-foot delta rapidly built outward into surrounding marshlands by riverbank rice cultivation (Buringh 1960: 187). Rice cropping is not thought to have been introduced before the late first millennium BC (Ghirshman 1954), although it was practiced in the Indus Valley at least a millennium earlier (Chakrabarti 1994). (B) Warka (ancient Uruk), straddling a relict bird's-foot delta extending into spring Euphrates floodwaters (black). As late summer heat dries surrounding marshes and lowers the water table, lower areas and infilled drainage are marginally wetter, and therefore darker. Less permeable, higher, and drier built-up areas, levees, and consolidated canal beds appear lighter in tone. Source: (A) USGS CORONA KH4B_1103-1A-D041-065 (May 1968); (B) KH4B_1107-2170DA-139 (August 1969).

Turtlebacks Rising

During the pluvial end–late Pleistocene Würm marine regression, rivers scoured channels of up to 40 meters in depth, leaving terraces (at former plain-level) protruding above the water surface and dumping the scoured sediments at delta mouths. Valleys between these terraces were infilled with silts from later alluviation, leaving the impression of a uniform surface. However, during mid-Holocene flood seasons, the tops of these relict terraces and sediment dumps, being of slightly higher elevation, would have remained dry whenever the surrounding plain became inundated by sheets of floodwater, like turtle's backs protruding from a silty tidal flat. In Egypt, systematic coring programs show that deltaic urban precursors clustered upon these features, safe above seasonal inundation (van den Brink 1993; Butzer 2001).

In the lower Mesopotamian alluvium, relict turtlebacks imaged during the spring spate, when floodwaters saturate lower-lying ground, can be identified by micro-drainage and differential dampening at their bases, making their slight relief above plain level detectable (Pournelle 2003a: figs. 75–66; 2003b: fig. 3).[6] These wind-scoured features are the loci for the oldest-known settlements in southern Mesopotamia (Figure 14).

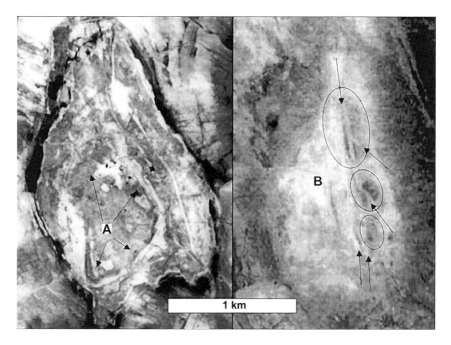

Figure 14. (A) Tello (ancient Girsu) appears to float on an island within irrigated croplands. The archaic city walls encompass one-third of the turtleback land area. (B) WS 230–232, arrayed along internal canals within a turtleback. The high water table following spring floods damps dust and reveals fine details of relief invisible at other seasons. The dark body at the left is a cloud shadow. Source: USGS CORONA KH4B_1103-1A-D041-057 (May 1968).

---

[6] Excavations at Tell Oueili (WS 460) confirm that the underlying geomorphology is analogous to similar sites in the Nile Delta. At Oueili, Pleistocene buttes punctuate a Holocene surface incised to several meters deep by the Shatt al-Kar east of the site. Oueili is situated atop one of these earlier surfaces, revealed by excavation as a buried turtleback, where it was most likely located for protection from seasonal flooding. A deep sounding showed 4 meters of alluvial deposition surrounding and eventually burying the channels that would have carried waters past its 'Ubaid 0 foundations (Porada et al. 1992: 86; Geyer and Sanlaville 1996; Plaziat and Sanlaville 1991).

A THIRD ECONOMIC PILLAR

The Holocene paleogeology of the lower alluvium suggests that a larger role must be given to littoral ecotones as a "third pillar" of the formative Mesopotamian economy. Interpretation of surface and excavation finds in light of the photographic evidence summarized above suggests a settlement progression beginning in the Neolithic ʿUbaid with opportunistic dependence on littoral biomass, and ending in the Bronze Age Early Dynastic, with intensive usage of what by then had become agriculturalized marsh zones. For the earlier Neolithic (ʿUbaid 0) periods, as sea levels slowly rose from 15 meters below to within several meters of their current levels (Sanlaville 1989), mid-Holocene (6000/5500–3500 BC) monsoon variations brought increased rainfall to the lower alluvium (el-Moslimany 1994; see Potts 1997: chap. 1, p. 52 passim). Because freshwater outflow to the Gulf is in any case constrained by the twin cones of the Wadi Batin and Karun-Karkeh drainages, even absent the effects of tidal forcing concomitant with later progradation of the Gulf head, these comparatively pluvial conditions would have increased the likelihood of seasonal flooding and marsh formation. Such evidence as exists from coring, excavation stratigraphies, and stratigraphic profiles drawn from regional wells uniformly shows marshy deposits underlying and/or mixed with earliest (ʿUbaid) occupation layers, suggesting that settlements were bordering on and/or subject to seasonal inundation (van Ess and Brückner, personal communication 2002; Nöldeke et al. 1932: 6, table 2; Eichman 1989: 197; Geyer and Sanlaville 1996; Woolley 1933: 328, 334–336, pls. 39, 42; Woolley 1956: pls. 76–78, 82, 83; Safar, Mustafa, and Lloyd 1981: 47, 58; Aqrawi 2001).

Buried Foundations

The little evidence available from excavation indicates a long period of Neolithic ʿUbaid adaptation to littoral conditions. No surface finds can be dated to ʿUbaid 0, but botanical finds from the deep sounding at Tell Oueili, which was situated on a low Pleistocene turtleback surrounded by infilled channels (Huot 1989; 1991; 1996; Forest 1996), suggest that water pooled near the site. These included edible sedge tubers *(Cyperus rotundus)* and giant reed *(Phragmites australis)* (Neef 1989). Near Ur, type site al-ʿUbaid was founded on a low sand knoll (H. R. Hall 1930; Hall and Woolley 1927), and site ES (Eridu Survey) 104 on a Euphrates levee. Comparison of ʿUbaid 1 pottery from al-ʿUbaid (H. R. Hall 1930) with ʿUbaid 0 type ware (Huot 1996) shows clearly the need for reseriation and reconstruction of early occupations, and the possibility of a much earlier origin for the ʿUbaid type site.

Similarly, the early foundations of the third-millennium BC city of Larsa bordered marshes fed by a great Tigris distributary running southward from Jidr.

Two additional ʿUbaid 1 sites (Haji Mohammed and W 267) were aligned north to south along a distributary dissipating into marshlands south of Warka. South of the present-day Euphrates, Eridu itself was founded on consolidated dune material, straddling the mouth of a branch of the Euphrates. Beneath later sacred areas were pedestaled mud structures, presaging a succession of temples with burnt offerings of fish (Safar, Mustafa, and Lloyd 1981; Porada et al. 1992), as well as a canoe model and numerous perforated clay ovoids, perhaps net weights (Lloyd and Safar 1948: 118, pl. III).

Four more so-called ʿUbaid 2 sites were also apparent on distributary levee back slopes, one of which, WS 247, overlooked (undated) westerly marshes. WS 242, the first of what would become a complex of sites characterized by surface finds of spools and net weights, was situated at the juncture of the Uruk levee with an anastomosing channel continuing southeastward to join the Tigris system. In marsh districts near al-Hiba (Lagash), characterized by a mixed agro-pastoral-fishing-reed manufacturing economy, similar spools and weights were used during the twentieth century to spin yarn and to weight fishing and fowling nets (Ochsenschlager 1993b). WS 298, a low mound located about 10 kilometers northeast of Uruk, was situated on a turtleback, in this case also facing a levee back slope.

During ʿUbaid 3, although Oueili itself appears to have undergone an occupation hiatus, WS 459 appeared adjacent to it. Surface finds were noted at Jidr, and at another new site, WS 275, located on a turtleback at the back slope of the Uruk levee. South of the modern Euphrates, ES 29, situated on a sand knoll at the Euphrates passage through the Hazim, was first occupied, as was ES 96, on a levee back slope. The Late ʿUbaid 3 site ES 141, 8 kilometers northwest of al-ʿUbaid, was similarly situated and had concentrations of freshwater mollusk on its surface. Wright noted an "expansion of settled areas up and down the developing levee system at this time" (H. T. Wright 1981b: 323). At Eridu, "temple platforms were raised, and clear evidence of mud brick directly associated with adjacent reed domestic construction was exposed" (Safar 1950: 28). This emphasis on levee colonization may have been directly tied to mastery and reliance on water travel as far away as the Persian Gulf, as evidenced by boat fragments and Mesopotamian-manufactured ʿUbaid-period pottery found among deep shell middens bordering Kuwait (Beech, Elders, and Shepherd 2000; R. Carter 2006; R. Carter and Crawford 2001; R. Carter et al. 1999; Frifelt 1989; Roaf 1996; Oates 1976; 1978).

Archaeological evidence from the southern alluvium throughout the later Neolithic is consistent with a riparian distributary system and concomitant marshy zone, shading from seasonal inundation to permanent lakes. At ʿUbaid-period Uruk, Haji Mohammed, al-ʿUbaid, Ur, and Eridu, the deepest soundings all revealed remains of reed platforms, traces of reed structures with plastered reed walls, and reed matting plastered with dung, earth, or

bitumen in addition to mud brick (summarized in Moorey 1994: 361). Inhabitants of the southern alluvium had liberal access not only to water supplies
and transport, but to littoral biomass. As in later periods, the area probably
provided food, including reed and other tubers, fish, shellfish, fowl, and pig
(Pollock 1999: 83; Desse 1983; Safar 1950; Safar, Mustafa, and Lloyd 1981);
construction material, including reeds and riparian woods (Salim 1962;
Thesiger 1964; Ochsenschlager 1993a; Potts 1997: 106–115); fodder and
browse, including reeds and sedges (Miller-Rosen and Weiner 1994; Miller-
Rosen 1995; Pournelle 2003b), and reeds as fuel for kilns and smoke-houses
(Englund 2002; Salim 1962; Thesiger 1964; Ochsenschlager 1993a).

Visible Settlement Trends

Thus far, the oldest period reached beneath the tens of meters of overburden at
Uruk dates to ʿUbaid 4/Terminal ʿUbaid. On surfaces exposed to Aeolian
scouring, settlement trends become somewhat more visible. Surface finds show
five new sites (WS 137, 160, 218, 260, 411) on turtlebacks, three abutting levee
back slopes. One, Raidu Sharqi, is added to a delta toe southwest of Uruk. At
Oueili, added to the earlier botanical constellation of tubers and reeds are cultivated date palm *(Phoenix dactylifera)*, water-loving poplar *(Populus euphratica)*,
and sea club-rush *(Scirpus maritimus)*, while faunal emphasis continues on cattle and pig (Neef 1989). Date cultivation suggests associated gardens and the
need for mechanisms to determine access to and control of the turtleback,
which was probably surrounded by marshes draining into seasonal lakes. Eridu,
12 hectares in extent, sported a temple on a raised terrace and, for some individuals, substantial brick tombs. Boat models indicate the use of sailing craft.
Bales of fried marine fish were recovered in the so-called temple precinct
(more likely, administrative storehouses), as well as from the altar, where they
were presumably laid as offerings. Botanical remains also included dates (Safar
1950; Gillet 1976; Safar, Mustafa, and Lloyd 1981; H. T. Wright 1981b).
Meanwhile, Ur and al-ʿUbaid had grown to about 10 hectares in size (H. R.
Hall 1930; Safar, Mustafa, and Lloyd 1981). Two sites (ES 73 and 134) were
added to the levee, and one (ES 5) to a large turtleback. Clay sickle distribution
indicates extensive harvesting along levee back slopes (H. T. Wright 1981b).
Wear pattern and phytolith analyses of similar sickles make intensive reed-har-
vesting for fodder and construction material likely (Anderson-Gerfaud 1983:
177–191; Benco 1992: 119–134).

    As rising sea levels reached (3800 BC) and then exceeded by 1 or 2
meters those of today (3500 BC), during the Early/Middle Uruk period the
Gulf head prograded as far north and east as modern Qurna. This marine
incursion would have resulted in tidal flushing as far northeast as Ur, and
perhaps as far as Uruk itself (Figure 12). This would have been accompanied
by at least seasonal marsh formation over all but the highest ground of the

Warka and Eridu survey areas, as the outlets of the combined Tigris and Euphrates discharge became flooded, slowing drainage to the sea. Not surprisingly, during this period, settlement was marked by a continuing colonization of turtlebacks.

Four new sites (WS 20, 22, 23, 24) clustered on the Uruk levee and its back slope in the vicinity of WS 42, all yielding fishing net weights and spools. Site WS 245exploits the same back slope locale as the 'Ubaid 2 site WS 247. In a completely new development, regularized waterways up to 12 kilometers in length may have extended south from the Tigris tributary levee to site WS 107, to site WS 109, and to sites WS 178-201-215. These are aligned respectively toward turtleback sites WS 137, 160, and 218. Similar village distributions are visible today, extending southward from the Euphrates as it wends through the eastern Iraqi marshes—for example, near Kabaish (ech-Chubayish) (Roux 1960; Salim 1962) (Figure 15), indicating that these waterways need not be interpreted as canals extending through arid zones. It is equally likely that they represent permanent boat transport routes between turtlebacks, with villages along their banks, kept clear of reeds during wet seasons and allowing access to the river during dry.

In the Eridu basin, only a few sites were classified as Early Uruk, and this was based on a handful of sherds and the absence of bevel-rim bowls. Assessing whether or not this indicates a hiatus in settlement foundation in the southern marshes depends upon better dating for sickle manufactures, and an assessment of the persistence (or not) of 'Ubaid pottery traditions. More likely, 'Ubaid-style levee exploitation either continues or dates to a somewhat later period. Spot elevations clearly show the Eridu basin (sloping northwest to southeast from 4 to 0.5 meters above mean sea level) separated from present-day Gulf waters to the west and south by the rising Arabian plateau. It is demarcated to the southeast by a 100-kilometer-broad expanse of sandy uplands standing over 24 meters above current sea level. Dune fields blanketing these uplands show no trace of intervening shorelines (General Staff of the Army 1941; Russian National Cartographic Authority 1991a; 1991b). To the east and northeast, the depression is flanked by a sandstone ridge (the Hazim), which *rises* from 3 meters to 46 meters above mean sea level from northwest to southeast (Safar, Mustafa, and Lloyd 1981: 30). Even at this period of maximum marine transgression, Eridu itself could have been situated on an ancient Gulf coastline. Imagery shows no evidence of seawater having either cut or surmounted this feature. Instead, there is much evidence of this depression having formed a closed, marshy basin, characterized by pooling, ponding, and drying of water, derived in part from wadis down-cutting from the Arabian plateau, but mostly from Euphrates flooding. A cut through the Hazim indicates outflow *toward* the Gulf, passing into a well-defined levee system skirting Ur and Tell al-Lahm.

Figure 15. Top: Suwaich (Kabaish; ech-Chubaish), extending several kilometers along a waterway in the Hammar marshes south of Qalat Salih. Only bright white spots are above the water surface. The name means "lace of built islands." In 1959, access was solely by water (black), through thick reed swamps (dark gray). Source: USGS CORONA KH4B_1107-2170DA-139 (August 1969). **Insets:** Bargat Bghadad was situated deep within the permanent marsh northeast of Suwaich. Drains emptied Lake Hammar, leaving the town high and dry. Now desiccated, house groupings appear situated along canals that were in fact waterways through the village. Source: Google Earth Digital Globe 2006. Below this, another example of a former waterway through the reed beds that now (erroneously) appears to be a chain of small settlements strung along a canal. Source: LANDSAT 1994. **Bottom:** East of al-Harb, drainage channels slice through the remains of raised-field gardens once located *within* Lake Hammar. Deprived of its livelihood, the population has fled. There is actually no association between the desiccated village waterways and what appears as a modern canal.

As sea levels and the Gulf shoreline fell back to approximately their present locations, these Early Uruk inroads presaged what at first review appears to be a site explosion during the Late Uruk. Over 100 new sites spread, fan-like, north and east from the emergent city at Warka, south from the levee system tying the Uruk and Tigris channels, and westward from the Tigris levee (no surveys having been conducted to the east). This site distribution has been interpreted as an opening up of land area amenable to grain cultivation. However, it is more an artifact of site visibility, indicating only the vertical limits of aeolian scouring through soft silts in exposing buried sites, and suggests that no *further* inundation occurred *after* the Late Uruk (see Pournelle 2003b: figs. 59, 77).

Until the Gulf head had fully withdrawn, despite a gradual shifting of the permanent marsh zone southward, we must assume that tidal flushing would have influenced cultivation regimes as far inland as Lake Hammar. This would be true even though summer rains were by this late date surely gone, and the climate had become more seasonal (as at present). The riparian regime appears to have been relatively stable until at least the late third millennium BC (Akkadian), when the Euphrates bed appears to have flipped into a southerly channel skirting the Eridu depression (depicted by H. T. Wright 1981b), perhaps obscuring earlier sites. Intensification of cattle production in riparian and littoral habitats would have simultaneously and steadily degraded browse, necessitating intensified fodder gathering and production (Belsky 1999). Contemporary protoliterate economic texts include dozens of ideographs for reeds and reed products, pigs, waterfowl, fish, dried fish, fish traps, dried and processed fish flour, as well as those for cattle and dairy products (Englund 1998). Palms, frogs, livestock emerging from reed byres, and hunting scenes with pigs stalked among reeds all appear on Late Uruk seals, sealings, and tablets recovered from Warka. Many tablets show the clear imprint of the reed mats upon which they lay as they dried (Boehmer 1999: 51–56, 66–67, 71–74, 90–104).

Notable is a match between the geographic clustering of sites around centers on turtlebacks with Adams's hypothetical Jemdet Nasr/ED I territories, based on site sizes and nearest neighbor analysis (Adams 1981: 20, fig. 8) (Figure 16). Among surface evidence, added to net weights, spools, and spindle whorls were a profusion of mace heads (Adams and Nissen 1972: 211–213), which could be indicators of local conflict (although they seem rather light in weight for this purpose) or local office. The profusion of visible Late Uruk small sites could therefore be evidence that, concomitant with intensified agricultural production, reed and other marsh products were becoming intensively harvested and administered to underwrite urbanizing consumption.

While protoliterate economic texts clearly show institutional control of marsh products, three site clusters strongly suggest that Uruk channel

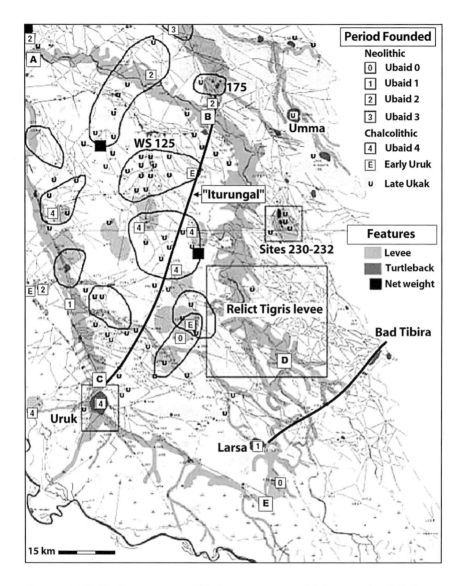

Figure 16. Relict levee systems, Warka survey area, with Iturungal and Bad Tibera waterways. Key indicates the earliest-suspected occupation for sites occupied during the Uruk (fourth millenium BC), with Jemdet Nasr/Early Dynastic nearest neighbor groupings. After Adams 1981; Steinkeller 2001.

management may have become integral to the management of the marshes themselves, as well as being a precursor to later irrigation technologies. Situated on a turtleback, sites WS 230–233 display an internal structure of modest, shallow waterways (Figure 14). These are unlikely to be natural, bearing a sharp resemblance to waterways ethnographically reported as being cleared during wet seasons and enlarged during dry, in order to extend boat transport through sites and to their surrounding marshes (Salim 1962; Thesiger 1958; 1964; see also Adams and Nissen 1972: 25). Site cluster WS 125 seems placed to control a series of modest offtakes from the west–east distributary, the 2-kilometer-wide fifth- to fourth-millennium BC levee of which underlies the modern trickle of the nearly abandoned Shatt al-Kar. Finally, multiple canal offtakes cut through the relict Euphrates levee abutting site ES 156 clearly directed water flow into the alluvial basin north of the site—but *not* into any apparent field irrigation system. Instead, the water flow seems designed to augment flood season catchment in what is now a desiccated wetland. The surface morphology of the area is directly comparable to desiccated habitation areas on the seasonally inundated edges of massive, permanent marsh reed beds such as those of the Al Khuraib marsh south of Amara (Figure 17).

Investigations of the Nile Delta (van den Brink 1989; 1993; Butzer 2001) and Chad (Holl 2001) suggest that in lacustrine borderlands characterized by seasonal marshes, such sites have long histories and comprise wet-season retreats for cattle herders who, as waters recede, moved animals downslope to graze resulting pastures. Site clusters WS 230 and WS 125 are examples that prefigure two predominant proto-urban locations: turtlebacks (Adab, Girsu, Oueili, Lagash, Nina, Eridu)[7] and levee-straddling cities, often sprawling over bird-foot distributary clusters (Jidr, Larsa, Shuruppak, Umma, Uruk, Ur) (Figure 18). Both site types comprised mid-Holocene "high ground" retreats, accessible by boat at least during the wet season. But, over time, given regional drying, only those along persistent distributaries would have continued to be accessible by water. Wilkinson notes that

> localized cleaning and management of [a] node of avulsion or bifurcation could have maintained flow in both channels . . . thereby substantially increasing the water supply and transportation network. . . . It is not clear which . . . large-scale canal digging or the semi-managed avulsion of anastomosing channels, produced the network that nourished the early cities. . . . Algaze's synergistic cauldron may therefore benefit from the consideration of these two human-environmental interactive systems. (Wilkinson 2001: 255)

---

[7] The Eridu location is difficult to classify, as it seems to have been situated on paleo-dunes embraced by distributary arms within an active alluvial basin. The point is that, compared with its surroundings, it embraced the (comparatively) high ground.

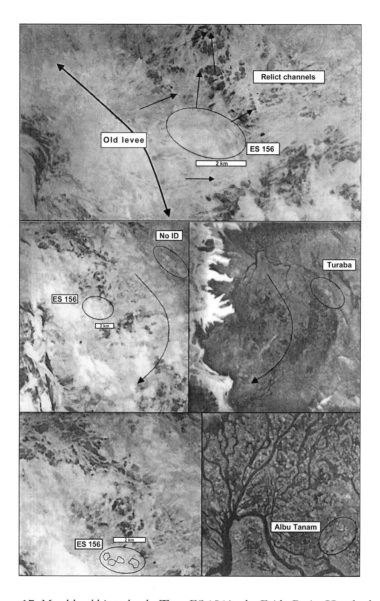

Figure 17. Marshland hinterlands. **Top:** ES 156 in the Eridu Basin. Hundreds of thread-like channels, 1.5–10 meters wide, extend between ES 156 and surrounding desiccated wetlands, suggesting levee cultivation combined with intensive marshland exploitation. **Middle:** (L) ES 156 (R) Turaba in the al-Khuraib (Tigris) marshes south of Amara. Water overtops banks and leaks through weak levees, draining slowly to eventually rejoin the fluvial system (arrows). **Bottom:** (L) Desiccated (white) water channels infilled with dry sand skirt ES 156. (R) Dendritic water channels (black) through reed beds skirt Abu Tanam. Source: (L) KH4B_1103-1A-D041-067 (May 1968); (R) KH4B_1107-2170DA-140 (August 1969).

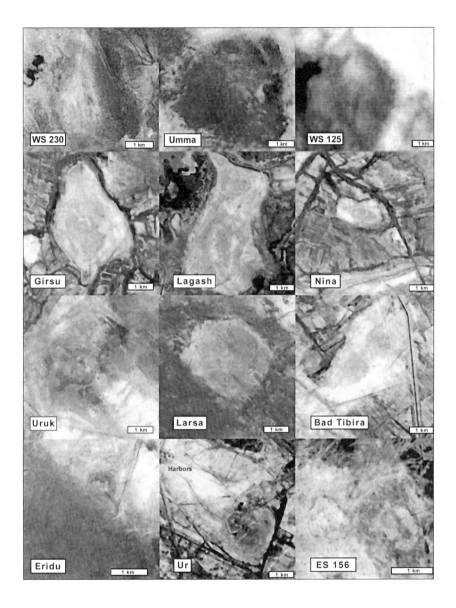

Figure 18. Deltaic Mesopotamian cities and surrounding wetlands, past and present. WS 125, Umma, WS 230, ES 156: USGS CORONA May 1968. All others: NIMA SPOT 1991. Scales approximate.

For example, the remarkably straight line of a posited route for the "Iturungal" connecting Uruk with the levee junction near site WS 175 (Steinkeller 2001) suggests an executed canal that also captured the water

traffic and produce of earlier, smaller-scale catchments dominated by turtleback settlements. The situation of a sweeping arc from Larsa to Bad
Tibira (Steinkeller 2001) suggests that this "canal" should be understood as
a transport waterway kept cleared for boat traffic through, and along the
edge of, marshy zones (Figures 15, 17).

Enduring Wetlands Capital

During the historical Early Dynastic III period (2600–2350 BC), sea levels
once again rose to 1 meter above present (Sanlaville 1989; Potts 1997: 33),
and thus in areas not yet transformed by state irrigation and drainage
schemes, a similar hydrologic regime to that of the late Chalcolithic probably
prevailed. All known third–second millennium BC (land) itineraries from
Sumer to Susa run first northwest to the Diyala region, and then southeast to
their destination, suggesting a requirement to circumnavigate a marine incursion. East of the Warka survey area, a relict levee, cut by modern canals,
extends into a seasonal flood zone. Ancient Lagash surmounts another levee
remnant, appearing as an island to the south surmounted by multiple occupation mounds (Pournelle 2003b: fig. 9). There, ED III faunal remains included
not only seven species of marine mollusk shell (which could merely have been
imported for bead manufacture; E. Carter 1990; Kenoyer 1990), but two of
marine fish, as well as duck, coot, cormorant, flamingo, gull, and spoonbill.
Spoonbill particularly prefer open marshes, shallow lagoons, and estuarine
mud flats (Mudar 1982: 29–30, 33–34).[8] Analysis of faunal remains from the
1970–1971 excavations of distinct temple and administrative/residential precincts showed a decided separation in their distribution. All fish, fowl, and
mollusk (shell) were found in the administrative/residential zone; none in the
temple area. This marked differentiation in consumption was also noted for
mammalian finds. In the temple precinct, as compared with the residential/
administrative precinct, ovicaprids represented a proportionally higher, cattle
a slightly higher, and pig a significantly lower percentage of finds (Mudar
1982). It is tempting to conclude that (elite) mutton and beef had become
appropriate as temple offerings and priestly food, while pork had become less
so, and fish inappropriate. If so, this reversal from the 'Ubaid precincts at
Eridu demarcates a transition from a time of Neolithic social integration

---

[8] Of note is the lack of 'Ubaid or Uruk finds, indicating that in Chalcolithic times
    the Gulf transgression either precluded permanent habitation altogether or con-
    fined it to relatively small areas, not subject to seasonal inundation, now deeply
    buried beneath subsequent occupation debris. That the earlier periods are repre-
    sented at nearby Tello (Girsu) and Shurgal (Nina) supports the latter probability.

served by fish as everyman's food, to one of Bronze Age social hierarchy marked by fish as poor man's food.

Although probably well above the mean, al-Hiba was hardly unique in its littoral reliance. Robert Englund has treated at length the regulation and management of late third-millennium Ur III fisheries (Englund 1990). Cylinder sealings from the ED III Seal Impression Strata at Ur depict reed structures (Amiet 1961: 333–344), cattle fed in and led from reed byres (Amiet 1961: 337, 342, 344), personages poled along fish-filled watercourses in high-prowed boats (Amiet 1961: 300), fishing from small watercraft (Amiet 1961: 310), and persons carrying tribute of fish and waterfowl (Amiet 1961: 302, 303). Umma texts record quotas for the production of reed, bitumen, boats mats, and standardized fish baskets (de Genouillac 1920: 603). Proto-Elamite lexical lists record 58 terms relating to wild and domestic pigs. "Professions lists" record offices including "fisheries governor" and "fisheries accountant" that endure one and one-half millennia to the Old Babylonian period (Englund 1998).

This administration of marshland resources was not a mere addendum to a better-studied agro-pastoral irrigation economy. Just as excavation overly focused on massive temple and administrative architecture has skewed attention to and perception of the scope and scale of Mesopotamian domestic settlement, osteological analysis overly focused on large mammalian fauna has skewed attention to and perception of the littoral component of the domestic diet. "For the vast majority of the working population, the primary dietary protein source was dried fish" (Englund, personal communication 2000). Its managerial origins in earlier hydrostrategies were *a priori* dependent upon a wetland landscape that endured in various forms for seven millennia, and one that only during the twentieth century AD finally was dammed, diked distributed, drained, and managed to extinction (Iraq 1956; Koucher 1999; Partow 2001). Early Dynastic foundations were, from a geographic perspective, well laid during the 'Ubaid 4 and were apparently predicated and dependent upon littoral communications with their hinterlands. During the Chalcolithic, 'Ubaid, and Early Uruk, palm groves, gardens, temples, kilns, and other institutions, long consolidated on turtlebacks and levees away from seasonal inundation by peoples accustomed to thorough exploitation of wetlands, became loci for Uruk political and economic transformations. These in turn laid the institutional foundations for subsequent Early Dynastic management, replication, and intensification of marshland production.

CONCLUSION: RESOURCES AND (SOCIAL) ENGINEERING

Exploitation of marshland resources made agricultural colonization of the southern Mesopotamian alluvium enduringly possible. Specialized communities harvested marsh fowl, fish, bitumen, shell, and reeds; grazed herds on and cut fodder from pastures watered by receding floodwaters; and traded boat cargoes with near-neighbors. Sixth- and fifth-millennium BC settlements initially took localized advantage of productive littoral ecotones. By practicing local, small-scale damming and diking to build up permanently habitable platforms and to control the rate and progression of flooding and runoff, they accumulated "hydrologic capital" that gave them possession of the most suitable landscapes, led to the invention of technologies for flood and irrigation control, and developed institutions for labor mobilization.

Resource complementarities would, of course, have provided local resiliency. But just as important would have been the replicability of these small, bounded, human-maintained ecosystems at each meander loop, on each turtleback, and at each levee junction. In such locales, locally shifting land usage brought minimal acreage into well-drained cultivation. Such specializations and complementarities thus could have been maintained beyond the reach of any locally destructive flood or drought. Communities sustained by marshland biomass and fed by the combination of farming, fishing, and husbandry could produce sufficiently consistent agricultural surpluses and sufficiently robust trade networks to tilt the balance toward consolidation of local management structures. This preceded the work of straightening and regularizing channels and building new canals that came to characterize and fuel urban growth during the third millennium.

Insightful Mesopotamian scholars have long considered the contribution of wetlands and water transport to pre-urban southern Mesopotamian material culture (Woolley 1929; 1955; 1956; Oates 1960; 1969; Potts 1997; Pollock 1999). However, only over the past decade has sufficient data accumulated to support the proposition that alluvial Mesopotamian cities grew from ʿUbaid precursors heavily participant in and reliant upon littoral subsistence and trade. Algaze's import substitution model (Algaze 2001a and this volume) must in this context be understood as a first delineation of the regional economic ramifications of this fundamental reassessment: a twofold "southern advantage" that may have overwhelmed the stability of supra-regional uniformity (or even advantages) in other social institutions. The first is the inexorable advantage of the riparian: it is simply easier to move bulky cargoes downstream than up, opening the possibility (from the southern Mesopotamian perspective) of downstream imports of bulk commodities in exchange for upstream exports of manufactured goods. The second is the inexorable advantage of the marsh, and not just in terms of its compounding the transportation advantage by opening pathways across the southern alluvium.[9] To be sure, Uruk's (and its sister cities') location would have conferred significant transportation advantages. But more importantly, in littoral ecotones, intensification of natural resource collection, hydrologic management, and cultivation are the primary mechanisms *both* for generating agronomic surplus *and* for buffering against its failure. By comparison, rain-fed grain farming is inherently more dependent on transportation advantages to overcome local or regional crop failures than wetlands exploitation and cultivation. In rain-fed zones, given comparable agricultural inputs, farmers can only increase production by enlarging the area under cultivation. During early urbanization and state formation, these marshlands—by 2001 almost fully destroyed, and therefore difficult to imagine in their former extent—would have acted as a nearly inexhaustible agro-pastoral buffer. Therefore, the greater resiliency here described is not merely a result of more varied resources (Wilkinson 2001), but of *more* resources.[10] To return to my opening comments, it is in this sense that one should understand Algaze's reference to greater fertility (Algaze 2001a: 200).

It was precisely at the time of increased local precipitation variability and during the general drying of the fourth millennium BC that the alluvial "Mesopotamian advantage" of higher resilience became crucial. This is true whether or not generally wetter mid-Holocene climate (Weiss and Bradley 2001; Cullen et al 2000; Bar-Matthews, Ayalon, and Kaufman 1997; Lemcke and Sturm 1997) or a summer monsoon effect deduced from paleobotanical data for the Arabian Peninsula (el-Moslimany 1994) positively affected Syro-Anatolia. In the south, the marsh littoral provided both a sustainable resource base and a model for hydrologic management, sustaining experiments in intensification that may well have sought to recreate and preserve previous natural conditions. These compounded geographic advantages fueled Algaze's "synergistic cauldron" and favored accelerated urbanizing processes.

---

[9] During the earlier Chalcolithic period, evidence for the movement of bulk goods is limited and (given the richness and perishability of available resources, unsurprisingly) local (H. T. Wright 1998). By the Late Uruk, when such evidence increases dramatically, routinized navigable routes would have been well established and, in a drying climatic regime, of heightened importance.

[10] Area-specific marsh resource productivity estimates for southern Iraq are at best fragmentary and will not be forthcoming, now that the marshes themselves have been consigned to oblivion (Partow 2001). A detailed demonstration of how productive the Mesopotamian marshlands might have been, given available technologies, will thus depend upon comparative proxies, for example, to the Ganges Delta or the (equally threatened) Florida Everglades. There, economic impact assessments show a dramatic decline in economic output following field drainage and the introduction of sugarcane monocropping (Hartmann 1994; McCalley 1999).

I do not mean to imply by this a crude environmental determinism. The situation of 'Ubaid towns, villages, temples, and associated temple economies on levees, turtlebacks, and marsh rims within the vast littoral created a kind of geographic circumscription-within-plenty. The high, dry ground itself, as well as associated permanent structures (temples, docks, ferries, kilns, and dwellings), could have become contested, but the resource base supporting them remained readily accessible. In considering early urbanization and the concomitant emergence of state-level institutions, this situation has profound scalar implications. "Northern 'Ubaid temples had the organizational technology to extract large-scale surpluses, but lacked the necessary resource base. Temples were thus a . . . critical factor in the development of Mesopotamian urbanism, but only when planted in the rich and diverse alluvium of the south" (G. Stein, personal communication to Algaze, 2001, emphasis added.)

Fish, shellfish, turtle, waterfowl, and pigs sustained human populations. Reeds, sedges, tubers, and seasonal grasses provided animal fodder and massive quantities of handicraft and construction material. Littoral ecotones constrained habitation. Annual floods replenished marshes and recessional gardens. The watery environment provided lines of communication that ensured rapid transmission of technologies, trade goods, and peoples themselves. All these factors concentrated resources, produce, institutions, and know-how into the hands of the few, setting the stage for hierarchy and heterarchy.

If adaptive flexibility explains the long history of cycling between urban agglomeration and ruralization in the southern alluvium, now that a voluminous body of investigations into the pastoral component of Sumerian agropastoral relationships have been undertaken (following Rowton 1973 and Adams 1981), the "third leg" of littoral resources must be carefully considered. Adams has long noted the role of marshlands as a place of flight from predatory rulership, and he never discounted their supplemental subsistence importance (Adams 1981; 2002). However, for the southern alluvium during the crucial sixth through fourth millennia BC, marshlands must be at the center stage of any nuanced discussion of adaptability and constraint. Proxies for specific "processes" of social organization and control are open to reinterpretation.

It could be charged that "ecological approaches . . . express an overriding concern for the adaptive features of societies" (Pollock 1992: 314), but emphasis on human ecology must be clearly distinguished from environmental determinism. Were marshlands sufficiently extensive to create a safe "inside passage" for primitive boat traffic eastward toward Susa? Is the cyclical history of Mesopotamian incursion along the Persian Gulf related to the same monsoonal cycle that alternatively encourages and discourages fishing and sailing?

It is precisely answers to these and similar questions that create "room for conscious manipulation and advantage-seeking behavior" (Pollock 1992: 314) that, at the close of the second millennium AD, obliterated the final vestiges of that ancient heartland of cities.

In this regard, in closing this short piece, I wish to lay down a marker toward further work on this bird's-eye view of cities like Uruk astride their bird's-foot deltas. As compared with rain-fed grain farming, which requires extensive landholdings, even absent any other (irrigated or otherwise) agricultural endeavor, exploitation of wetlands capital is especially dependent upon associated control of human capital. While reed crops have the advantage of virtually unlimited regenerative capacity, that capacity is dependent on hand-harvesting. Reed beds subjected to mechanical plowing, chopping below the waterline, or desiccation to allow easier access quickly die (Westlake, Kvet, and Szczepanski 1998). Wetland successor crops such as rice and sugarcane are notorious for their dependency on slave labor to establish and maintain profitability (Carney 2001; Galloway 1989; Rehder 1999; Seavoy 1998). As 'Ubaid towns grew, burgeoning demands for reed as food, animal fodder, fuel, and construction material would have, from a political-economic perspective, created selective pressure for labor intensification, with concomitant labor control by ideological, administrative, or other means. Indeed, administrative texts for the later Ur III period show that reed harvesting constituted a significant component of labor debt (Englund 2003); that reed transport constituted a significant component of boat cargoes (Sharlach 2004); that reed, along with fish and sheep, was an integral component of the bala exchange system (Sharlach 2004); and that, as for other foodstuffs (cereals and containers of fish), reed was probably a designator of an archaic metrological system (Chambon 2003).

While beyond the scope of this paper to fully explore, only a small intellectual leap is required to hypothesize that burgeoning reed-cutting sickle scatters are material evidence of such labor intensification in the hinterlands as early as the 'Ubaid period. The predominance of reeds, reed bundles, and reed structures as components of the very ideograms of Uruk protoliterate texts point to their major role in fourth-millennium tributary economies. It may well yet be proven that the lasting importance of those marsh-grown reeds was not only as a commodity per se, but in the way the demands of their production structured the political-economic underpinnings of urban-centered labor control. In short, when assessing labor requirements, along with the work involved in producing the barley that presumably filled the bevel-rim bowl, one must add that required to deliver the reeds to fire the kiln. In addition to the labor behind every woven wool textile, one must consider that behind the harvesting of the reeds that fed the sheep. In addition to the work that went into building every mud-brick wall, one must picture the productive effort that delivered the supports between the courses, the filler within the roof, and the matting that lined the walls and floors. From a bird's-eye view, that picture becomes compelling.

Cycles of Settlement in the Khorramabad Valley in Luristan, Iran*

Frank Hole

Abstract

This paper reports on an archaeological survey carried out in the Khorramabad Valley in the Luristan province of western Iran in the 1960s. The rugged topography of this region, with parallel mountain ridges, narrow valleys, and few passes, created small isolated pockets of favorable land for settlement with little potential for internal growth, but extensive forests and pastures. Until the nineteenth century, Luristan remained largely beyond the reach of history, despite its proximity to the literate civilizations of Mesopotamia and Iran. Lacking either unique resources or good routes, Luristan was isolated from the outside world as well as internally from one valley to the next. For long stretches of time, it is likely that the predominant mode of occupation was transhumant pastoralism.

Although relatively good archaeological sequences are known from adjoining regions, there is no single sequence of occupation for Luristan. Indeed, it appears that most sites were small and short-term, and for long stretches of time, Luristan may have lacked permanent settlements. When sites were

---

* I happily acknowledge the companionship of Kent Flannery and our government representative, Mohammed Khorramabadi in 1963, and in 1965 of John Durham and Jahangir Yassi. I am grateful for the assistance provided by the Ministry of Education and the Archaeological Service of Iran and for funding from National Science Foundation grants GS 67 and 724, Rice University, and the Smithsonian Institution. Help with various aspects of the ceramic analysis was provided by Yale students Yukiko Tonoike, David Fabricant, and Scott Gorman.

present, their ceramic parallels came from diverse regions, possibly reflecting shifting social, economic, and political alliances. Despite such hints of interaction, most of the material found in Luristan is unique to the region, a reflection of its prevailing isolation and unique modes of adaptation. In particular, there is the recurring domination by nomadic people who sometimes built forts at strategic locations, but otherwise left few remains other than tombs that have been discovered so far.

INTRODUCTION

Bob Adams pioneered the use of surface survey to write the history of several regions of Mesopotamia and adjacent Khuzistan, Iran. By their nature, such surveys reveal only a superficial outline of visible and recognizable remains, leaving much of the "history" to be filled in from written sources, archaeological excavation, and geographic contexts. While no region in the heartland of Mesopotamia has been thoroughly and comprehensively investigated through both survey and excavation, at least the major historical events, dynasties, and players are known over some 5000 years. For much of this time, there are rather detailed records that document economic activities, agricultural practices, religious rites, mythology, climatic events, political intrigue, and warfare. Moreover, where there have been detailed studies of modern soils, hydrology, and land use practices, it is often possible to make shrewd inferences about the ways these may have varied in the past. In short, when many strands of evidence are available, they can be woven together to construct a plausible history. Bob Adams was the first to draw on all these sources, and his studies have guided all who have followed.

Because of its rich documentary sources and abundant archaeological remains, Mesopotamia serves well as a model. However, in most of the Near East, one—or even many—of the sources that enriched Adams's research is lacking. Mesopotamia enjoyed fertile, highly productive soils and a large population, factors that permitted a relatively unbroken, internally consistent yet dynamic civilization to persist through the millennia. This picture contrasts in nearly every particular with the central western Zagros Mountains.

In this chapter, I relate the results of my survey of the small Khorramabad Valley in Luristan, Iran, conducted in 1963 and 1965, to events recorded in Mesopotamia and elsewhere.[1] While records of major political events in

---

[1] This is the first installment of the publication of our surveys in western Iran, to be followed by a comprehensive, extensively illustrated monograph that will describe our collections from the Saimarreh, Kuh-i Dasht, and Borujerd Valleys, as well as sites in the Solduz region of northern Iran. With technical studies of paste that we expect to carry out, as well as information from comparative material in the other valleys, we may be able to further refine our dating and reconstructions of interaction zones.

Mesopotamia are relatively complete, they are virtually nonexistent for Luristan. Moreover, as I shall discuss, there are long stretches of time for which we have no evidence of settlement. Archaeologists have a tendency to think in terms of continuity as in Mesopotamia, but abandonment of sites and even regions is part of a normal cycle in civilizations throughout the world (Marcus 1998; Minnis 1985; de Miroschedji 2003; Yoffee 1988), and we should expect gaps in the sequence of occupation, particularly in regions like Luristan that are marginal for agriculture and incapable of sustaining sufficiently large populations to remain viable in the face of external pressures. Pressures would include excessive climate variability such as drought, prolonged cold, torrential rain and flooding, as well as incursions by peoples from outside seeking resources (natural, livestock, and human), trading opportunities, or refuge from starvation, hostilities, and/or political oppression. The mountain and valley geography of Luristan relegates it to a marginal position with little potential for internal growth. In fact, one might characterize Luristan as an enclosed periphery, one that has no center and whose valleys are impacted differentially by events from outside. If we had complete information, we would probably find that each valley holds evidence of a unique history. It is difficult and not a little frustrating to attempt to link these various histories through comparisons of ceramics recovered only from the surfaces of sites, and without further survey and especially excavations, it may be impossible. Levine and Young (1987: 16) note that there is no single sequence for the central Zagros. They see the Mahi Dasht and Kangavar Valleys, both along the High Road, as being relatively isolated from each other through the Late Chalcolithic. A similar point is made by Haerinck and Overlaet (2002) who describe three regional variants during the third millennium along the Zagros front range, including southern Luristan. In short, Luristan, identified today by the language spoken by its recent tribal people, may have lacked social, political, or even ethnic or linguistic unity for much of its past. Teasing evidence of this from survey data is probably impossible, but recognition of the potential complexities is a first step.

GEOLOGY AND GEOGRAPHY OF LURISTAN

As Bob Adams made clear in his work in Mesopotamia and Susiana, survey results are meaningless unless they are placed firmly within their environmental context. I therefore set the scene here by means of a discussion of the geology and geography of Luristan. Surrounded by the regions that spawned centers of civilization, Luristan lay largely outside their orbit and beyond the reach of written history such that only archaeology can hope to illuminate its past (Figure 19). Indeed, Luristan remained in prehistory until the nineteenth century. Owing to the absence of cities, a paucity of permanent villages, and its transhumant tribal populations, much of Luristan has often been effectively vacant at

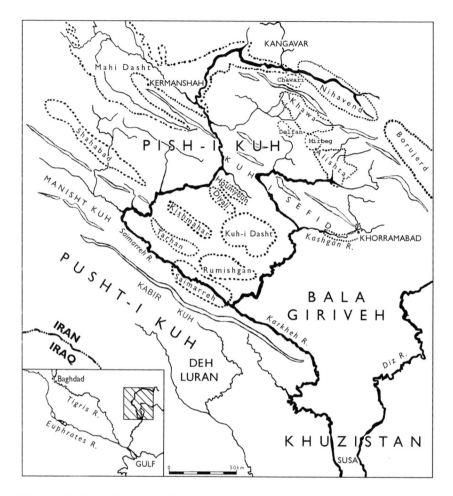

Figure 19. Map of Luristan showing the main mountain valleys and geographic regions (adapted from Meade 1968).

one season or another. Moreover, for its land area, Luristan has been thinly populated even in the best of times. Luristan owes its relative isolation to its physical geography. The climate and topography encourage seasonal movement and discourage agriculture. It is a rugged and perversely difficult landscape to penetrate, marked by a series of anticlinal mountain ridges breached by few easy passes. Such a landscape favors hardy, independent, and combative people.

Edmonds's succinct description serves well to characterize Luristan: "[I]t consists of a series of remarkably regular parallel ranges running from north-west to south-east, with fertile valleys, each more elevated than the last, between them" (Edmonds 1922: 335). That is, the valleys and ridges rise in a series of steps from the Kabir Kuh eastward to the plateau of Iran. Oberlander, a physical geographer, who studied the Zagros in the 1960s, names it the Luristan Folded Basin in which "lacustrine plains, such as those at Hulailan, Kuh-i Dasht, and Mahi Dasht, offer the best agricultural possibilities to be found within the central Zagros; accordingly they are heavily populated in comparison with the rest of the region" (Oberlander 1965: 43). The Bala Gariveh section, the Luristan Saddle, is a more tightly folded region with "much wilder scenery than the neighboring Luristan Basin" and lacks broad plains (Oberlander 1965: 44). While the central Zagros drainage has three major rivers, some of the plains lack flowing water (Hole 1962), and only the cold, high plain of Alishtar is blessed with numerous springs (Black-Michaud 1986). As Oberlander notes, "south of the thirty-fourth parallel, agriculture dependent on rainfall is almost everywhere marginal, and irrigation is practiced in valleys throughout the highland" (Oberlander 1965: 15). Black offers a somewhat different view of central Luristan. "The vast majority of cereal growers are . . . forced to rely on rainfall alone," an undependable strategy (Black-Michaud 1986: 15). The anticlinal ridges that separate the valleys are often tree-clad and in the higher elevations may hold a substantial cover of snow in the winter. In short, the region is well suited to transhumant pastoralism and less desirable for subsistence agriculture, let alone dense settlement. Even though some valleys may be suited to agriculture, fields and stores are vulnerable to migrating tribes. Edmonds remarked that "at the time of my visit [to Khorramabad in 1917], many roofs were yellow with maize spread out to dry; owing to the insecurity the owners harvest it at the earliest possible moment, leaving the final separating and drying processes to the security of their houses" (Edmonds 1922: 443).

Within the folded zone, Goff sees Kuh-i Sefid, a long mountain ridge, as creating a boundary between *garmsir*, the warm, winter pastures in the southwest, and *sardsir*, the upland, summer pastures in the northeast. This ridge runs from near Kermanshah to Khorramabad, broken by several passes through which tribes migrate. She notes that this region "can contain widely differing cultures within a single period" because of the confining nature of the mountains and the restricted possibilities of moving between them (Meade 1968: 108). Luristan is the "land of the Lurs," an Indo-European–speaking people whose language is closely related to both Kurdi and Farsi. We have no direct knowledge of the time when these people entered the central Zagros, but Levine sees Indo-European place names becoming widespread in the early first millennium BC (Levine 1987: 231–232).

Luristan is often divided into Pusht-i-Kuh, including the Kabir Kuh, Saimarreh, and land "outside" the mountain; Pish-i-Kuh, the land "inside" the mountain; and Bala Gariveh, eastward of the Kashgan-Khorramabad Rivers. We will follow this convention here, with the following further subdivisions. *Southern Luristan (Pusht-i-Kuh)*, bounded by Kabir Kuh and the Saimarreh River, consisting primarily of the Saimarreh Valley and the adjacent lowlands;

Central Luristan (Pish-i-Kuh), consisting of many small valleys including Khorramabad, Rumishgan, Tarhan, and Kuh-i Dasht, bounded on the north by
Kuh-i Sefid; and *Bala Gariveh* to the south, separated from central Luristan by
the Kashgan River; *Northern Luristan*, consisting of high valleys north of Kuh-
i Sefid, including Khawa, Chawari, Alishtar, Delfan, and Mirbeg; *Western
Luristan*, consisting primarily of Hulailan Valley and upper drainages of the
Saimarreh River (see Figure 19). Although a two-dimensional map suggests
the close proximity of these valleys, and the overall distances as the crow flies
are not great, the entire region covers approximately 65,000 square kilometers
of rugged terrain. According to Schmidt (Schmidt, van Loon, and Curvers
1989: 2), it was about a two-day horseback ride to travel along a relatively
smooth route from Khorramabad to Rumishgan in the 1930s.

It is instructive to read Schmidt's accounts of Luristan between 1934 and
1938. Entering Rumishgan, he "saw the broad flat alluvial valley, with its
clusters of brush villages and a few cultivated patches interrupting the
monotony of the tan-colored plain" (Schmidt, van Loon, and Curvers 1989:
1). "Clusters of brush shelters and nearby winter villages marked the dwellings of the Rumishganis. Hundreds of little depressions, wells, and storage
pits were to be seen close to each settlement. There were hillocks and faint
garden enclosures extending down from the mountain slopes" (Schmidt, van
Loon, and Curvers 1989: 2). The only source of water was from wells "ten to
twenty meters deep" (Schmidt, van Loon, and Curvers 1989: 3). Schmidt
traveled shortly after the tribes of Luristan had been defeated by the Persian
military and many had been settled in villages. Less than two decades earlier,
Luristan was described by C. J. Edmonds, a British officer who attempted to
travel from Khuzistan to Khorramabad and Borujerd in 1917, as follows:

> The Lurs are all nomads, living in black tents and moving with all their
> belongings between their winter and summer pastures. . . . The only town
> in the province is Khurramabad. [Edmonds estimated that about 4000
> people lived there.] There were a number of villages in the Kurrehgah or
> the Khurramabad plain, but they were all ruinous and deserted when I was
> there in 1917. Indeed it is almost possible to say there are no villages what-
> ever in Pish-i Kuh and Bala Gariveh, if occasional collections of huts, in
> which Lurs remaining in the very high country for the winter may take
> refuge during the snows be excluded. In the summer the Lurs build them-
> selves bowers of branches, called *kula*, which are cooler than tents.
> (Edmonds 1922: 340)

Edmonds also refers to the "chronic state of anarchy" that made travel in
Luristan nearly impossible for outsiders in the nineteenth and early twentieth
centuries. Indeed, he was held hostage in Khorramabad for several months
(Edmonds 1922: 342, 447).

Kuh-i-Dasht is an immense plain, at an altitude of about 4000 feet, measuring about 10 miles by 8, as flat as a billiard table. It is wholly devoid of
trees, and has comparatively little water. There are a few mounds said to
cover ancient ruins. Truffles are found, and the plain abounds with
gazelle. Camps of various sections of the Dilfan were dotted over it (in
January). Nazar Ali was building himself a new fort to replace one
destroyed by the Vali of Pusht-i Kuh three or four years before.
(Edmonds 1922: 450)

Of Hulailan, he remarked, "The district is said to produce three crops of
maize in a year, but owing to locusts no wheat had been grown for seven or
eight years. Truffles in large quantities are found in spring. . . . The following
day we marched north-westwards up the valley, *past several villages, a pleasant
reminder that we were out of Luristan*" (Edmonds 1922: 451, my emphasis). As
we review the archaeological evidence, we should keep these images of
Luristan in mind.

THE SURVEY AND ANALYSIS

I surveyed the Khorramabad Valley in 1963 and 1965 when I was excavating
two Paleolithic cave sites, Kunji and Ghamari. It is worth briefly describing
how we did the survey and the sources we had to work with. Where Adams
was able to use aerial photographs, we had only topographic maps made for
the British Army at a scale of 1/4" = 1 mile, or 1:253,440, published in 1942.
These maps were largely based on a survey made in 1934 by a plane table
team that in six months covered 11,000 square miles (J. V. Harrison 1946).
Although this was an improvement over an earlier map about which Freya
Stark said, "Its streams are dotted blue lines on the map and the position of its
hills a matter of taste" (Stark 1934: 3), still it lacked details that would be useful in survey. Where villages were named and still present in the 1960s we
could use them as points of departure, but where there were no convenient
landmarks we resorted to triangulation by compass, attempting to sight on
eminences that were only imperfectly recorded on the topographic maps.
Our problem was precise recording of site locations, not the discovery of
sites. On the ground, modern villages reduced the areas where we could collect pottery, but this was usually only a minor inconvenience, particularly as
village children enthusiastically scoured the sites for handfuls of sherds for
our approval and kept the guard dogs at bay.
    The long time between collection and study of the material allowed me to
benefit from the publication of comparative material and thus to be able to
make more accurate assessments. I was surprised, nonetheless, at how difficult
it actually was to find diagnostic comparanda, in part because I had expected to
find more continuity than apparently exists. Lacking these, I seriated ceramics

by treating homogeneous assemblages from small or short-term sites as representing short periods of occupation. When sites had more than one period
represented, unknown sherds were assigned according to paste and manufacturing details, or left as unknown when ready fits could not be found. In this
way, I have been able to construct a succession of ceramic assemblages that will
ultimately require verification through targeted excavations at key sites.

Apart from my excavations in the two caves, there are *no* excavated sites in
the valley. Moreover, there are few excavated sites in all of Luristan, and the
most important of these are in widely separated valleys. In Hulailan, there is
Tepe Guran (Meldgaard, Mortensen, and Thrane 1964; Mortensen 1963;
Trane 2001); in Mahi Dasht, Sarab (McDonald 1979), Siahbid, Chogha
Maran, and Jameh Shuran (Levine and Young 1987); in Kangavar, Godin Tepe
and Seh Gabi B and C (McDonald 1979; Young 1969; 1975; Young and Levine
1974); in Khawa, Baba Jan (Goff 1976; 1977; 1978; 1985); and in the Malayer-
Jawkar plain, Nush-i Jan (D. Stronach and Roaf 1978; R. Stronach 1978). The
old French excavation at Giyan near Nehevand has long been used as a stan-
dard for comparison (Contenau and Ghirshman 1935). The excavations by the
Holmes Expedition in Rumishgan and Kuh-i Dasht (Schmidt, van Loon, and
Curvers 1989), as well as Aurel Stein's (1940a; 1940b) collections in Kuh-i
Dasht, Rumishgan, Saimarreh, Hulailan, Alishtar, Delfan, Mahi Dasht, and
Kermanshah, add some comparative material. Despite such seemingly wide
coverage, no valley has a complete sequence, and each valley has a different set
of material, albeit with some sharing of diagnostic types. This underscores the
broken nature of Luristan and the relative isolation of valleys within it. It
seems that impacts from outside as well as indigenous developments affected
each valley somewhat differently and at different times.

A number of excellent overviews of central Zagros archaeology, based on
survey and excavation, exist (Goff 1966; 1971; Levine and McDonald 1977;
Levine 1987; Levine and Young 1987; M. A. Stein 1940a; 1940b; Young 1965;
1966; 1967; 1975; Young and Smith 1966). Particularly informative, especially
for southern Luristan, is an up-to-date summary of finds made by the Holmes
Expedition (Schmidt, van Loon, and Curvers 1989). Various summaries are
also included in *The Archaeology of Western Iran* (Hole 1987b).

THE ARCHAEOLOGICAL SEQUENCE

My intention here is twofold: (1) to report the results of my analysis, and (2)
to relate these to broader social, political, and ecological processes in surrounding regions. For the sake of comparability and consistency with previous work, I use a standard chronological framework, although I have devised
phases of local significance to indicate the unique nature of the ceramic
assemblages and to underscore the variability within and beyond Luristan.

This has not been an easy process, since each author seemingly has a unique periodization based on either a local archaeological sequence (for example, Godin Tepe), or on a historically derived Mesopotamian sequence. In local usage, period names such as Late Bronze or Iron III may be offset some hundreds of years from another chronology using the same terms. In the absence of radiocarbon dates or historical sources, chronological precision in Luristan may be on the order of ± 250 years or more.

Neolithic

Agricultural settlements began in the Near East 11,500 years ago in the Levant, but the oldest agricultural sites in Iran date back only to the late ninth–early eighth millennium at Ganj Dareh, Abdul Hosein, Guran, Ali Kosh, and Sarab (Braidwood, Howe, and Reed 1961; Hole, Flannery, and Neely 1969; Mortensen 1963; Pullar 1990; P. E. L. Smith 1983; P. E. L. Smith and Young 1983). These preceramic and ceramic Neolithic sites lie outside Luristan, and at this time Khorramabad was apparently not occupied, at least by people who left traces in either lithics or ceramics. In our preliminary survey report (Hole and Flannery 1967), we attributed some chaff-tempered, red-slipped sherds found in Kunji Cave to possible transhumant pastoralists who had migrated from the region of Deh Luran. Such sherds are commonly found in the Mohammad Jaffar phase of the ceramic Neolithic at Ali Kosh and Chogha Sefid (Hole, Flannery, and Neely 1969), but it now seems more likely that these sherds actually pertain to the later stages of the Chalcolithic, as I discuss below. So far as we can tell, the Khorramabad Valley entirely missed the era of the finely made microblades typical of the Zagros Neolithic (Hole 1994b; Kozlowski 1994; 1998).

Early Chalcolithic

The oldest mounded site on the valley floor in Khorramabad is Bagh-i No (KR-20), first recorded by Cuyler Young (Young 1966: 231) (Figure 20). From a borrow pit made by villagers, we recovered a particularly crude ceramic ware there, as well as seeds and enough charred material for a radiocarbon date of ca. 5000 cal BC. Eleven sites in our collection have this ceramic or its immediately derived successors. Young (1975) reports finding similar sherds in valleys north of Khorramabad, and Pullar (1990) found Bagh-i No sherds in Abdul Hosein. This suggests a northern distribution in the high valleys for this particular ware. McDonald (1979: 525) sees parallels with the ceramics of Seh Gabi C and thus a late sixth-millennium date, roughly contemporary with Bagh-i No. The early Khorramabad ceramic becomes finer, and other wares are added to the assemblage over a span of perhaps some hundreds of years. Among the new wares are some with grit temper seemingly similar to some found by Goff (1971) in central northern Luristan. In broad terms, the Bagh-i No phase is contemporary

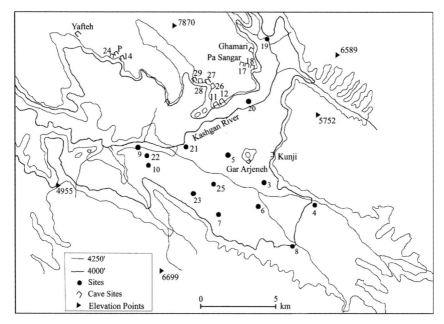

Figure 20. Sketch map of sites in the Khorramabad Valley, based on surveys of
1963 and 1965. Map based on 1/4": 1 mile British series. Elevations are in feet.
The 4000- and 5000-foot contours are shown, along with drainages, all of which
(except the Kashgan River) are seasonal.

with Samarra and Early 'Ubaid in Mesopotamia. The fact that there are many
sites suggests that they were permanent agricultural settlements, although herders may have moved seasonally to higher pastures.

Both the Neolithic and Early–Middle Chalcolithic occurred during the
climatic optimum, a period during which both temperature and precipitation
may have been higher (Rossignol-Strick 1996). This may help explain the
presence of Neolithic sites in the higher valleys, such as Abdul Hosein and
Ganj Dareh, as well as sites in valleys where today precipitation is too low to
support subsistence agriculture. This favorable period came to a close, perhaps rather quickly, at the end of the fifth millennium, as implied by the
widespread abandonment of settlement in many regions (Hole 1994a).

Middle Chalcolithic

Our next phase, Daurai, is named after KR-6, a multiperiod site from which
we collected the greatest amount of pottery. The pottery from this period is
untempered, relatively thin, well fired, and generally has black paint on a
salmon-colored paste. These changes in temper and firing suggest that there
is a temporal gap between the Bagh-i No and Daurai phases, although perhaps not of long duration. The closest comparisons for the Daurai phase

come from Seh Gabi B in the Kangavar Valley on the High Road (outside Luristan proper), where a chaff-tempered black-on-buff ware, in the context of Dalma sherds, shares some motifs with the Khorramabad sites (Levine and Young 1987). The apparent movement south of Dalma wares from northern Iran stops at the edge of central Luristan and does not reach Khorramabad. The Godin Tepe (X–IX) dates encompass 4500–3800 BC (Hole 1987c: table 2), although I estimate a range of 4800–4200 BC for the Daurai phase.

Eleven sites—two of good size (KR-6 and KR-8) and both with large numbers of sherds—were settled at this time. There is enough variability in the motifs and other slight differences in the ceramics between these sites (for instance, the introduction of a buff slip) to suggest a temporal change, but this cannot be demonstrated from surface collections where some sites produced only a handful of sherds.

Late Chalcolithic

Following the Daurai phase, in addition to a site on the valley bottom, there is evidence for occupation in two caves, Ghamari (KR-1) and Kunji (KR-2), both of which we tested through excavation. The post-Pleistocene layers in these caves contain abundant sherds as well as remnants of stone enclosures. That these enclosures represent herding camps is suggested by their similarity to structures built in Shanidar Cave by Kurdish pastoralists in modern times (Hole 1987c; Solecki 1979; 1998). A herding focus may also be indicated by the extensive ash layers, perhaps resulting from the burning of dung. This pastoral adaptation may have been built on an earlier tradition manifest in the cemeteries at Hakalan and Parchineh in southern Luristan (Haerinck and Overlaet 1996; M. A. Stein 1940a; Vanden Berghe 1973; 1975).

Although the Late Chalcolithic occupation of the caves was of relatively short duration, the ceramics recovered from our test trench in Kunji Cave clearly indicate two phases. I refer to the earlier as the Ghamari phase, contemporary with the late or terminal 'Ubaid (H. T. Wright and Johnson 1975). In a change from the previous phase, the Black on Salmon ware is largely absent, the Black on Buff ware is chaff tempered, and there are red-slip wares and scraped-sided bowls. While I regard the change from untempered to chaff-tempered ceramic as sequential and hence a separate phase, it remains possible that what actually occurred was an intrusive pastoral group occupying the caves during part of the Daurai phase. Neutron activation or petrographic analysis might settle whether the pots were made locally. Goff (1971: 143) notes that the scraped-sided bowls have a distribution in northern Mesopotamia (compare Çoba bowls). We have referred to the period in which these bowls occur as "post-'Ubaid" in northern Syria where it has a date of 4566–4320 BC (2 sigma cal) (Hole 2001).

The Kunji phase follows the Ghamari phase. This phase at Kunji Cave, and probably also at KR-6, is denoted by the appearance of typical early Uruk forms, including bowls with beveled rims, club rims, and incurving sides, as well as jars with short vertical spouts. These types provide the first indication of contact with lowland Mesopotamia. This was noted by Wright and his colleagues (H. T. Wright and Johnson 1975) who demonstrated that the Kunji ceramics compare closely with those from two sites on the edge of the Deh Luran plain as well as with Godin VI. The Kunji assemblage mostly consists of local wares with beveled-rim bowls, a combination seen at the same time— probably early to mid fourth millennium—in a number of other sites from Anatolia to Iran where Uruk types mingle with local wares (Algaze 1993a; E. F. Henrickson 1994; G. Stein 1994a). Goff (1971: fig. 7) finds a similar assemblage in Baba Jan V, including fine buff ware jars identical to those found in Kunji and Ghamari. According to Goff, this ware is restricted to eastern Pish-i Kuh, whereas the scraped-sided bowls have a western Pish-i Kuh and northern Mesopotamian distribution. The ceramics of Godin VI also show some parallels to those in the Kunji phase (H. T. Wright and Johnson 1975). It is possible that the most characteristic form, beveled-rim bowls, represent containers for goods that were distributed from Godin or elsewhere to the remote valleys. Petrographic analyses of these vessels may show whether they were made locally or imported. In any event, the occupation of the caves suggests that at least some elements of the population were involved in transhumance and may have acquired ceramics on their travels.

Sherds from KR-5 and KR-14, both with mica in the temper, may be an "eastern variety of early Uruk" (Goff 1971: 144). The fact that sherds from these sites are grit tempered but not otherwise specifically diagnostic suggests that they might fit more readily in the middle Uruk, as described below.

Middle Uruk Period

Three sites (KR-7, -20, -25) have assemblages that can be attributed to Middle Uruk. Although the finger-impressed bowls look superficially like the older ones, now they are tempered with grit rather than with chaff, and there is a range of other vessels that compare with Middle Uruk. There are no sites unequivocally to be dated to the Late Uruk. If we may actually speak of contacts between Mesopotamia and Luristan at this time, they must have been tenuous. It seems more likely that the ceramics derive from the movement of, or contact with, indigenous transhumant groups who adopted ceramics found at the edge of the Mesopotamia plain. Goff notes that "each of the large plains in western Luristan—Tarhan, Kuh-i Dasht, and Rumishgan—are dominated by one or more major tepes" (Goff 1971: 145) at this time, a pattern that could imply, using ethnographic analogy, forts/manors of semi-sedentary pastoralists. KR-25, strategically located and with extensive later occupations, might have been such a site.

As we have seen, Godin VI has some parallels with the Kunji phase. Godin V, occurring at the end of Godin VI and incorporating much of its ceramic inventory, also has a wide range of lowland Uruk ceramics that probably date to the Middle Uruk, or around 3500 BC. These ceramics include a range of jars with incised shoulders, twisted handles, and droop spouts, conventionally thought of as Late Uruk styles, but more likely Middle Uruk, in common with other sites where a similar mix of ceramics has been found. This "Uruk" enclosure at Godin has been termed a Susian trading post handling shipments of goods between the plateau and Susa, perhaps following the Khorasan Road rather than going through Luristan (Weiss and Young 1975).

Without firm dates it is hard to assign very specific estimates for the duration of the Late Chalcolithic in Luristan, but it is reasonable to guess that the Ghamari and Kunji phases are primarily late fifth to early fourth millennium, unless we assume a substantial lag in the diffusion of vessel forms from northern Mesopotamia and Susiana to Luristan. This assessment differs significantly from that of E. F. Henrickson (1994: 97), who sees the "Uruk" presence as dating primarily to the second half of the fourth millennium. Whatever the case may turn out to be, it is remarkable that for the entire fourth millennium we have evidence of only four occupied sites in the Khorramabad Valley. An absence of sites would, however, correspond to the widespread abandonment of regions in western and southern Iran toward the end of the fourth millennium, a shift in settlement that could be linked to climatic change, whose effects in Luristan have been neither verified nor quantified (Hole 1994a; Rossignol-Strick 1996; Weiss 2000), or to political realignment and consolidation taking place in southern Mesopotamia (Johnson 1988-89). It is worth noting that Mortensen (1975) found no sites in Hulailan from the mid-fourth through the first half of the third millennium, and Uruk is absent from the Pusht-i-Kuh (Haerinck and Overlaet 2002: 168).

Hiatus in Settlement

If we assume that Middle Uruk is roughly dated to 3500 BC, our next evidence of occupation comes some 600 to 700 years later in the Early Bronze Age. This does not imply that there are *no* sites in Luristan of Late Uruk age; rather that the Khorramabad Valley was not settled. Kamtarlan in Rumishgan has Uruk vessels similar to those found in Godin V; but apart from these sites, other occurrences are only of the ubiquitous bevel rim bowls, a type that enjoyed long use. An abandonment may have taken place at the time of a climate change 5200 years ago, as implied by a variety of proxy indicators (de Menocal 2001; Rossignol-Strick 1996; Weiss 2000), but since we have neither accurate control over the dates of the Khorramabad sites, nor actual knowledge of climate changes in Luristan, this remains speculative. It appears that the abandonment of settlement in Khorramabad and in Luristan generally preceded this climatic event and must require another explanation. Goff notes that Uruk sites were abandoned and new ones established, along with new pottery and grave types, all suggesting a "radical break with the past" (Goff 1971: 149). A similar "gap" between Uruk and the Early Bronze Age is seen in Rumishgan (Van Loon and Curvers 1989). Levine and Young (1987: 40) find the arrival of Transcaucasian Culture Gray Wares at Godin a signal of "a massive foreign invasion" between 2950 and 2400 BC. Weiss (2003: 601) refers to this as the classic signature of population movement, but this seemingly occurred later than a climate event.

Early Bronze Age

KR-5, Masur, has ceramics reported to include "beveled-rim bowls, heavy-rim trays, and solid footed cups of rough chaff tempered ware as well as body sherds of wheel-thrown straw and crushed calcite tempered buff ware with painted dark bands" (H. T. Wright 1987: fn. 8). These compare with Godin V and Banesh in Fars (Voigt and Dyson 1992: 141) and imply a post–Late Uruk occupation. Two other sites, KR-23 and KR-25, are attributed to the Early Dynastic (ED) I–II/Jamdet Nasr period, perhaps indicating that the valley was unoccupied for some hundreds of years following the Middle Uruk. The small sites on the valley floor display sherds of characteristic ED I/II form and style, similar to those from Godin III:6 (R. C. Henrickson 1986: 21). By mid-third millennium there are a number of additional sites (KR-3, -5,- 8, -9, and -22), and excavations in Kunji Cave by John Speth (Emberling, Robb, and Speth 2002) yielded elite burials of this period. The vessels—both ceramic and lead—are dated to 2700–2600 BC, contemporary with the *libaq* tombs of Luristan, many of which were recorded by Goff (1971), who notes their Elamite associations. A probable tomb of this age was reported by Herzfeld (1929–30) at Gilwaran, Khorramabad, and other comparable tombs have been excavated in Guran in Hulailan (Trane 2001) and at Kamtarlan I and Chigha Sabz in Rumishgan (Schmidt, van Loon, and Curvers 1989). These imply a strong component of pastoral nomadism, coupled with at least seasonal villages in Khorramabad at this time. The burials in Kunji and in the other valleys, with both ceramic vessels and metal, reflect the growing appropriation of wealth by individuals in the Early Dynastic period, a phenomenon seen throughout the Near East. Goff (1971) remarks on a movement of villages toward the edges of plains, enabling people to indulge in mixed agriculture and stock breeding. The picture in Khorramabad is different in that the sites are centrally located and, perhaps not coincidentally, some are at the locations of recent tribal forts as shown on the British Army map. Of these, KR-5 is the only valley bottom site with painted ceramics of this period, and it is possible these came from a tomb.

While all the sites can be attributed to the Early Bronze Age, they display so much variability from one to another as to suggest either rapid stylistic change or influences and intrusions from different regions. The influences at this time seem to emanate most strongly from the southwest, perhaps, as Carter suggested, due to Elamite influences. However, "written sources, differing burial customs, settlement patterns, ceramic styles, and ethnographic analogy confirm the presence of various ethnic groups and political alliances in the central Zagros during the third millennium but do not as yet permit any certain identifications" (E. Carter and Stolper 1984: 143). The distribution of tombs dating to this period is also heavily weighted toward Pusht-i-Kuh, northwest of central Luristan.

The latter half of the third millennium, including the Akkadian/post-Akkadian period (2200–1800) is represented by only one site in Khorramabad, so far as I can tell. We did not recover the late third-millennium pottery so characteristic of other regions, although a single site does have comb-incised sherds. Since these are the only "diagnostics" of this period that we have, we must admit that comb impressions are also found on Islamic wares and that these latter are also represented at KR-25. It is, therefore, questionable whether the end of the third millennium is actually represented. R. C. Henrickson (1986) observed the same absence in the Godin region. We note that Naram-Sin led an expedition into the mountains against the Elippi, probably taking the High Road into the Mahidasht, the presumed heartland of this polity. He probably felt no pressure from the Khorramabad region if he even knew it existed. Moreover, Luristan held no natural resources that could not have been obtained more easily elsewhere.

Hiatus in Settlement

Approximately 700 years elapsed before we have evidence of resumed settlement in the Khorramabad Valley. A devastating drought around 2200 BC affected most of the ancient world and led to political turmoil (Weiss 1997), perhaps accounting for the lack of late third-millennium sites in Khorramabad. One might have expected an incursion of people into Luristan at the end of the third millennium, driven by drought from agricultural pursuits elsewhere. Instead we find, as is true elsewhere, that we miss an influx of people and that settlement only resumed after a prolonged hiatus. We should admit, however, that finding sites of economic refugees is problematic and our survey was not designed to look specifically for such traces. Clearly we need to find ways to discover ephemeral sites as well as accurate information on the climate history of this region.

Late Bronze Age

We regain settlement in the first half of the second millennium. There are four sites (KR-5, -21, -22, -25) that are probably contemporary with the Khabur-related settlements that turn up in the central Zagros (Goff 1971) at Surk Dum

Luri in Rumishgan and in the boulder ruins described by Schmidt (Schmidt, van Loon, and Curvers 1989). The sparse evidence thus indicates some settlement from roughly 1800 to 1400 BC. Across eastern Luristan, Goff reports that patterns of settlement "would appear to have been almost identical with those prevailing today" (Goff 1971: 150), with farming and pastoralism and many small sites, often in defensible positions. Moreover, in both eastern and western Luristan, "the end of the second millennium seems to have been characterized by a general shift to the mountains—the end of a process started by the *lihaq* users 1500 years earlier, and a reflection of the increasingly disturbed conditions prevailing over all of the Middle East at this period" (Goff 1971: 151).

Carter says that the "towns of Luristan and southern Kurdistan appear to have been culturally distinct and their political role in the Elamite state unknown" (E. Carter and Stolper 1984: 179). She sees a "strong Elamite influence" in the bronze work of Pusht-i-Kuh (as does de Miroschedji), and she believes that the Elamite interest in the mountain regions stemmed in part from their need to secure routes for trade in metal. However, as I have noted before, the principal route (the High Road) circumnavigates central Luristan; moreover, there was a shift to trade via southern Iran (de Miroschedji 2003: 23, 33).

Hiatus in Settlement

Once again there is a gap in occupation of perhaps 600 years. This does not appear to have any climatic implications, and it remains unexplained except through sociopolitical events that are outlined below.

Iron Age

Levine divides the first millennium into three parts: the first 350 years are dominated by Assyria, and the second saw the rise of the Medes and Cyrus's accession to the throne in 559 that ushered in the third, Achaemenian period. After Alexander's defeat of Darius III in 330, there was "political fragmentation" to end the millennium (Levine and Young 1987).

Luristan was home to the provincial Elippi Kingdom but, despite repeated Assyrian incursions into the region, "Elippi is hardly mentioned in the sources" (Levine 1987: 230). It appears that most Assyrian attention was focused on the Mannean kingdom, located west of the High Road in Kurdistan. The limited historical sources indicate that the central Zagros was inhabited throughout the millennium by peoples speaking diverse languages. Following the collapse of the Assyrian Empire, the Zagros kingdoms were eventually incorporated into the Median Kingdom and in turn absorbed into the Achaemenian Empire.

Iron I (1400–1100 BC) is not represented by excavated material in the central Zagros other than, perhaps, by gray wares at Tepe Giyan. The type fossils are "the button or pedestal based Early Western Gray Ware goblet, and the 'Elamite' or 'Kassite' goblets" (Levine 1987: 236), neither of which was recovered in our survey. In fact, Levine's review lists only graves at Godin and Giyan and a possible settlement at Guran, and he raises the possibility that the "Early Western Gray Ware" found in the graves represents a transhumant element from the north, whereas the goblets at Guran denote a settled population. Unfortunately, we recovered neither type of vessel and thus can contribute nothing to this discussion. Two graves in Chigha Sabz are attributed to Iron I by Van Loon and Curvers (1989). Goff mentions that major sites were abandoned and "not a sherd of Iron Age I ware has so far been found [west *sic*.] east of the Kuh-i Sefid. The desolation may be attributed either to the raids of the Elamite kings in the late thirteenth and early twelfth centuries BC or to counter raids of invading Iron I people across the Nehavand passes" (Goff 1971: 151). The general absence of evidence other than these tombs, for the latter half of the second and the first centuries of the first millennium, may truly reflect unsettled political conditions.

Iron II/Neo-Elamite (1100–500 BC) encompasses the period of the famous Luristan bronzes (800–700 BC), most of which were derived from cemeteries farther west in Kurdistan and in southern Luristan. The tombs are evidence that there is a strong nomadic presence in the Zagros under the leadership of wealthy chiefs. E. Carter (1984: 188) refers to Iron II in Luristan and Kurdistan as a period of prosperity that coincided with the decline of Susiana. Historical sources tell of severe food shortages around the turn of the millennium and raiding by seminomadic populations (E. Carter and Stolper 1984; de Miroschedji 2003; Schwartz 1995). By the mid-second millennium, the Elamite state had become a major power along with Babylonia and Assyria, with capitals at Anshan in Fars—known archaeologically as Tepe Malyan—and a corresponding "winter" capital at Susa in Khuzistan. This link between Fars and Khuzistan continued into the Achaemenid period and is a reflection of the environmental imperative that fosters transhumance. While movement between lowland and highland was natural, the only good routes circumvented Luristan, enclosing it in a sense, but leaving it isolated from direct interaction with the major polities.

Levine notes that it is "only in the reconstructed sequence of graves from Tepe Giyan that we have anything approaching a sequence. . . . The Iron II period in the Zagros and Khuzistan is, therefore, characterized by a number of relatively distinct and non overlapping ceramic assemblages, which are considered to be contemporaneous because they fit between earlier and later periods where better interregional correlations are possible" (Levine 1987: 237).

The local ceramic assemblage is early Genre Luristan (Baba Jan III) which occurs in the valleys closest to Khorramabad and may represent "evidence of nascent Elippi . . . assuming that ceramic distribution is a measure of social and, in this case, political integration" (Levine 1987: 241). Goff mentions "the sudden appearance of Baba Jan B wares all over the 'tribal region' of the eastern Pish-i Kuh which presumably indicates the arrival of a new racial group" (Goff 1968: 127). The valleys she mentions are on the edge of the central plateau and not in Luristan proper. The manor house at Baba Jan dates to this period, as does the fortified building that contained a large columned hall at Godin (Young and Levine 1974). After a short period of use, both of these structures were abandoned and, curiously, the Godin fort lost its militaristic features during renovations. A "sanctuary" at Chigha Sabz in Rumishgan dates to this period as well. Together these sites suggest increasing social stratification and religious activity (Van Loon and Curvers 1989).

According to Levine:

> The first two thirds of the first millennium B.C. witnessed changes in western Iran as dramatic as any the area has undergone since the Neolithic. At the turn of the millennium, the three great historical rivals in lowland Mesopotamia—Elam, Babylonia, and Assyria—were still playing out a drama that had begun almost two thousand years before. By the end of the period, not only had these three powers disappeared, but the Achaemenid Empire was in the hands of the Macedonian Alexander, bringing the last of the great oriental empires of antiquity to its conclusion. (Levine 1987: 229)

Despite these political changes that must have impacted Luristan, we have no archaeological traces of any activity in Khorramabad until *Iron III, the Median period, (850–500 BC)*, at which time we have four sites (KR-3, -6, -7, -23). Historical sources indicate that the Median Kingdom was composed of people of diverse ethnic backgrounds. Herodotus referred to them as "people living in villages," meaning that they were not urban (Herodotus 1987: I.95–130). A combination of settled and pastoral occupation is compatible with our evidence.

The archaeological evidence consists of "micaceous buff wares" associated with many sites just beyond our region, as well as Gray Wares that are associated with Iron III tombs in Pusht-i-Kuh (Haerinck and Overlaet 1998; 1999; 2003). We found none of the latter—not surprising, perhaps, because they are found in graves of transhumant people—but we do have other ceramics that can be attributed to Iron III. There are good parallels with Baba Jan II in the fine red-slipped ware and with both Nush-i Jan I and Baba Jan plain wares (Goff 1985: 3). The fortified palace at Godin was built by a Median khan or chief, one of many rulers of the Medes, "a very diverse people in terms of culture and social and political organization" (Young 1997: 449).

The Persian Empire was formed when Cyrus defeated the Medes and made them his principal allies in his quest for world domination. Again we have no archaeological evidence from our area, perhaps because most of the able-bodied men were conscripted into serving in foreign wars. Alexander's defeat of the Persians and the sacking of Persepolis in 323 BC ushered in the *Parthian Period (210 BC–AD 225)*, and at this time we find a characteristic, highly fired "cinnamon" ware with a dark core, at three sites (KR-3, -6, -7). Clearly by now there was ample skill and technology to carry out agriculture by irrigation, and the small villages on the Khorramabad plain may reflect this.

Levine (1987: 239) speaks of an "Early Parthian," or Iron IV, which is characterized by the introduction of the painted ceramics that precede the clinky wares assigned to the Parthian period, but we have no examples of this ware in Khorramabad.

Sasanian/Islamic/Historic and Ethnographic

The subsequent archaeological record of the Islamic and modern eras is sparsely represented in our collection, and I cannot as yet report on specifics. Rather, I will end with the recent era. I quote from C. J. Edmonds, a British officer who traveled on a difficult migration route from Khuzistan to Khorramabad. Luristan, he says,

> has been in a chronic state of anarchy, certainly during the last century and probably throughout their history, with only brief intervals of comparative order under an occasional strong governor. Lord Curzon quotes Quintus Curtius and Pliny, who described how the tribes of Elam "set at nought the authority of the Medes and Persians, defied Alexander, and provoked Antiochus." Local tradition states that the ancient city of Khurramabad was destroyed by Chingiz as a reprisal for a series of treacherous attacks in his rear. In more recent times the Lurs have set at nought the authority of the Persian Government. For some years past no Persian Governor has been able to penetrate from Burujird to Khurramabad. The last to attempt it was the powerful Nizam-us-Sultaneh, whose army, including a large force of Swedish trained gendarmerie, was completely defeated at Khurramabad in 1915. (Edmonds 1922: 36)

It seems that over the centuries, Luristan has been home to many tribes, most recently Luri, each with its khan who built forts in strategic places. From the sixteenth century, these tribes were governed by the wali of Luristan, an Ottoman appointment that became hereditary, and gave the wali absolute power over the people of Luristan. By the twentieth century, his power had been split into southern (Pusht-i-Kuh) and northern (Pish-i-Kuh) regions under two governors, both of whom were deposed by the Reza Shah's forces. Similar shifting fortunes, some locally engendered, others imposed, may have characterized Luristan since the end of the Chalcolithic.

CONCLUDING REMARKS

The attempt to understand the history of the Khorramabad Valley has high-lighted the need for excavations, both for refining the ceramic chronology and, more importantly, to document the nature of the settlements. On the sole basis of surface remains and the distribution of sites, we have gained only the most superficial impression of the dynamics of occupation. It is clear that the Khorramabad Valley was not always isolated, because at various times it received ceramic and probably population inputs from outside Luristan, yet the Khorramabad Valley was beyond the reach of Dalma, Halaf, classic Late Uruk, and Transcaucasian Gray Wares, and locally made ceramic styles pervaded the valley throughout its history. We have as yet no good way to assess the degree to which Luristan was actually utilized during the periods when ceramics are not present.

This study has also pointed up the need to consider Luristan broadly rather than valley by valley, because it is unlikely that any of the valleys sufficed to support a minimal social and reproductive population except during unusually favorable climatic periods and when peace prevailed. If this is the case, we should consider any valley as only a small part of a group's sustaining area, which would have included the surrounding hills and ridges as well as seasonal pastures. While we may imagine this situation, we cannot know with any accuracy how the sizes of local groups and of their territories varied through time, although we might gain some insight into the political structure through the excavation of forts and manors. We can imagine that the valleys on the edges of Luristan are more likely to have been impacted by peoples outside of Luristan, such as Susiana, than by those in the interior. Unless archaeologists one day can carry out a comprehensive survey of all the valleys, we will not know for sure whether there were region-wide disruptions of occupation, nor will we be able to disentangle the zones of interaction at each period. The knowledge that there were substantial, repeated gaps in occupation in at least some valleys encourages us to seek explanations, whether climatic, political, or other.

I close this short paper by noting that the pastoral mode of adaptation that has characterized much of the history of the region has been brought to an end, first by the forcible settlement of nomads by the Reza Shah in the 1920s and 1930s, and more recently by the inexorable crush of population that has spread agriculture and villages onto pasture land. Luristan is no longer geographically isolated, and modern agricultural technology and industry have overcome the former environmental limitations of settlement and agriculture. It remains to be seen whether the fragile landscape of Luristan is capable of sustaining the unprecedented stresses of this newly intensive occupation.

HARAPPAN GEOARCHAEOLOGY RECONSIDERED: HOLOCENE LANDSCAPES AND ENVIRONMENTS OF THE GREATER INDUS PLAIN

JOSEPH SCHULDENREIN, RITA WRIGHT, AND
MOHAMMED AFZAL KHAN

ABSTRACT

The emergence of complex societies in the Indus Valley is largely documented through the archaeological records of its two primary urban centers: Harappa in the north and Mohenjo-daro in the south. The dynamic geography of linked settlement and subsistence environments remain incompletely understood. This presentation begins with a summary of fundamental site and landscape relationships across the Harappan culture core. A baseline landscape chronology for the pivotal middle to late Holocene is generated. Reconstructions are synthesized by merging geological and archaeological sequences for the Lower and Upper Indus floodplains and terraces. Lower Valley Harappan sequences are characterized by changing settlement distributions in response to migrations of the main stem of the Indus channel. Recently developed Upper Valley chronologies have integrated depositional and soil-forming sequences with stable surfaces, climate change, and periods of intense settlement in the Harappan hinterlands. Convergent upstream and downstream landscape records for the Indus point to discrete climatic intervals that may have influenced the broader course of Harappan settlement. A period of Middle Holocene desiccation, based on monsoon circulation patterns, preceded initial Harappan occupations prior to 5000 BP. Significantly, the interval of Harappan-era florescence is accompanied by mixed climatic signals, based on equivocal interpretations of the geomorphic and paleoenvironmental record. The decline of the Harappan heartland may be related to a change in the precipitation regime as well as more intensive human manipulation of the floodplain environment.

INTRODUCTION AND OBJECTIVES

It is widely recognized that the earliest state societies of the Old World flourished in part because of their locations on the fertile floodplains and terraces of the world's most extensive rivers. Between 5500 and 3500 years ago, complex societies emerged in the valleys of the Nile (Egypt), Tigris-Euphrates (Mesopotamia), Yangtze (China), and Indus (Pakistan and India). The archaeological record of the evolution, fluorescence, and collapse of these societies is as varied as it is complex, but the chronicle of the Harappan civilization is perhaps the least known because its script remains undeciphered.

Archaeological explorations of the Indus civilization of Pakistan, India, and northeastern Afghanistan, are rich and compelling, but uneven. Although the major urban centers of Mohenjo-daro and Harappa are generally included in evolutionary syntheses of state societies, much less is known about the greater landscapes and environmental backdrop to Indus cultural developments. Until recently, paleoecological approaches were not widely incorporated in Indus studies, unlike the case in Mesopotamia (Adams 1965; 1978; 1981; Adams and Nissen 1972) where site–landscape relations were at the core of developing an understanding of the regional settlement network of irrigation-based economies and polities. Reconstructions of the human and environmental dynamic of the Indus culture have been hindered in part because landscape studies have not extended beyond its major urban areas.

Over the past decade, geoarchaeology has shown promise for modeling settlement and landscape dynamics for the Indus civilization. Geoarchaeology explores systematic relationships between sites using methods and techniques of the earth sciences (for instance, in the study of soils, sediments, drainage nets, and topographic settings) (Butzer 1982; M. R. Waters 1999). For complex societies, geoarchaeology examines broad parameters of climatic and environmental change, but even more importantly, it sheds light on how natural terrain and landscapes were modified by polities confronting population pressure and resource stress. Adaptive hallmarks of the Indus culture include water management systems, complex mound construction, and use of domesticated plants and animals. The relatively sudden collapse of the Indus civilization remains a mystery but is likely attributable to combinations of climatic, hydrographic, geological, and human impacts. Geoarchaeology is a means for sorting out these factors, linking them chronologically, and tracking landscape changes that may help account for cultural transformations in South Asia during the Middle Holocene.

This paper reviews the current state of Indus geoarchaeological research. The chronology of Indus occupations is initially considered with respect to the calibrated radiocarbon record. Extant site–landform correlations are then viewed as a backdrop to deciphering Middle Holocene site geography. Sites are unevenly distributed across the landscape and reflect complex geomorphic processes that have biased the site distribution records. Geomorphic maps provide some insights on site distributions, but the most ancient sites with information on human ecological dynamics are those that can be tied to alluvial geomorphology and the linked soil and occupation stratigraphies of the greater Indus floodplains. Stream behavior and sedimentation regimes differ between the Indus's Upper and Lower Basins, and each is discussed in terms of its archaeological implications. For the pivotal Middle Holocene, floodplain histories that order cycles of environmental stability and settlement geography suffer from a lack of radiocarbon dates and inattention to soil chronologies and sediment stratigraphies. A recent pilot study of an Upper Indus Valley sequence points the way to filling this gap (Schuldenrein et al. 2004; R. P. Wright, Khan, and Schuldenrein 2002; R. P. Wright et al. 2005a; 2005b). Finally, some hypotheses exploring the climatic and environmental evidence for Middle Holocene cultural expansion and Late Holocene collapse are entertained.

GEOGRAPHY AND ARCHAEOLOGY OF THE INDUS HEARTLAND

Indus Chronologies

The Harappan or Indus culture has traditionally referred to the complex of sites centered on the Indus River and tributaries that culminated in urban adaptations between ca. 3200 BC and 1900 BC (Allchin and Allchin 1982; Possehl 1997b; 1999; 2002). Key settlements are also centered along the Ghaggar-Hakra in Cholistan (Mughal 1997) and northwest India (Francfort 1986). Figure 21 illustrates key sites by cultural component, with respect to primary drainages, geographic features, and regions of the greater Indus culture area. Harappan manifestations are densest in semiarid Pakistan but extend well into India. They are also culturally related to early agricultural communities in the western piedmont of Baluchistan and Afghanistan (Jarrige and Lechevallier 1979). At least seven regional Harappan core areas have been identified (Joshi 1984; Possehl 1999), with the result that cultural chronologies vary between areas. For the purpose of this paper, an overarching cultural sequence is utilized (Table 1). The major developmental divisions are between the Early Harappan (Period 2/ Kot Diji phase) and Mature Harappan (Period 3/Harappan Phases A, B, and C). Early Harappan marks the transition from village farming communities into "formative urbanism," an adaptive shift that included the building of walled settlements, the growth of regional trends in pottery manufacture and ornamentation, the development of writing, and the spread of trade networks (Kenoyer 1998). The subsequent

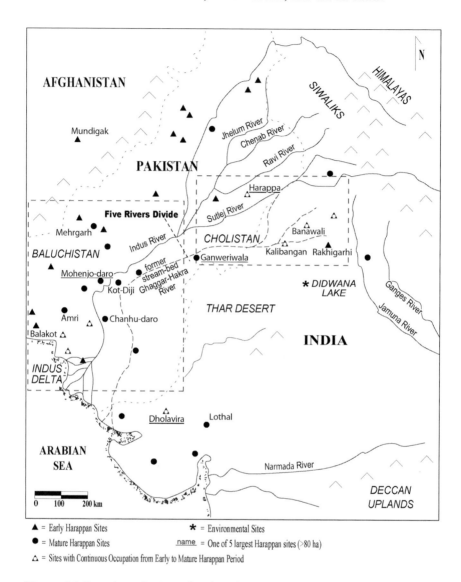

Figure 21. Location of principal archaeological sites, paleoenvironmental sites, and geographic regions mentioned in the text. The Upper Indus refers to the area east of the Five Rivers Divide, while the Lower Indus is the area to west and south.

Mature Harappan signaled the integration of regional traditions into systems of networked cities with satellite communities, and the emergence of socio-economic and political hierarchies that managed industrial-scale production, a standardized system of writing, systems of weights and measures, and increased trade. The Early Harappan lasted to ca. 2600 BC, the Mature

TABLE 1. Indus Valley Chronology for the Harappan Era

Years BP	Period		Phase	Period Intervals
5800			*Early Food Producing Era*	
5500				
	Period 1	Early	*Regionalization Era* Ravi (aspect of Hakra) Phase	(>3300–2800 BC)
5000				
	Period 2	Early	Kot Diji (Early Harappa) Phase	(2800–2600 BC)
		Mature Harappan	*Integration Era*	
	Period 3A	Mature Harappan	Harappa Phase A	(2600–2450 BC)
4500				
	Period 3B	Mature Harappan	Harappa Phase B	(2450–2200 BC)
	Period 3C	Mature Harappan	Harappa Phase C	(2200–1900 BC)
4000			*Localization Era*	
	Period 4	Late	Harappa/Late Harappa Transitional	(1900–1800 BC)
	Period 5	Late	Late Harappa Phase	(1800–1300 BC)
3500				

Source: After Shaffer (1992), Possehl (1999), and Meadow et al. (2001)

Harappan was eclipsed by ca. 1900 BC (Late Harappan), and the civilization was in decline by 1700 BC.

In the past decade, Harappan chronologies have been substantially refined on the strength of calibrated Holocene ^{14}C determinations that accommodate the disjuncture between radiocarbon years and solar years (de Vries effects; see Stuiver et al. 1993; Taylor 1997). The significance of the calibrated sequences cannot be underestimated, since together the Early and Mature Harappan lasted only about 1400 years, and correlating sequences within such a limited time frame is dependent on the accuracy and convergence of absolute dates and cultural sequences. Harappan-age radiocarbon dates have been compiled in several publications (Allchin and Allchin 1982; Kenoyer 1991a; Possehl 1997b; 1999), but the majority of samples (> 60 percent) are derived from only three sites—Harappa, Mohenjo-daro, and Kalibangan (Schuldenrein 2002).

The dates largely corroborate successions generated from typological and archaeological analyses and attest to the pan-regional reach of the culture. Harappan civilization spans the Middle to lower Late Holocene, with site frequencies highest for the Mature Harappan, between 4600 and 4000 BP (ca. 2600–2000 BC). A recent inventory of Harappan-age sites assigns

976 to Mature and 477 to Early phases, approximately a 2:1 ratio (Possehl 1999: 714 and app. A).

Combining the absolute chronologies with the archaeology underscores several spatio-temporal trends:

1. There is sparse evidence for occupation on the Indus alluvial plain prior to 3300 BC; radiocarbon evidence suggests that earlier sites are most likely to have occurred in the Upper Indus Valley (Schuldenrein 2002).

2. The end of Harappan occupation is dramatic, given the fall-off in radio-carbon dates after 1900 BC

3. Deterioration of both the northern and southern urban centers—Harappa and Mohenjo-daro, respectively—may have preceded the decline in satellite communities, which may have outlasted the two hub communities by 200 to 400 years (Kenoyer 1991a; 1991b; Schuldenrein 2002: fig. 2).

HARAPPAN LANDSCAPES AND SITE GEOGRAPHY

The Indus River is the central geographic feature for the distribution of Harappan sites. It rises in the Himalayas, initially flowing north and west through its mountainous segments, then turns southwest to drain the foothills (Siwaliks) and ultimately flows the length of Pakistan before emptying into the Arabian Sea through the Indus Delta (Figure 21). The densest Harappan distributions begin south of the Siwaliks, where the greater Indus tributary net begins; site clusters intensify progressively downstream, in the graded terrain of the Punjab and in the Lower Indus in Sindh.

Separation of the Upper and Lower Indus Basins is a function of a major structural fault, the Sulaiman Foredeep, at the Five Rivers Divide (Figure 21). The Upper Basin refers to the catchment north and east of the confluence of the Five Rivers (Jhellum, Chenab, Ravi, Beas [buried and not shown], and Sutlej), while the Lower Basin extends to the stream mouth at the modern Indus delta and coast (Figure 21). Large sites are dispersed along coastal reaches north and south of the Indus Delta as well. The highest site densities occur in the abandoned desolate segments of the Ghaggar-Hakra Plain (to Cholistan and to the east; Figure 21), a landscape greatly altered by channel abandonments and subsequent dune activity (Courty 1995; Mughal 1992). Early researchers recognized that the present alignment of sites does not nec-essarily conform to either the Harappan-age Indus alluvial geography or the reach of the culture core (Mackay 1945; Mughal 1990; 1992; Raikes and Dales 1977; Wilhelmy 1969). Further impeding systematic reconstruction of site–landform relationships is the absence of a reliable site inventory as a result of disparate regional and local records, limited dissemination of much of the Pakistani and Indian literature, and lack of documentation for inaccessible areas (although see Possehl 1999). Such considerations notwithstanding, the available site distributions suggest that alluvial histories are linked to site formation chronologies. As discussed below, the alignment of earlier Harappan sites in the Upper Valley and later Harappan settlements in the Lower Valley argues that the Holocene histories of each segment account for human–landscape interactions constrained by more localized cultural and environmental influences.

More generally, landform chronologies suffer from a lack of pre- and non-cultural radiocarbon dates and a near absence of soil development histories (paleo-pedology). For the Middle Holocene, the identifications of stable surfaces, through soil sequences, establishes those periods of landscape stasis when flooding was minimal and extensive floodplain reaches were available for settlement (Schuldenrein et al. 2004; R. P. Wright, Khan, and Schuldenrein 2002; R. P. Wright et al. 2005 a; 2005b). Thus the establishment of soil-based timelines is a critical barometer of the environmental and climatic conditions favoring settlement at around 5500 BP. Dating difficulties have been partially overcome by LANDSAT- and aerial photograph-based mapping and paleochannel modeling of the Lower Indus near Mohenjo-daro (Flam 1993; Harvey and Schumm 1999; Jorgensen et al. 1993), and by site formation and soils investigations at both Mohenjo-daro (Balista 1988; Cucarzi 1984; Jansen 1999) and Harappa (Belcher and Belcher 2000; Pendall and Amundson 1990a; 1990b; Schuldenrein et al. 2004; R. P. Wright, Khan, and Schuldenrein 2002; R. P. Wright et al. 2005 a; 2005b).

A broad picture of settlement and landscape patterning can be obtained with the help of two separate maps of surface geology (Government of Canada 1956; Mian and Syal 1986). These maps complement each other, as the former links landforms topographically and the latter utilizes soil groups as an organizing principle. Table 2 correlates landform categories and cultural chronologies, presents an assessment of site expectation, and summarizes the characteristics of the seven primary landform complexes. The main depositional processes for each complex are identified, along with estimates of age based on the limited geomorphic, sedimentological, and soil studies performed to date. The antiquity of the landforms generally grades to younger in a seaward direction, a function of increased downstream alluviation compounded by rising sea level along the coastal plain. While it might be expected that age-dependent geomorphic dynamics are also reflected in the site distributions—younger sites expected closer to the coast and better preservation upstream—such an assessment is premature.

Table 2 is thus at best a crude guideline for site expectation. This is because the ages of the landforms are unreliable, based on relative landform

TABLE 2. Landforms of the Indus and Harappan Site Distributions

Landform	Description	Depositional Process	Age	Upper Basin	Lower Basin	Harappan Site Expectation
Sandy deserts	Laterally zoned complex of dune and terrace meso-environments	Alluvial valleys dominated by flooding and stream migration, but punctuated by protracted intervals of aeolian activity and tectonic displacements	Pleistocene to Holocene	Southeastern margins of Ghaggar Plain in Cholistan	Similar to Cholistan in upper Thar Desert; southern reaches not widely known	High
Bajadas	Coalescent aprons and alluvial fans	Fan progradation of coarse, stony gravels and sandy gravel sedimentary suites	Late Pleistocene to Holocene	Discontinuous fan complexes along piedmont edge (to western margin of Indus)	More extensive, semi-continuous fans grading directly onto alluvial terrain	Medium
Undulating sandy terraces	High escarpment interfluves with irregular surfaces	Interglacial and post-glacial outwash intercalated with massive angular boulders (tectonic origin?) and capped by loess	Middle to Late Pleistocene	Semi-continuous landform between Jhelum and Indus	NA	Low
Bar uplands (doabs)	Extensive terraces 2–9 m high; also referred to as tablelands since they span extensive interfluves between drainages	Massive outwash deposits laid down by post-glacial melting and resorting of coarser fills from Himalayan core area	Late Pleistocene–Early Holocene	Older and more extensive at upstream ends of Chenab, Ravi, and Sutlej drainage where they extend across interfluves; irregular remnants near channel confluences	NA	Medium
Terrace (T-1)	Low-relief terrain generally used for contemporary agriculture and flood control	Protracted seasonal and irregular overbanking; episodic sheet flooding, meandering, and braiding	Middle to Late Holocene (Early Harappan to post-Harappan)	Semi-continuous bands running parallel to principal flow axes of the Five Rivers; Meso-landforms include level plains and (isolated) infilled channels. Periodic sheet flooding has destroyed/modified landform in recent times	Localized basins, levee remnants, and infilled ancient stream channels of the former meandering Indus trunk stream; low relief of basin preserves extensive buried segments between Thar Desert and western mountains	Medium–High
Floodplain	Near level to mildly undulating surfaces. These are ellipsoid to more laterally extensive segments of alluvium dispersed irregularly along proximal margins of active drainages	Cut and fill deposits inset into T-1 banks	Late Holocene, contemporary to Historic (post-Harappan)"	Localized point bar deposits along outside banks of meandering segments of primary drainages; dominant accretion along major confluences (Indus, Chenab, Sutlej, and Jheulum)	Attenuated in downstream direction; disappears immediately north of Indus Delta where it grades into deltaic sediments	Low
Indus delta and estuarine plain	Coastal plain aggradation of pro-deltaic and marine sediments	Level surfaces dominantly silty; basins are infilled with clays; tidal flooding and riverine sedimentation attest to highly variable geomorphic process in littoral setting	Holocene	NA	Sediment complex of spill flats, basins, spill heads, meander bars, and levees	Medium

elevations and on scaled degrees of soil development on the more stable and older terraces. Thus, in the Five Rivers area (see Figure 21), the prevailing alluvial chronology projects floodplain and terrace surface ages on classic cut and fill models (Brinkman and Rafiq 1971; see discussion in Flam 1993). The Bar Uplands—the higher areas (or interfluves) between the rivers—are considered to be Pleistocene terraces that were downcut, their margins subsequently aggraded in the Early Holocene to create what will be referred to here as Terrace T-1 (see Figure 22 for the area around Harappa; elsewhere called subrecent floodplains; see Flam 1993). A second cycle beginning with the dissection of the T-1 landform and culminating with construction of the floodplains is assigned to the Contemporary/Historic period (or Late Holocene). There are no absolute dates or soil sequences anywhere to confirm these associations (although see Schuldenrein 2002).

Table 2 shows that the highest concentrations of sites are contained in sandy deserts and first terraces (T-1 landform). Preservation conditions and contexts are different for the two. In the sandy deserts of the Ghaggar-Hakra region, for example, site exposure is the product of Cholistan's dynamic geomorphic environment in the recent past. Landscapes now consist of a series of low-relief dune and desert landforms that did not exist in Harappan times when this part of the Ghaggar-Hakra drainage sustained a lush alluvial biome. Aeolian sedimentation has overridden the former riparian environment, virtually masking it and obscuring the evidence of a biotically differentiated floodplain that sustained an environment suitable for agriculture and broadly based subsistence economies.

The other context, T-1 landforms, is more typical for well-preserved Harappan sites. These are former floodplains whose archaeological environments are either sealed by later Holocene alluvium or consist of mounds built on that older floodplain. In the Upper Basin, the more prominent topography underscores the correspondence between mounds and elevated terrace environments. A typical setting is shown in Figure 22. Here Harappa and two smaller satellite mounds, Chak Pirbane Syal and Lahoma Lal Tibba, occupy the terrace landform (T-1) positioned between more dynamic, currently active floodplain (T-0) segments which are now subject to extensive inundation (Schuldenrein et al. 2004). The T-1 is also known locally as a *doab*, and in the Upper Basin it refers to elongated Late Quaternary terraces, parallel to stream flow and forming the interfluves between adjacent trunk streams; elevations can extend to 15 meters above floodplains (T-0) but are more typically less than 5 meters high. Site positioning on the doab between the Ravi and Beas Rivers was optimal for exploiting riverine resources and for farming the well-drained raised fields of the flanking rivers. The present topography preserves evidence of the Middle Holocene physiography. Elsewhere in the Upper Valley, bajadas, gently sloping plains of unconsolidated rock debris at

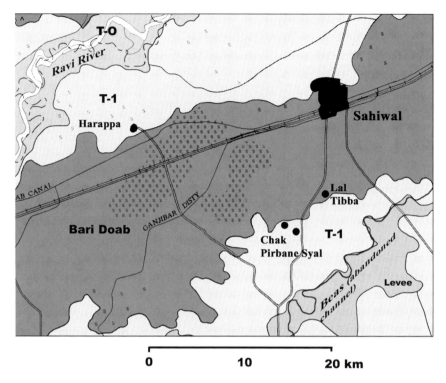

Figure 22. The Bari Doab and landforms in its immediate vicinity. Note the first terrace (T-1), floodplain (T-0), and levee segment flanking the Doab. Present locations of Harappan-period sites are shown on margins of Doab and T-1 (modified from Government of Canada 1956).

the mountain fronts—effectively desert pavements that are resistant to erosion—are likely to preserve nonstratified evidence for recurrent Harappan occupations. The more complex depositional features (Indus Delta) contain clustered landscape segments of variable age with similarly variable preservation potential. Low site expectation is characteristic of areas where both landforms and sites are poorly investigated or where there is no apparent relationship between landform and site selection. Table 2 indicates that the highest expectation for preserved, stratified sites is in the T-1 landform category. Moderate to high site expectation is noted for the Upper and Lower Basins because of the unique geomorphic processes associated with the channel geometry and flooding behavior of each segment, as summarized below.

As previously stated, the absence of an absolute Holocene landform chronology remains an impediment to understanding the environmental history of the Harappan landscape. However, it is still possible to systematize associations between Harappan site clusters and landform complexes on a broad scale (refer to Figure 22 and Table 2). Accordingly:

1. There is a high density of Early Harappan (Kot Diji phase) sites on the bajadas grading down from the Piedmont Plain. Major sites generally occur along major drainages but smaller ones do not. The coalescent alluvial fans upon which the latter sites are found are difficult to bracket stratigraphically, since such fans are erosional surfaces of uncertain Pleistocene age.

2. Markedly lower site densities in the Upper Valley may reflect the dynamism of the Upper Indus drainage system and the dearth of systematic archaeological and geoarchaeological exploration of this region. The discrepancy in site frequencies between the Lower and Upper Valley is pronounced. The majority of known Upper Valley sites are associated with either Bar Uplands or T-1 surfaces.

3. Early and Late Harappan sites along the distributaries emptying into the mouth of the Arabian Sea attest to extensive deltaic progradation (buildup) during the Middle to Late Holocene. The Harappan coast may have been tens of kilometers inland of its present location, although coastline configurations of the Harappan-age littoral landscape remain speculative.

4. The proliferation of lineally configured Late Harappan sites in the Lower Valley signifies pronounced channel migration along the downstream reaches of the Indus in the Middle and Late Holocene. At Mohenjo-daro, the Indus flowed up to 25 kilometers to the west of its present course. Sites span several geomorphic units, including the T-1, bajadas, and undifferentiated piedmont segments. Former channel courses have been extensively mapped and relatively dated based on geomorphic features.

5. The preservation of extensive Harappan site complexes in the sandy deserts of Cholistan—the Ghaggar-Hakra Plain—reflects a major paleogeographic shift during the Late Holocene. The primary landscape modification involved stream capture and the westward migration of the drainage net, most dramatically the Sutlej, between ca. 1500 BC and AD 1500. Both climatic and tectonic mechanisms account for attendant landscape overhauls.

In sum, while the geomorphic record is useful for sorting out relationships between site selection, preservation, and landform types, its potential for establishing the synchroneity of occupation and landscape history is constrained by the lack of dated subsurface stratigraphic evidence. The impact of tectonics may be the most difficult to chronicle. Nevertheless, the aforementioned landform complexes (Table 2) accommodate nearly 90 percent of known Harappan sites, based on a general correspondence between landform units and recent site distribution maps (in Possehl 1999). Primary sources for environmental and Harappan-aged sequences are stratified alluvial records whose deep flood sets are separated by developed soils signifying stable landforms with archaeological potential.

ALLUVIAL GEOMORPHOLOGY OF HARAPPAN SITES

As the above discussion stresses, the key measures of landscape change for the critical protohistoric period are extant landform configurations and stratigraphic sequences. Landform configurations (and by extension, site–landform correlations) are only indicators of preservation. Stratigraphic sequences preserve depositional histories and are more complete, finer-scale proxies for environmental succession. The alluvial geomorphology of the Indus is therefore an optimal backdrop for ordering human ecological events.

Pre-Quaternary dynamics of Indus stream flow, hydrography, and topography were initially fashioned by structural elements (Friend et al. 1999) and, as noted above, the Sulaiman Foredeep is the feature that separates the Upper and Lower Indus Basins (Kazmi and Rana 1982; Haghipour, Ghorashi, and Kadjar 1984; Biswas 1987) (Figure 21). However, there is considerable debate as to the influence of tectonics versus other environmental factors—climate, paleohydrology, runoff, erosion, stream migration, and alluvial landform construction—in modifying those Late Quaternary landscapes contemporaneous with earliest settlement. Lateral channel migration is characteristic of most of the Indus, such that meter upon meter of Late Quaternary sediments have built up extensive, low-relief, alluvial plains (Harvey and Schumm 1999; Jorgensen et al. 1993). It is often impossible to differentiate buried channels because of the depth of sediment burial and the uniformity of sediment type (typically in the fine sand or silt loam size grade). Depositional uniformity has obscured Harappan settlement topography and complicated attempts to synthesize stream and valley histories. Massive flooding, breaches in channel flow due to monsoon-generated runoff, and overhauls of the contemporary and perhaps earlier irrigation networks (Wescoat 1998) have collectively reduced gradients to the point where visible landform separation is possible only in select reaches of the drainage. The vast majority of Harappan sites are situated within this typically undifferentiated alluvial terrain, with sites occupying terrace or basin segments at elevations below 1200 meters (Schuldenrein 2002). It has been estimated that the Harappan civilization encompasses nearly half a million square kilometers (Agrawal 1992).

In general, the rivers above the Five Rivers Divide flow below the levels of the adjacent floodplains. This is not so for the Indus trunk stream to the south. The Upper Basin is characterized by a series of high-order tributaries separated by the low-relief *doabs* cited earlier (Figure 22); these were the loci of mound sites immediately flanked by laterally extensive alluvial basins (Khan 1991). In contrast, the Lower Basin has sustained a more freely migrating stream—between the Thar Desert and the Western Mountains—that eventually progrades into the coastal delta (Figure 21). The differences between Lower Valley and Upper Valley landscape relations and associated geomorphic processes are discussed below.

Lower Valley

Early attempts at modeling relationships between site location and environment were begun at Mohenjo-daro in order to address the reasons why this enormous, 250-hectare city was abandoned. It was thought that the site was either obliterated by a series of floods that created a semipermanent dam or lake, or that frequent channel shifts depleted soil moisture recharge and agricultural productivity of the fields fronting the floodplain. Arguments in support of the dam theory were given prominence in the 1960s and 1970s, with the recognition of presumed alluvial and paludal (that is, swamp or marsh-related) deposits ranging 8 to 12 meters above the existing floodplain (Raikes 1964, 1965; Dales and Raikes 1977; Raikes and Dales 1977). Damming of the Lower Indus that resulted in such sedimentation was attributed to tectonism. An alternative hypothesis raised doubts that field relations and sedimentology implicated a relict dam landform (Lambrick 1967). Instead it was argued that the disposition of the deeply stacked fine sands, silts, and clays was of aeolian origin.

The Raikes hypothesis has subsequently been questioned on a variety of grounds, most notably whether the impermeable source alluvium could retain floodwaters without dam failure (Jorgensen et al. 1993; Harvey and Schumm 1999). Revised assessments are based on geomorphological work that has linked lateral stream movement to depositional suites near Mohenjo-daro, effectively confirming the Lambrick hypothesis. By quantifying rates of sedimentation, stream slope, and channel displacements through time, they concluded that Indus River dynamism is best explained by channel migration, perhaps initiated by tectonics but ultimately perpetuated by segmentation of the various reaches of the lower drainage basin. Segmentation of channel reaches may have accounted for the partitioning and zonation of agricultural fields for finite durations, thus accounting for limitations on Harappan settlement, patterns of land use, and longevity.

LANDSAT and aerial photographic mapping of relict paleochannels and levee remnants in lower Sindh bolsters this hypothesis (Flam 1993; 1999).

Flam mapped two major and numerous minor courses of the former Lower Indus between 4000 and 3000 BC. Figure 23 shows that both the major channel courses—the Sindhu Nadi to the west and the Nara Nadi to the east—flank the present locations of major Harappan sites. The complex migrations of the ancestral stream left meanders that isolated landscape segments which may have been functional over several decades or longer. Such extensive meandering at Mohenjo-daro resulted in the long-term dis-

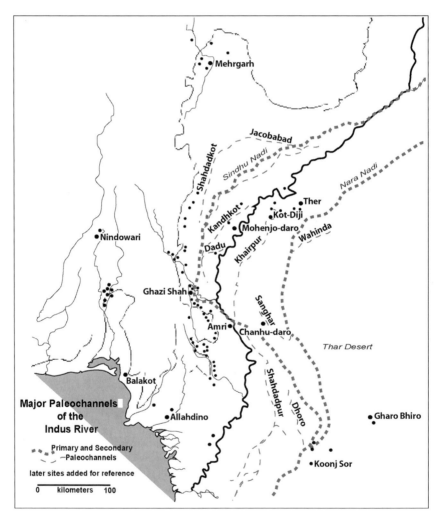

Figure 23. The ancient drainage net of the Lower Indus Valley in the vicinity of Mohenjo-daro. Principal paleochannels—Sindhu Nadi and Nara Nadi—as well as key tributary segments are shown. Key archaeological sites are depicted. (Map modified from Flam 1993 and Possehl 1999: 296, 309).

placement of the active Indus channel to its present position, approximately 25 kilometers southeast of its original course, during peak Harappan occupation. Changes in the flow regime of the major channels would have promoted sheet flooding whose effects extended throughout the drainage net in Sindh. The relatively short and irregularly dispersed irrigation channels suggest that only limited irrigation agriculture was practiced (Flam 1999) and its role at Mohenjo-daro has been minimized (Jansen 1999). Ultimately full-scale abandonment of complete settlement networks may have occurred as flood subbasins were reconfigured and cultivable tracts inundated. Lower Basin research has also demonstrated that progradation of the delta has systematically extended the shoreline southwestward into the Arabian Sea. The complex alignments of the primary Harappan centers south and west of Mohenjo-daro are consistent with arguments tying progressive channel migration to shoreline displacements (see Figure 23).

This hypothesis has not been verified by either landform relations or by the stratigraphic record. A critical gap is the chronology of Holocene terraces and the cut and fill cycles that produced the *doabs* (Figure 22 and Table 2). In the Lower Valley, lateral migration produced relatively shallow terraces, on the order of < 1 meter, but it remains difficult to establish firm landform associations with Harappan sites aligned with such subdued surfaces flanking contemporary channels (Schuldenrein 2002). Terrace chronologies remain uncertain and must be considered relative in the absence of more refined mapping bolstered by radiocarbon dates and soil sequences. Beg (1993: 258–263), for example, has proposed a soil taxonomy for the terraces and subrecent floodplains that postdates the landform chronology of Mian and Syal (1986; see Table 2).

Some critical chrono-stratigraphic information can be gleaned from Mohenjo-daro itself. Jansen (1999) noted that the replacement of mud brick by burnt brick for retaining walls between the Early and Mature Harappan was a technology designed to stabilize foundations against rising groundwater. It is now estimated that original (Early) Harappan landforms were up to 10 meters below present surfaces, while groundwater is only 5 meters below. Groundwater would have migrated from excess discharge laterally (by channel movements, as noted) or from increased discharge from the Indus. It is known that siltation increased drastically during the Holocene—on the order of 10 centimeters per century (Haitken 1907). The variable location of water sources is also indicated by the proliferation of over 600 wells in the city. Such needs were clearly related to a time when the river was considerably more distant from its present position.

Upper Valley

As in the case of the Lower Valley, both climatic and tectonic mechanisms were major influences in fashioning Upper Valley landscape histories, but the lines of evidence are more varied and several areas have been investigated.

The Ghaggar-Hakra Area. It is striking that the highest densities of sites in the Upper Valley were associated with the Ghaggar-Hakra Plain in Cholistan (Figure 21; Mughal 1982; 1989). That area is now traversed by a series of dry distributaries linked to the primary channel bed. An early study (Wilhelmy 1969) offered initial indications that site abandonments were related to stream capture of the Sutlej during the Late Harappan and the culture's subsequent collapse (1500 BC–AD 1500) when the Indus and Ganges drainages assumed their present configurations. Flam (1999) suggests that an upstream change of this magnitude resulted in the increased flow to the Sindhu Nadi.

The Ghaggar-Hakra research has benefited from contributions from archaeology, historiography, geomorphology, and sedimentology, much of which has been recently summarized by Possehl (1999: 359–387). The density of Harappan sites and their intricate associations with complex stream migrations is illustrated in Figure 24. Some researchers have associated the Ghaggar-Hakra drainage with the ancient Sarasvati, which was the holiest of Indian rivers in Vedic times (Wadia 1966). References to the stream's significance during the time of Alexander the Great are noted historically (Tod 1829). Archaeologically related investigations of the dry streambeds have been undertaken since the late nineteenth century (Oldham 1893; S. Bhan 1973; Pande 1977).

There is some question as to the chronology, morphology, and evolution of the Indus and Ganges systems and the pivotal role of the Ghaggar-Hakra in explaining such developments. It has been proposed that, at various times in the Holocene, the Ghaggar belonged either to the Jamuna/Ganges watershed, or to the Indus—via the ancient Hakra—since the modern river Sutlej is located between them (Figure 21). The preponderance of the evidence now favors a west-southwest (that is, Indus net) flow during Harappan times. The primary channel was gradually displaced northwestward, initially captured by the Sutlej, and then by the Beas, subsequently emptying into the primary Indus stem (Mughal 1997; Pande 1977; Possehl 1999; 2002; Wilhelmy 1969). By 1500 BC the stream channels shown in Figure 24 were effectively bereft of water, except for pockets sustained by recharge during seasons of intense monsoon rains.

The emergence of stream networks since the Middle Holocene has been modeled on alignments of Harappan sites (Figure 24). Site distribution data for the Cholistan Desert sites along the abandoned bed of the Hakra are presented in Table 3. The data report provides information on site size and more

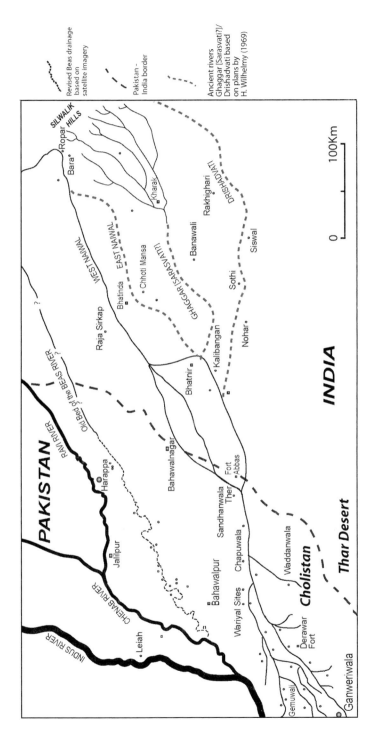

Figure 24. The ancient drainage of the Upper Indus Valley in the vicinity of Harappa and south and west to Cholistan. Note the complex streambed and settlement configurations of the Ghaggar-Hakra along margins of defunct channels. The old Bed of the Beas is shown along with principal sites investigated during the recent Beas Survey (see text). (Map redrawn from Possehl 1999: 382).

detailed measures of settlement frequency by site category (such as camp, residential, industrial, cemetery) for the periods from 3500 BC through 1000 BC (data assembled from Mughal 1982; 1990; 1992). While a comprehensive analysis of site function and settlement trends is beyond the scope of this study, the data illustrate that site densities (by count) and site sizes (by area) are highest during the Mature Harappan. They are preceded and succeeded by lower site densities and smaller site sizes during the emerging and declining phases of the Harappan culture. The exception to this trend is during the Early Harappan, where high site frequencies but relatively small site sizes mirror pre-state, nomadic-pastoral settlement patterns that favored clustering in well-watered settings not tied to perennial stream flow (Kenoyer 1998). Thus the high stream density (larger proportion of stream arteries relative to land area) modeled for the Mature Harappan reflects a dynamic stream network that must have been, in part, manipulated by polities of a stabilized state society. To what extent this development represented human engineering (drainage and irrigation nets) versus climatic influences (higher or better distributed rainfall) or tectonic shifts (displacements of the entire drainage net) remains uncertain. What is clear is that the landscape was such that the available rainfall and water sources, including springs and seasonal aquatic basins, favored the long-term survival of the state-based organization. The Mature Harappan represented the era of optimal balance between human exploitation and availability of water resources.

The situation to the north and east of Cholistan is of equal interest. To date, the only studies of the subsurface geological record are those of Courty

TABLE 3. Distribution of Sites: Sindh and Cholistan

Site category	4th millennium BC	3100/3000– 2500 BC	1500–2000/ 1900 BC	1900– 1500 BC	1100/ 1000– 500 BC
	Hakra	Early Harappan	Mature Harappan	Late Harappan	Painted Gray Ware
Camp sites	52	3	10		13
Residential sites	45	23	50	14	14
Industrial activity	2	14	33	14	
Exclusively industrial			79	9	
Cemeteries			2		
Total number of sites per period	99	40	174	50	14

Source: After Mughal 1990; 1992.

(1995) who addressed the chronologies of sedimentation and soil formation as proxies for the interplay between dynamic flood-prone environments and stable landscapes that would have preserved soil horizons and archaeological sites associated with their upper profiles. She concluded that the widely accepted Early Holocene moist phase in South Asia initiated the multiple channel configurations in the Ghaggar-Hakra. The last major phase of alluviation ended prior to 5000 BP. Subsequently, progressive narrowing of floodplains created the segmentation of discrete river reaches (shown in Figure 24). By Harappan times the various stream segments sustained small lakes, seasonal swamps, and minor basins. Thus, scarcity of water accounted for the general configuration of the earliest Harappan sites. Floodplain terrain prone to systemic flooding promoted clustering of populations on rises above the seasonal impoundments and in interdunal settings. The appearance of aeolian sands and loess and layered silts and clays in the upper sediment columns are indicative of siltation and encroaching dune migration (Courty 1995: fig. 5). Irrigation canals have been identified (Courty 1990), suggesting that some flooding occurred and that, as in the Lower Valley, small-scale diversions were built in response to high-frequency, high-impact climatic events. The lowest-lying settings (marshes) were also drained by Harappan farmers. Salinization became a serious problem, again (as in the Lower Valley) because of rising water tables and increasingly poor drainage. Winter wheat may have ceased to be a major crop. The belief is that devegetation may have promoted slope stripping, erosion, and the acceleration of dune development. The decrease in soil moisture content was the main finding for the Harappan-period sediment analysis (Courty 1995). Progressive desiccation and salinity eventually forced the abandonment of the Ghaggar-Hakra Plain.

Harappa. The only other area in which significant geoarchaeological studies have been performed is at the site of Harappa itself. Here there is excellent evidence for a different landscape concurrent with the original settlement. The site occupies a relict Pleistocene terrace overlooking an abandoned reach of the Ravi River (Whitehead 1932; see also Schuldenrein et al. 2004). Site stratigraphy (Kenoyer 1991a: figs. 4.5, 4.10, 4.11, 4.14) reveals precultural deposits at depths in excess of 4 meters below surface. Recent studies of the geomorphology indicate that, like the Ghaggar-Hakra, the earliest Harappan occupants settled on a landform within a meander channel that eventually became an oxbow lake (Belcher and Belcher 2000). The landscape evolved into a terraced river plain overlooking a rich aquatic setting.

A robust program of paleosol mapping in the late 1980s by Amundson and Pendall (1991; Pendall and Amundson 1990a; 1990b) produced a map of the Holocene soils that surround the site and demarcate the ages and magnitudes of weathering environments radiating away from the mound proper (Amundson and Pendall 1991: fig. 3.4). Their research determined that after stabilization of the late Pleistocene terrace, a succession of soils formed on varied landscape segments and parent materials which was tied to the migrating channel and its surrounding floodplain. Stable isotope analysis (for carbon and oxygen) offers the possibility that during Harappan times an extensive tropical grassland was sustained by cooler and moister climates (Amundson and Pendall 1991). The oldest (Pleistocene) soils were recognized on the strength of the diagnostic calcic soil horizon (Bk, characterized by carbonate nodules or *kankars*) and were dated to > 7000 BP. Buried soils implicated four intervals of weathering at 5000–15,000 BP; 2000–5000 BP; < 4500 BP; and recent. Since then, new radiocarbon dates have been obtained for the terminal alluvial episode preceding the Early Harappan occupations. Age determinations of 11,270 ± 40 BP (Beta-133921; organic sediment; $\delta^{13}C$ = –19.7‰) and 13,090 ± 40 BP (Beta-133922; organic sediment; $\delta^{13}C$ = –23.‰) date a well-developed soil formed on overbank alluvial silts (Schuldenrein et al. 2004). The dates confirm that stable environments and well-drained landforms emerged at the end of the Pleistocene in the better-drained segments of the Upper Valley.

In contrast with that at Mohenjo-daro, geoarchaeological work at Harappa has stressed the chronology of stable environments (through soil studies) while underplaying reconstructions of the depositional environments. Thus there is an excellent baseline study of the surfaces contemporaneous and even predating the Harappan occupation, but there is minimal information on the changing stream environments during the Middle Holocene. More extensive geomorphological studies are warranted to develop a comprehensive landscape chronology.

Beas River. Harappa's setting on the Bari Doab (Figure 22) indicates that at various times its resource environment would have incorporated both the Ravi and Beas floodplains (Figure 24). Reconstructions have demonstrated Harappa's logistic dependence on the Ravi, but the magnitude of Holocene channel migrations underscores the potential significance of the Beas as part of an economic landscape for Harappa and its satellite communities. Earlier studies suggested that subsequent to the Harappan collapse, the Beas—as the ultimate conduit for the Sutlej—may have functioned as the trunk stream for the Upper Valley (Mughal 1997: see fig. 4). A recent survey of the Punjab province disclosed a broad representation of prehistoric, protohistoric, and historic sites (Mughal et al. 1996), dispersed on various landforms aligned with the ancient Beas. The Beas Survey was designed to link a population of Harappan-age sites with their landforms, occupation chronologies, and land-

scape histories using dates and sedimentological histories derived from stratigraphic profiles.

RECENT DEVELOPMENTS IN
UPPER VALLEY GEOARCHAEOLOGY

The Beas Survey

The Beas River Survey was the first study in the Upper Indus designed to
establish a regional stratigraphic framework bridging environmental and
mound formation histories. The survey focused on a population of eighteen
Harappan sites spanning the buried margins of the ancient channel for a 200-
kilometer stream segment (Figure 24) (R. P. Wright, Khan, and Schuldenrein
2002; R. P. Wright et al. 2005 a; 2005b; Schuldenrein et al. 2004). The Beas
alluvial setting lent itself to modeling baseline stratigraphies because the
Harappan sites are relatively large and alluviation was shallow, facilitating
access to stratigraphic interfaces between cultural and floodplain deposits.
Moreover, the Beas is the trunk drainage intermediate between the Ghaggar-
Hakra, the axis of the densest cluster of known Harappan sites, and the Ravi,
the location of Harappa.

While currently defunct, the Beas preserves numerous stratigraphic
exposures even though most of its ancient course and floodplain margins
have been infilled, overridden, and sealed. The disposition of sites flanking
the inner and outer channel banks is evidence that during the Holocene, the
Beas was an active stream and the lifeline for settlements in much the same
way that the ancient Ravi was for Harappa (Belcher and Belcher 2000). Two
sites in the upper end of the drainage—Lahoma Lal Tibba and Chak Purbane Syal—facilitate chronological connections between occupations and
environmental histories. They are the basis for comparisons with Harappa
because of their proximity and geomorphic setting (Figure 22).

Developmental Histories at the Upper Beas Sites. A guiding principle
for structuring the environmental chronologies for the Beas sites was the use
of the available Harappan soil stratigraphy to document periods of landform
stability (Amundson and Pendall 1991; Pendall and Amundson 1990a;
1990b). A second strategy was to probe, and subsequently date, the interface
between the natural surface of the mounds (that is, the alluvium) and the initial intact occupation horizon. This was designed to enable identifications of
the time frame between the stabilization of the floodplain (namely, the soil
formation) and its initial settlement.

Cultural chronologies were established by test excavations within the
mounds (R. P. Wright, Khan, and Schuldenrein 2002; R. P. Wright et al.

2005a), and continuous stratigraphic records—from occupation through the latter phases of floodplain alluviation—assembled by extending mound profiles into the natural substrate. Here hand-driven 30-millimeter-diameter cores were extracted to depths of > 3 meters into the soils and alluvium. It was thus possible to bracket the periods of terminal alluviation, initial soil formation preceding the cultural occupation, and the nature of the occupation. Finally, alluvial sequences subsequent to occupation were obtained by sampling and dating floodplain segments away from the mounds. The composition of that alluvium would inform on the channel geometries and flooding patterns that resulted in site abandonment. Most significantly, radiocarbon dates were secured from soil horizons within these sites, a strategy that had not been utilized before for ordering environmental events.

Detailed descriptions of site archaeology are presented elsewhere (R. P. Wright, Khan, and Schuldenrein 2002; R. P. Wright et al. 2005a; Schuldenrein et al. 2004). For present purposes, it is noted that Lahoma Lal Tibba consists of two mound segments, located about 4 kilometers north–northwest of a prominent meander loop of the former Beas channel (Figure 22). Maximum elevation is 4.5 meters at the apex of both mounds, and assemblages consist of dense concentrations of Harappan pottery, pyrotechnical refuse, architectural foundation materials, and mud-brick fragments. The assemblages suggest an initial Early Harappan occupation (2800–2600 BC) that extends to the Mature phase (Period 3, 2600–1900 BC) (Table 1; Meadow, Kenoyer, and Wright 2001). Exposures revealed the interface between a moderately well-developed soil profile—an intact Cambic paleosol with a diagnostic calcic ("Bwk") horizon—and initial Harappan occupation, at approximately 0.9 to1.0 meter above the general levels of the alluvial plain (Figures 25 and 26). The composite profile registered 3 meters of cultural sedimentation capping 4 meters of pre-occupation stream deposits and soils. Analysis of sediments supplemented by radiocarbon dates identified five stratigraphic units for the composite section as follows: 3 meters of separable cultural horizons (Unit 1); a Middle Holocene soil immediately underlying the initial occupation (Unit 2); an Early Holocene soil that is more deeply weathered (Unit 3); a deep alluvial fill of terminal Pleistocene age (weakly weathered) (Unit 4); and an older, coarser Pleistocene flood deposit (Unit 5).

The second site, Chak Purbane Syal, 6 kilometers southwest of Lahoma Lal Tibba (Figure 22), is variously eroded and has been known for over half a century (Vats 1940). The two surviving mound segments are 1 to 2 meters high, and both mounds are capped by one to three cultural levels in their uppermost meter. The cultural stratigraphy is subtle, and microstratigraphic analysis indicates local episodes of sheetflow and mound collapse over the course of occupation. As at Lal Tibba, the lower exposures disclosed a sharp

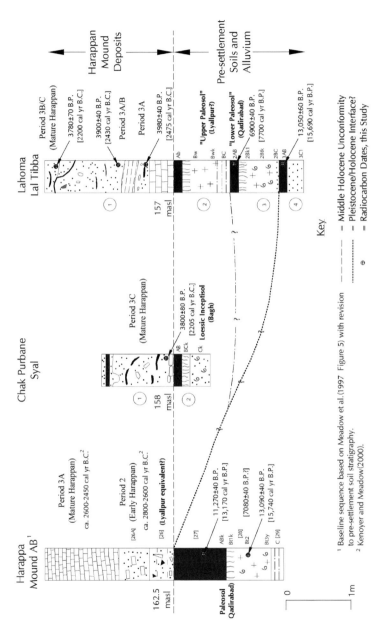

Figure 25. Site-specific and regional stratigraphies of Harappa, Lohoma Lal Tibba, and Chak Purbane Syal. Note the Middle Holocene unconformity marking the interface of cultural and natural sequences (also indicated by absolute elevations). Conventional (^{14}C) and calibrated (cal BP or BC) dates are presented as available.

stratigraphic boundary between the initial occupation and a moderate to weakly developed paleosol (Figures 25 and 27). The western mound was underlain by a silty inceptisol that graded to a coarser, mixed sandy but still weathered silt exposed at the eastern mound section. Soil horizonation varied considerably across the site. The upper weathering horizons—AB–BCk-featured weak to moderately developed subangular blocky structures that were dominated by silts with limited amounts of translocated clays (Figure 27). These properties are suggestive of a cumulic profile, one in which weathering dominates over reduced sedimentation. Progressive calcification was persistent in the soil profile, well into C horizons, and carbonate nodule sizes and densities increased. The nearly pure silt composition in the AB soil horizon is indicative of single-source wind deposition typical of a loess profile. Radiocarbon determinations postdate the primary occupations at Lahoma Lal Tibba, but are consistent with that site's uppermost component and are equivalent to the Mature to Late Harappan transition at Harappa (Schuldenrein et al. 2004; R. P. Wright, Khan, and Schuldenrein 2002. R. P. Wright et al. 2005a.).

It is possible to bridge the soil chronologies and geomorphic histories across Harappa, Lahoma Lal Tibba, and Chak Purbane Syal, as the Bari Doab is their common landform (Figure 22) and has been relatively stable since early Holocene times. Figure 25 presents composite site stratigraphies for each of the three locations, indexed by key radiocarbon dates. The section underscores the significance of the Early to Middle Holocene unconformity which marks the passage from the earliest cultural to terminal natural sequences at each site. Key soil, alluvial, and occupational stratigraphic breaks are shown, together with dates obtained for sediments and/or cultural features. In the case of Harappa, dates for individual cultural periods are averaged from recently published determinations, and the column is taken from AB Mound, HARP Trench 42 (Meadow, Kenoyer, and Wright 1997). Only the lowermost 2 meters of cultural deposits at Harappa are illustrated.

Figure 25 places the age of the soil at the interface of the earliest occupation (Early Harappan) and terminal alluviation ($[^{14}C]$ 11,300–13,100 BP [13,200–15,800 cal BP]). The soil, also known as the Qadirabad (after Pendall and Amundson 1991), is typically preserved on the margins of the landform only, since northward migrations of the Ravi (away from the *doab*) resulted in younger landscapes—and soil chronologies—closer to the present abandoned channel. Lahoma Lal Tibba's equivalent soil is dated $[^{14}C]$ 7000–13,000 BP [7,800–15,700 cal BP] based on the ages obtained from the bracketing A-horizons between Units 3 and 4. The terminal alluvial soil at Harappa—at $[^{14}C]$ 11,300–13,100 BP—is coincident with the Pleistocene–Holocene transition and is marked as a discontinuity at both Lahoma Lal Tibba and Harappa, despite some uncertainty as to the reliability and correlation of dates. For these reasons, it is provisionally proposed that the upper portion of the Qadirabad soil dates to at least [^{14}C] 7000–10,000 BP and that it marks the initial phase of regional landscape stabilization during the Early Holocene. It may extend into the Pleistocene (that is, > [^{14}C] 11,500 BP) because of the apparent antiquity of the Qadirabad soil at Harappa proper.

The second major paleosol is that registered by Unit 2 at Lahoma Lal Tibba (Figure 25). It is probably equivalent to the Lyallpur soil of Pendall and Amundson (1991) which underlies the initial (4000 BP) Harappan occupation at that site. This is a Middle Holocene soil that dates to the interval [^{14}C] 7000–4000 BP. Finally, the soil profile at Chak Purbane Syal developed on parent materials somewhat different from those at Harappa and Lahoma Lal Tibba, including a significant, albeit thin, loess contribution. The chrono-sequences are not immediately transferable, but the fact that the soil is weathered and underlies the occupation everywhere across the terrain suggests that it is only slightly younger than the Lyallpur.

Changing channel flow and alluvial geography are implicated by the contrasting sedimentary suites at Lahoma Lal Tibba and Harappa (Figure 25). At the base of the Lal Tibba sequence, the deposits of Unit 4 are substantially coarser than the overlying alluvial fills and provide evidence of the dynamism of the Late Pleistocene Beas. It and the terminal alluvium at Lahoma Lal Tibba are capped by entisols. This is evidence of limited soil formation and dominant alluviation. Such a pattern is consistent with channel sedimentation and considerable lateral migration. It has been discussed elsewhere that Unit 4 marked the onset of a fining upward sedimentary suite that is a signature depositional index of a meandering stream (Schuldenrein et al. 2004). Eventually, the migrating stream moved toward stabilization or eventual channel entrenchment within the Beas channel, only irregularly discharging sediments onto the higher *doab* surfaces (in Unit 3). Soil formation then dominated over flooding, signified by the more strongly developed profiles of Units 2 and 3. The transition from active alluviation to dominant soil formation would appear to coincide with the earliest Holocene (ca. [^{14}C] 10,000 BP)

The alluvial chronology is somewhat more complex at Harappa since the Ravi probably drained a broader catchment (even in earlier Holocene times), and changes in its fluvial regime were more dynamic than those of the Beas. Moreover, the size, logistic placement of Harappa, and land use practices of the (presumably) greater population would have resulted in larger-scale stream migrations and more complex landform configurations than at Lahoma Lal Tibba, whose smaller size may be consistent with a less dynamic stream and more subdued floodplain topography. Nevertheless, at Lal Tibba, most of the main mound is underlain by the Middle Holocene (Lyallpur) soil. At Harappa, an overhaul of the site environment also occurred during the Middle Holocene, when meanders formed oxbows, channels were laterally migrating,

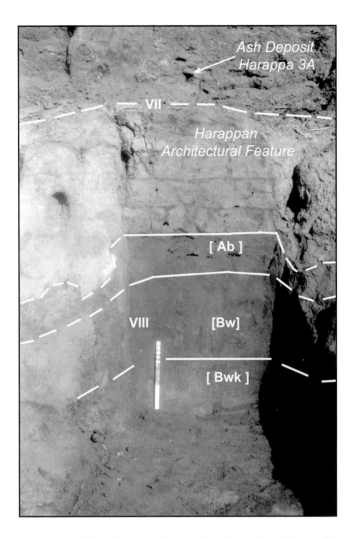

Figure 26. Contact of initial occupation surface Period 3A (Mature Harappan) and Mid-Holocene paleosol at Lahoma Lal Tibba, North Mound (see Figure 25). Roman numerals refer to field levels. Adjacent soil horizons are shown in brackets. Note the four courses of bricks associated with the Harappan architectural feature. The whitened color at the base of the profile highlights calcic soil horizon (Bwk). Scale 30 cm.

and the primary drainageway moved north. The concentric banding of soils of progressively younger age and weakly developed soil profiles away from the primary mound are evidence that the Ravi channel shifted nearly 20 kilometers over the past 4000 years (Belcher and Belcher 2000). Finally, the limited expo-

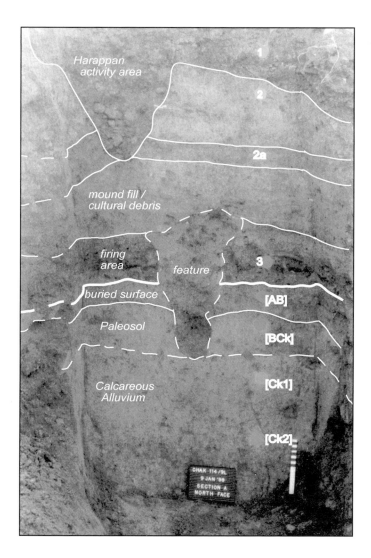

Figure 27. Contact of initial occupation surface Period 3 (Mature Harappan) and Mid-Holocene paleosol at Chak Pirbane Syal, also referred to as Chak 114-9L (see Figure 25). Arabic numerals refer to cultural levels (above paleosol). Adjacent soil horizons are shown in brackets. Note the whitened calcic horizons (BCk, Ck1, Ck2). Scale 20 cm.

sures at Chak Purbane Syal show that deflation was probably a considerable factor later in the Holocene. It is possible that the ongoing displacement of streams exposed large silty tracts along the recently abandoned floodplain, thus providing fresh sources of sediment that were mobilized by wind action.

Taken together, the alluvial histories of all three sites provide unique windows on regional Holocene developments. Both Harappa and Lahoma Lal Tibba illustrate a stabilization of landscapes in the Early Holocene as the Pleistocene stream courses gradually adjusted to new channel geometries. Finer sediments in post-Pleistocene deposits are deeply weathered in both sequences (Qadirabad soils), providing reinforcing evidence for optimal climatic conditions (such as stabilized rainfall regimens and moderate evapotranspiration rates) during the Early Holocene. Thinner Middle Holocene soils (Lyallpur) and renewed channel migration (principally registered in the Ravi) are evidence of some destabilization of environments at around the time of the initial pre-Harappan (Period 1[Ravi phase]) and Early Harappan (Period 2) occupations (Table 1).

Synthesis of Landscape Records

The landscape records for both the Upper and Lower Indus converge around full-scale overhauls of the drainage basin in the postglacial period. These developments can be expected to mirror broader climatic and environmental changes for most of South Asia because of the pervasive impacts of the Asian monsoon. The key element in understanding climatic succession is the variability, intensity, and periodicity of monsoon circulation patterns over the duration of the Holocene (Bryson 1996; Swain et al. 1983; Wasson 1995). The effects and the timing of climatic cycles are variously registered across the physiographic regions of South Asia. To obtain a measure of understanding of transformation bearing on Harappan landscapes, it is appropriate to summarize the reconstructions that focus on (1) the semiarid and arid Indus landscapes in which the Harappan sites are clustered; and (2) the critical later Middle Holocene period during which climatic and environmental changes bear most directly on Harappan settlement.

Table 4 is a synopsis of Holocene landscape and paleoclimatic trends across the Indian subcontinent with data sets associated with the Harappan phases highlighted (ca. 5500–3500 BP). The types of settings for which information has been assembled include aeolian mantled terrain; coasts (estuaries and drainage mouths); lake beds; fluvial features and valleys; buried soil (paleosol) localities; and low-lying areas with evidence for structural movements (tectonics). Because the monsoon was such an overarching mechanism for climatic change across the subcontinent, its manifestations should be represented across most geographic subdivisions (although see Wasson 1995 for an alternative viewpoint).

It cannot be overstressed that the stratigraphic records across South Asia are spotty and uneven because of the relatively recent incorporation of the latest paleoclimatic and environmental methodologies. Soil sequences remain woefully undocumented, and the tectonic record has not been widely investigated (compare columns in Table 4). It is nevertheless possible to discern converging lines of paleogeographic evidence. Most striking is the evidence for Early Holocene moisture associated with the establishment of post-Pleistocene monsoon circulation. Reduction in aeolian activity (Ghaggar-Hakra) is consistent with renewed alluviation and submerged coastlines for many regions of the subcontinent, highest lake levels in Rajasthan, and subsequent delta progradation as rising base levels reflect stabilization of transgressive coastlines. The formation of the most deeply weathered soil profiles in the Harappa area (Amundson and Pendall 1991; Schuldenrein et al. 2004) signifies that well-drained surfaces flanked the major rivers of the Punjab at that time.

A gradual turn to desiccation, ca. 7000–6000 BP, may be indicated by resumption of loess sedimentation in the Ghaggar-Hakra Plain, a reduction in the scale of alluviation and incision of some of the main river valleys, and stabilization (and initial lowering) of lake levels. Soil chronologies have not been documented for this time frame, although it is not clear whether or not this is a function of increased erosion or insufficient research. Wasson (1995) infers that reduction in lake levels across the southern hemisphere's monsoon belts is proxy evidence for the decline of southwest monsoon intensity coupled with high evapotranspiration ratios.

For the 2000 years of peak Harappan settlement in South Asia, the paleoenvironmental record is somewhat ambiguous (Table 4, shaded band). Cessation of dune activity in the Ghaggar-Hakra and optimal freshwater influx at Didwana and coastal transgressions (+3 to +6 meters) may be measures of increased moisture, but such developments as channel migrations, westward drainage displacement, and abandonment and desiccation of the Ghaggar-Hakra Plain midway through the interval are more equivocal. Here again, the degree to which tectonics account for drainage realignment is both pivotal and uncertain. If existing reconstructions of channel desiccation are correct (Possehl 1999; Wilhelmy 1969), then the 4000–2500 BP interval resulted in net displacements of flow lines on the order of 100 to 150 kilometers northward, coupled with desiccation in abandoned channel lines. Evidence for north and westward channel migration has been noted for the Ravi at Harappa (Belcher and Belcher 2000), for the Sutlej-Beas (Wilhelmy 1969; Possehl 1999; 2002; this study), and along the Lower Indus at Mohenjo-daro (Flam 1993). However, even extensive structural dislocations should not have resulted in realignments of topography and drainage to such a degree that all signs of hydric conditions in the ancient depressions are absent. Courty's (1995) sedimentological study of the abandoned depressions in the Ghaggar-Hakra Plain argues for reduced seasonal flooding and dune encroachments and a turn to drier conditions, an argument that is in opposition to widely held concepts of increased moisture during the Harappan (Singh et al. 1974;

TABLE 4. Synopsis of Holocene Landscape and Paleoclimatic Trends in the Indian Subcontinent (with peak Harappan era highlighted)

Years BP	Aeolian Activity	Coastal Changes	Lacustrine Record	Fluvial Sequences	Soil Chronology	Tectonics	Climate
0				Reduction of swamps and channel activity; lowered water tables, Ghaggar			Reduced precipitation
1000	Moderate aeolian activity, Ghaggar	2m regression in Saurashtra; accelerated pro-deltaic aggradation at mouth of Arabian sea (lower Indus)	Progressive desiccation and salinity, Didwana	incision in Deccan Uplands; aggradation exceeds subsidence in lower Indus		Upwarping promoting stream capture and westward drainage (lower Indus) with episodes of eastward avulsion	High precipitation levels with contemporary rainfall patterns
2000				Peak flood stages-Narmada R.; reduced seasonal flooding and siltation of channels, Ghaggar	Soil formation in Nepal		
3000	Cessation of dune build-up: Thar Desert; localized sand dunes, Ghaggar	Maximum sea levels (+3 to +6 m transgression)	Optimal fresh water influx and highest lake levels, Didwana	Sandy alluviation of Belan River; moderate aggradation in Deccan Uplands	Sultanpur soils at Harappa (Bk, Bw horizons)	Structural deformation leading to eastward and westward stream capture in Punjab (Ghaggar-Hakkra)	Generally decreased monsoonal precipitation punctuated by moister pulses
4000				Reduction in aggradation and channel avulsion along lower Indus			
5000	Loess sedimentation, Ghaggar plain	Onset of marine transgression	Moderately deep freshwater, Didwana	Incision of Belan River into Pleistocene fills; reduced alluviaton; slackwater formations, Ghaggar			Stabilization and gradual decline of southwest monsoon intensity; high evapotranspiration
6000							Maximum winter monsoons
7000		Southwestward migration and sedimentation of Indus delta	Fluctuating dry/saline and deep/freshwater conditions, Didwana; high water levels and freshwater Bap Malar, Thob	Rejuvenation of alluviation in valleys of Deccan uplands; massive seasonal flooding, Ghaggar plain	Nevasa; soil formation in Nepal; Gamber, Lyallpur soils at Harappa (Bk, Bw, By horizons); weathering of E. Indian soils		
8000	Limited extent and reduced rates of dune construction, Thar Desert						
9000		Still-stands, submerged terraces in Goa (−92m, −85m, −75m and −55m)		Rapid aggradation of lower Indus			Establishment of post-Pleistocene monsoon circulation
10000	Terminal loess deposition in interior Gujarat		Rising lake levels, Didwana	Alluviation at foot of Siwaliks			

References

Aeolian: Gujarat loess (Chamyal and Merh 1995); Ghaggar (Courty 1995)

Lacustrine: Thar Desert and Didwana (Chawla et al. 1991; Misra, 1995; Singh et al. 1972, 1974, 1990; Singhvi et al. 1982; Wasson et al., 1983, 1984; Wasson 1995); Kajale and Deotare (1997); Deotare et al. (1998)

Sea levels: (Juyal et al. 1995); Sarma (1971); Marathe (1995); Flam (1993); Snead (1993a, 1993b)

Fluvial sequences: Narmada River (Baker et al. 1995); central India (Williams and Clark 1995); Pappu (1974; 1995); Korisettar (1979); Ghaggar plain (Courty 1995); Indus (Jorgensen et al. 1993)

Soils: Nepal & Siwaliks (Corvinus 1995); Nevasa soils (Misra 1995); "red dunes" (Gardner and Martingell 1990); Pendall and Amundson (1990a, 1990b)

Tectonics: Wilhelmy (1966); Jorgensen et al. (1993); Agrawal and Sood (1982)

Climate: Nigam & Hashimi (1995); Von Rad et al. (1999); Bryson (1996); Brinkman and Rafiq (1971); Singh et al. (1974); Swain et al. (1983); Wasson (1995)

Bryson and Swain 1981). Courty's position is that Harappan environments and rainfall distribution patterns were analogous to those of the present. This argument is compelling insofar as traditional landscape indicators of reduced moisture (such as lowered water tables and broader dune expanses) are linked to agricultural practices during the Harappan period. But a major concern in Courty's analysis is the absence of any consideration of tectonic influence as a mechanism accounting for the initial displacement of the drainage lines despite the fact that the stream displacements near Harappa and Mohenjo-daro during the Late Harappan would appear to lend some credence to structural displacement mechanisms. The soil reconstructions at the Beas sites do not offer unequivocal indications of stable environments after 7000 BP, although identifications of two cycles of low-magnitude alluviation capped by thin soils is indicative of a controlled floodplain environment for the period 7000–4000 BP.

Recent offshore coring on the Makran coast sheds new light on the ambiguous climatic proxy data (von Rad et al. 1999). Here marine cores were used to infer paleoclimatic conditions based on relative thicknesses of turbidite varves (that is, continentally derived monsoon deposits) (Figure 28). Thicker varves signal greater precipitation, while thin varve deposits denote less precipitation and drier circulation patterns. Figure 28 shows that during the peak Harappan phases, mean varve thicknesses spiked twice within the period 4000–3500 BP, suggesting that high and widely fluctuating levels of precipitation may have characterized the latter part of that occupation. High periodicity may also indicate that the distribution of rainfall or the frequency of overbanking would have accelerated at that time. It may have been that the

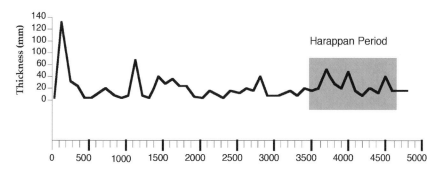

Figure 28. Late Holocene climatic signals inferred from the thickness of turbidites in the oxygen-minimum zone off Makran Coast, Pakistan (after von Rad et al. 1999). Note the pronounced variations for turbidite thicknesses during the Harappan period.

successes of the Harappan agriculturalists in managing the rainfall—specifically constructing and maintaining effective irrigation and drainage systems—extended their ability to function in a climate in which rainfall was abundant but erratic. However, erratic precipitation, salinization, and mismanagement of the water control systems could have hastened the civilization's downfall. It is not clear whether or not moister climates are implicated (as varve thickness may also reflect human-induced mobilization of sediment), but precipitation intensities and regimes may have been different then than at any other time. Increased rainfall may have disrupted water management systems and dictated changes to Harappan adaptive strategies.

Depositional records of the past 3000 years suggest that the effects of human modifications to the landscape may have been as critical as any natural processes of sedimentation. The Late Holocene lake records suggest increased desiccation as water levels decrease, while reinitiation of dune activity also points to higher wind activity and less vegetation cover. Shoreline regression (by 2 meters) is also consistent with the reduction in available moisture. Von Rad et al. (1999) imply that over the past few thousand years, low precipitation values are characteristic and are interspersed with aperiodic rainfall regimes that have minimal effects because of their limited durations. Paleo-circulation models argue for high precipitation after 3000 BP, the effects of which are tempered by the stabilization of contemporary seasonal rainfall distribution patterns. Thus, despite increases in net moisture, the distribution of precipitation may have had deleterious environmental effects—for example, catastrophic inundations of farmed fields—conceivably exacerbated by population increases and stress on natural landscapes. Here again, the paleoclimatic record is not unequivocal.

CONCLUSIONS

An abundance of geoarchaeological and Quaternary research across South Asia is beginning to make possible broad environmental chronologies across a range of physiographic zones. Regional investigations focusing on the locations of sites along landforms and the assembly of alluvial histories for the Upper and Lower Valleys of the Indus enhance understanding of the critical Middle Holocene period in this key cultural area. Larger-scale climatic events—immediately antecedent to Harappan occupation—are preserved in the depositional histories of the valleys sealed beneath Harappan mounds. Soil sequences distinguish those periods favorable to settlement. It is thereby possible to document changing thresholds in stream energy levels and floodplain morphologies, to date them, and to link floodplain histories along the length of contemporary drainage lines. In this way, it may also be possible to calibrate the relative impacts of tectonics and climatic mechanisms regionally, thus structuring chronologies for Holocene floodplain transformations.

In summary, the following working hypotheses can be generated regarding Holocene paleo-landscapes and circulation patterns for the greater Harappan countryside:

1. Continental and littoral geomorphic histories and soil sequences converge around moister climates during the Early Holocene (ca. 10,000–7000 BP), during which time post-Pleistocene monsoon circulation patterns were established; they stabilized toward the end of this period.

2. There is more limited stratigraphic evidence for the lower Middle Holocene, although general indications are that southwest monsoon intensities diminished and drier climatic cycles were initiated (ca. 7000–5000 BP).

3. The record for the Middle Holocene contemporaneous with peak Harappan occupation (ca. 5000–3000 BP) is ambivalent; mechanisms accounting for fluvial cut and fill cycles, moisture budgets, coastal terrace cutting, and aeolian events may reflect tectonic influences and human manipulation of alluvial and even perimeter environments (due to agricultural practices).

4. The later Holocene stratigraphic record (prior to 3000 BP) preserves increasing evidence for anthropogenic sedimentation, underscoring human landscape manipulation; critically, present patterns of rainfall (seasonal precipitation) had been clearly established, although there are some indications of greater precipitation between 3000 and 2000 BP.

ACKNOWLEDGMENTS

The work of Robert McCormick Adams continues to be an inspiration for Wright and Schuldenrein, both of whom participated in Bob's classes at the University of Chicago and at Harvard. His work formed a baseline in our conception of the Beas project. In our field research, we wish to thank Saeed ur Rahman, Director General of the Department of Archaeology and Museums, Government of Pakistan, for permission to conduct the survey and to work on these important materials. We owe a great debt to the Punjab Archaeology Survey, and Rafique Mughal during his tenure as Pakistan's Director General of Archaeology and Museums. Muhammad Hussain, Field Officer, accompanied us during our first season. Members of the Beas Survey team Susan Malin-Boyce, Suanna Selby, and Mark Smith provided invaluable assistance in all stages of the work. We also thank Dr. Richard Meadow and

Dr. J. Mark Kenoyer, co-Directors of the Harappa Archaeological Research Project. The project was supported by grants from the National Endowment for the Humanities, the National Geographic Society, and the Wenner-Gren Foundation for Anthropological Research.

REPRESENTING ABUNDANCE: A VISUAL DIMENSION OF THE AGRARIAN STATE*

IRENE J. WINTER

ABSTRACT

The symbolic systems and representational strategies of the early agrarian state in ancient Mesopotamia remain relatively unexamined. One important rhetorical device in text is the assertion of, or hope for, abundance as the result of divine beneficence brokered by the state apparatus. It is argued here that the use of visual motifs such as repetitive friezes of domesticated plants and animals—often dismissed as merely ornamental—not only paralleled textual references to abundance, but actually offered an independent and highly charged articulation of the same governing concept.

Analysts of the early agrarian state have stressed the agricultural and pastoral surplus necessary to sustain the specialized labor force and social hierarchy characteristic of an urban population, while field archaeologists have sought remnants of large-scale storage facilities, increased scale of irrigation systems, and other features to document the production and accumulation of such surplus (Childe 1951; Adams 1960; Sherratt 1980; Hunt 1987; 2000; Dolce 1989; Pollock 1992; H. T. Wright 1994; Breckwoldt 1995–96; Smyth 1996; Algaze 2004; Rothman 2004; M. E. Smith 2005; Steinkeller, this volume). Remaining underdocumented, however, are the symbolic systems and representational

---

* I am grateful to Jeffrey Hamburger, Robert Hunt, Ann Kuttner, Naomi Miller, Alex Nagel, Nicholas Postgate, John Russell, Gil Stein, Piotr Steinkeller, and Elizabeth Stone for stimulating conversations on this topic. Robert Hunt also gave generously of his expertise and critical acuity in a reading of an early draft.

strategies that mirrored such necessities, or even—dare one say!—actively served to create a receptive social environment in which the authority structures needed for a requisite surplus could be reinforced.

In the present paper, I wish to pursue ways in which the accumulation of such a surplus, through the production of domesticated plants and animals and the yield of the Tigris-Euphrates Rivers, was reinforced through visual representation in the early stages of the agrarian state. I shall argue that surplus in our terms was in Mesopotamia equated with a concept of "abundance" in natural production, and that the representation thereof constituted a virtual "iconography of abundance." This iconography was then consciously deployed to signal the surplus that on a practical level permitted the maintenance of an urban, specialist population. At the same time, on the rhetorical level the iconography also served to lay the foundations for social cohesion through a shared visual vocabulary for success issuing from a projected cosmic/natural order.[1]

Such a study could not have been undertaken by an art historian until relatively recently, and on many levels, it owes its conceptual base to the work of anthropologically trained archaeologists, notably Robert McCormick Adams, whose focus on early state formation significantly changed the sorts of questions one asks of artifactual and archaeological materials. From *Land Behind Baghdad* (1965) to *The Uruk Countryside* (Adams and Nissen 1972) and *Heartland of Cities* (1981), Adams helped to sensitize the field to think beyond the immediate locus of excavation to broader issues of region and system. His work—and subsequently that of his students and the field at large—demanded that one consider site distribution with respect to the sustaining area of agricultural and animal production, themselves essential components in the dynamics of state development and maintenance. More recently, with the development of the subfield of "landscape archaeology," the study of topography, region, and space have focused attention on these broad issues (such as Wilkinson 2003; A. Smith 2003; Gleason 1994). Their work further opens the door to seeing artistic production not as separate from, but in conjunction with, the particulars of a given land/environment, as a locus for both biological and social reproduction.[2]

---

[1] The present paper has grown out of a presentation in a symposium honoring Bob Adams at the meetings of the American Oriental Society in Toronto in 2001. A portion of that presentation, pursuing the rhetorical component of this claim for the Neo-Assyrian period, has recently been published as Winter 2003.

[2] Indeed, as noted by Adam T. Smith (2003: 10, 54), the land provides the conditions for aesthetic as well as pragmatic pleasure. In the visual domain, a very specific case was noted in a recent study by Trudy Kawami (2001), which demonstrates a correlation between the introduction of a new variety of milk cow in the Uruk period and the appearance of the same breed of bovine figurines on stamp seals.

Indeed, this conjunction between agrarian and artistic production from the Uruk to the Neo-Sumerian periods, fourth to third millennium BCE, argues for continuity of a central theme of "abundance," despite changes in representational strategies over time. I shall argue it is no accident that an iconography of abundance appeared precisely at a moment in history when, although domestication had been under control for millennia, the need for sufficient surplus to both provision the city/state and afford a medium of exchange in long-distance trade was of primary importance in both the rhetoric and the governance structures of the stratified state and its agrarian-based economy.[3]

The rhetorical aspect was instantiated in both text and image. To date, the textual components have been better integrated into the broader picture. Virtually every literary text attributes "abundance"—Sumerian $he_2.gal_2$, $he_2.nun$; Akkadian *ḫegallu, nuḫšu, tuḫdu*—directly to one deity or another. And virtually every Mesopotamian ruler who left royal inscriptions has at some point declared himself to be the "provider" of abundance for the land, thanks to the privileged relationship he enjoys with a god, or the gods. Clear from the context is that this abundance issues from the natural world—water, plants, animals, fish—rather than from material wealth or manufactured goods.

The agency of gods and rulers with respect to provisioning the land was articulated most explicitly by Gudea, ruler of the city-state of Lagash in the Neo-Sumerian period (ca. 2110 BC). Preliminary to building a temple for the state god, Ningirsu, the ruler is visited in a dream by the deity, who makes a promise [Cyl. A, xi 1–17; Edzard 1997: 75–76]:

---

[3] Congruent with more recent archaeological studies of domestication, the Sumerians themselves seem to have preserved a memory of bringing domesticated species into the Tigris-Euphrates Valley. In the literary composition, "How Grain Came to Sumer" (ETCSL t.1.7.6), we are told of a time when men did not know barley or flax, and then barley was brought down from the mountain and introduced into Sumer. The text breaks off at this point, but as a story of origin, it is clear that the introduction of these two species was taken as generic for the bringing of "civilization," since, before that time, "Men used to eat grass with their mouths like sheep. In those times, they did not know grain: barley or flax" (lines 1–2). Modern scholars have argued for one variable or another as the prime mover in the process toward urbanization—most recently, Algaze (2004) sees trade as the principal engine in what he calls the "Sumerian takeoff." The issue of what produced the urban phenomenon in southern Mesopotamia in the fourth millennium BC is beyond the scope of the present study. What I would insist upon is that, whatever the accountable factors (and I emphasize the plural; similarly, Wilkinson 2003: 71), the rhetorical strategies employed to maintain the system had to have been polyvalent, and the assertion of abundance (read surplus) with respect to agricultural/pastoral production was one of them.

When you, true shepherd Gudea, will start (to build) my House . . .
then I will call up to heaven for a humid wind, so that surely abundance [ḫe₂.gal₂] will come to you from above and the land will increase in abundance.
When the foundations of my House will be laid, abundance will surely come at the same time:
the great fields will "raise their hands" to you . . . ; water will . . . rise . . . where it never reaches;
. . . more fat will be poured, more wool will be weighed in Sumer (than ever before). . . .

The trope of promised abundance is woven through the entire account, ending with the point when the temple has not only been physically completed, but has begun to function as a cultic center, the deity installed within. As part of the temple equipment, (images of) the seven daughters of Ningirsu and his consort, the goddess Bau, are placed near the deity to offer permanent prayers on behalf of the ruler, and these daughters are explicitly identified as the ones who "create/provide abundance for the people" [ḫe-gal₂-lu₂-šar₂] (Cyl. B xi 15–23; Edzard 1997: 95).[4]

. . . that the vast fields might grow rich, that the ditches and canals of Lagash be full to the brim, that in the plain . . . the grain goddess . . . might proudly look up . . . , that after the good fields have brought barley, emmer and all kinds of pulses, enormous grain heaps, the whole yield of the land of Lagash might be heaped up. . . .

Finally, the account closes with a series of summary refrains on the same theme (Cyl. B xix 12–15; xxii 19; Edzard 1997: 98–99, 100):

The earth makes mottled barley grow for him (Gudea), and the abundance of the land of Lagash increases under (its) ruler.
May the people lie down in safe pastures under your reign, (enjoying) abundance. . . .

No other ruler of the second half of the third millennium offers as complete an account. However, Shu-Suen of the later Third Dynasty of Ur designates the god Enlil as the "lord of abundance" [en ḫe₂-gal₂-la], and then asks that he himself be granted "years of abundance" [mu ḫe₂-gal₂-la] (ETCSL t.2.4.4.a, lines 21, 31), while the text known as "Erra and Naram-

---

4   This episode is followed immediately by the introduction of the inspector of fisheries of the Gu-edenna to the deity [Cyl. B xii 7–15], and his intervention that the birds and animals and fish of the steppe might also produce abundantly (Edzard 1997: 95).

Sin" associates the earlier Akkadian ruler with a "reign of abundance" [*pa-la-i nu-úh-ši*] (Westenholz 1983: 199), suggesting that this was not limited to a Sumerian topos.[5] In addition, as evidenced in various Sumerian literary texts known from Old Babylonian–period copies, almost all of the great gods, including An, Enlil, Enki, Utu, Nanna-Suen, Inanna, Nisaba, Dumuzi, Ninurta, and Nanše, are credited with providing this same abundance (he_2-gal_2) in the land.[6]

At least a millennium separates the Neo-Sumerian royal inscriptions and the largely Old Babylonian–period copies of literary texts from the early phases of urbanization at Uruk/Warka. The Uruk period has received the lion's share of attention in political analyses of the early state (for example, Algaze 1993a; G. Stein 1999a; Rothman, ed. 2001; see on this also, the historiographical perspective provided by Bernbeck and Pollock 2002), due to interest in the formative phase of urban processes. Not surprisingly, this same theme of desired abundance, particularly with respect to domesticated animals and plants, is to be found referenced extensively from the beginning. It is not yet explicit verbally in the archaic texts from Uruk (Nissen, Damerow, and Englund 1993), but is attested visually, in the cultic objects associated with the temples of the Eanna precinct of Uruk, dedicated to the goddess Inanna.

The theme may be demonstrated in the low-relief decoration on a rectangular alabaster trough found in the Eanna, for example (Moortgat 1969: pls. 17–18; our Figure 29). On each long side, a biological couple—male ram and female ewe—flank a reed hut that may well correspond to the "sheepfold" or "birth hut," since from it there emerges a pair of lambs, one in each direction, toward each couple. That this is not merely a single occurrence, but rather represents a known motif in the period, is demonstrated by a pair of stone bowls, one from Khafaje (Hansen 1975: pl. 71b), the other in the Louvre (Figure 30). In these cases, the flanking animals are cows or bulls, and

---

5 Jacobsen's discussion (1993: 72–73) of the term **lú** argues that "provider" ("suggesting the responsibility of providing food for others") is part of the meaning of the term, usually translated as "man." He cites Shulgi Hymn G, which indicates that the Ur III ruler himself was considered such a provider by the god Enlil, thereby implying an equivalence between the notion of providing abundance and the provider thereof, which constitutes a major rhetorical trope of kingship.

6 ETCSL t.1.1.4, line 2; t.1.2.2, lines 159–70; t.1.1.3, lines 52–60, 71b, 90; t.4.32.e, line 34; t.1.5.1 lines 186–97; t.4.16.1, line 33; t.4.08.01, lines 53–56; t.1.6.2, lines 362–64; Sjöberg 1975; Jacobsen 1993: 72. The theme also recurs in the Old Babylonian debate texts. In the text known as "The Hoe and the Plough," the hoe claims that "the abundance I create spreads over all the land" [he_2-gal_2-gu_{10} **kur-kur-ra šu-bi**] (ETCSL t.5.3.1, line 79); and in the debate between Sheep and Grain, before grain is accorded victory in the debate, *both* are credited with bringing abundance [he_2-gal_2] to the assembly of the gods (ETCSL t.5.3.2, lines 52–54). (All ETCSL texts in this note were accessed on 04/12/2004.)

Figure 29. Alabaster trough, Uruk period, probably from Warka; height 16.3 cm; length 1.3 m (British Museum, London, WAA 120000).

Figure 30. Stone bowl fragment, Uruk period (photograph courtesy Département des Antiquités Orientales, Musée du Louvre, AO 8842).

the emerging animals immature calves, but the parallel is clear. On the Louvre vessel, two strap-handled pitchers are shown in the upper field, on either side of the hut, suggesting a reference to the important new breed of milk-producing cattle appearing in the Uruk period (Kawami 2001). On the trough, pairs of reed bundles at the far left and right, associated with the cult of Inanna (Szarzynska 1987–88), serve as frames to the whole scene, and also, as on the stone bowls, rise from the roof of the reed hut, towering above the emerging young. These reed bundles are repeated on the two short sides of the trough as well, along with free-floating rosettes, another element associated with the goddess, adjacent to two ewes or lambs. The juxtaposition of reed bundle, rosette, and domesticated quadruped echoes similar juxtapositions on cylinder seals of the same period, also from the Eanna precinct at Uruk (see, for example, Moortgat 1969: pl. B1). For the trough and the bowls, at least, it is not unlikely that depiction of the nuclear units of reproduction (male, female, and offspring), along with references to the divine power generating reproduction, actually have significance with respect to their functions as containers: the trough possibly used to water animals intended for the temple, the bowls possibly holding milk as divine offering.[7]

The cereal component is as well documented as the animal. On a fragmentary limestone stele from Warka, dated stylistically to the Uruk period, for example (Figure 31), we see in the upper register several empaneled boxes that may be a convention for indicating agricultural fields, containing what look like young stalks of grain (followed in the second and third registers by work scenes employing nude (?) and bald male figures; Becker 1993: pl. 39 no. 785). Unfortunately, the stele was found in a secondary context, reused in antiquity in a later water channel (Becker 1993: 58). However, the imagery seems especially appropriate to Warka and the goddess whose powers govern fertility in the plant as well as the animal domain.[8] Thus, from the beginning of the early Mesopotamian state, there is a well-structured cosmology of reproduction in which gods, their temples, rulers, and rituals are set in an active relationship to living things.

On several occasions, domesticated animals are actually paired with domesticated plants in repeating motifs. For example, on a stone vessel of the Uruk period found at Ur (Strommenger 1964: fig. 28; Hansen 1975: fig. 71a; see Figure 32), one sees a repeated pairing of a sheaf of grain behind a standing bull, which reflects visually the dual domains of agricultural and animal productivity referred to in the Gudea text cited above. Both plant and animal represent not just any species, but domesticates. Their duplication—echoing the grammatical reduplication of nouns, adjectives, and verbal stems in the Sumerian language used to indicate the plural/scale/quantity/intensity—seems to announce in visual terms the necessary multiplicity (read abundance) of reproduction and its resultant surplus, upon which the agrarian state was founded.

---

[7] Joy McCorriston (1997) has shown that one of the important by-products of the particular breed of wool-bearing sheep introduced into southern Mesopotamia was a fourth-millennium textile industry of woven woolen fabrics, complementary to earlier flax-made textiles. Algaze discusses this industry in terms of the dynamic between imports and the stimulation of indigenous production (2004). It is important to note that plants and animals may carry meaning on more than one level. However, it may also be the case that one level of meaning tends to be privileged in particular instances of representation—in the present case, for example, the wealth/abundance represented *by* the herd encompassing the wealth/abundance available from the produce *of* the herd.

[8] Representatives of the Iraq Board of Antiquities found another stele fragment in the Spring of 2004, which seems to belong to the same stylistic period, if not monument; but until it is published, this cannot be determined for certain.

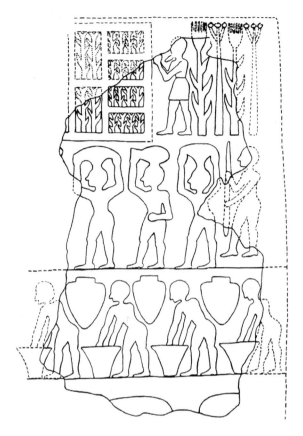

Figure 31. Drawing, stele fragment, Uruk period, found Warka; height 79 cm (after Becker 1993, #785; Iraq Museum, Baghdad, IM 6842).

Figure 32. Stone bowl, Uruk period, found at Ur; height 5.5 cm (Iraq Museum, Baghdad, IM 11959).

The emphasis on production and reproduction of both plants and animals is also found in the conjunction of grain and domesticated quadruped on a number of cylinder seals of the period (for example, Amiet 1980: nos. 396–399; see Figure 33) and is most evident on the lower portion of the alabaster cult vessel known as the Warka Vase, also of the Uruk period (Heinrich 1936: pl. 36; Moortgat 1969: pls. 19–21; discussed by Winter 1983; Bahrani 2002; Bernbeck and Pollock 2002: 187–190; see Figures 34 and 35). Above a pair of wavy lines indicating water,[9] two bands are joined by a narrow dividing strip: the bottom shows the alternation of stalks of grain, most likely barley,[10] with what can now be identified

Figure 33. Cylinder seal impression, Uruk period (photograph courtesy Département des Antiquités Orientales, Musée du Louvre, MNB 1906, A25).

---

[9] Identification of these paired wavy lines as water conforms with the ideographic sign for water in early Uruk tablets and is replicated visually on a Uruk-period cylinder seal that shows such a band running through a terrain marked by drilled blobs to indicate "land" (see, for example, Moortgat 1969: pl. A2). The presence of a water channel immediately below the grain and animals suggests a hierarchy, with water as the source for the growth in the registers above. This would represent the symbolic, and even cosmic, rendering of the importance of water management known to have been of primary concern in the early state, and with which a good deal of recent scholarship has been concerned. See, in particular, the various papers published in the proceedings of the Sumerian Agriculture Group (for example, Postgate and Powell, eds. 1988).

[10] The extensive scholarly discussion of the increase in ratio of barley to emmer/wheat from the Uruk period through the third millennium may be found summarized in Powell 1985; and more recently, in A. Cohen 2003.

Figure 34. Alabaster vase, Uruk period, found at Warka; height 1.10 m after restoration (Iraq Museum, Baghdad, IM 19606).

as flax;[11] the upper shows five alternating pairs of identical rams and ewes.[12] The two bands are bound into a single register with a minor subdivision. Their repetition around the circumference of the vase calls to mind H. Groenewegen-Frankfort's eloquent description of a prehistoric beaker from Susa, where the form of the vessel is iterated and reiterated through the repetitive decorative program (Groenewegen-Frankfort 1987: 146–147 and pl. I). Yet, for the Warka Vase, the repetitive nature of the lower register has led most Western viewers to pass over the bands quickly, in a rush toward the more dynamic and linear narrative of the upper register.[13] I would argue, however, that this repetition was carefully planned and highly charged with meaning. Predating by millennia the Neo-Platonic elevation of the circle as the perfect geometric form because it has no beginning and no end, the procession of plants and animals is acephalous and inexorably conveys the eternal nature of the productivity depicted. Just as in Mesopotamian literary texts, drama is actually achieved through a tension built up by repetition, it is suggested that pictorial repetition, too, serves to raise a scene from the level of the actual, or temporal, to the (hoped for) perpetual, or recurrent.[14]

In order to understand the nature of repetitive imagery in the ancient Near East, it is essential to resist the Western relegation of pattern and repetition to the merely "decorative" (see, on this, Winter 2003). The union of

---

[11] Groenewegen-Frankfort (1987: 151) had earlier associated the plant with the date palm. Flax has now been identified independently by H. Crawford (1985) and the present author (Winter 1983)—the former on morphological grounds, where she then discusses the likelihood of flax fiber production by this period; the latter both on morphological grounds and also by virtue of the frequent pairing in literary texts of Sum. še and **gu**, "barley and flax" as the two paradigmatic archetypes of agricultural production (for example, Enlil and Sud, version B, line 20 = ETCSL t.1.2.2; Enlil and Ninlil, line 147 = ETCSL t.1.2.1; A Hymn to Utu, line 34 = ETCSL t.4.32.e; The Debate between Winter and Summer, line 6 = ETCSL t.5.3.3—all accessed 04/12/2004). See also the images and discussion in Ertuğ 2000: esp. figs. 3 and 4, for visual comparanda with the actual plant.

[12] The rams and ewes are obviously gendered, and this parallels the reference on the Warka trough to the biologically reproducing nuclear couple. I argue elsewhere that the barley and flax also have gendered associations, the shaft of barley reading "male" for Dumuzid, consort of Inanna; the flax connected to fabric and the weaving of the sheets for the bridal bed, as in the text of Dumuzid-Inanna A (ETCSL t.4.08.01, accessed 04/19/2004), hence female. For now, I am persuaded that the base of the vase echoes the cultic event signaled in the upper register, on which see Hansen 1975: 180.

[13] Even the perspicacious Groenewegen-Frankfort, while lauding the Susa vessel, dismissed such repetition in Mesopotamian art in terms of a loss of "vigor," stating that in the reduction to pattern, the "temporal aspects of action and . . . space . . . (are) robbed of their truly dramatic character" (Groenewegen-Frankfort 1987: 162).

[14] Noted in Winter 1976, a review of Groenewegen-Frankfort 1951 [1987] (upon its initial reissue in 1974).

Figure 35. Detail, lower portion, alabaster vase.

not just any plants and animals, but domesticates, in the lower registers of the vessel makes clear that several millennia following upon Neolithic break-throughs, those responsible for the program of the Warka Vase were not unaware that the economic and subsistence base for urban society lay in the surplus possible through that very domestication.[15] I would even go so far as

---

[15] Adams himself emphasized early on that the agricultural "revolution" of the Neolithic was what ultimately made it possible for both specialization and the aggregation of communities into urban centers (Adams 1960). What is interesting for our purposes is that this development and dependence was not unremarked by the Sumerians of the fourth/third millennium BC.

to suggest that the repeating figures of plants and breeding animals circling the lower portion of the vessel with no apparent beginning or end can be read symbolically as fundamental (basic) to the urban enterprise—representing that perpetual chain of productivity, that very *abundance*, in which the state (as well as its rhetoric) was grounded, and upon which it depended.[16]

The middle zone of the Warka Vase also often gets short shrift. There, a fairly homogeneous row of nude, bald men moving from right to left carry vessels, again in an acephalous procession . The roll-out drawing of that register makes clear that at least three different vessel types are represented: a shallow bowl of uncertain material, the contents of which are not visible; a spouted pitcher, of a type known from pottery of the period, presumably containing a liquid of some sort; and a basket with at least two sorts of contents visible mounded above the rim. A palm frond in one of the baskets, as well as in the baskets of the upper, narrative register representing a scene oriented to the goddess Inanna, suggests that the contents of at least those baskets would be dates—entirely fitting, considering the association of Inanna with the fruit of the date palm.[17] Given the presence of a nude, bald male in the upper register identical to those in the middle register, who offers a basket directly to the goddess, it would seem that the unending procession of the middle zone is meant to conceptually culminate in the offering of all of the contents of the various vessels, that is, the productivity of the land, to the goddess above in a cultic setting.[18]

This fits well with the cult offerings recorded in the reign of Ibbi-Suen of the Ur III period to the moon-god Nanna/Suen at Ur, in which festival offerings of fruit, especially dates (Sum. su_{11}-lum), are presented in baskets of 3-sila capacity, sometimes accompanied by beer and animals.[19] Although

---

[16] Although in the literary text, "The Debate between Sheep and Grain," grain is ultimately declared by Enki to be predominant, the whole debate tradition—"hoe and plough," "palm and tamarisk," "bird and fish," "farmer and shepherd" "winter and summer"—tends to pair sets that are in fact essential dyads, one hardly more important than the other. As noted above, in the Sheep and Grain text, before the ultimate judgment is made, the two protagonists are brought before the gods, where it is made clear that both of them "brought abundance ($he_2.gal_2$) to the assembly" (ETCSL t.5.3.2, line 54); and in "The Debate between Winter and Summer," as well, both protagonists are credited with providing abundance: winter in terms of water and planting, summer in terms of harvest (ETCSL t.5.3.3, line 23; both texts accessed 04/12/2004).

[17] For the association between Inanna and the date palm, see Abusch 1995, with reference to Jacobsen 1976: 34–36. For the presentation of dates to the deity, see the reference in the poem "Inanna and Šu-kale-tuda" (ETCSL t.1.3.3, lines 83–84, accessed 04/17/2004) to ". . . dates . . . fit for the temples of the great gods." In yet another Hymn to Inanna (Sjöberg 1988: 169, col. ii, line 7), the goddess is called "the one who makes the dates be alluring in their panicles/baskets."

here the recipient is the late third millennium moon-god at Ur, whereas it is the earlier Inanna of Uruk who is depicted on the vase, one may assume that the broad pattern of offerings within a Sumerian cultic context would be similar (see Szarzynska 1997). This picture is consistent with a point made by Nicholas Postgate (1987) that, in general, third-millennium references to fruits are largely contained in offering lists of materials supplied to temples for use in cultic contexts. In addition to mention of "Dilmun dates in baskets," such texts also refer to nuts, apples/pomegranates, figs, and grapes, and to dates, grapes, and pomegranates in jars—suggesting that they have been rendered as syrup (see, for example, the poem "Enlil and Sud" = ETCSL t.1.2.2, lines 118–123, where the produce is dispatched by Enlil to Ereš as marriage gifts). While most of these texts are again Neo-Sumerian in date or Old Babylonian in copy, there are also Early Dynastic references to both figs and apples/pomegranates, so it may well be that the differential sizes of round objects in the baskets of the Warka Vase also represent some of these other fruits, along with a predominance of dates. And while it is impossible to determine, without an extensive study of liquid offerings in cultic settings plus archaeological sampling and analysis of residues found in appropriate contexts in the field, what liquids (from beer to fruit syrups to water) might

---

[18] For the cultic setting of offerings to Inanna in archaic Uruk, including liquids in jars and various comestibles in bowls, see Szarzynska 1997. The paired elements that are gathered behind the goddess on the upper register of the vase presumably also represent received offerings, including animals, vessels, and baskets. Indeed, one wonders whether the assemblage represents not just numerical pairs, but actually, as with reduplication in Sumerian verbs and adjectives to indicate myriads/plurality, might in fact stand for a general visual category of "multiples," hence to be read as "abundance." That abundance was signaled in royal texts as having been provided by individual rulers to the temple of a particular god is apparent in later hymns of the Third Dynasty of Ur: for example, in the text known as Shulgi A (ETCSL t.2.4.2.01, line 51), where the king is made to state in the first person: "I filled with abundance the temple of Nanna/Suen" [e_2 ^{d}suen-na . . . he_2.gal_2-la he_2-bi_2-dug_8]. In addition, in the text known as "Enki's journey to Nibru" (ETCSL t.1.1.4, line 50), Enki's temple in Eridu is described as one "whose inside is full of abundance" [$šag_4$-bi he_2.gal_2 sug_4-ga]. If one understands the reed bundles behind the goddess on the Warka Vase as representing her shrine (compare Szarzynska 1987–88), then the presentation of these offerings to the goddess at her shrine could well link the Uruk-period cultic practices in urban temples with those reflected in later texts.

[19] See the discussion in M. G. Hall 1985: esp. 260–95, where different types of offering are enumerated; also Sallaberger 1993. The other fruit most frequently mentioned in offerings is Sum. ḫašḫur, "pomegranate" or "apple" (M. G. Hall 1985: 291), and this could account for the other type of basket content depicted on the vase. Beer is also mentioned in conjunction with offerings to the sun-god in the Hymn to Utu cited above (ETCSL t.4.32.e, line 42, accessed 04/12/2004).

have been contained in the spouted vessel on the Warka Vase, the point remains that the offerings mirror primary agrarian production.

What we see on the Warka Vase represents the inverse of the abundance desired *from* the goddess, she who is described as "keeping the abundance of the land in her hands" [ḫe₂-gal₂-kur-kur-ra šu-še₃ la₂ /-a-e (Sjöberg 1988: 167, col. i, line 16)]; it is the offering back *to* the goddess of the fruits of her proffered abundance, manifest in the previous harvest. There is a retrospective aspect to such offerings, comparable to the offering of harvest fruits in the Jewish festival of Sukkoth (Schauss 1973: 170). A similar ceremony is also attested for ancient Mesopotamia—for example, in the "Debate between Winter and Summer" (ETCSL t.5.3.3, line 60l, accessed 04/12/2004), which makes reference to "the harvest, the great festival of Enlil." But there is also a prospective aspect: the offerings, like Gudea's construction of the temple itself, constitute service to the deity which will then stimulate the next round of positive response(s), in an unbroken chain of reciprocities. In just this way, in the temple bathing festivals (Sanskrit *abhishēka*) observed in Hindu India, ritually offered materials are proffered not just symbolically, but in great abundance. Furthermore, the bathing festival to Krishna Rādharāmana-ji in his Vrindaban temple, as but one example, is celebrated both at the beginning and at the end of the monsoon season that will determine the next harvest, and so may be seen in relation to the fertility of the agricultural year to come (Winter 2000).

Robert Hunt (1987) has discussed the "provisioning of cities" from the perspective of what is necessary at the physical and practical level for the city/state to be maintained; and also (2000) the technology plus labor force required to successfully manage natural resources. His analysis complements the textual evidence for cultic offerings in the context of ritual activity, which works at the symbolic and cosmological level to maintain the same system (see Sallaberger 1993). And I am arguing here that similar principles may be observed in the visual sphere, marked on cultic objects like the Warka Vase and also on public monuments like the fragmentary stele mentioned above.

Similar themes are referenced throughout the third millennium BC, from the Early Dynastic period through the Third Dynasty of Ur. On the silver vase inscribed by Enmetena of Lagash, for example (Moortgat 1969: pl. 113; see Figure 36), attention has been largely focused on the major imagery around the body of the vessel: the lion-headed eagle viewed frontally, his claws grasping the hindquarters of pairs of heraldic lions and ibexes. This composite bird-creature is the familiar of the god Ningirsu, to whom the vase is dedicated, and it is clear that the principal iconography is tailored to the deity in whose cult the vase would presumably have been used. Still, incised above the main panel, around the shoulder of the vessel, is a continuous frieze of couchant calves facing left, ordered like the rams and ewes of the Warka Vase, with no clear

Couchant
cattle

Couchant
cattle

Figure 36. Silver vase of Enmetena of Lagash, Early Dynastic III period, found at Tello (photograph courtesy Département des Antiquités Orientales, Musée du Louvre, AO 2674).

beginning or end. One wonders, therefore, whether there is not more to be read from the iconography of the vase as a whole when the two registers are combined: the lion-headed eagle of Ningirsu controlling the wild animals of the steppe, in order that the domesticated breed depicted on the shoulder should be able to reproduce abundantly and enduringly. That this is not a unique juxtaposition is suggested by an Early Dynastic seal in the Louvre (Figure 37), where in the lower register, along with a combat scene, the lion-headed eagle has its talons into the backs of couchant ibexes, while in the upper register bovids emerging from a hut appear with a milking scene. This motif, on both vase and seal, would then provide the visual equivalent of the "safe pasture" cited in Gudea's Cylinder B above. In the text, the safe pasture is used as a metaphor for the security of the people, but underlying it is the importance of security from human and/or animal predators that will permit the herd to flourish, multiply, and produce.

Related plant and animal motifs appear regularly on works dated to the Early Dynastic period: for example, on a number of objects from the Royal Cemetery of Ur, including vessels, gaming boards, and personal jewelry (Zettler and Horne, eds. 1998: esp. pls. 29–30; Miller 2000; Gansell 2004; see Figure 38); in the representation of the goddess Ninhursag on a basalt vessel inscribed by Enmetena of Lagash from Tello, on which the goddess holds a date spathe in her right hand (Moortgat 1969: pl. 115; see Figure 39); and in the several examples of priests or rulers pouring libations into a potted plant, usually some form of date frond with clusters, before a seated deity (for example, on a limestone plaque from Tello: Moortgat 1969: pl. 114). This motif continues well into the Third Dynasty of Ur, as seen on the Stele of Ur-Namma from Ur (Canby 2001: pl. 10; see Figure 40). Semi-divine figures

Figure 37. Cylinder seal impression, Early Dynastic III period (photograph courtesy Département des Antiquités Orientales, Musée du Louvre, AO 10920).

Figure 38. Jewelry assemblage from PG 1237, Early Dynastic period, found at Royal Cemetery, Ur (photograph courtesy The University of Pennsylvania Museum).

holding a flowing vase on Akkadian seals (Boehmer 1965: 232, 280, 502, 523, 525) or the fish depicted in the streams that flow as attributes from the shoulders of the god Ea/Enki (Boehmer 1965: 377, 488, 493–499, 508–513, 520) may also fall into this same category of referencing natural abundance, especially as produce in the rivers, from fish to reeds, is frequently mentioned within the literary topos of Sumerian he_2-gal_2, Akkadian *hegallu*.[20]

---

[20] The flowing streams with leaping fish are not only a visual attribute of Enki; they also appear as a literary trope, as in the text "Enki's journey to Nibru" (ETCSL t.1.1.4, line 80, accessed 04/17/2004), where it is stated: "When Enki rises (from the Abzu), fish leap before him like waves." The Akkadian seals cited in our text, plus those explicitly representing some sort of grain/vegetation deity (Boehmer 1965: 536–52), make as clear as the citation above relating the Akkadian ruler Naram-Sîn to Akk. *nuhšu*, "abundance/prosperity," that these concepts were not solely Sumerian.

Figure 39. Basalt bowl fragment, dedicated by Enmetena of Lagash to Ninhursag; height 25 cm (photograph courtesy Staatliche Museen zu Berlin, VA 3164).

Clearly, the visual motifs change over the two millennia from early Sumerian urbanization and the city-state to Neo-Sumerian territorial expansion of the fully developed and bureaucratized nation-state, and for purposes of classification, the iconographer would be likely to put the themes into different categories (animal files, repeating plant chains, libations before deities, semi-divine figures with flowing vases). What I am suggesting, however, is that once one identifies the textual continuity of claims to and desire for abundance, then the general theme of an "iconography of abundance" also becomes apparent, with multiple ways to signal the concept.

This variation in the visual repertoire is parallel to the literary component, which also employs variant imagery in how abundance is ascribed and described.

Figure 40. Stele fragment of Ur-Namma, Third Dynasty of Ur, second register of obverse, found at Ur (photograph courtesy The University of Pennsylvania Museum, CBS 116676).

In Ur-Namma C, for example, a hymn celebrating Nippur and its god, Enlil, the king is made to proclaim: "Anu opened his pure mouth and rain was produced for me, He made it fall right into the deep earth, and abundance came forth to/ for me" (Flückiger-Hawker 1999: C 20–21). Ur-Namma goes on to state that he is "the faithful shepherd who has increased his flock" (Flückiger-Hawker 1999: C 76), declaring his "enormous harvest which raises itself high" (Flückiger-Hawker 1999: C 80). The hymn ends with libations to Enlil, and the paean: "thanks to him (Ur-Namma) abundance entered the Royal Canal and the temple of Enlil" (Flückiger-Hawker 1999: C 103). In Ur-Namma D, the hymn describes the king as having been provided with broad wisdom by Enki, digging a "canal of abundance" in his home city of Ur, which then produces plentiful fish, birds, and plants, as well as watering large arable tracts where barley sprouts like reed thickets (Flückiger-Hawker 1999: D21–22; 33'–36').

While royal hymns celebrate abundance, lamentations mourn what has been lost, thereby providing us with the same value system through inversion. In the lament known as the "Death of Ur-Namma," the king is made to complain, rather like Job: "Despite having made abundance manifest to the Anuna-gods (that is, having made prolific offerings?) . . . no god assisted me, nor was my heart relieved!" (Flückiger-Hawker 1999: A158–160). And yet, the lament ends with the reassurance that the canebrakes which the king has drained, and the vast barley fields which he has produced, will ultimately be productive and looked upon with admiration (Flückiger-Hawker 1999: A227–230). These references in Ur-Namma A and D may well provide the key to the elusive reverse of the Ur-Namma stele in Philadelphia, where we know a small fragment of text makes reference to the canals dug in the reign of that ruler, while the second register shows elements of a canebrake (Canby 2001: pl. 11). A variety of other laments, including *The Lamentation over the Destruction of Sumer and Ur* (Michalowski 1989) and several of the texts known as the *Canonical Lamentations* (M. Cohen 1988: 511, line 1; 589; 637, lines a+11 and 12) equally provide the inverse of abundance in the negative tropes of floods that drown the harvest, sheep and goats that cry out, and forests and orchards that have been destroyed. The catalog of disasters in the *Lamentation over the Destruction of Sumer and Ur*, for example, includes the loss of cattle, palm trees, and fertile reeds (Michalowski 1989: lines 411–418); while the more encouraging restoration promised by Enlil at the end envisions full rivers, good rains, abundant grain, fish and fowl in the marshes, plentiful reeds, and fruit-bearing trees in the orchards (Michalowski 1989: 498–505)—in short, along with plentiful herds, all that a good agrarian state needs to be fully functional.

The visual repertoire, despite its variations, was more limited than the textual; but I would argue that paired tropes of grain and flax, male and female sheep/goat/cattle, domesticated plant plus animal, along with libations into palm plants and flowing streams, all serve iconically to reference the same semantic range of the productivity of the land. Whether this selection is a question of visual economy, with signs standing for an understood whole, and/or whether it was a symptom of the separation of the urban community/cult from the rural sphere (as per Bernbeck and Pollock 2002: 186), thereby reducing the range of productivity to the level of symbol, the fact remains that the city was as dependent on agrarian production as was the countryside. The key to the power of these motifs in the Mesopotamian universe lies in the very phenomenon that has led to their dismissal by Western analysts: repetition. If one of the primary characteristics of the fourth millennium was an "unprecedented focus on duration" (Bernbeck and Pollock 2002: 189–190), then repeating bands of plants and animals, especially in a frieze around a circular vessel, represents precisely that which endures and recurs, that which is *not* subject to temporal variability or limitation.

Nor is it surprising that the positive is what is represented visually, since the objects on which such representations occur are largely cultic, reflecting not so much the "real" natural world, and surely not its inversion, but rather an ideal world order. The works therefore articulate the desired "best-case scenario," in a repeating, hence infinite, sequence, leaving the negative for historical accounts and paradigmatic "Lamentation" literature. At the same time, it is important to emphasize that one must see the visual repertoire as no less rhetorical than the textual. Abundance is both necessary and desired; and, as on the Warka Vase, the luxuriance of natural production is what undergirds the ordered cosmos as well as the urbanized city-state. In this universe, an "iconography of abundance" lends itself to a "cultural rhetoric of abundance," with the agricultural and pastoral landscape as much a component in the state apparatus, and as political, as the urban landscape.

If (as per A. T. Smith 2003: 10) the land provides the ground for a culture's values and aesthetic response as well as its practical produce, then what becomes interesting is precisely *which* aspects of the natural landscape a given culture or period selects for representational and symbolic purposes. For the Tigris-Euphrates Valley, from the earliest phases of the Sumerian city-state, the underlying concept of desired abundance in the natural world was clearly articulated in text and image through the representation of often-repeated domesticated plants and animals, the rivers and the life they sustained, all of which remained a constant theme for millennia.

In short, what modernity has relegated to "mere ornament" was in fact highly charged, through the very principle of repetition, to stand as a sign of eternal and unending productivity—provided by the gods as part of the cosmic order and actualized through the ruler. Visual rhetoric was likely to have been a deliberate strategy of the center, and so should then not be underestimated as an artifact of the early state.

RESISTING EMPIRE: ELAM IN THE FIRST MILLENNIUM BC

ELIZABETH CARTER

ABSTRACT

Early in the first millennium BC, the Elamites were on the periphery of the powerful Assyrian Empire; by the last half of the millennium, they became part of the Achaemenid core, their political power and "cultural capital" subsumed within the Persian imperial style. This paper documents how the Elamites maintained their cultural and political independence despite intense Assyrian pressure and discusses the subsequent acculturation[1] of the Elamites into the larger, international Iranian world of the last half of the first millennium BC. The Elamites adjusted and adapted their customs over the millennia and maintained a cultural presence in southwestern Iran long after their political demise (Potts 1999).

HISTORICAL BACKGROUND

During the late second millennium, the Elamites of southwestern Iran formed a union of highland and lowland folk, who came together to defeat the Babylonians. This combination of local powers carried the seeds of its own destruction, as small polities grew increasingly independent. The former union crumbled under pressure from Nebuchadnessar I (1125–1104). The capitals of Susa in Khuzistan and Anshan in Fars had already declined in importance by 1100–1000 BC (E. Carter 1994; de Miroschedji 1990). Textual sources for the period from 1000 to 744 BC are absent from Elam, and it is

---

[1] For a review of the definitions of acculturation and the distinctions between assimilation and acculturation, see B. J. Stone 1995. Here the term is used to describe the process that takes place when cultures come into direct and continuous contact with subsequent modifications in the original cultural patterns of either or both groups.

only in the mid-eighth century that written documents provide any significant information (Waters 2000).

The Elamites of the late second millennium, possibly pushed by a prolonged drought (Neumann and Parpola 1987), apparently turned increasingly to pastoralism and plunder for their livelihood (E. Carter 1984). In Babylonia, Chaldea, and Iran, the first centuries of the first millennium BC are periods of tribal growth and urban decline. Scattered Mesopotamian sources show that Chaldeans and Aramaeans had moved into the areas of southwestern Iran formerly under Elamite control, especially along the river Ulai (the modern Karkheh) and in the Pusht-i Kuh (western Luristan) (Brinkman 1984b; 1986; Cole 1996a; 1996b). To the southeast in the territory of Anshan, the Persian tribes appear to have entered Fars at this time (E. Carter 1994; Stronach 1974), and the Medes were consolidating their power base in northwestern Iran (Roaf 1995).

Elamite territory lay in the midst of these forces in the middle plains of central Khuzistan, the upland valleys of southeastern Khuzistan, and western Fars (E. Carter 1994). To the northwest of Susa, particularly on the upper reaches of the Karkheh River, Elamite cultural traditions remained alive in Luristan, but our sources are mute on the ethnic background of the population. Tribal boundaries were permeable, and Kassite, Elamite, and Aramaean groups frequently moved between highlands and lowlands in the Pusht-i Kuh (Brinkman 1986). Layard's description of the relationship between the Arabs of the Trans-Tigridian corridor and the Lurs of the Pusht-i Kuh in the nineteenth century offers a reasonable ethnographic parallel to the fluid situation sketched from the texts:

> During the summer the tribes [Beni Lam Arabs] congregate near that river [Tigris] and on the borders of the vast inland marshes formed by its waters. In the winter and spring they usually encamp in the sandstone and gypsum hills running parallel to the great range, or in the plains at the foot of the mountains. They mix with the Feili tribes of the Pusht-i-Kuh, and pasture their flocks on their lands for which they yearly pay a small sum to the Wali Ali Khan. They are usually on good terms with the inhabitants of the mountains, whose chiefs continually take refuge in their tents when opposed by the government or expelled by their own tribes. The Arab Sheikhs at the same time frequently seek asylum among the I'liyáts of the hills. Thus it is for their mutual interest to be on friendly terms. (Layard 1894: 46–47)

In the eighth century, a shift of the Euphrates River course back toward the old centers of settlement in Babylonia was in part responsible for a rebirth of urban life. The southern and eastern trade routes increased in importance at this time. Wool, livestock, and slaves from the Zagros, metals from the Iranian

Plateau and Oman, camels, purple dyes (?), and incense from Arabia were among the essential commodities of this trade. Babylonia's cities managed the trade and reaped the profits (Cole 1996a; 1996b).

Babylonian advancement meant that Elam gained as well—a pattern observed over the millennia (de Miroschedji 2003). Renewed international trade traversed Elamite territories, and these regions profited since they produced wool, supplied pack animals, and controlled access to the metal sources. Susa, the most famous of the Elamite cities, also prospered (see below), but we have little direct evidence of its role in the larger transregional economy documented for Babylonia.

Until 750, the Assyrians had limited interest in the Zagros, and the Elamites remained sheltered in their mountain valleys. There is no evidence that the Assyrians had any expansionary goals toward the east, nor did the Elamites want to come into direct conflict with the Assyrians.[2] Later in the eighth and seventh centuries, when the Assyrians and Elamites did fight, it was "nearly always the direct result of Babylonian efforts to maintain or regain its independence from Assyria" (Gerardi 1987: 256). These circumstances suggest that the southern trade routes had become important alternatives to the western trade routes controlled by the Assyrians and their vassals. The Elamites provided military aid to the Babylonians not only for direct monetary gain, through bribes and a share of the booty, but also to maintain the commercial advantage they had when the Babylonians controlled the international trade routes.

Elam was unstable—nineteen kings ruled Elam during the reign of Sargon II (721–705 BC) alone (Gerardi 1987: 257, 259, fig. 9)—and the Assyrians used Elamite disunity to keep them under control. The Elamites, nevertheless, were successful up to a point in avoiding the full force of the Assyrian army. Even after the destruction of Elam by Assurbanipal in 646 BC, the persistence of the mountain polities in southeastern Khuzistan and the resiliency of Susa between 646 and 550 BC bear witness to the success that Elamites had against the Assyrians (Potts 1999: 259–308).

THE LANDSCAPE OF RESISTANCE IN ELAM

The Archaeological Record in Susiana

Because textual sources for the Neo-Elamite I (1000–775 BC) period are lacking, archaeology perforce plays a large role in our discussion of the early Neo-

---

[2] The Elamites avoided direct confrontation with the Assyrians by occasionally making treaties with them and resisted them by selectively giving political refuge to the Babylonian opponents of Assyria (Gerardi 1987; Stolper 1984).

Elamite period. First in this chain of evidence is R. McC. Adams's survey in the Khuzistan plain (Adams 1962) (Figure 41). One of the major results of his survey was to identify a sharp population drop during the middle of the first millennium BC. He linked this desertion of the plain directly to the Assyrian conquest. Subsequent surveys (E. Carter 1971; de Miroschedji 1981c) and excavations at Susa (de Miroschedji 1981a; 1981b) and the reexamination of excavated materials from Al Untash Napirisha (E. Carter 1992) show, however, that the desertion of the plain was a longer and more complex process.

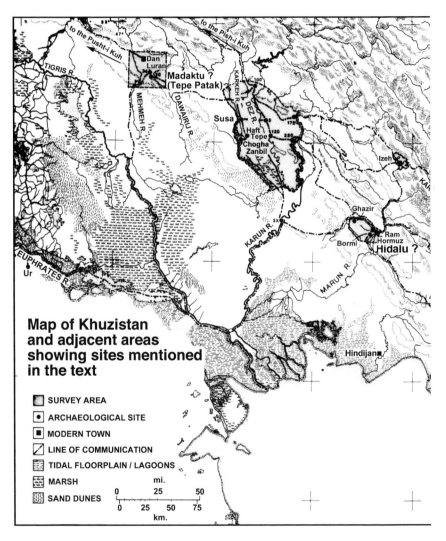

Figure 41. *(FACING PAGES):* Map of Khuzistan and adjacent areas showing sites mentioned in the text.

The Elamites, instead of facing the Assyrians, appear to have moved out of their path—creating their brand of a "landscape of resistance." De Miroschedji (1981a) outlined a ceramic chronology through his excavations in the Ville Royale II (Neo-Elamite: NE I 1000–775 BC; NE II 774–522 BC)[3] and resurveyed sites in the northern portions of the Susiana plain (de Miroschedji 1981c) (Figure 42). Around Susa, the number of settlements had already begun to decline during the Late Middle Elamite period (ME II–III, ca.1350–1000 BC) (E. Carter 1994). On the northern Susiana plain by 1000 BC or so, over

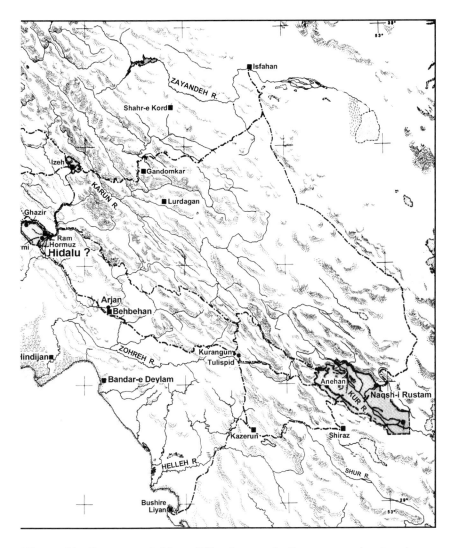

Figure 41. *(CONTINUED)*: Map of Khuzistan and adjacent areas showing sites mentioned in the text.

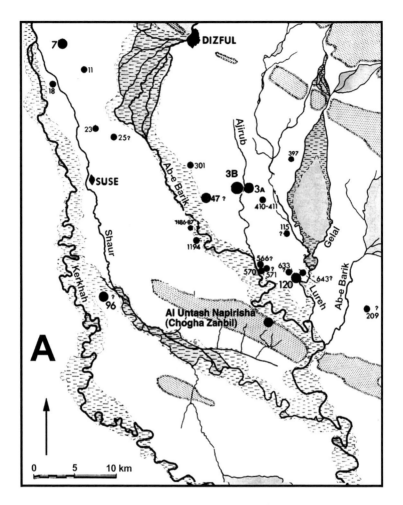

Figure 42. *(FACING PAGES):* (**A**) Northern Khuzistan in the Neo-Elamite I period (ca. 1000–775 BC), after de Miroschedji 1981c.

half the twenty-one Neo-Elamite I sites were new foundations, and ten of the thirteen new sites were on the east side of the Diz River. The foundation of sites KS-633 and KS-643 near KS-120, Deh-i Noh, may be linked to the fractionalization of the major Middle Elamite settlement there. Likewise, the establishment of new settlements (KS-566, -570, -571) may reflect the breakup of the large (100 hectare) Middle Elamite settlement at Al Untash Napirisha,

---

[3] Historic periodization based on linguistic and historic criteria generally uses three phases: NE I = 1000–743 BC; NE II = 743–653 BC; NE III = 653–550 BC. For a discussion of the various schemes, see Waters 2000: 3–4. Archaeologists can distinguish only two phases on the basis of the excavated ceramic materials.

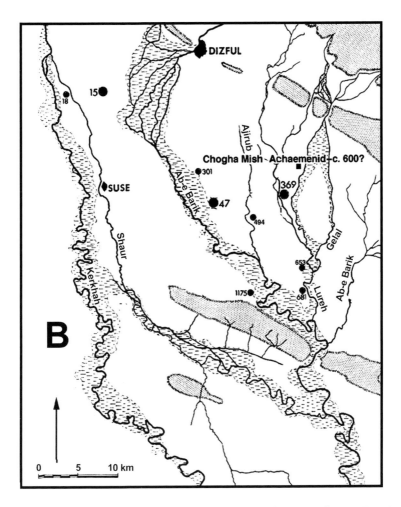

Figure 42. *(CONTINUED):* (**B**) Northern Khuzistan in the Neo-Elamite II period (ca. 725/700–520 BC), after de Miroschedji 1981c.

where only squatter occupations and a few impoverished burials can be dated to the early first millennium (E. Carter 1992; Ghirshman 1968). The southern portion of the Susiana plain appears to have produced very little Neo-Elamite material, but needs to be reexamined in the light of new ceramic data.

In the Neo-Elamite II period (774–522 BC), the population on the Susiana plain declines even further. The two largest Neo-Elamite I sites, KS-3A-B and KS-7, are abandoned. De Miroschedji's (1981c: 169–172) work identified only six sites of the period in northern Susiana. The most important was KS-369 (12 hectares), which is situated 5 kilometers southwest of Chogha Mish (KS-1) (Figure 42b). Chogha Mish might offer a partial explanation for the precipitous drop in Elamite settlement in northern Khuzistan. The ceramic assemblage identified there as Achaemenid contains a number of earlier types that find parallels with Godin II and Nush-i Jan Late Median types dated around 600 BC (Delougaz and Kantor 1996: 10–18; R. Stronach 1978). These materials suggest that contemporary, but ceramically distinct groups may have occupied part of the Susiana during the Neo-Elamite II period and remained unrecognized by researchers looking for Elamite materials.

De Miroschedji (1981c: 172)[4] suggests that, given the politics of the period, the foundation of Elamite sites in northern Khuzistan should be dated before Assurbanipal's conquest in 646 BC. If his reconstruction is correct, then the Susiana conquered by Assurbanipal can be seen as a region whose population had declined but which included a group of settlements on the southeastern edge of the Susiana plain. The survey data show a continued development of the area on the lower course of the Lureh between it and the Diz (Figure 42b). The growth of this sector of the plain on the road to the Ram Hormuz possibly should be seen as an effort to expand in the direction of the Elamite settlements in southeastern Khuzistan.[5]

At Susa, the state-sponsored buildings of earlier times are conspicuous by their absence (Malbran-Labat 1995: 205) in the Neo-Elamite I period. Monumental works of metal sculpture, so distinctive of the Middle Elamite period (see, for example, Harper, Aruz, and Tallon 1992), are unknown during the Neo-Elamite I period. A comparison of the archaeological assemblages earlier and later than the Neo-Elamite I period show that luxuries were few and far between around the turn of the millennium in Susa. But by the middle of the eighth century, as noted above, prosperity returned to lowland Babylonia, and Susa appears to have been part of that mini-renaissance.

The best-known ruler of the time, Shutruk Nahhunte II (717–699 BC), took the name and title: King of Anshan and Susa, enlarger of the realm (Waters 2000: 111–116). This act appears to have been an attempt to tie his rule to the powerful Middle Elamite dynasty founded by Shutruk Nahhunte I (ca. 1165 BC). The early excavations at Susa revealed a small temple decorated with glazed tiles and inscribed with the name of Shutruk Nahhunte II, which reuses earlier construction materials and is possibly recycled from Middle Elamite II–III (ca. 1350–1000 BC) times (Amiet and Lambert 1967;

---

[4] De Miroschedji's (1981c: 172) suggestion that mobile pastoralists, recent Aramaean immigrants, formed a high percentage of the population in Khuzistan appears unsupported.

[5] Perhaps it is not accidental that Assurbanipal's annals record that the Elamite, Ummanaldas, fled south from Madaktu and used the Diz as his line of defense (Gerardi 1987: 195–196).

Heim 1992). One of Shutruk Nahhunte II's texts also records that he rein-stalled statues of earlier Elamite rulers before the cult image of Inshushinak (Montagne and Grillot-Susini 1996: 24–25).

In short, the revival of the Elamite language (or at least inscriptions), along with the use of an older royal titulary and the continuity of architec-tural and artistic traditions, point to a conscious Elamite revival in Susiana during the Neo-Elamite II period. These references to the past do not mean that the population of Susa was fundamentally Elamite,[6] but it does show that the local rulers of an ethnically diverse city sought to associate them-selves with an earlier period when the Elamites were masters, not servants of the Babylonians. Vallat (1980) has argued that it is only at this time that low-land Susiana became a province of highland Elam. Regardless of whether his view is correct, the use of Elamite in royal inscriptions tied Susa to its glori-ous past, linked it to the increasingly powerful highland polities to the north and east, and distinguished the Susians from both their Assyrian enemies and Babylonian allies.

Seen in this light, the reintegration of Susa with the adjacent mountain polities, which were bound to them by tradition and trade, becomes a means of resisting empire. By the eighth century BC, and probably earlier, a new political and social landscape emerged in Elam. Susa was no longer the polit-ical center of Elam, but remained an important symbol of Elamite identity. The towns of Madaktu and Hidalu (Figure 41) now appear frequently in the Assyrian sources as the foci of political and military activity. The flight of Kudur Nahhunte (693–692 BC) from Madaktu to Hidalu also hints at the importance of the upland regions to Elam's political structure (Waters 2000: 31–33) and underscores the links among the mountain strongholds in the Zagros.[7] De Miroschedji (1986b) has suggested that Tepe Patak in the Deh Luran plain (60 kilometers northwest of Susa) should be identified as Madaktu.[8] Hidalu probably lies in the Ram Hormuz (150 kilometers to the southeast) or in the adjacent Behbehan region (E. Carter 1994).

Renewed contacts with the highlands set Susiana apart from the powers that surrounded Elamite territory: the Assyrians and Babylonians to the west; the Medes to the north; and the Persians to the east. The effectiveness of

---

[6] Stolper 1992: 259–260; the slightly earlier Neo-Hittite revival in north Syria (Dodd 2002) may offer a parallel to the Elamite revival in Khuzistan.

[7] M. A. Stein's (1940b) road from Behbehan to the Pish-i Kuh completely bypasses Susa and it seems likely that these mountain roads were well used in the Neo-Elam-ite period to connect the various highland regions that comprised the country.

[8] The identification is not generally accepted; compare Vallat 1993: 162. It seems more likely that Madaktu lay in the upland valleys of Luristan, but its location is still unknown.

Elamite strategy is attested by its resiliency. Urban life in Susa survived and even revived in the short period between the Assyrian conquest in 646 BC and the total takeover of the city by Darius in 522 BC (Potts 1999: 297–307).[9]

The Northwest Highlands

Surveys and excavations in Luristan show the appearance of numerous cemetery sites dating to the early first millennium BC, but permanent settlements are very poorly attested (Vanden Berghe and Tourovets 1995). These burial grounds are located along rivers and streams, primarily along the upper courses of the Karkheh, the Saimarreh, and the Gar Ab.[10] Likewise, Vanden Berghe (1973a: 28) found sites along the smaller streams traversing the Zagros and leading to the foothill road such as the Cham Ab, the Gulgul, and the Dawairij. Most are isolated cemetery sites and were very likely the burial grounds of mobile pastoralists (Figure 43).

Looted tombs in this region have yielded a large number of metal objects, making precise dating difficult. Even excavated tomb groups are difficult to date both because of the custom of reusing tombs (Vanden Berghe 1973a) and the lack of comparative materials. Likewise, inscribed pieces[11] are limited in their usefulness in establishing a date for the burials since they have a long use life and were often heirlooms by the time they were included in a burial. Nevertheless, the military character of many of these funerary assemblages—swords, daggers, maceheads, quivers, and shields—is clear, and they are common features of the Luristan Iron Age burials.

The recent publication and analysis of comparative materials suggest that the Luristan cemeteries range in date between ca.1200 and 600 BC. The materials from the Iron Age I and II (ca. 1200–800 BC) cemeteries like Bard-i Bal and Gulgul show cultural ties with the Elamite regions, but few parallels with Mesopotamia (Vanden Berghe and Tourovets 1995). For example, an idol with two rampant mountain goats from Bard-i Bal shows a clear affinity with older and contemporary Elamite artistic styles known from Susa

---

[9] I suggest that the most logical date for the founding of the *Village perse-achéménid* (the area in the *Ville des artisans* of Susa, east of the main tell) (Ghirshman 1954) is just before the rebuilding of the older areas of the mound by Darius, since the leveling required for the new structures on the Apadana would have displaced people from this area of the site.

[10] Vanden Berghe (1971; 1973a) originally dated these burials somewhat earlier than the bulk of the comparative material now suggests. This article was completed before I received Overlaet 2003.

[11] Brinkman (1968: 9–12) studied the inscribed pieces, Luristan bronzes from the antiquities market, and found them to date between the twelfth and tenth centuries.

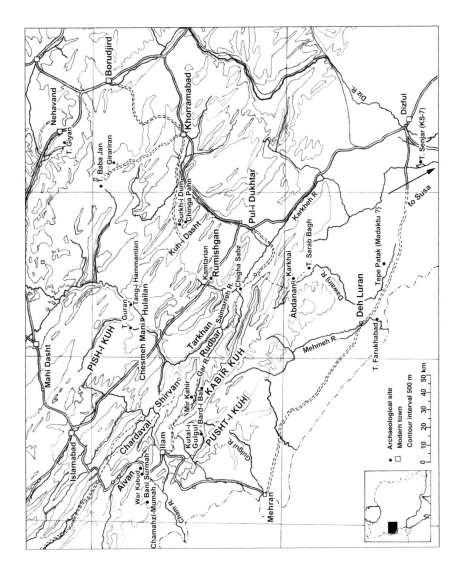

Figure 43.
Archaeological sites in
Luristan (after Haerinck
and Overlaet 1998).

(Vanden Berghe 1971: 20, fig. 14; compare Amiet 1988: figs. 39 and 71). At Karkhai in the Abdanan region, just north of the Deh Luran plain, the grave goods included a faience box (compare Amiet 1966: fig. 375, p. 498), a composite pin (de Miroschedji 1981a: fig. 40: 4-5), and an ink-pot metal vessel (de Miroschedji 1981a: fig. 40: 12)—all items closely paralleled at Susa in the Neo-Elamite II period.

On the other hand, near Aiwan in northwestern Luristan, burial goods of Iron III date (ca. 800–600 BC) show close ties to Assyria and north Syria and not to the adjacent Elamite areas to the east and south (Haerinck and Overlaet 1998; 1999; Vanden Berghe and Tourovets 1995). We have no certain way to identify the ethnicity or politics of the people buried in scattered graveyards of Luristan, nor can we be sure who made these items. Are the Assyrian-style objects found in Luristan imports, local work made in emulation of imperial styles, or brought by some deported population from the north?

The distribution of the funerary assemblages and burial types nevertheless appears to make a certain amount of historical sense. The grave goods found at the northwest edge of the Trans-Tigridian corridor east of the Zagros front show closer connections to Assyrian and north Syrian styles; those found farther to the east and southeast appear local and/or Elamite. In the Pish-i Kuh (the eastern side of the Zagros front), two Iron Age sanctuary sites have been identified on the eastern branches of the Saimarreh River. Both are situated in large valleys and may have been places of pilgrimage and/or passages for peoples from the east and west of the Kabir Kuh. One is in the Hulailan Valley, near the site of Tepe Guran at a place called Tang-i Hamamlan (Thrane 1964); and the other, called Surkh Dum, is located in the Kuh-i Dasht. Tang-i Hamamlan was looted, and the rescue excavations could only tentatively confirm the presence of a shrine.

Numerous finds, however, came from the sanctuary at Surkh Dum (eighth to seventh century BC) (Muscarella 1981; Schmidt, van Loon, and Curvers 1989). At Surkh Dum, the persistence of Elamite artistic and religious traditions in the mountains is clear. Votive pins stuck into the interstices of the walls are reminiscent of the tombs excavated in Luristan with Elamite-related metal objects stuck in their walls (Vanden Berghe 1971: 18). The use of cylinder seals as votive offerings is also an Elamite practice well attested at Al Untash Napirisha (Porada 1970). Faience and bone carvings are manufactured in local styles but may share some features of Elamite traditions (Muscarella 1981; Schmidt, van Loon, and Curvers 1989: 245–254, 363–379). Some of the metalwork also shows close Elamite ties; particularly striking is the goddess on the coiled serpent throne (Calmeyer 1995).

The site may have been an administrative center in the mountains for mobile pastoralists moving between northern Susiana and the Pish-i Kuh during the eighth and seventh centuries BC (Schmidt, van Loon, and Curvers 1989: 489). The ethnographic data suggest that the shrine[12] was possibly a spot to make offerings and to perform oaths for the nomads on their biennial migration. Other interpretations of this unique building are possible, but the ties to Elamite cultural traditions are clear. The metalworking that flourished during the first part of the first millennium in Luristan was a development with a background in earlier Middle Elamite craft traditions (Moorey 1971: 302–309; Porada 1965: 45–73). Surely some of these people were Elamites, while others must have belonged to different ethnic or linguistic groups but nonetheless appreciated Elamite artistic styles. The archaeological record alone does not allow us to specifically distinguish Elamite from non-Elamite in the mountains of Luristan.

The Southeastern Highlands

Surveys in the Ram Hormuz plain and small-scale excavations at the site of Tall-i Ghazir show that occupation there continued throughout the late second millennium BC well into Achaemenid times (E. Carter 1994; H. T. Wright and Carter 2003). Instead of declining in population like the middle plains of central Khuzistan, population rose during this period. Surveys (H. T. Wright, ed. 1979) in the Izeh region, 80 kilometers to the north of Ram Hormuz, have failed to discover any settlements of the period, but I suspect that the modern town itself may cover the occupation. Rock reliefs at Shikaf-i Salman, 3 kilometers south of Iseh, and Kul-i Farah, 7 kilometers northeast of the city, carry inscriptions in Elamite that identify the region as part of a small state called Aapir ruled by Hanni, a contemporary of Shurtur Nahhunte, son of Idadu (not Shutruk Nahhunte II 717–699 BC) (De Waele, 1981; Vanden Berghe 1986; Waters 2000: 111–116). The original reliefs appear to have been carved in the late Middle Elamite period (1300–1000 BC) but the inscriptions added later. The one exception to this is the relief called Kul-i Farah I, where the image and the inscription are apparently roughly contemporary. The panel shows the king, Hanni, with his general, Shutrutu, and his cupbearer, Shuturututa, musicians and priests participating in a sacrifice. The text, although difficult, seems to recount the brilliant career of the ruler, including a suppression of a revolt and the construction of a temple (Calmeyer 1990; Stolper 1990; Waters 2000).

The mention of Elamite divinities in the inscriptions and the scenes of sacrifice and religious processions accompanied by musicians demonstrate that the Kul-i Farah reliefs were part of an important outdoor sanctuary.

---

[12] For an overview of shrines in Luristan in the recent past and some of their ethnographically attested functions, see Mortensen and Nicolaisen 1993: 121 ff.

Likewise, the spring sanctuary at Shakaf-i Suleiman appears to have been a sacred spot. It is significant that a nonroyal personage—and supposed vassal of the Elamite king in Hidalu—could decorate the cliffs with his history and those of his family and associates. The use of these reliefs in the Neo-Elamite period also suggests a need to continue and elaborate Elamite traditions in the highlands.

In addition to the rock reliefs from Izeh, two other much earlier rock reliefs appear to have had additions made to them in the Neo-Elamite period: the first at Kurangun (Vanden Berghe 1986: 163), and the second at Naqshe Rustam near Persepolis in Fars (Seidl 1986). The latter addition was more certainly made in that period since the dress of the figures is visible, identifiable, and roughly datable.

The chance discovery of an extraordinarily rich tomb made near Arjan, 10 kilometers north of the modern city of Bebahan (Alizadeh 1985) has produced another Elamite inscription. The tomb was a stone-built underground chamber, situated outside the settlement and constructed in the style of the highlands, but with plastered walls like an Elamite burial. It contained a U-shaped bronze coffin of a type used in Mesopotamia and Iran; metal objects and vessels were found inside and outside the coffin. The objects inside the coffin included an inscribed gold ring, 98 round gold discs that were originally sewn on a garment, a dagger, some fragments of textiles, and a silver rod. Outside the coffin on the floor of the tomb chamber were an elaborate bronze stand, lamp, silver jar, bronze jar, bronze cup, and ten cylindrical vases. A gold ring, which can be described as Achaemenid in style with an Elamite inscription, was found. Vallat (1984) dates the inscription (Kiddin Hutran, son of Kurlash) to the period between 640 and 525 BC—post-Assyrian conquest and pre-Darius.

The mixture of Iranian, Assyro-Babylonian, Syrian, and Elamite identifiable in the artworks placed in the burial are representative, I believe, of the beginnings of the international, imperial Achaemenid style. The "Phoenecian" bowl (Majidzadeh 1992) illustrates Elamite participation in the larger international world of the time and the close ties of the Elamites to the Achaemenid world (Briant 2002: 20–21; E. Carter 1994; D. Stronach 2003).

Much of what is known from southeastern regions of Elam appears to postdate the Luristan finds with an overlap in the seventh century when the Elamites were able to resist Assyria. Both historical and archaeological records show that the Elamites were mobile, fragmented populations unable to mount a real challenge to the Assyrians. When threatened, they abandoned the lowlands of Khuzistan, possibly first moving northwest into Luristan and then turning southeast to eastern Khuzistan. Further publication of materials from Luristan and future excavations in eastern Khuzistan and western Fars will no doubt allow a more detailed evaluation of this proposal.

THE UNIQUE CASE OF THE ASSYRIAN RELIEFS

Thus the most pardoxical evidence of Elamite resistance to Assyria is from the city of Nineveh in the heartland of Assyria. Assurbanipal's detailed records of his Elamite wars saved for posterity the people he most wanted to eliminate from historical memory. Indeed, Assurbanipal's inclusion of the Elamites in his records of conquest elevated Elamite status. In 653 BC, King Assurbanipal of Assyria attacked the Elamite forces at an unknown location along the River Ulai (the modern Karkheh) in the province of Khuzistan. The sculpted walls of Room XXIII in the southwest palace of Sennacherib, Assurbanipal's grandfather, record the events before, during, and after the battle.[13] These reliefs have been thoroughly studied (most recently by Curtis, Reade, and Collon 1995; Kaelin 1999), and the purpose of the remarks below is to examine them as documentation of Elamite resistance to Assyria.

Even though Assurbanipal was victorious, the prominence[14] given to the battle with Te-Umman (Elamite, Tepti Humban Inshushinak, 664?–653 BC) tends to emphasize Elam's dogged resistance to, rather than its destruction by, the Assyrians. The details of the setting, the method of attack (lightly armed Elamites and Babylonian allies racing down a hillside to attack the Assyrian army), and the identification of the actors in the drama by epigraphs make it one of the most mimetic narratives in all of Assyrian art. The Elamites are still generic enemies; but their leaders are named and their family relationships mentioned in the epigraphs. These labels focus the attention of the viewer, literate or not, and provide specificity (Gerardi 1987: 94).

The images and their local details were designed to impress Elamite and other visitors to the palace and to illustrate the futility of revolution (Russell 1991: 223–240). The portrayal of the Elamites as humans, without a divine mission to rule, is clarified in the epigraphs. Above the figure of a man being beheaded in the Till Tuba relief is written:

> Te-Umman, king of Elam, who in fierce battle was wounded, Tammaritu, his eldest son, took him by the hand and to save (their) lives they fled. They hid in the midst of a forest. With the encouragement of Assur and Ishtar I killed them. Their heads I cut off in front of each other. (Gerardi 1987: 276)

---

[13] The walls were of a fossiliferous limestone imported by Sennacherib but carved or recarved by Assurbanipal (Russell 1999: 157).

[14] In addition to the reliefs in Sennacherib's palace, a rendering of the same events was found in Assurbanipal's north palace (Barnett 1976: 6–8, pls. 24–26).

Throughout the epigraphs Te-Umman calls on his son-in-law and his son, but Assurbanipal, of course, only relies on Ashur and Ishtar—a confirmation of Assurbanipal's divine right to rule.

Assurbanipal (668–627 BC) had used various means to control the Elamites throughout his reign: foreign aid, installing local puppet rulers, making treaties, and finally his formidable military machine (Gerardi 1987: 250–258). Assurbanipal records in his annals the destruction of Susa and Elam in graphic detail. He describes how he looted the city and desecrated its temples. He destroyed the ziggurat of Susa, ripped off its bronze horns, and cut down the trees in its sacred groves. Equally humiliating for the Elamites was Assurbanipal's violation of the royal tombs at Susa.

> I pulled down and destroyed the tombs of their earlier and later kings, who had not revered the deities of Ashur and Ishtar my lords, . . . and I exposed them to the sun. I took away their bones to Assyria, I put restlessness on their ghosts, I deprived them of food-offerings and libations of water. (Translation Saggs 1984: 114)

The destruction of the royal tombs sends a clear message to the Elamites, one that is also illustrated on the upper left of the Till Tuba relief where the Gambilu, Elamite allies, are shown as captives grinding the bones of their ancestors (Russell 1999: fig. 60). In short, Assurbanipal tried to detach the Elamites and their allies from their heritage, just as the Elamites had tried to nurture these links to past glory. His publicly displayed hatred of the Elamites may well have been a factor that pushed them into the arms of the rising Persian dynasty.

THE ACCULTURATION OF THE ELAMITES
BY THE PERSIANS

How trustworthy are the reports of Assurbanipal? Elamite deportees turn up as far afield as Samaria and Egypt. There is even a letter that records the names of administrators sent to Elam, although the exact date of the document is disputed (Potts 1999: 288–289). The textual and archaeological records outlined above show that the Elamites remained in their mountain valleys and at Susa even after Assurbanipal's conquest (Potts 1999: 289–308). Faced with the rise of the Neo-Babylonian dynasty on the west and the Medes on the north, the Elamites were left with little other choice than to throw their lot in with the Persians. The situation appears to have been mutually advantageous. The fragmented Elamite armies needed protection from their enemies. The Persians needed the Elamites' knowledge and possibly sought to coopt their prestige,[15] gained from many years of battling the Assyrians as allies of the Babylonians and along the Trans-Tigridian corridor.

The archaeological and historical records relating to Elam in the early first millennium BC are complex and diverse. Taken together, they provide a picture of how one peripheral state resisted a powerful empire only to become part of the imperial core of another dominant state. The archaeological record indicates that the Elamites of Susiana left their lowland cities when faced with political and environmental pressures. Settlement in the lowlands are abandoned and older centers such as Al Untash Napirisha and Deh-i No appear to fragment in the Neo-Elamite I period (1000–775 BC). By the end of the eighth century BC, the beginning of the Neo-Elamite II period (774–522 BC), Susa sees a revival linked probably to the renaissance evidenced in Babylonia, although the surrounding plain remains sparsely settled. The Elamite language reappears in Susa in royal inscriptions at this time, and these texts were perhaps a conscious effort to tie the local Susian ruler to a glorious past. The use of Elamite might well have been an act of defiance against both the Babylonians and the Assyrians.

The Elamites, according to Assyrian sources, used a wide range of tactics to resist the Assyrian efforts to control them, including guerilla warfare, ambush, and flight. Most apposite is the retreat from Madaktu (perhaps northwest of Susa) to Hidalu in southeastern Khuzistan by Kudur Nahhunte (ca. 693–692 BC) or Humban Haltash III (648?–645? BC) (Waters 2000: 32, 71) (Figure 41). To the Assyrians and the Babylonians, the Elamites presented a more or less united front from the mid-eighth century into the reign of Te-Umman (ca. 664?–653 BC). But after this time, the Assyrians increased their involvement in Elamite internal affairs, and the period is one of increasingly unsettled conditions and factional strife for Elam.

The impact of Assurbanipal's defeat of Susa and other Elamite cities in 646 BC is difficult to judge. The surprisingly rapid recovery of Susa between 646 and 522 BC suggests that the blow may have been less than the Assryian records would have us believe. Also, by this time the Elamites were in close and productive contact with the rising Persian Empire. When Assyria fell in 612 BC, the Elamites had thrown their lot in with the Persians.

The early Achaemenids' use of indigenous Elamite traditions in the formation of the new imperial culture was a means of gaining control over the Elamites "cultural capital." The placement of the new Achaemenid capital cities and the decentralized political organization of southwestern Iran may

---

[15] Persian links to the Medes are shrouded in legend but were of importance in establishing the northwestern half of the empire and consolidating Central Asia. A very similar process of acculturation perhaps took place there as well (Briant 2002: 31–106).

well have been based on Elamite practice (de Miroschedji 2003). The use of
Elamite as the first official language of the empire and administration, and
the persistence of Elamite religious personnel and cults supported by the
crown, also became essential parts of the newly emerging Achaemenid imperial identity in Fars (de Miroschedji 1986a; 1990).

In the Cyrus cylinder, celebrating his capture of Babylon in 539 BC, the
king portrays himself as the successor of Assurbanipal and reiterates his support for the god Marduk. But Cyrus also refers to himself as king of Anshan
and includes a list of his ancestors at this point in the inscription, stating his
family ties to an Elamite past (Brosius 2000: 10–11). Under Darius, the use of
Elamite as an official language in inscriptions and administration persisted,
but these were minor elements in the newer and more international Achaemenid imperial practices.

The reconstruction of Susa, the old Elamite capital, is an indication of
the thoroughness of Achaemenid control and illustrates its importance as a
regional center. Susians are shown on the Persepolis reliefs, and some Elamites are listed among the once rebellious peoples in the Bisitun inscriptions.
But the Elamites are now shown as supporters of the new regime, part of the
Achaemenid imperial core, not the defiant Elamites that resisted the Assyrian
armies for nearly a century.

THE LATTIMORE MODEL AND HATTI'S KASKA FRONTIER

PAUL ZIMANSKY

ABSTRACT

As barbarians on the northern border of the Hittite Empire, the Kaska played a role reprised by the Germans on the edge of the Roman world and by various groups along the inner Asian frontiers of China. Politically amorphous, ethnically ambiguous, and economically inconsequential, they were a perennial threat to the dominant imperial power of their time, frequently defeated in battle but never controlled. Although archaeological and textual evidence on many key points is meager and inconclusive, much of what we know of the Kaska and their relationship with the Hittites suggests that the ideas on frontiers developed by Owen Lattimore are applicable here. Ecological factors may have determined the location and nature of the contact between imperial authorities and the Kaska, and the frontier was certainly porous in both directions. The Kaska themselves may have been, to a certain extent, the creation of the Hittite Empire. Their interactions with the Hittites shed light on the mechanisms by which one of the first territorially extensive polyglot empires in history was created and maintained.

More than thirty years ago I enrolled in a course entitled "Ecological Approaches to Culture History" taught by the then Dean of Social Sciences at the University of Chicago, Robert McCormick Adams. It was a heady experience for a beginning graduate student, with the professor's innovative inquiry penetrating every cranny of the dense and stimulating list of readings on the syllabus. In the end, I was perhaps a little too awed: the primary basis for the grade was a major research paper, and one was under some pressure to produce something worthy of acute decanal scrutiny. The thesis of the present contribution occurred to me about midway through the course, and I actually wrote a few pages before succumbing to despair that I needed to know a great deal more about the archaeology of a region in which no archaeology had been done. The upshot, not surprisingly, was an "incomplete" that dogged me for longer than I care to admit in print. Eventually I cleared my record by cobbling something together on Urartu, which turned into a doctoral thesis and my first book. But the original question has lingered in the back of my mind ever since, and it seems an appropriate essay for the festschrift of the teacher who set me to thinking about this and so many other things—better thirty years late than never.

At the time of the course, Adams himself was considering the nature of frontiers as interfaces of adaptive strategies, in particular the case of internal frontiers of ancient Mesopotamia (Adams 1974b). His work was informed by models that Owen Lattimore (1940; 1962) had developed for Central Asia and China, which saw frontiers as social configurations, zones of marginal populations with conflicting allegiances, not as lines on a map or fixed geographical entities (Lattimore 1962: 469–471). An empire can conquer a larger territory than it can administer, and at some point it comes up against the law of diminishing returns as it attempts to append marginal lands to an economic, military, and bureaucratic system that was developed for, and best suited to, the conditions of its core territory (Lattimore 1962: 503). There was, of course, a strong environmental component in determining where a frontier might be established, but one also must recognize human choices and varying adaptive strategies:

> Over vast areas in Asia, from the earliest times, the following choice has been well understood: "If we stay here and dig (or plough) and plant, the harvests will be uncertain and we shall always be poor farmers. If, instead of submitting to that fate, we use the same land for grazing animals, we can become rich herdsmen. Better a rich herdsman than a poor farmer. Let us, therefore, improve our herding techniques, and if that requires changes in the organization of our society, let us make the changes accordingly." What this means is that the concept of geographical determinism must be modified by an understanding of the human ability to choose alternative methods of production, taking control of the environment instead of submitting to it. (Lattimore 1979: 35)

Lines were indeed created between barbarian (that is, external) and civilized (internal) populations in such material form as Hadrian's Wall or the Great Wall of China, but these were never impervious boundaries.

> [B]oth the Great Wall of Chinese and the fortified frontiers of the Roman empire, though they may always have been described as necessary to "keep out the barbarians", were in fact constructed by the Chinese and Romans to limit their own expansion. . . . In all such cases, the establishment of the frontier marks the zone beyond which the further extension of the empire

would cost more in military and administrative expenditures than could be paid for by increased revenues. (Lattimore 1979: 37–38)

The periodic appearance of "barbarians" as external threats to sedentary populations within the imperial jurisdiction, in this understanding, is not seen as an independent variable, but rather a contingency in which internal conditions of the empire played an important role:

> Civilization itself created its own barbarian plague; the barbarian terror that harried the northern frontiers of civilization did not erupt from a distant, dark and bloody ground that had nothing to do with civilization; it was an activity of peoples who were the kind of people they were because their whole evolution had been in contact with, and had been molded by, the advance of civilization. (Lattimore 1962: 504–505)

Since our historical sources tend to reflect the viewpoint of those who inhabit the cities and centers of power within the empire itself, the symbiotic and interactive factors shaping frontier life are apt to be obscured, particularly when operating in a vacuum of archaeological evidence. In considering the Lattimore thesis, Adams noted:

> The periodic crises of Chinese dynastic history, viewed by rulers and chroniclers alike as massive incursions of external barbarians, thus turn out in Lattimore's view to stem in large part from the decomposition of Chinese society itself. Subsistence patterns, market orientations, political loyalties, and effectiveness of administration were all linked together in a complex web. The main sources of collapse were periodic shifts or strains in this web of internal patterns, although naturally the urban elite and its apologists sought to externalize the source of their disaster in the great fortifications they erected and in the historical records that they only maintained. (Adams 1974b: 11)

More than a decade and a half after his death, Lattimore remains a towering and revered figure. A paperback biography of Genghis Khan currently in bookstores praises him as "a man unrivaled in his experience and expertise" and "the best possible inspiration" for the author (Man 2004: 274). Although Lattimore's ideas on frontiers have not gone unchallenged by cultural anthropologists working in Central Asia, they continue to have a broad impact, which is not limited to Asia alone. For example, one historian of Roman frontiers credits Lattimore's work as a factor currently reshaping his own field:

> Lattimore's influence has been widely recognized by European historians, although it is true that the model is only strictly relevant to pre-industrial societies. For the reinterpretation of Roman history, however,

it has provided a dramatic, new instrument. He has also inspired more recent studies of Chinese spacial identity and the historical interface between frontier ideology and practice, which read uncannily like descriptions of the frontiers of the Roman Empire. (Whittaker 2004: 191)

The idea that Lattimore's ideas might productively be applied to an academically more obscure boundary, much closer to the dawn of imperialism in the historical record, seems worthy of consideration. To the Hittites, the Kaska[1] play a role of northern frontier barbarians so conventionally scripted that one might accuse the writers of our primary historical sources of lacking originality, were they not among the first to confront this problem in a large, enduring, polyglot empire.[2] For three centuries, the disunified and unruly Kaska, living not far from the imperial capital at Hattusa, constituted a perennial threat. They rose up and raided Hittite territory on numerous occasions when the central authority was weak, and sometimes even when it was otherwise apparently strong. During the reign of Muwatalli, who is celebrated for his confrontation with the Egyptian army at the Battle of Qadesh in southern Syria, Hattusa itself was burned by the Kaska, and the imperial capital moved to the south. The Kaska are also suspected of being key players in the destruction of Hattusa at the end of the Hittite Empire, although there is no specific textual evidence for this. The imperial government tried various strategies for dealing with them, none of which appears to have solved the problem of the "barbarian menace" for long. Parallels with Germans and the Roman Empire have been noted in the general literature on the Hittite Empire, as in this example:

> [The Kaska] took every opportunity to sweep across the frontiers of Hatti, and occupy territory within the Hatti land, on one occasion capturing and sacking the capital itself. When they did venture to commit themselves to

---

[1] The term is also rendered Kaška or Gašga in the literature on the subject. The Hittites themselves were inconsistent on whether the stops were voiced or voiceless, and it is generally accepted that the Hittite sibilant conventionally transcribed as a š was actually pronounced as s. I have chosen the alternative without diacritics in part for simplicity and in part because it seems to have become the convention in English-language scholarship. On the negative side, an Internet search for "Kaska" takes one directly to the Yukon and studies of the modern people of that name who reside there; only when coupled with "Hittites" does one reach the hemisphere with which this article is concerned. My apologies to those who have been thus misled, but I trust that the detour was for them, as it was for me, not without interest.

[2] One can invoke the Guti in the Akkadian Empire, and the MAR.TU for the Ur III kingdom as antecedents, but the Hittite Empire was an empire of greater geographical extent and a higher degree of internal complexity than these polities, and Kaska were no wave of invaders, but a perennial, well-neigh static problem for almost all of Hittite imperial history.

pitched battle, they were generally no match for a Hittite army. But a total conquest of the Kaska people forever eluded their Hittite adversaries. Like the Germanic tribes who constantly harassed, invaded, and occupied the frontier regions of the Roman empire, the Kaskans had no overall political organization and lived and fought as independent tribes. They could not be conquered *en masse*. (Bryce 2002: 114)

Could there be an ecological explanation of, or at least an ecological dimension to, Hatti's long and troubled relationship with the Kaska? Is there a way in which the Hittites themselves can be said to have created this "barbarian plague"? Were Kaska incursions the result of strains and imbalances in the web of relationships in the empire itself? These questions seem worth asking, although formidable barriers stand in the way of answering them in the current state of research. On the positive side, there is a good deal more material to work with now than there was thirty years ago. While the Kaska remain archaeologically invisible, the problem has recently been addressed both from the perspective of ethnoarchaeology (Yakar 1980; 2000) and on the ground (Glatz and Matthews 2005;[3] R. Matthews, Pollard, and Ramage 1998; R. Matthews 2000). There are also new Hittite texts to work with as provincial archives have been unearthed for the first time, at Maşat (Alp 1991) and Ortaköy (Ünal 1998).[4] Both of these sites were near the Kaska frontier, and the archives of the former (in the absence of a publication of the latter) show that both were intimately involved with the Kaska at many levels. Despite continuing controversies over many of the details of Hittite geography, this new work makes it possible to be a little more confident of the location of the northern outposts of Hittite power, and thus of the environmental and geographical conditions of the zone in which its effectiveness waned. Let us therefore review what is known of the Kaska historically and geographically to at least frame the question of an ecological approach for further research.

---

[3] I am most grateful to Roger Matthews for making this article available to me in proofs prior to its publication. When it reached me two days before the submission deadline for my own manuscript, I was delighted to have the new information it contained as well as its review of textual evidence on the relationship of the Kaska to the Hittites, which reached conclusions very similar to the ones for which I was striving, albeit without reference to Lattimore. This reinforcement came at the price of making much of my own article redundant. Therefore, I have cut it back in favor of frequent references to Glatz and Matthews, and perhaps moved own my suggestions toward more tentative and insecure ground than they would have occupied had more description been included

[4] A full, authorized publication of the Ortaköy tablets has yet to be made, but this unauthorized preliminary study gives a flavor of the archive, which is considerably larger than the one from Maşat.

THE ORIGINS OF THE KASKA

There is an undeniable degree to which the Kaska must be conceived as some sort of ethnic category, although the rigor with which any modern definition of ethnicity may be applied to them is highly questionable. We do not know, for example, whether they themselves had any concept of collective self-identity. It is through the eyes of scribes connected to the Hittite imperial government that we learn most of what we know of them. They are designated LÚ^{MEŠ} ^{URU}*Kaška* (that is, men of the "city" Kaska) and their territory KUR ^{URU}*Kaška* (land of the "city" Kaska) or KUR.KUR^{MEŠ} ^{URU}*Kaška* (lands of the "city" Kaska) (von Schuler 1976–80: 461), but this is merely a convention for indicating peoples—there is no city of Kaska. The Kaska make occasional appearances in Egyptian records, where they are treated as a people with distinctive cultural associations (Moran 1992: 1, 101). A century after the fall of the Hittite Empire, they turn up in Assyrian records well south of their original homeland in the context of invading tribes.

None of this rules out the possibility, however, that who the Kaska were might well have been largely the result of interaction with the Hittite Empire. A parallel with Germans can be invoked here as well. Hachmann has commented (1971: 36) that "the Germanic peoples were almost a political invention of Casear's: almost but not quite" because he defined them by the creation of a boundary on the Rhine.

> For Caesar the Rhine was the boundary between the geographical areas of Germania and Gallia, and the Germani were the inhabitants of Germania. In this respect linguistic conditions were of no significance. No Roman— not even Caesar himself—would ever have enquired whether the Germanic peoples all spoke the same language or what that language was. To them the Germani were, quite simply, the people who lived on the right bank of the Rhine. (Hachmann 1971: 46)

There are two separate issues here: when do a people called Kaska appear, and when do they start behaving like Kaska? With regard to the former, they are not mentioned in any of the texts of the Assyrian Trading Colony period (nineteenth and eighteenth centuries BC),[5] nor do they appear

---

[5]　Mellaart (1974: 499–500) says: "It is tempting to ascribe the destruction of the Central Anatolian cities at the end of the 'Colony period', and the disruption of the Cappadocian trade to the first invasions of these turbulent elements onto the C. Anatolian plateau." This is in turn based on the assumption that Hattusili I transferred of the Hittite capital north from Kuššara to Hattuša (Boğazköy) to bring it closer to a frontier already threatened by the Kaska. Burney (2004: 150) opines that the Kaska tribes may have come from across the Black Sea and triggered the ethnic movements associated with the end of the trading colony period. All of this is speculation.

in documents composed in the Hittite Old Kingdom (late seventeenth and sixteenth centuries BC). According to records of Hattusili III, written in the thirteenth century, the loss of significant amounts of Hittite territory to the Kaska took place the reign of Hantili (sixteenth century BC). Von Schuler, noting that many Old Kingdom documents show continuing Hittite control of areas that were in Kaska hands during the Empire, urges skepticism on this point (von Schuler 1976–80: 461–462). The vividness of the first contemporary references to the Kaska in the prayers of Arnuwanda and Asmunikal suggests that they relate quite recent events:

> In the country of Nerik, in Hursama, in the country of Kastama, in the country of Serisa, in the country of Himuwa, in the country of Taggasta, in the country of Kammama, in the country of Zalpuwa, in the country of Kapiruha, in the country of Hurna, in the country of Dankusna, in the country of Tapa[panu]wa, in the country of Tarugga, in the country of Ilaluha, in the country of Zihana, in the country of Sipidduwa, in the country of Washaya, in the country of Parituya the temples which ye, the gods, possessed in these countries, the Kashkeans sacked them. They smashed the images of you, the gods. They plundered silver (and) gold, rhyta (and) cups of silver (and) gold, (and) of copper, your implements of bronze (and) your garments; they shared out these things among themselves. They scattered the priests and the holy priests, the mothers-of-god, the anointed, the musicians, the singers, the cooks, the bakers, the plowmen (and) the gardeners and made them their slaves. They also scattered your cattle (and) your sheep. They shared among themselves your fields (and) lands, (the source) of the sacrificial loaves (and) the vineyards, (the source) of the libations. Those the Kashkeans took for themselves. . . . Here, to the Hatti land, no one brings tribute (and) treasures for you anymore. (Goetze 1969: 399)

While modern authorities conventionally accept the notion of a Kaskan "invasion" of the Pontic region during or immediately after the Old Kingdom, it is not entirely clear that these "invaders" actually came from outside this area.[6] Von Schuler cautions that linguistic evidence tells us nothing about Kaskan origins. The place names in the regions in which the Kaska were known historically predate the "kaškäische Landnahme," and personal names follow the patterns for Hittite lands, with a slightly greater preponderance of

---

[6] The definitive study of the Kaska history in which all of the primary sources available at the time of its publication were presented is von Schuler 1965: 19–70. Issues about the dating of many of the key texts arose shortly after this work was published (Klinger 1995: 83–84, n. 33). For an up-to-date English-language overview in which Kaska campaigns are treated within a reign-by-reign political history of the Hittites, see Bryce 1998.

names of (proto)Hattian ancestry than in central Anatolia. He concludes: "Die Frage, ob die K. anatolische Autochthonen, veilleicht soger Hattier, oder aber Einwanderer aus Ost oder West gewesen sind, muß einstweilen unbeant- wortet bleiben" (von Schuler 1976–80: 463). The possibility that their mate- rial culture was to some extent autochthonous is also raised by an argument based on pottery found in Boğazköy in the aftermath of the imperial collapse that seems to pick up traditions of the Early and Middle Bronze Age. Since Kaska are presumed to have participated in the site's destruction and may have briefly inhabited it, this pottery could conceivably have been associated with them. If this hand-made tradition is indeed to be considered Kaskan, then its putative absence in the Late Bronze Age requires an explanation—perhaps a consistent misdating of survey materials in the absence of stratified excava- tions in the Kaska area (Glatz and Matthews 2005: 30–31).

There is much less uncertainty about when Kaska begin behaving like Kaska, and the date corresponds rather well with the point at which Hittites start governing like Hittites. In the Hittite Old Kingdom, before the Kaska make their appearance in written records, the sources suggest that rulers of the Hittite state sought to make the Black Sea itself the northern frontier, but this is perhaps better conceived as the limit of a sphere of raiding rather than administered territory.

> But was this [Old Kingdom expansion] really "empire-building"? In their zest for military adventure these early kings completely outran their resources. An empire pre-supposes some degree of organisation. We are told only that the seven cities of the plateau were assigned to the king's sons to govern "when he returned from a campaign". . . . [T]his part-time administration of the Anatolian plateau is hardly what is usually meant by the Hittite Empire. We should think of it more as a first step in the unifi- cation of the Hittite homeland. (Gurney 1979: 154–155)

It is after this phase of freewheeling conquests and dramatic collapse that the land deeds and other administrative mechanisms characteristic of impe- rial administration come to the fore. Not long after the formal means of gov- ernment appear, the prayers of Arnuwanda and Asmunikal represent the loss of northern cult centers like Nerik to the Kaska as a *fait accompli*. In the Hit- tite New Kingdom/Empire (fourteenth and thirteenth centuries BC), the Kaska are repeatedly attested in their role as northern barbarians. Gurney characterizes the relationship over the following centuries as follows:

> Hittite garrisons were posted in the main centres, but they do not seem to have been strong enough to hold down the Kaska-folk who now inhabited these Pontic valleys. There is no hint whatever that the tribesmen were receiving help from beyond the borders of the Hittite world; yet the king

was obliged every few years to lead his imperial army into the northern hills to pacify the country. Mursilis records such campaigns (again in great detail) for years 1, 2, 5, 6, 7, 9, 13, 24, 25, 26 of his reign. Each campaign seems to have been successful, yet no finality was achieved; the tribes were always ready to break out afresh at the slightest sign of weakness. Thus it is difficult to avoid the suspicion that the causes of unrest lay deeper than the Hittites themselves knew. (Gurney 1990: 26)

Table 5 presents an overview of the chronology of relations with the Kaska as presented in the surviving records from Boğazköy. The specifics of individual campaigns in this prolonged military interaction need not concern us here. Among the more dramatic moments were the recovery of some of the territory by Mursili II, the Kaska's sack of the vacated Hittite capital Hattusa in the time of Muwatalli, and Hattusili's subsequent recovery and resettlement of Nerik (Haas 1998–2001: 230). Although the Kaska make no appearance in the records for the final years of the Empire, it is often assumed that they were responsible for the violent destruction of Boğazköy that marked the end of both the empire and cuneiform literacy on the Anatolian Plateau (Bryce 1998: 379).

In short, from the perspective of chronology, it is not improbable that the "Kaska" were "almost but not quite" created as barbarians on the frontier by administrative decisions of Hittite rulers.

THE GEOGRAPHY OF THE KASKA FRONTIER

While there is much controversy about the specific location of many cities and the connotations of geographical referents in Late Bronze Age Anatolian geography, the general arena of the Hittite/Kaska interface is agreed to lie on the southern fringes of the Pontic range. Yakar, for example, presumes the eastern Kaska tribes were to be found in the Çarşamba plain as well as the lower Yeşilırmak and Kelkit Valleys; central Kaska areas lay in the Bafra plain (including the lower Kılızırmak Valley), the districts of Durağan, Kargi, and the hilly territory south of the Bafra plain; and the western tribes in Sinop and Kastamonu provinces, including the valleys south of the Isfendiya Mountains, and perhaps also the valleys south of the Ilgaz Mountains (Figure 44).

Identifying where the Kaska were archaeologically seems best accomplished indirectly, by finding the northern limits of the Hittites. Here the work of Roger Matthews and his colleagues is particularly important (Glatz and Matthews 2005; Matthews, Pollard, and Ramage 1998; R. Matthews 2000). In the Paphlagonia (Kastamonu) survey, they have been able to give material confirmation of a line of Hittite fortresses that in fact constituted the *limes*. Beyond that, there is almost nothing to observe, and the general impression from archaeology is that the regions beyond the area of Hittite frontier are virtually deserted. While this picture is not as complete as it

TABLE 5. Chronology of Hittite-Kaska Interaction

Kings	Approximate Dates	Relations with Kaska and Other Historical Events
Hantili II Zidanta II Huzziya II Muwatalli I	15th century BC	Loss of north to the Kaska, according to Hattusili
Tudhaliya I/II Arnuwanda I Hattusili II?	1400–1360	First contemporary references to Kaska Kaska attack while king is in Assuwa First treaties with Kaska
Tudhaliya III	1360–1344	Maşat texts Loss of more territory to Kaska Kaska threat to capital
Suppiluliuma I	1344–1322	Numerous campaigns against Kaska
Arnuwanda II	1322–1321	
Mursili II	1321–1295	Numerous campaigns against Kaska Defeat of Pihhuniya, Kaskan who atypically ruled as "king" Resettlement of Tiliura with prisoners King visits Nerik but does not keep it
Muwatalli II	1295–1272	Kaska burn Hattusa after Hittites move capital Hattusili III as border commander Kaska contingent in Hittite forces at Qadesh
Urhi-Teshub	1272–1267	Nerik restored to Hittite control
Hattusili III	1267–1237	Treaty with Tiliura and second resettlement with natives Tudhaliya IV campaigns against Kaska before accession
Tudhaliya IV	1227–1209	
Kurunta	1228–1227	
Tudhaliya IV	1227–1209	
Arnuwanda III	1209–1207	
Suppiluliuma II	1207– End of empire	Destruction of capital. Kaska involvement?

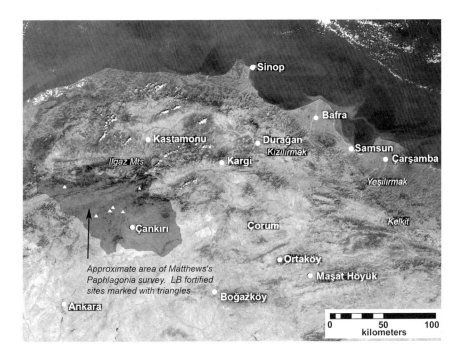

Figure 44. Map of Khuzistan and adjacent areas showing sites mentioned in the text.

might be were we better informed on the material associations of Kaska culture,[7] it seems clear that there were no major population concentrations in the area in the Late Bronze Age.

Farther to the east, the documents found at Maşat—which are the first major group of texts discovered and published from a place other than the capital—show that the site was in close proximity to the frontier. They also show that there were quite a few people living beyond it, and they were in constant interaction with the site's inhabitants.

---

[7] Noting suggestions that Kaska pottery is unknown, or might be indistinguishable from Hittite pottery, Glatz and Matthews comment: "In fact, the position is even bleaker: we do not even know whether the Kaska were using pottery at all" (Glatz and Matthews 2005: 30). In the caption to a photograph of a modern permanent village in the Black Sea regions, Yakar claims: "If the houses are abandoned they will decay and the remains will disappear in the thick vegetation cover. The Kaska also probably built their villages and most of their household utensils from wood and thus became largely invisible in the archaeological record" (Yakar 2000: 288, fig. 106). Even were there a more substantial archaeological record to work with, it is improbable that the frontier would provide any material means of separating Kaska from Hittite populations (Lightfoot and Martinez 1995: 481).

Geographically, of course, this is a quite different set of conditions from what defines Lattimore's inner Asian frontier zone, or the frontiers of the Roman Empire. In place of increasing aridity, there is actually an increase of precipitation as one moves northward from the Anatolian Plateau. The Pontic region is certainly not one that encourages long-distance nomadism, so the choice between being a rich herdsman or a poor farmer is not one between pure sedentism and continuous mobility, but rather the degree to which one is committed to a lifestyle of annual transhumance and living in smaller communities that exploit the modest pockets of arable land only part of the year.

> The economic strategies of Bronze or Iron Age communities in the Black Sea region could not have been very different from those still practiced by traditional rural communities today. In this region intensive animal husbandry and cultivation of various food plants for self-consumption exploit two or more vertically different habitats. Winter habitats at low elevations allow the sowing of cereal fields in autumn while summer habitats at higher altitudes afford freegrazing for cattle, sheep and goats for more than half the year. In high altitude plateaux barley rather than wheat is planted in cleared patches of forests at elevations not exceeding 2000 m. (Yakar 2000: 286–287)

There are conflicting indications on the extent to which the Kaska were indeed heavily invested in transhumant pastoralism, and this may well reflect differences in subsistence strategies among the Kaska themselves. The booty taken from them by the Hittites in their campaigns is overwhelmingly in the form of sheep and goats. There are references to the Hittites destroying harvests and seizing Kaska grain as well. It is also noted that when attacked by the Hittites, they did not defend their "cities," and if these were destroyed would either return to rebuild them or build new ones elsewhere. Von Schuler notes: "Dieser Art von Beweglichkeit is nicht die Eignetümlichkeit städische gebundener Kulturen" (von Schuler 1965: 75). The annals of Mursili, however, contain an oft-quoted parenthetical remark that the Kaska were swineherds and weavers of linen (Goetze 1969: 396). As pigs are not particularly mobile, this would indicate a measure of sedentism. Von Schuler (1965: 77) downplays the association of Kaska with pigs, noting that pigs never appear among the things taken from them by the Hittites. Glatz and Matthews (2005: 31–32), however, find both the pigs and the linen have long histories in the Pontic region and see more merit in the characterization, recognizing that the area was celebrated in the Byzantine Empire both for its swineherds and for its bacon. In any case, there is general consensus that the transhumant model works well for at least some of the Kaska, particularly those who caused the Hittites the most trouble.

Would a shift to this kind of environment create some sort of dynamic barrier into which the administrative capacities of the Hittite Empire diminish the farther they were projected? One can certainly imagine that the forests and broken terrain would have impeded an army that measured its power by the numbers of chariots. One can also appreciate that the rewards of raiding small, seasonal villages would have been small and that any agents of the state left behind to maintain order and collect taxes might feel their talents were not being put to the best use. The larger enigma of how the Hittites could be so effective in creating an empire of diverse peoples and environments, embracing so much of Anatolia and Syria, yet fail so conspicuously so close to home on their northern frontier continues to present many challenges, which we can only take on with a better understanding of the economic integration of the core territory than we currently possess.

HITTITE-KASKA INTERACTION ON A POROUS BOUNDARY

The Hittites, who recognized the legitimacy of governments other than their own to an extent uncharacteristic of other Near Eastern empires, such as Egypt and Assyria, were preoccupied with the idea of defined boundaries between states. Borders were an essential part of the way they governed, as transfers of land from disloyal subordinates to loyal ones was a fundamental policy of their leadership (Wazana 2001: 696–697). Instructions for border guards found in the archives at Boğazköy make it clear that the frontier was conceived as a zone of danger in which watchmen and spies were constantly on the alert for movements of the enemy. Hittite forces operated from fortified locations, into which they moved dependent populations at night (Beal 1992: 275–276). The Maşat letters show the actual application of these principles and make it clear that the central government in Hattusa was directly concerned with the Kaska frontier and regarded it as a dangerous place (Hoffner 2002: 66).

Treaties, which first appear in the final years of the Old Kingdom—that is, about the same time as the putative Kaska invasion—were another important tool in imperial policy and have been called the "ideological glue which held the Hittite empire together" (Beckman 1999: 3). It is clear enough that both the environment and the political makeup of the Kaska lands would frustrate their application in this area. The notoriously fragmented political configurations of mountainous areas generally would defeat a political system that was based on treaties that required the personal attention of a king and a staff of historically-minded scribes to keep each unit in place. For the most part, there was no government on the Kaska side with which to sign a treaty (Gurney 1990: 26). That did not stop the Hittites from trying, and fragments of several treaties with the Kaska are known (von Schuler 1965: 109–151; Neu 1983).

These legal mechanisms, ultimately, drew their effectiveness from the power of the Hittite army. The normal campaigning practice of employing a large force under the leadership of the king would be relatively ineffective in an environment where power was shared among many small, mobile units, and a short campaigning season did not help matters (Glatz and Matthews 2005: 29).

The primary point to be made with regard to the Lattimore hypothesis, however, is that despite the fortifications and the surveillance of the border zone, the frontier was in fact quite porous. Most informative on this matter are the treaties, in particular the one drawn up by Hattusili III with the resettled town of Tiliura. Bryce summarizes the Hittite policy as follows: The Hittites tried to keep Kaska out of the border towns but allowed them to move around the countryside. They recognized some Kaska, bound by treaty, as friendly and allowed them to graze their flocks beside those of the Hittites. These allied Kaska were enjoined to keep enemy Kaska away and compensate Hittites for any loss of cattle to them (Bryce 1986–87: 93). It is also clear that trade with the Kaska was allowed, with certain limitations, although the people involved were not dignified with the title of "merchant":

> [T]he king allowed certain Kaškaeans to buy and sell in designated cities along the northern border. Not all Kaškaean tribal groups entered into treaty alliance with the Hittite state. So only persons from allied groups (called *takšulaš* "those of a peace treaty") were granted this access to Hittite cities. The text reads: "In addition: If a person of an allied (Kaškaean tribe) comes into Hatti, he may conduct business (*happar ... ieddu*) in whatever city the Commander of the Border Provinces assigns to him. But he must not do business in any other city (just) because he wishes to." (Hoffner 2001: 183)

Another form economic activity is revealed in some detail by the Maşat documents: hostage taking and ransom. It is interesting that the ransom that Hittites demanded for their Kaska prisoners took the form of cattle and quantities of unnamed people:

> The tablet that Alp published as HKM 102 is a list of persons captured in battle who are made available to be ransomed by their peoples. Several in the list are said to be "blind" and of others it is said that "they see." The persons are listed by name. After most of the names in the list a ransom price is set. For example: the ransom of Mr. Tāmiti of Taggašta, who has not been blinded, is "two boy hostages and one man" (line 3). The ransom of Mr. Šuganaili of Kaštaharuka, who has been blinded, is "one man, one

woman, one child, eight oxen, and three goats" (lines 4–5). The ransom of Mr. Pihina of Kutuptašša, who has been blinded, is "two men, and three oxen" (lines 6–7). The ransom of Mr. Himuili of Kamamma, who has not been blinded, is "two hostage girls and one man." (Hoffner 2002: 67–68)

One would assume that the Kaska themselves were making similar demands for the bounty of their own raiding activities. There were also fugitives moving in both directions, and if for some reason a Hittite living in or around the capital fell afoul of his or her own government, the Kaska frontier would be the obvious one to head for.

Another indication of mobility is seen in the service of Kaskan contingents in Hittite armies. One group fought against Egypt on the Hittite side in the Battle of Qadesh. Another served with Hattusili III in a civil war (von Schuler 1965: 74). It is probable that Hattusili's military power came from the northern frontier area generally, since that is where he served during the time his brother, Muwatalli, was ruling the empire from a new and ultimately temporary capital in the Lower Land.

In summing up the situation, Glatz and Matthews point out that what we see in the treaties and other documents on the Hittite side is probably only part of the picture. Here, as with the textual record everywhere else in the ancient Near East, it is the atypical rather than the routine that gets written down.

There is evidence for mobility between the two sides, as well as for one party recruiting factions of the other side for its own ends. It is highly probable that other aspects of social fluidity between Hittites and Kaska, such as intermarriage and peaceful cohabitation, were commonplace and, for that reason, failed to find their way into the highly attenuated historical record (Glatz and Matthews 2005: 29).

CONCLUSIONS

If we apply some of the principles of Lattimore's analysis of the inner Asian frontiers to China, recognizing the ways in which they have stimulated recent reconsiderations of Roman frontiers (Whittaker 1994), do we have grounds for a more sophisticated understanding of the Kaska? We would be less inclined to worry about the ethnicity of the Kaska and the putative migrations that brought them into prominence. Instead, the key issues in their emergence would be explored in the spheres of cultural ecology and Hittite imperial capacities.

In the end, what does define someone as being Kaska? Not belonging to a specific polity, certainly, since the Kaska in the Late Bronze Age never belonged to one. Nor was it residence in a non-Hittite land, since whatever the realities of the extent of their authority, the Hittites continued to regard the Kaskean countries as belonging to the land of Hatti (Goetze 1969: 396). The personal names of Kaska betray no particular linguistic affiliation or even linguistic consistency (von Schuler 1965: 89–91). While von Schuler (1965: 91) warns against interpreting the meager onomastic evidence as an indication that the Kaska were merely inhabitants of a northern region distinguished by their independence, one not need go that far to see them as a group that accommodated diverse and dissident elements who, for one reason or another, had crossed over from Hittite control.

The Kaska frontier would be the zone in which the reach of the Hittites' military power exceeded its grasp, where, as one moved farther north into more mountainous terrain, the costs of inclusion of more territory and peoples into the empire would dramatically increase as the benefits diminished. The Kaska themselves, as ungovernable, unsophisticated, and perennially dangerous threats from outside the empire would largely be, in fact, a creation of the empire itself. Although the kings at Hattusa would construct a *limes* (Houwink ten Cate 1995: 264), its purpose would be less to wall the Kaska out as to define the sphere of Hittite authority and administration. Across the frontier there would be a continuous interchange of peoples. With their divided and shifting loyalties, the population of this zone was probably what provided the Kaska with the manpower to threaten the Hittite state in times of stress[8]—not people bred in some more remote Kaska homeland.

There is certainly some evidence for all of this in the meager records that survive both in the form of Hittite texts and archaeological discoveries. There is the promise of more detail in newly discovered cuneiform archives outside of the capital, and the potential for finding more texts as interest shifts from the capital to provincial sites. Virtually anything excavated in a Late Bronze Age context in the Pontic region of Turkey will provide new insight on the Kaska, as this area constitutes the largest lacuna in reconstructing a picture of the actual situation as opposed to one based entirely on the biases of people in the employ of the Hittite central government. The rewards of any study of the Kaska will count less as an ethnography of an obscure people on the fringes of the Near East than as a contribution to our understanding of the prime achievement of the Hittites themselves, an appreciation of the essential elements through which they created their empire.

---

[8] It is hard to image where else the Kaska would have found the 800 chariots they marshaled against Hattusili III (von Schuler 1965: 74).

ANCIENT AGENCY: USING MODELS OF INTENTIONALITY TO UNDERSTAND THE DAWN OF DESPOTISM*

HENRY T. WRIGHT

ABSTRACT

This contribution takes up Adams's challenge to archaeologists to study individual agents of change. Here, the potentials and pitfalls of such an endeavor are illustrated with three case studies from the late fourth and early third millennia in Southwest Asia. First is the case of a tomb from the gateway center of Arslantepe in south-central Anatolia, where it is possible to discuss leaders, their strategies and tactics of domination, and their successes or failures. Second is the case of special contexts in a sequence of residential units at the central town of Susa in southwestern Iran, where it may be possible to discuss individual roles and identities. Third is the case of artifacts iconically associable with one or a few individuals in a sequence of short-term trash deposits at the small rural settlement of Sharafabad near Susa, where we can discuss the efforts of low-level local authorities to deal with year-to-year agricultural problems. In spite of the many potential difficulties, this endeavor suggests that it is likely that, with the development of new and more careful methods, we will be able to directly evaluate agent-based theoretical constructs using archaeological evidence from Mesopotamia.

* Acknowledgments: I am indebted to Marcella Frangipane and Alain Le Brun for keeping me abreast of ongoing work on the evidence from Susa and Arslantepe. The paper has profited from comments from Jane Buikstra. Finally, I thank Elizabeth Stone for her ceaseless efforts to bring this to fruition. The errors are entirely my own.

Introduction

From his first overview volume (Adams 1966) and breakthrough papers of the 1970s (Adams 1974a; 1978) to his most recent presentations (Adams 2005), Robert Adams has reminded us of the importance of including agency and intentionality in our efforts to understand the rise of urban societies. He has also forcefully emphasized the difficulties of using such perspectives before the development of writing systems capable of recording individual identities and actions. In this contribution, I would like to argue that the future evaluation of the roles of agents is not as bleak as it has seemed. Consideration of three examples from protohistoric periods in the greater Mesopotamian world allows us to evaluate constructions about the past in which the actions of individuals are important, although determining that a number of demonstrated actions were undertaken by one actor is difficult. To use agent-based approaches will require not only new ways of thinking about archaeological evidence, but new ways of recovering, recording, and analyzing such evidence.

It is important to note that Adams's long-standing conceptions of agents in the past has a solid foundation in material and social relations. His ancient actors produced, exchanged, and consumed the material bases of life, built social relations with others, made many kinds of decisions, engaged in conflicts, performed rituals, and so on. Though very aware of their relevance, Adams does not focus on issues of perception and symbolism. If actors are so solidly grounded in material reality, surely we can define the archaeological traces of their acts.

Agency in Theories of Complex Societal Development

Approaches to the rise of complex societies have long focused on the actions of early paramount chiefs (Barker and Pauketat 1992; Pauketat and Emerson 1997; Sahlins 1981; Webster 1975; H. T. Wright 1994) and heads of state (Engels 1972 [1884]; Kus and Raharijaona 1998; 2000; Sagan 1985; H. T. Wright 1977). But, how, in the absence of written records, can such ideas be evaluated with the evidence from the earliest emergence of political complexity?

We can begin by arguing that even if we cannot monitor the individual in prehistory, we can use concepts of agency and intention in the building of theoretical constructs as long as these constructs have testable implications. Thus, a construct about competition between and among paramount chiefs and subchiefs has implications for the periodicity of competition and the periodic abandonment of centers which can be tested with the impersonal archaeological evidence of destruction and settlement pattern shifts (H. T. Wright 1994).

Such testing of general implications may, however, leave core linkages in such constructs unevaluated if we cannot find evidence of past actors and acts. We could be more confident regarding propositions about competition between chiefs if we knew whom the competition was between or among, and in whose favor the competition was resolved. In at least some past processes, such issues can be resolved if we view archaeological sites as accumulations of the material consequences of individual acts. Each cooking pot can be viewed as a record of individual decisions and movements to make the pot (Sinopoli 1991; van der Leeuw and Pritchard 1984), and individual meals prepared in the pot, and individual action in breaking the pot and throwing away its pieces (Skibo 1992). Each burial records a ritual performed by people associated with the dead person to memorialize that person and lay claim to his or her social accomplishments (O'Shea 1984). With hard work and careful thought, we can determine, for some archaeologically attested cultural systems, the contributions of actors.

The accumulations of settlement debris found in archaeological surveys and the associated sets of artifacts and ecofacts found in excavated loci are treated in the aggregate, at worst as records of culturally normative behaviors and at best as records of intercorrelated variation in past cultural processes. There are, however, many examples of archaeologists defining the actions of agents, even without the benefit of an associated textual record. A few examples from recent work in Mesopotamia will show the possibilities, the difficulties, and the potential of such efforts.

THE EVIDENCE OF A MORTUARY RITUAL: ARSLANTEPE, CA. 2950 BC

The site of Arslantepe, in the basin of Malatya in the Taurus Mountains of south-central Turkey, was a flourishing local ritual and administrative center during the fourth millennium BC, overseeing relations with both upper Mesopotamia to the south and Transcaucasian peoples who had moved into central Anatolia. The excavation at Arslantepe by the Università di Roma "La Sapienza," Istituto de Palentologia, initiated by Salvatore Puglisi and Alba Palmieri and continuing under Marcella Frangipane, is the most innovative current research on early complex societies in Southwest Asia. Careful stratigraphic and architectural excavation have demonstrated the occupation of the abandoned palace area by "transhumant pastoralists of Transcaucasian origin" (Frangipane et al. 2001: 106). In 1996, the Arslantepe team found a large tomb (Figure 45) cut into the layer marking the destruction of the center at the beginning of the third millennium BC. This tomb transforms our understanding of "power and authority. . . after the collapse of centralised Mesopotamian-type structure . . . north of the Taurus" (Frangipane et al. 2001: 107). The central figure in the tomb was a robust adult male accompanied by a horde of

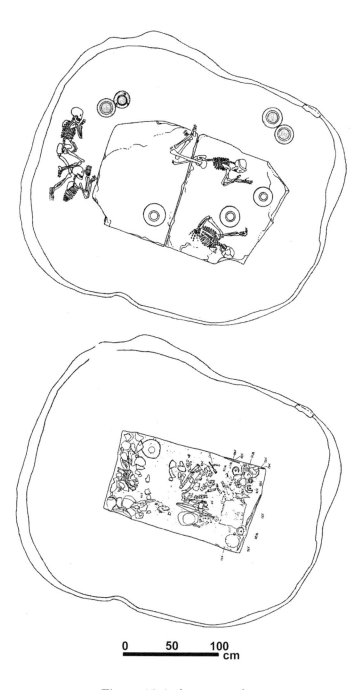

Figure 45. Arslantepe tomb.

weapons, tools, and ornaments of copper-arsenic and a copper-silver alloys, many of Transcaucasian stylistic affinity (Frangipane et al. 2001: figs. 18–21). These weapons and a group of almost identical weapons cached in the preceding palace during its heyday (Frangipane and Palmieri 1983) have negligible nickel traces and most closely match known copper sources near the Black Sea in northeast Anatolia (Hauptmann et al. 2002: 61–62). A copper-silver diadem or headband had designs known from Early Bronze Age sites in the Transcaucasian region (Frangipane et al. 2001: 115). Pitched onto the slabs that covered the tomb of this man were the bodies of four young people, three females and one male. The females had been severely beaten in the weeks before their deaths (Frangipane et al. 2001: 123–129). The young man and one of the young women had diadems similar to that found with the central burial. Accompanying the remains of these individuals were large jars of traditional Arslantepe manufacture and Transcaucasian-style jars and bowls (Frangipane et al. 2001: figs. 14–15).

At the time of this funerary ceremony, the site of the Mesopotamia-related citadel seems already to have been partially reoccupied by a campsite of herders with material remains of purely Transaucasian cultural affinity. One can therefore propose a narrative of the events: after a long period as a gateway community mediating relations between the towns of upper Mesopotamia and the Transcaucasian peoples who had established themselves in central Anatolia, conflict broke out, Arslantepe's citadel was destroyed, and the survivors were subjugated by new immigrants. When a Transcaucasian leader died, a number of the survivors from the earlier regime were killed, preventing the reestablishment of the former elite. However plausible his participation may seem, we have no way of demonstrating whether or not the interred warrior was involved in the destruction of the citadel. Likewise, we have no way to know whether the slain young people were involved in resistance to Transcaucasian rule. If efforts to analyze trace elements in the remains of the five individuals are successful, it will be possible to demonstrate whether they grew up near Arslantepe or elsewhere (Buikstra et al. 2003). It would also be helpful to know whether these dead individuals were genetically related or not. Although ancient DNA has so far proved to be poorly preserved in samples from Bronze Age Mesopotamia, it is possible that a more classical study of discrete dental and cranial traits would be helpful. Such evidence would sharpen our understanding of the strategies used to conquer Arslantepe and the place of such strategies in the broader movement of mountain people from Anatolia and Iran into the fringes of Mesopotamia at the turn of the fourth millennium BC. Whether the death of the warrior signaled the failure of the strategies used to take over the area or whether communities with a culture derived from the Caucasus succeeded in establishing an enduring control of the

Malatya basin may be determined by intensive archaeological survey and further excavation in the area.

The Evidence of Household Accumulations: Susa, ca 3200 BC

The site of Susa, on the Susiana plain in the foothills of the central Zagros Mountains of south-western Iran, was also a flourishing local political and economic center during the fourth millennium BC, closely related to the network of centers in lower Mesopotamia to the southwest. Almost a century of excavation by successive French archaeological missions culminated in a series meticulously executed campaigns directed by Jean Perrot from 1968 to 1978. Most important for understanding the later fourth millennium center are the superb excavations of Alain Le Brun and Odile Duane at Acropole I (Le Brun 1971; 1978; 1985; Le Brun and Vallat 1978). These exposed a sequence of modest buildings (Figure 46), the domestic uses of which were indicated by hearths, bins, and many ordinary ceramic vessels. This sequence shows much continuity in architecture and portable technology, not necessarily indicating the same families lived here over several generations, but indicating that a sequence of people with similar ideas about domestic living occupied the area. Important for an agental perspective are concentrations of objects left in small chambers or parts of larger chambers at the time each successive building was rebuilt. It is true that these represent a series of "snapshots" taken every few decades, and incomplete snapshots at that, since objects with a perceived future value may have been removed before the old walls were leveled to begin a new building. Nonetheless, they provide evidence that our ideas about the specialization of actors in Uruk societies may be somewhat ethnocentric. We often speak of farmers, craftspeople, scribes, or priests, but what—beyond the serving and drinking of liquids, indicated by the cups, small jars, and tall jars or bottles found in all concentrations—did the people in this succession of houses actually do?

In the earlier structures for which this kind of information is available, Layer 17B2, there are two of these concentrations with arrays of items, one in each unit. As seen in Table 6, Locus 797 is especially distinguished by the quantity of evidence for manufacturing, including both an unfinished mace head and the grinding and polishing stones that may have been used for their production. Indeed, with the exception of the numerical tablet, the objects associated with personal ornament and administration are also of stone, and thus their presence in this area could indicate their production rather than their use. The objects from Locus 757, by contrast, show little connection with production. Instead, items of personal adornment and administration are common.

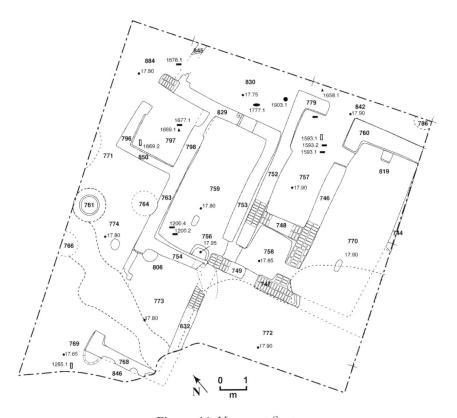

Figure 46. Houses at Susa.

In a later structure, Layer 17B1, there are three of these concentrations in the two units. One, Locus 751, has only the usual ceramic vessels. Otherwise, only an animal figurine is reported. Locus 750 has the usual ceramic vessels and several tablets with numbers and seal impressions, related to administrative activity. Other than the evidence for domestic and limited administrative activity, there is no indication of other actions or identities. In contrast, Locus 780 has, in addition to the usual ceramics, necklaces, beads, pendants, and mace heads related to costume, and a group of spindle whorls used in spinning.

Even with the full publication of the careful Acropole I excavation, there will be questions we cannot answer. There must have been many years during which these houses were cleaned frequently, and associated objects were not left in place. In addition, unfortunately for us, the occupants of these buildings were not regularly interred under the floors, which might have given us a way to tell which of a person's activities were deemed most important and most defining of identity, as well as to assess their biological life histories.

Finally, current political circumstances have prevented members of the Susa team from studying the recovered artifacts with modern analytical methods. Even were these data available, there would be questions we would find diffi-

TABLE 6. Artifacts in Concentrations: Suse Acropole I:17

Layer		17B2		17B1		
Locus		757	797	750	751	780
Containers	Coarse bowls			+ +	+	+ +
	Conical cups	+	+ +	+	+	+ +
	Bowls	+ +	+ +		+ +	+ +
	Small globular jar	+ +	+	+	+ +	+
	Small four-lug jar	+			+	
	Small spouted jar		+	+		+
	Medium–large jars	+			+	+
	Tall jars and bottles	+	+	+	+ +	+
	Bottle stoppers		+			
	Other vessels	+	+ +		+ +	+ +
	Stone bowl or basin		+			+
	Stone jar	+				+
Costume	Beads and spacer beads	+ +	+ +		+ +	
	Pendants		+			+
	Metal pin	+				+
	Bone pin	+				
	Macehead		+ +			+
Administration	Stamp seal	+				
	Cylinder seal	+	+			
	Counter	+				
	Numerical tablet	+ +	+	+ +		
Craft	Polisher or grinder	+	+ +	+		
	Long pebble	+	+			
	Unfinished macehead		+ +			
	Spindle whorl		+			+ +

Note: "Coarse bowls" include both mold-made beveled rim bowls and wheel-made "flower pots."

cult to answer. Unlike burials, we cannot be certain such bounded concentrations of artifacts are left by one or a group of actors in the domestic unit. If they are from one person's "closet," they suggest that the individuals had different mixes of identities. The only activity that all the people represented by these "snapshots" seem to have engaged in was, not surprisingly, eating and drinking. Some had formal costumes perhaps related to ceremonial roles, and two of these also appear to have been more involved in craft work, in one case spinning and in the other the making of stone mace heads. Some concentrations had items of accounting technology, in two cases with evidence of elaborate costumes and in one case without. This evidence suggests that, at the time later Uruk states flourished, activities may have been specialized, but individuals, or at least households, were engaged in different mixtures of activities and were not engaged exclusively in one profession.

THE EVIDENCE OF OFFICIALS AT WORK:
SHARAFABAD, CA. 3350 BC

Even before the formalization of writing, participants in the early stages of cultural complexity were identifying themselves with distinctive signs, which we often recover in diverse contexts. In early Mesopotamia, actors were identified by their seals.

At the site of Sharafabad on the plain of Susa, excavation revealed evidence of a small rural center from the third quarter of the fourth millennium BC. The buildings were poorly preserved, but much has been learned from a deep refuse-filled pit (H. T. Wright, Miller, and Redding 1980; H. T. Wright, Redding, and Pollock 1989). The pit had a well-preserved microstratigraphy that preserved the trash deposited over two and half years, including an earlier, relatively good year with copious harvests in which there appear to have been much harvest labor on the site and much export of goods, followed by a later, relatively poor year—perhaps a drought year—in which little was exported but many storerooms were opened (H. T. Wright, Redding, and Pollock 1989: 108–111). Since the basketloads of trash coming from as many as 100 people were dumped into this pit, many of our observations are relevant only to the aggregate behavior of this small community. One group of sealings (Figure 47), however, can be used to identify the activities of one or two people who were in a position of local authority during these two years. These are stamp seals with related iconography. One is an oval stamp seal with evident wear and chips on the edge. It has a design of a kneeling anthropomorphic figure with a bushy tailed fox leaping above its back (H. T. Wright, Miller, and Redding 1980: fig. 6.3). The other is a rectangular seal with a design showing a similar anthropomorphic figure with

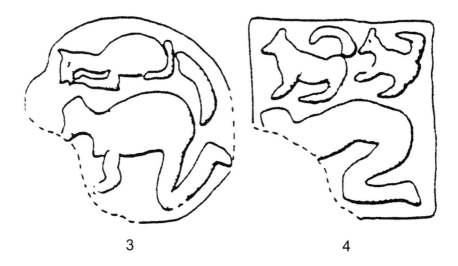

3   4

Figure 47. Sealings from Sharafabad.

two curly tailed dogs leaping above its back (H. T. Wright, Miller, and Redding 1980: fig. 6.4).

During the first, prosperous year, two sealings from the worn older seal
on containers, one a cloth-wrapped bale and the other indeterminate, were
discarded in the pit. During the second, poor year, two heavy "peg and string"
sealings, of a kind thought to be used to lock the doors of storage rooms at
Sharafabad, were discarded. One had an impression of this older oval seal, but
the other had the impression of the newer rectangular sealing. A basket sealing with the impression of this newer seal was also discarded during this second, poor year (H. T. Wright, Miller, and Redding 1980: fig. 7).

In my initial presentation of these data, I suggested that one individual
was involved and that this person had replaced the worn oval seal with the
fresh rectangular seal. If so, we can say that in the first, prosperous year, this
individual was authorizing the closure (and by implication the opening) of
small lots of goods, and the sealing of doors. In the second, poor year, there is
some opening of goods sealed with the new seal and of some storerooms
opened, some sealed earlier and some sealed more recently. However, colleagues have suggested that these might be the seals of two different people
with iconically similar seals, perhaps from the same family or social institution, one replacing the other. If so, the bearer of the old seal handled minimal
duties with small lots of goods in the first year, and his or her replacement
dealt with the crisis created by the poor year, opening more storerooms.
These people, or perhaps their intermediaries using their seals, were clearly
at the little settlement dealing directly with the consequences of the crisis.

The number of seal-users and even their relationships might be elucidated with study of fingerprints on the sealings (Elizabeth Stone, personal communication 2005).

If these inferences are correct, we have some knowledge of the actions of local authorities in different economic circumstances. If we had the evidence of the seal bearers' residences, not possible at badly disturbed and eroded Sharafabad but expectable at other sites, we could know more about their other concerns and about the extent to which they profited from their positions of authority. If we had their burials, which is unlikely given the rarity of Uruk burials, we would be able to answer more questions about such local authorities, who were modest but essential to the operation of early Mesopotamian economic and political formations.

FUTURE STUDIES

This contribution has asked whether there are systematic ways of learning about individual actors before written records are available.

- In the case of a tomb with multiple burials, well fixed in a sequence of settlement and artifactual changes, it is possible to discuss leaders, their strategies and tactics of domination, and their successes or failures.

- In the case of a sequence of possibly personal "closets" in a sequence of residential units, it is possible to infer clusters of activities from clusters of artifacts types, but the effort to talk about individual roles and identities is vitiated because we cannot tell whether these relate to one person or to several members of a residential unit, and we cannot be sure what was removed from these contexts before they were sealed.

- In the case of artifacts iconically associable with one or a few individuals—stamps seals and sealings in a sequence of short-term trash deposits—we can discuss the efforts of low-level local authorities to deal with year-to-year agricultural problems, although the lack of associated domestic architecture makes it hard to determine to what extent these individuals profited from their efforts.

All of these examples are drawn from preliminary reports, and subsequent analyses may improve our understanding.

One form of individual action that Adams argued was particularly important is that of fringe agents and entrepreneurs—for example, long-distance traders—who provide innovation and stimulus to change (Adams 1974a). I have been unable to provide an archaeological example in which such agents could be discussed. The Persian Gulf, where so much outstanding archaeology has been completed in the past four decades, has yet to produce burials or residences of pre- or protohistoric traders of the fourth or early third millennia. One might expect a shipwreck to provide the structured and temporally well-bounded contexts needed to discuss such traders as agents, but so far preliminary underwater surveys have yet to record early wrecks. We can hope the future will bring such discoveries.

Archaeologists reading these words know that most of us have been using a mélange of 1930s methods designed to study culture history and 1960s methods designed to study culture process. This mélange is ill suited to document the actions of past agents. We need contexts that are both more precisely defined temporally and better understood socially. Certainly, the kind of excavations needed will be slower if we are to accurately remove and record micro-contexts, and more expensive, primarily because of the use of more complex analytical techniques, than the conventional archaeology of today, but they will be necessary if we are to understand the emergence of complex cultural formations.

Even with more precise methods, the examples discussed above indicate that there are limits on what can be known about ancient agents. The inadequacy of artifactual preservation, particularly of burials, and the cleaning up and redeposition of most trash in mixed deposits insure that few cases of action by individuals will be documented, and they may not be the cases we need to evaluate theoretical constructs about social dynamics. Even when iconic evidence pointing to individuals is available, we may not be able to correctly interpret it. Nonetheless, the very existence of dynamic social constructs that must be tested demands that we try.

CITY AND COUNTRYSIDE IN THIRD-MILLENNIUM SOUTHERN BABYLONIA

PIOTR STEINKELLER

ABSTRACT

Thanks to the extraordinarily detailed information on the topography of the province of Umma in Ur III times (2100–2000 BC), deriving both from ancient written sources and modern surface surveys, this geographical region offers a unique opportunity to study settlement patterns and population density in southern Babylonia toward the end of the second millennium BC. This paper presents preliminary results of the ongoing investigation of the province of Umma, concentrating on the questions of rural settlements and the relationship between the countryside and urban centers. Apart from demonstrating that the rural settlements were much more common than suggested by the results of surface surveys, it is also argued that the relationship between the urban and the rural spheres, rather than representing a sharp and antagonistic dichotomy, formed a continuum, dominated by the presence of "rural" features, as regards both the physical and the socioeconomic landscape.

INTRODUCTION

This communication[1] presents preliminary results of my investigation into the settlement patterns and population density in southern Babylonia during the Ur III period (roughly the last century of the third millennium BC). The

---

[1] This is an expanded version of a paper read at the 211th meeting of the American Oriental Society, Toronto, March 30–April 2, 2001, as part of the special session honoring R. McC. Adams.

185

focus of this project, on which I have worked off and on for the last seventeen years, has been the province of Umma.[2]

The reason for selecting that particular region as the object of my investigation is the simple fact that Ur III Umma provides the best textual evidence available both on the settlement patterns in a single geographical region of ancient Babylonia and on the sizes of populations resident in its towns and rural areas. In terms of its quality, this evidence—a single archive numbering in excess of 15,000 individual tablets which cover a period of roughly forty years—is absolutely without parallel among the voluminous economic and historical documentation from ancient Mesopotamia (Steinkeller 2003). Umma sources are unique in that, unlike any other cuneiform corpora surviving from this or any other period, they document in astonishing detail the agricultural and other activities taking place in the countryside. As such, they offer an almost photographic view of Umma's hinterland and, as a consequence, provide an excellent index of all settlements in the province, as well as of its waterways, fields, orchards, forests, and other topographic features.

Yet another advantage in focusing on Umma is that the geographic extent of this particular region in Ur III times—as regards its borders, overall size, and main topographical points—is known with a high degree of accuracy. This fact too sets Umma apart from all the other provinces of the Ur III state, and applies even to the neighboring Girsu/Lagash area, which has bequeathed to us an equal (if not a larger) number of cuneiform tablets, making it, next to Umma, the best-documented Ur III province. However, a reconstruction of the borders and total land area of Girsu/Lagash is impossible, primarily because of the fact that there is no way of determining how far it extended to the north and east—not to mention that its written sources do not contain even remotely comparable information on the countryside.

One of the central issues addressed by this study is the nature of the relationship between the urban sphere and its hinterland. In this context, the question of rural settlements is of particular interest, since it is thought by most archaeologists that villages represented a strikingly rare feature in the settlement pattern of third-millennium southern Mesopotamia. This view, as is well known, is based primarily on the results of surface surveys that were conducted in southern Iraq by Robert McC. Adams and other scholars (Adams 1965; 1981; Adams and Nissen 1972; Gibson 1972; H. T. Wright 1981b). Indeed, rural settlements identified by these surveys are scarce, and so a generalization to this effect seems to be justified. The whole matter is much more compli-

---

[2] The results will appear as a book, provisionally entitled "Population Density, Settlement Patterns and Rural Landscape in southern Babylonia under the Ur III Dynasty: The Case of the Province of Umma."

cated, however, since the percentage of urban as opposed to rural settlement in the third millennium varied significantly from one period to another. According to Adams's (1981: 136–141) own analysis of the survey data, following a sustained growth of settlements during the second half of the fourth millennium, there took place, at the very beginning of the third millennium (Early Dynastic I), a rapid growth of urban centers. This happened, apparently, at the expense of rural sites, which almost completely disappeared. From that point on, the number and total occupied area of rural settlements steadily increased; Adams even uses the words "dramatic progression" to describe this trend (Adams 1981: 138, table 12). In more specific terms, while in the Early Dynastic II and III periods, rural settlements, according to Adams's calculations, represented only 10 percent of the total occupied area, this figure rose to 18.4 percent in the Akkadian period, reaching as much as 25 percent in Ur III and Isin/Larsa times. Thus, even on the strength of survey data, which unequivocally indicate a sustained rise in the number of rural settlements during the third millennium, it is difficult to talk of the "absence" of villages in the Ur III period (though such a characterization may be an apt description of the situation existing in ED times). Surprisingly, this view is equally widespread among philologists. A classic example here is Wilhelmus Leemans (1982: 246), who, writing twenty years ago, maintains that in the Pre-Sargonic and Sargonic periods, "the land between cities like Girsu and Umma was uninhabited," and that, based on the alleged rarity of references to villages in Ur III sources, "the settlement pattern remained the same in the Ur III period [as earlier]." Even as astute and well-informed an Assyriologist and historian as Mario Liverani (1999: 45) thinks, much more recently, that there existed exceedingly few rural settlements in southern Babylonia in all the phases of third-millennium history. He attributes this fact to the peculiarity of the farming regime in that geographic region, which had led to the creation of "a 'Sumerian' landscape landmarked by large cities that burn out (so to speak) the surrounding villages." The sole dissenting voice is G. van Driel (2001: 110), who, in an article published recently, suggests a radically different picture. Relying to a large extent on the data from Ur III Umma, van Driel suggests that the small settlements located by Adams's survey for the territory of Umma in Ur III times "constitute little more than one or two percent of the total that can be assumed to have existed (perhaps: 'at a given time') on the basis of the equally incompletely available written evidence."

Although van Driel's conclusion is based on the study of a highly limited set of data, his recognition of the great importance of this evidence for the question of rural settlements is right on target. On the most basic level, the textual data provide a test of evidence derived from surface surveys. More importantly, however, the existence of this huge body of data permits a truly synthetic and cross-disciplinary approach to key questions of settlement and population density in early Babylonia. My study aims to be the first extensive application of such an approach.

The absolutely fundamental importance of Adams's work for this project cannot be overstated. Without his survey data and analytical studies, none of the problems I am specifically concerned with could begin to be formulated or contemplated. Thus, I gratefully and happily acknowledge the dependence of my investigation both on his findings and on the general intellectual orientation of his scholarship. As a personal note, I wish to add that one of the most memorable and truly formative experiences of my university days was Adams's course on the natural environment of the Mesopotamian floodplain, which I was privileged to attend at the Oriental Institute in the early seventies. This paper is meant to repay my debt to him in at least some measure.

THE SETTLEMENTS AND THE RURAL LANDSCAPE
OF THE PROVINCE OF UMMA

It may be estimated that the territory of the province of Umma formed a square with sides approximately 45 kilometers in length (see Figures 48 and 49), with a resulting area of roughly 2,000 kilometers.[3] The western and eastern sides of this square are particularly well defined. To the west, the Umma territory adjoined the province of Adab, with the border between the two running near the town of Karkar (Tall Jidr = Warka Survey 004), which was still within Umma's borders (Steinkeller 2001: 72). The eastern border ran just to the west of Girsu, the capital of the Girsu/Lagash province and Umma's neighbor to the east. The terminal point there was Apishal, Umma's second largest urban center, which is probably identical with the site of Muhalliqiya (Steinkeller 2001: 54–55).

The course of the southern border, which Umma shared with the province of Uruk, can be traced with nearly the same exactitude (see Figure 49). Assuming, as appears very likely, that the site of Nasiriya is identical with an Umma dependency GARshana (and a close neighbor of the Girsu/Lagash province), the Umma-Uruk border must have extended to the south of Nasiriya but to the north of Bad Tibira (Uruk Survey 451), which belonged to Uruk (or, alternatively, to Larsa).

The extent of the province to the north is considerably less clear. As an educated guess, I assume that its northern border ran only a few kilometers north of Karkar (see Figure 48). However, since it is clear that an extensive

---

[3] Van Driel (1999/2000:81) speculates that the Umma province embraced a considerably smaller area: 1225 square kilometers—"a kind of lozenge or square with sides of 33–35 km." However, this estimate (or guess, more correctly) is based on a very limited (and often erroneous) understanding of Umma's hydrology and topography.

canal system along the east bank of the Tigris must have existed (whose extent, however, is exceedingly difficult to gauge with the textual data available), it cannot be excluded that the Umma province controlled additional territories beyond that line, especially in its northeastern corner (the region of Apishal = Muhalliqiya). If so, this would obviously increase the total area of the province but probably by an insubstantial amount.

A systematic study of the extant textual evidence permits the compilation of a catalog of 158 settlements that may be assigned to the province of Umma in Ur III times with a high degree of assurance. An absolutely positive determination to that effect is possible in some 110 cases. The status of the remaining places (roughly one-third of the total) remains uncertain, since it cannot be fully demonstrated either that the places in question were permanently inhabited settlements or that they in fact belonged to the Umma territory rather than to one of the neighboring provinces of Girsu/Lagash, Adab, Uruk, or Shuruppak.

As defined in my study, *settlement* is a locus of continued human habitation characterized by the presence of more than one permanent dwelling. It is further understood that *continued* is longer than one year, and that *permanent dwelling* means other than living arrangements of a clearly temporary nature, such as tents and shepherds' encampments.

A few words of explanation need to be said about the procedure by which this catalog of Umma settlements was created. In the initial step, place names designating discrete localities were separated from other types of toponyms (such as the names of waterways, temple names, and the like). It was then determined which of those localities may confidently be identified as Umma dependencies. In most instances, the textual context and the frequency with which a given locality is named in Umma sources are sufficient grounds to decide this point, although some cases inevitably remain ambiguous. Finally, an assessment was made whether a given locality was a settlement (as defined above), and, if so, what was its estimated size in terms of population and the number of dwellings. For this purpose, a four-rank settlement classification was constructed: (1) "hamlet", comprising all settlements from hamlets through small villages with a population between 10 and 250 persons and with 2 to 50 dwellings; (2) "large village," comprising all settlements from large villages through small towns with a population between 250 and 1000 people and with 50 to 200 dwellings; (3) "town," with a population over 1000 and with over 200 dwellings; and (4) "city," with a population over 20,000 and with over 4000 dwellings.

The decision to assign a settlement to one of these four categories was made based on the availability of various size indicators, such as (1) site size as determined through archaeological surface survey; (2) the presence in a given settlement of textually documented architectural structures, such as grain silos, storehouses, temples, palaces, private dwellings, and the like; (3) titles and professional designations of individuals associated with a settlement; (4) the documented numbers of inhabitants; (5) the settlement's general reputation as a political, religious, and administrative center; and (6) the name of the settlement itself, at least in the case of the toponyms employing the words **é-duru₅** ("hamlet"), **é** ("estate"), and **uru/ālu** ("town"). Among the Umma settlements, the majority fell into the "hamlet" category. At least 85 of those can be positively identified, and the actual total of such settlements may have been as high as 110 to 120.

This classification is certain in the case of 45 settlements whose names identify them either as **é-duru₅** ("hamlet") (43), or as **é** ("estate") (2). Otherwise, the threshold diagnostic feature permitting such a determination is the existence at a given place of grain-storing facilities, which are designated by the terms **guru₇** and **ì-dub**, both of which describe the same kind of a structure, a grain silo or storage bin.[4] As shown by the relevant textual data, **guru₇** and **ì-dub** were large, permanent structures capable of storing very substantial volumes of grain[5] and used continuously from year to year. Since it is inconceivable that a facility of this kind would have been left in the countryside unattended and without permanent protection, one may assume, therefore, that any locality with either a **guru₇** or an **ì-dub** must also have contained other buildings, which would have housed the caretakers of the grain silo.

Although this procedure assumes that the threshold size indicator permitting a completely certain "hamlet" (or higher) classification is a documented record of grain-storing facilities, it appears that already the presence of a threshing floor (**ki-sur₁₂**) is sufficient to allow such a ranking. This assumption rests on my experience in working with the Umma sources, which has taught me that if a threshing floor is attested for a particular locality, a reference to its **guru₇** or **ì-dub** may be expected to turn up in other sources, almost as a matter of course.

The conviction that the localities with threshing floors were regularly equipped with grain silos becomes even stronger when one considers the very nature of Umma's rural organization. As described in detail below, a key

---

[4] It is characteristic that, save for a few exceptions, the Girsu/Lagash sources use only the term **ì-dub**. On the other hand, at Umma both **guru₇** and **ì-dub** are employed, with the former term being favored. Despite the wealth of information available for these structures in various periods of Babylonian history, a systematic study of them is as yet wanting. The only treatment available is by Tina Breckwoldt (1995–1996), who discusses the Old Babylonian grain-storing facilities.

[5] See, for example, a record of 330 bushels of barley that was expended from the silo situated in front of the hamlet Eduru-ašag-lamah (330.0.0 **še gur guru₇ igi É-duru₅-a-šag₄-lá-mah-ta**—Sigrist 2000: text no. 601:11–12).

element of this organization (in particular, as it functioned within Umma's institutional sector) was a rural domain: a concentration of agricultural and other resources centered around a single support settlement. Such a domain operated largely as an autonomous economic unit, with its agricultural produce normally processed and stored in its associated settlement. Although it is possible that two different domains, each with a separate threshing floor, may on occasion have shared the same grain silo, the norm, as is strongly indicated by our data, appears to have been the opposite: each domain stored its produce separately, in its own storage facility.

One may be quite confident, therefore, that the overwhelming majority of the Umma localities for which the only diagnostic indicator available is a threshing floor (25 cases) were settlements of at least the "hamlet" rank. In this connection, one might recall the dual sense of the Akkadian word *maškanu*, which means both "threshing floor" and "hamlet," as if the two concepts were virtually synonymous. However, since the status of the localities in question cannot be demonstrated beyond doubt, I classify them as unconfirmed cases and exclude them for this reason from the overall statistical evaluation.

An examination of the data on these "hamlets" shows that they do not represent a uniform phenomenon. Instead, a wide divergence, both in terms of settlement size and internal complexity, can be found. The majority of Umma "hamlets" appear to have been minimal, highly specialized agricultural outposts which functioned merely as grain-processing and grain-storing centers. As far as can be ascertained, such a center was comprised of a grain silo, a threshing floor, and—although this is largely a supposition—a couple of dwellings housing the silo's caretakers. Also included there occasionally was a small temple or chapel, a feature normally associated with larger, more complex settlements.

The specialized settlements of this type appear to have been characteristic of Umma's rural landscape, at least within Umma's institutional economy. A clear pattern of separate, individually named units can be discerned, among which all the land resources managed by the governor of Umma and his organization were more or less evenly distributed. Each such unit, which can be compared to a domain, included a similar range of components: an arable field, a support settlement, plots of land under vegetable cultivation, a date-palm orchard, and grazing land. Many of the Umma domains also possessed their own micro-canal systems, as well as forests and even marshlands—productive of fish, waterfowl, reeds, and grasses.

The administrative focus of the domain was its support hamlet, as seen best from the way cereal production was organized. We have abundant sources that demonstrate that, following the harvest in the domain field, the grain was transported to the hamlet, where it was processed and placed in a silo. The bulk of the grain was then transported by boat to Umma and other towns of the province, with the remainder being stored in the hamlet to support its resident population and the local cult (if there was a temple there) and to be used as seed grain, animal fodder, and food rations during the next agricultural season.

What these support settlements may have looked like is nicely illustrated by Tell al-Raqa'i, a third-millennium site in the middle Khabur Valley (Schwartz and Curvers 1992; Schwartz and Klucas 1998). Raqa'i was a specialized agricultural hamlet, involved in grain processing and storage. Although in Level 3 it was only 0.17 hectare in size, it was divided into four distinctive areas, containing at least fourteen separate houses, a very large and complex grain-storing facility, and a small temple. Importantly, Raqa'i was not an isolated site but, very much like the Umma hamlets, was part of a regional system. This system, which included the neighboring sites of 'Atij, Kerma, Ziyadah, and perhaps others, embraced the lower section of the Khabur Valley and served to mobilize and store cereals throughout this region.

Another apt analogue for the Umma hamlets is Tell Karrana, an early third-millennium rural site in northern Iraq (Wilhelm and Zaccagnini 1993), which consisted of no more than a single inhabited building and a granary. Its excavators concluded, "there can hardly be any doubt that the remains of Karrana 3 point not to a small village, but rather to some sort of isolated agricultural complex (a farm-house, a 'villa rustica' or such like) which served the purposes of processing and storing cereals as well as meat and other products produced from livestock breeding" (Wilhelm and Zaccagnini 1993: 251).

Different types of small, specialized settlements are represented by the places named Anzagar, kar (Umma), and Ka'ida (Umma). The first, whose name means "fortified farmhouse" or "tower," was the site of a roadhouse whose function was to provide messengers and other state officials in transit with food provisions and animal fodder, and probably with overnight accommodations as well. This roadhouse, which must have resembled fairly closely the caravansaries of much later times, was staffed with a permanent personnel (**gìr-sì-ga**) and possessed its own threshing and grain-storing facilities.

By contrast, kar (Umma), "the quay (of Umma)," functioned as the principal harbor of the city of Umma (Steinkeller 2001: 51–52). Located a short distance away, it contained a storehouse, a weaving establishment, and probably also various other structures typical of a port. Judging from the huge volume of traffic and cargo known to have passed through it, the storehouse of kar (Umma) must have been a very large building. Perhaps what the sources refer to as a "storehouse" was actually a complex of riverfront warehouses and silos.

A similar type of settlement was Ka'ida (Umma), which served as a key relay point in the boat traffic between the city of Umma and the Tigris (Steinkeller 2001: 49–51, 53, and 50, map 2). Although direct evidence to that effect is lacking, Ka'ida too very likely contained extensive storage facilities.

Next to these highly specialized kind of minimal settlements, which appear to have formed a fairly uniform group and must have accounted for the majority of the "hamlets," there is evidence of larger settlements with more diversified economies and a greater variety of architecture, which should be classified as full-fledged villages. The structures known to exist in these settlements are storehouses (**gá-nun**—16 attestations), palaces (**é-gal**—7 attestations), sheep-fattening establishments and sheepfolds (**é-udu**—7 attestations), and, documented singly, shipyards (**mar-sa**) and weaving establishments (**é-uš-bar**).

In addition, in at least sixteen of these localities, one detects the presence of temples or chapels, as indicated by the references to deities and their associated cultic personnel. In some cases, more than one deity is documented per site, suggesting that multiple temples existed there. Such temples, which Umma sources include under the broad category of **èš dil-dil ma-da** ("various shrines of the countryside"), appear to have been but small (probably one-room) chapels, with only a handful of attendant personnel attached to them. Such personnel usually consisted of a **gúda** priest and a couple of female servants; in one instance, a high-ranking **egi-zi** priestess is documented (**Ašag-du-nunuz**).

The architectural features I have just described tend to occur in clusters, indicating a significant complexity of the settlements in question. Thus, for example, storehouses and palaces—accompanied by grain silos, threshing floors, and other structures—are attested jointly in Eduru-gu'edena, Eduru-IŠ.U.U, and Id-lugal. The settlements of Ašag-lugal, Eduru-du-kugsig, Emah, and Girgish each contained a temple, a storehouse, a grain silo, and, only in the case of Emah, also a palace. Other documented clusters of architectural features include a palace + sheepfold + grain silo (Eduru-ašag-lamah and Kamsala), a palace + grain silo (Eduru-ašag-manu), a chapel/temple + storehouse + sheepfold (Eduru-A'abba), a chapel/temple + grain silo + sheep-fattening establishment (A'uda), and a chapel/temple + grain silo (Id-sala).

Turning our attention now to larger settlements, these fall, as already noted, under three categories: "large village," "town," and "city." Of these categories, "city" is the most distinct and obvious one. Its sole representative is the city of Umma, which, owing to its size (200 hectares) and an estimated population of 20,000 to 25,000 individuals, stands out among the Umma settlements as a sui generis phenomenon.

Under the "large village" category, which I reserve for the settlements ranging from large villages through small towns, twelve settlements may be classed:

A'ebara, Al-bura, Al-Šu-Suen, Amrima, Dintir, Gishabba, Gishgigal, Hardahi, Kamari, Ṣarbat, Tim-KU.KU, and Uṣar-atigini. Most of them had temples.

The same number of settlements (12) may be assigned to the "town" category, which designates in my scheme the upper spectrum of "urban" settlements below the "city" ceiling, with a population of over 1,000. The places in question are Apishal (= Muhalliqiya?), Aṣarum-dagi, GARsuda, GARshana (= Nasiriya?), GuSAHAR.DU, Id-dula, Karkar (= Tall Jidr, Uruk Survey 004), Ki'an, Kisura (Umma), Mashkan, NAGsu (= Uruk Survey 175), and Zabalam (= Ibzaykh, Uruk Survey 169). With the exception of Gu-SAHAR.DU and Kisura (Umma), all of these settlements had temples, often with the **egi-zi** and **ereš-dingir** priestesses and the majordomos (**sabra**).

The distribution of settlements among "large villages" and "towns" is generally only approximate; in some instances, there is simply not enough evidence to assign a settlement to one of the two categories with certainty. Nevertheless, it appears fairly certain that, as in the case of "hamlets," neither "large villages" nor "towns" constituted uniform categories. Among the "towns," only Apishal, GARshana, Karkar, Ki'an, NAGsu, and Zabalam appear to have met the definition of a bona fide town, with the remaining ones probably being closer to a "large village" type. The "large villages" too appear to have varied in size, with some of them perhaps sharing more affinity with the "hamlet" category than with the true large villages.

A very special phenomenon that must finally be discussed in this connection is the evidence of a more dispersed mode of habitation in the Umma countryside. There survive records of large groups of individuals who appear to have lived outside of nucleated settlements, apparently in isolated farmhouses. Thus, for example, we read of 116 men (**éren**) residing "at the inlet of the Gishgigal canal," and of 119 men (**éren**) living "at the outlet of the Umma canal." The real populations behind these figures must have been quite substantial. Even if one uses the conservative factor of three to include dependents of the men in question, the total population figures would have to be put at 348 and 357 individuals, respectively. If the factor of five—still quite realistic—is employed, the respective figures rise to 580 and 595.

It must be noted at this point that it is very difficult to pigeonhole Umma settlements into a few distinctive size- and type-categories. It is even harder to draw a sharp distinction between the "rural" and "urban" features in their composition. Both the smaller and the larger ones show the same types of architectural structures and very similar elements of administrative and socioeconomic organization. It is usually only an aggregation of architectural features and a larger resident population that permits one to characterize a given place as a predominantly "urban" rather than a "rural" settlement. It seems more appropriate, therefore, to describe the Umma settlements, with the possible exception of the city of Umma, as a rural continuum, which was punctuated along the spectrum with an increasing presence of the seemingly "urban" characteristics.

The data from Umma make it absolutely certain that the view of the alleged rarity of rural settlements in third-millennium Babylonia needs to be revised. Moreover, it cannot be argued that the province of Umma was an anomaly in that respect, since the same situation existed during the same period in the province of Girsu/Lagash. Simply by perusing the indexes of the main editions of Girsu/Lagash sources, it is possible to compile a list of some 160 hamlets. The actual total of such settlements must have been considerably higher, since, based on what we know about the size of that province's institutional economy, the territory of Girsu/Lagash was larger than that of Umma by at least a factor of four.

To be sure, the Ur III period was not representative of the entire third millennium, since it constituted the peak of a millennium-long population growth. In Early Dynastic times, Babylonia's population must have been significantly smaller, as can be gathered from the fact that the economy of Girsu/Lagash in ED IIIb, in terms of both population and resources, appears to have represented only one-fifth of that recorded for Ur III times. One must assume that this enormous expansion was the direct result of a dramatic population growth throughout the alluvium. In this light, the population figures named in the inscriptions of the Girsu/Lagash rulers UruKAgina and Gudea probably deserve to be given serious consideration: while UruKAgina claims to have been divinely selected from among a population of 36,000, the corresponding number given 150 years later by Gudea is 216,000—a sixfold increase.[6]

Indeed, the survey data corroborate this conclusion very closely. According to Adams, the population of the alluvium increased by a factor of three between ED I and Ur III (or by five between late Uruk and Ur III). As he describes it, for most of the millennium there was little change. "Then, within a relatively short period at the end of the millennium, there was a sharp increase in the numbers of sites in every size category [and in the total occupied area]" (Adams 1981: 143).[7] Thus, Early Dynastic rural settlements were much fewer in number than at the end of the millennium. In fact, this conclusion is fully supported by the textual data, since such sites are comparatively rare in the sources from Early Dynastic Umma and Girsu/Lagash. Nevertheless, their total number was undoubtedly much higher than indicated by the surveys, and, as I will argue in detail later on, the relationship between the urban and rural spheres in Early Dynastic times was clearly the same as in the Ur III period.

---

[6] See Steible 1982: 298–299 Ukg. 4 vii 29–viii 6; Edzard 1997: 32 Gudea Statue B iii 6-11.

[7] See also Adams (1981: 151), where he talks of the "prodigious growth of population between Early Dynastic and Ur III times."

It will be useful at this point to compare the figures on Umma's settlements as derived from texts with those supplied by Adams's surface survey (see Table 7). The latter covered approximately 66 percent of the area that, according to my reconstruction, constituted the province of Umma in Ur III

TABLE 7. Settlements of the Umma Province in Ur III Times

A. *Based on archaeological survey data*

Settlement Type	#	Size	Name	Uruk Survey #
Urban Center	1	200 ha	Umma	197
	3	100 ha	Zabalam	169
			Karkar	004
			GARshana?	213
Town	1	30 ha	NAGsu	175
	2	15 ha		
	6	7 ha		
Village	6	2 ha		
Total	19	614 ha		

Total population: 61,400/76,750 (100/125 persons per ha). Assuming that the surveyed area represents roughly 66 percent of the total area of the Umma province, the total number of sites could be put at 28/29: 19/20 urban settlements + 9 villages. This results in a total population of ca. 100,000.

B. *Based on textual data: 110 confirmed settlements (158 including uncertain cases)*

#	Type	Population	Total Population
1	City (Umma)	20,000–25,000	20,000–25,000
12	Towns	5,000	60,000
12	Large village/ small town	600	7,200
85	Hamlet/small village	50	4,250
Total			91,450–96,450

Classification used:
(1) Hamlet through small village: population 10–250; dwellings 2–50
(2) Large village through small town: population 250–1,000; dwellings 50–200
(3) Town: population 1,000–10,000; dwellings 200–1,000
(4) City: population over 20,000

times (see Figures 48 and 49). Within those two-thirds of the province, the survey identified nineteen sites that may be dated to Ur III and Isin/Larsa times. Assuming that this figure represents about 66 percent of the sites that a complete survey would have uncovered in the entire area, the total may be put at 28/29. As can be seen in Table 7, the number of large sites is roughly the same in either calculation: 19/20 in the survey against 25 in my reconstruction. However, there is a dramatic difference in the number of smaller sites. While the survey indicates 9 villages (6 real + 3 extrapolated), my findings show at least 85 villages, with an actual total that may have been as high as 110/120.

The failure of the survey to identify these villages is not surprising. Indeed, Adams recognized this fact himself: "substantial settled areas around the cities, not to speak of the small, impermanent villages or encampments of those who were at a given time semi-sedentary, accumulated little debris. Thus it would not be surprising if many have been lost from sight beneath aeolian deposits or alluvium" (Adams 1974b: 8).[8]

A good illustration in point is the case of the third-millennium rural settlement Sagheri Sughir near Ur, which was partly excavated by Henry Wright. Here is how Wright describes the present condition of that site, measuring 230 × 70 meters or about 1.5 hectares in size: "Two processes have all but obliterated the mound: irrigation of the first and second millennia B.C. deposited silt on the plain and raised its surface about two meters. Erosion lowered its summit, leaving only the peripheral dumps of the later occupations. The site is virtually invisible" (H. T. Wright 1969: 43).

The majority of the Umma hamlets appear to have been minimal, one-period settlements. Moreover, it is even possible that many of the smallest, purely agricultural hamlets may have moved from place to place with the fallowing cycle and overall changes in land utilization. If this were the case, then, one might find multiple physical manifestations the same "hamlet" within a single agricultural area. In other words, what is described as a single hamlet in our sources could actually have been several different settlements, between which the same group of residents moved back and forth as the changing conditions of cultivation required.

A useful analogy here is provided by the modern villages of tenant farmers, such as existed until recently in the Daghara region of southern Iraq.

---

[8] Compare van Driel (2001: 111–112): "It is safe to assume that small settlements, especially if they were only occupied for limited periods, will be easily overlooked in a large scale car-based archaeological survey. The small settlements have little relief, are easily covered by silt or dunes, deflated or even ploughed under. Many may have disappeared completely." (See also Brinkman 1984a: 170–171; Pollock 1999: 55; Wilkinson 2000: 223–232.)

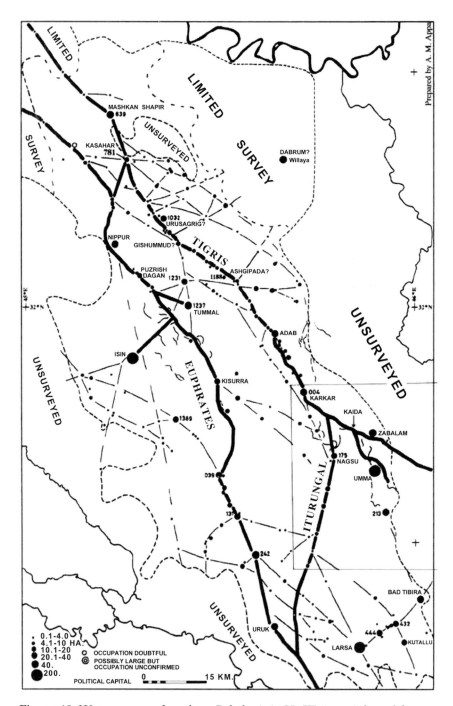

Figure 48. Watercourses of southern Babylonia in Ur III times (adapted from Adams 1981: 163, fig. 31).

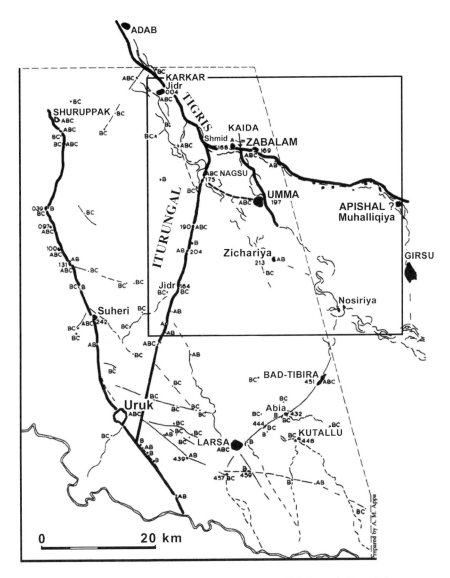

Figure 49. Watercourses in Umma province in Ur III times (adapted from Adams and Nissen 1972: 36, fig. 17).

These settlements, ranging in size from five to fifty family compounds, were superficially similar to those occupied by tribal farmers. But the homes of tenant farmers were simpler than those found in tribal villages, reflecting "the residents' unwillingness to invest money and effort in property which, at any time, they may choose or be obliged to abandon. Since in this area the larger estate owners had more land than sharecroppers to farm it, tenant farmer settlements tended to shift about from area to area or plot to plot. This is true even when the same family continues to work year after year for the same estate owner, who will alternate cultivation of his lands, following the area's system of fallowing" (Fernea 1970: 16). The tenant farmer "characteristically carries his wooden roof beams with him and may simply rehabilitate the walls of an abandoned mud hut near his newly assigned plot of land" (Fernea 1970: 15). As for the rural dispersed dwellings, whose presence in Umma's hinterland is strongly indicated by our data (see above, p. 194), there is no possibility whatsoever that traces of such habitations could ever be discovered by a surface survey.

The question now arises as to the significance of these "missed" or "overlooked" hamlets. For the overall demographic picture, these settlements, which may have numbered as many as 120, were not very important. Even if one assigns to them an average population of as high as 100 (the figure I use in my study is 50), this would add only 12,000 individuals to the total population estimate[9]. But the existence of these settlements changes dramatically—and this point cannot be overemphasized—the very nature of the relationship between the urban and the rural spheres: that is, how rural space was physically organized and how it related to and interacted with the urban center.

It must be remembered here that the alleged absence (or at least the great scarcity) of rural settlements in the third-millennium survey data has had a significant impact on the way archaeologists tend to visualize the relationship between the towns and countryside in early Mesopotamia. The prevailing view is that there existed an essential dichotomy between these two spheres. The posture of cities vis-à-vis their hinterlands is thought to have been invariably exploitative and predatory. According to this view, villages were rarely part of an articulated system for administration, since cities showed little interest in them, except as a source of agricultural products. Those were extracted from the hinterland in an ad hoc and always a coercive manner, with virtually nothing being offered in return. This intermittent exploitation was met with a resolute resistance of the rural population, which resorted to the use of various self-defensive strategies, the most important among them being the institution of "rural community."[10]

The data from Umma, however, offer a radically different picture, a picture that is not limited to the Ur III period but appears to apply equally to the entire second half of the third millennium. Let me begin with its purely physical aspects. Assuming that the total area of the Umma province was roughly 2000 square kilometers (45 × 45 kilometers), and that the total num-

[9] The question of the population estimate is too complex to be discussed here. I will deal with this issue at length in my book.

ber of settlements was roughly 110 (25 towns and large villages + 85 hamlets), the settlement density was one site per each 16.6 square kilometers. This translates into a median distance of about 4 kilometers between individual sites, and a median distance of roughly 9 kilometers between large villages and towns.[11] There was hardly any site within the Umma territory, therefore, from which another site, whether large or small, could not be seen. This fact alone indicates a high degree of connectedness and mutual dependence among the settlements of all types.

Rather than representing two different, sharply contrasted phenomena, at Umma the urban city and its countryside form a continuum, as regards both the physical and the socioeconomic landscape. In my reconstruction of Umma's physical landscape, there was no dichotomy, no fixed barrier between the town and the countryside; the two blend into each other. Urban space gradually and almost imperceptibly becomes countryside. The central, densely built-up section of a settlement thins out into suburbs; from there, it is only a couple of kilometers to the first hamlet; along the way, here and there one sees a single farmhouse; then another hamlet, followed by a village, and finally, another town. And so on.

---

[10] See the following two statements, which are typical of this position: "Historically, successful urban centers often maintained a parasitic or predatory relationship with their hinterlands, siphoning off as many assets as possible, while stopping short of undermining rural infrastructure. . . . Rural community organization in the face of urban demands must have taken a variety of forms, some of which may have predated the intrusion of state into the countryside" (Schwartz and Falconer 1994: 3–4); ". . . the evolution of cities entails also the evolution of the countryside, ruralization being the counterpart of urbanization. . . . This process of ruralization means that the 'countryside' of city-states is quite unlike the countryside of the same area before city-states. The countryside is made into 'a chaotic and brutish landscape' by city-states, who fear its wildness (from their perspective), as they depend on its resources" (Yoffee 1997a: 260–261).

[11] This agrees surprisingly closely with the settlement distribution that existed about the same time in the rain-fed upper Mesopotamia. As concluded by Tony Wilkinson, "in the wetter parts of Mesopotamia the Bronze Age landscape was dominated by nucleated tells, occurring at a fairly regular distribution every 10 to 15 km across the plains, with small tells at lesser distances" (Wilkinson 2000: 237). A survey of the surroundings of Tell Hamoukar in the northeastern corner of the Khabur region, which was carried out by Jason A. Ur (2002), yielded similar results. This survey, which covered an area of 125.6 hectares with a 5-kilometer radius, identified a total of fourteen third-millennium sites (= one site per roughly 9 square kilometers). Excluding Hamoukar, which measured 105 hectares, those were either between 2 and 4 hectares (four sites) or below 1 hectare (nine sites) in size. An inter-settlement distance of 10/15 kilometers roughly corresponds to the Babylonian "mile" (**danna/bēru**), which was 10.8 km in length. Is it possible, therefore, that the Babylonian "mile" is a native definition of the median "urban" distance?

What is more, textual data make it clear that the urban and the rural spheres were very closely integrated with each other, both economically and socially. City-based institutions embraced even the most marginal parts of the countryside (Steinkeller 1987a; 1999: 291–295), while elements of the rural social organization were present in force in "urban" environments. Indeed, it can be argued that it was precisely this exceedingly high level of urban–rural integration—the absence of sharp borders between the town and the countryside—that was largely responsible for the success of the southern Babylonian city-state as a political, social, and economic institution.

In fact, the alleged urban–rural dichotomy is shown to be false not only through the testimony of written records. It is equally indefensible from a broader socio-historical perspective. If any universal generalization about urban–rural relationships can be made, it is that cities always dominate the countryside (and not the opposite), and that cities depend on the countryside for their support. However, that domination may take a variety of forms; it does not always need to be coercive and exploitative. In the words of Moses I. Finley, "hypothetically, the economic relationship of a city to its countryside . . . can range over a whole spectrum, from complete parasitism at one end to full symbiosis at the other" (Finley 1973: 125). At the root of the city–countryside relationship, there lies a simple economic question: how can a town dweller induce the rural population to share with him their agricultural products, or, in other words, how does the city acquire an agricultural base for itself? This can be achieved either through coercion or through a strategy of various incentives, such as, for example, trade or participation in a shared ideological system. In third-millennium southern Babylonia, that goal was achieved through the use of various integrating mechanisms, chief among them being the "temple community" or "temple estate" as a cross-ecological social and economic institution (Steinkeller 1999: 290–295).

The notion of the urban–rural dichotomy,[12] which is deeply entrenched in ancient Near Eastern scholarship, is clearly dependent on comparisons with the late classical, medieval, and later Western urbanism. But such analogues appear to be quite inappropriate, since most of Near Eastern urbanism—and this is particularly true of third-millennium Babylonia—fits the Western model neither in economic nor in social terms.

From the perspective of human geography, a settlement qualifies to be called "urban" when the majority of its dwellers are not concerned with primary food production.[13] Such a definition certainly does not fit Babylonian

---

[12] For an extensive and cogent critique of this view, see now Schloen (2001: 101–104, 194–199).

[13] "Implicit in all definitions [of an urban settlement] is the accepted fact that an urban population is a permanent sedentary group of people who are not mainly concerned in primary food production" (Jones 1965: 162).

settlements, since the majority of the residents of even the largest among them, such as Umma for example, were directly involved in agriculture. Babylonian cities also fail to meet the modern sociological definition of the city because they had none of the social hallmarks of the Western city, such as, for example, what Ferdinand Tönnies called the substitution of *Gesellschaft* for *Gemeinschaft*, or, in other words, the replacement of a "face-to-face" society by the impersonal world of contracts and rationalizing behavior (Morris 1991: 37; Tönnies 2001). Nor do we find there any trace of independent city governments. Instead, as pointed out long ago by Max Weber, "self-administration" was an exclusive feature of villages and professional associations (Weber 1978: 1226–1231).[14] Thus, the "self-government" bodies one encounters in third- and second-millennium Babylonian towns (such as **babtu**, "town quarter," **ḫazannu**, "village headman, mayor," and **šību**, "elder") were in reality elements of the rural social organization.

To be a city in the sociological sense, the settlement should also show some form of urban "citizenship," and that feature too is completely absent in Babylonia, at least after the first millennium, when the phenomenon of **kidinnūtu** ("protection" or "special/exempt" status), which could arguably be interpreted as an incipient form of citizenship,[15] comes into being. Finally, it is self-evident that physical aggregation should not be confused with the growth of the city in a sociological sense (Martindale 1958: 62),[16] nor can one speak of urbanization "in the sense of the increasing separation of the city from the countryside" (Morris 1991: 36). In other words, the presence of seemingly "urban" physical features and the settlement's overall size in terms of acreage and population are not in themselves sufficient criteria for an urban designation. For example, modern Asian villages often have populations of 5000 and more, which is double the urban threshold current in the United States. In China, villages "range from tiny hamlets through villages of several thousand people, and they grade imperceptibly into agricultural or market towns, which are even bigger. *Indeed small towns here, as elsewhere in advanced communities, must be accepted as part of the rural settlement pattern* [emphasis added], and the pressure of population is such that they may be found at intervals as small as a mile" (Jones 1965: 120–121).[17]

---

[14]   In more general terms, this means the absence of urban autonomy: "Historically speaking, the significance of the city lies not in numbers of inhabitants or in the intensity of economic activity . . . but in the acquisition by its residents of judiciary, fiscal, and administrative autonomy" (Pipes 1995: 203).

[15]   Since such a status implies a shared complex of duties, rights, and privileges by qualified urban dwellers, it broadly meets a definition of "citizenship."

[16]   See also Schloen (2001: 196), who takes to task the "ahistorical functional assumption that . . . differences in the quantitative scale of human settlements necessarily correspond to qualitative difference in the structure of social relations."

As I noted earlier, the Umma settlements refuse to be fitted into a neat, bipolar urban–rural scheme. Thus, one encounters in villages characteristics that are usually associated with urban environments, such as the presence of temples and palaces. On the other hand, towns, even the largest among them, display in their physical makeup and social organization features that must be analyzed as rural. To reiterate, these facts argue that the third-millennium settlement pattern is best described as a rural continuum. A settlement with a population between 5000 and 10,000, the overwhelming majority of which was directly engaged in agriculture, was hardly a city; a classification "large village" or "rural town" is definitely more appropriate.[18] I would consider that even a settlement like Umma, with its estimated population of more than 20,000, was more correctly a large rural town. The same was true, I believe, of other Babylonian settlements customarily referred to as "cities," such as Uruk, Ur, Larsa, Girsu, Lagash, Adab, Nippur, and Shuruppak (here, of course, I do not mean the first-millennium urbanism represented by cases such as Babylon and Uruk since, both quantitatively and qualitatively, this was a completely different phenomenon).

But even if one excepts Umma and classifies it as a city, the fact still remains that it was the rural towns and villages that were the characteristic and determining feature of the southern Babylonian settlement pattern. Assuming that the total population of the province of Umma was in the range of 100,000, only 20 to 30 percent of that number lived in a true urban setting (Umma). And it goes without saying that if one wants to draw any meaningful conclusions about the urban–rural relationship in third-millennium Babylonia, one must see the whole relationship in a historical perspective. First of all, it is clear that the settlement pattern was the result of an uninterrupted organic development that went back to prehistoric times. There is no question that, in Babylonia, urbanization—and, more specifically, the formation of settlement networks—was essentially a bottom-up development. In other words, towns grew up from villages (Steinkeller 1999: 307). Historically, therefore, towns were but greatly expanded prehistoric villages. While some of the earliest villages became cities (if that is how one decides to call the largest settlements), others reached only the size of towns, while still others continued as villages (or ceased to exist altogether, to be

---

[17] For where the town works as an enlarged village, which relates to the countryside as simply as a village to its fields, town and country are indivisible, and questions of feeding the town or of exchange between town and country simply do not arise" (Osborne 1991: 120).

[18] See Schloen (2001: 197), who proposes, for the Bronze Age, "a model of the city as an overgrown agricultural village, or rather an agglomeration of similarly structured villages."

replaced by new villages, and so on). But much of the original interrelationships that already existed among all those settlements in prehistoric times continued in force well into the second millennium.[19]

Third-millennium southern Babylonia, at least when seen from the textual vantage point, is characterized by a network of traditional, time-sanctioned inter-settlement connections—economic, social, and religious—that must have been in existence since at least the mid-fourth millennium (Steinkeller 1999: 307). These interrelationships were manifested most visibly in the institution of the city-states. The southern city-state is best described as a hierarchically structured grouping of urban and rural settlements, which functioned as an autonomous political and economic entity. Accordingly, southern Babylonian city-states need to be understood as complete systems which were kept together by networks of mutual rights and obligations, operating equally in socioeconomic and religious realms.

In creating that pattern, one factor was of basic determining significance: the natural environment of the Babylonian floodplain, in particular, the complete dependence of this region on artificial irrigation. One of the obvious consequences of this fact was that any prospects of agricultural activity in the hinterland were entirely dependent on the acquiescence and cooperation of the major settlements, which controlled all the major watercourses and canals simply by virtue of being located on the main waterways and because they had the necessary resources to maintain the respective canal systems. Thus, the very existence of an artificial canal system fostered—if not made mandatory—a high level of social and economic integration between towns and the countryside. At the same time, this fact alone precludes any possibility of the existence in the countryside of agriculturally based "rural communities" that were politically and economically independent from the central institutions.[20]

The importance of religion cannot be overestimated as a key element that made the southern Babylonian city-state work. This point was aptly recognized by Adams, who, in critiquing another scholar's model of state formation, forcefully argued for "a special role for religion and religious institutions" (Adams 1981: 77). What I mean by "religion"—and I am sure that Adams understood it in the same way—is a symbolic manifestation of social behavior (or "social action" if you will), that is, a means through which

---

[19]   Accordingly, the view that during the formative stages of Mesopotamian history, "ruralization" was an evolutionary consequence of the earlier "urbanization" (Yoffee 1997a: 260–261, cited above in n. 10)—in other words, cities came first, villages appeared only later—is completely mistaken. To be sure, Babylonian cities always played an active role in establishing rural settlements, but only after they themselves had come into being.

social and political relationships are expressed, negotiated, and further refor-
mulated.

Indeed, it was religion (specifically: cult) that cemented and perpetuated
social and economic relationships between the settlements within individual
city-states. Thus, for example, the relationship that existed between the city
of Umma and its dependency Apishal had an economic as well as a religious
aspect and was based on traditions that must have been very ancient, going
probably as far back as prehistoric times. For various kinds of reasons, geographical and other, Apishal appears to have been better suited to be an economic partner of Umma than of Girsu/Lagash, perhaps because as a close
neighbor of Girsu/Lagash, Apishal may have enjoyed more economic and
political independence in an alliance with Umma. In the sphere of religion,
this relationship manifested itself most visibly in the fact that the gods of
Apishal were an integral part of the Umma pantheon. In the same way, the
ties that existed between the city of Umma and many of her villages must also
have been the product of a long historic development which had followed the
parallel socioeconomic and religious courses.

It must be understood that much (if not most) of the cultic activity of a
southern Babylonian city-state took place in the countryside, not just immediately outside the city-walls, but in a real rural space. As part of festivals,
town-based deities would travel to the countryside to inspect their rural
estates and to pay calls on local gods—their country cousins, so to speak. And
at the same time, rural populations and their deities visited towns in order to
take part in central festivals and other forms of cultic celebration.[21] The
function of these rituals clearly was to perpetuate traditional connections
between towns and the countryside, to maintain the sense of corporate identity between the city dwellers and the rural population. For all practical purposes, therefore, both groups formed a single extended socio-religious
community.

---

[20] This applies only to the "internal" countryside, that is, the alluvial hinterland
within the Tigris and the Euphrates systems. The situation in the "external" countryside, by which I mean the outlying territories along the left bank of the Tigris
and the right bank of the Euphrates, may have been quite different, since, even in
Ur III times, the political and economic control that the central government exer-
cised over those regions must have been considerably less. As a matter of fact, we
have textual indications that it was precisely there that the Amorites permanently
settled in large numbers for the first time. Adams's recent work on the western
branch of the Euphrates (ancient Araḫtum) in the area of Ur and Eridu, which is
based on satellite images, indicates a very extensive network of sites and fields in
that area at roughly the end of the third millennium (Adams, personal communication). It would not be surprising if this network turned out to be vestiges of that
early Amorite occupation.

An excellent illustration of how the cult integrated southern Babylonian towns with their hinterlands is provided by Gudea's building project on the Eninnu,[22] the temple of Ningirsu and the most important sanctuary of the Girsu/Lagash city-state. It is characteristic that the countryside was actively involved in each stage of this operation. When the plan of the rebuilding of the Eninnu is conceived, Gudea undertakes a boat trip to visit the main deities of the province (in particular, the goddess Nanshe, whose domain embraced the southern portions of the city-state, along with the towns of Nimin, Sirara, and Gu'abba) in order to consult them about the feasibility of the project and to obtain their cooperation. Only when this is accomplished may the project begin in earnest. Various ritual preliminaries then take place, culminating in the symbolic ground-opening ceremony in which the representatives of the three rural groupings or territorial clans (**im-ru-a**) of Girsu/Lagash[23] play a central part. Once the old structure is torn down in preparation for the new construction, Ningirsu and his divine court move out to his country estate for the duration of the project. The whole undertaking ends with a triumphant return of Ningirsu from the countryside and his occupation of the new Eninnu.

It should be noted here that the recent scholarship on Classical Greek city-states has reached a closely similar understanding of the urban–rural relationship. For example, Robin Osborne (1985; 1987; 1991) attributes the strength of the polis of Athens to its success in incorporating its villages and rural towns in its political and social structures (compare Wallace-Hadrill 1991: xiii), and stresses the inherently rural character of Classical Greek cities:

What is distinct about the Greek city is best revealed by the contrast between that city and the cities of the Roman, medieval, and early modern periods. The Greek city is not just a town, it cannot be divorced from its countryside. By the Roman period this was no longer true even in Greece itself. By the later Roman era the countryside ran itself almost independently of the town: village markets obviated the need for travel to the town to exchange goods; men thought of themselves as from a village rather than from a city and recorded villages as their places of origin; village and city politics had little or nothing to do with each other. The later Roman

---

[21] For the ritual activity in the countryside, see extensively Sallaberger 1999, who restricts his discussion to the Ur III period and uses mainly the data from Umma and Girsu/Lagash. Identical rituals are documented in Pre-Sargonic times at Girsu/Lagash, although a systematic study of topic is still lacking.

[22] Edzard 1997: 30–38 Statue B, 68–101 Cylinders A and B.

[23] These three groupings probably reflect the original division of Girsu/Lagash into three separate political units or proto-city-states. See Steinkeller 1999: 291 and n. 7, 307 and n. 68.

city foreshadows the enclosed medieval city of which Pirenne has written: 'Once outside the gates and the moat we are in another world, or more exactly, in the domain of another law.' . . . Urbanization was unknown in Greece. . . . None of the conditions necessary to encourage a significant proportion of the population to devote themselves to non-agricultural occupations were met in any city in Classical Greece. . . All Greek cities were overwhelmingly agricultural, with a very restricted range of manufacturing. . . . The Classical city was embedded in the countryside. Agriculture made the Greek city possible and established its limits. The agricultural production of the countryside shaped the social structure. Patterns of residence and land-holding played a major part in establishing the political framework and the nature of political crises. . . . The connection between the city as independent political unit and the city as countryside was intimate. Once the Greek city lost its political autonomy, the pattern of exploitation and occupation of the countryside began. The loss of city autonomy led directly to the development of urban units and the independent life of the countryside characteristic of the Roman period . . . [then] the process of differentiation had began which led eventually to the birth of the urban city and rustic countryside out of the inseparable unit of town and country which was the Classical Greek city. (Osborne 1987: 193–196)

Or, as it was argued by another author, "a strong network of rural settlements should be seen as supporting, not antithetical to, the polis," and "the corollary of a strong urban center is not an empty countryside, but one with a dense network on intercommunicating settlements for which it provides the common focus" (Wallace-Hadrill 1991: xiii). As for the integrating role of religion in early Greece, it will suffice to cite François de Polignac's (1995 [1984]) *Cults, Territory, and the Origin of the Greek City-State*, in which the author convincingly demonstrates that the Greek polis developed its political and social identity through an intimate relation with its hinterland.[24]

---

24   Note, in particular, the following conclusion: "In the bipolar view of the city presented here, the idea of a central point is thus not abolished but complemented by that of a median point. The two were linked through the axis of relations by means of which the city was elaborated and around which the secondary cults, whether of gods or of heroes, in the settlement or on its fringes, within the territory or on its boundaries, delineated and defined the function of appropriation, delimitation, interconnection, and integration and affirmed the city's identity and sovereignty as a polis. Some of these concepts were coordinated and synthesized in the great sanctuary out in the territory, others in the great sanctuary in the heart of the town" (de Polignac 1995 [1984]: 154).

SOCIAL CONDITIONS IN THE UMMA COUNTRYSIDE

I wish to close this paper with a brief discussion of the social conditions in the Umma countryside in Ur III times. It can be shown that all the people who settled in the Umma province were state dependents, either directly, as members of the royal sector (essentially: the royal military organization, represented by the **šhaginas**, "generals"), or indirectly, as subordinates of the local provincial economy (headed by the **énsi**, "governor," and corresponding roughly to the old city-state economy).[25] At least two-thirds of Umma's rural population were members of the royal sector. Best described as military colonists, they cultivated about two-thirds of the available arable land. Key information on the social organization of Umma's rural population is provided by a number of sources, in which a unit of military settlers is described by the kinship term **im-ri-a** (a variant spelling of the earlier-discussed **im-ru-a**), meaning "territorial clan" or, as it is used specifically in this context, "extended family." Clearly, some sense of common descent (real or fictitious) must have been shared by the members of such a group to warrant this appellative. This fact strongly suggests that the organizational patterns of Umma's military reflected kinship relationships where in part indigenous familial groupings had been absorbed wholesale by the state structures. What happened, apparently, is that rural communities were reorganized and transformed into semi-military settlements under the guidance of the central government; their male members were pressed into military units, assigned commanders, and made part of the overall state organization. As royal dependents, these military colonists were provided with subsistence fields. The source of these fields seems to have varied; some of them probably represented newly developed holdings, while others very likely came from the land that had originally been utilized by the very same rural groups, but was later "nationalized" by the Ur III kings.

It appears that such semi-military groupings, although firmly embedded in the state structures, at the same time functioned with a considerable degree of autonomy—either inherited from a pre-Ur III past or acquired secondarily—which manifested itself in the presence of a self-government, headed by an executive officer called *ḫazannu* ("village headman, town mayor"). The *ḫazannu*s operated on the level of towns, but we find them also in large villages. Significantly, the *ḫazannu*, though not a member of the military organization *sensu stricto*, fell under the authority of the local military commander, rather than that of the governor of the province. Thus, he could

---

[25] For the administrative and economic organization of the Ur III provinces, see Steinkeller 1987b; 2002a: 114–116.

act as a general's representative, and might even to lead the men from his native settlement on a corvée project. As such, he served as a direct link between the rural structures and the crown, to the almost complete exclusion of the governor and his administration.

Although such self-governing bodies are never mentioned specifically, their existence may be gathered from the label "a completed case/transaction of the citizens of GN" (di-til-la dumu GN), which is appended to a number of Umma legal documents. The places named in this context are A'ebara, GARshana, and NAGsu. What this evidence indicates is that the residents of the settlements in question were treated by law as collective bodies, in turn implying that they had their own representatives, probably groups of elders (ab-ba / šību), who either validated or witnessed the cases in question.

While the majority of the royal settlers who lived in the Umma countryside probably stemmed from the indigenous local population, there were also numerous newcomers among them. In a group of sources illustrating the operations of a royal rural estate situated near the town of GARshana, the personal names are almost exclusively Akkadian (David I. Owen, personal communication 2006). This and other data indicate a considerable influx of population from northern Babylonia, a process that had very likely begun in the Sargonic period, when we find the earliest evidence of a significant Akkadian colonization in southern Babylonia. Foreigners were brought there too, as shown by the mentions in Umma sources of the Elamites, Amorites, and men of Huhnuri being assigned subsistence fields. In the neighboring province of Girsu/Lagash, one even finds villages that apparently were entirely settled with foreigners.[26]

We can see, therefore, that the social organization of the Ur III countryside was the product of a very complex development. To a large extent, this development was steered by the central government. It appears that, when the founders of the Ur III state turned the former city-states into a uniform provincial system, they made a concentrated effort to preserve as much as possible of the original structure in order to minimize social disruption. In this way, the governor's domain (that is, the original city-state) survived in a virtually unchanged form, although some of its landed resources appear to have been absorbed by the royal sector. The same policy was employed within the royal domain, which consisted mainly of newly developed agricul-

---

[26] The evidence here comes from the toponyms such as Lulubuna, "(village of the men from) Lulubum," Ebih, "(village of the men from) Ebih = Jebel Hamrin," and Eduru-Elamene, "village of the Elamites." Similar settlements are documented in other provinces of the Ur III state (such as the village of the men from Shimanum near Nippur).

tural areas but also included confiscated lands. There, the crown absorbed the existing rural groups while at the same time brought in large numbers of new settlers. All of these people, the indigenous population and the newcomers, were turned into a uniform category of semi-military colonists, settled on royal land, and organized into military units along extended-family lines.[27]

Thus, there did indeed exist "rural communities" in southern Babylonia, but these were clearly secondary adaptations sponsored by the state, and not the vestiges of a pristine "village sector," such as was postulated by Diakonoff—and I hardly need to point out that the difference between these two concepts of the "rural community" is quite dramatic.

Such an understanding of the social matrix of rural Babylonia agrees very closely with what was said nearly twenty years ago about the Near Eastern peasant society by Henry Rosenfeld. As Rosenfeld (1983: 154) argued, peasants are, historically, "tribal peoples who, as rural cultivators, in one way or another had been incorporated into, or made to serve, state ends." As a result, "very often 'traditional,' seemingly indigenous, folk patterns of behavior are in reality the outcome of state-sponsored devices of control over the folk" (Rosenfeld 1983: 158). And, even without the benefit of the Umma data, Rosenfeld was able to reach the following—in my view, quite prophetic—conclusions about the early Mesopotamian sociopolitical development:

> As soon as, or soon after, the early states incorporated tribal groupings, then as now, we should be speaking of a structure that consistently was allowed to reproduce itself in order to meet state ends, and whose "kinship" is the end result of that state-made structural unit. That is, the early Mesopotamian city-states sapped the tribal kin lineage of its content once and for all. What remained, and what we can find, is a recreated adapted structure fabricating its "kinship," as best as it can, out of the structures imposed and maintained by successive regimes. (Rosenfeld 1983: 168)

---

[27] FA closely similar development took place in the settlements that were established by the Ur III kings in the periphery of their state (Steinkeller 1987a). As in Babylonia, the population of those settlements was turned into military colonists, provided with subsistence fields, and subjected to a uniform taxation system. Although some of those colonists may have been brought from Babylonia, it seems certain that the majority of them stemmed from the local population. Characteristically, these peripheral settlements show the presence of an identical self-governing body, represented by the *ḫazannu* and the elders.

THE MESOPOTAMIAN URBAN EXPERIENCE

ELIZABETH C. STONE

ABSTRACT

This paper pulls together both textual and archaeological data to present a picture of the southern Mesopotamian city, focusing on the third and early second millennia BC. Beginning with a look at houses and households, the view moves out to include neighborhoods, the major institutions of palace and temple, and eventually the city as a whole. The paper ends with a discussion of the relationship between city and countryside, using data from both small excavated sites and from high-resolution satellite imagery. The thrust of this contribution is that it was the face-to-face communities that made up the building blocks of Mesopotamian society, creating a flexible structure capable of moving between Adams's modes of maximization and resilience.

INTRODUCTION

Of the various early civilizations studied by anthropologists and archaeologists, Mesopotamia is not only arguably the oldest, but more importantly to my mind, it is the civilization that provides us with the best tools for arriving at a real understanding of how it operated. The range of data sources is unparalleled: the broad survey work undertaken by Robert Adams, the century or more of excavations at its many large and impressive urban sites, and the large number of cuneiform inscriptions which provide the details of daily life are unmatched elsewhere. Yet in some ways, this very wealth of data has led to something of a cacophony, where differences in both the nature of the data studied and their temporal resolution impede the development of a coherent view of ancient Mesopotamian society. This paper will try to resolve these many voices into a more unified view of the building blocks of Mesopotamian cities and city-states. I am trying here to follow in the footsteps of Robert Adams, who always advocated the integration of archaeological and textual sources, of humanities and social scientific approaches, as the way toward developing a clearer understanding of past behavior.

It is the work of Adams and his students and colleagues (Adams 1965; 1972b; 1981; Adams and Nissen 1972; Gibson 1972; H. T. Wright 1981b) that has provided the broadest view. Adams's surveys have shown how the pattern of urban growth and decay was the result of a complex interplay between environmental factors—shifting watercourses, salinization of land—and human factors—the ebb and flow of political relations in the area. However, in the process of documenting changes in individual settlements and even settled areas over time, this work also provided a sense of the "longue durée" of Mesopotamian history, where the exigencies of life in the southern plain shaped both settlement and society in much the same way over the millennia. In general, the survey data shifted the focus from city to city-state—the network of numerous settlements of varying sizes, tied together by political and economic ties and a complex irrigation system. But the picture provided by the survey work was also somewhat impressionistic because the "type fossil" ceramics used to date the sites did not allow an assessment of settlement patterns that even approximated the temporal resolution of data recovered from excavations, whether textual or artifactual. For example, two periods that are seen by Assyriologist and archaeologist alike (although for different reasons) as radically different—the Ur III and Isin-Larsa periods—are grouped together in the survey data (Adams 1981: 163, fig. 31).

The wealth of cuneiform documentation recovered from Mesopotamian sites provides a picture that is almost antithetical to the results of settlement surveys. The vast majority of the written corpus comes from urban centers rather than from small sites—most of which remain unexcavated. Written documents appear to have been plentiful at times of centralization and rare in the intervening periods of fragmentation, with significant genre changes between periods as different types of transactions enter the written record. These genre changes have resulted in a view of Mesopotamian society as lurching from warring city-states to imperial domination, from intense bureaucratic activity to private enterprise. Moreover, the philological background of most Assyriologists has left them bereft of the historical, sociological, or anthropological models of ancient society that might have helped place the written documents within broader frameworks, resulting in a field dominated by narrowly framed descriptive publications rather than the kinds of broad, integrative works that have characterized Adams's books and articles.

There are, however, some exceptions. For those interested in the topic of Mesopotamian urbanism, the 1970s and 1980s saw a move toward examining private documents organized not by genre but by site, and in some instances relating those documents to the archaeological record. Urban-focused studies of third-millennium documents have not come as quickly, but we await with anticipation Piotr Steinkeller's forthcoming work on the city of Umma. In the 1990s, the publication of Nicholas Postgate's *Early Mesopotamia* (1992) and Jack Sasson's *Civilizations of the Ancient Near East* (1995) succeeded in replacing the old emphasis on a hierarchical temple-centered society with a stress on the flexibility of Mesopotamian social institutions, on its entrepreneurial character, and on the interplay between hierarchy and heterarchy which characterized its political relations.

Fortunately, our knowledge of ancient Mesopotamia is not limited to the written sources and the results of surface surveys. Archaeological excavations have been undertaken in southern Mesopotamia for over a century. Although the focus of many of the early excavators—and even some modern ones—was on narrow issues of chronology, the crucible of the Diyala Project brought together Assyriologists, art historians, and archaeologists—most notably Thorkild Jacobsen, Henri Frankfort, and Seton Lloyd—in ways that allowed them to approach a real understanding of life in ancient Mesopotamia as they debated their work around the dig house fire. To a large extent, our understanding of Mesopotamian urbanism is built on their work at Tell Asmar and Khafajah (Delougaz 1940; 1952; Delougaz and Lloyd 1942; Delougaz, Hill, and Lloyd 1967; Frankfort 1939b; 1943; 1955; Frankfort, Lloyd, and Jacobsen 1940; Hill, Jacobsen, and Delougaz 1990), as well as on the contemporary excavations at Ur (Woolley 1974; Woolley and Mallowan 1976) and the later work at Tell Harmal (Baqir 1946; 1959), Nippur (McCown and Haines 1967; E. C. Stone 1987), and Haradum (Kempinski-Lecomte 1992). More recently, research interests shifted toward intensive intrasite surveys at sites such as Abu Salabikh (Postgate 1977; 1978; 1980; 1982; 1983; 1984; 1990; Postgate and Moorey 1976; R. Matthews, Postgate, and Luby 1987; W. Matthews et al. 1994), el-Hiba (E. Carter 1990), Mashkan-shapir (E. C. Stone 1990; 1996a; E. C. Stone and Zimansky 1992; 1994; 1995; 2004), and Larsa (Huot, Rougeulle, and Suire 1989), and to a certain extent at Uruk (Finkbeiner 1991) and Nippur (Gibson 1992).

How then do we draw these very different strands of evidence together. I believe that the same variety that has led to what I described above as a cacophony can be used to present a single voice. All three of the data sets—from settlement pattern studies, from excavations, and from textual evidence—are biased, but they are biased in different ways. The survey data loses the chronological precision of our other sources but provides the big picture within which all other data sets should be addressed. The textual record is certainly biased toward those whose activities were deemed worthy of transcription and against the poor and the weak. It is also dominated by records of the activities and points of view of urban residents, and not so much of those who lived in more modest settlements. But to a large extent, the latter are offset by the results of the excavations, which have included domestic areas as well as public buildings, and within the former, small modest structures as well as the houses of the well-to-do. Moreover, the source of all cuneiform texts are excavations, whether conducted by archaeologists or looters, and thus the archaeological record provides the contexts that define the textual record. For example, I have argued elsewhere (E. C. Stone 2002a) that the stark difference between the Ur III written record and that of the subsequent Isin-Larsa period reflects more the differential preservation of public and private contexts for the two periods than any truly dramatic revolution within Mesopotamian society. Thus, when an active interplay is maintained between the survey, textual, and archaeological data sets, it should become possible to present a sense of the key factors in Mesopotamian society, albeit with a focus on urban centers as a result of the bias of our excavated data.

I will limit my remarks to southern Mesopotamia, and to the third and early second millennia, because it is in this area that we have the extensive survey work of Adams and his students and colleagues to inform our understanding of changing patterns of settlement, and it is for this period that we have the city-specific textual studies and the intensive intrasite surveys that have done so much to reveal details of the Mesopotamian urban experience. Little is known beyond temple plans of the organization of late fourth-millennium sites in the southern alluvium; and if the housing areas excavated at Habuba Kabira (Vallet 1996) were typical of settlements in the south, it would appear that we see here more a continuation of residential patterns established in fifth-millennium village sites such as Tell Abada (Aboud 1984) than the dense housing that characterizes districts dating to fully historic periods. Urban life also continued in southern Mesopotamia much later than the mid-second millennium, but both textual and archaeological data are limited except in the Neo-Babylonian period. In terms of organization, I will look at the city from the inside out, beginning with an examination of Mesopotamian houses and households and ending with a consideration of the relationship between the city and its hinterland.

HOUSES AND HOUSEHOLDS

While the archaeological surveys provide the framework within which to view ancient Mesopotamian cities, as *Evolution of Urban Society* (Adams 1966) had stressed, it was the internal workings of these settlements that drove the

Mesopotamian experience, and so it is to the excavation data and the texts derived from them that we must turn for illumination. Excavations in the Diyala, Ur, Nippur, and elsewhere have provided detailed evidence of the houses of average Mesopotamian citizens, full of the bric-a-brac of daily life and often containing both the graves and written records of their inhabitants. Studies such as those by Elizabeth Henrickson (1981; 1982) on the house areas in the Diyala, by Edward Luby (1990) on the houses and graves at Ur, and my own work at Nippur (E. C. Stone 1981; 1987) all made clear that Mesopotamian residential districts were composed of large, well-appointed houses with smaller houses nestled between them, and occasional shops and shrines. The differences between these largest and smallest houses are not based solely on size. It is only in the larger houses that we find special-purpose rooms such as kitchens, bathrooms, and household shrines, and it is within these houses that the richest of the intramural graves are to be found. This pattern was found everywhere (see Figure 50): in the walled precinct around the Temple Oval (Delougaz, Hill, and Lloyd 1967: pl. 14), in the priestly quarter near the Ur Temenos (Woolley and Mallowan 1976: pl. 122; Charpin 1986), and in the less exalted residential districts excavated at Tell Asmar (Delougaz, Hill, and Lloyd 1967: pl. 28), Nippur (McCown and Haines 1967: 34–68; E. C. Stone 1987), Ur (Woolley and Mallowan 1976: pls. 124, 128), Sippar (Al-Jadir and Abdulla 1983), Tell Harmal (Baqir 1946; 1959), and Haradum (Kepinski-Lecomte 1992).

The size range of these houses is identical to that of modern apartments in European and American cities, between 40 and 500 square meters, with the majority between 60 and 200 square meters. House sizes are comparable in all excavated areas, whether they are in the same site, between sites, or between sites dating to different periods.

House *plans* are also similar across both space and time. The exceptionally large houses usually have multiple courtyards, and have been found in third-millennium Tell Asmar (Delougaz, Hill, and Lloyd 1967: pl. 26, House II) and in second-millennium Ur (Woolley and Mallowan 1976: pl. 124, 13 Church Lane and 11 Paternoster Row) and Larsa (Calvet 1996: 204, fig. 7). The medium-sized houses from all sites and periods, those between around 100 and 200 square meters in size, tend to approximate the typical courtyard house in which a central space is surrounded by rooms on all sides (see, for example, Moorey 1982: 198). Meanwhile, many of those houses less than 100 square meters in size are long, narrow, and found in groups of two or three (E. C. Stone 1996b: 232–233). It seems likely that the largest houses represent the amalgamation of more than one courtyard house and the smallest their breakup into smaller units. Although the findspot evidence for the tablets is somewhat questionable, this seems to have been the case for the small structures in Paternoster Row at Ur (van de Mieroop 1992: 153–156).

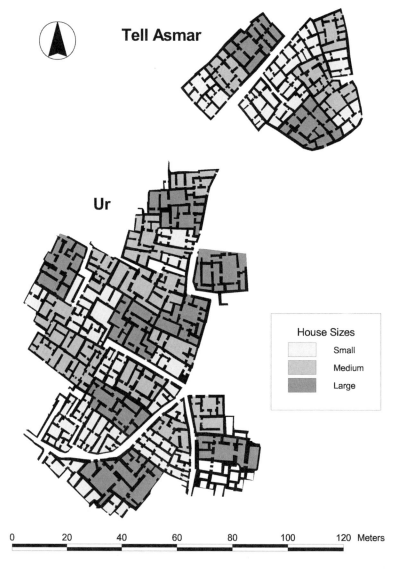

Figure 50. Domestic areas at third-millennium Tell Asmar and second-millennium Ur (after Delougaz, Hill, and Lloyd 1967: pl. 28; Woolley and Mallowan 1976: pl. 124).

The important point here is that the consistency of these patterns over both space and time suggests significant stability in Mesopotamian social relations. Moreover, the similarity of house sizes with those occupied by modern urban residents, the proximity of houses of the rich and the poor, plus the wealth of objects recovered from these contexts, all suggest that earlier views of Mesopotamian cities—where exploitation by religious and political elites were seen to result in the impoverishment of the bulk of the population—can no longer be sustained.

Our changing view of domestic districts in Mesopotamian cities was enhanced by studies—all based on early second-millennium private documents—that focused on texts from individual cities. This endeavor, initiated by Leo Oppenheim (1969), was primarily carried out by Rivkah Harris (1975) on the texts from Sippar but was soon followed by studies of Tell Sifr (Charpin 1980), Ur (Charpin 1986; van de Mieroop 1992), and Nippur (E. C. Stone 1987). These private texts allow us to reconstruct genealogies and analyze the economic fortunes and social relations of families by examining real estate transactions, letters, and other texts. Moreover, in the case of some of the texts from Nippur and Ur, their archaeological contexts were preserved, allowing a direct link to be drawn between the history of the family and their domicile.

These texts provide a glimpse into the private economies of the time, indicating that, in addition to owning their own houses, the residents of these districts usually owned date orchards and sometimes grain fields; or they might hold religious offices or be engaged in professions. The picture they provide is of urban residents who were both independent and connected to the public sector. It also seems to have been a very literate society, with scribal schools found in almost every district, and school texts recovered from almost every house.

Where genealogies can be reconstructed, a pattern consistent with high levels of social mobility can be determined. Often these genealogies illustrate the slow decline of families over time. Successive generations can be shown to be increasingly impoverished as large family size and partitive inheritance combine to erode family wealth (see E. C. Stone 1987: 41–53; see also Figure 51). Sometimes, however, other individuals suddenly show up in the textual record, allying themselves with the older families through adoption, and they can be seen to reconstitute large estates through successive purchases of property (E. C. Stone and Owen 1992; see also Figure 52). The pattern revealed in these texts is strikingly similar to the rise and fall of both princes and notable families described by Ibn Khaldun (1969).

One of the most important aspects of these texts is their usefulness in documenting differences between residential districts. At Ur, clear differences can be seen between the Area EM, which was dominated by the clergy (Charpin 1986), and AH, which had a more entrepreneurial character (van de Mieroop 1992). In a similar vein, at Nippur, TA was occupied by small farm owners, whereas those living in TB seem to have had a stronger tie to a state

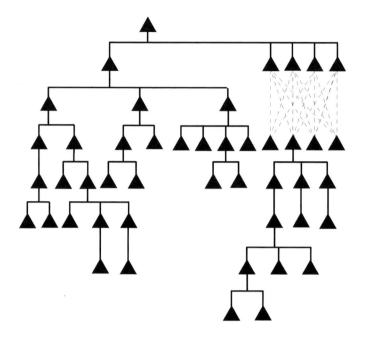

Figure 51. Ninlil-zimu genealogy (after E. C. Stone 1987: fig. 1).

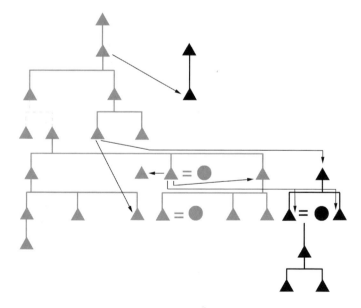

Figure 52. Manum-meshu-lissur genealogy (after E. C. Stone and Owen 1992: fig. 2). The genealogy shown in gray is the family whose fortunes descended over time. The genealogies shown in black are the families who were connected to this family through adoption. Each adoption is shown by a black arrow.

institution (E. C. Stone 1987). These data, when combined with the results of intramural surveys to be discussed later, suggest an urban landscape made up of numerous small, face-to-face communities. In structure, these seem very similar to those documented from Islamic cities. The Islamic neighborhood in Damascus illustrated by Sauvaget (1934: 452) was the center of daily activities and contained all the necessities of life, including a small market, a fountain providing fresh water, a bakery, a mosque, and a bath house. Like their Mesopotamian predecessors, the Islamic neighborhood consists of a mixture of large, medium, and small houses. The Mesopotamian textual and archaeological data suggest that differences in wealth existed within such neighborhoods rather than between them, and again the similarities seen between the Mesopotamian evidence and the data from Ottoman Islamic cities suggest significant continuity. Even though detailed Islamic data are only available from the nineteenth century, after the introduction of capitalism had begun to change the high levels of social mobility typical of late medieval Islamic cities, a map of residential neighborhoods in Aleppo demonstrates that *all* neighborhoods included both rich and poor (David 1975: fig. 12).

Thus, the combination of textual and archaeological data from residential districts within urban centers in Mesopotamia suggests not only long, unbroken traditions of domestic life, but also that those traditions were characterized by strong neighborhood development, high levels of social mobility, and the domestic context of officeholders, small farmers, and the like. But cities are not just large residential areas, they are defined both by their concentrated populations and, perhaps most importantly, by their institutions. Recent research has also witnessed significant growth in our knowledge of palaces and temples, again the result of detailed publication of the archaeological contexts combined with the study of the associated epigraphic and other finds.

PALACES AND TEMPLES

So far, the excavated palaces have been associated with independent rulers of cities, rather than with provincial governors. Thus, buildings like the palace at Mari (Parrot 1958–1959) would not have been features of most cities; instead, more modest administrative structures, such as the Palace of the Rulers at Tell Asmar (Frankfort, Lloyd, and Jacobsen 1940) and the many other administrative buildings that have been excavated, would have been more common. Nevertheless, the rich architectural, artifactual, and epigraphic finds from Mari provide a unique window into the lifestyle and the concerns of Mesopotamian royalty (Parrot 1958–1959). The residential apartments for both the royal family and guests are comparable in organization but almost double the size of the largest known houses (Figure 53), and the elaboration of the bathrooms and kitchens are certainly unmatched in such contexts. But palaces are much more than royal residences; large-scale storage areas and administrative quarters were also found. But the heart of the palace lies in the audience hall, the place where the ruler fulfilled his role as the arbiter of justice. The large size of such rooms suggests, to me at least, the modern *mudhif*, the tribal guest house where the sheikh performs a very similar role. If this analogy can be drawn, then royal judgments would have been made in public, making acts of favoritism or revenge difficult. Such a process would be in

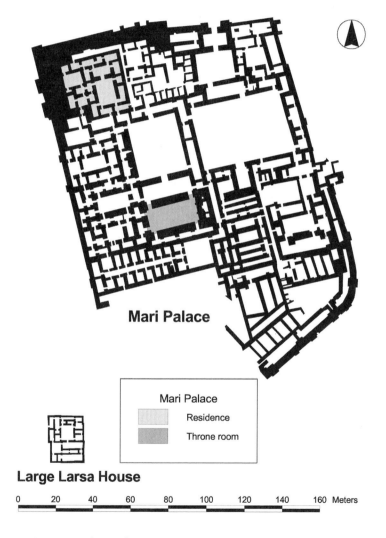

Figure 53. Mari Palace (after Margueron 1982: fig. 148). A large house from Larsa is included for comparison (after Calvet 1996: fig. 7).

keeping with more recent assessments of royal power in Mesopotamia. Our written sources tell us that the king was chosen by the gods from the broad citizenry of the city—this in the face of numerous, short-lived royal lineages. They also demonstrate that he was expected to maintain the peace, stabilize the economy, satisfy the gods, and protect the weak from the strong. Postgate (1992: 269–270) has suggested that the city assembly may have been the means by which the gods indicated their choice. If so, this would also be similar to the way in which new tribal sheikhs are chosen—or were before the British registered all land in Iraq in the name of the then sheikh (Fernea 1970: 105–106). Local governors, of course, were appointed by the king, but it seems probable that such appointments must have followed a process similar to that used to choose village or neighborhood leaders, which in both ancient Mesopotamian (van de Mieroop 1997: 232) and medieval Islamic times (Lapidus 1984: 92) involved some combination of election from within and appointment from above.

The kings, governors, and other royal servants were by no means the only institutional forces within Mesopotamian cities. Every city had one or two temples dedicated to the city god or gods and numerous other smaller religious establishments. The latter varied in size from tiny shrines tucked away within the residential matrix to large important temples, such as that excavated at Ischali (Hill, Jacobsen, and Delougaz 1990). The rich textual record from the Inanna Temple at Nippur (Hallo 1972; Zettler 1984; 1987; 1992) and the Ischali Temple (Greengus 1979; 1986) suggests that, like other aspects of Mesopotamian society, kinship relations were critical. The important offices in the Inanna Temple were held by members of a single family who also played an important role in the Temple of Enlil, the temple dedicated to the city god. Richard Zettler (1992: 82–86) argues that this family was resident within the Inanna Temple, and he has identified that residential zone. Similar residences associated with temples are also known from earlier examples, such as the house attached to the Temple Oval at Khafajah (Delougaz 1940). But, whereas the Khafajah residence is almost double the size of the largest known domestic structure, the residential apartments in the less important Inanna Temple (Zettler 1992) and in the temple at Tell Agrab (Delougaz and Lloyd 1942: 261–265) are comparable in size and organization to the average house (Figure 54).

Temples seem to have been the main landowners in ancient Mesopotamian cities, and they managed these lands through a mixture of land grants to officeholders and the provision of "rations." Those who received rations used to be described as a semi-free component of society (Gelb 1965), but today the term used, *gurush*, is now translated simply as "man" (Steinkeller 1987a; Waetzoldt 1987); and since the monthly payments of 60 liters of barley are

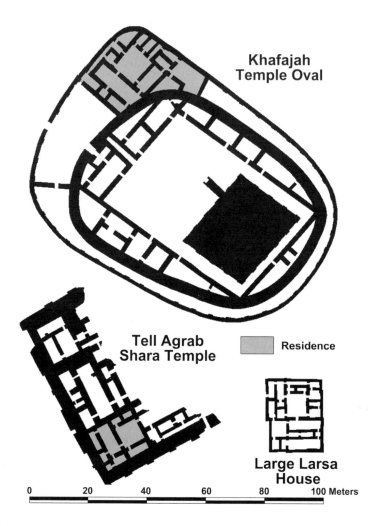

Figure 54. Residential areas within the Temple Oval at Khafajah (after Delougaz 1940: pl. III), and within the Shara Temple at Tell Agrab (after Delougaz and Lloyd 1942: pl. 26).

more than double the basic subsistence needs, perhaps the term "salary" would better identify the economic position of the *gurush*.

Adams long ago pointed out that communal management of agricultural land is the optimal way to handle the Mesopotamian environment (Adams 1978). Data from 1950s Iraq make clear that small farm owners were considerably worse off than the sharecroppers or tribal groups who operated where the landowners or sheikhs provided large-scale management (Poyck 1952). Thus, the role played by the temples, and to a lesser extent the palaces, in managing agricultural land should be seen not so much as indicating an exploitative economic system than as the most efficient means of promoting economic well-being.

URBAN PLANNING

Now that we have the building blocks of Mesopotamian urban centers, it is time to come to grips with a picture of the city itself. Here we will turn to the intrasite surveys that were conducted to answer some of the questions on urban organization that Adams's regional surveys tackled for overall settlement on the Mesopotamian plain. A number of such surveys have been conducted: the program of surface scraping and sample excavations at Abu Salabikh (R. Matthews, Postgate, and Luby 1987; W. Matthews et al. 1994; Postgate 1977; 1978; 1980; 1982; 1983; 1990; 1994; Postgate and Moorey 1976; Postgate and Moon 1982; 1984), the intensive surface and aerial survey at Mashkan-shapir (E. C. Stone and Zimansky 1995; 2004), the less detailed surveys at Larsa (Huot, Rougeulle, and Suire 1989) and el-Hiba (E. Carter 1990), and the surveys of settlement area over time conducted at Uruk (Finkbeiner 1991) and Nippur (Gibson 1992).

Since our work at Mashkan-shapir was specifically designed to provide a general view of that Mesopotamian city (Figure 55), I will focus on that project here, using data from the other surveys as appropriate. The most striking aspect of this survey was that it showed the degree to which Mesopotamian cities were broken up into different sectors, both by canals and by internal walls. Similar canals can be seen in the aerial data from Larsa (Huot, Rougeulle, and Suire 1989)[1] and Uruk (Becker and Fassbinder 2001) and are clearly visible as undisturbed areas in the recent helicopter photographs of looted urban sites in southern Iraq. In the Mashkan-shapir aerial photographs, internal walls can be identified separating administrative and cemetery areas from the residential districts (E. C. Stone and Zimansky 2004: 325). Similar walls were seen between residential districts in the course of surface scraping on the much earlier West Mound at Abu Salabikh (Postgate 1983: fig. 354), and surrounding the residential district attached to the Temple Oval at Khafajah (Delougaz, Hill, and Lloyd 1967: pl. 14). The internal canals—which resulted in the multi-moundedness characteristic of Mesopotamian urban sites—together with these walls served to divide the cities into a number of sectors. Moreover, the areas that housed the main temples and the administrative or palace sector are usually on the periphery of the cities and not in the

---

[1] Huot and his colleagues (1989) describe these as streets, but not only do they resemble canals identified elsewhere, but an examination of SPOT and CORONA imagery of the area around Larsa shows them continuing beyond the city as canals.

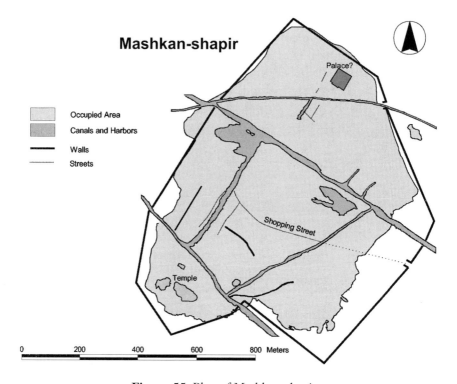

Figure 55. Plan of Mashkan-shapir.

center (E. C. Stone 1995: 238–239), such that the residential districts lay at the heart of the Mesopotamian city.[2]

These broad surveys have also allowed us to test the impression provided by excavated house areas that they were not segregated by wealth and power but rather reflected different kinship or occupational groups (E. C. Stone 1981; 1987). Objects that can be associated with wealth and power—such as the Mesopotamian badges of office, cylinder seals, and the key imported item, copper/bronze—are found in all parts of Mashkan-shapir and are not concentrated in only a few areas (E. C. Stone and Zimansky 2004: 343, 358). Moreover, the large amount of copper/bronze recovered from the surface of Mashkan-shapir suggests an overall level of wealth. A total of more than 6

---

[2] In our work at Mashkan-shapir, we identified the western part of the site as an administrative zone on the basis of the sealings found in our excavations there (E. C. Stone and Zimansky 2004). However, a recent Digital Globe Quickbird image, taken now that the area has been irrigated and salinized, identifies a large, 50-meter square public building in the far north of the site (see Figure 67) that bears a strong resemblance to the contemporary palace excavated at Larsa (Margueron 1982: fig. 260).

kilograms of copper alloy was recovered from the surface of the site, compared with only 32 chipped stone tools (E. C. Stone and Zimansky 2004: 127). Since the site has a fourth-millennium component from which the stone tools may well have derived, these data present an overwhelming case to suggest that *all* inhabitants of second-millennium Mashkan-shapir, be they ever so humble, had access to metal for tools.

Another feature of the survey data—again including the distribution of metals and metal slags—is the light it sheds on the activity of artisans, an arena poorly documented in the written record. It is clear that most artisans were private, although some could be contracted by the large institutions, but we have little further documentation of their activities.

The first pattern identifiable in all intrasite survey data is the concentration of smokestack industries, especially ceramic production. Mashkan-shapir (E. C. Stone and Zimansky 2004: 340–341), Abu Salabikh (Postgate 1990: 103–104), Larsa (Huot, Rougeulle, and Suire 1989: 51), and el-Hiba (E. Carter 1990) all evidence areas where pottery production, and perhaps other pyrotechnic activities, were concentrated. But perhaps the most intriguing aspect of the Mashkan-shapir survey is the distribution of small concentrations of copper fragments and copper slag, almost certainly indicators of the presence of small smithies. Although one or two are found elsewhere, most are located along the main east–west street that runs across the center of the site to the large eastern gate (E. C. Stone and Zimansky 2004: 342). These data, together with evidence recorded in the texts that artisans in different crafts tended to be neighbors, might suggest that Mesopotamian cities had an ancient equivalent of "Main Street," with only the copper workshops leaving identifiable surface indications. The central location of this street might suggest that in ancient Mesopotamian cities, as in the later Islamic examples, their precursor of the *suq* also lay at the heart of the city.

The last question that may be solved by the survey data is the identification of places for the exchange of goods. Written sources, especially from early second-millennium Sippar (A. L. Oppenheim 1969: 12), suggest the presence of squares located close to city gates as the primary locus of trade and exchange. We also know that groups of foreign merchants, organized into a guild-like structure, lived in Mesopotamian cities and were associated with the *karum*, or city quay, which may or may not have been located within the city walls.

A number of city gates have been identified at both Mashkan-shapir (E. C. Stone and Zimansky 2004: 376) and Larsa (Huot, Rougeulle, and Suire 1989: fig. 9a). Perhaps the absence of dense settlement at Mashkan-shapir in the vicinity of the eastern end of the main street and (already discussed) may indicate the locus of one of the squares mentioned in the texts. But at Mashkan-shapir, Ur, and Uruk, there are also intramural harbors associated with the canal system (E. C. Stone and Zimansky 2004: 376; Woolley and Mallowan 1976: pl. 116; Margarete Van Ess, personal communication), and the aerial photographs of Larsa (Huot, Rougeulle, and Suire 1989: 22) suggest that there was at least one there also. It seems likely that these harbors must have played some role in trade and exchange.

MESOPOTAMIAN CITIES

How, then, can we draw together these data on the Mesopotamian city? The typical Mesopotamian family would have consisted of a male head of household, his wife, sons, their wives and children, and unmarried daughters. The family would have been supported by the ownership of a small orchard plot and/or officeholding and/or work as artisans. I suggest that the grown sons, who had no independent economic existence until their father died, might have been those listed as receiving rations from the temple or palace. Put a pig in the courtyard and the family should have been able to afford to acquire the pottery, grinding stones, terracotta plaques, and copper/bronze tools which are so ubiquitous a feature of residential districts.

There is only rare evidence for political competition within the family—and that is mostly between brothers following the family's breakup occasioned by the death of the father—but such competition existed at all other levels within the city. The heads of households would have been engaged in a struggle for dominance in the neighborhood and in the larger urban assemblies, with kinship, clientage, and possibly even scribal education (as was the case in later Islamic cities) all playing a role. Rivalry also existed between the private sector and the public sector and, in at least some instances, between the temple and the palace. Beyond the urban framework, contention between city-states was rampant during the early to mid-third millennium and certainly played a significant role in the interregna between the times when Agade, Ur, and Babylon dominated the southern plain. But even during times of secure imperial rule, it seems likely that the city-states still competed over the general population, tempting some to change allegiance by building new canals and opening up new land. I would argue that it was this competition over people and resources that drove the high levels of social mobility seen in our texts and which resulted in the lack of evidence for extreme poverty and exploitation visible in either the textual or archaeological record. Apart from the slaves, who never formed a large sector of the population, people could vote with their feet. The evidence that they did so is seen both in the pattern of shifting settlement documented by Adams in his regional surveys, and by the evidence for changes in urban density and occupation documented for Nippur and Uruk, the two long-lived sites where such surveys were carried out. When things worked well, this process served to make

Mesopotamian cities some of the wealthiest and most successful in the ancient world, but if competition among elites resulted in an abandonment of their obligations to their clients and kinsmen, urban flight by the latter was the likely result. It seems probable that a combination of these factors and long-term degradation of arable land led to the periods of turmoil that intervened between the prosperity associated with the Akkadian, Ur III, and Old Babylonian periods.

CITIES AND HINTERLANDS

But, as seen so clearly in Adams's surveys, Mesopotamian cities, with their houses and neighborhoods, administrative centers and temples, artisans and merchants, did not exist in a vacuum; the rural hinterland was replete with settlements varying in size from small towns to hamlets. Our difficulty, of course, is that most of these have remained unexcavated, and some of the smallest settlements—probably those where reed huts rather than mud-brick houses dominated—could not be identified in the regional surveys. But we do have two early second-millennium village-sized sites, both less than 2 hectares in size, which have been largely excavated: Tell Harmal (Baqir 1946; 1959) and Haradum (Kepinski-Lecomte 1992). Both are surrounded by walls, both have administrative buildings, temples, and workshop areas, and both have houses containing tablets indicating both literacy and the same kinds of economic concerns as the contemporary urban residents (Figure 56). Their house patterns differ slightly in that they lack both the rare, very large houses and the very small houses found in the urban districts. But a comparison of object classes from Haradum and Mashkan-shapir shows that the only types of objects found in the latter and absent in the former are the inscribed nails and cylinders that testify to royal building projects at Mashkan-shapir.

The data from Haradum and Tell Harmal—and indeed also from the somewhat larger Tell Mohammed (about 10 hectares; Metab 1989–1990) and Tell edh-Dhubai (4 hectares, Hammoudi 1989–1990)—which include numerous cuneiform tablets, suggest that the rural landscape of Mesopotamia, at least in the early second millennium, was much more complex than had been previously thought. The question remains whether these represent a momentary spread of literacy and urban ideals to the rural hinterland, or if, as suggested by Steinkeller's article in this volume, instead we should consider the many small sites identified by Adams as representing not so much peasant village life, but rather a rich tapestry of settlement types, some as elaborate as palaces and temples, a complexity already suggested by Adams's (1981: 77–80) review of surface indications of manufacturing and other debris from Uruk-period sites. Until now, excavation has been the only way to identify the internal workings of Mesopotamian archaeological sites, and

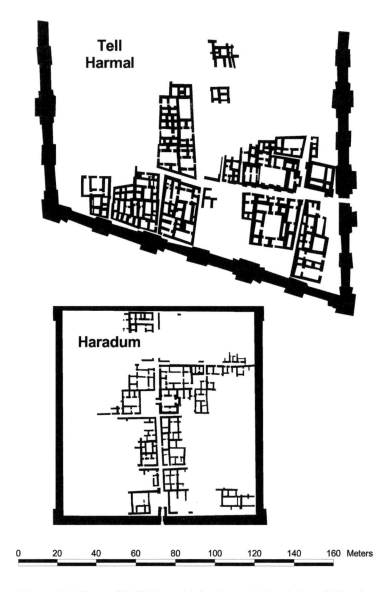

Figure 56. Plans of Tell Harmal (after Baqir 1946: pl. 1) and Haradum (after Lepinski-Lecomte 1992: pl. V).

few small sites have been judged to merit such investigation. Recent commercially available satellite imagery may now change all this. Digital Globe images, with their 0.60-meter resolution and good saturation in desert areas, often record details of ancient fortifications, internal canals and harbors, and even whole building plans within archaeological sites.

So far we have had access to only two small images, one of the area around Mashkan-shapir and one of the northern portion of the Eridu Survey area (H. T. Wright 1981b), which also includes areas not covered in the survey. Architectural traces are preserved in the now-irrigated Mashkan-shapir area as a result of rising salts in mud-brick walls. In the Eridu area, they are very clear at some sites because, we believe, they were destroyed by fire.[3] In the Mashkan-shapir area, in addition to architectural details visible at Mashkan-shapir itself, two of the small Partho-Sasanian sites in the area seem to have consisted of perhaps no more than a single large building (Figure 57). In the Eridu area, not only can we map all of Eridu survey Site 34, a 60-odd-hectare site dating to the early second millennium (Figure 58), but two other sites in the vicinity show similar traces.[4] One is a 5-hectare site which consists of a main mound organized on a grid pattern like Haradum, but with two subsidiary mounds, at least one of which seems to have included a substantial public building (Figure 59). The other is a tiny site, less than a half hectare in size, dominated by a 20 × 30 meter courtyard building and surrounded by a wall and probably a moat (Figure 60). None of these sites resemble the agricultural villages that dot modern Iraq and that have, consciously or unconsciously, served as our models for their ancient counterparts.

These data support the conclusion that, just as the population of Mesopotamian cities seems to have been very agrarian, with well over 50 percent of the population making their living through agriculture, so too does the rural sector look very urban. Indeed, I will close with the suggestion that Mesopotamian households, and the neighborhoods or villages that they form, were the real building blocks of society, but it was the ability of the urban centers to provide both a larger political arena and an efficient resource base that led to their popularity. Such a view amplifies the Adams's (1978) argument that the rural sector of Mesopotamia offered a degree of resilience necessary for providing continuity in Mesopotamian civilization in the face of the boom and bust economies of the larger cities. This resilience is most easily effected when the elements necessary for urban life are also part of rural existence.

---

[3] I was able to visit Eridu Survey Site 34 in May 2003, and both the surface and the sections of looting holes exhibited clear signs of burning.

[4] It seems likely that these two sites date to the same period as Site 34, but this cannot be established without collecting sherds from their surfaces. However, although these are located beyond the Eridu survey area, it is clear that they were on a river system that was active during the early second millennium. Whether water flowed there at other times is less clear.

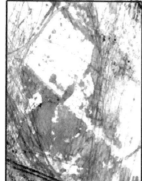

Figure 57. Digital Globe imagery, taken July 31, 2003, in the Mashkan-shapir area. Sites with traces of architecture outlined by salt concentrations include Sites 637 (top), 641 (left), and 639 (right, now identified as ancient Mashkan-shapir). See Adams 1981.

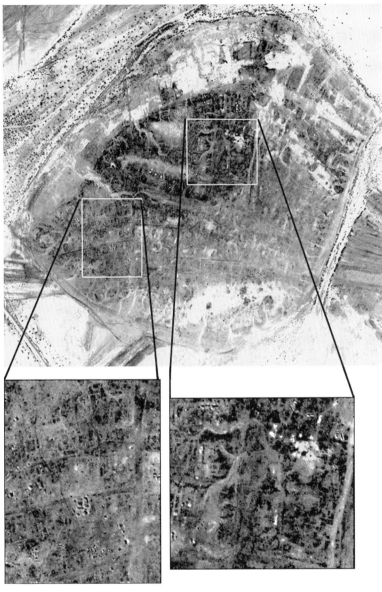

Figure 58. Digital Globe imagery, taken February 9, 2003, of Eridu survey Site 34 (H. T. Wright 1981b), perhaps to be called Tell Dahalia.

Figure 59. Digital Globe imagery, taken February 9, 2003, of the area just to the north of the Eridu survey (H. T. Wright 1981b). The main mound of this site is some 4 hectares in size.

Figure 60. Digital Globe imagery, taken February 9, 2003, of a site less than a half hectare in size in the area just to the north of the Eridu survey (H. T. Wright 1981b).

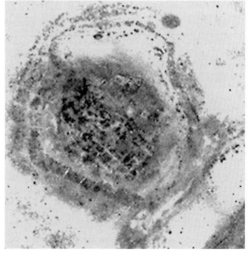

THE ARCHAEOLOGY OF EARLY ADMINISTRATIVE SYSTEMS IN MESOPOTAMIA[*]

MITCHELL S. ROTHMAN

ABSTRACT

One of the key problems addressed by anthropological archaeologists over the past three or four decades is the origin of societal complexity, especially as represented in the so-called primary and secondary state. In many ways, Adams catalyzed this search with his groundbreaking work, The Evolution of Urban Society, in 1966. Those studying this evolution do not always agree on how best to understand it. Some, like Henry Wright, argue that the scale on which we must measure cultural evolution itself consists of the decision-making mechanisms or the administrative core of increasingly complex societies. Others emphasize the broader social and environmental conditions under which broad social changes occur. All agree that we need to find a means to investigate the administration of evolving ancient societies. This article reviews some of those theoretical approaches to studying the origin of ancient societal and administrative development. Utilizing examples from Tepe Gawra and Arslantepe, it describes attempts by anthropological archaeologists to use the information content of seals and the earliest writing to discover the origin, elaboration, and functioning of administrative organizations. The origin and role of earliest writing systems are also briefly discussed in this context.

---

[*] The degree to which I have been able to understand the evolution of complex societies in Mesopotamia and beyond, and to recover and to apply archaeological data to this class of problems, is related to the wisdom and experience shared with me by my teachers: Henry Wright, Kent Flannery, and Robert Dyson, Jr. Although I have met Adams only a few times, I count him as one of my teachers, because again and again I find the words of his articles stay with me as guideposts.

INTRODUCTION

The goal of archaeology in the latter part of the twentieth century was to understand cultural and societal evolution per se. This is very different from the goal of archaeology and anthropology a hundred years ago, when the West was in the midst of its age of colonial expansion. In the earlier part of the twentieth century, archaeological fieldworkers were concerned with documenting ancient human cultures as a way to find proof of a progressive ascent to civilization. Often, archaeology in the Classical or biblical worlds was intended to show how the foundation of Western civilization was undergirded. Artifacts as relics and cultures as units defined by commonalities of artifact style were the foci of investigation for most of this past century (Childe 1929).

Specifically, the focus of archaeology in the late twentieth century was the evolution of organization and group behavior. As Fred Plog wrote a quarter-century ago, "For me the critical component of the concept of organizational change is the term organization. Organization refers to the components of a system and the interaction between the components. In this sense, human behavior at all levels—individual, group, and societal—is organized" (Plog 1977: 24).

A number of hallmarks or trends have marked change not only in degree, but also in the kinds of organizations that evolved. One of those hallmarks is the beginning of urbanization and the state, subjects in which Adams has been a pioneer.

SEALS, SEALINGS, AND TABLETS

Within the broad scholarly concern with urbanization and the state, the core issue has been to understand the administrative organization of both urban systems and state societies. However, anthropologists realized that administrative organization must also be understood in the larger cultural context of social stratification, broader power relationships, economic production and exchange, and ideology, all within a regional framework (see, for example, Algaze 1993a; Adams 1974b; 1981; Hole 1983; H. T. Wright 1969).

Among the data sources tapped for analysis of administration in the ancient Near East are seals, sealings, and writing systems. Early scholarship on seals and sealings in the Near East reflects the earlier concern with culture history and progressive cultural change. In Henri Frankfort's groundbreaking book, *Cylinder Seals*, he reflects that earlier orientation (Frankfort 1939a). The titles of the chapters of that book are "The Achievement of the Uruk Period," "The Decline of the Jemdet Nasr Period," "The Stylistic Development of Early Dynastic Glyptic," "Subjects of Early Dynastic Seals," and so forth. Even the chapters on the subjects of the seals are merely description of subjects and analysis of their renderings, not an attempt to make sense of how and why those images were used by particular individuals or the organizations they represented. Interestingly, seals are seen as a primary way to understand ancient religious ideology. Stylistic similarities in seal design are more important than the use of seals. Writing, beginning with cuneiform on clay tablets, is merely one more trait on the list of the requirements necessary to be included on the honor roll of "civilizations."

In the remainder of this paper, I discuss the attempts by anthropological archaeologists to use the information content of seals and the earliest writing to discover the origin, elaboration, and functioning of administrative organizations. That discussion, of necessity, will require some analysis of the theoretical problems of and perspectives on understanding ancient complex society. The geographical focus is Mesopotamia, and the temporal focus is the sixth through the very early third millennium BC—that is, prehistoric times.

Seals were used to impress clay as early as the late Neolithic period (roughly the eighth–seventh millennia BC). Seals and their clay sealings functioned to restrict access to goods or raw materials locked in jars, boxes, baskets, sacks, or rooms (Ferioli and Fiandra 1979; 1983; 1994; Rothman 1994a; 1994b). Much later, after writing became the primary administrative tool, seals were still used to convey authentication of authority on messages, much as a signature does today. Seals as objects were also used in religious and magical practices and were occasionally buried with their owners. Ancients valued them and their designs as reflections of ethnic, religious, and other forms of identity, although that subject is tangential to this paper.

Writing in Mesopotamia was intimately associated with administration. There can be little doubt that at its earliest appearance, writing was utilized as a more information-rich version of the system of the seals and sealings used before its invention (Nissen, Damerow, and Englund 1993). The system of writing, once invented, quickly developed other uses, from recording political propaganda, myths, literary genres, religious rituals, and divinatory texts to writing private letters and leaders' orders to subordinates. However, it is the origin of writing specifically in administration that is of interest here.

Before seeing how these administrative data have been interpreted, and what the future might hold for these data sets, the theoretical question of how we understand administration within a society must be addressed.

STUDYING ADMINISTRATION IN COMPLEX SOCIETY

Ethnographers and ethnologists see three basic modes or forms of social organization: kinship, community, and administration. "Kinship structures define boundaries of membership by relationships of marriage and parentage.

. . . Community structures define boundaries of membership primarily by common residence in a territory (or, metaphorically, by common adherence to a profession). . . . Administrative structures define boundaries of membership largely by contract (as in bureaucracy) or by traditional claims to personal service . . . and depend on a hierarchical branching structure of super- and subordination to channel communication downward of plans and upward of reports" (Wallace 1971: 1). Clearly, Wright and Johnson's definition of the state fits Wallace's definition of an administrative form of social organization: "[A] state . . . will be defined as a society which is primarily regulated through a differentiated and internally specialized decision making organization which is structured in minimally three hierarchical levels, with institutionalized provision for the operation and maintenance of this organization and implementation of its decisions" (Johnson 1973: 2). Although Adams finds the use of concepts of administrative organization like those of Wright and Johnson limiting in their explanatory power, he does see a qualitative change in the organization of the first true cities of fourth-millennium BC Mesopotamia such as Uruk-Warka. He writes, "Status display, ritual, and administrative requirements surely reached their highest levels [in the late fourth millennium BC]—always remembering that the three were 'embedded' in one another rather than differentiated" (Adams 1981: 80).

Efforts to understand evolutionary change in Mesopotamia and elsewhere, particularly in terms of the origin of administrative forms of social organization, have proven difficult and controversial (Feinman and Neitzel 1994; McGuire 1983; Yoffee 1993a). Administrative forms of social organization and their evolution are more varied, complex, and harder to unravel than the earlier ideas of civilization with their trait lists of kingship, bureaucracy, monumentality, writing, and the like. The goal of unraveling the evolution of state society itself has given way to that of understanding the functioning of state institutions within particular societies over the long term (G. Stein 1998: 10), an approach that Adams had proposed a decade earlier (Adams 1988).

In order to discover the nature of administrative forms of social organization and the processes of change that led toward increasing elaboration of such forms, we must first understand how administrative structures articulate with the rest of the organizational systems of a society. As a number of scholars have asserted, administrative organizations are but one of a number of sometimes competing, and sometimes cooperating, institutions. Stone has made the point that the administrative core of the city is but one modality for organizing behavior (E. C. Stone and Zimansky 1995). Certainly, there is evidence of all three forms of organization—kinship, community, and administrative—in ancient Mesopotamia from 3500 BC even to today. For example, the administrative core of ancient southern Mesopotamia was defined by the institutions of palace and temple. However, the ancient city had some sort of citizens' council as well. This early organization, "[c]onstituted as an assembly, the community of citizens, though as a rule [made up of] only the old, rich, and privileged [citizens], administered the city under a presiding official" (A. L. Oppenheim 1977: 111–112). This was not a democracy like the town meetings of New England, but was distinct from the institutions of kingship and state religion, yet not totally independent of them. It was also distinct from clearly kinship-organized clans or lineages inside, and even more outside, the city. To further complicate the issue, some social groups, especially among food producers, moved from one organizational and residential pattern to another in times of political or economic disruption. To survive the crises that arose in the many cyclical periods of consolidation and decline, individuals had to be resilient. They moved in and out of the administrative or community-based structures found in the urban areas (Adams 1978).

The distinction here is encapsulated by the idea of "heterogeneity" (G. Stein 1998). "While hierarchy undoubtedly characterizes power relations in some societies, it is equally true that coalitions, federations, and other examples of shared or counterpoised power abound" (Crumley 1995: 3). Even within the confines of a society typified by administrative forms of social organization, there can be a series of different administrative organizations. Where these types of organization existed, they may also have had different goals and different strategies, even if in some sense they were at the same level of administrative elaboration. This idea of different goal-oriented types of organization is called "dual evolution" (Blanton et al. 1996). It has been has been applied with mixed results to early Mesopotamian administrative organizations (Rothman and Peasnall 1999). It states that there are broadly two sets of goals and their concomitant strategies used by administrative organizations: corporate, on the one hand, or exclusionary and network, on the other hand. In corporate strategies, the administrative organization is a necessary coordinating or regulating body that is nonetheless dedicated to the common good rather than taking advantage on behalf of its own socially and economically stratified members. An exclusionary or network strategy emphasizes the amassing of status, privilege, wealth, and political power for a limited "elite" group, in part by reaching beyond their political boundaries to establish economic relations of direct benefit to their in-group and in part by mobilizing the labor of their local population. Another, in my mind, similar approach is Flannery's idea of "system-serving" versus "self-serving" orientations (Flannery 1972; Frangipane 2000).

So where do we stand theoretically on the issues of the origin and operation of administrative forms of social organization, and how do we begin to analyze the data? Going back to basics, when we talk about administrative forms of social organization, we are clearly talking about polities, and beyond those, regions. Whatever one's opinion of the utility of world systems theory as it is applied to ancient societies, it has shown us that we must understand the structure and function of societies, particularly their economic administration, in terms of the broadest geographical reach of their economic and political systems (Algaze 1993a). Certainly, we must heed the words of Adams (1974b), Feinman (1994), Blanton et al. (1996), Chase-Dunn and Hall (1991), and others that the scale of polities and their boundaries must be specified, because those related factors have a determinative effect on transformations in organizational forms and arrangements.

A second and probably the most important factor to understand is that of function. It is clear that no administrative organization controls all activities or even a large proportion of the activities engaged in by the members of any society or region. Each administrative, community, or kinship organization is created as the answer to specific needs and continues or is modified as those needs change (Nissen 2001). Their particular structure must, at least initially, be based on the requirements of coordinating or regulating a specific set of functions. That list of functions can be expanded or contracted over time, as conditions change or as the organizational and technical abilities of various social mechanisms become elaborated and administrators strive to expand their sphere of control. This factor is directly relevant to sorting out what the relationships are among various heterarchically arrayed organizations and groups.

A third factor is the nature of the leadership. To the degree that there are hierarchies, how are they structured? How is authority expressed and reinforced within the group? Are the primary means of legitimization economic, political, religious, or social? Wallace proposes that every administrative organization, however simple, has three elements: "the owners on whose behalf and under whose auspices certain work is done; a target population, for whom or upon whom the work is done; and the administrative organization proper, which is the action group. In general these three groups overlap in personnel" (Wallace 1971: 1–2). We have tended to talk in very general terms about "elites," but as owners, how are they positioned vis-à-vis the action group? Are they the same as the action group, or do they control the action group? Certainly, the sometimes cooperative and sometimes confrontational relationship between government and business in the current day illustrates both the complexity and the potential explanatory power of viewing these groups as analytically separate, however intertwined they seem.

ARCHAEOLOGICAL INVESTIGATION

The archaeological investigation of administrative forms of social organization as social phenomena, particularly those of states, actually began in the latter part of the twentieth century through regional surveys, not with seals or writing. Adams's surveys in some part were seen, though not planned, as an attempt to explore Wittfogel's idea that irrigation management was the vehicle through which strong, centralized, in Wittfogel's terms "despotic" administrations evolved (Wittfogel 1981). Wright, who more than anyone championed the idea that the state was essentially a decision-making, administrative body controlling economic activity, began his search by trying to get inside the administrative core of Mesopotamian societies (H. T. Wright 1969). In his dissertation, he wanted to explain the relationship between food production and administrative control mechanisms. In part, he explicitly set out to understand Adams's rejection of Wittfogel's theory and Sander's whole-hearted acceptance of it (H. T. Wright 1969: 1).

That early work, following Adams's survey in Iran, was extended to the Susiana plains. Wright and his student, Greg Johnson, found in the literature of economic geography a way to apply the theory of state as a hierarchical, information-processing agency to site distribution maps (Wright and Johnson 1975; Johnson 1973; 1980). The idea that a "central place" was the largest and the most administratively important node in a settlement system could then be discovered through survey. If site size hierarchies equaled administrative organization, then a site distribution of central cities, towns, and villages verified the existence of a society that was a state.

Adams still found this formulation of the state as the action group "too narrow" (Adams (1981: 76f). It did not permit one to include religious ritual; it was not specific enough about what was being administered; and it mixed the more general idea of politics, which certainly happens outside of the action group, with the structure of the action group. The axiom that central sites have to be large and that every settlement system with a tri-modal distribution by size represented a three-tiered hierarchy of administration has been questioned (Rothman 2002a: 5–6; and, in fairness, by Henry Wright himself [personal communication]).

Alternative theories on the relationship of irrigation works to administration are also possible. It has been suggested that irrigation may not be important for administrative elaboration because of its managerial requirements. Rather, control of choke points on dendritic irrigation systems gave the "owners" and their action group at centers like Susa a way of promoting an exclusionary strategy (Rothman 1987). The creation of complex, unequal power relationships became an essential cause of administrative elaboration (Yoffee 1995).

If a settlement system approach leaves such questions open, it becomes necessary to delve into the structure and function of the action group itself, as Wright recognized long ago (H. T. Wright 1969). The only way to do so directly is through the two administrative technologies mentioned above: seals and tablets. Of course, these independent variables must be coordinated with other traditional archaeological data, such as evidence of the structure of economic production, variations in social status, scalar stress, religious ideology, and so forth. It has long been assumed that the presence of seals and especially sealings necessarily indicates administration (Figure 61); however, the fact that seals and sealings existed at a period, the Halaf of the sixth millennium BC, that most scholars feel had a fairly simple, barely hierarchical organization, should provide a caution (Pittman 2001; von Wickede 1990). It is not the presence of sealings, but how and in what contexts they were used that is the critical datum. There can be little doubt that over time, what may have originally been a marker of private ownership took on more clearly administrative

Figure 61. Seals and sealings from ancient Mesopotamia.

functions (Ferioli and Fiandra 1979; Fiandra 1979; Frangipane 2000). The overall number of seals and sealings increased. Scholars further discovered that an increasingly formal, administrative system was represented in seal and sealing use as time went on. As early as the 1950s, Leo Oppenheim (1958) recognized that seals were bureaucratic tools, but it was Ferioli and Fiandra (1979) who began the systematic study of their use in administration. It was they who recognized that wherever administrators used sealings as locks, they were retained for audits (Ferioli and Fiandra 1994). Similarly, after tablets came into use *parallel to* (not entirely replacing) sealings, the seal took on the role of verifying the authority of the goods distributor or, in private matters, the recipient (Fiandra 1979: 31). These devices did not merely seal the goods or raw materials against unauthorized access, but were actually counting devices whereby administrators could record inputs of goods and raw materials from particular sources—persons or offices— and also regulate outflows. The development of the bulla or sealed clay ball with counting tokens makes this clear (Figure 62; note the numerical marker holes). This practice was

Sealed bulla with tokens

Godin Tepe Counting Tablet

Accounting tablet with signs

Tablet with cuneiform writing

Figure 62. Bullae, early tablets, and tablets with writing.

nowhere clearer than at Arslantepe (Ferioli and Fiandra 1979; Frangipane 1994; Frangipane and Palmieri 1983), where excavators found clumps of seal-ings in the size and shape of ancient baskets, dumped in an abandoned room of its palace near sealed storerooms (Figure 63:A206).

What, however, was being regulated by the action group? How was the action group structured? For the answers to those questions, it is necessary to map the distribution of seals and sealings against the various activity areas of a site or set of sites. Luckily, such sites exist, covering a critical period of pre- and early development of administrative forms of social organization in northern Mesopotamia.

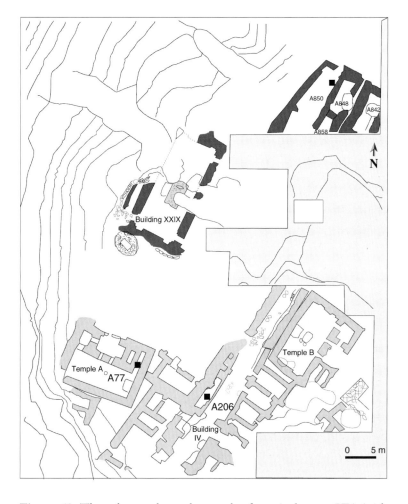

Figure 63. The palace and temple complex from Arslantepe VIA (with the storerooms and sealing dump area marked by filled-in squares).

TEPE GAWRA, ARSLANTEPE, AND THE
FUNCTIONS OF ADMINISTRATIVE ORGANIZATIONS

One site was Tepe Gawra, located not far from the Tigris River in the piedmont of northeastern Iraq (Rothman 2002a). Aside from the number of seals and sealings recovered, its unique advantage is the breadth of its horizontal exposure: 100 percent of Levels VIII–X, 66 percent of XI/XA–XI/A/B, and 50 percent of Level XII.

From Level XII at the intersection of the 'Ubaid and Uruk period levels (ca. 4300 BC, LC 1 in the Santa Fe chronology [Rothman 2001]) to Level VIII, at the beginning of the so-called Uruk Expansion (3700 BC), development and change in the administration of the site is evident. Excavated areas of Level XII include a series of extended family houses, a central storehouse (perhaps for grain), and an area for the sorting, storage, and presumably exchange of craft goods (Rothman 2002a: fig. 5.13). In other words, although the primary organizing principle of the settlement was extended family- or kinship-based, evidence of exchange networks beyond the site, and even beyond the immediate area, is clear (see Frangipane 2000: 226f for comparison). This is demonstrated by the presence of storage areas with manufactured goods, many of which are from materials exotic to the immediate Gawra area. In addition, a recent chemical analysis of sprig ware and what I call impressed bubble ware (Rothman 2002a: 55–56, pls. 7, 9, 13, and 15) indicates that a central manufacturing center or centers of these pottery types existed. Exchanges were conducted between Gawra and, on the one hand, Shelgiyya on the Tigris north of modern Mosul (sprig ware) and, on the other hand, Tell Brak in the Khabur (bubble ware) (Rothman and Blackman 2003). The distribution of seals and sealings, however, is very generalized, covering all functional areas. In other words, there is little that looks like hierarchy or regulation; instead, a corporate or system-sustaining organization on the edge of something new is evidenced. By Phase XI of Level XI/XA (early LC 2), a marked difference in function and organization is evident (Figure 64). A central temple facing out on the countryside indicates a role for the site in its larger polity. Houses as a rule are smaller, and excavators recovered clearly specialized activities in buildings that were obviously not houses. These specialized functions include a dedicated weaving shop, a woodworking shop, and a building with military and social functions. Unlike Level XII, the distribution of seals and sealings in good provenience is limited to the special-function buildings. There also seem to have been some design subjects (predation scenes, lines of herd animals) that are associated with manufacturing, on the one hand, and with religion and chiefly authority, on the other (Rothman 1994a). Levels X and IX (late LC 2) at Gawra reveal a diminution of specialized economic activity and the dominance of Gawra's religious and social—perhaps these are chiefly— functions at this small center. The distribution of seals and sealings, including for the first time an often-repeated single seal (Rothman 2002a: pl. 51, seal

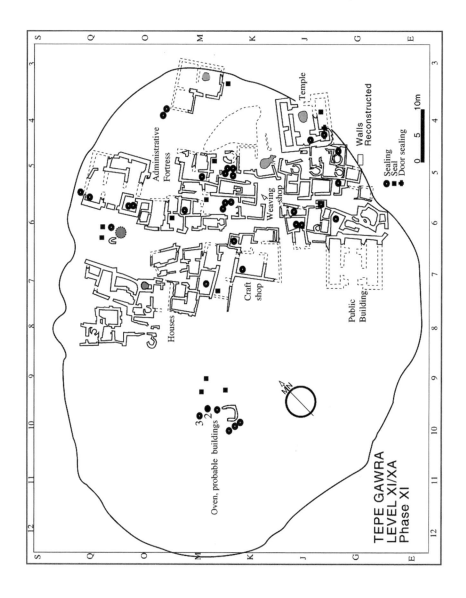

Figure 64.
Distribution of
seals and sealings at
Tepe Gawra, Level
XI/XA, Phase XI
(ca. 4000 BC).

2003), are clustered around those two functions (Rothman 2002a: fig. 5.53). Few seals or sealings were recovered from the clusters of small residences with small-scale craft and domestic activity (Rothman 2002a: fig. 5.53). This suggests that one of the functions of the site nearer the beginning of the fourth millennium later became the catalyst for a newly elaborated administrative structure. That structure would undergo a marked a change in Gawra Level VIII (Figure 65). There, religious and social functions continued, but were isolated on the eastern half of the mound. On its western half, economic production, presumably for exchange—especially exotic obsidian knapping—was revitalized. Residences all but disappeared, leaving only the specialized functions of a center, including a central warehouse. The distribution of seals and sealings reflected this change, including what looks like a new hierarchical level of control associated with a central storehouse. Sealings with the same seal impression of a bull, dog, and snake were recovered from every institution on the mound (Figure 61) but were concentrated near the warehouse (Figure 65). One of these sealings was recovered in two pieces, one found by the warehouse, the other in the temple's side room, as if it were a modern tear-off receipt. In other words, what the distribution of these sealings implies is that central administrators or comptrollers were receiving sealed goods at the warehouse, opening them, repackaging them, and then sending them to each religious, sociopolitical, and economic institution. The comptroller that broke the sealing would keep one piece, and the other piece would be sent to its allotted destination as verification of payment and as a record of the source.

Tepe Gawra burned at the end of Level VIII, now dated to the beginning of the Early Middle Uruk or LC 3 period (ca. 3700 BC). Another site, Arslantepe, continued and became an even more administratively sophisticated center along the Upper Euphrates River near the Taurus Gates.

Arslantepe VIA (Figure 63) represents the apex of administrative development at the end of the fourth millennium (Frangipane and Palmieri 1983; Frangipane 1994; 2000). Although we have only the administrative core—the temple-palace complex—this administrative center was clearly involved in the collection and directed redistribution of staples (goods used for immediate consumption or in exchange for political favors by the "owners" group) obtained as tribute (H. T. Wright 2000). This centralizing trend is represented in large storehouses at the center of sites such as Arslantepe in northern Mesopotamia, as well in Adams's "heartland of cities"—namely, Uruk-Warka and Susa. As Frangipane writes,

> In the later [late fourth millennium] period of economic and political centralization, it was probably the elites who used the clay-sealing control system in their own family environment who then employed it centrally. By doing so, they gave this technology an enormous impetus, enabling it to

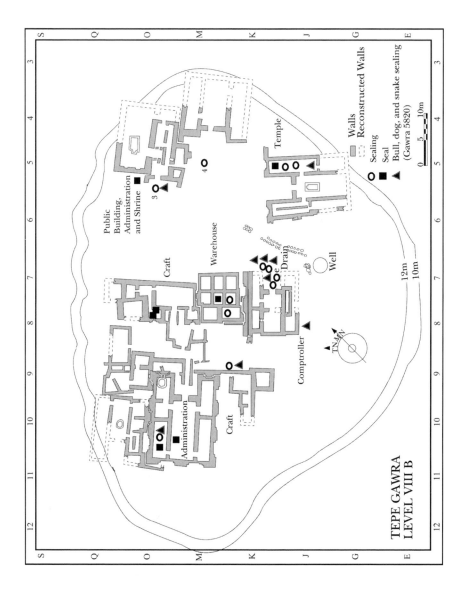

Figure 65.
Distribution of seals and sealings at Tepe Gawra, Level VIII (ca. 3700 BC).

achieve its full potential with the addition of new instruments (spherical bullae, complex tokens, tablets [Figure 62 above]). Evidence of the relation that existed between the adoption of these procedures in the family environment, their particular development in elite contexts, and their further enhancement into the public early state sphere comes not only from the large concentrations, often associated with mass-produced bowls in the Late Uruk centers, like Uruk [Warka] itself, Susa, and Arslantepe, but also from the substantial quantities of these materials found in the residential quarter of elites on the sites of Jebel Aruda [a city of southerners planted in Northern Mesopotamia in the late fourth millennium]. (Frangipane 2000: 228–229)

In the absence of other, contemporary functional areas, we cannot know for certain whether we are seeing the agents or the owners (elites), nor can we know if the ways in which the religious institution coupled with the palace reflect modes or rationales for hierarchical behavior. However, the complexity and efficiency of the Arslantepe VIA sealing system as compared with that of earlier Tepe Gawra shows a marked increase in the power of this simple system of sealing for managing increasingly hierarchically organized polities.

Arslantepe also gives us an unparalleled view of how the administrative system based on sealing worked. The bowls, referred to above by Frangipane, are called variously Beveled Rim Bowls, Wide Flower Pots, or conical bowls. They are quickly produced, roughly fired bowls that have been associated with rations (Johnson 1973; Nissen 1970). Despite other interpretations of their use—they clearly are multipurpose vessels like the various disposable plastic containers of modern times—these types are found in such great numbers and in such proveniences that it is hard to deny that one of their uses was as ration bowls. For example, at Gawra VIIIC, in the so-called West Temple (none of whose contents mark it as a building for religious ritual), field notes speak of stacks of Wide Flower Pots lying in a side room in "decimeters of grain" (Rothman 2002a: 65). The directed redistribution at Arslantepe was carried out through two storerooms in the palace: A340 and A365 (Frangipane 1994). Room A365 was filled with large pithoi but had no sealings, whereas Room A340 had various sized vessels, as well as 200 sealings, sealing clay blanks, and bunches of conical bowls (as well as cooking pots and grinding stones). One room, A365, was surely a storeroom accessible only by officials. They would have restricted access to it by sealing the door peg with clay and stamping it. One whole section of dumped sealings in Room A206, an abandoned room used as a trash dump, are of the door lock type (Ferioli and Fiandra 1994: fig. 6). The other room, A340, was the disbursement station, with large pithoi in one corner and the broken sealings, clay sealing blanks, and the like in another. Those sealings were mostly attached to sacks or basketry and rope originally, which probably means that vessels had been sealed. Among the 220 sealings recovered, 70 had "readable" designs. Of those, only 32 different seals were used. These same designs were found on the top of the Room A206 trash, and only two were found elsewhere on the site. In other words, we are probably seeing the remains of the office of the comptroller of rations. Esin (1994a: 142) demonstrates that the design may match the office rather than an individual person, since the same design is found on different sized seals at Değirmentepe.

The formality of the sealing process is also evident at Arslantepe. Ferioli and Fiandra (1994: 150) demonstrate the step-by-step procedure: First, the seal was impressed on the controlled items in their containers. This probably happened in some central place—a storehouse or other centrally controlled locale. Second, when the items in sealed containers reached their final destination, an authorized official removed the sealings and placed them in a container. That this happens is clear from the Room A206 dump, in which sealings are not scattered randomly but appear to have been dumped in rounded clusters. From later, historic times, we know that documents of certain types were placed in baskets with a subject sealing tag. Third, these containers were removed to another location for auditing, as demonstrated by the auditing rooms found at Mari and Hamad in Syria. Finally, after the audits the sealings were discarded. In Wright's terms, we certainly are seeing at least three hierarchical levels of control represented in this system: the initial sealers, the disbursement department, and the head of the organization who sets the policies on what is to be collected from whom and what is then to be redistributed to others.

Clearly, when we look at how administrative hardware correlates with function, we have a powerful way to see a variety of organizations, their purpose, and their structure. The other sources of inside information on administrative organization and functions lie in two other elements of seals and sealings: design and shape. There can be no doubt that if we understood how the iconography of seal design relates to institutions, occupations, status, place, ethnicity, and so forth, we would be much closer to the understanding of the variability in this behavior (Rothman 2002b).

MESSAGE CODES AND WRITING

That such codes clearly are contained in seal designs is further evidenced by Winter's (1987) work with Ur III royal seals of the late third and early second millennia. She was able to show that slight variations in design—such as how many horns a god had or whether the human was introduced to a god through an intermediary—signal the rank of the sender/sealer within the palace. These subtle variations in design are comprehensible to officials far from the capital and those not in face-to-face contact. Common people would have had no idea what these variations meant, only that this was from a royal source and that they should therefore keep their hands off. Nissen proposes that the change in the shape of seals from the earlier stamp to the later cylinder had a similar goal:

> [The cylinder seal] allowed the entire surface to be imprinted, making it very obvious from a short glimpse whether the fastener had been tampered with. In other words, when stamp seals were used, protection was tied to the general familiarity with everyone who used a seal—and a high degree of familiarity is characteristic of small groups. In contrast, the new kind of protection was an impersonal one. . . . The appearance of cylinder seals indicates that more people than before were engaged in economic life. (Nissen 2000: 212)

Going back to questions of administrative structure and complexity, these innovations certainly indicate a new scale in the geographical area administered by leadership groups. It also indicates that regulating a more complex series of tasks in that wider area of necessity requires increases in administrative hierarchy, that is, new levels of bureaucracy to monitor other bureaucrats.

The coming of tablets at the very end of the fourth millennium or the beginning of the third millennium in southern Mesopotamia marked a period of transition. In terms of its initial appearance, "writing" did not represent a quantum leap, but a logical next step (Fiandra 1979). Note, for example, the similarity between the early tablet and the bulla shown in Figure 62. The information contained in bullae was now put into a more compact and more easily archived form.

The question of whether these earliest tablets are writing is a topic of debate. Schmandt-Besserat (1992) argues that the system of writing that emerged in or about Uruk-Warka IV—the very end of the fourth millennium—was a natural outcome of the use of bullae. She has found many small object-shaped clay pieces that, she argues, are the glosses of the earliest pictographic images on tablets. Although Nissen (1986a) argues that the dating of the Uruk-Warka tablets is far from firm, he, too, sees that the cuneiform-based system of rendering these images developed over a period of time from earlier administrative forms. However, Lieberman (1980) points to problems with Schmandt-Besserat's analysis. Among his points are that many of the tokens that were shaped like later pictographs are pierced like beads, and that the tokens actually found in bullae do not look like the pictograph-shaped tokens. Those that have been seen in situ, largely by using X-rays of intact bullae, include pyramidal, disk, and round shapes. These are the shapes of numbers impressed on the outside of bullae and early tablets. Almost none of the more complex "pictograph" tokens have been found inside bullae.

To my way of thinking, writing is defined as the recording of natural speech. "The Uruk IV script was, then, a completely new communicative device that did not render language but was related to it in a distant way" (Michalowski 1990: 59). For the topic of understanding administration, however, whether it is writing or not is of secondary importance.

Whether writing in the strict sense or not, Nissen (2001) has argued that tablets, as well as all of the other administrative tools invented throughout the fourth millennium, served very specific needs. "It is agreed that writing is an outcome of the new arrangements of labor and management within late Uruk city-states. However, whereas Schmandt-Besserat holds that writing was but a small step in the use of tokens to record goods, Michalowski—harkening to the very idea Schmandt-Besserat claims to refute—contends that writing was an invention, a complete transformation of methods of communication and record keeping" (Yoffee 1995: 286).

These tablets are of great interest to us: why they were invented, how they were used, and what they can tell us about administrative structure and function are all questions that concern us. However, one caveat is necessary. Perhaps more so than at any later time, Uruk IV and related Susa tablets reflect not the heterogeneous nature of society, but only its core political institutions and administrative practices. What we find in them are records of disbursement and receipt of a variety of goods—among them grains, vegetables, libations, oil, domestic animals, clothing, and so forth—often tied to specific tasks to be performed for compensation (Nissen, Damerow, and Englund 1993: fig. 43).

As students began to learn the craft of a scribe, they wrote out many lists of words. Each "exercise" contained words in the same semantic domain. One of those lists is the so-called Professions List from Uruk-Warka, undoubtedly the largest and most complex city-state of the late fourth and early third millennia BC (Englund, Nissen, and Damerow 1993). It includes all sorts of profession names, from cooks to leaders. What is stunning is the implication that all of these professions have formal ranking, from the Leader or Head of a bureau to the laborers who work for that leader (Nissen 2000: 215). This list must reflect a clear hierarchy of tasks and organizations already established by the end of prehistoric times.

The early tablets further explain why this system of record keeping became essential. "Judging by the items that are listed on the tablets, besides keeping tight control of the flow of goods into and out of the central stores by means of daily accounts, the administration apparently was also interested in long-range developments such as the total grain delivery over several years, or were interested in obtaining planning data" (Nissen 2000: 214). As Adams (1966; 1981) has pointed out over and over, this question of risk in agricultural production, the cornerstone of life on the southern Mesopotamian alluvium, had a catalytic effect on the development of social organization. What we are seeing here is not merely the control of the movement and access to particular goods. What these tablets represent is a kind of administrative elaboration that has evolved into sophisticated planning organizations. To plan, to archive data, to analyze it, to have the mechanisms at hand to put those plans into effect and make sure that they are carried out represents a high plateau in the evolution of administrative organizations. This trend would grow with the further elaboration of administrative structure, leading in less than a millennium to territorial states and empires.

ANALYTICAL TRENDS AND PROSPECTS

As the discussion of intellectual approaches to societal cultural evolution above indicates, the subject of pre- and early historic administration is but one aspect of a larger class of problems. For example, as Adams has shown us, we must see the development of Mesopotamian society in a broad environmental context, natural and human. What were the elements of the natural environment that directed and limited the sorts of settlement systems, institutions, and organization that typified the periods of Mesopotamian development? How did human population density, the demands of population on productive and administrative systems, and the nature of human interactions affect the dynamics of these ancient societies? He opened the geographical perspective of researchers, emphasizing a regional framework for analysis of these problems.

Because archaeology, even with the availability of later cuneiform documents, is limited in its ability to answer questions of complicated human cultural systems in all their various iterations, we must utilize a comparative method (Rothman 2004). This means creating an intellectual yardstick to make comparison appropriate. Adams's student, Henry Wright, championed the state (and its predecessor organizations—namely, tribes and simple and complex chiefdoms) as such a benchmark. We must also look at the systems for which administration is created in the first place. Another of Adams's students, Guillermo Algaze, focused on questions of cross-cultural interaction and economic exchange, in the creation of the cities, economies, social status differentiation, *and* administrative organizations. Yet a third student of Adams's, Elizabeth Stone, saw the dual nature of governance in these ancient polities (E. C. Stone 1987).

In some ways, an emphasis on the *functioning*, as opposed to the *origin* of complex societies and administrations, represents a return to Adams's original paradigm. To this analytical trend others added a post-processual emphasis on ideology and the role of those elements of society usually ignored in earlier analyses. Adams's interest in technology represents another new direction in understanding ancient society (Adams 1996).

In other words, the study of ancient administration and societal evolution has reached a crossroads, which will require a reexamination of theory, methods, and potential co-investigators. One task is to refine our terminology. We need to define more clearly terms like "elites" in order to understand better who the policymakers, controllers of resources, recruiters of labor, and interest groups of states were, those that Wallace defines as the "owners" (see above, p. 240). We need to know how they functioned and how they interacted with those who implemented their wishes (the "action group" [see above, p. 240]). We must discover various kinds of centralization that can occur in a complex society (heterogeneity)—that is, various kinds and modalities of administration. We need to agree on what exchange, trade, and bureaucracy mean. This clarification will make our comparisons apt in terms of the questions we ask. We must, in general, continually reassess our assumptions about the ancient world.

In our excavations, we must fit our methods to the kinds of information needed to understand administration and the larger societal and environmental contexts of the societies we investigate. The cost of excavation is rapidly rising, but wherever possible, we must emphasize broad horizontal excavation to uncover larger samples of the settlements (and functional areas) that existed in antiquity. My analysis of administration at Tepe Gawra would be impossible with the kinds of horizontal samples excavated nowadays. We need to publish our data fully—many of the most critical data sets remain unpublished in notebooks and on museum shelves. We must work together to establish minimal standards for recovery and publication that guarantee the availability of the information necessary to approach a variety of research questions.

As new approaches and new questions emerge, we must seek new partnerships with other specialists. So-called new or anthropological archaeologists brought life sciences—ecology, ethnozoology, and ethnobotany—into their projects. As we incorporate ideas from the post-processual school with its emphasis on ideology and refine our earlier theories, we must develop new ways of working with old and new collaborators. We must find new common ground with art historians, whose rich body of iconographic data holds extraordinary potential for understanding ideology, an indigenous point of view. We must forge a new bond with those who deal with documentary evidence, bringing them into our research designs and plans before excavation and survey begin.

In all of this, Adams has shown us the rewards of thinking big and of synthesizing many sources of information. Without his vision, we would probably be far behind where we are in understanding the evolution of ancient administration and society in general.

ISLAMIC ARCHAEOLOGY AND THE "LAND BEHIND BAGHDAD"

DONALD WHITCOMB

ABSTRACT

This paper uses the research activities of Robert Adams to illustrate the stages of the nascent field of Islamic Archaeology. His Land Behind Baghdad *(1965) is remarkable among archaeological reports in its detailed inclusion of Islamic periods. Islamic historians have cited this book with amazing frequency; obviously, this research resonates with historians who otherwise look to archaeology only for a few pictures. This book represents a movement, though perhaps not intentional, toward a methodology for this historical archaeology, providing vital evidence for the development of society and economy in Islamic contexts.*

Archaeology and history are intertwined from the earliest explorations in the search for monuments and documents. For Islamic Archaeology, a beginning might be set with the visit of Kaisar Wilhelm II to Palestine in 1898, the same year as the beginning of the Berlin–Baghdad railroad (Bernhardsson 2005: 53). Among the many Ottoman firmans resulting from this gesture was permission for Sarre and Herzfeld (1911–1920) to survey the length of the Euphrates and Tigris in 1905. Their method of detailed observation of archaeological ruins at Raqqa was used as a means of explicating minimal geographic texts. Herzfeld extended the research potential of this methodology in excavations at Samarra from 1911 to 1914 (Herzfeld 1923; 1927; 1930; 1948; Leisten 2003; Northedge, Wilkinson, and Falkner 1990; 1991). His mapping of a site stretching over 23 miles (35 kilometers) was facilitated by the use of remote imaging (aerial photographs), which revealed palaces and mosques, streets and residences, race tracks and *hayrs* (enclosures). Excavations revealed that these buildings, both official and residential, were embellished with elaborate stucco and fresco decorations. The artifacts recovered featured beautiful ceramics, both locally produced and imported from China; Samarra ceramics became an immediate and continuing source of fame for this site in Islamic art and archaeology. Thus, the urban archaeology of Samarra was hijacked by the sensational artistic discoveries, which placed the Abbasid capital of the ninth century in tyrannous control of standards and sequences throughout Islamic studies. The continuing search for art works mined from urban sites is another result of the Samarra excavations, a pattern also found in Byzantine archaeology (Rautman 1990).

Samarra set a very visible model of Islamic Archaeology for both historians and other archaeologists. It was soon after this excavation that James Henry Breasted discovered frescoes at Dura Europos, which resulted in one of the first publications of the Oriental Institute, *Oriental Forerunners of Byzantine Painting* (1924).[1] One may see in this publication an interest in field evidence for delineating broad historical concerns. This approach does not fare well in the view of a new book by Tim Insoll entitled *The Archaeology of Islam*. He castigates Islamic Archaeology with being excessively concerned with evidential typology to the detriment of socially aware syntheses. When Insoll turns to landscape archaeology, he declares that "archaeological studies of settlement, landscapes and environments have until recently infrequently considered . . . social, sacred or symbolic factors of great importance" (Insoll 1999: 201). Thus, while Wilkinson's work on Sohar is mentioned, Adams's more comprehensive research on irrigation systems of Mesopotamia is not included in the discussion.[2] The detailed inclusion of Islamic periods in *Land Behind Baghdad* (Adams 1965) has been cited by Islamic historians with amazing frequency; obviously this research resonates with historians who otherwise look to archaeology only for a few pictures.[3]

Adams's stated purpose anticipates the popular Braudelian vision, in examining "not the ebb and flow of the historical record, but the underlying, more slowly changing relation of man to land in a . . . marginal part of the Mesopotamian alluvium" (Adams 1965: vii). The research consisted of field reconnaissance in 1957–1958, mapping and collecting surface materials (sherds) from 867 sites. A sophisticated game of connecting the dots resulted in the identification of chronological phases of the irrigation system and

---

[1] Breasted made this discovery while riding with the British army in an armored car, not an imitative model for contemporary research programs.

[2] Wilkinson 1975; 1976; 1977. Adams should not feel slighted by this, since this archaeology of Islam does not mention either Herzfeld or Sarre (Sarre and Herzfeld 1911–20) either; see Whitcomb 2000.

[3] When I asked various people why this is so, the first response was "Baghdad"; given the felicitous title, perhaps a reprint might soon be appropriate and timely.

associated settlements. This clever research design originated with Thorkild Jacobsen (Adams 1965: viii, 119–125) and is advanced with a full listing of caveats: problems of erosion, alluviation, sampling error, and imprecise dating criteria. The last difficulty stemmed from an exclusive reliance on "fossil" indicators, compounded by the utilization of only Samarra (for the early Islamic) and Wasit (for the Middle Islamic) comparanda.

While the accuracy of Adams's survey has been challenged repeatedly in its archaeological details, the cumulative picture is persuasive and leads to testable hypotheses. Adams (1965: 89) describes urban sites in which textual evidence is "supplemented" by surface reconnaissance, and he notes that the majority of sites found through survey are rarely, if ever, mentioned in textual sources. One may note that this archaeological method is essentially comparative, but Adams also reaches specific conclusions that are counter to historical ones: "The greatest degree of urbanization, prior to modern times, . . . came not as a concomitant of the greatest intensity of land usage but as *the sequel to a decline* in provincial settlement, irrigation, and agricultural production" (Adams 1965: 99, emphasis added; see Jundi Shapur, below).

The archaeological use of material culture can thus lead to better historical understanding. These positivistic resulting hypotheses can be of great relevance to historians.[4] But a more immediate attraction may have been the utilization of medieval Arabic geographers, who produced a large corpus of literature with information surprisingly underutilized by traditional historians, especially in a systematic manner.[5] Adams augments the geographers' observations with lists of revenues and other economic data, which gives a certain cliometric modernity to the arguments. The result is a mélange of medieval description, medieval accounts, and modern fieldwork, each of which may be questioned as to its degree of accuracy. Cumulatively, these data provide a convincing "big picture" which has seemed unassailable.

The relationship of history and archaeology has been dealt with on a global scale by Anders Andrén (1998). He notes that "all meaning springs from contexts," or more explicitly, "from a methodological point of view, much of the theoretical debate in today's archaeology can be seen as a search for new contexts" (Andrén 1998: 155). As a part of this search for context, Adams (1970) conducted a series of soundings at a small nameless mound, dubbed Tell Abu Sarifa, in the vicinity of Nippur. This excavation attempted to address

---

[4] Archaeological materials must be used with caution, however; the identification of Islamic ceramics with a Muslim population suggested by Bulliet (1980) was effectively criticized as an erroneous zero-sum game by Morony (1994: 225–226; see Whitcomb 1995).

[5] See Wenke and Pyne 1990, for caveats in the proper utilization of these resources.

the imprecisions of ceramic typology to delineate a sequence of ceramic types spanning the Partho-Sasanian into the Islamic period. It would seem safe to say that few historians have utilized these contextualizations, since the textual referents are entirely absent. Indeed, the ceramics found in these excavations had to be tied to the relative chronology based on Samarra, as well as Wasit and Kish, before they became meaningful (Adams 1970: 118–119).

As an example of history and archaeology following Adams's surveys in the Diyala and southwestern Iran (Adams 1962), one may turn to his research at the site of Jundi Shapur (Adams and Hansen 1968). In the late Sasanian and early Islamic periods, Jundi Shapur was known variously as a Sasanian royal residence, the seat of the Nestorian Metropolitan for Khuzistan (under the name of Bet Lapat), and a center for academic knowledge, especially its famed medical school. The city was apparently founded under Shapur I in the third century CE, whence the common etymology of the name, meaning the military camp of Shapur (see Potts 1989, for a discussion of this term). Nabia Abbott provided this and other historical information, unfortunately without documentation, in a brief note to accompany the archaeological report of Adams and Hansen (1968).

We have a report of the series of soundings into this cityscape in 1963.[6] The historical structuring of the town seems to rest on a grid of ridges of an orthogonal town (measuring about 3 × 1.5 kilometers). Two hypotheses seem to have driven the research: (1) that within the many mounds were "monumental buildings suitable for a Sasanian capital"; and (2) its subsequent history was one of gradual impoverishment into a small "provincial Islamic town sorely beset by the corruption, violence and intrigue" of a post-Abbasid political collapse (Adams and Hansen 1968: 54). This latter characterization is later refined, being seen as the result of the Zanj rebellion and occupation of Ya'qub ibn Layth, both within the Samarra period. The excavated soundings could confirm neither of these urban conditions; rather, the projection of "a long period of deterioration of the city" (Adams and Hansen 1968: 57) prejudices the complexity of the phases of its history. One may acknowledge the difficulty in assessing the observations of medieval geographers (Adams and Hansen 1968: 58) and must note the continuing quality of glazed ceramics in Middle Islamic (and especially post-Samarran) periods. In a more abstract sense, this oversized town may represent a state of hyperdevelopment (like many of the irrigation projects of the Sasanians). Thus, the subsequent history of Islamic Jundi Shapur may be better viewed not as a decline, but rather a restitution to a more balanced and sustainable urban system.

---

[6] Jundi Shapur is roughly the same size as Antioch, which may give some credence to the etymolology advanced by Frye, "better than Antioch [has] Shapur [made this city]"; see Abbott 1968: 71, n. 1.

Conclusions

This paper has used the research activities of Robert Adams to illustrate various stages of the development of the nascent field of Islamic Archaeology. Through this cumulative experience, one may recognize movement, though perhaps not intentional, toward a methodology for this branch of historical archaeology. The beginning in each new region to be investigated is usually a high-profile, large site of symbolic importance. This role in Khuzistan is filled, in a sense, with the French excavations at Susa, though the Islamic aspects have received emphasis only relatively recently (Kervran 1985; Whitcomb 1985). A similar instinct may have guided the preliminary investigations at Jundi Shapur, attractive in its size and historical importance, not to mention its potential for aesthetically significant discoveries.

The next stage in the development of Islamic Archaeology is the multiplication of investigations of specialized sites; instead of common tells, investigation turned to citadels, ports, and especially "desert castles," as classes of comparable examples. Again, an underlying inspiration would seem to be art historical and—seen at another scale—in the multiplication of monument types under study (mosques, palaces, baths, and the like). Perhaps a distinctive feature of such research is the treatment of the monument, or settlement type, as an isolated phenomenon pursued for its own internal logic or combination of features. The archaeological alternative, to which Adams made a major contribution, is to place such data into a regional system or, in other words, the contextualization of elements into a broadly functional logic. Thus, the data provided by archaeological survey provides information that is critical to the understanding of fully historic as well as prehistoric periods. A structural limitation to such research lies in interpretative precision, particularly in its chronologies; hence, the necessity of excavating one (or more) representative sites. This is the logic of Tell Abu Sarifa, useful but not terribly exciting digging.

Another stage for Islamic Archaeology will be the focus on socio-cultural or historical problem solving. While this is an implied constant in earlier archaeological programs, the professionalization of a discipline of Islamic Archaeology requires such a methodological concentration. Thus, for Insoll, the definition of the field is found in the explicit archaeology of religion, but he does not make the case that material culture may consistently be seen through cultic or spiritual influences of this alternative archaeology. Islamic Archaeology is practiced, by Adams and more specialized scholars, as a historical archaeology providing vital evidence for the development of society and economy in Islamic contexts. The growth and direction of this discipline owes much to Samarra and more to the *Land behind Baghdad*.

THE URBAN ORGANIZATION OF TEOTIHUACAN, MEXICO*

GEORGE L. COWGILL

ABSTRACT

Teotihuacan, in the highlands of central Mexico, grew rapidly from ca. 150 BC to ca. AD 200, by which time it covered about 20 square kilometers, with a population of roughly 100,000. Thereafter, its size may have changed little until a decline began ca. AD 550, ending in collapse ca. AD 650. During much of this time, it was the capital of a regional state covering 25,000 to 100,000 square kilometers, and influential far beyond that. An orientation of 15.5 degrees east of astronomic north was followed closely throughout the entire city, with certain exceptions, suggesting a strong central authority early on. At the same time, there is evidence of "bottom up" as well as "top-down" processes. The interplay of these processes is traced at increasingly large scales, ranging from the walled multi-apartment compounds in which most inhabitants of the city lived, through small neighborhoods and ethnic enclaves, and up to large districts of the city. Evidence about craft production (ceramics, obsidian, textiles, lapidary materials) suggests that some was carried out by specialists on behalf of the state or other large institutions or wealthy patrons, and some was carried

---

* In addition to their publications that I have cited, in preparing this paper I have profited much from discussions with Dr. Ian Robertson and ASU graduate students Oralia Cabrera, Destiny Crider, and Kristin Sullivan. Elizabeth Stone, René Millon, and Joyce Marcus made useful comments on an earlier draft.

*out by independent units working on their own. No unequivocal rulers'
palaces have been identified, though there are several good candidates.
Rule may have shifted over time from highly concentrated authority to a
more oligarchic system of shared elite power, and the location of the physical seat of government may have shifted over time. The orientation and
key distances in the spatial layout of major features of the city may have
had cosmic significance.*

INTRODUCTION

Ancient cities vary considerably in the degree to which they exhibit regular
layouts. The early urban settlements of Mesopotamia, for example, tend to
have winding streets without a hint of a grid pattern (not unlike Rome or
London or the earliest European settlements in Boston or the tip of Man-
hattan), while major Harappan settlements look more orderly (more like
many new settlements planted by imperial Rome or the colonial nucleus of
Philadelphia or early nineteenth-century Washington). It may be that settlements created by already strong regional states or empires tend to be more
planned than those "pristine" cities that came into being in the context of
societies only just in the process of creating highly organized institutions
and practices of statecraft—but this seems at best only a general tendency
rather than a rule.

Issues concerning the meanings of orderly layouts, the reasons for them,
and their effects on the lives of inhabitants deserve cross-cultural investigation. I will not attempt that here, and will instead concentrate on Teotihuacan,
a metropolis in the highland Basin of Mexico that flourished from ca. 150 BC
to ca. AD 650 and that, at least after ca. AD 200, exhibited an exceptional
degree of ordered layout that must represent planning imposed from above.
At the same time, there may have been a good deal of structure that was the
result of "bottom-up" self-organizing processes (Robertson 2001). I have
touched briefly on these issues elsewhere (Cowgill 2000a; 2003; 2005), and in
other publications I have tried to say a little about everything at Teotihuacan
(Cowgill 1997; 2000b). Here I cover in more depth topics concerning Teotihuacan as a city, especially the planned and unplanned aspects of its spatial
structure, residential units, ethnic and craft neighborhoods, identifiable larger
districts, and some of their sociopolitical implications.

However, by way of a bit of comparison, sociocultural resemblances
between Teotihuacan and Harappan society, other than the relatively ordered
layouts of settlements, seem very limited. Harappan society, at least in its
material manifestations, looks austere and almost ascetic, somewhat reminiscent of the material culture of the nineteenth century Shakers in the United
States. At Teotihuacan, to be sure, images possibly celebrating specific named

individuals are rare and controversial (Cowgill 1997; 2000b; Pasztory 1997), but overall the material culture was exuberant and colorful, some house interiors and pyramid exteriors were richly ornamented with polychrome murals, some ceramics were highly decorated, and many lines of evidence attest to a wide range of lifestyles, from the sumptuous to the impoverished. Perhaps a higher proportion of people than in most ancient societies enjoyed an intermediate level of comfort, and there may have been a smaller proportion in the lower range, but this is one of the innumerable conjectures that needs further investigation. Also, of course, Teotihuacan has far more imposing civic-ceremonial structures in spacious configurations than seems to be the case at Harappan sites.

BACKGROUND

Teotihuacan grew rapidly from about 150 BC to ca. AD 100–200, after which growth probably ceased, and there seems to have been little further change in size until about AD 550, after which there was probably a substantial decline in population before the central part of the city was burned in around AD 650. I refer to the interval from 150 BC to AD 650 as the Teotihuacan period. Teotihuacan was the capital of a regional state that covered the Basin of Mexico and at least the immediately surrounding areas for an average distance of 90 kilometers (an area of about 25,000 square kilometers), and perhaps an area two to four times that (that is, possibly an average radius of 130 to 180 kilometers). Within this area, it was a "primate" center—that is, far larger than any secondary center. Beyond this radius, it probably set up a few key outposts as far away as the Pacific Lowlands and highlands of Guatemala, and it seems to have intervened briefly in the politics of major Maya centers such as Tikal and Copán (Braswell 2003; Fash and Fash 2000; Stuart 2000).

Figure 66 is a chronological chart that includes the names of relevant ceramic phases. All these absolute dates are rough estimates based on an insufficient number of sometimes contradictory calibrated radiocarbon dates and some cross-ties with the Maya Lowlands (a thousand kilometers to the east) and should be understood as having a 95 percent confidence interval of plus or minus a century or more.

After the central core of Teotihuacan was burned, at the end of the Metepec phase, ca. AD 650, the city may have been briefly abandoned. At any rate, subsequent occupants had a markedly different material culture, including ceramics of a style called Coyotlatelco that has affinities with traditions to the northwest of the Basin of Mexico (Crider 2002). Some of these people may have been descendants of the earlier occupants, but it is likely that there was significant inmigration. The peripheral parts of the ancient

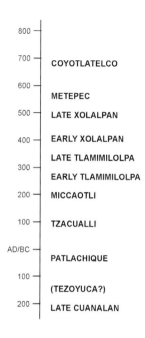

Figure 66. Teotihuacan chronology.

city have had substantial occupations ever since, but their connections with the Teotihuacan tradition have been tenuous.

Thanks to the massive Teotihuacan Mapping Project—a comprehensive surface survey directed by René Millon in the 1960s—we know that during the centuries that it flourished, Teotihuacan covered about 20 square kilometers—that is, around 2000 hectares. Figure 67 reproduces the map of René Millon, R. Bruce Drewitt, and George Cowgill (1973) at a reduced scale. René Millon (for example, 1976: 212) estimates a peak population on the order of 100,000 to 200,000, but estimates of prehistoric population sizes are notoriously difficult. Millon's are based on good archaeological evidence of more than 2000 substantial residential structures occupied simultaneously, most of which contain more than one apartment, plus much less certain estimates of the likely number of occupants of such structures. A careful reassessment of these population estimates is desirable. Until that is done, I am more comfortable with a guess in the lower part of Millon's range, or even a bit lower, possibly 80,000 to 100,000 inhabitants. Estimates upward of 200,000 that occur in the secondary and tertiary literature, seeming to grow with decreasing familiarity with the data, should be ignored.

No other Mesoamerican city was so populous until the Aztec capital, Tenochtitlan, grew to around 150,000 to 200,000 by the early 1500s (Calnek 1976: 288). Nevertheless, a number of other Mesoamerican cities were quite large, on the order of 30,000 to 60,000 inhabitants. Early Old World cities, with the probable exception of north China, seem considerably smaller in both area and population. I do not know what this means, but it is worth noting.

Teotihuacan was not exactly a pristine city. It grew to unprecedented size, and previously there had been no settlement larger than 1000 to 2000 people in the Teotihuacan Valley, which is the northeastern part of the Basin of Mexico. However, there were some quite large earlier settlements elsewhere in and near the Basin of Mexico, including Cuicuilco in the southwestern part of the basin, about 52 kilometers away, and Cholula, 95 kilometers to the east in the Valley of Puebla. Both of these are very little known, the former buried under several meters of basalt from a volcanic eruption, and the latter under the modern city of Cholula. However, Cuicuilco, at least, probably covered several hundred hectares before Teotihuacan was founded, and William Sanders, Jeffrey Parsons, and Robert Santley (1979: 97) estimate its population as roughly 5,000 to 10,000 even before Teotihuacan began. Thus, the founders of Teotihuacan did not start from scratch—they may have had no idea of how large their city would become, but they already had knowledge of settlements that had populations on the order of several thousands. This experience may have predisposed Teotihuacan's founders to imagine the possibility of laying out a grid over a large area that as yet had little population and consequently few people whose interests were adversely affected. On the other hand, although an orderly layout was applied early to major civic-ceremonial structures, it may be that it was only extended to residential areas after these had become quite populous. If so, imposition of the layout must have run counter to many interests and given rise to a great deal of resistance, which the central authority would have had to overcome. Barry Kemp (2000) cites the example of London after the Great Fire of 1666, where a number of orderly plans for rebuilding were quickly discarded in favor of something very close to the previous layout, inherited from medieval times. This surely relates to the fact that by the late seventeenth century, English royal authority was not in a position to override collective interests of wealthier merchants and property owners in London. It contrasts markedly with, for example, the way that nineteenth-century developers in Chicago laid out largely imaginary grid patterns on the prairies well outside the actually built-up area, a phenomenon ridiculed by Anthony Trollope but one that had a strong impact on the subsequent layout as it materialized.

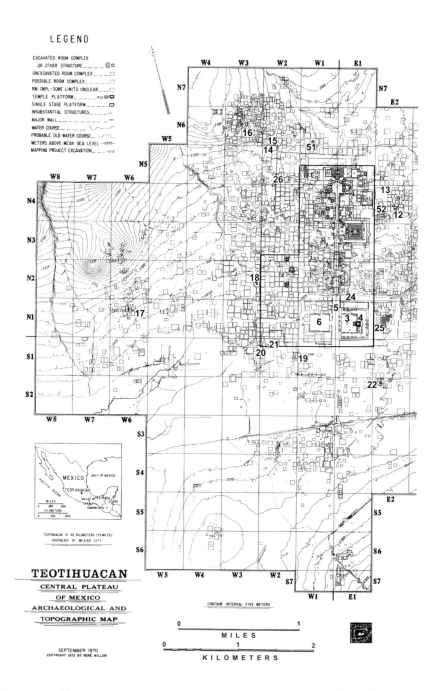

LEGEND

EXCAVATED ROOM COMPLEX
  OR OTHER STRUCTURE _ _ _ _
UNEXCAVATED ROOM COMPLEX _ _ _
POSSIBLE ROOM COMPLEX _ _ _ _ _
RM. CMPL - SOME LIMITS UNCLEAR _ _ _
TEMPLE PLATFORM _ _ _ _ _ _ _
SINGLE STAGE PLATFORM _ _ _ _ _
INSUBSTANTIAL STRUCTURES _ _ _ _ _ _
MAJOR WALL _ _ _ _ _ _ _ _ _ _
WATER COURSE _ _ _ _ _ _ _ _ _
PROBABLE OLD WATER COURSE _ _
METERS ABOVE MEAN SEA LEVEL _ _ _
MAPPING PROJECT EXCAVATION _ _ _

TEOTIHUACAN
CENTRAL PLATEAU
OF MEXICO
ARCHAEOLOGICAL AND
TOPOGRAPHIC MAP

SEPTEMBER 1970
COPYRIGHT 1972 BY RENÉ MILLON

CONTOUR INTERVAL FIVE METERS

MILES

KILOMETERS

Figure 67. *(FACING PAGES; INSET ON FOLLOWING PAGE):* A map of Teotihuacan at its height (reproduced with permission of René Millon).

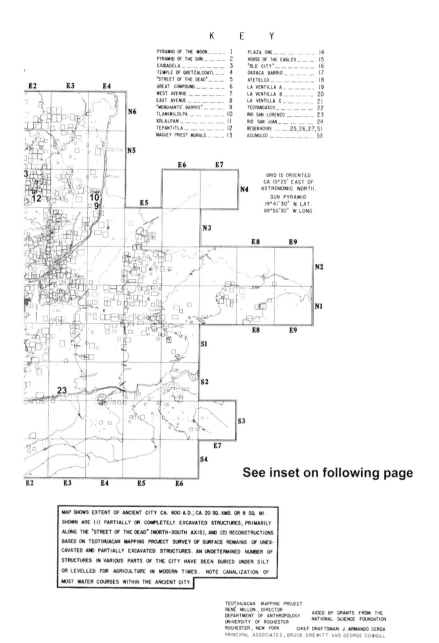

See inset on following page

MAP SHOWS EXTENT OF ANCIENT CITY CA. 600 A.D.; CA. 20 SQ. KMS. OR 8 SQ. MI.
SHOWN ARE (1) PARTIALLY OR COMPLETELY EXCAVATED STRUCTURES, PRIMARILY
ALONG THE "STREET OF THE DEAD" (NORTH-SOUTH AXIS), AND (2) RECONSTRUCTIONS
BASED ON TEOTIHUACAN MAPPING PROJECT SURVEY OF SURFACE REMAINS OF UNEX-
CAVATED AND PARTIALLY EXCAVATED STRUCTURES. AN UNDETERMINED NUMBER OF
STRUCTURES IN VARIOUS PARTS OF THE CITY HAVE BEEN BURIED UNDER SILT
OR LEVELLED FOR AGRICULTURE IN MODERN TIMES. NOTE CANALIZATION OF
MOST WATER COURSES WITHIN THE ANCIENT CITY.

TEOTIHUACAN MAPPING PROJECT
RENÉ MILLON , DIRECTOR
DEPARTMENT OF ANTHROPOLOGY   AIDED BY GRANTS FROM THE
UNIVERSITY OF ROCHESTER   NATIONAL SCIENCE FOUNDATION
ROCHESTER , NEW YORK   CHIEF DRAFTSMAN J. ARMANDO CERDA
PRINCIPAL ASSOCIATES , BRUCE DREWITT AND GEORGE COWGILL

Figure 67. *(CONTINUED; INSET ON FOLLOWING PAGE):* A map of Teotihuacan at its height (reproduced with permission of René Millon).

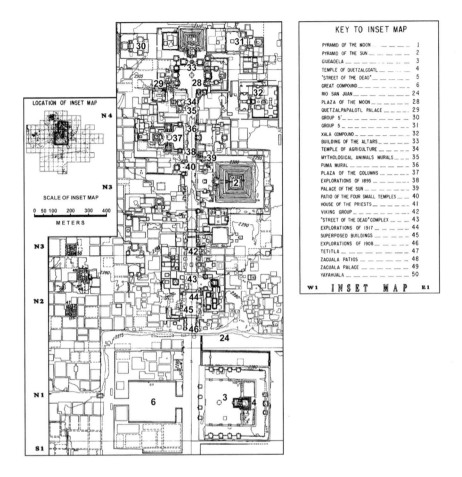

Figure 67. *(INSET):* A map of Teotihuacan at its height (reproduced with permission of René Millon).

A PERVASIVE STANDARD ORIENTATION

Many structures and other features at Teotihuacan have north–south orientations extremely close to 15.5 degrees east of astronomical north. It is important to emphasize that many of these are not merely within a degree or so of this orientation, but within five or ten minutes of it. This is probably about the limit of what is possible with naked-eye surveying methods (and rather better than some present-day layouts in the Phoenix metropolitan area, where orthogonal intentions make minor deviations painfully obvious). A prime example is the great Avenue of the Dead,[1] which runs for over 5 kilometers from the Moon Pyramid (Figures 67:1; 68:1) in the north to the southernmost outskirts of the city. The northernmost 2 kilometers have the immense Sun Pyramid (Figures 67:2; 68:2) and the great 16-hectare Ciudadela enclosure on the east (Figures 67:3; 68:3), and the "Great Compound" on the west (Figures 67:6; 68:11). It is lined on both sides by a continuous series of lesser pyramid groups, platforms, and elite residences. South of the Ciudadela, the remaining 3-kilometer stretch is detectable, but only occasional platforms and pyramids of modest size, separated by wide intervals, adjoin the southern avenue.

Many other north–south streets are also extremely close to 15.5 degrees east of astronomic north, as can be seen in Figures 67 and 68, which follow this orientation, and even today a number of field boundaries have the same alignment, as shown in the 1962 topographic map prepared for the Mapping Project (R. Millon 1973: map 3; 1976: 208–209). The channel of the Río San Juan, a modest and seasonally intermittent stream that traverses the city from northeast to southwest, was altered so that segments conform to the Teotihuacan orientation, while other segments form 45-degree diagonals.

This north–south orientation was also followed for some distance outside the city itself. For example, a present-day road running north–south for about 1.5 kilometers near the east sides of Squares S1W5 to S4W5 of the Millon map follows this orientation very closely, as does a deeply entrenched watercourse in Squares N2W8 and N1W8. To judge from published maps, a single canonical orientation is followed more strictly at Teotihuacan than in Harappan cities or other ancient "orthogonal" cities of the Old World.

Nevertheless, there are some complications. A number of important east–west features, including the north and south sides of the Sun Pyramid, are quite exactly perpendicular to the canonical north–south axis—that is, 15.5 degrees south of astronomic east. But there are other major east–west features that run around 16.5 to 17 degrees south of east. A particularly notable example is the Ciudadela enclosure, about 400 meters on a side, which was built in a single operation in about AD 150–200, but as a parallelogram rather than a rectangle. The long stretches of surviving original outer enclosing platforms permit very accurate measurements, and while the east and west sides follow the 15.5-degree orientation, the north and south sides are skewed by about 1 to 1.5 degrees (Drucker 1974). It is unlikely that Teotihuacan builders were unaware of this deviation (for one thing, if they had not

---

[1] It is more commonly called "Street" of the Dead (Calle or Calzada de los Muertos in Spanish, derived from the sixteenth-century Aztec name for this feature, Miccaotli), but I prefer "Avenue" of the Dead, since this more adequately suggests its breadth, approximately 60 meters for much of its length. It bears repeating that the name seems inappropriate, since no mortuary monuments or major tombs have been discovered along it.

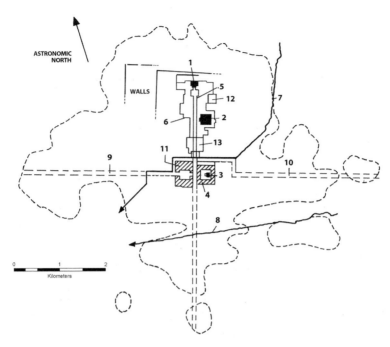

Figure 68. A simplified map showing some principal features and approximate limits of Teotihuacan at about AD 500. 1: Moon Pyramid; 2: Sun Pyramid; 3: Feathered Serpent Pyramid; 4: Ciudadela; 5: Avenue of the Dead; 6: approximate limit of the northern civic-ceremonial zone; 7: Río San Juan; 8: Río San Lorenzo; 9: West Avenue; 10: East Avenue; 11: Great Compound; 12: Xalla; 13: Avenue of the Dead Complex.

been able to measure angles rather accurately, the Ciudadela would probably have been a slightly irregular four-sided polygon, rather than a parallelogram). This skewing is also present in the Feathered Serpent Pyramid within the Ciudadela and even in that pyramid's interior structure and in pits outside it. I know of no compelling explanation for this skewing.

Some other features, notably some of the long freestanding walls outside the ceremonial core of the city, are closer to 17 degrees east of astronomic north in their north–south stretches and 17 degrees south of true east in east–west sections. These walls are not well dated, and it is possible that they are relatively late in the Teotihuacan period. Their orientations are closer to those reported for many post-Teotihuacan structures in Mesoamerica. A segment of the Río San Juan on the northeastern margin of the city, running from Square N6E4 to N3E4, also deviates eastward of the 15.5-degree orientation.

Most strikingly, another small watercourse, the Río San Lorenzo, in the southern part of the city, runs straight for at least 4 kilometers, from map Square S2E3 to S4W6. It is highly implausible that a stretch of a natural stream could run that far without meanders, and I feel sure that its course has also been intentionally altered. But it runs 8 degrees north of west, just half the canonical orientation (Figures 67 and 68 suggest that it runs slightly south of west, but this is an illusion caused by the fact that these figures are themselves oriented about 15 degrees and 25 minutes east of north). This can scarcely be accidental, but the reason for it is an unsolved puzzle. Possibly it will somehow prove a key to the reason for the canonical orientation.

I think the reason for the canonical orientation is still not fully understood. Perhaps the best explanation so far is that, if the currently accepted correlation between the European calendar and the "Long Count" of the Classic Maya is correct (there are still some doubts about this), then the mythical starting date for the Long Count would be 11–13 August in 3114 BC (R. Millon 1981). On those days of the year, at Teotihuacan the sun sets 15.5 degrees north of west. However, there is little else to suggest that Teotihuacanos attached much importance to the Long Count, except that it is attested by inscriptions as close as La Mojarra, a site in the Gulf of Mexico lowlands, over 300 kilometers away, which has no evidence of any interaction with Teotihuacan. Since north–south is more prominent than east–west in the layout of Teotihuacan, I suspect that the alignment may be related to some object in the northern sky. Since the direction of the earth's rotational axis precesses with a period of about 26,000 years, the possible shift in the canonical orientation might perhaps be explained by use of a northern celestial object as a point of reference. It is certainly not accidental that, viewed from the Avenue of the Dead, the Moon Pyramid is nicely framed by Cerro Gordo, the extinct volcano that forms the northern edge of the Teotihuacan Valley (Tobriner 1972), but the same framing could have been achieved by using a somewhat different orientation and a somewhat different east–west location for the Avenue of the Dead.

Saburo Sugiyama (1993) questions the existence of significant east and west major streets, and, thus, the existence of a quadripartite structure in the Teotihuacan urban layout. However, the Mapping Project found enough evidence for major east and west avenues to establish their existence beyond reasonable doubt, at the latitude of the Ciudadela and the Great Compound. Nevertheless, they are not lined by platforms or pyramids, and the twofold east–west division marked by the Avenue of the Dead is far more prominent, at least materially, than the north–south division marked by east and west avenues. Probably the most conspicuous features of these east and west avenues are low platforms running across them, situated symmetrically about 2750 meters east and west of the Avenue of the Dead centerline (Sites 11:N1E6 and 34:N1W6; see R. Millon, Drewitt, and Cowgill 1973 for locations of these and other sites mentioned). There is also a possible transverse platform about 2250 meters west of the avenue (Site 1:N1W5). Site 11:N1E6 was recently excavated as a salvage project of the Instituto Nacional de

Antropología e Historia, which verified that it was indeed a platform rather than a residential structure and recovered a unique ritual deposit composed primarily of female and infant figurines, dating stylistically to the Early Tlamimilolpa subphase (Fernández Mendiola and Jiménez Hernández 1997; Rodríguez and Rubio 1997). It is possible that this platform and its companion on the west marked some sort of socially significant boundaries of the city, although substantially built residential compounds extend hundreds of meters farther in both directions.

I must also mention figures composed of small dots poked into the soft plaster of newly laid floors or pecked into rock outcroppings. These often represent crosses set into concentric circles, but Maltese crosses and other forms occur as well. They are found widely in central and northern Mexico, and even occur in the Lowland Maya area. It has been suggested that they are of calendrical significance and that they may also be reference points for city planning (Aveni 2000). Some, indeed, are positioned to relate to solar events, as at the site of Alta Vista in the state of Zacatecas, very close to the Tropic of Cancer (Aveni, Hartung, and Kelley 1982).[2] Also, the first two found at Teotihuacan, one in the floor of a room on the Avenue of the Dead and one pecked into a rock on a hill several kilometers to the west, were almost exactly perpendicular to the avenue. However, many more have since been found at Teotihuacan, including a concentration on the platform just south of the Sun Pyramid. Although they are quite variable, many contain configurations of 260 dots, which are very likely related to the Sacred Round of 260 days that is very widespread in Mesoamerica, consisting of all permutations of twenty day names and thirteen day numbers. Thus, these pecked figures may well have had calendrical and divinatory significance, but, at least at Teotihuacan, probably not astronomical significance.

It is interesting that figures comprised of dots pecked in bedrock occur at the sixteenth-century capital and pilgrimage center of Vijayanagara in southern India, where they were used as game boards (Mack 2002: 117). Anthony Aveni (2000: 257) suggests that some of the pecked figures at Teotihuacan may also have been used for games, and I think this especially may have been the case for the concentration found near the Sun Pyramid. This need not be inconsistent with their possible use in divination, since outcomes of games can predict future events. However, there are also graffiti in Teotihuacan floors that are quite different from these pecked figures, and considerably more like the designs used for the ethnohistorically known Mesoamerican game of *patolli*. Hence, the suggestion that the pecked figures at Teotihuacan

---

[2] There is, however, no compelling or even persuasive reason to link this site to Teotihuacan.

and elsewhere in Mesoamerica might be related to games is highly speculative. The suggestion that they may have been related to calendrical ritual is more plausible, but they remain enigmatic. I think, however, that most of them had little or nothing to do with city planning.

Whatever the reason for it, the *pervasiveness* of a single plan at Teotihuacan is important. It differs from, for example, Highland Maya centers where each large district has a plan but different districts follow different plans. This implies that the orientation of major features of Teotihuacan was *very* meaningful, controlled by a very strong and centralized overarching authority, or both.

A STANDARD UNIT OF MEASUREMENT

Several researchers, some of whom worked independently, have produced evidence for the widespread use of a unit of measurement varying from 80.5 to 83 centimeters at Teotihuacan (Drewitt 1987; Drucker 1974; Sugiyama 1993), and my own unpublished investigations have added some further evidence for this unit. This Teotihuacan measurement unit, or TMU, is manifested both in the dimensions of features of individual residences and pyramids, and in long-distance relationships. Within this 2.5-centimeter range, several variants fit best in specific cases. This may mean that the unit varied somewhat over time or among various builders, that it was difficult for Teotihuacanos to measure long distances with high accuracy, or both. One particularly striking example is that the distance from the Moon Pyramid to a point on the Avenue of the Dead in front of the Sun Pyramid is 1000 TMU, from that point to where the Río San Juan crosses the avenue is 1000 TMU, and the distance along the avenue from the Río San Juan to the Río San Lorenzo is 2000 TMU. That is, the distances between these points stand in the ratio 1:1:2. The slightly skewed north–south wall that runs for over 800 meters in Squares N5W2 and N4W2 is 1000 TMU west of the Avenue of the Dead, and the north–south watercourse in Square N2W8 is 4500 TMU west of the avenue. This is a conservative listing of some of the most obvious examples. There are suggestions that this TMU may even have been used to situate small rural sites up to 15 kilometers or more outside the city, but these need further study.

There is no obvious religious significance to multiples of 500 or 1000 TMU, and these long-distance patterns may simply reflect mundane orderliness. Even so, their wide prevalence in the city is another sign of centralized planning based on a single reference point. The persistence of some of these features up to the present day, about fourteen centuries after the collapse of Teotihuacan and nearly five centuries after the Spanish Conquest, is presumably not because they have remained very meaningful for much of that time, but simply because once they were established, there was never any good reason to change them.

In the case of individual structures, smaller multiples of the TMU may have served primarily as a convenience for builders. They could, for example, have been useful in calculating quantities of materials needed. In a later section, I discuss other TMU multiples proposed by Sugiyama (1993; 2005) that may correspond to symbolically significant numbers.

I now turn to a discussion of kinds of spatial units at Teotihuacan, beginning with individual apartment compounds and moving to small neighborhoods and larger districts, after which I consider possible palaces.

APARTMENT COMPOUNDS

These are substantial structures, each with multiple apartments, whose walls have rubble and adobe cores faced with approximately 5- to 10-centimeter-thick calcareous concrete layers, in turn covered by a thin layer of white plaster, sometimes decorated with fresco murals. Floors are also often of plastered concrete, although floors composed of small rounded river cobbles and earth floors are also not uncommon, often in the same compounds as the plastered floors. Most compounds were begun between ca. AD 200 and 300, and nearly all earlier structures were quite thoroughly razed in preparation, so we know almost nothing about earlier structures, although the abundance of redeposited ceramics from earlier occupations attests to their presence. Very likely, earlier residences were something like the earth and adobe structures recently found buried by volcanic ash at Tetimpa, not far away in the state of Puebla (Plunket and Uruñuela 1998), but we cannot be sure of this. In future work, we must intensify our search for the rare traces of earlier residential structures, especially to determine whether the substantial compounds known from excavations simply repeated earlier patterns in more durable form, or whether they represent disruptions of them.

The Mapping Project found Teotihuacan-period ceramics on some tracts without evidence of substantial architecture, especially toward the margins where substantial structures tend to be more widely spaced. However, these ceramics comprise a very small fraction of the total, and most Teotihuacanos must have lived in substantial compounds of the kind just described. Yet, occupants of many of these compounds were not of particularly high status. The Tlajinga 33 compound, discussed further below, is a good example of something close to the lower end of the status spectrum.

Once built, these apartment compounds typically went through at least two or three significant rebuildings. Floor levels were raised somewhat with each rebuilding (but not nearly to the extent seen in southwest Asian tells), and the depth from the current ground surface to archaeologically sterile subsoil usually ranges from 50 to 150 centimeters and is rarely over 2 meters except near the Avenue of the Dead, where some floors may be 5 meters or more above subsoil. Some apartment compounds, such as Zacuala "Palace"[3] (Figures 69; 67:49), have a highly integrated internal plan, while Jorge Angulo (1987) argues that Tetitla (Figures 70; 67:47) is the outcome of enlargements and alterations in what began as at least two separate units. At Tlajinga 33, a compound in the southern part of the city (Figures 71; 67: southwest corner of Square S3W1), excavations demonstrate a complex history of changes in size and shape (Storey 1992; Widmer 1987; Widmer and Storey 1993). In general, interior walls of apartment compounds are fairly close to the canonical orientation of 15.5 degrees east of north, but, at least in less well-built compounds, the alignments are only approximate, as seen in Tlajinga 33.

Exteriors of apartment compounds conform quite well to the canonical orientation. Most are rectangular, often nearly square, and often roughly 60 meters on a side, but they are not very standardized in size, and many are considerably smaller than this and a few are much larger. For example, Techinantitla (Figure 67: southwest part of Square N5E2), interpreted before excavation as several apartment compounds, after partial excavation appears to be a single enormous compound about 80 × 100 meters (R. Millon 1988: 97). Within apartment compounds, a limited number of modular ideas are expressed in highly varied ways, as can be seen from Figures 69–71 and 73. These include nearly square central courtyards, often with an altar in the center, surrounded on three or four sides by platforms a meter or so high on which rooms fronted by porticoes face the courtyard, with the eastern (that is, west-facing) platform being larger than the others. The platforms have *talud-tablero* profiles, that is, a basal sloping apron is surmounted by a somewhat overhanging vertical panel (Figure 72). Stairways, often with broad, plain, low balustrades, lead from the courtyard to the platforms. In addition, there are passageways and room groups, which form identifiable apartments and which themselves often have smaller interior patios. The number of rooms in a single apartment is generally consistent with its occupation by a single household. Thus, there would have been several households in a single compound. Interior walls tend to be around 30 to 50 centimeters thick, but the outer walls bounding the whole compound are much thicker, often over a meter. Usually two or three doorways give access to the compound from outside. Teotihuacan apartment compounds are not standardized or barracks-like. The state

---

[3] Names of excavated Teotihuacan structures come from a variety of sources. Many, such as Zacuala, are Nahuatl names still in use for the plots of land they occupy.

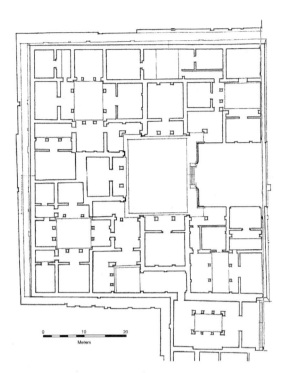

Figure 69. The Zacuala "palace" apartment compound.

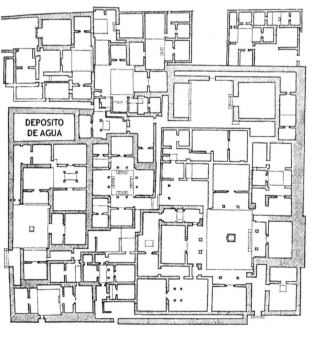

Figure 70. The Tetitla apartment compound.

Figure 71. The Tlajinga 33 apartment compound.

may have subsidized their construction and probably had some control over their exterior dimensions, but it clearly did not dictate internal arrangements. Network analyses by Mary Hopkins (1987a; 1987b) demonstrate this variability in layouts.

The social units that occupied compounds have often been termed "lineages," but the concept of "house" is probably better (see, for example, Carsten and Hugh-Jones 1995; Joyce and Gillespie 2000). Although graves are mostly simple unlined pits in subsoil under compound floors, a few have unusually rich offerings suggesting that the deceased was a founder, and the choice to put burials under compound floors itself suggests that key survivors

Figure 72. A profile of typical Teotihuacan *talud-tablero* platform construction. The thick black lines represent tabular stone slabs.

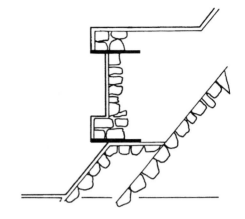

of the deceased expected to reside in the same place for some time to come. It is thus likely that apartment compounds tended to have a fairly stable core of persons considered to be linked by real or fictive kin ties. Beyond that, other individuals and small family units may well have shifted residence expediently, depending on space availability; social relations such as marriage, apprenticeship, and possibly clientage or servitude; and to escape from compounds where internal relationships were troubled. As Millon pointed out long ago, such residential flexibility seems the only way to make the fixed dimensions of apartment compounds compatible with the inevitable fluctuations in compositions over time of individual domestic units. Annabeth Headrick (1999) proposes that, at a much higher level, there may have been large internally ranked clans. If so, head families may have resided on or near the Avenue of the Dead, while lower-ranked clan members may have been spatially dispersed or to some extent concentrated in specific districts of the city. Evidence concerning such possible clan units is very scanty at present, but perhaps these conjectures can some day be tested.

Everywhere in the city, apartment compounds have interconnecting systems of subfloor drains that lead rainwater outside. In the more crowded parts of the city, compounds are separated by narrow streets, often no more than 2 to 3 meters wide. Without wheeled vehicles or beasts of burden, these would have been quite adequate for foot traffic. Open drains often run down their centers. Deep deposits of ceramics and even apparent earth floors have been observed in some streets but not adequately reported (for example, Séjourné 1966). It seems that these deposits would have markedly affected movement, and possibly they belong to a late stage in the city's history when public services were in decline.

Where apartment compounds are more widely spaced, they still follow the canonical orientation, and in most districts they are within the same general ranges of size and shape as in the more densely occupied districts. I suspect that garden plots occupied many of the intervals between these more widely spaced compounds.

POSSIBLE SMALL NEIGHBORHOODS OR BARRIOS

Outside the central civic-ceremonial core of Teotihuacan, there is occasional evidence of some spatial clustering of apartment compounds. There is, for example, a block of about 350 meters on a side (that is, about 12 hectares) in map Square N4E2 that includes the excavated Tepantitla compound (Figure 67:12). This block contains about 35 apartment compounds, with a small temple platform near the center of the block. I would very roughly guess the population of this block at around 1500 to 2000 persons. It is tempting to interpret it as a socially meaningful neighborhood, or *barrio*, and to think that the small temple might be a *barrio* temple, conceivably associated with the residence of a *barrio* leader. Millon has produced an unpublished and highly tentative subdivision of the whole city into approximately a hundred spatial units of about this size. Nevertheless, there are serious difficulties in identifying many hypothetical *barrios* of this size throughout the city. Except for a few ethnic enclaves and areas of craft specialization, which I discuss below, we have not so far been able to identify spatial units of this size on the basis of materials collected during the full-coverage surface survey of the Mapping Project or the few and generally spatially scattered cases of apartment compounds that have been excavated by technically adequate methods. In particular, the suggestion that scattered three-pyramid complexes served as *barrio* temples does not hold water. There are fewer than ten of these three-pyramid complexes outside the central core, far too few to match up with the hundred or so spatial units tentatively suggested by Millon, and nearly all these three-pyramid complexes occur in the northwestern quadrant of the city, leaving very large districts of the city without such pyramid complexes (which are prominent enough that they cannot be missed on survey).

If *barrio* headquarters existed at all, they are far more likely to have been like the Yayahuala apartment compound, where access to the large central courtyard is unusually direct and an unusually large platform faces this courtyard on its east side (Figures 73; 67:50). R. Millon (1976) suggests that Yayahuala may have been the residence of a *barrio* head. This may be so, but we know so much about Yayahuala because it has been excavated, and it is unlikely that it would have been recognized as unusual on the basis of surface survey alone. This means that if there were special residences of *barrio* heads, they are still nearly all unidentified. Thus, it is uncertain whether *barrio*-level units were important in the sociopolitical organization of Teotihuacan. The multi-apartment compounds are an unusual kind of residential unit, and they imply that there were important social units comprised of several households sharing the

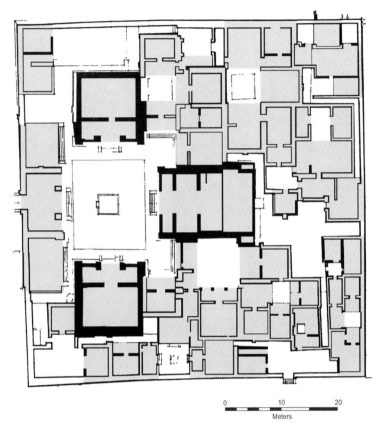

Figure 73. The Yayahuala apartment compound.
Shaded areas were probably covered by roofs.

same compound, as discussed above. Jeffrey Altschul (personal communication) suggests that apartment compound social units may have made *barrio* units unimportant.

ETHNIC ENCLAVES

We are on much firmer ground in talking about small ethnic enclaves and small neighborhoods of craft specialists, and in considering larger city districts on the order of 100 hectares and up in size. A spatially compact enclave covering 6 to 10 hectares and consisting of roughly ten apartment compounds, in map Square N1W6, not far from the western margin of the city, showed an unusual proportion of Oaxaca-like ceramics in the Mapping Project survey. A number of excavations have been carried out in some of these compounds (Rattray 1987a; 1987b; 1993; Spence 1976; 1986; 1989; 1992; 1996). The residential architecture in these compounds is typically Teotihuacano, somewhere in the intermediate range of quality, and the majority of the ceramics are typically Teotihuacan wares. However, a significant fraction were locally made (as determined by instrumental neutron activation analyses) but close copies of the wares of the Oaxaca region, including Monte Albán, the capital of the independent Zapotec state, some 375 kilometers from Teotihuacan. Many of these locally made imitations are utilitarian types, suggesting persistence of Oaxacan culinary and other domestic practices. A still smaller fraction are actual imports from Oaxaca, including Monte Albán–style ceremonial censers that are very different from the "composite" censers of Teotihuacan. Mortuary practices differ sharply from those of Teotihuacan (where most burials are flexed and in simple oval pits under house floors) and resemble those of Oaxaca in the use of stone-lined rectangular tombs that could be entered and periodically reused. Analyses of stable isotopes of oxygen in bones and teeth suggest that some of the persons buried in this enclave were residents of Teotihuacan, some came from places unknown, and none of those so far tested had spent any appreciable time near Monte Albán (White et al. 1998). There are still some puzzles about the chronology, but it is likely that this enclave was founded in the Early Tlamimilolpa phase (ca. AD 200) and maintained its ethnic identity until the collapse of Teotihuacan.

The impression that emerges, then, is of a group of a few hundred people from Oaxaca whose descendants maintained their ethnic identity for several centuries and lived in a compact enclave, but received few newcomers from Oaxaca after the founding generation. What brought them to Teotihuacan and what kept them there are puzzles. Their location far from the city center and the modest quality of their architecture imply that they were not high-status emissaries. To date, the most plausible suggestion is that they were masons. This is supported by the fact that Oaxaca-related materials have also been found at Teotihuacan-related sites in the vicinity of the later, Early Postclassic center of Tula, about 60 kilometers away, where the nearest significant occurrences of the limestone needed to make lime for Teotihuacan building are found (Crespo and Mastache 1981).

Another very clear ethnic enclave is the so-called Merchants' Enclave, at the northeastern margin of the city, covering a few hectares in Map Squares N3E4 and N4E4, just south of the extensively excavated Tlamimilolpa complex (Linné 1942). Test excavations were made by the Mapping Project in two structures in this enclave, and they were subsequently excavated more extensively by Evelyn Rattray (1987a; 1987b; 1989; 1990). Here, again, the great majority of the ceramics are local Teotihuacan wares, but about 6 percent are fine-paste imports from the Gulf Lowlands of Mexico, and about 3 percent are imports from the Maya Lowlands of northern Guatemala and the Yucatán Peninsula. Many of the earlier structures in this enclave are circular, a form that is otherwise rare at Teotihuacan but is believed to have been prevalent in the Gulf Lowlands. Later structures are architecturally typical of Teotihuacan. It is likely, though not certain, that the occupants of this enclave were, indeed, merchants. Since fine ceramics imported from the Gulf Lowlands and the Maya area are found scattered in small quantities throughout Teotihuacan, part of their trade may have been in ceramics. However, it is likely that most of the trade was in perishable materials, such as cotton textiles. At the altitude of Teotihuacan, where winter frosts are normal, cotton does not grow. Maguey cactuses (agaves) do grow there and produce a coarse fiber, but finer materials must have been imported, as raw cotton, spun yarn, or woven textiles. Some of the cotton may have come from the nearby and lower Valley of Morelos, but much may have come from the Gulf Lowlands, where there is abundant evidence of a cotton industry (B. Stark, Heller, and Ohnersorgen 1998). A review of data bearing on textile production at Teotihuacan (Cabrera Cortés 2001) has turned up little evidence of spinning or weaving (admittedly, both these tasks can be carried out with only perishable materials, but in post-Teotihuacan times, ceramic spindle whorls are abundant in the Teotihuacan Valley), but a considerable number of bone needles suitable for embroidery and other techniques for ornamenting already woven fabrics have been found at Teotihuacan. It seems likely, then, that occupants of the Merchants' Enclave were involved in importing cotton textiles, probably in large quantities, in addition to other things. It is unlikely that Teotihuacan exerted enough political influence in the Gulf Lowlands to have demanded these items as tribute, but what the Teotihuacanos could have offered in exchange remains unclear. A distinctive greenish kind of obsidian, whose source, near Pachuca, is about 55 kilometers from Teotihuacan, was, beyond reasonable doubt, controlled by Teotihuacan. It occurs widely in small amounts in Teotihuacan-period Mesoamerica. However, at least in the south central and southern Gulf Lowlands, this green obsidian is rare, and most of the obsidian is from closer sources, unlikely to have been controlled by Teotihuacan (B. Stark et al. 1992).

There are also suggestions of an enclave with west Mexican affiliations, not far from the Oaxaca Enclave, but so far little of the evidence for this has been published. Karl Taube (2000), expanding on earlier work by Clara Millon (1973), discusses iconographic and glyphic evidence for a strong Maya connection at the Tetitla compound, although no concentration of Maya ceramics has been reported there, and there are as yet no studies of Tetitla skeletal data bearing on this question.

CRAFT-SPECIALIST NEIGHBORHOODS

We have some evidence about localized concentrations of craft specialists, though far less than one would think from the secondary literature. In particular, the belief that around 400 workshops have been securely identified has little foundation. It stands to reason that there were many workshops at Teotihuacan, but we still have no good quantitative estimates. Perhaps most is known about production of a particular ceramic utility ware, San Martín Orange, which comes mainly in two forms, amphoras suitable for transport and storage and open craters suitable for food preparation by boiling or stewing. It is a sturdy and serviceable ware, well made but with little or no decoration, popular from the beginning of the Xolalpan phase (ca. AD 350) to the destruction of the city. The Mapping Project survey found high concentrations suggestive of its manufacture in the Tlajinga district, south of the Río San Lorenzo and rather separated from the main part of the city, in Map Squares S3W1, S3W2, S4W1, and S4W2. Subsequent excavations at one site in this district, Tlajinga 33, confirmed its manufacture there, as well as some evidence for lapidary production (Storey 1992; Widmer 1987; 1991; Widmer and Storey 1993). James Sheehy (1992) and Mary Hopkins (1995) have conducted a variety of archaeometric and compositional studies of this distinctive ware. Most recently, Kristin Sullivan (2006) has reexamined Mapping Project surface collections to determine which sites in this district were producing San Martín Orange ware most intensively and the degree of standardization in vessel sizes. She concludes that producers were working as independent specialists with little or no state intervention, although there may have been some local organization above the apartment compound level.

In contrast, producers of composite ("theater") incense burners—and the mold-made ornaments that rather flamboyantly adorned them—in a large walled enclosure attached to the north side of the Ciudadela (Site 2:N1E1), were probably working under state or at least institutional supervision and sponsorship. However, numerous censer fragments were also collected during the Mapping Project survey in and near Square N6W3 at the northwestern margin of the city, in quantities suggestive of local manufacture. If so, the distance from the civic-ceremonial core suggests little state control. This is also true of some definite or probable ceramic figurine workshops identified by Warren Barbour (1975), especially at Site 23:N5W3.

For other parts of the city and for other ceramic wares, there are known concentrations suggestive of local manufacture, but none have yet been adequately studied. Just outside the southeastern edge of the city, there is a site with an exceptional number of pottery-making tools, and we hope that before long excavations can be carried out there.

Michael Spence (1981; 1984; 1986; 1987; Spence, Kimberlin, and Harbottle 1984) has published a number of articles on obsidian at Teotihuacan. John Clark (1986) has questioned the scale of production of obsidian objects and the scale of their export elsewhere in Mesoamerica. Clark's estimates are probably too low. Nevertheless, earlier claims about the scale of Teotihuacan obsidian working and its export were surely exaggerated (for example, Santley

1983). None of the many suspected obsidian workshops at Teotihuacan has yet been excavated, although a structural complex adjoining the west side of the Moon Pyramid (Site 6:N5W1) that contains huge amounts of debris from the production of obsidian bifaces is now being excavated by David Carballo of the University of California, Los Angeles. Its location suggests that the refuse may be from obsidian workers attached to whatever community was identified with the Moon Pyramid. Some of the other sites in the city with strong evidence of specialized production of obsidian bifaces or prismatic blades are located far from any major civic-ceremonial structures and are more likely to have been occupied by independent artisans. It is difficult to say much more about the organization and scale of obsidian production at Teotihuacan with any confidence until we have more and better data.

Much the same applies to the organization of work in fine lapidary materials, such as green stone (usually fuchsite and serpentine, rarely jade) and marine shell. The Mapping Project found unusual quantities of fragments of such objects, including pieces broken during manufacture, at a cluster of six or eight apartment compounds in map Square N3E5, on the city's margins, and further evidence came from a small excavation there (Turner 1987; 1992). Evidence of lapidary work also came from fine screening at Tlajinga 33 (Widmer 1991). In both cases, it is likely that the artisans were independently organized. On the other hand, recent excavations in the La Ventilla district have revealed apartments of rather low construction quality in which there is considerable evidence for lapidary working, and adjoining apartments occupied by persons of much higher status, not far southwest of the Great Compound (Gómez Chávez 2000). In this case, the context suggests that the artisans were probably clients of wealthier patrons.

M. Oralia Cabrera Cortés (2001) has recently reviewed evidence for textile production at Teotihuacan. As indicated above, there is little evidence for spinning or weaving, but considerable evidence, in the form of bone needles, for embellishment of already woven textiles. Occasional bone needles are found widely in excavations, but notable concentrations occur in a La Ventilla compound near the place where there is evidence for lapidary work (Romero Hernández 2003), and in the north "palace" of the Ciudadela. This last suggests that some fine textile working may have been carried out in elite households, a practice that has parallels in other societies. Most recently, another concentration of bone needles has been found in excavations in the Teopancaxco apartment compound (Site 1:S2E2; Figure 67:22) (Linda Manzanilla, personal communication 2002). The walls of this compound have mural paintings, and its occupants were probably of above-average status.

In sum, to judge from the close proximity to or distance from major civic-ceremonial structures, it looks as if, for each craft, some workers were attached to powerful institutions and others were working independently.

Further studies of differences and similarities in products of less and more independent workshops will be interesting.

LARGER DISTRICTS

A few large districts are fairly obvious at Teotihuacan. One such is the central civic-ceremonial core, covering very roughly 250 hectares and largely enclosed by freestanding walls (Figure 68:6). It is worth pointing out that the Avenue of the Dead does not look like a major access-way for commerce and other mundane activities. Its northern terminus is blocked by the Moon Pyramid, located well south of the northern margin of urban settlement. Movement along its northern part would have been slowed and possibly controlled by a series of six transverse platforms with stairways that cross the stretch of the avenue between the Sun Pyramid and the Río San Juan (Figure 67). East and West avenues and lesser streets look more suitable for ordinary trafficking, and the Avenue of the Dead looks best fitted for ritual processions, access to religious and administrative structures, and perhaps the movements of pilgrims.

Another well-defined district is the Tlajinga area, discussed above. Yet another is the so-called Old City, which roughly corresponds to the region now called Oztoyahualco, in the northwestern part of the city. There are, however, two distinct subregions here. One, centered on Map Squares N6W3 and N6W2 and extending into the southern parts of N7W3 and N7W2, was recognized as different during the Mapping Project survey. In particular, apartment compounds are smaller and closely crowded. Linda Manzanilla's (1993; 1996) excavation at 15B:N6W3 found architecture somewhat different from most excavated Teotihuacan apartment compounds, although multiple apartments exist here also. If I understand correctly, René Millon suspects that residences in the subdistrict may preserve the style that prevailed generally at Teotihuacan before the massive program of apartment compound construction began in the Tlamimilolpa phase, and this was probably one of his reasons for labeling the whole district the "Old City." However, the highest densities of early ceramics (Patlachique and Tzacualli phases) are found in surface collections from another part of the Oztoyahualco region, 500 meters to a kilometer southeast of the northwesternmost part, centered on Map Squares N5W2 and N4W2. It included Plaza One, an early three-pyramid complex partially excavated by Millon and others in the late 1950s (R. Millon 1960; R. Millon and Bennyhoff 1961). Densities of early ceramics peter out in the northern part of N6W3.[4] In my opinion, the northwestern part of the district labeled "Old City" on the Mapping Project maps is better thought of as different,

---

[4] Because of the amount of recycling of earlier fill in subsequent building at Teotihuacan, tracts that have any cultural material at all on the surface have strong representations of ceramics from all periods of nearby occupation.

rather than earlier. The very high densities of materials collected from the surface in this subdistrict suggest that many craft workshops may have been located here. However, Manzanilla's is so far the only controlled excavation in this far northwestern subdistrict, and further excavations are urgently needed. The facts that this subdistrict lies outside major freestanding walls and contains two relatively large three-pyramid complexes suggest that it may have been partially independent of the central authority, although the structures conform closely to the canonical orientation.

Sophisticated multivariate spatial statistical studies by Ian Robertson (1999; 2001), utilizing Mapping Project electronic files, have gone far beyond earlier studies (for example, Cowgill, Altschul, and Sload 1984) and have revealed additional patterns, many of which could not have been discerned by simpler methods. Using ceramic categories pertaining to the Miccaotli phase, Robertson identified four major kinds of assemblage, interpretable as segments of the continuum from high to low socioeconomic status. These show marked differences in their spatial distributions, though with much overlap. Not unexpectedly, sites attributable to relatively high status occur most frequently near the city center, those attributable to low status are found most often near the margins, and those of intermediate status tend to be in between. However, there is a great deal of overlap and interdigitation in the locations of sites assigned to each category. The pattern is concentric only in a very broad-brush sense. Within any specific district, there are mixes of sites attributable to quite different socioeconomic statuses. This heterogeneity of neighborhoods confirms and extends René Millon's (1976) earlier observations, based on a small number of excavated compounds.

Robertson has gone beyond this, however, to consider the different *mixes* of kinds of sites in different neighborhoods. That is, in addition to considering the spatial distributions of types of *sites*, he has looked at types of *neighborhoods*. Here the spatial pattern is even clearer; types of neighborhoods with many high-status sites are more prevalent toward the center, and neighborhoods with many low-status sites are more typical of the peripheries, although, again, there are important exceptions. These patterns may have been to some degree imposed by top-down regulations, but they may easily be the result of bottom-up self-organizing processes based on individual residential decisions.

Robertson has carried out comparable analyses for the subsequent period, the Tlamimilolpa phase. The results are broadly similar but suggest decreasing heterogeneity within neighborhoods and increasing socioeconomic segregation. He suggests that this could have led to increasing tensions that may have played a role in the eventual destruction of the city. It will be important to see the results of extending his analyses to the Xolalpan and Metepec phases.

No discussion of districts at Teotihuacan could be complete without mentioning various long, freestanding walls detected by the Mapping Project. These are shown in Figure 68, with uncertain cases marked by dashed lines. There may well be others, yet undetected. No evidence of massive gates has been found and, in the absence of heavy siege apparatus in Mesoamerica, they should not be expected. In any case, the walls were more likely for regulating movements within the city than for defense. They do not surround the city, and they are little more than 2 meters thick at their bases, built of the same materials as apartment compound walls. The sole case with evidence of the original height of a wall is where one abuts the northwest corner of the Moon Pyramid (Mapping Project excavation 5). It was originally about 5 meters high. The absence of monumental gates means that we do not know how many openings there were in these walls, nor where openings were located. So far, except for the fact that the "Old City" is extramural, no obvious simple relations between these walls and districts identified by other criteria have been identified. These walls remain another important but still poorly understood feature of Teotihuacan.

PALACES

Much confusion about palaces has been caused by the rather broad meanings of this term in both English and Spanish and the generous application of this term to Teotihuacan apartment compounds (for example, Séjourné 1959; Flannery 1998). This was not unreasonable when it was believed that there were only a few large and architecturally substantial apartment compounds at Teotihuacan, but now that we know that there were more than 2000 such compounds, the use of this term at Teotihuacan must be reconsidered. The term should mean more than simply a residence of unusually fine quality. I define a palace as the residence of a ruler or at least holder of high political office, associated with which, in addition to residential quarters, there are facilities for carrying out various activities pertaining to the office of the chief occupant, such as feasting, entertainment and housing for visiting dignitaries, conducting business with members of the local population, judicial activities, and storage of food and perhaps other goods for distribution on suitable occasions. This is a polythetic definition: a palace need not provide for all these activities, but it should contain at least some of these in addition to residential quarters. By this definition, few if any Teotihuacan apartment compounds qualify as palaces.

Within the central civic-ceremonial core of the city, however, several complexes deserve serious consideration as possible palaces. In the great Ciudadela compound, there are two apartment compounds of above-average size and unusually symmetrical plan, flanking the north and south sides of the Feathered Serpent Pyramid (also known as the Temple of Quetzalcóatl) and

facing a large enclosed plaza within the Ciudadela and extending about 4.4
hectares in area (Figure 74). The northern compound is connected by stairways directly to a large walled enclosure attached to the north side of the
Ciudadela (Site 2:N1E1), which is still largely unexcavated but within which
partial excavation has revealed abundant evidence for specialized production
of composite ("theater") censers and the mold-made ornaments that pro-
fusely decorated them, discussed above as a likely workshop for "attached"
artisans. Long ago, Armillas (1964: 307) and Millon (R. Millon 1973: 55)
suggested that the heads of the Teotihuacan state resided in the compounds
within the Ciudadela. I (Cowgill 1983) agreed with this, although I pointed
out that the earliest stages of these compounds are not earlier than Miccaotli,
and heads of state must have resided elsewhere during the Patlachique and
Tzacualli phases, when Teotihuacan was growing most rapidly, early stages of
the Moon Pyramid were being built, and the Sun Pyramid reached nearly its
present size. I also pointed out that these two compounds do not provide the

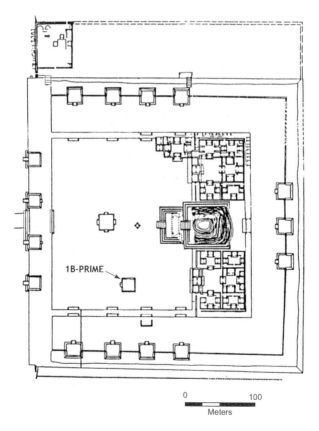

Figure 74. The Ciudadela, including residential compounds
that may have been palaces.

amount of facilities for governmental business that I would expect, although the close connection of the northern compound to the large walled enclosure attached to the north side of the Ciudadela might partially offset this. I suggested, tentatively, that, following the early growth of the city, centered on the Sun and Moon Pyramids, the Ciudadela might have been deliberately constructed by a very powerful ruler as the materialization of a new regime.

I further suggested that his successors might have found the Ciudadela residences awkwardly lacking in facilities for governmental activities and shifted to the Avenue of the Dead Complex, midway between the Ciudadela and the Sun Pyramid (Figures 75; 67:43). Most of the perimeter of this 12- to

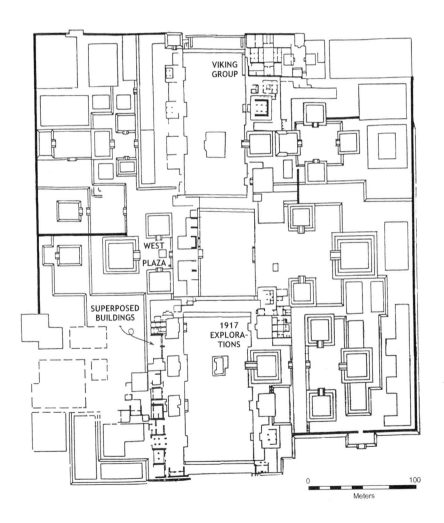

Figure 75. The Avenue of the Dead Complex.

13-hectare complex is surrounded by a wall, and within it there are a number of three-pyramid complexes, platforms, apartment compounds (including the "Viking" group), plazas, and possible office and storage structures. Burials are notably absent. Although it straddles the Avenue of the Dead, access from the avenue is limited. A sizable fraction of the western half was excavated in the early 1980s (Cabrera Castro, Rodríguez, and Morelos 1982a; 1982b; 1991; Morelos 1993). To me, it is suggestive of a city within a city, a little like the Forbidden City of Late Imperial Beijing. It seems to offer both residential facilities (some of very high quality) and the multitude of facilities for other functions and functionaries that I expect of a palace. In 1983, I suggested that the residence of the heads of the Teotihuacan state may have shifted from the Ciudadela to the Avenue of the Dead Complex, perhaps around the Late Tlamimilolpa subphase, while the Ciudadela compounds continued to have symbolic and religious significance.

This scenario still seems to me to be among the reasonable possibilities, although many alternatives are also reasonable. Excavations at the Feathered Serpent Pyramid have revealed that around 200 sacrificial victims were associated with its construction, but major pits had been looted and we do not know whether the pyramid was a funerary monument (Cabrera Castro, Sugiyama, and Cowgill 1991; Cowgill 1997; 2000b; Sugiyama 1998; 2005). Perhaps no more than a century after the pyramid's construction, the temple atop it was burned and fragments of it were thrown into the fill of a stepped platform built over the face of the pyramid; the pyramid itself was battered and allowed to fall into ruin. It is possible that the Ciudadela and the Feathered Serpent Pyramid were built by a highly autocratic ruler (and his successor, if the pyramid was indeed built upon this ruler's death), and its destruction and desecration may mark a turn to a more collective political system (in the sense of Blanton et al. 1996). This is very much what René Millon (1992) proposed. It is not inconsistent with the possibility that the Avenue of the Dead Complex became the new seat of central government.

The picture is further complicated, however, by the Xalla Complex, currently being excavated by Manzanilla, López Luján, and others. This is a walled complex in Map Square N4E1, a few hundred meters north-northeast of the Sun Pyramid and a few hundred meters southeast of the Moon Pyramid, covering about 4.5 hectares (Figures 76; 67:32). It contains a mix of plazas, platforms, room groups, and pyramids (in sets of four, rather than the more typical sets of three). Whatever else can be said about it, it is both monumental and architecturally unique at Teotihuacan. Its construction began in the Early Tlamimilolpa subphase, which means it is probably a little later than the earliest phase of the residences that flank the Feathered Serpent Pyramid. It may have been a palace for rulers, or it may have served some other special purpose.

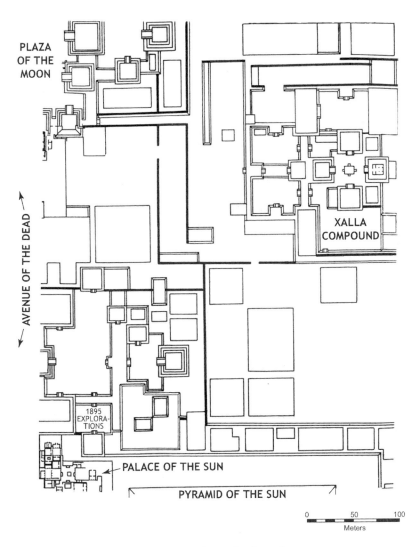

Figure 76. The Xalla Complex.

The Great Compound is formed by very large but low platforms in Map Square N1W1, just across the Avenue of the Dead from the Ciudadela (Figures 67:6; 68:11). Inside it is a large plaza which Millon has suggested may have been the principal marketplace of the city. It should be understood that this is so far merely a suggestion, not the definite identification often assumed in secondary literature. Nevertheless, it is quite plausible. On the surfaces of both the large platforms of the Great Compound are a number of structures of the same general shape and size as apartment compounds. None have yet been excavated, and at present we can only speculate about their nature. Nothing suggests to me that any of them were ever palaces. They may well have served intermediate level administrative functions, and it is conceivable that some were state storage facilities (the absence of good evidence for state storage facilities at Teotihuacan has been a persistent puzzle).

Thus, even after eliminating the Great Compound and apartment compounds outside the civic-ceremonial core, we are left with an embarrassment of riches, with at least three candidates for palace complexes. It could be that these served as palaces at different times or that some were not palaces at all, but it is also possible that the Teotihuacan political system, at least by the Late Tlamimilolpa subphase, was heterarchical as well as somewhat collective. That is, there may have been two or three somewhat independent political hierarchies (Ehrenreich, Crumley, and Levy 1995). This could help explain the muted monumental commemoration of individual rulers. However, at present this is sheer speculation.

CENTRAL TEOTIHUACAN A COSMOGRAM?

By the sixteenth century, Mesoamerican ideas about Teotihuacan were largely in the realm of mythology, and they perhaps tell us little about the thought, society, and history of the Teotihuacanos. Nevertheless, it is quite possible that the names of the Sun and Moon Pyramids derive from their Teotihuacan-period meanings. A colossal stone monument in female dress and extremely damaged remnants of a second were found near the Moon Pyramid. These have been variously identified as a water goddess and as manifestations of a pervasive "Great Goddess" that supposedly was the principal deity of the city (for example, Pasztory 1997).[5] There are problems with both these identifications, and I think these figures may well represent a Moon goddess. Fallen sculptures found in front of the Sun Pyramid include skulls and jaguars. At first sight, these do not seem to have obvious solar connections, but they may have to do with the Mesoamerican concept of the night sun of the underworld, with which jaguars are associated. Perhaps the Sun Pyramid, which faces toward the setting sun, was associated with the daily passage of the sun through the heavens and then through the underworld during the night. As to the Feathered Serpent Pyramid, by the sixteenth century the god or culture-hero Quetzal-cóatl was associated with both the feathered serpent and the planet Venus, and this may have been so even in Teotihuacan times. A case can be made, then,

---

[5] As the only general book-length treatment of Teotihuacan in English, Esther Pasztory's *Teotihuacan: An Experiment in Living* (1997) is, in many ways, a useful introduction, and I agree with many of her interpretations. However, there are a few factual errors, parts are already outdated, and some of her interpretations are very questionable.

that this triad composed of the three largest pyramids at Teotihuacan may have represented the Moon, Sun, and Venus, all of which were prominent astronomical objects in Mesoamerican thought.

Another pervasive Mesoamerican concept is the notion of four principal world directions, plus a vertical axis at their intersection that runs through various horizontal layers of the underworld, emerges at the earth's surface, and rises through multiple layers of the heavens. This cosmological model, the "Pivot of the Four Quarters" (Wheatley 1971), is, of course, found far beyond Mesoamerica, in North and South America, East Asia, and perhaps elsewhere. In Mesoamerica, the vertical axis is sometimes represented by a tree or large pole, but it can also be materialized on the ground as a horizontal axis, with north at the top (Ashmore 1991; Coggins 1980). It is highly likely that this was the case at Teotihuacan, and that the Avenue of the Dead was thought of as just such an axis. This would, to be sure, place the Moon in the highest layer of the heavens, but this may not have posed a serious problem for Teotihuacanos. Sugiyama (1993; 2005) proposes that the Feathered Serpent Pyramid and the Ciudadela, being south of the Río San Juan and bearing some watery symbolism such as marine shells, represented Venus in the watery underworld.

The details of these models need substantiation, and far more needs to be done with Teotihuacano iconography and symbolism, but I have little doubt that the Avenue of the Dead and the civic-ceremonial structures associated with it were viewed, at least on ceremonial occasions, as sacred rather than mundane space. Even today, walking northward along the avenue, it is easy (possibly deceptively easy) to feel that one is ascending through increasingly higher layers of sacred space (a feeling aided by the gentle upslope of the physical terrain). This concept was probably never far from people's minds, even when they were carrying out more secular business in the civic-ceremonial core. Outside that core, a more mundane attitude toward space may have been more prevalent, except for the ritual performances that certainly occurred at times there also, in contexts ranging from individual devotions, through households, apartment compounds, and districts.

In addition to the largest civic-ceremonial structures, a number of other freestanding platforms and pyramids were recorded by the Mapping Project. Some of these are single platforms or relatively small single pyramids, but more than a score are "three-pyramid" complexes, formed of a pyramid facing a plaza that is flanked on two sides by somewhat smaller pyramids. Their physical configuration suggests that they were dedicated to some triad of deities, but nothing suggests to me that these also represented the Sun, Moon, and Venus, and I have little idea what three gods were represented. Along the Avenue of the Dead, most three-pyramid complexes occur in matching pairs facing east and west; that on the east side (thus facing west) a little the larger of the two. The west-facing Sun Pyramid (arguably part of a three-pyramid complex if much smaller nearby pyramids are taken into account) is the major exception, for it has no western counterpart. The Moon Pyramid (also arguably part of a three-pyramid complex) and most of the few three-pyramid complexes outside the civic-ceremonial core face southward. Some of these south-facing three-pyramid complexes were already important places by the Tzacualli phase or earlier (for example, Plaza One, Figure 67:14), and thus predate the Ciudadela/Feathered Serpent Pyramid Complex and were at least coeval with the Sun and Moon Pyramids. All this points toward an early emphasis on south-facing pyramid groups, with the Moon Pyramid preeminent among them. Yet, by the Tzacualli phase, the Sun Pyramid faced west, and this westward emphasis is seen also at the slightly later Feathered Serpent Pyramid. This shift from south-facing to west-facing must be meaningful, but it remains a puzzle.

Sugiyama (1993; 2005) argues that a number of distances within the built environment of Teotihuacan are calendrically or astronomically important multiples of the TMU. For example, the sides of the Sun Pyramid are 260 TMU long, the eastern edges of the platforms surrounding the Sun Pyramid and the Ciudadela are both 2 × 260 TMU east of the central axis of the Avenue of the Dead, and the distance from the east edge of the Great Compound to the east edge of the Ciudadela is 584 TMU (584 is the average number of whole days in one Venus cycle). He also argues that all the principal features of the layout of the civic-ceremonial core were conceived as a single master plan from the beginning, although he acknowledges that they were not all built at once. It is certainly the case that the final configuration is coherent, rather than the jumble seen in many modern cities. Nevertheless, both Millon and I think that the layout evolved somewhat over time and was probably not planned in its entirety from the beginning.

One particularly enigmatic feature is Structure 1B-prime:N1E1, a small platform with a room atop in the southern part of the Ciudadela plaza (Figure 74) (Cabrera Castro 1982). Teotihuacan layouts are usually highly symmetrical, but there is no evidence that this platform ever had a counterpart in the northern part of this plaza. Mural designs painted on the walls of the room (Figure 77) are suggestive of later Mesoamerican cosmograms in codices (for example, Aveni 2000) and also of designs interpreted as Venus symbols on a structure at Tikal that has Teotihuacan-like *talud-tablero* architecture, near a composite stela that is very distinctively Teotihuacan in form and symbolism (Taube 2000). The location and imagery of this rather unimposing structure in the Ciudadela are a major unsolved puzzle.

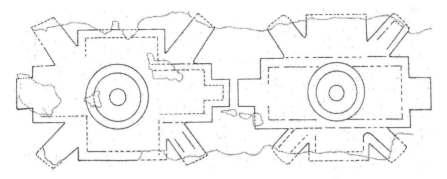

Figure 77. Mural designs on structure 1B-prime: N1E1 in the Ciudadela plaza.

CONCLUSION

In this paper I have tried to summarize what is known of Teotihuacan as an urban society and to offer interpretations I think warranted. I hope to have corrected some misunderstandings about Teotihuacan and to offer a sound basis for studies comparing Teotihuacan and other early urban societies. Necessarily, however, my review emphasizes not only how much we have learned about Teotihuacan, but also how much more remains to be learned before too much of the city (much of which is outside protected zones) is destroyed by modern developments.

THE HARAPPAN SETTLEMENT OF GUJARAT

GREGORY L. POSSEHL

ABSTRACT

The modern Indian state of Gujarat has emerged as the Sorath Domain of the Indus civilization (ca. 2500–1900 BC), an area with a material culture that shares much with the Mature Harappan known from Mohenjo-daro and Harappa, but also has distinctive material elements that set it apart from the other Indus domains. Approximately 400 of the 1500 known Indus sites are found there. Archaeological data suggest that during the Early Harappan (ca. 3200–2600 BC) and the Early Harappan–Mature Harappan Transition (ca. 2600–2500 BC), there was a migration of agro-pastoralists of the Indus cultural tradition into this region. The routes are not precisely known, but there is evidence that they crossed the Ranns of Kutch and also traversed the dry land around the northern edge of the Great Rann and moved south onto the North Gujarat plain. The peoples of the Early Harappan and the Early Harappan–Mature Harappan Transition met and interacted with a diverse set of peoples who were already present in Gujarat, as documented at the sites of Loteshwar, Nagwada, Padri, and Somnath. The economy of these "aboriginal peoples" of Gujarat was a combination of hunting, gathering, and pastoralism, and possibly some farming as well. During the second half of the third millennium BC, the Sorath Domain emerges as a complex cultural mosaic of peoples. This paper reviews the archaeological data supporting this hypothesis and offers a general model for the eastern expansion of the Harappan peoples out of Sindh and the Punjab.

INTRODUCTION

In the course of his career, Robert McC. Adams made many contributions to the study of ancient settlement patterns, in terms of both theory and field exploration. Over the past twenty years, his approach has also produced many insights into the lives of the prehistoric peoples of Gujarat. Since this article will appear in a volume not intended for South Asian specialists, and since it is impossible to fully appreciate the material reviewed in this paper without the benefit of a general chronology, one for the Greater Indus Region is presented as Table 8.

TABLE 8. A Chronology for the Greater Indus Valley

Stage and Phase	Dates
Stage One: **Beginnings of Village Farming Communities and Pastoral Camps**	
Kili Ghul Mohammad phase	7000–5000 BC
Burj Basket-marked phase	5000–4300 BC
Stage Two: **Developed Village Farming Communities and Pastoral Societies**	
Togau phase	4300–3800 BC
Kechi Beg/Hakra Wares phase	3800–3200 BC
Stage Three: Early Harappan	
Four phases thought to have been generally contemporaneous	
Amri-Nal phase	3200–2600 BC
Kot Dijian phase	3200–2600 BC
Sothi-Siswal phase	3200–2600 BC
Damb Sadaat phase	3200–2600 BC
Related material:	
Aceramic Northern Neolithic	2800–2500 BC
Stage Four: The Early–Mature Harappan Transition	
Early–Mature Harappan Transition	2600–2500 BC
Stage Five: Mature Harappan:	
Five phases thought to have been generally contemporaneous	
Sindhi Harappan phase	2500–1900 BC
Kulli Harappan phase	2500–1900 BC
Sorath Harappan phase	2500–1900 BC
Punjabi Harappan phase	2500–1900 BC

Stage and Phase	Dates
Eastern Harappan phase	2500–1900 BC
Three phases in adjacent regions	
Quetta phase	2500–1900 BC
Late Kot Diji phase	2500–1900 BC
Mature Northern Neolithic	2500–2000 BC
Stage Six: Post-urban Harappan	
Jhukar phase	1900–1700 BC
Early Pirak phase	1800–1000 BC
Late Sorath Harappan phase	1900–1600 BC
Lustrous Red Ware phase	1600–1300 BC
Cemetery H phase	1900–1500 BC
Swat Valley Period IV	1650–1300 BC
Late Harappan phase in Haryana andWestern Uttar Pradesh	1900–1300 BC
Late Harappan-Painted Grey Ware Overlap phase	1300–1000 BC
Early Gandhara Grave Culture phase	1700–1000 BC
Late Northern Neolithic	2000–1500 BC
Stage Seven: Early Iron Age of Northern India and Pakistan	
Late Pirak	1000–700 BC
Painted Grey Ware	1100–500 BC
Late Gandharan Grave Culture	1000–600 BC

The past decade has seen significant changes in our understanding of the Indus civilization. Exploration in India and Pakistan has vastly increased the documentation of sites from the beginnings of food production to the Early Iron Age (summarized in Possehl 1999: 555–567), and the study of settlement patterns and landscapes is beginning to come of age. Long-term excavations at places such as Harappa (Meadow 1991), Mehrgarh (Jarrige et al. 1995), Rojdi (Possehl and Raval 1989), and Dholavira (Bisht 1999) complement this exploratory work (Figure 78).

The Environment of Gujarat

Gujarat is made up of four distinct regions: Kutch, Saurashtra, and North and South Gujarat. Kutch is dominated by massive salt flats called "ranns" and the pasturelands of the higher ground, especially a rich area known as "Banni" (Figure 79). Saurashtra is a peninsula of basaltic, Deccan trap jutting into the

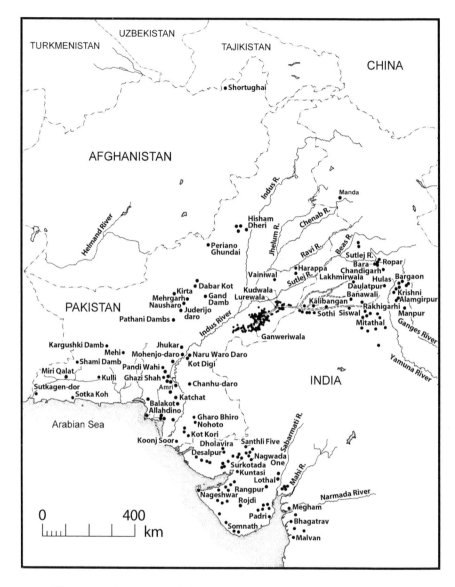

Figure 78. Some sites of the Indus Civilization and its predecessors.

Arabian Sea. Known as Kathiawar in British colonial times, this is a land of many rivers disposed in a radial pattern around the higher land in the center of the region. There is just enough monsoon rainfall for dry cropping to be done in the summer months, and the rivers provide a reasonably dependable water supply for humans and their animals. Vast stretches of rich pasture lie in the "doabs" between the many rivers. The long seacoast of Saurashtra has given the peoples living there ready access to maritime resources, probably

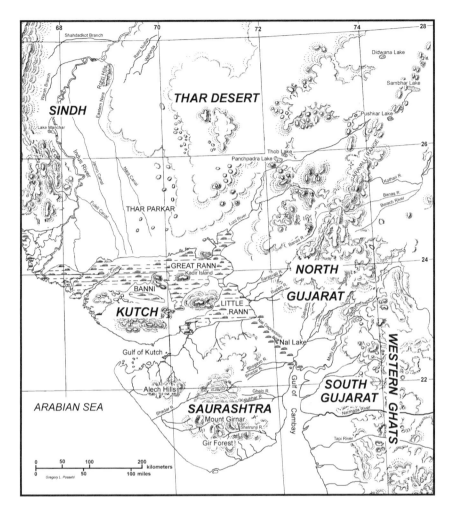

Figure 79. Some geographical features of Gujarat.

since the early Holocene. Reconstructions usually portray Saurashtra in the Holocene as a savannah grassland, with thick deciduous forests, including teak, in the upper elevations of the hills. North Gujarat is an almost feature-less sandy plain, crossed by several important rivers which drain into the Ranns of Kutch, or the Gulf of Cambay. The sandy soils do not retain much monsoon moisture; the slightly higher rainfall here, as compared with Sau-rashtra, makes dry cropping just possible. Also like Saurashtra, this is a vast pastureland of good grass, especially during and following the monsoon. South Gujarat is a relatively wet, thickly vegetated region, including the mountains of the Western Ghats and the coastal plain fronting them. There is more farming than pastoralism in this region. The coast of the Gulf of Cambay provides access to the sea and maritime resources.

There is a rich archaeological record in Gujarat generally, beginning with the Lower Palaeolithic (Sankalia 1987), but while the area is suitable for farming and pastoralism, it did not play a role in the early domestication of plants and animals because it is well outside their native ranges in Baluchistan and the Northwest Frontier. Farming and pastoralism seem to have come to the area from the northwest, with a migration of peoples from Sindh, accompanied, it seems, by a process of acculturating an indigenous population of hunter-gatherers to the arts of agriculture and pastoralism. The story of these two anthropological processes is the principal theme of this paper.

THE FIRST EXCAVATION OF A HARAPPAN SETTLEMENT IN GUJARAT

Father Henry Heras of Bombay University conducted the first excavation at a site of the Harappan Civilization in Gujarat (Figure 80). This excavation took place in 1930 near the famous town of Vallabhipur in eastern Saurashtra (Heras 1938). Heras's published recollection of this work was made as a part of his note on the Indus graffiti he found there. Whether the place Heras excavated is the Sorath Harappan site of Valabhi, later excavated at Vallabhipur by R. N. Mehta (1984) of the M. S. University of Baroda, is not known.

The second excavation of a Bronze Age site in Gujarat was conducted in 1934–1935 at Rangpur by M. S. Vats at the invitation of the Thakore Sahib

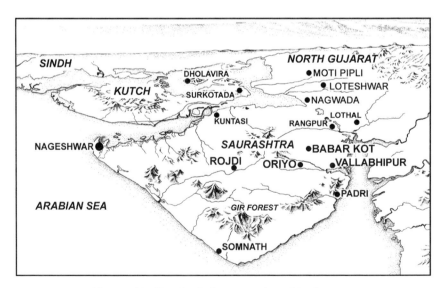

Figure 80. Sites in Gujarat mentioned in the text.

of Limbdi State. Vats dug three trenches at this huge site and found a great deal of pottery but little architecture. Vats opined that the pottery was Indus black and red ware, with the presence of triangular terracotta cakes and perforated vessels reinforcing his conclusion. But he also noted that some of the ceramics appeared to be more "evolved" than those found in the Early and Intermediate periods of Mohenjo-daro or Harappa. It was on this basis that Vats (1934–1935) suggested that the part of Rangpur where he excavated might correspond to the Late period of the Indus civilization or perhaps fall between that time and the period of Cemetery H at Harappa. Thus began the myth that the Bronze Age sites of Saurashtra were "Late Harappan."

We have known for many decades that there are Mature Harappan sites in the Kutch District of Gujarat. I call these "Sindhi Harappan" because of their close geographical and cultural affiliations with Mature Harappan sites in the lower Indus Valley. Records are available on 54 of these sites, as enumerated in Table 9.

S. R. Rao's (1963) excavations at Rangpur from 1953 to 1956 are also important in documenting the Indus civilization in Gujarat, but it was his work at Lothal (1954 to 1963), the southeasternmost Sindhi Harappan site, that most thoroughly clarified the point that there were Indus settlements in Gujarat outside of Kutch (S. R. Rao 1979; 1985). Later excavations demonstrated that there is even a Sindhi Harappan site called Nageshwar at the very northwestern tip of Saurashtra (Hegde et al. 1990), which seems to have been seasonally occupied for the harvesting and working of shells, especially the conch.

TABLE 9. Mature Harappan Sites in Kutch

Site	Coordinates	Excavated
Bhachau		
Chitrod	23° 24' 00" N – 70° 40' 00" E	
Desalpur	23° 37' 00" N – 69° 08' 00" E	Excavated
Dholavira	23° 53' 10" N – 70° 13' 00" E	Excavated
Gadhwaliwadi	23° 30' 00" N – 69° 08' 00" E	
Gunthai	23° 28' 00" N – 69° 09' 00" E	
Jatavadar	23° 45' 00" N – 70° 40' 00" E	
Jhangar, Anjar	23° 19' 00" N – 70° 05' 00" E	
Jhangar, Khavada	23° 53' 00" N – 69° 44' 00" E	
Juna Chopadwa	23° 16' 00" N – 70° 15' 00" E	

Site	Coordinates	Excavated
Kanmer	23° 29' 00" N – 70° 29' 00" E	
Kanthkot		
Katasar	23° 34' 00" N – 70° 29' 00" E	
Kerasi	23° 40' 00" N – 70° 44' 00" E	
Khakhra Dera	23° 34' 00" N – 70° 29' 00" E	
Khandariya		
Kharika Khanda	23° 27' 00" N – 70° 19' 00" E	
Khavda		
Khedoi	23° 03' 00" N – 69° 57' 00" E	
Kotada Bhadli One	23° 22' 00" N – 69° 26' 00" E	
Kotada Bhadli Two	23° 22' 00" N – 69° 26' 00" E	
Kotada Bhadli Three	23° 22' 00" N – 69° 26' 00" E	
Kotada	23° 18' 00" N – 70° 06' 00" E	
Kotahra		
Kotara	23° 58' 00" N – 69° 47' 00" E	
Ladai		
Lakhasar One	23° 14' 00" N – 70° 41' 00" E	
Lakhasar Two	23° 14' 00" N – 70° 41' 00" E	
Lakhpar	23° 33' 00" N – 70° 28' 00" E	
Lakhpat	23° 50' 00" N – 68° 47' 00" E	
Luna	23° 40' 00" N – 69° 15' 00" E	
Luna Mandvi	22° 50' 00" N – 69° 24' 00" E	
Mandriyara Mohra	23° 30' 00" N – 70° 16' 00" E	
Meghper	23° 50' 00" N – 70° 42' 00" E	
Morvo	23° 29' 00" N – 69° 09' 00" E	
Mulu		
Narapa		
Navinal	22° 50' 00" N – 69° 35' 00" E	
Nenuni Dhar	23° 51' 00" N – 69° 44' 00" E	

Site	Coordinates	Excavated
Ner		
Netra Khirasara		
Pabumath	23° 37' 00" N – 70° 31'00"E	Excavated
Pirwada Khetar	23° 20' 00" N – 70° 00'00"E	
Rampar Vekarano Timbo		
Rampara	23° 30' 00" N – 70° 45' 00" E	
Ramvav	23° 32' 00" N – 70° 28' 00" E	
Samagogha	22° 55' 00" N – 69° 40' 00" E	
Sapara		
Selari	23° 42' 00" N – 70° 37' 00" E	
Shikarpur	23° 07' 00" N – 70° 35' 00" E	Excavated
Surkotada	23° 37' 00" N – 70° 50' 00" E	Excavated
Todia Timbo		
Todio	23° 05' 00" N – 68° 55' 00" E	
Vada	23° 29' 00" N – 69° 07' 00" E	

ROJDI 1982–1986: THE EMERGENCE
OF THE SORATH HARAPPAN

When the renewed excavations at Rojdi began in 1982–1983, the research team had a working hypothesis that deep in the core of the mound, there should be a settlement that dated to the third millennium, contemporary with the Mature Harappan. We expected to find Sindhi Harappan–type artifacts, probably "provincial" in style, distinctive of the Indus peoples who inhabited Saurashtra. The artifacts should have included the Indus stamp seals, cubical weights in the Mature Harappan metrical system, etched carnelian beads, faience artifacts, baked brick buildings, brick-lined wells, a drainage system, and Sindhi Harappan pottery, especially some of the distinctive black painted red ware.

There are three phases of occupation at Rojdi. Rojdi A and B can be securely dated to the third millennium BC, contemporary with the Indus civilization. Rojdi C is "Post-urban" and dates to roughly 1900–1700 BC. This chronology is based on a long series of radiocarbon dates (Table 10) and confirmed by dates from three other third-millennium sites in Saurashtra:

Babar Kot, Padri, and Kuntasi, as seen in Table 11. The suite of artifacts that were actually found in the course of our excavations at Rojdi proved to be at variance from this "working hypothesis" (Possehl and Raval 1989).

TABLE 10. Rojdi Radiocarbon Dates

Lab No.	5730 Half-life	Calib-3 dates	Period
PRL-1704	5710 ± 90 bp	[1] cal BC 4687 (4535) 4459 [2] cal BC 4780 (4535) 4354	Late Sorath Harappan
PRL-1084	3700 ± 150 bp	[1] cal BC 2289 (2120, 2084, 2042) 1884 [2] cal BC 2489 (2120, 2084, 2042) 1683	Rojdi C Late Sorath Harappan
BETA-61767	3570 ± 60 bp	[1] cal BC 1973 (1892) 1780 [2] cal BC 2114 (1892) 1742	Rojdi C Late Sorath Harappan
BETA-61768	3520 ± 60 bp	[1] cal BC 1914 (1875, 1836, 1818, 1800, 1785) 1745 [2] cal BC 2013 (1875, 1836, 1818, 1800, 1785) 1682	Rojdi C Sorath Harappan
PRL-1870	3470 ± 160 bp	[1] cal BC 1973 (1748) 1529 [2] cal BC 2197 (1748) 1414	Rojdi C Late Sorath Harappan
PRL-1081	2360 ± 210 bp	[1] cal BC 790 (399) 181 [2] cal BC 911 (399) cal AD 76	Rojdi C Late Sorath Harappan
PRL-1083	3875 ± 120 bp	[1] cal BC 2481 (2390, 2389, 2333) 2141 [2] cal BC 2844 (2390, 2389, 2333) 1974	Rojdi B Sorath Harappan
TF-200	3810 ± 110 bp	[1] cal BC 2455 (2272, 2258, 2204) 2041 [2] cal BC 2563 (2272, 2258, 2204) 1924	Rojdi B Sorath Harappan
PRL-1088	3770 ± 120 bp	[1] cal BC 2397 (2190, 2160, 2145) 1981 [2] cal BC 2553 (2190, 2160, 2145) 1789	Rojdi B Sorath Harappan

TABLE 10. Rojdi Radiocarbon Dates (cont.)

Lab No.	5730 Half-life	Calib-3 dates	Period
TF-199	3590 ± 100 bp	[1] cal BC 2112 (1926) 1772 [2] cal BC 2197 (1926) 1679	Rojdi B Sorath Harappan
PRL-1281	3520 ± 110 bp	[1] cal BC 1973 (1875, 1836, 1818, 1800, 1785) 1686 [2] cal BC 2138 (1875, 1836, 1818, 1800, 1785) 1527	Rojdi B Sorath Harappan
PRL-1282	3470 ± 140 bp	[1] cal BC 1944 (1748) 1612 [2] cal BC 2140 (1748) 1435	Rojdi B Sorath Harappan
PRL-1091	4150 ± 110 bp	[1] cal BC 2886 (2859, 2815, 2693, 2672, 2670) 2504 [2] cal BC 2924 (2859, 2815, 2693, 2672, 2670) 2457	Rojdi A Sorath Harappan
PRL-1085	4020 ± 110 bp	[1] cal BC 2853 (2558, 2530, 2497) 2405 [2] cal BC 2882 (2558, 2530, 2497) 2200	Rojdi A Sorath Harappan
PRL-1087	4010 ± 110 bp	[1] cal BC 2850 (2553, 2543, 2493) 2363 [2] cal BC 2880 (2553, 2543, 2493) 2196	Rojdi A Sorath Harappan
PRL-1093	3920 ± 110 bp	[1] cal BC 2563 (2455, 2412, 2409) 2203 [2] cal BC 2857 (2455, 2412, 2409) 2041	Rojdi A Sorath Harappan
PRL-1089	3870 ± 120 bp	[1] cal BC 2474 (2328) 2140 [2] cal BC 2837 (2328) 1972	Rojdi A Sorath Harappan
PRL-1284	3810 ± 100 bp	[1] cal BC 2453 (2272, 2258, 2204) 2045 [2] cal BC 2553 (2272, 2258, 2204) 1942	Rojdi A Sorath Harappan
PRL-1285	3740 ± 140 bp	[1] cal BC 2393 (2137) 1935 [2] cal BC 2558 (2137) 1745	Rojdi A Sorath Harappan

TABLE 11. Radiocarbon Dates from Babar Kot, Padri, and Kuntasi

Babar Kot Radiocarbon Dates

Lab Number	5730 Half-life	Calib-3 dates	Period
PRL-1490	3233 ± 165 bp	[1] cal BC 1683 (1512) 1315 [2] cal BC 1888 (1512) 1047	Late Sorath Harappan
BETA-43245	3660 ± 70 bp	[1] cal BC 2135 (2026, 1997, 1985) 1924 [2] cal BC 2201 (2026, 1997, 1985) 1784	Sorath Harappan
BETA-43246	3700 ± 60 bp	[1] cal BC 2179 (2120, 2084, 2042) 1976 [2] cal BC 2278 (2120, 2084, 2042) 1905	Sorath Harappan
WIS-2235	3730 ± 60 bp	[1] cal BC 2197 (2135, 2071, 2063) 1989 [2] cal BC 2290 (2135, 2071, 2063) 1942	Sorath Harappan
WIS-2234	3775 ± 120 bp	[1] cal BC 2399 (2192, 2157, 2147) 1983 [2] cal BC 2556 (2192, 2157, 2147) 1827	Sorath Harappan
PRL-1487	3850 ± 110 bp	[1] cal BC 2464 (2289) 2137 [2] cal BC 2582 (2289) 1972	Sorath Harappan
WIS-2232	3900 ± 105 bp	[1] cal BC 2551 (2450, 2446, 2401, 2372, 2365) 2198 [2] cal BC 2837 (2450, 2446, 2401, 2372, 2365) 2038	Sorath Harappan
PRL-1493	3980 ± bp	[1] cal BC 2611 (2468) 2327 [2] cal BC 2873 (2468) 2142	Sorath Harappan
PRL-1492	4030 ± 120 bp	[1] cal BC 2859 (2563, 2524, 2500) 2405 [2] cal BC 2888 (2563, 2524, 2500) 2197	Sorath Harappan

Padri Radiocarbon Dates

Lab Number	5730 Half-life	Calib-3 dates	Period
PRL-1784	3660 ± bp	[1] cal BC 2179 (2026, 1997, 1985) 1887 [2] cal BC 2317 (2026, 1997	Sorath Harappan, Period II
PRL-1786	3940 ± 90 bp	[1] cal BC 2285 (2137) 1976 [2] cal BC 2460 (2137) 1881	Sorath Harappan, Period II
PRL-1536	4010 ± 140 bp	[1] cal BC 2861 (2553, 2543, 2493) 2321 [2] cal BC 2907 (2553, 2543, 2493) 2048	Sorath Harappan, Period II
PRL-1785	4390 ± 90 bp	[1] cal BC 3260 (3022, 2985, 2928) 2905 [2] cal BC 3347 (3022, 2985, 2928) 2784	Pre-Harappan, Period I
PRL-1787	4820 ± 90 bp	[1] cal BC 3699 (3636) 3387 [2] cal BC 3792 (3636) 3363	Pre-Harappan, Period I

Kuntasi Radiocarbon Dates

Lab Number	5730 Half-life	Calib-3 dates	Period
PRL-1370	3710 ± 160 bp	[1] cal BC 2328 (2128, 2080, 2045) 1884 [2] cal BC 2563 (2128, 2080, 2045) 1680	Sorath Harappan
PRL-1371	3650 ± 140 bp	[1] cal BC 2197 (2019, 2003, 1981) 1780 [2] cal BC 2457 (2019, 2003, 1981) 1674	Sorath Harappan

The artifacts from Rojdi are not always strikingly Mature Harappan in style (Figures 81, 82). There are no Indus stamp seals at Rojdi, nor at any other Harappan site in Gujarat, save for those that can be called "Sindhi Harappan." But there is a great deal of Indus writing on pottery in the form of graffiti (Figure 82:6–13) as well as cubical stone weights that follow the

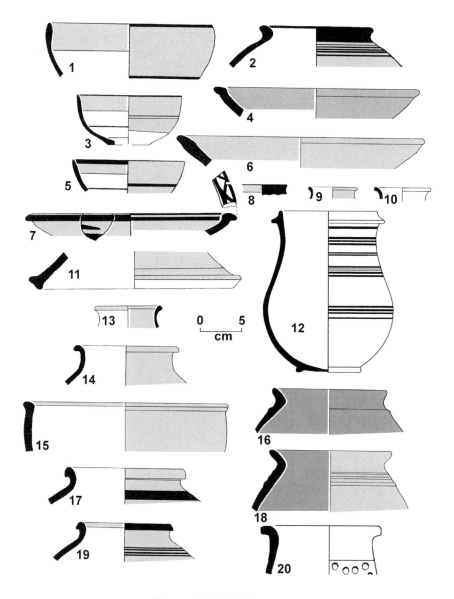

Figure 81. Rojdi A pottery.

Mature Harappan metrical system (Figure 82:17). We also have Mature Harappan–style etched carnelian beads (Figure 82:1–5) and some faience, but no baked bricks, let alone entire buildings of this material. Rojdi has none of the facilities for managing water that are found at a place like Mohenjo-daro—not even a well. Moreover, Rojdi is quite small by Mature Harappan

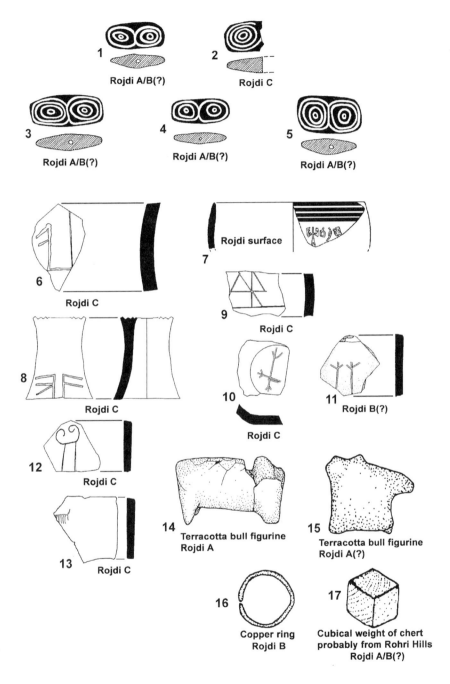

Figure 82. Artifacts from Rojdi A, B, and C.

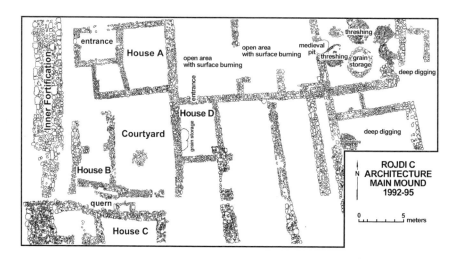

Figure 83. Plan of the Rojdi C settlement on the Main Mound of Rojdi.

standards (about 7.5 hectares), but it appears to have been a well-planned set-tlement, with clear traces of regular planning and alignment, although it must be admitted that these data come from the second-millennium occupa-tion of Rojdi C (Figure 83).

As can be seen in Figure 81, the ceramics of Rojdi A are stylistically akin to those of the Sindhi Harappan, with dishes on stands, perforated ware, and considerable overlap in the shapes of jars, bowls, and large storage contain-ers. There are also many differences. The Rojdi ceramic corpus does not include the Mature Harappan goblet or beaker, for example, and the S-form jar is represented by two examples from Rojdi that are relatively squat, com-pared with Sindhi Harappan examples, and "provincial" in style (Figure 81:12). The Mature Harappan black-on-red ware painting style is not found at Rojdi, but there is a local style that includes the representations of both plants and animals. Rojdi is therefore a mixed bag of characteristics, suffi-ciently different that I have come to call Rojdi, and the other sites like it in Saurashtra, "Sorath Harappan" settlements (Possehl 1992a; 1992b; Possehl and Herman 1990). Clearly contemporary with Mohenjo-daro and the Indus civilization, there is enough of the Mature Harappan world there to keep Rojdi as a part of a larger Indus civilization, but the differences are important too, especially the lack of stamp seals and the kind of facilities that managed water for the Harappans, especially in Sindh and the Punjab.

Rojdi was not the only Sorath Harappan site. There are now records of 327 sites of the Rojdi A/B type in Saurashtra as compared with 198 sites of the early second-millennium Rojdi C.

Perhaps the most powerful reason to think of Rojdi as a part of the Harappan civilization is not related to the material culture found there, but to what we are learning about the culture historical roots of its people. This is the principal reason that I find it quite off the mark to think that the peoples of the Sorath Harappan are not "Harappans" at all (Varma and Menon 1999).

THE ANARTA TRADITION OF NORTH GUJARAT

It is now clear that by the end of the fourth millennium, farmers and/or herders had made their way into Kutch, North Gujarat, and Saurashtra. These peoples remain somewhat shadowy, but their earliest documented occurrence has been defined at Loteshwar. Period I was an aceramic hunter-gatherer camp, but Period II was a camp for people who made pottery and kept domesticated sheep and goats, some cattle, and also hunted wild mammals. We do not know the role that cultivation played in their subsistence activities. Two radiocarbon dates from Period II at Loteshwar calibrate to ca. 2900–3700 BC (Sonawane and Ajithprasad 1994: 136).

The majority of the pottery of the people of Loteshwar II seems to be local wares, not clearly a part of the Harappan or Early Harappan cultural tradition (Figure 84). They consist of a Fine Red Ware, Gritty Red Ware, Burnished Red Ware, and a Burnished Grey/Black Ware (Ajithprasad and Sonawane, in press). However, there are also some shapes and fabrics that do look more like those of the Early Harappan, but these are in the minority. This entire pottery corpus has been dubbed the "Anarta Tradition" (Ajithprasad and Sonawane, in press).

We do not have a full report on the excavations at Loteshwar, so details of this important site are lacking. Nevertheless, there is nothing in either the proposed chronology or the material culture that runs counter to established facts. It can certainly be argued that 3700 BC is rather early for the beginnings of the Early Harappan, but this can be easily explained if it is to the peoples of the Hakra Wares Phase that we should ascribe the origins of the Harappan cultural tradition. This is an important detail but does not compromise the proposition that there is substantial archaeological evidence for food-producing peoples in North Gujarat in the fourth millennium BC.

The people(s) of the Anarta Tradition lived alongside an "aboriginal" population who subsisted on hunting and gathering, using microlithic tools and living in small camps like those at Akaj and Langhnaj (Sankalia 1965). As far as we know, the peoples represented by these sites, of which there are hundreds in North Gujarat (K. K. Bhan 1994: 73–74), kept no domesticated animals and did no farming.

Pottery of the Anarta Tradition has also been found at Nagwada, Surkotada, and Lothal (Sonawane and Ajithprasad 1994: 135), although at the latter

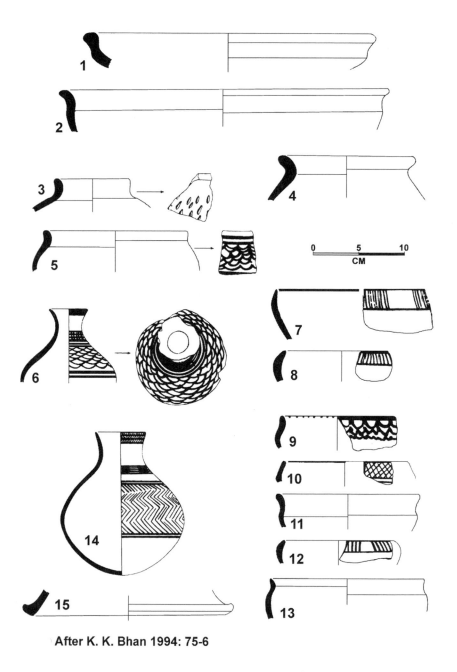

After K. K. Bhan 1994: 75-6

Figure 84. Pottery from Loteshwar.

two sites, Anarta pottery is not a prominent part of the ceramic corpus. Thus, it is evident that the "local wares" of the Anarta Tradition had a long life, beginning in the fourth millennium and extending in time to at least the second half of the third millennium, where they are contemporary with the Indus civilization.

The culture historical roots of the people(s) of Loteshwar II are not entirely clear and are probably anything but simple. As a working hypothesis, it can be postulated that their deep history relates to the early food-producing economies of Sindh, but this may be quite distant and/or indirect. Such a relationship would account for the presence of domesticated sheep, goat, and cattle. However, their "cultural distance" from the early food-producing peoples of Sindh appears to be rather pronounced, since they came to make their own types of pottery and also used the microlithic tool technology of the hunter-gatherer peoples of Gujarat and Rajasthan. It is entirely possible that the people(s) of the Anarta Chalcolithic were indigenous to North Gujarat and took to food production, at least the use of domesticated animals, through a process of acculturation.

EARLY HARAPPANS IN GUJARAT

By the very late fourth millennium (ca. 3200 BC) or early third millennium, the peoples of the Anarta Tradition were joined by others who used the ceramics that we can associate with the Early Harappans of Sindh: Amri-Nal and Kot Dijian. This has been reasonably well documented at three sites: Nagwada, Moti Pipli, and the small group of cairn burials at Surkotada.

Nagwada

Prof. K. T. M. Hegde and a team from the M. S. University of Baroda have found one extended and three pot "burials" at Nagwada, a site in the estuary of the Rupen River in North Gujarat (Hegde 1989; Hegde et al. 1988; 1990). The pottery from the Nagwada graves, especially the pot burials—which were in fact cenotaphs rather than burials—is very much within the Amri fold, made up of hard pink to red fabrics with shapes like those from Amri Period I, including tall vases with featureless rims (Figures 85, 86). There is also a small, red slipped pot with white painting that bears a striking similarity to something out of a Sothi-Siswal assemblage (Figure 87). All of the interments were sealed below a stratum with Mature Harappan material, indicating that they belong to the early period at the site (Hegde et al. 1988: 58).

Moti Pipli

Small-scale work at the site of Moti Pipli in the Banaskantha District of North Gujarat has also produced Early Harappan ceramics (Figure 88). Once again, there is no final report on this excavation, but we do know from A. Majumdar

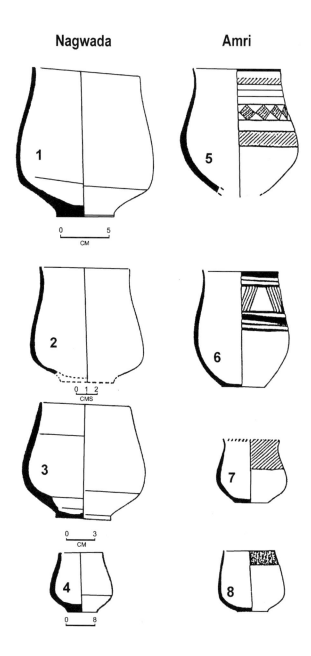

Figure 85. Early Harappan pottery from Nagwada and Amri.

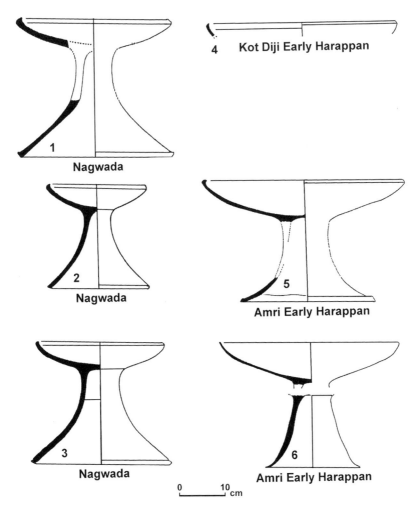

Figure 86. Early Harappan pottery from Nagwada, Amri, and Kot Diji.

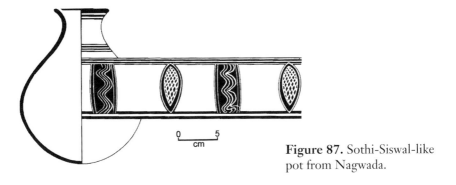

Figure 87. Sothi-Siswal-like pot from Nagwada.

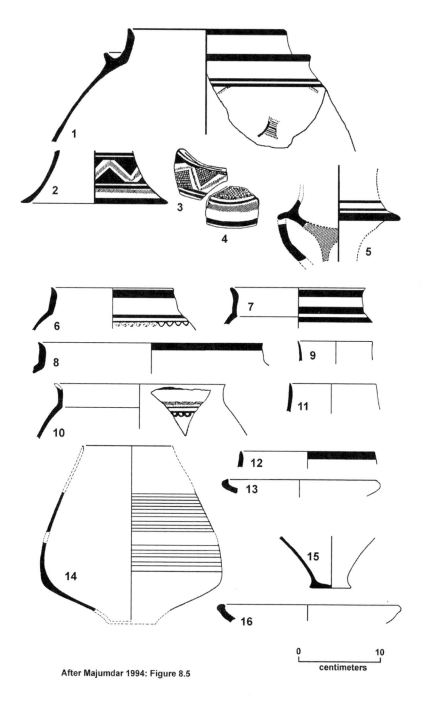

After Majumdar 1994: Figure 8.5

Figure 88. Early Harappan pottery from Moti Pipli.

(1994) that the ceramics come from graves—once again cenotaphs. The ceramics in Figure 88 are clearly Early Harappan in character—generally what I would associate with the Amri-Nal assemblage—but the flange rim of Figure 88:1 looks quite Kot Dijian.

Surkotada

Surkotada is a prominent archaeological site in Rapar Taluka of Kutch District (Joshi 1990). The principal mound there is a fortified, Mature Harappan settlement. In general, it is a "standard" Sindhi Harappan site, but there are some interesting ceramics, especially those of the Anarta Tradition.

The excavator uncovered four burials near Surkotada. These were secondary interments located in a small cemetery 300 meters northwest of the main mound (V. V. Rao 1990; Possehl 1997a). There is no systematic report on the skeletal material from these interments, but their ceramics are clearly a part of the Amri-Nal assemblage of southern Sindh. I have given exact comparisons elsewhere (Possehl 1997a), but the key element here is the frequency of high, featureless rims on these pots, which is typically Amrian. The dish on stand from the Surkotada cemetery (Figure 89) also has an exact comparison with one from Amri.

THE EARLY HARAPPAN/MATURE HARAPPAN TRANSITION IN KUTCH

Dholavira is the name of a modern village on the western end of Kadir Island in the Great Rann of Kutch. It is just opposite the shore of the Thar Parkar area, some 75 kilometers northwest of Surkotada. The archaeological site, known locally as Kotada (Large Fort), lies adjacent to the village, and its excavation has provided much interesting information on the movement of ancient Sindhis into Kutch. In 1990, R. S. Bisht of the Archaeological Survey of India initiated excavations there (Bisht 1989a; 1989b; 1991; 1994; 1997), in the course of which he found what he has termed a "pre-Harappan" occupation (Bisht 1991: 76) which he attributes to the Early Harappan–Mature Harappan Transition. This is a 100- to 150-year period of change that has been hypothesized by Shaffer and Lichtenstein (1989) and myself (Possehl 1990; 1993; 2002: 50–53) as the time when there was a paroxysm of culture change during which most of the distinctively urban features of the Indus civilization were developed. The "Transition" is generally dated to ca. 2600–2500 BC.

The ceramics of Period I at Dholavira have been described only in a preliminary way but include wheel-made red to pink wares, comb-incised wares, and a "reserved slip" ware. Deep dishes and jars have been reported, and slips

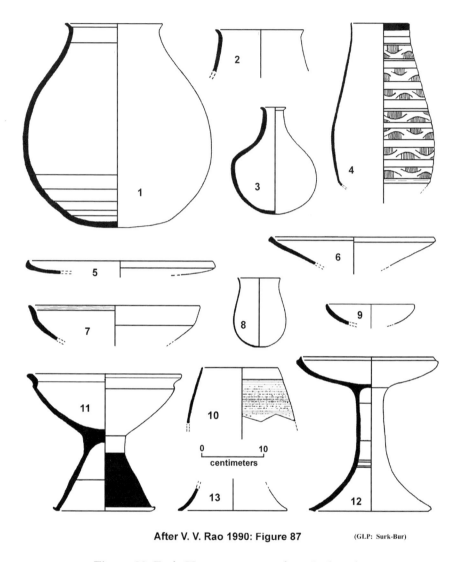

After V. V. Rao 1990: Figure 87   (GLP: Surk-Bur)

Figure 89. Early Harappan pottery from Surkotada.

are present in red and darker tones. Painting, also in dark colors, is sometimes highlighted in white—one of the hallmarks of the Early Harappan.

Bisht has allowed me to handle some of this material, and I concur that the ceramics of Period I at Dholavira have close parallels with materials from Amri II, the transitional period that Jean-Marie Casal postulated as the bridge between the Early Harappan of Period I and the Mature Harappan of Period III (Casal 1964). In addition to Dholavira, there are two sites in Saurashtra that also impinge on this discussion: Somnath and Padri.

VILLAGE SITES IN SAURASHTRA PRIOR
TO THE INDUS CIVILIZATION

Somnath

The ancient Nagara Mound of Somnath lies on the east bank of the Hiran (Hiranya) River on the southern coast of Saurashtra. The site was first excavated in the 1950s under the direction of the late P. P. Pandya, with the cooperation of the Maharaja Sayajirao University of Baroda (Nanavati et al. 1971), and later by Deccan College and the Gujarat State Department of Archaeology (*Indian Archaeology, A Review* 1971–1972: 12–13; 1975–1976: 13; 1976–1977: 17–18; Dhavalikar and Possehl 1992).

The first occupation at Somnath, referred to as the "Pre-Prabhas period," was found in the earliest excavations (Subbarao 1958: fig. 36:135), but its significance was not recognized at that time. Renewed work in the 1970s reexposed the Pre-Prabhas levels, which cover roughly 75 square meters and rest on a sterile deposit of marine sand at about 3 meters below the modern ground surface. The material from the Pre-Prabhas levels consists of pottery, a few chalcedony blades, and beads of faience and steatite, some of which are segmented. Most of the artifacts came from Stratum 15, associated with a fragment of wall plaster with reed impressions, suggesting simple wattle-and-daub architecture. The pottery includes an incised coarse grey/red ware and red slipped ware (Figure 90), red ware (Figure 90:1–6), and black and red ware (Figure 90:7–15). There are types shared between Pre-Prabhas Somnath and the Pre-Harappan Anarta Chalcolithic of North Gujarat, seen, for example, in the open dish in red ware on Figure 90:4–5. Occasional well-fired red-ware sherds of apparent Sorath Harappan affiliation were recorded in association with these wares.

Although the pottery from Period I is mostly fresh and unrolled, the presence of a yellowish silt suggests a flood during Pre-Prabhas times. It is possible, therefore, that the area in which the excavation took place was a secondary deposit resulting from this flood and that the original habitation was elsewhere under the mound. There is a hiatus between the Pre-Prabhas and the Prabhas levels.

The two radiocarbon dates from the Pre-Prabhas levels are remarkably consistent and calibrate to ca. 2900 BC (see Possehl 1988: TF-1287 and PRL-90). This caused some concern when they were first published, since they were early and seemed to run counter to the notion that the Harappan sites in Saurashtra were "Late Harappan." But now that similar dates have come from Rojdi, Babar Kot, Kuntasi, and Padri, they are much more acceptable to the general archaeological community.

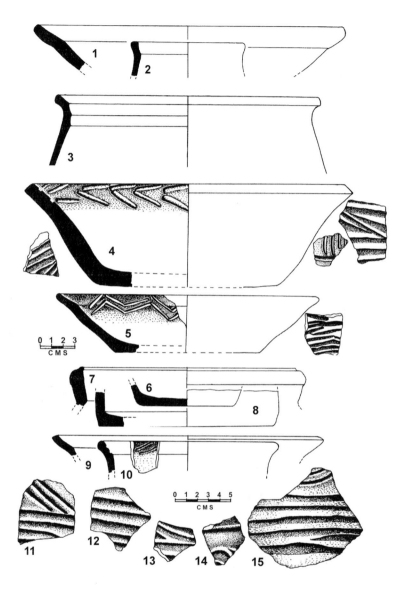

Figure 90. Pre-Prabhas pottery from Somnath.

Little is known of the people who made and used the Pre-Prabhas ceramics. It seems clear that they are dated to the early third millennium BC and that their pottery lies outside of the Amri-Nal tradition. The first step in resolving these points should be a thorough survey of the Saurashtran coast, with the aim of locating more sites with Pre-Prabhas ceramics. An excavation at one or two of these would take us a long way toward understanding this material.

Padri

Excavations at the ancient settlement at Padri village, located south of Bhavnagar City and on the eastern coast of the Gulf of Cambay, have uncovered what seems to be a small village of the mid to late fourth millennium (Shinde 1992a; 1992b; Shinde and Kar 1992). This date is based on two radiocarbon determinations (see Table 11). There is as yet no subsistence information for this period at the site, but the inhabitants lived in small houses of pressed clay. They also made a distinctive ceramic that has been called "Padri Ware" (Shinde and Kar 1992) (Figure 91), a thick—compared

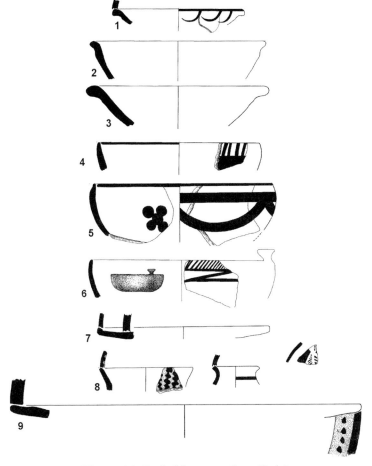

Figure 91. Period I pottery from Padri.

with the finer Sorath Harappen ceramics—coarse ceramic to which a fair amount of sand has been added. There are two forms: convex-sided bowls and globular pots, and the outer—and sometimes the inner—surfaces of these pots were coated with a thick red slip which has a tendency to crack. The painting is geometrical and in black (Shinde and Kar 1992: 107). Padri Ware is said to share many features with the Gritty Red Ware of the Anarta Tradition (Sonawane and Ajithprasad 1994: 133).

There are many interesting things to be learned from Padri, but one thing is certain: it gives us more documentation for pottery-using (probably food-producing) villagers in Saurashtra prior to Mature Harappan times, an adaptation wholly in keeping with the evidence from Somnath, the North Gujarat sites, and Kutch.

These observations on the early settlers of Gujarat, along with other data, suggest that we should begin to develop a working hypothesis on the movement of peoples and/or the early food-producing technology out of the ancient "Neolithic homeland" in the hills and piedmonts of the eastern edge of the Iranian Plateau, into Gujarat and peninsular India.

THE GENERAL MODEL OF EXPANSION

Diffusion and acculturation, the spread of peoples and their cultures, is one of the oldest topics in archaeology. In consideration of the early food-producing settlers of Gujarat, we need to understand how they moved there from the "old Neolithic homeland" of Baluchistan and its eastern piedmonts. This is the area within which the wild progenitors of the early domesticated plants and animals were native, and, consequently, the area within which the earliest food-producing communities of the subcontinent are found. The Early Harappan sites on the North Gujarat plain, and the contemporary settlements at Padri and Somnath, are far removed from this "homeland" and are well outside the native ranges of the sheep, goats, wheat, and barley that sustained them.

Elsewhere (Possehl 1999: 427–429, 473), I have made a case for the emergence of pastoralists as part of the food-producing revolution. The agricultural village and the pastoral camp can be imagined to be on a multidimensional continuum. This sees village farming communities as reliant more on agriculture and plants than on mobility and animals, while the pastoral camp is more mobile and dependent on pasture and animals. Despite these differences, both forms of adaptation tend to utilize both domesticated (and undomesticated) plants and animals. Very few traditional farmers in settled villages keep no animals as a part of their subsistence strategy, especially in the ancient Near East, Iran, Central Asia, and the Greater Indus region. The same principal applies to the pastoral nomads, who regularly undertake some agriculture themselves, while at the same time relying to a very great degree on their animals for their livelihood. The notion that pastoral nomads do not engage in agriculture is an anthropological misunderstanding.

The general hypothesis for the expansion of food-producing peoples out of the aforementioned "old Neolithic homeland" holds that pastoral peoples were usually the lead element in exploring new territory in the Greater Indus region (Allchin 1972; Possehl 1979). Some of the reasoning here has to do with the ecology and mobility of these people and their need for new pasture, as well as the economic rewards and prestige that come with the discovery of new mineral and lapidary resources. But we cannot discount more human motivations in this as well—the pleasure and adventure of travel and exploring new territory, meeting new people, even if possible conflict might be involved.

What we see most clearly in the archaeological record of early farming and herding peoples in the Greater Indus region are the settled, village communities. These places were more or less permanent facilities, and architectural debris accumulated along with trash: broken pots, figurines, terracotta cakes, and the other flotsam and jetsam of human existence. These places are easily identified, and the artifacts allow us to give them a relative chronology. What is not seen nearly as clearly are the herders, the pastoral and other kinds of nomads, be they full time, seasonal, or otherwise itinerant. Since these people travel light and are not necessarily in the same place twice, they do not leave a robust archaeological record. But, there is enough archaeological data to support the theoretical stance outlined above, so that we can be assured that they were present and probably in large numbers, possibly even outnumbering the settled farmers. We are not in a position to estimate the size of the population with this adaptation, so these comments are merely suggestions, but the ancient pastoral nomad is securely documented at places such as Bagor in Rajasthan (Misra 1973) and in the camp sites that M. R. Mughal (1997) found associated the Hakra Wares Phase in Cholistan.

These nomadic peoples should probably be thought of as more or less full-time specialists or as transhumants who may have been settled farmers for part of the year and pastoral nomads for the other (Barth 1961; Leshnik and Sontheimer 1975; Prasad 1994). Even within these norms there is great variation and sociocultural dynamism—where full-time pastoralists settle down to become full-time agriculturists in groups or as individuals, or farmers increasingly rely on animals and end up being mobile pastoralists. These subsistence strategies have a diversity of forms, which shift and change over time. We should not imagine that there was necessarily a continuity in adaptation from father to son, mother to daughter. "Once a farmer, always a farmer" or "once a pastoral nomad, always a pastoral nomad" simply does not hold when we use the ethnohistorical record and principles of human ecology as a guide to understanding the peoples of the Indus Age. Nor is it wise to think in terms of "typical" farmers and "typical" pastoral nomads, since there is so much room for variation, the utility of these typological categories is moot.

People adapted to the mobile management of domesticated animals would have been allied to and symbiotic with village farming communities. But, pastoralists can also operate independently of these villages, and it is in this mode that the resilient explorer of the Greater Indus region was probably to be found. Enough is known from Gujarat and the Punjab and Haryana to believe that pastoral peoples were in these areas prior to settled farming communities, possibly by a millennium or more—witness the Anarta Chalcolithic found at Loteshwar. This begins to document the thought that, in general, it was the pastoralists who first explored and "discovered" new lands, living there on a seasonal basis and returning from time to time when the needs of their animals and their own dispositions decreed. Over time, this led to the intrusion into the eastern region and the southeastern areas of the Greater Indus region by food-producing peoples.

Those pastoral communities that were relatively free from village farming communities would have had to engage in some agriculture, which implies at least a seasonal permanency of settlement with storage facilities, a stable occupation of one small spot of earth, further implying the buildup of an archaeological midden. It also seems to be true that the village farming communities followed behind the nomads, at least chronologically. This growth in the spread and number of village farming communities probably reflects both the migration of farmers and their families and the settling down of people who were once mobile pastoralists.

This leads to the notion that there was a succession of interrelated processes at work. First, the initial exploration by pastoralists, followed only later by the settling in of some of these folk, along with the beginnings of seasonal agriculture. A third stage would have involved full-time occupation of the newly explored lands by the pastoral *cum* farming peoples in these frontier areas, at first quite mobile within their new lands, but some gradually settling over time into permanent villages. There is also documentation for the progressive encroachment of village farming communities into the new areas, as more and more territory was taken under cultivation, perhaps to accommodate the increasing population of the region.

These food-producing peoples of the Indus Age were not the first to use the new lands to the east and south of the Indus Valley. There was a historically deep indigenous population of hunter-gatherers there, and we can expect that the explorers of the Indus Age would have come into contact with them. It would seem unlikely that all of these encounters were peaceful, happy ones, as the fortification of sites of the Indus Age in Kutch might document. But, there are signs in the archaeological record of acculturation having taken place, most notably in the archaeological record at Langhnaj and Lothal (Possehl and Kennedy 1979). Some of the encounters, at least, were sufficiently amiable for this process of cultural exchange to have taken place. While there is a chronological sequence to this model, it is not linear and there is overlap in time between the various cultural processes.

The older chapters of the archaeological record inform us that by the beginning of the Early Harappan stage, all of northern India and Pakistan, outside the Kechi Beg and Hakra Wares areas, were inhabited by peoples who might be thought of as "aboriginal." In the course of exploration and land use, the herder and farmer of the Indus Age would have met, engaged, even fought with these peoples, some of whom were surely quite foreign to them, not part of the peoples of the Indus Age. Other aboriginal groups, however, may have taken what they wanted from those of the Indus Age, such as domesticated animals, pottery, and copper artifacts, but maintained their own identity, as those at Bagor seem to have done. Still others may have become refugee populations, staunchly defending their own way of life from the dreaded farmers and pastoral nomads, while some probably failed to compete effectively with their new neighbors and became extinct. There could, of course, be many more reasons, and I leave it to the fertile mind of the reader to create the myriad possibilities of mixing and matching that a culture historical setting such as the one described here makes feasible.

This conception is a model, or image, of the forces driving the expansion of peoples during the Indus Age. There were other explorers—traders, itinerant craftsmen, tinkers, bards, travelers, and the like. But the cumulative effect of all of these "others" could not have matched the impact of thousands of pastoral nomads. Thus, when considering how or what led the peoples of the Anarta Chalcolithic and those of the Amri-Nal/Kot Diji phases into Kutch and Gujarat, think in terms of pastoral nomads leading the way, probably in Stage Two (Togau or Kechi Beg phase), or maybe as early as Stage One, drawn to the area because of its immense value as a rich pastureland for their vast herds of cattle, sheep, and goats.

Sites from the pioneering stages, prior to the appearance of villages, do exist. Some have probably been discovered, but we lack the sophistication to know them for what they are. It takes careful exploration and hard work to recognize them, but these settlements can be found and they will document the pioneering of early food-producing peoples—a clear challenge for those of us who enjoy archaeological survey.

Robert McC. Adams (1978) has dealt with these kinds of sociocultural/historical issues in a systemic way. He thinks of sociocultural stability as a propensity for systems generally to return to some sort of equilibrium after a temporary disturbance. The propensity for disequilibrium is a sort of sociocultural rigidity or brittleness. Other aspects of sociocultural systems are more resilient and reflect a primary concern with long-term survival. Behavioral qualities that can be associated with resilient sociocultural systems are an abilities to deal effectively with contingencies of many sorts. Some of this resilience comes from the alliances and relationships that these peoples have with those who surround them, especially peoples with significantly different forms of adaptation from their own. Such sociocultural systems survive because they are able to successfully negotiate within a dynamic historical setting, in a world that is constantly in flux.

The sociocultural system I have described for prehistoric Gujarat includes those on the "farming-pastoralist" continuum as well as the hunter-gatherers. This was a system with great resilience, or survivability, since it is still in evidence today.

A TALE OF TWO *OIKUMENAI*: VARIATION IN THE EXPANSIONARY DYNAMICS OF 'UBAID AND URUK MESOPOTAMIA*

GIL J. STEIN AND RANA ÖZBAL

ABSTRACT

The last few decades of research have documented two major periods of expansion by the earliest complex societies of Mesopotamia—the 'Ubaid ranked polities of the sixth and fifth millennia and the Uruk states of the fourth millennium BC. In both periods, Mesopotamian material culture styles were broadly distributed in neighboring regions of Syria, southeast Anatolia, and Iran. In each case, architectural, ceramic, and artifactual commonalities of the 'Ubaid and Uruk horizon styles help define an oikumene or interaction sphere. Although some researchers argue that both periods can be explained as eras of Mesopotamian colonial expansion, we argue here that each oikumene had a fundamentally different expansionary dynamic and mode(s) of socioeconomic organization. A contextual analysis comparing different regions shows that the 'Ubaid expansion took place largely through the peaceful spread of an ideology, leading to the formation of numerous new indigenous identities that appropriated and transformed superficial elements of 'Ubaid material culture into locally distinct expressions. Volumes of interregional trade were low, and population movements

---

* This article is a revised version of a paper presented at the 100th annual meeting of the American Anthropological Association in 2001. The session, "Theoretical Foundations in the Dust: The Past and Future of Mesopotamian Archaeology" (co-organized by Gil Stein and Guillermo Algaze), was held to honor Robert McC. Adams for his contributions to our understanding of ancient Mesopotamian complex societies in their ecological, social, and economic settings. We would like to thank Geoff Emberling and Susan Pollock for their insightful comments on an earlier draft of this paper. All remaining errors are our own.

329

were minimal. By contrast, the Uruk expansion was an actual colonial phenomenon, involving the founding of Mesopotamian trading enclaves among preexisting local polities and emulation by local groups in the so-called peripheral areas. Relations between Uruk colonists and local polities varied from coercive to cooperative, depending on the distance from Mesopotamia and the degree of preexisting indigenous social complexity. Once the basic differences between the ʿUbaid and Uruk oikumenai are recognized, we can develop more accurate models of variation in the political economies of early Mesopotamian complex societies.

INTRODUCTION

Among Bob Adams's greatest contributions to the anthropological-archaeological understanding of ancient Mesopotamia have been his emphasis on broad regional syntheses (Adams 1966; 1972b) and his clear focus on the need to explicitly examine the development of complexity in this area as a series of historically grounded social transformations (Adams 1981; 1989; 2004). In that spirit, we offer the following essay as a tribute to a scholar who has inspired us and strongly influenced the orientation of our research.

EARLY MESOPOTAMIAN HORIZON STYLES/ INTERACTION SPHERES/OIKUMENAI

The last few decades of research have documented two distinct major periods of expansion by the earliest complex societies of Mesopotamia: the ʿUbaid ranked polities of the sixth and fifth millennia and the Uruk urbanized states of the fourth millennium BC. In both periods, southern Mesopotamian material culture styles spread far beyond their region of origin in the southern alluvium and were broadly distributed in neighboring regions of north Syria, southeast Anatolia, and western Iran. In both cases, architectural, ceramic, and artifactual commonalities of the ʿUbaid and Uruk horizon styles have been used to identify geographically extensive and long-lived interaction spheres or oikumenai, covering more or less the same territory. Although some researchers argue that both periods can be explained as eras of Mesopotamian colonial expansion (for example, Oates 1993; J. Oates and Oates 2004b), we argue here that each interaction sphere had a fundamentally different expansionary dynamic marked by strikingly different effects on the social identities of the indigenous groups who participated in these networks. In this paper, we show the contrasts between the ʿUbaid and Uruk oikumenai by examining the social contexts in which these two Mesopotamian styles of material culture were selectively used and translated into local cultural schemes.

THE 'UBAID (CA. 5800–4200 BC)

In the arid alluvial zone of southern Mesopotamia, the 'Ubaid assemblage first developed in the early sixth millennium BC and lasted until about 4200 BC. Best known from the sites of Eridu (Safar, Mustafa, and Lloyd 1981) and more recently Oueili (Huot 1983; 1987; 1996b), the 'Ubaid material cultural assemblage (Figure 92) includes brown-painted and reduction-fired (often greenish) ware ceramics made on a slow wheel, large baked clay "nails" or "mullers," clay sickles, and highly distinctive cone-head clay figurines (Perkins 1949: 73–90; Redman 1978: 247–250). 'Ubaid houses have a characteristic tripartite form with a T-shaped or cruciform central room (Aurenche 1981: 201; Forest 1983). The 'Ubaid period sees the earliest appearance in southern Mesopotamia of clearly ritual public architecture in the form of standardized rectangular temples oriented to the cardinal points and constructed with niched facades, buttresses, altars, and offering tables (Roaf 1984; Safar, Mustafa, and Lloyd 1981: 86–114; but compare Forest 1987 for an alternative interpretation of temples).

In sociopolitical terms, several lines of evidence suggest that 'Ubaid Mesopotamia was organized as a series of small-scale ranked societies that we can characterize as chiefdoms, grounded in corporate (Blanton et al. 1996) or communal modes of leadership (Akkermans 1989; G. Stein 1994b). Broad horizontal clearances at the central Mesopotamian 'Ubaid site of Abada suggest a pattern of community organization with freestanding houses showing a great deal of variation in economic status, as inferred from both house sizes and artifact inventories (Jasim 1985: 202–203; 1989).

In the early to mid-fifth millennium BC, the distributions of southern 'Ubaid pottery, architectural styles, and other artifact classes spread widely beyond the southern alluvium, forming a horizon style that extended across an astonishing distance of 1800 kilometers, from Cilicia on the Mediterranean coast of Turkey, across southeast and south-central Anatolia, north Syria, and the Iraqi Jazira, into southwest Iran, and down the western shore of the Persian Gulf into what is now Saudi Arabia (Oates 1983; J. Oates and Oates 2004b; Yoffee 1993b) (see Figure 93). 'Ubaid styles can be found together across this broad area at sites along the Persian Gulf (Frifelt 1989; Oates 1983: 255–256, e.g., H3; Carter et al. 1999; Carter and Crawford 2001; 2002; Masry 1974; Roaf 1976), as well as at numerous northern sites in Iraq, Syria, and southeast Anatolia including Tepe Gawra (Tobler 1950), Hama (Fugman 1958: 14–22; Thuesen 1988: 90–93;), and Değirmentepe (Esin 1989; 1998; Esin and Harmankaya 1986; 1987; 1988).

The stylistic similarities in 'Ubaid pottery as well as the floor plans of public and private buildings excavated at 'Ubaid sites in the southern Mesopotamian heartland, and in the northern sites led early researchers to view the 'Ubaid as two slightly varied renditions of a homogeneous culture complex

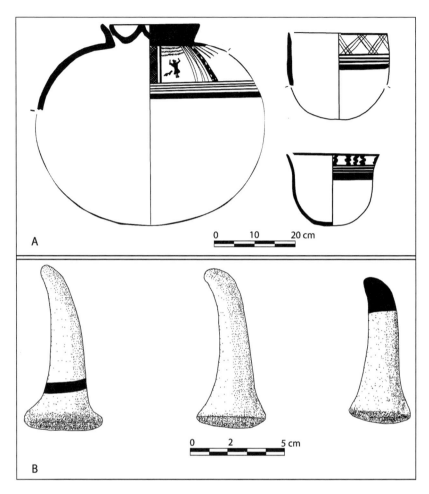

Figure 92. Examples of ʿUbaid material culture. (A): After Roaf 1989: figs. 4, 10; (B): after Jasim 1985: fig. 58b, f, g.

(Oates 1960; J. Oates and Oates 2004b: 180; Perkins 1949; Roaf 1990: 51–56). In addition, the spread of ʿUbaid assemblages was perceived as originating from a single identifiable south Mesopotamian source to the northern peripheries and replacing the preceding local Halaf culture (Mallowan and Rose 1935: 14; Mellaart 1982: 7; Redman 1978: 251–253). This perception led some researchers to suggest that northern ʿUbaid sites were in fact southern Mesopotamian colonies, established for the asymmetrical exchange of raw materials and most probably inhabited by an immigrant southern population who maintained close ties with the parent societies of lowland Mesopotamia (Esin 1985b: 257; 1989; Oates 1993: 409–410; J. Oates and Oates 2004a: 184; 2004b: 95–99; Yakar 1985: 336; but compare Thuesen 2000).

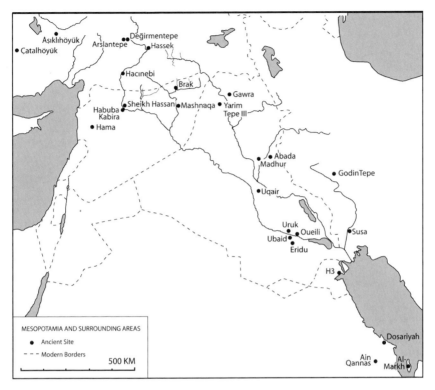

Figure 93. Map showing the location of sites mentioned in the text.

Traditional archaeological models of colonization assume that artifacts or architectural types define a cultural entity that is more or less identical wherever it occurs (for example, Mellaart 1975). The "colonial" material assemblage has been viewed as a series of discrete items without regard for variability in the interrelationships or the social context of their form, practice, and meaning.

However, more recent developments in the comparative archaeology of culture contact processes (Cusick 1998; Lightfoot, Martinez, and Schiff 1998; Lyons and Papadopoulos 2002; G. Stein, ed. 2005) suggest that the appropriation and use of material culture is complex, selective, and contextually dependent. In the case of the spread of ʿUbaid material culture, when one examines the social contexts of artifact use, the resultant picture shows great regional variation in the forms of contact and their material correlates. At the actual boundary between lower and upper Mesopotamia in the Syrian steppe, we may well have limited evidence suggestive of migration at the site of Mashnaqa (Thuesen 2000) and possibly other sites in the Khabur (Hole 1997: 43). It is also possible that southern migrants were present at Brak as well, since this site functioned in later periods as a "gateway community"—what we might call the northernmost outpost of southern Mesopotamia (Oates 1987: 193; J. Oates and Oates 2004b: 95). However, a contextual approach suggests that in most other cases, 'Ubaid material culture spread to the north peacefully through some combination of trade and the local appropriation of 'Ubaid social identity and ceremonial ideology rather than actual colonization. It is becoming clear that the so-called Northern 'Ubaid sites show far more sociocultural, ritual, ideological, and stylistic continuities with the pre-existing Halafian culture than was previously recognized (Breniquet 1989: 334–336; Davidson and Watkins 1981: 9; Nissen 2001: 167–170; Thuesen 1992: 14). In fact, some north Mesopotamian idiosyncrasies that are rare or even unknown in the alluvium are found in both the pre- and post-'Ubaid of the north. This includes, for example, the widespread use of seals and sealings (Akkermans and Duistermaat 1997; Breniquet 1989: 335; Esin 1994b; Perkins 1949: 87; Tobler 1950), smaller nuclear family–sized houses (Bernbeck 1995; but see Nissen 2001: 170), and the persistence of tholoi in 'Ubaid levels (Breniquet 1991: 25; Edens and Yener 2000: 200–201; Tobler 1950; Wilkinson, Monahan, and Tucker 1996; and possibly Nishiaki et al. 2001: 58–59).

Our analysis focuses on two key sites, Tepe Gawra in northern Iraq and Değirmentepe in southeast Anatolia, to illustrate that:

- 'Ubaid styles of material culture spread gradually and were selectively appropriated by northern communities; and

- those elements of 'Ubaid architecture and other classes of material culture that spread to the north were transformed and used in everyday practice in ways that were fundamentally different from superficially similar sites with 'Ubaid material culture in southern Mesopotamia.

The site of Tepe Gawra in northern Iraq provides one of the best data-sets with which to understand the nature of the 'Ubaid *oikumene* (G. Stein 1991). Gawra is a small, 2.5-hectare mound whose long stratigraphic sequence documents the transition from Halaf to 'Ubaid (Tobler 1950). Stratum XX is the Halaf occupation. In the succeeding Strata XIX to XII, 'Ubaid material increases in frequency, while Halaf artifacts become progressively scarcer, and eventually disappear.

To understand the significance of both the selection of elements of the southern Mesopotamian 'Ubaid assemblage and the rate of their acceptance, it is useful to separate the *public* from the *personal* components of cultural identity (Bentley 1987; see, for example, Wiessner 1983 for a comparable discussion of archaeological style). The perception of self in relation to the larger community can be viewed as a form of *public* identity, conveyed through highly visible social domains (Wiessner 1985: 161–162; Wobst 1977) as reflected in ceramics, architecture, ritual paraphernalia, or badges of rank and accessible to many people at an intermediate social distance. *Personal* identity, on the other hand,

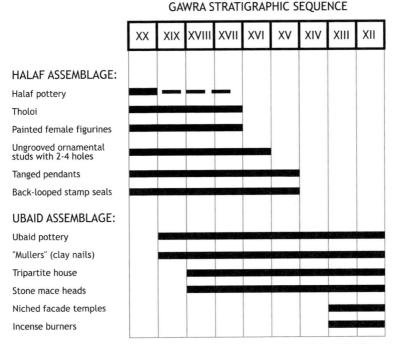

Patterns of Change in Material Culture at Tepe Gawra (N. Mesopotamia) in the Fifth Millennium BC

Figure 94. Patterns of change from Halaf to 'Ubaid material culture at Tepe Gawra (northern Iraq) from Stratum XX to XII.

refers to the definition of the self in the more circumscribed or domestic domain and is conveyed through small items of personal adornment often found in contexts involving minimal social distance.

Interestingly, the first markers of Halaf identity to disappear at Tepe Gawra and become replaced by their 'Ubaid counterparts are Halaf ceramics and house form, both reflecting community affiliation as an aspect of *public* identity (G. Stein 1991). Similarly, larger, highly visible stone mace heads—badges of rank indicative of 'Ubaid *public* identity (G. Stein 1994b)—also appear at a relatively early date in Level XVIII. However, it is significant that the most persistent and longest lived Halaf artifacts are smaller-sized markers of *personal* identity—seals, sew-on ornamental studs, and tanged pendants, items that were most visible in face-to-face interaction (G. Stein 1991:7, Figure 94).

In short, the public and domestic aspects of cultural identity at Gawra seem to have changed at different rates. People quickly took on markers of 'Ubaid identity in the public domain, especially in contexts relating to community affiliation and hierarchical social status. However, at the same time, the inhabitants of Gawra retained a distinctively Halaf personal identity, which they expressed primarily in the private or domestic domain. There need not be any contradiction in having an 'Ubaid public identity while retaining a traditional Halaf conception of self, since these two aspects of cultural identity were expressed in different social contexts (G. Stein 1991).

Surprisingly, the last items of southern 'Ubaid material culture to be adopted at Gawra were temple architecture and cult artifacts related to religious ideology (G. Stein 1991: 8). One reason may be that the 'Ubaid form of temple-based religion had no precedent in traditional Halaf society (Akkermans 1993: 298). The Halaf sites of the north do not have formal temples, suggesting that the ritual and the domestic spheres were not seen as conceptually and spatially distinct. The alien nature of this 'Ubaid ritual innovation suggests that the spread of 'Ubaid material culture was gradual and selective, rather than the sudden, wholesale replacement to be expected if the traditional colonization model had been correct.

The site of Değirmentepe in southeast Anatolia provides additional evidence that 'Ubaid material culture cannot automatically be seen as reflecting colonization (Özbal 2000). Instead, architectural patterning and the use of space show that 'Ubaid styles were completely transformed in order to fit into preexisting indigenous cultural schemas. Değirmentepe is a small 2.5-hectare mound near Malatya in the upper Euphrates of eastern Turkey. Excavations between 1979 and 1986 exposed a broad area of the site dating to the end of the second half of the fifth millennium BC (Esin 1981a; 1981b; 1983a; 1983b; 1984; 1985; Esin and Harmankaya 1986; 1987; 1988). Değirmentepe Level 7 yielded 'Ubaid pottery and fourteen mud-brick buildings, of which at least eight are typical 'Ubaid-style tripartite houses. While the actual house plans closely resemble their 'Ubaid counterparts in southern Mesopotamia, the use of space in the Değirmentepe houses, and their relationship to one another, show fundamental differences in both community organization and in the meanings and uses of domestic space (Özbal 2000).

In southern Mesopotamia, 'Ubaid domestic and ritual spaces were clearly distinct, so that we can easily differentiate temples (Safar, Mustafa, and Lloyd 1981) and domestic residences (Jasim 1985: 1989; Mallowan and Rose 1935: 11–12; Roaf 1989). Although they conform to the same floor plans, temples are more symmetrically planned and have elaborately decorated niches and buttresses, offering tables and altars (Perkins 1949: 87–88; Roaf 1984: 88; Safar, Mustafa, and Lloyd 1981). As stated by Roaf (1984: 88), the similarity in floor plans between 'Ubaid temples and houses is probably no coincidence, as "the temple was the house of God" and 'Ubaid ritual architecture exhibits the earliest beginnings of the historic-period temples.

However, Değirmentepe lacks the clear functional differentiation between the sacred and the residential of the southern 'Ubaid (Özbal 2000: 12). Instead, nearly all the central court areas of the tripartite structures, although clearly domestic, yield ritual evidence as well (Esin 1998; Esin and Harmankaya 1988). This is suggested by the presence of features such as offering podia, monumental hearths, altar tables, wall paintings, and burials as well as nearby pits containing ash and sacrificial offerings (Esin 1998; Esin and Harmankaya 1988: 92–93, 104–105; Helwing 2003: 68). The recurrence of a similar repertoire of ritual objects in nearly all the tripartite buildings suggests that rituals were conducted at the level of the household and that the sacred structures were jointly used as residential dwelling spaces (Özbal 2000: 18). Thus, Değirmentepe uses a local Anatolian tradition, found at some Ceramic Neolithic and Chalcolithic sites, of incorporating ritual space within the residential sphere (Naumann 1971: 433–434; Özdoğan 1999: 230; for example, Alkım 1979: 201; Düring 2001: 9–11; Duru 1999: 176–179; Hodder 1999: 179; Silistreli 1989: 62; 1991: 96).

Even more striking is the transformation of 'Ubaid style tripartite architecture in this eastern Anatolian context (Özbal 2000:19). In southern and south-central Mesopotamia, 'Ubaid tripartite houses were freestanding (Jasim 1985; 1989; Lloyd and Safar 1943: 149; Roaf 1989; Safar, Mustafa, and Lloyd 1981; Youkana 1997: fig. 9) (see Figure 95). However, at Değirmentepe, the tripartite houses are contiguous, in an agglutinative pattern of community organization with adjacent houses sharing walls (Figure 96). This reflects a fundamental difference in the cultural construction and meanings of public and private space. Agglutinated settlements are typical of

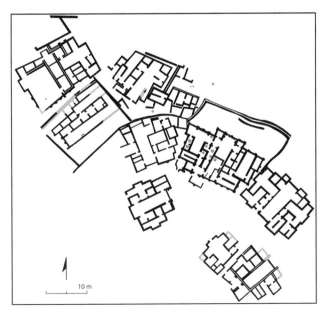

Figure 95. Tell Abada (central Iraq): 'Ubaid house plans in freestanding settlement layout (after Jasim 1985: fig. 2).

Figure 96. Değirmentepe (southeast Turkey): 'Ubaid-style house plans in agglutinative settlement layout (after Esin and Harmankaya 1987: fig. 2).

both north Mesopotamian (compare Bernbeck 1995: 14; Sievertsen 2002) and Anatolian traditions (Özbal 2000: 9) and are exemplified at sites such as Chatal Höyük (Mellaart 1975: 101), Aşıklı Höyük (Esin 1991; 1999: fig. 104), Yarim Tepe III (Merpert and Munchaev 1993), and Gawra (Tobler 1950). The redefinition of southern 'Ubaid tripartite buildings into this northern syntax at both Gawra and Değirmentepe represents a transformation of both the local and the foreign to create a hybridized identity (Bhaba 1992; Van Dommelen 2002; 2005) rather than an 'Ubaid colonial imposition.

These examples demonstrate not only how 'Ubaid elements actively became part of existing and well established repertoires of culture and meaning (as in the Değirmentepe case) but also show how various aspects of southern elements are selectively adopted at different rates (as in the Gawra case). Overall, this highlights the importance of recognizing the site-specific nature and the differential appropriation of 'Ubaid characteristics and the unique ways in which they are transformed into local and cultural repertoires.

URUK (CA. 4200–3000 BC)

The fourth-millennium Uruk assemblage represents a second, distinct Mesopotamian horizon style, almost as widely distributed as the 'Ubaid in roughly the same areas of the Near East. During the early to mid-fourth millennium BC, urbanized state societies had emerged over much of the alluvium in southern Mesopotamia and southwestern Iran (Adams 1981; Nissen 2000; Pollock 1992; H. T. Wright and Rupley 2001). The elites of these highly stratified polities had developed centralized institutions to mobilize surplus labor and goods from their hinterlands in a meticulously administered political economy (Algaze 2001b; H. T. Wright 2001a).

The economic sphere of Uruk Mesopotamian state societies quickly expanded to form an extensive interaction network connecting the southern alluvium with the less urbanized polities in the neighboring highlands to the north and east (Algaze 1993a; 1993b; 2001b; Rothman 2001; H. T. Wright 2001a). Several sites in the latter areas have been identified as Uruk trading colonies, apparently established to gain access to trade/communication routes while extracting metals, semiprecious stones, lumber, or other commodities from the resource-rich highland zones, in what many researchers consider the world's earliest known colonial system (Algaze 1993a; Lupton 1996; Sürenhagen 1986). This process by which southern Mesopotamian societies travel to so-called peripheral regions for colonization and intense commercial contact is often called the "Uruk Expansion" (G. Stein 1999a: 91-101). Sites recognized as Uruk "colonies" have been identified across a vast area along key trade routes from Hassek Höyük in the Turkish upper Euphrates, across north Syria and northern Iraq, and into the Zagros Mountains of western Iran (see, for example, Behm-Blanke et al. 1981; 1983; 1984; Boese 1995; Strommenger 1979; 1980; Sürenhagen 1986: 10–12; van Driel 1977; van Driel and van Driel-Murray 1979; 1983; Weiss and Young 1975; Young 1986). At these sites, the full range of Uruk material culture styles appeared suddenly in the archaeological record in a pattern quite different from that of the earlier 'Ubaid oikumene (Lupton 1996; Sürenhagen 1986) (see Figure 93).

The southern Mesopotamian Uruk colonies are quite distinctive as intrusive sites, established rapidly in the midst of local Iranian, Syrian, and southeast Anatolian cultures. Three different forms of Uruk material culture occurring together serve to identify the Mesopotamian implanted settlements while distinguishing them from contemporaneous local settlements (G. Stein 1999b). This can be seen best at the site of Habuba Kabira on the Syrian middle Euphrates (Strommenger 1979; 1980). Sites identified as colonies have the full repertoire of Uruk ceramics (Sürenhagen 1986: 26–27). These same sites also have distinctive south Mesopotamian Uruk domestic or public/ritual architecture such as the "middle-hall" house and niched facade temples, often decorated with baked clay wall cones (Heinrich 1982; Özten 1984; Sürenhagen 1986: 10). Culturally specific aspects of technological style such as brick dimensions and bricklaying patterns exactly match the practices in the southern homeland (Schwartz 2001: 252). A third distinctive feature of the Uruk colonies is the presence of the full range of south Mesopotamian administrative technology such as cylinder seals, bullae, tokens, and clay tablets with numerical inscriptions used to monitor the circulation of goods (Ferioli and Fiandra 1983; Pittman 1993; 2001; van Driel 1983) (see Figure 97).

In some cases, the colonies were founded from scratch on uninhabited land (Strommenger 1980; van Driel and van Driel-Murray 1983). However, at the outer reaches of the exchange network in the highland resource zones, Uruk colonies took the form of small trading enclaves within preexisting indigenous settlements such as Godin (Weiss and Young 1975; Young 1986) and Hacınebi (G. Stein 1999a; 2001; 2002). In these latter settlements, not just the *forms* of material culture, but also behavioral patterning, food preferences, and technological styles are all aspects of daily practice that identify south Mesopotamians as an ethnically distinct alien minority. At Godin, the Mesopotamians lived within a clearly defined residential quarter (Weiss and Young 1975; Young 1986). At Hacınebi, for example, comparisons of fauna between the Uruk and Anatolian parts of the site show differences between the two groups in food preferences, so that sheep and goats were 49 percent of the local meat consumption, but provided 80 to 90 percent of the Uruk diet. This matches exactly the known food preferences in the south Mesopotamian heartland (G. Stein 1999a: 145–146; Stein and Nicola 1996). At the same time, butchery practices show clear differences between Uruk and local contexts, in both the locations and the widths of cut marks, suggesting that the two groups used different butchering tools (G. Stein 1997; 1999a: fig. 7.14). Chipped stone tools show similar differences in technological style, so that even when Uruk and local specialists made the same tool forms, the proportions of the tools differed significantly. Blade tools from Uruk areas at Hacınebi are significantly narrower than their local counterparts and match closely the dimensions of blades from south Mesopotamian Uruk sites (Edens 1996; 1997; 1998a; 1998b).

These differences within and between sites remind us that we must view fourth-millennium Greater Mesopotamia as a complex mosaic composed of an Uruk heartland, Uruk colonies in the outlying regions, indigenous settlements such as Arslantepe that traded with these colonies while remaining politically and culturally autonomous (Frangipane 2001b; Frangipane and Palmieri 1989), and indigenous settlements such as Gawra that remained outside the system, having only minimal interaction with Uruk southern Mesopotamia

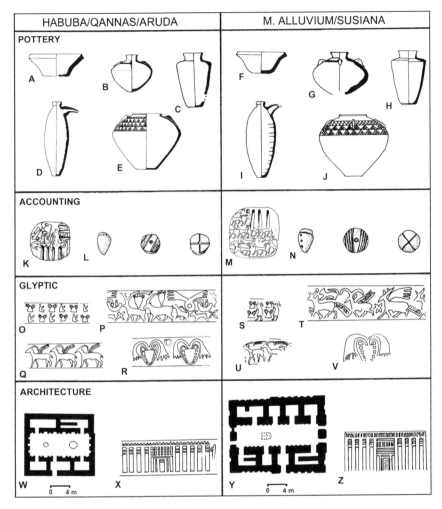

Figure 97. Examples of classic Uruk material culture from southern Mesopotamia and from Uruk expansion sites (reproduced with permission from Guillermo Algaze, after Algaze 1993b: fig. 17).

(Rothman 2002a). The colonies themselves differed significantly from one another, depending on such factors as distance from the homeland, the size of the neighboring local population, and the degree of social complexity in the neighboring indigenous polities (G. Stein 1999a; 1999b; 2001; 2002).

The power of the Uruk states over other parts of the interaction network appears to have declined with increasing distance from the alluvium (G. Stein 1999a; 1999b; 2001; 2002). Thus, for example, a comparison of (a) the city of Uruk itself; (b) large colonies such as Habuba Kabira; and (c) small, distant colonies such as Hacınebi or Godin shows a tremendous degree of variation in social and economic organization as one moves outward from the urban core to its periphery. In the south Mesopotamian heartland, cities such as Uruk and Susa controlled their rural hinterlands, exacting taxes and administering the most basic subsistence activities. In the "near periphery"—the sparsely populated areas of Syria closest to southern Mesopotamia proper—Uruk colonies such as Sheikh Hassan and Habuba Kabira were large, fortified settlements that apparently used coercion to control the local Syrian communities around them (Boese 1995; Strommenger 1979; 1980). In more distant regions, Uruk settlements such as Godin V in highland Iran and Hacınebi in southeast Turkey took the form of small outposts located inside the preexisting towns of local polities. The small numbers and vulnerable position of the south Mesopotamian colonists at sites such as Hacınebi and Godin meant that they could survive only by remaining on good terms with their more powerful indigenous neighbors.

Processes of interaction at any given point in the Uruk trading network were thus structured by a combination of parameters, including distances to the core as well as various environmental, cultural, and economic factors. Nonetheless, "colonies" and even "enclaves," which are less coercive ports of exchange, are archaeologically clearly identifiable through a broad range of material cultural and architectural correlates that are identical to those of another region but are located in spatially discrete occupations surrounded by settlements of local culture.

Conclusions

This comparison of the horizon styles associated with the two earliest Mesopotamian complex societies points to a number of important contrasts between the so-called expansionary dynamics of the ʿUbaid and Uruk periods. It is clear that while the Uruk expansion was a case of actual colonization, the spread of the ʿUbaid into neighboring regions reflects the gradual, peaceful spread of an ideological system that was translated into a variety of different local cultural schemes, forming what are, in effect, new, hybrid social identities in these outlying areas. The ʿUbaid case shows convincingly that even though the external forms of ʿUbaid houses and pottery styles were more or less identical in both the heartland and the highlands, the ways that these items were used and conceptualized in daily local practice reveal profound cultural differences within this oikumene.

At a broader level, this comparison reminds us that a widely distributed horizon style cannot be assumed to reflect an underlying uniformity of cultural, social, or political systems. Significantly, this is true in both the ideological expansion of the ʿUbaid period, and in the elaborate commercial-colonial network of the Uruk urbanized states. It is precisely this variation in Near Eastern complex societies that we need to recognize, model, and explore in the second century of anthropological archaeology between the Tigris and the Euphrates.

THE SUMERIAN TAKEOFF*

GUILLERMO ALGAZE

ABSTRACT

The emergence of early cities in the alluvial lowlands of southern Meso-potamia during the fourth millennium BC must be understood in terms of both the unique ecological conditions affecting the area at the time, and the enduring geographical framework of the Mesopotamian lowlands which allowed for the efficient movement of commodities via water trans-port and facilitated interaction between diverse social units. These condi-tions promoted evolving long-term trade patterns that, inadvertently, differentially favored the development of polities in the southern Mesopot-amian alluvium over contemporary societies in neighboring regions.

More specifically, by the final quarter of the fourth millennium, the social and economic multiplier effects of trade patterns that had been in place for centuries (if not millennia) had brought about substantial increases in population agglomeration throughout the southern alluvial lowlands. Concurrent with these increases, and partly as a result of them, important socioeconomic innovations started to appear in the increasingly urbanized polities of southern Mesopotamia. These were unachievable in

* Earlier drafts of this article were read and criticized by Robert McC. Adams (UCSD), Elise Auerbach (University of Chicago), Alex Joffe, David Jordan (UCSD), Philip Kohl (Wellesley College), Richard Meadows (Harvard), Joyce Marcus (University of Michigan), Joy McCorriston (Ohio State University), Joel Robbins (UCSD), Morris Silver (CCNY), Piotr Steinkeller (Harvard), and Donald Tuzin (UCSD). Each offered substantive criticism, important editorial comments, and cru-cial missing references. Their invaluable contributions are acknowledged with grati-tude, even though, occasionally, I chose to disregard their advice. For this reason, remaining errors of omission and interpretation are entirely my own.

343

other areas of the ancient Near East, where urban grids of comparable scale and complexity did not exist at the time. Most salient among these innovations were (1) new forms of labor organization delivering economies of scale in the production of subsistence and industrial commodities to southern societies, and (2) the creation of new forms of record keeping in southern cities that were much more capable of conveying information across time and space than the simpler reckoning systems used by contemporary polities elsewhere.

More than any other factor, these socially created innovations help explain why complex, regionally organized city-states emerged earlier in southern Iraq than elsewhere in the Near East, or the world.

. . . without the wool for textiles to be traded for natural resources that were wholly lacking in the alluvium, it is difficult to believe that Mesopotamian civilization could have arisen as early and flourished as prodigiously as it did.

Adams 1981: 11)

INTRODUCTION

Robert McCormick Adams, as evidenced in the preceding quotation, always emphasized the critical role played by trade in the processes that gave rise to early Mesopotamian (Sumerian) civilization in the alluvial lowlands of the Tigris and Euphrates Rivers. In this article, I build on this theoretical foundation and try to elucidate, however roughly, the reasons behind the centrality of trade in the emergence of the world's earliest fully urban, state-level societies. My ideas owe much to a close reading of Adams's many seminal contributions on this and related subjects, as well to continued interaction with him over the years.

Economic geographers argue that the substantial variations in population concentration and economic activity present today are the inevitable result of cumulative processes whereby socially created technologies and institutions increase the natural advantages of specific sites or areas by delivering increasing returns to scale. This involves self-reinforcing processes of accumulation, exchange, population growth, agglomeration, and innovation that ultimately determine the varying developmental trajectories of different regions and the location, number, and rate of growth of cities within them (Krugman 1991; 1995; 1998; Pred 1966).

These processes are not limited to the modern world, but instead have been operative at least from the time of the earliest cities and states. The emergence of early Sumerian civilization in the alluvial lowlands of southern Iraq during the Uruk period—roughly spanning the fourth millennium BC—is very much a case in point. This was characterized by the creation of a thriving heartland of multiple competing but culturally unified city-states, a form of social organization that was hitherto unparalleled in the human career. Often singly and certainly in the aggregate, these emergent early Mesopotamian states greatly surpassed contemporary polities elsewhere in Southwest Asia in terms of their scale and their degree of internal differentiation, both social and economic (Adams 1981; Algaze 2001a; 2001b; Pollock 2001). A particularly noteworthy aspect of this process is that it followed centuries, if not millennia, in which the growth trajectory of polities in the alluvial lowlands of the Tigris-Euphrates system hardly differed from those elsewhere in the Near East (Oates 2001; Wilkinson 2001; H. T. Wright 2001a).

The crystallization of Sumerian civilization in the Uruk period thus represents a dramatic "takeoff"—a decisive shift in favor of southern Mesopotamia in the balance of early Near Eastern urbanization, sociopolitical complexity, and economic differentiation. Why did this shift take place? Could a comparable shift have occurred anywhere in the ancient Near East, or were there factors specific only to southern Mesopotamia at this time that made it more probable that the takeoff would occur there rather than elsewhere? If the latter, what specific processes help account for the emergence of civilization in the south?

THE NEED FOR MODELS

Archaeological evidence for the emergence and growth of early cities in the southern Mesopotamian alluvium throughout the various phases of the Uruk period (ca. 3900–3200/3100 BC) is of varying reliability, resolution, and coverage[1]. The formative phases of the Early Uruk period (ca. 3900–3600 BC) are, for all practical purposes, known only through survey data (Nissen 1993). The Middle (ca. 3600–3400 BC) and Late Uruk (ca. 3400–3200/3100 BC) periods are somewhat better understood, since pertinent data are provided not only by settlement pattern surveys, but also by excavations at a few sites and some texts. However, existing exposures remain unrepresentative beyond the central administrative areas of major sites such as Warka, and available texts remain difficult to interpret (Englund 1998) and date only to the final stage of the Uruk period.

The scarcity of representative data bearing on the emergence and growth of early cities and states in fourth millennium southern Mesopotamia means that if we are to generate testable propositions about those processes, we need to use models illustrating how comparable phenomena unfolded elsewhere in

---

[1] For the chronology of the Uruk period, see now H. T. Wright and Rupley 2001.

the world. One obvious source is provided by the work of economic historians and geographers seeking to understand why, where, and how cities have emerged in modern times. These scholars take it as given that trade is a key factor in the evolution of social complexity and that cities serve as the most efficient way to manage regional and interregional exchange in situations marked by asymmetries in resource endowments, commodity production, and access to transportation across the landscape (for example, Hicks 1969; O'Sullivan 1996; Pirenne 1936).

In contrast, discussions in ancient Near Eastern studies about the why, where, and how big of early urbanism (when they occur at all) proceed as if Adam Smith's (1954 [1776]) work on the social ramifications of trade and David Ricardo's (1971 [1817]) analyses of the role of comparative advantage between regions as a spur to trade had never existed, and as if later refinements of their pioneering work by economic geographers and development economists (summarized in Krugman 1995) had never occurred. Particularly lacking in our field are discussions about how differences in access to transportation and the technologies of communication affect the process of urban growth. Worse still is the almost total absence in our discussions of other key causal agents highlighted in more recent economic analyses of urban dynamics. Without question, the most crucial of these is the role of urban institutions in creating organizational efficiencies that yield significant economies of scale in the production and distribution of commodities (North 1991).

The general lack of an economic focus in research on ancient Near Eastern urban origins is a direct consequence of the difficulty of characterizing, let alone quantifying, the data recovered from the earliest Mesopotamian cities. However, there are other complicating factors, both theoretical and methodological. On the theoretical front, many in our field assume, following the work of Karl Polanyi (1957a; 1957b) and Moses Finley (1985), that ancient socioeconomic phenomena were of a fundamentally different character from those in operation today, with the corollary that the forces underlying the emergence and growth of early cities in antiquity must also have been substantially different from those at work in more recent historical periods.

But is this really the case? I suspect that in many cases the answer is a clear no, and that this would be generally acknowledged if we only had the ability to precisely quantify and accurately characterize the types of economic activity in many urban societies of the premodern era. The historic periods of Mesopotamian civilization are a case in point. Polanyi's insistence, for example, that price-making markets subject to laws of supply and demand did not exist in early Mesopotamia has now been convincingly refuted by work that shows how exchange ratios for different commodities in some Mesopotamian cities varied according to changes in supply resulting from the ebb and flow of political and military circumstances during the Isin-Larsa and Old Babylonian periods of the early second millennium BC (Farber 1978; Silver 1995). Equally relevant is recent work clarifying the entrepreneurial and profit-seeking nature of contemporary Mesopotamian trading enterprises. Cases in point include Old Assyrian trade with Anatolia (Adams 1974b; Dercksen, ed. 1996; Larsen 1976) and Old Babylonian trade in the Persian Gulf (Leemans 1960; A. L. Oppenheim 1960). Less well attested but possibly similar in structure were independent merchant colonies sent beyond Mesopotamia proper by individual Sumerian city-states in the second half of the third millennium (Foster 1993). The cumulative weight of this evidence makes it clear that wealth-maximizing behaviors by individuals, kin groups, and institutions played a role in spurring and maintaining Mesopotamian urbanism in the historical periods. Under these circumstances, can we truly discount the possibility that comparable motivations may also have played a role in the inception of Mesopotamian urbanism?

Another problem is methodological. Central Place theory, the tool most commonly used in approaching ancient Near Eastern urbanism, is inherently ill equipped to address questions of origin. In essence, the locational theories put forth by twentieth-century successors of von Thünen—most notably Walter Christaller (1966 [1933]) and August Lösch (1954 [1940])—seek to understand the forces that spread economic activity *away* from a center. This involves a tradeoff between economies of scale which provide an incentive to concentrate production, and transportation costs which provide an incentive to disperse production and managerial functions to multiple sites close to consumers/workers. Central Place models help us understand how hierarchies of function are maintained across a landscape. However, because the models simply assume the a priori existence of a central urban market, they tell us nothing about why population and economic activity become concentrated *in the first place*, as noted by John Marshall (1989) and Paul Krugman (1995).

URBAN DYNAMICS: WHY, WHERE, AND HOW?

To understand the deeper causes of why and where cities emerge, we need to go back to the concept of comparative advantage, articulated by the great economist Ricardo almost two centuries ago. From a Ricardian perspective, cities invariably represent nodes in wider transportation networks and are the most efficient way to mediate sustained trade between places with varying degrees of comparative advantage in the production of both necessary and desirable resources. Such advantage is created by differences in productivity between polities, caused by the naturally uneven distribution of resources in different areas, differences in access to transportation, and social factors such as organizational and technological efficiencies delivering increasing returns to scale.

Since cities form as a response to regional imbalances in comparative advantage, they should preferentially emerge either at natural passage points between regions involved in exchange or at the end points of natural transportation routes between such regions (Burghardt 1971; Hirth 1978). They should also form at critical nodes along such routes, such as intersections or transshipment points where goods need to moved between routes served by different types of transport—for example, from water to land transport (Bairoch 1988; Burghardt 1979). Further, because of the multiplier effects of trade on social evolution (below), cities should concentrate in areas possessing the greatest positive productivity differential along a transportation route which in turn ensures larger amounts of fungible surpluses usable for trade.

The central role of trade as a spur to processes of urban origins and growth is explained by the iconoclastic urban expert Jane Jacobs (1969; 2000). She argues that urbanism is a natural form of human organization once a threshold of population density and social complexity has been reached, and that social complexity and population density, in turn, are functions of economic differentiation. By implication, the question of urban origins thus devolves into the question of how economic differentiation is created initially, and the question of growth becomes that of how and at what rate differentiation expands. This is where trade comes in.

According to Jacobs, economic diversity is first created as a result of positive feedback created by a settlement's capacity to generate exports by combining some of its imports and/or preexisting resources with human labor and capital. This generates economic diversity at the same time that it makes possible the acquisition of more and different imports, some of which can again be used to generate additional exports. This process creates co-developments in the form of an increasingly large, skilled, and diverse workforce (that is, human capital), and this, in turn, creates the potential for further economic diversification by adding new types of work and new ways of working. As both work and diversity expand, so does population density within the affected settlements. This increase commonly takes place at the expense of nearby rural populations, which is why developing cities are always the economic and physical shapers of their hinterlands.

Once founded, the key concept for understanding how cities grow is that of Circular and Cumulative Causation. This is an idea first articulated in the 1950s by the economist Gunnar Myrdal (1957) and later elaborated, expanded, and formalized by Allen Pred (1966). At its simplest, it involves the recognition that forces of production and urbanization are interlocked in a circular process whereby a change in one causes changes in the other which "move the system in the same direction as the first change, but much further"

(Myrdal 1957: 13). As explained by Krugman (1995: 49) and Jacobs (1969; 2000), the most important mechanism whereby this takes place is import substitution.

After a regional economy grows beyond a critical point by means of the mechanisms described by Jacobs, it becomes profitable to replace imports of some commodities that are amenable to economies of scale, with, for instance, mass production of local manufactures. This substitution will further expand urban employment, drawing in workers from the countryside and other regions, and in so doing will also increase the size of the local market and the range of skills possessed by the population. As this process unfolds, a number of multiplier effects come into play, resulting in increases in productive capacity. These include the creation of new industries that provide production inputs to the initial industry ("backward linkages") or of activities that either add further value to semi-finished goods or provide services connected to, and made necessary by, the production of such goods ("forward linkages") (Pred 1966: 25–26).

In the Mesopotamian case, one of the most important of these forward linkages must have been the expansion of the managerial classes required to organize the larger number of workers, store and distribute their enhanced production, and keep accurate records of these various activities. This expansion is likely to have been quite substantial, as may be inferred from recent studies of the relationship between changes in population density and the extent of bureaucratic superstructures in modern urban societies. These studies show that expanding population density consistently leads to a disproportionately large growth in the size of the communicative components of managerial institutions in a city. Why this is the case is explained by John Kasarda (1974), a sociologist, who notes that in human societies, as in biological organisms, increasing size exacerbates particular systemic problems and normally results in disproportionate growth in sectors serving to solve these problems. The most critical problem faced by large-scale social systems, according to Kasarda, is articulating communication among its parts. For this reason, as they grow increasingly large and diverse, complex societies must divert an ever larger proportion of their human resources to collecting, processing, and transmitting information.

In due course, these interrelated multipliers combine to create the enlarged population and market size necessary to induce more import substitution. In turn, as the process is repeated at an ever increasing scale, a spiral relationship is created between population growth, market size, the range of productive activities that a region possesses, and the efficiency level of those activities. Production is highest and most efficient where population and markets are larger, but markets increase where production is greater, so that city-led regional growth (or decline) always takes the form of a self-reinforc-ing snowball or cascade effect (Krugman 1995: 49).

EARLY MESOPOTAMIAN CITIES: WHY?

What can we learn from these modern economic models of urban process that will help us better understand the forces at play at the onset of early Mesopotamian civilization? Two lessons come to mind. First, as they have in modern times, trade and changes in commodity production and labor orga-nization are likely to have played fundamental roles in change. Second, pro-cesses of Circular and Cumulative Causation are also likely to have been as consequential in antiquity as they are today, so that if a region gained an ini-tial advantage, those processes would have concentrated new growth and its multiplier effects in the already expanding region rather than elsewhere (Malecki 1997: 49–50). Under these circumstances, what is left to be eluci-dated are the forces that set trade (and its multiplying ramifications) into motion in the first place.

In the case of early Sumerian civilization, the trigger was provided by the combination of the enduring geographical framework of the Mesopotamian alluvium and the unique environmental conditions that prevailed in the area during the late fifth and throughout the fourth millennium BC. Geography was important because it provided southern Mesopotamian societies with an enduring and irrevocable advantage over their neighbors in the form of the low shipment costs made possible by water transport. The cities of the allu-vium were, in effect, at the head of an enormous dendritic transportation sys-tem created by the north–south flowing rivers. This allowed them to procure information, labor, and commodities from areas within the vast Tigris-Euph-rates watershed more efficiently than any potential upstream competitors or rivals away from the rivers. The crucial edge of the southern cities lay in their ability to import needed commodities *in bulk* from resource areas in the sur-rounding highlands by means of low-cost river transport by raft or boat. Of equal importance, the network of canals surrounding Mesopotamian cities and connecting them with the main courses of the rivers allowed them to move bulky agricultural commodities across their immediate dependent hin-terlands with great efficiency.

Environment, in turn, also gave southern societies important advantages in the productivity, variety, and resilience of their subsistence and exportable resources as compared with those available to surrounding polities. These advantages would have been particularly pronounced at the time of early urban emergence in Mesopotamia. As I have recently discussed these data elsewhere in some detail (Algaze 2001a), only a brief summary of the perti-nent information is offered here.

A variety of paleoenvironmental data suggests that the climate was wetter for much of the fourth millennium BC. This means that marginal areas of the Mesopotamian alluvium that are today unproductive because of insufficient water or lack of drainage would likely have been integrated into fluvial networks draining into the sea. In addition, at least for the Late 'Ubaid period and, possibly, into the Early Uruk period, parts of the alluvium which today receive no summer precipitation whatsoever would have been affected by summer monsoonal rains. These rains would have greatly expanded the availability of animal forage at precisely the time of greatest need, and would have enhanced the productivity of both summer crops and date palm groves.

Also more propitious for human settlement were the regimes of the Tigris and Euphrates Rivers through the fourth millennium. New remote sensing work at UCSD by Robert McC. Adams and Jennifer Pournelle (this volume) shows that the rivers formed a single dynamic and complexly intertwined network of anastomosing channels throughout the fourth millennium, creating much vaster areas than was the case later on when various types of high-value crops and grain could only have been produced by means of simple flood-recession irrigation.

Last but not least was the enhanced availability in the fourth millennium of resources from bio-mass-rich marshes, lagoons, and estuaries brought into close proximity to Uruk population centers by temporary mid-Holocene sea level rises. These resources included dried, salted, and smoked fish, various types of fowl, numerous reed products, and dairy products from herds of cattle kept at the margins of greatly enlarged marshes and lagoons (Pournelle, this volume).

The consequences of the geographical and environmental advantages just noted are clear. On the one hand, advantages in the productivity and resilience of their environmental framework meant that Uruk elites could extract larger surpluses per unit of labor than their counterparts elsewhere, and they could do so with greater reliability and predictability. In addition, inherent advantages of water transport would have allowed Uruk elites to mobilize surpluses from their immediately dependent hinterlands at lower cost than their competitors. This also meant that the extent of those dependent hinterlands would naturally be larger than those of their landlocked competitors, and that southern elites and institutions could procure resources and information from a much vaster area at much lower cost than their contemporaries. Taken together, these advantages gave emerging Uruk polities substantial comparative advantages over their peers in neighboring areas in the amounts and variety of information and resources at their disposal, the size of the labor force at their command, and the productivity of those laborers. Under these conditions, as Ricardo reminds us, trade is the logical outcome.

EARLY MESOPOTAMIAN CITIES: WHERE?

It should be clear from the foregoing discussion that many of the key underlying assumptions of Central Place theory are simply unsuitable to the analysis of the conditions prevalent in the alluvial lowlands of the Tigris-Euphrates fluvial system when the early cities first emerged. First, the model assumes that access to agricultural land is the most important economic variable affecting the location of early cities and, therefore, that the movement of agricultural products is the main factor structuring the spatial relationship between settlements in any given region. Second, the model assumes that transportation costs increase steadily with distance. These assumptions are perfectly compatible with conditions prevalent across much of the Mesopotamian periphery, but they fail to account for the complexity of the situation in southern Mesopotamia. The first assumption misses the mark in that it underestimates both the degree of ecological variability of the southern alluvial plain in the fourth millennium BC and the importance of marshes, lagoons, and estuaries at the time. Further, it discounts the probability that resilience strategies based on access to multiple resources (Adams 1978) within the alluvium or the desire to maximize access to trade and communication routes in and out of the alluvium (Algaze 1993a) were factors of equal or even greater locational importance for early cities in the Mesopotamian alluvium than access to agricultural resources. The second assumption has always been irrelevant to conditions in southern Mesopotamia because transportation costs for bulky, locally produced agricultural commodities would not have increased exponentially with distance within the alluvial delta of the Tigris-Euphrates system as presumed by Central Place models. Rather, as explained earlier, such costs were kept in check by networks of natural and artificial canals and marshes surrounding early settlements.

Available surveys of the Mesopotamian alluvium show that multiple urban centers emerged in the area during the fourth millennium (Adams 1966; 1981; Adams and Nissen 1972; Gibson 1972; H. T. Wright 1981b). Each of the sites in question is located along one of the main courses of the Tigris and Euphrates Rivers as they existed at the time. Access to (irrigable) agricultural land was no doubt a factor here, but, above all, the large Uruk sites (Nippur, Uqair, Kish (?), Abu Salabikh, Site 1306, and Site 1172) of the northern part of the Mesopotamian alluvium were also located along the natural transportation routes in and out of the alluvium, which follow the rivers. The southernmost Uruk-period centers (Uruk, Umma, Eridu, Ur, Girsu [Tello], Site 125), in turn, were all situated at logistical transshipment points between different types of routes. They were (1) at the end of the vast north–south transport route created by the rivers, (2) within reach of the lateral routes created by extensive marshes and lagoons at the encroaching head of the Persian Gulf in the fourth millennium (Pournelle, this volume), and (3) at the head of overland routes into the Arabian Peninsula and maritime routes into the Persian Gulf and Indian Ocean. These uniquely privileged positions naturally lessened the transportation costs of these sites and maximized their access to information and products from various far-flung areas and catchments.

EARLY MESOPOTAMIAN CITIES: HOW?

The concept of Circular and Cumulative Causation, discussed earlier, allows us to visualize a still speculative though ultimately testable scenario to account for the precocious urban takeoff of southern Mesopotamian societies in the fourth millennium. For heuristic purposes, this evolving process is divided here into a number of discrete stages, although substantial overlaps clearly existed between them.

The initial stage in the growth of southern economies would have taken place during the late fifth and early fourth millennia—a time when the Mesopotamian alluvium was a mosaic of very different but easily exploited resource areas. In its northern portions, gravity flow irrigation and increased water tables would have made grain cultivation and horticulture more profitable, whereas areas nearer the gulf were better situated to exploit its biomass-rich marshes, lagoons, and estuaries. Inadvertently, this setting provided the initial impetus for burgeoning trade between communities exploiting these varied economic resources. Each of these centers would have specialized in the production of those few crops or commodities best suited to its location within the alluvial ecosystem. Products traded in this initial stage would have included (1) woven and dyed textiles, goat-hair products, leather goods, dairy fats, and other pastoral resources distributed by communities situated at the margins of the better-watered parts of the alluvium where they would have enjoyed preferential access to pastoral and nomadic groups; (2) flax-based textiles, garden crops, and grain produced by polities in the northern portion of the Mesopotamian alluvial plain where the combined flow of the Tigris and the Euphrates made irrigation agriculture and horticulture both more likely and more profitable; and (3) dried, salted, and smoked fish, various types of fowl, reeds, and other marsh or littoral resources preferentially produced by centers immediately by the Persian Gulf littoral.

A second stage in the process may have started already by the Middle Uruk period and would have been marked by an emerging elite awareness of the social implications of the trade patterns already in place. In this stage, technologies and practices initially developed by individual centers exploiting their own specialized niches would have come to be perceived as highly advantageous by many of the competing centers. This naturally would lead to a decrease in regional specialization within the alluvium, as each competing polity used the material surpluses and human skills acquired during the initial stage to replace some imports from nearby centers, or possibly even from foreign areas, by creating their own productive capacities for those products, thus setting in motion the further growth spurt that accrues from import-substitution (see above).

The third stage of the process, datable to the Middle and Late Uruk periods (ca. 3600–3200/3100 BC) would have been characterized by heightened competition between alluvial polities that had by now achieved broadly comparable productive capabilities. Since such polities no longer had much to offer each other in terms of exchange, this stage was characterized by a significant expansion in external trade between individual cities and neighboring areas. Here, the ongoing import substitution processes in the south would have begun to focus more on the replacement of foreign commodities. Increased foreign trade was also enhanced at this point by the domestication of donkeys, which made overland communication across the ancient Near East possible (H. T. Wright 2001a: 127), and likewise, for the first time, provided the physical capacity to export alluvial goods in bulk.

As external trade became increasingly important in the Middle and Late Uruk periods, various types of southern outposts were established at locations strategic for transport across the Mesopotamian periphery (Algaze 1993a; 2001b). These outposts were principally, but not solely, situated at the intersections of the north–south flowing rivers and the principal east–west overland routes across the high plains of northern Mesopotamia (Algaze 1993a; 2001b; but see Rothman, ed. 2001). While these outposts may have served in part as outlets for displaced populations from the south (Johnson 1988–89; Pollock 1999; Schwartz 2001; H. T. Wright 2001a), their carefully selected locations suggest that they also served as collection and transshipment points for the increasing amounts of commodities imported into the alluvium in the later part of the Uruk period, and as distribution points for alluvial exports.

The role played by these trade patterns in the emergence of Sumerian civilization is made clear if we focus our attention on the long-term multiplier effects of import substitution. These processes can be easily documented in the archaeological record of ʿUbaid- and Uruk-period Mesopotamian societies. Perhaps one of the earliest examples in the record is the partial replacement of imported flint by locally manufactured clay sickles, a process that began in the Late ʿUbaid period and continued through the various phases of the Uruk (Benco 1992). Another example is provided by metals, first attested in the south by the end of the ʿUbaid (Moorey 1994: 221, 255–258). Initially, metal goods must have been brought into Southern Mesopotamia as fully finished products imported from the metal-producing highland regions of Iran and Anatolia where metallurgical technologies were first developed (Kohl

1987: 16; G. Stein 1990). By the Middle–Late Uruk periods, however, Uruk societies had already created their own metal-processing industries that relied instead on imports of only lightly processed ores and of semi-processed ingots of smelted copper as opposed to fully processed tools, artifacts, and objects of personal adornment. Evidence of this shift from metal consumers to value-added producers in the south (still using, of course, partially processed imported resources) is provided by ores recovered at Warka and ingots recovered at Jebel Aruda, an Uruk colonial enclave along the Euphrates in Syria, as well as by metal-processing installations identified in Uruk sites both in and out of the alluvium (Algaze 2001a: 208–209 for specific references). In addition, by the final phase of the Uruk period, we also get textual corroboration for the shift in the form of the pictogram used in the earliest Archaic Texts to denote a smith, which shows a smelting furnace with attached blowpipes (Moorey 1994: 243).

By far the most important case of import substitution in the south is provided by the adoption, sometime by the Late 'Ubaid, of wool-bearing breeds of sheep that had been initially developed in the highlands surrounding Mesopotamia (Davis 1984; Sherratt 1997: 539). Because such sheep are not indigenous to the lowlands, wool must have been initially introduced into the south as an import from the surrounding highlands. But wool and woolly sheep did not remain imports for long. As Joy McCorriston (1997) has recently noted, archaeobotanical, zooarchaeological, and textual data from various Uruk sites show that by the second half of the fourth millennium, these once imported commodities had been thoroughly integrated into the southern economy. This took the form of a fast-growing indigenous textile industry based on woven woolen textiles capable of being dyed which, for all practical purposes, replaced the less efficient and less colorful flax-based textiles that had constituted the bulk of local production in the south until that time.

In spite of their late start, southern producers of woolen textiles soon surpassed their highland predecessors and competitors in both scale and efficiency. Several factors may account for this. The first is that by integrating the sheep into the agricultural cycle of grain, the south possessed as much fodder as the highlands, so that no dietary disadvantages accrued to the sheep as a result of their introduction into their new man-made habitat. The second is that the south had the comparative advantage of easy access to many natural dyes. This is another point recently raised by McCorriston (1999; 2001: 222, and personal communication 2001), who notes that many of the dyes used to color Near Eastern wool in antiquity could be derived from desert or garden plants available in or around southern Mesopotamia or from products only obtainable via the Persian Gulf, such as various types of marine gastropods and indigo.

The third factor is that southern Mesopotamian societies possessed larger pools of labor available for textile work. From the beginning, these workers appear to have been organized in ways that allowed for greater efficiency and superior craftsmanship in the production of textiles. Contemporary depictions of female workers (pig-tailed figures) attending horizontal looms (Amiet 1972: nos. 673–674; 1980: nos. 319–320) suggest that already by the Late Uruk period the woolen textile industry of the southern lowlands was based on centrally administered weaving establishments exploiting the labor of various categories of dependent women in both cities and the countryside, such as we know existed in most Sumerian and Babylonian polities during the third and early second millennia BC (Jacobsen 1970 [1953]; Maekawa 1980; Waetzoldt 1972).

The shift from linen to wool as the primary material for textile manufacture in the south and the closely related development of state-sponsored weaving establishments during the fourth millennium present us with a textbook case illustrating the many multiplier effects that commonly attend the introduction of new industries and increases in productive capacity. Particularly noteworthy are the forward and backward linkages related to the start of industrial-scale weaving in the south. Examples of the former are provided by the fulling of semi-finished woven textiles with oils and alkali and the dyeing of fulled cloth. Both of these practices are well attested in written record of the later third millennium, and both require a substantial input of value-adding labor and new resources (McCorriston 2001: 222; Potts 1997: 95). Under Mesopotamian conditions, an equally important forward linkage is the shift to industrial-scale textile production which would have required scores of bureaucrats to record, store, and redistribute the output, and also to supervise the distribution of subsistence rations to workers. Examples of backward linkages, in turn, are provided by a variety of labor-intensive activities that contributed necessary inputs to the weaving establishments, but largely took place away from them. Minimally, these include pasturing the sheep, washing, plucking and/or shearing, combing, and spinning the wool, separating the wool by quality, and delivering it to the various urban and rural locations where state-organized weavers labored.

THE EVIDENCE FOR TRADE

The foregoing discussions presume that trade, both internal and external, was the engine of early Mesopotamian urban growth. Nevertheless, substantial disagreement remains on the importance of long-distance trade to the processes of urban and state formation in southern Mesopotamia.

Many scholars reviewing the data for southern Mesopotamian economies of the fourth millennium properly highlight the importance of local tribute extraction and intraregional distribution of resources as key elements in that economy, but either minimize the overall importance of long-distance trade to the socioeconomic processes at work at the time (for example, Frangipane 2001a; Pollock 1999; Schwartz 2001; Weiss 1989) or presume that the increase in long-distance exchange was a consequence of urbanism rather than a cause (H. T. Wright 1981a; 2001a). Such views are flawed on two accounts. First, they fail to acknowledge the evidence for valuable imports in both the textual and archaeological record of Uruk sites. The case of metals and precious stones is particularly instructive. The earliest Archaic Texts, for instance, already include numerous references to metals which must have been imported into the south either as finished products or, most likely at this point, manufactured in place from imported ores and ingots (above). Similarly, some of the Middle and Late Uruk–period southern colonial sites on the Euphrates yielded evidence for the import and in situ processing of various types of exotic stones, including lapis (for specific references, see Algaze 2001a: 208–209), all presumably for re-export to larger Uruk centers in the south. Those centers, in turn, have also yielded some evidence for this wealth. Nowhere is this clearer than in the so-called Riemchengebäude structure found in the Eanna Precinct at Warka (Late Uruk: Eanna IV), which was literally brimming with many categories of imported exotic materials (for a full inventory, see now Forest 1999: 67–73).

The second problem is that those who minimize the early importance of trade consistently overestimate how representative the archaeological record really is. Must we believe that the Riemchengebäude was an exceptional find that bears no relationship to elite activities at the site? On the contrary, it is more parsimonious to think that this is not a case of unusual wealth but rather one of unique preservation, since the building was buried after being consumed by fire. Most likely, one reason why wealth on the scale found at the Riemchengebäude is not well attested in other excavated areas of Warka, save for scattered buried hoards such as the Sammelfund (Heinrich 1936), is because so many of the Uruk-period structures cleared in the Eanna Precinct represent no more than the foundations of buildings that were carefully and purposefully cleaned and emptied in antiquity (Eichmann 1989).

An equally important reason for the paucity of evidence for Uruk-period exchange is that so many of the articles traded at the time would have left few traces in the archaeological record. This includes, of course, both the principal exports (finished textiles) from the alluvial lowlands at this time and the principal imports, either because they do not preserve (timber), or because, except in destruction levels, they are commonly recycled (metals, precious stones, and the like).

Andrew Sherratt (2004) also notes that in truly complex societies, sumptuary goods will be distributed more widely across social hierarchies than in simpler societies, as such commodities become a medium of exchange capable of being converted into a wide range of goods and services. This naturally increases the likelihood that such commodities will be kept longer in circulation, that they will be transformed more often (for example, metals by melting), and that they will be passed on across generations more consistently. As commodities circulate more broadly across wider social networks, excavations at single central sites, or, worse still, at the core of such sites, would be unlikely to produce a representative sample of the scale and type of sumptuary commodities in circulation at any one time. Regretfully, the kind of broad sampling strategy needed to document the spread of sumptuary commodities in regionally integrated societies has not been part of the excavated record for the Uruk period in the alluvium.

A further problem is that in complex societies, a high proportion of exotics would also naturally get withdrawn from circulation for use as burial gifts. One suspects that the continuing and still puzzling dearth of mortuary evidence from southern Mesopotamia for the Uruk period may be responsible to a greater degree than is generally acknowledged for the view that imports of sumptuary commodities into fourth-millennium Mesopotamia were relatively rare.

ISSUES OF SCALE:
SOUTHERN VERSUS NORTHERN MESOPOTAMIA

Where trade flows, its ramifications soon follow in the form of increasing social complexity and urbanism. Thus, the precocious development of southern Mesopotamia throughout the fourth millennium BC comes as no surprise. How unique development in the south was at this point becomes clear when we compare available survey and excavation data for both the nature of sites and patterns of settlement in the alluvium against comparable data from neighboring regions, particularly from upper Mesopotamia.

For the south, available survey data (Adams 1981; Adams and Nissen 1972; H. T. Wright 1981b; for a reworking of the data, see now Kouchoukos 1998: 230–249; Pollock 2001) reveal that both absolute population levels and relative agglomeration rates were significantly higher throughout the various phases of the Uruk period than they were in any one coherent area of the Mesopotamian periphery (Kouchoukos 1998: tables 5.4–5.6, fig. 5.9).[2] In

---

[2] Note, however, that Wilkinson's detailed and particularly systematic survey of the upper Jezira plains west of the Tigris in northern Iraq show what appear to be higher overall regional population densities in that area than in the south (Wilkinson 2000: fig. 5). It is unclear whether this represents a real pattern or whether it is a consequence of depressed site counts in the south due largely to sedimentation (Wilkinson 2000: 244). Although I am inclined to the latter position, it is certain that, in either case, the south still had a much greater proportion of its overall population living in agglomerated settlements and that these settlements were situated at much shorter distances from each other than their northern counterparts.

fact, surveys document multiple interacting urban sites (40+ hectares in extent) within the surveyed portions of the alluvium throughout *every* phase of the Uruk period, all situated alongside canals and within relatively short distances of each other and each positioned at the apex of a variegated settlement structure. Development in the area reaches its peak by the final phase of the Uruk period, when the site of Warka grew to the extraordinary size of 250 hectares (Finkbeiner 1991) and was surrounded by numerous dependent villages and towns, totaling a minimum of 280 hectares of further occupation (Adams 1981; Adams and Nissen 1972).

The sites just discussed are likely to be only the tip, so to say, of the Uruk-period settlement iceberg in southern Mesopotamia because a number of sites exist outside of the thus far surveyed areas that were occupied during one or more phases of the Uruk period. These sites are not considered in recent reviews of the nature of Uruk-period settlement in southern Mesopotamia (for instance, Algaze 2001a; Pollock 2001; Wilkinson 2000), but several are likely to have been quite substantial at the time. Foremost among these are Umma and the nearby site of Umm al-Aqarib.[3] Numerous Archaic tablets recently plundered from either (or both) of those sites appear immediately comparable with the earliest examples from Warka (Robert Englund, personal communication 2001). At a minimum, these tablets attest to the economic importance of the Umma area in the Late Uruk period, but since at Warka these tablets are part of a wider urban assemblage of great extent and complexity, their presence in the Umma area argues for a similar context. Though circumstantial, this evidence suggests that Umma may have been second only to Warka itself in terms of urban and social development in the Late Uruk period.[4]

The long sequence of growth in the south throughout the Uruk period contrasts starkly with the overall developmental trajectory of contemporary

---

[3] Both Umma (WS 197) and Aqarib (WS 198) were at the edge of Adams's 1968 survey area but could not be properly surveyed at that time because of extensive sand dunes covering both sites (Adams and Nissen 1972: 227–228). The dunes have since cleared the area.

[4] At present, the settlement data for Late Uruk southern Mesopotamia is anomalous in that it shows a central site (Uruk) that is four times as large (that is, populous) as second-tier settlements (such as Site 1306). Analyses of modern urban systems (Krugman 1996) leave little doubt that urban populations arrange themselves in rank order by size in ways that are both patterned and predictable ("Zipf's Law"). The behavior of such modern systems suggests that a tier of settlement may actually be missing from our southern Mesopotamian data. If urban rank-size rules apply to the Mesopotamian case, as I would expect, the missing settlement(s) should be roughly about half the extent (population) of Warka. I expect that Umma represents the missing tier and that further work at that site will eventually show it to have been somewhere in the range of 120 hectares in the Late Uruk period.

northern Mesopotamian societies. To be sure, as Henry Wright (2001a: 145) has noted, both have an initial burst of settlement growth and expansion of social complexity in the earlier part of the fourth millennium, but in the north this lasts only until about 3500/3400 BC. This has become evident only recently in upper Mesopotamia as a result of new excavations at Tell Brak (J. Oates and Oates 1997; Emberling et al. 1999) along the Jagh Jagh branch of the upper Khabur River in Syria, new excavations at Nineveh along the upper Tigris River in Iraq (Stronach 1994), new surveys at both Tell el-Hawa (Wilkinson and Tucker 1995) and Tell Hamoukar (Gibson 2000; Gibson et al. 2002; Ur 2002a; 2002b; Reichel 2002) and their environs in the Jebel Sinjar plains of northern Iraq and Syria, and older surveys of Samsat and its environs (summarized in Algaze 1999) in the upper Euphrates area of southeastern Turkey. This new work shows that the scale of individual sites in disparate areas of the northern Mesopotamian plains during the first half of the fourth millennium was roughly comparable to that of contemporary sites in the southern Mesopotamian alluvium. Tell Brak, for instance, grew to 65 hectares (Emberling et al. 1999) in the so-called northern Middle Uruk period and may have been even larger at the time, depending on whether or not the intervening area between the main site and nearby contemporary suburbs was occupied (H. Wright, personal communication 2004; J. Ur, personal communication, 2003). Brak was thus broadly similar in extent, if not slightly larger than, Uruk itself and Site 1306 (Adams's "Early/Middle Uruk" phase: Adams 1981). Nineveh too is likely to have been substantial at this time. Its most recent excavator, David Stronach (1994), gives a preliminary estimate in the 40-hectare range. Hawa is reported to have been in the 30+-hectare range at this time, and Samsat and Hamoukar were about half that size.

Similarities in the scale of individual sites in northern and southern Mesopotamia, however, mask important differences in the complexity of the overall settlement systems of both areas. Even at their peak in the "northern Middle Uruk" period, these Late Chalcolithic societies hardly equaled their southern counterparts. This is reflected in both the density and the hierarchy of settlement grids surrounding large settlements in the two areas. Pending the publication of recent surveys around Brak conducted by H. Wright and his colleagues (Lawler 2006), the best data we have for the north is derived from systematic surveys for the Hawa and Samsat environs by Tony Wilkinson, which show that during the first half of the fourth millennium, both sites were surrounded by a corona of uniformly small village or hamlet-sized sites (Wilkinson 1990a; Algaze 1999; Wilkinson and Tucker 1995: fig. 35, top). This compares unfavorably with the more complex settlement grids of variously sized dependent settlements that surrounded contemporary (Early/Middle Uruk) urban centers in the south (Adams 1981; Pollock 2001). Further, surveys of the Hawa and Samsat environs show that a more complex three-tiered settlement pattern structure appears in their vicinity only *after* the onset of contacts with the Uruk world, not before (Algaze 1999; Wilkinson and Tucker 1995: fig. 35, bottom).

A further noteworthy difference is a consequence of the geographical constraints affecting human settlement in northern and southern Mesopotamia. Large Late Chalcolithic settlements in the northern plains such as Nineveh, Hawa, Brak, and Samsat were situated in different drainage basins and were separated from each other by hundreds of kilometers. They were thus largely isolated one from the other in terms of day to day contacts. This was not the case in the south, where multiple competing settlements connected by waterways existed within short distances and easy communication (via water) of one another.

In light of the above, it should not be surprising to find sharp differences in the overall developmental trajectories of both areas through the fourth millennium. Most salient among these is that in the north, unlike the south, the initial burst of growth and development was not sustained for long. Data from Nineveh, Hawa, and Samsat are unreliable on this point, but new excavations at Brak and Hamoukar show that those settlements contracted in the second half of the fourth millennium (Emberling 2002; Emberling et al. 1999: 25–26; Gibson 2000; Gibson et al. 2002; Ur 2002a; 2002b), just as the expansion of southern sites such as Warka reached their Late Uruk peak. Brak was the largest and most impressive of the Late Chalcolithic centers in northern Mesopotamia identified thus far, and its contraction in the final quarter of the fourth millennium meant that Late Uruk urban centers in the alluvium were significantly more developed than contemporary Late Chalcolithic polities in the Mesopotamian periphery. In fact, at 250 hectares, Late Uruk Warka is likely to have been exponentially larger than any contemporary peripheral competitor. The fact that this huge differential developed at precisely the time of the maximum expansion of the Uruk colonial network is unlikely to be a mere coincidence.

Survey evidence from various areas across northern Mesopotamia (summarized in Algaze 1999: table 3; Wilkinson 2000) shows that the area was effectively ruralized by the end of the fourth and the transition to the third millennium. The indigenous centers that existed in the region in the preceding period had vanished, and comparable indigenous centers did not reappear in the area until the final phases of the Ninevite V period, sometime in the second quarter of the third millennium (Schwartz 1994a; Weiss 1990; Wilkinson 1994). In contrast, urbanism in the southern alluvial plains continued to flourish and expand not only though the Late Uruk period, but throughout the fourth–third millennium transition (Jemdet Nasr) as well (Adams 1981; Postgate 1986). The urban spiral of the south continued unabated well into the first quarter of the third millennium (Early Dynastic I): older sites such as Ur, Kish Nippur, Abu Salabikh, Warka, and, possibly, Umma grew further, and new cities were founded across the alluvium, including most notably Lagash (al-Hiba) and Shuruppak (Fara) (Adams 1981; Gibson 1972; H. T. Wright 1981b). Warka reached 600 hectares in extent at this point (Finkbeiner 1991), but this was no longer exceptional; al-Hiba, situated at the edge of the easternmost marshes in the alluvium, was almost as large (E. Carter 1985).

THE SYNERGIES OF CIVILIZATION

Multiple socio-evolutionary synergies would have arisen from the differences in rates of population agglomeration and the distance between polities typical of southern Mesopotamia and areas on its periphery throughout the second half of the fourth millennium, outlined above.

The first synergy arises from the greater concentration of polities that existed in the Mesopotamian alluvium throughout the roughly 700-year duration of the Uruk period, as compared with neighboring areas. As Colin Renfrew and his colleagues (Renfrew and Cherry 1986) have repeatedly argued, the long-term presence of multiple polities within relatively short distances of each other invariably engenders important processes of competition, exchange, emulation, and technological innovation. The impact of these mutually reinforcing processes has been explained by Robert Wright (2000: 165–168), who notes that in situations where antagonistic but mutually communicative polities exist, social and economic innovations that prove maladaptive in any one society are likely to be weeded out more quickly than in less competitive settings. Conversely, innovations that prove advantageous are more likely to spread quickly across the various polities, thus accelerating the pace of change of the system as a whole.

The second synergy arises from the greater proportion of the population of southern Mesopotamia that lived in towns and cities and their immediate hinterlands through the Uruk period as compared with the more dispersed settlement typical for neighboring areas at the time. This had many consequences. First, as Adam Smith (1954 [1776]: book I, chaps. 1-3) noted more than 200 years ago, the assemblage of a critical mass of both producers and consumers is a necessary precondition for the division of labor and resulting economies of scale (below). In addition, proximity between workers and employers lowers training costs and increases labor flexibility (Malecki 1997: 49), thus providing southern institutions quicker access than their competitors to skilled workers/builders/soldiers in times of growth or need.

Increasing population density in towns and cities would also have compounded the natural transportation advantages of the alluvial environment by the development of further efficiencies in shipping and communication arising from the increasingly compact arrangement of the inhabitants of the area throughout the fourth millennium. One compounding efficiency was provided when artificial canals began to be built across portions of the southern alluvium in the Uruk period (Adams 1981; Pournelle, this volume), expanding the communication network to areas beyond the natural flow of the rivers. In so doing, the new canals also served to reinforce ongoing urbanization processes in the alluvium. This effect, no doubt inadvertent, is suggested by studies that clearly link reductions in transport costs of agricultural commodities in traditional societies to the movement of population into cities (Fujita and Krugman 1995: 520).

The third synergy is closely related to the preceding and again arises from increasing density and compactness. This inevitably led to a multiplication of interactions between individuals in cities. As interactions multiply, information flow is enhanced. This has two crucial interrelated effects. The first is that it exponentially increases the possibility that technological improvements and inventions will take place in urban settings. Why this should be so is explained by Gerhard Lenski (1979: 16), a sociologist, and Joel Mokyr (1996: 71), an economist, who note that technological innovation is essentially a process of recombining existing elements of information, so that the rate of innovation rises as the store of information increases. This increase will always be logarithmic, since the possibility of new combinations increases many times faster than the basic elements of information. The second effect of enhanced information flow is one noted earlier: innovations, once created, would naturally diffuse faster.

As the web of interpersonal communications became increasingly dense in the southern cities that were growing many times larger than neighboring population centers by the second half of the fourth millennium, the likelihood that advantageous inventions and innovations would arise and be quickly diffused was greatly enhanced. In the Mesopotamian case, this found expression in a variety of revolutionary technologies of social control that fall in the realm of what the eminent social anthropologist Jack Goody (2000) has termed "technologies of the intellect."

Perhaps the most salient of these technologies of the intellect was the *systematic* use of various types of dependent laborers receiving rations for the production of subsistence and sumptuary commodities and for building activities. Evidence for this is provided by millions of ration containers themselves found at a variety of Uruk sites (Nissen 1988), by hundreds of attestations of signs for various categories of dependent laborers in the known corpus of Archaic Texts from Warka, and by at least one tablet that summarizes food rations given to different groups of male and female captives (Englund 1998: 70, 178–179, fig. 66). This means that elites in fast-growing Uruk cities had more laborers at their command than competing elites elsewhere, that they could extract more energy from those laborers, and that they were better able to move them around as needed at little cost—an ability often identified as a key factor in economic development (Krugman 1995: 19). More importantly, it also means that Uruk elites could also organize laborers in nontraditional ways so as to take advantage of increases in productivity and other economies of scale arising from the specialized production of commodities.

The clearest material evidence for this organizational quantum leap in how labor was organized is provided by the well-documented shift to standardized, mass-produced ceramics throughout the Uruk (Nissen 1974), but comparable changes can be seen in the way other commodities, such as wool (Green 1980; Nissen 1986b) and metals (Nissen 1988), were produced or procured at that time. These patterns leave no doubt that economies of scale based on task specialization were being introduced in a variety of Uruk-period productive activities.

A second technology of the intellect appearing at this time in the south consisted of new forms of information processing and record keeping that were more capable of conveying information across time and space than the simpler reckoning systems used by contemporary societies elsewhere. This process started in earnest in the Middle Uruk period with the introduction of devices such as impressed hollow balls filled with tokens capable of conveying information by combining numbers and images, and culminated in the development of pictographic writing by the final phase of the Uruk period. Writing was arguably the most important consequence of the disproportionate expansion of the communicative sectors in growing Mesopotamian cities which resulted from their need to articulate their ever more diverse and ever larger components. What writing gave to early Mesopotamian decision makers (and the urban institutions they worked for) was a flow of varied and reliable economic information that allowed them to deploy available labor and resources so as to maximize their revenues and extend their power. In so doing, writing provided southern Mesopotamian societies of the Late Uruk period with a further substantial competitive advantage over contemporary polities elsewhere in which similar breakthroughs in accounting, accountability, classification, and access to information were absent (Algaze 2001a).

These various synergies represent multiple facets of a single phenomenon: advances in the efficiency and intensity of social interactions possible within and between southern societies of the fourth millennium above and beyond those practicable in neighboring areas at the time. These advances are key to understanding the Sumerian takeoff because, as the sociologist Amos Hawley (1986: 7) notes, human settlements have historically exhibited a tendency to grow to the maximum size afforded by the technology for communication and transportation possessed by the population. Improvements in the ability to move materials, people, or information inevitably lead to increases in mean aggregate settlement size. This has been understood by economists since the time of Adam Smith (1954 [1776]: book I, chaps. 1–3), who observed that gains in the efficiency of transportation and communication always act as a spur to economic growth in human societies. The reasons for this are explained by Hawley (1986: 65–66), who notes that social units engaged in specialized functions are necessarily spread over space, which naturally decreases the efficiency of information flow and increases the cost of value-added production and services. Thus, increases in communication efficiency and reductions in mobility costs always result in gains in specialization and differentiation—processes that, as noted earlier, are central to the origins and growth of urban societies. It is not difficult to see how all of this relates to the Sumerian case. The Uruk-period takeoff correlates both with enhanced communication efficiency in the form of new reckoning and writing systems and with reductions in mobility costs as population became concentrated, production facilities consolidated, and production standardized.

CONCLUSIONS: THE MESOPOTAMIAN CONJUNCTURE

Why did the balance of urbanization and social complexity in the ancient Near East shift decisively to the southern alluvial lowlands of Mesopotamia in the second half of the fourth millennium BC? Early on, the stage was set by advantages in productivity, reliability, and ease of transportation inherent to the "natural landscape" of southern Mesopotamia. Absent in neighboring regions, these advantages can be considered as the necessary conditions in the conjuncture that resulted in urban development. No doubt, the most important of these advantages was ease of transport. Whereas geography in the south both permitted and encouraged linearly arranged agglomerations based on intensive agriculture and on boat and raft transport, the geography of areas outside the Tigris-Euphrates alluvial lowlands instead encouraged population dispersal so as to maximize the amount of territory under (dry farmed) cultivation. Under these circumstances, a critical mass of compact and closely interacting polities such as existed throughout the Uruk period in alluvial Mesopotamia failed to form in neighboring areas in the fourth millennium. Accordingly, polities in those areas were not likely to significantly enhance their productivity in and of themselves, because they lacked the critical mass of population to permit much specialization of labor or to encourage the development of new, more complex technologies of communication, such as proved fundamental for the Sumerian takeoff.

Indigenous city-states comparable (in complexity, if not always in scale) to those that had thrived in the south since the fourth millennium did emerge across the upper Mesopotamian plains sometime just before the middle of the third millennium (Weiss 1990; Wilkinson 1994), 800 years or so after the Sumerian takeoff. However, it was only by adopting forms of social and economic organization and writing systems derived from southern models (Postgate 1988) that these upper Mesopotamian polities were able to marshal the organizational efficiencies needed to overcome the difficulties of overland transportation that had prevented their Late Chalcolithic predecessors from forming enduring complex societies. Bluntly put, urbanism in the Mesopotamian periphery was only possible as an engineered landscape; it only became viable as a result of innovations in communication and labor control created first in the Sumerian heartland.

In the end, it turns out that Karl Wittfogel (1957) was right, but for the wrong reasons. Rivers were indeed central to the development of early Mesopotamian civilization as he argued, but not so much as a source of irrigation water as in their role as conduits of transportation for subsistence commodities, building materials, necessary resources, and sumptuary goods. After all, in Mesopotamia as elsewhere along other river basins where pristine civilizations formed, cities emerged not at random along the courses of the rivers, but rather in fertile areas downstream, where a minimal threshold of access to local agricultural resources was ensured and where, more importantly, transport costs were lowest and access to diverse resources within the river's watershed was highest (Bairoch 1988: 12). The importance of rivers to the emergence and growth of many urban societies is elegantly explained by Felipe Fernández-Armesto, a historian, who notes that "civilizations of scale can only be built with concentrated resources. Resources can be concentrated only by means of good communications. And for almost the whole of history, humankind has depended for long-range communications on waterways" (Fernández-Armesto 2001: 182).

Nevertheless, natural advantages derived from geography and environment do not explain in and of themselves the crystallization of early Mesopotamian civilization—or, for that matter, that of any other pristine civilization. In the final analysis, environmental and geographical factors are only permissive, not prescriptive. Whether individuals and groups react to environmental conditions and take advantage of geographical possibilities, and how they do so, are always constrained by culturally determined perceptions of opportunities and threats. Moreover, the present is also shaped by the past through inherently unpredictable accidents and innovations that add an element of indeterminacy to any attempt at historical prognostication or explanation.

Seen in this light, the natural advantages of the southern Mesopotamian landscape merely provided a backdrop wherein some social responses became more likely than others. Given the diversified but dispersed resources prevalent in southern Mesopotamia throughout the late fifth and fourth millennia BC, and the naturally low mobility costs of the area, one of the most probable of these responses was for pre- and proto-historic elites to specialize in the production of a limited number of commodities best suited to their location within the alluvial environmental mosaic and to engage in trade with differently specialized local rivals. By the same token, the absence of important resources from the Mesopotamian environment, most notably roofing-grade timber, stone, and metals, also made it likely that early southern elites would seek to engage in trade with their foreign counterparts in areas where such resources occurred naturally.

In turning to trade earlier and more intensively than those in neighboring societies, elites in alluvial Mesopotamia surely had no understanding of the long-term developmental consequences of the actions they were undertaking. Rather, trade simply became an efficient way to accomplish what elites do in all human societies—namely, sanction existing social inequalities, extend the amounts and varieties of commodities and labor at their disposal, and increase their political power. In this light, the Sumerian takeoff was, in effect, an unanticipated consequence of long-term trade patterns that differentially favored the development of societies in the alluvial lowlands of Mesopotamia over polities in neighboring regions.

At first, the trade was spurred by differences in productivity that favored the south and that were largely the result of geographical and environmental factors. Once a significant measure of exchange was in place, however, conditions that further expanded the comparative advantage of Sumerian societies arose primarily as a result of conditions created in large part from the social ramifications of the trade itself. Rapidly urbanizing Uruk polities possessed ever larger markets and pools of skilled and unskilled labor, usable, as needed, for commodity production, building, or agricultural activities, as soldiers engaged in warfare against local rivals or as colonists and emissaries sent to faraway lands. Synergies derived from the greater population density and larger labor pools were compounded by socially created organizational efficiencies delivering ever increasing returns to scale. These came principally in the form of new ways of organizing labor and in more efficient and more accurate ways of conveying information across space and time that southern societies developed through the Middle and Late Uruk periods, culminating in a formal writing system. Social innovations such as these ultimately explain why complex, regionally organized city-states emerged earlier in southern Iraq than elsewhere in the Near East, or the world.

Transformative Impulses in Late Bronze Age Technology:

A Case Study from the Amuq Valley, Southern Turkey

K. Aslihan Yener

Abstract

This article explores one of the many topics Robert McCormick Adams has addressed: the relationships between social institutions and technology. Adams has long focused his attention on interpreting the growth of complex political confederations in the ancient Near East, regional production disparities brought on by varying skills, and semi-commercial trade and its institutions. Many of these factors played major developmental roles during the rise and indeed collapse of empires in this region. I emphasize here a very particular kind of knowledge that became closely guarded by regions in high-resource zones, that of technological know-how—the specialized skill not only to make high-status items, but to organize the strategic production and trade of artifacts that concentrates privilege on certain sectors of the population. A number of scholars studying the role of metallurgical technologies have begun to understand that certain techniques detected in the manufacture of artifacts actually contain information about social relations. That is, discovering the ways of making things and organizing production could reflect more about social characteristics than previously thought. The production of metals in the Amuq region, especially in the territorial capital Alalakh, may hold clues to these important relationships.

Introduction

While many are familiar with Robert McCormick Adams's surveys in Iraq and his theoretical contributions on the rise of complex social institutions, his more recent research on the social contexts of accelerated technological change has reached a broader range of scholars outside the field of the ancient

Near East. *Paths of Fire*, published in 1996, fueled debate among those interested in the transformative impulses that link the sociocultural sphere and
technology. This paper focuses on information from a different part of the
debate on technology—specifically, ancient metal technology—and draws on
the work of a 2002 University of Chicago seminar on the archaeology of
technology at which Adams was a guest. Using preliminary results of archaeological field research in the Amuq Valley in southern Turkey, integrated with
metallography, I aim to steer further investigation into the rapid technological shift from the use of bronze to iron contextualized before and during the
collapse of palace economies in the middle of the second millennium BC, a
topic that Adams (2000) has recently addressed. The goal of these two lines of
inquiry—that is, the first contextual and the second technical—is to define
the socio-technical systems of production, and the relationships of these systems to wider political and social contexts.

THEORETICAL AND COMPARATIVE BACKGROUND

One of the most difficult issues that archaeologists face in practice is inferring
broader sociocultural processes from mundane artifacts, over and above the
important insights that can be made on how they pattern across a landscape,
settlement, or within a building. While textual resources are sometimes available, these often reflect a narrow viewpoint, often with an elite bias, and at
best carry only faint echoes of the larger, ethnically diverse, but mute populations. Adams (2000: 98–99) correctly noted that this "restricted range of
actors and behaviors" needs amplification if any cogent conclusions are to be
reached about the dynamics of ancient polities. Moreover, given the vagaries
of excavated evidence, Adams points out that technical change is comparatively well represented in the archaeological record, and that archaeological
priorities should therefore focus on this issue. Indeed, since technology has
often been implicated in creating and defining social relations and social distance through production, exchange, consumption, display, and related activities, a nuanced understanding of change in technology could provide
important clues to sociocultural organization.

  Augmenting these themes, Adams (1996: 6) states that "technological
innovations have a role reminiscent of genetic mutations in biology in terms
of supplying the raw materials for change, but they differ in that they are less
random, are more context dependent, more prone to occur in closely interrelated clusters and likewise more transformative in the scale and scope of their
consequences." Nevertheless, Adams cautions against the notion of drawing
too many parallels to biological and adaptationist approaches to human social
evolution, despite the recent wide popularity of this theme (for example, see
Diamond 1999). One of the disturbing features of such approaches, accord-

ing to Adams, is that they do not see "a further, equally qualitative leap beyond mere biological life involved in the distinctively human capacity for intentionality, experiment, symbolization, directed and self conscious and surely 'autonomous' but not necessarily 'adaptive' agency. And the irregularities of technological evolution, moving upward from early agriculture, may be the best place we have from which to view this process of emergence" (Adams email, personal communication). I was encouraged by this suggestion, and in a recent University of Chicago Interdisciplinary Archaeology Workshop discussion (February 2002), Adams urged the archaeological community to seek an understanding of social and technical change, which is precisely what archaeologists are best qualified to do.

Archaeologists have generally regarded metal technology as peripheral and often relegate these data to appendixes in excavation reports. In addition, researchers of metals have been hampered by the controversy generated from technological deterministic models best exemplified by Childe (1951 [1936]) and other linear evolutionary schemes. Turning the prevailing pattern of technological discussion around, Adams has linked technological change to cumulative socioeconomic forces that can be understood within a historical context (Adams 2001). That is, technology alone has not been the agency of change. Change-producing stress and transformative impulses come from a diversity of directions, such as the environment and, especially, the people themselves.

If, as Adams urges, socio-technical changes need to be closely examined to further the construction of broader theoretical models of ancient civilizations, new breakthroughs in scientific instrumental analysis and recent studies of technological processes provide important methodological and theoretical frameworks. Indeed, scholars working with metals within the growing field of the anthropology of technology have shifted their emphasis toward deriving a better understanding of agency and production parameters in the process of developing new formulations, developed by Pierre Lemonnier (1986; 1993) and Francois Sigaut (1994), among others. These ideas, coupled with insights gained from methodologies developed for metallography by Cyril Stanley Smith and others (Scott 1991; C. S. Smith 1981), have augmented the theoretical foundations of accelerated technical change, as outlined by Adams.

One of the most influential new studies of technological processes comes out of Lemonnier's reassessment of operational sequences, that is, *chaîne opératoire*, an idea developed originally by Leroi-Gourhan (see summaries in Pfaffenberger 1999). Lemonnier (1993) used a general concept of technological systems—or ways of doing something—called "styles of technology," which are "signifying systems" present not only in socio-technical systems but in broader social contexts as well. The artifact, according to this notion, provides information beyond style and function, and also informs on techniques developed within a culturally mediated system of technological knowledge. This idea was outlined in an influential article by Sigaut (1994) who discussed his idea of "technical facts," which are the biological, chemical, and environmental parameters that limit the ways artifacts are made within a single social context. He presented a detailed study of the operational pathways or production steps that are used in any technology. While there may be several possible paths taken by a smith to make a bronze blade, each of these processes would be, according to Sigaut, significantly limited by the natural constraints of the pertinent "technical facts." Approaching the problem through the perspective of how natural constraints are mediated through culture, Lemonnier (1993) noted that if there is no technical logic behind particular methods of manufacture, there is a cultural logic that can be even more enlightening for reconstructing a larger social scale and may reveal human choices among alternative routes (Pfaffenberger 1992). Hence, these sociotechnical systems will tell us much about the culture of the artisans and their relationships with an artifact and its technology (Harper 1987; Pinch and Bijker 1987). Indeed, as Tim Ingold (1997: 107) notes, "technical relations are embedded in social relations." Thus, artifacts and techniques of manufacture do not just reflect culture, they are embedded in culture, and enact cultural transmission (see especially Gordon and Killick 1993).

A third significant contribution was made by a materials scientist, Cyril Stanley Smith (1981), who suggested that the analysis of an artifact can inform on the particular technical paths taken by the metalworker, giving a rare glimpse into that smith's cognitive experience. By utilizing metallography on archaeological finds, he revealed the vivid, microscopically detectable landscape of techniques used in Damascus steel, Japanese Samurai swords, Neolithic beads, and the sophisticated bronze alloys of later periods in the ancient Near East. Through the techniques of materials science, he added new methodological rigor to artifactual studies and demonstrated that the complex microstructure of metal objects represents a record of their past. While not explicitly connecting his metallographic analysis to social phenomena or political history, the implications were there for others to follow (see, for example, Epstein 1993; Pigott 1996). These studies extend Smith's analysis to demonstrate how some regions had particular ways of viewing and organizing the production of materials (Lechtman 1984; 1988). Glimpses can be caught of how shared cognitive codes and cultural experiences might shape ways of making artifacts (Appadurai 1986; Eliade 1978 [1956]).

Problem Orientation: Late Bronze and Early Iron Age

How, then, does this relate to the arrival of iron in the ancient Near East? At issue is the beginning of the generalized use of iron in the later second millennium BC. Utilization of iron metal from meteoric sources and the use of iron ores as pigments, stone hammers, and, significantly, in the smelting of copper had already existed for millennia, as outlined in several important surveys by Waldbaum (1980; 1999). Given the facts that (1) bronze annealed to the hardness of low carbon steel outperforms a wrought iron, and (2) complex pyro-technological skills and resources are needed to make iron, the reason behind the transition to iron during the mid-second millennium BC has eluded researchers to date. Various attempts have been made to explain this accelerated change. Speculations about a tin shortage brought about by disruptions of the tin trade at the end of the Late Bronze Age (see references in Wertime and Muhly 1980) have been discounted, given the dramatic drop in the price of tin in the Late Bronze Age reflected in Ugaritic texts (Heltzer 1978); indeed, this suggests an oversupply in the market and not the reverse. Certainly fluctuations do occur, but scant evidence exists that the "world system" was tightly integrated prior to the first millennium BC. The Hittites have also been credited with developing the use of iron, however nebulous and unproven this notion may yet be (Muhly et al. 1985; see also a summary of Anatolian iron in Yalçın 1999).

Middle Bronze Age texts from eighteenth-century BC Kanesh reveal that iron was valued as power embedded in social, religious, economic, and political contexts. Providing intriguing insights into early iron use, the texts mention two traded commodities, *Amatu* and *Asiu*, tentatively translated as iron (Maxwell-Hyslop 1972). Iron is not only protected by the Anatolian kingdom of Kanesh, but its trade is forbidden. In fact, one such merchant, Pusu-Ken, gets put into "jail" for having smuggled iron (Larsen 1976). Clearly, as Helms (1993) has written, trade is initiated by and for political elites whose goal is not only the accumulation of materials, but also the accumulation of specific kinds of power, in this case through the control of iron. This relationship between iron and power is illustrated by textual references to an iron throne given to King Anitta of Kanesh, of exceptional size in spite of the fact that iron was worth eight times as much as silver (Košak 1982; 1985). Iron was also found (Table 12)[1] at the trading colony Kültepe Ia, and fragments of high iron-copper[2] were found together with a hoard of copper bun ingots in the Sarikaya and Hatipler palaces at another important colony, Acemhöyük. These data suggest that the Middle Bronze Age palace economies may have played an important role in the early control and exchange of iron.

---

[1] Analyses by Professor Hadi Özbal; samples courtesy of Professors Kutlu Emre, Nimet Özgüç and Aliye Özten.
[2] Analyses by Professor Hadi Özbal: 70.4% iron, 2% copper; sample no. Ac-93, V/33.

Table 12. Kültepe Ia Iron Samples

Au	Ag	Sn	Pb	As	Sb	Ni	Zn	Co	Fe	Cu
11	0.05	0	0.03	0.02	0.03	0.03	0.04	0.01	42.3	1.04
7.5	0.03	0	0.02	0.04	0	0.04	0.03	0.01	29.1	2.36

Note: All measurements are in percents, except for gold, which is in parts per million.

Decades of analysis of copper artifacts from Anatolian sites, particularly at Ikiztepe in the Black Sea area, have prompted new insights into technological change over time (Özbal et al. 2002). This accumulated evidence (see also Yener 2000 and references) suggests that the third millennium BC was typified by the exploitation of local ores—each with differing compositions—and the use of localized alloying components. Thus, this technology reflects long-held production traditions situated within a politically Balkanized matrix of semi-independent Early Bronze Age Anatolian state polities. Local production parameters are especially evident, as contemporary and stylistically similar artifacts from different sites reveal markedly heterogeneous compositions. This tradition changes, according to Özbal et al. (2002), in the second millennium BC, when copper began to be distributed over long distances as evidenced by standardized bun and ox-hide ingots reflecting more or less homogeneous compositions (Pulak 2000). This suggests that a more standardized, industrial mode of metal production appears within the context of the sociopolitically and economically integrating empire of the Hittites. Thus, this period sees a diminishing role of "ma and pa" mining and household production systems, as the local extraction of ores and more centralized distributive systems of ingots takes their place. Analysis of the metal artifacts from these empire-mediated exchange nodes should reflect this homogeneity, although a comprehensive analytical program of this sort has not yet been undertaken for Late Bronze Age Anatolia.

Bringing new insight into the process of societal change and its role in the coming of iron, Adams raises important interpretive possibilities about intense transformative impulses, or relatively rapid innovations resulting in the change from a bronze- to an iron-based technology. Adams calls attention to a period of "change-inducing stress" and accelerating technological change at the end of the Late Bronze Age social landscape in the Near East.

A brief summary of the history of the Amuq area in southern Turkey indicates that the rise of large territorial states in the Late Bronze Age (1600–1200 BC Amuq Phase M) marks an important transformation in the Near East.

Here the main players are Anatolia, Syro-Mesopotamia, and Egypt, all of which are engaged in a global political struggle. The Hittites (see Bryce 1998) exemplify a quintessential expansionist state in Anatolia which arose, competed with, and coexisted with its expansionist counterparts. The majority of the historical data for the Late Bronze Age comes from the archives found at the site of Tell Atchana, ancient Alalakh. Alalakh was the capital of a small regional state, the sub-kingdom of Mukish, situated in the Amuq Valley, inconveniently in the path of expansionist superneighbors to the north and south. Indeed, archival sources suggest that Alalakh Level VII was destroyed by one of the earliest Hittite kings, Hattusili I, during his second Syrian campaign (Gates 1981; Klengel 1992). In subsequent centuries, the city eventually emerged as part of the Hittite Empire, with the burning of Level IV attributed to the Hittite Great King Suppiluliuma I. Egypt, the other superpower in the Near East, also had a long, abiding interest in this area, as witnessed by the events surrounding the Kadesh war and its aftermath (Klengel 1992). The cities in the Amuq Valley and their vassal villages shifted allegiances according to immediate political expediency, and in some periods became independent.

Tell Atchana, ancient Alalakh, is a 9-meter-high, 23-hectare mound located on the levee of the Orontes River (Figure 98) and was initially surveyed by Robert Braidwood and his colleagues as part of the University of Chicago, Oriental Institute Syro-Hittite project (site no. AS [Amuq Survey] 136; Braidwood 1937). The survey mapped 178 sites, and of these, Chatal Höyük and Tells Judaidah, Ta'yinat, and Kurdu were extensively excavated by

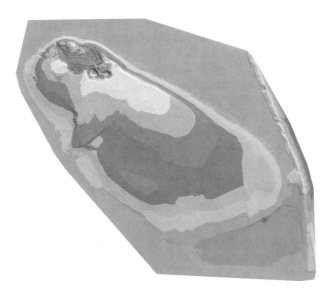

Figure 98. Tell Atchana (ancient Alalakh). Topographic map by S. Batiuk.

the Oriental Institute to complete a sequence dating from about 6000 BC to AD 600 (Braidwood and Braidwood 1960; Haines 1971; Swift 1958). Tell Atchana was subsequently excavated in 1936–1939 and 1946–1949, under the direction of Sir Leonard Woolley (Woolley 1948; 1953; 1955a). Archives and multiple temples, palaces, private houses, and city gates were uncovered in seventeen levels roughly dating between the late third millennium and 1200 BC. After a long pause of sixty years, the Oriental Institute began a new era of investigations in the Amuq Valley in 1995 (Yener et al. 1996; 2000; Amuq Valley Regional Projects, hereafter AVRP).[3] Coincident with the hope to contextualize the significance of these sites—and especially the capital Alalakh—within the broader Amuq Valley and eastern Mediterranean, during the first few years the project focused on the regional scale with a series of geoarchaeological and archaeological surveys. These have supplemented the regional database, which now includes information on 346 sites (Wilkinson et al. 2001; Yener 2005).

Although Alalakh was the capital city of the kingdom of Mukish, it was also a vassal of the powerful kingdom of Yamhad (Aleppo) during the eighteenth/seventeenth century BC. Yamhad was ruled by King Abban I, who gave Alalakh and its various affiliated villages in the Amuq to his brother Yarim-Lim (Astour 1992; Kuhrt 1995; for other interregional relations, see Magness-Gardiner 1994). In Level VII, a new temple, a monumental palace, and a city gate were constructed by Yarim-Lim. Exotic items such as ivory, metal, precious stones, and ceramics were found in these major public buildings and testify to a particularly lively interregional trade. Prestige items from Egypt, as well as Aegean-styled ceramics and wall paintings, perhaps represent the distribution of imported commodities and the maintenance of new value systems through elite households.

Aside from the storage of imported goods, however, there is considerable evidence that there were workshops within the palace (Woolley 1955a), where localized metal production took place (Klengel 1979: 439). Figure 99a is a distribution map of metal finds from Level VII contexts, which reveals a surprising amount of metallurgical residues such as lumps of copper, slag, and crucible fragments (after Müller-Karpe 1994: 94–95; Woolley 1955a: 272–387), as well as artifacts of gold, silver, lead, and copper within and in the vicinity of the palace. The main conclusion to be drawn from this sub-

[3] This research has had consistent, generous, and greatly appreciated funding from countless private individuals, the Oriental Institute members, the Institute of Aegean Prehistory, and the National Geographic Society. I would like to especially thank the efforts of the Turkish American Amuq Valley Archaeological Projects committee for their untiring support.

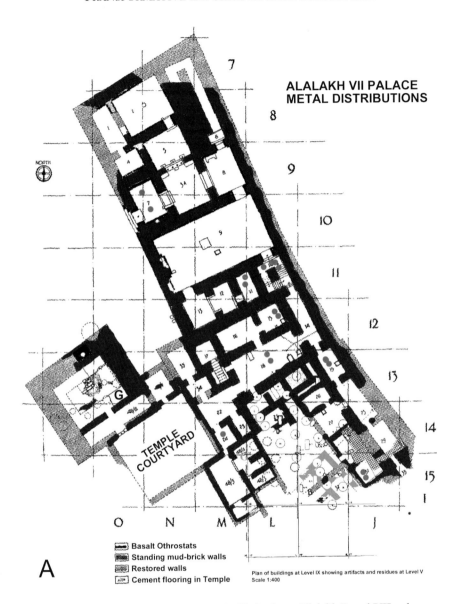

Figure 99 (*CONTINUED ON NEXT PAGE*). (A) Atchana/Alalakh Level VII palace showing locations of metallurgical artifacts and residues (after Müller-Karpe 1994, with additions).

stantial evidence of craft production is that it was clearly associated with the domain and geography of the palace and the so-called private houses nearby.

The production of metal within palace workshops continues in the subsequent Late Bronze Age Palace Level IV (Figure 99b). In the mid-fifteenth century, Alalakh, with Idrimi at the helm, was a vassal of Barrattarna, king of the

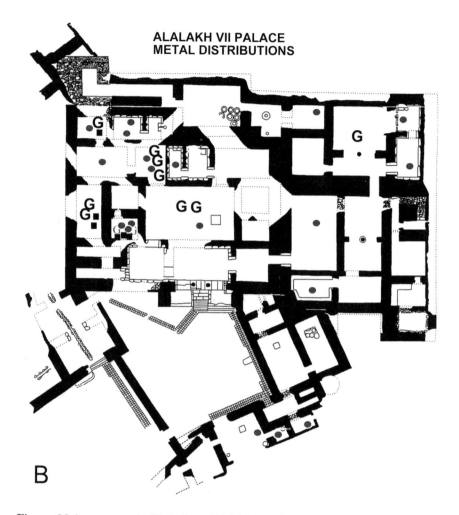

Figure 99 (*CONTINUED*). (B) Atchana/Alalakh Level IV palace showing locations of metallurgical artifacts and residues (after Müller-Karpe 1994, with additions). Legend: Circles showing locations of copper based, lead, silver, and iron metal and slag residues. G = Gold.

Hurrians and Mitanni. With new assessments amending Woolley's attribution (Gates 1981; 1987; Heinz 1992), Idrimi is now seen as the architect of the southeastern wing (C1-9) of the palace and the triple gate, both assigned to Level VB. His son, Niqmepa, a vassal of Saustatar of Mitanni, may have built the Level IV palace, which was destroyed during the reign of his son, Ilim-ilimma (according to various authors, with dates ranging from late fifteenth to late fourteenth century).[4]

The palace and temple of Level IV yielded a whole constellation of cop-per-based artifacts, as well as molds, and fragments of iron, lead, and silver. A distribution map of metal and metal residues from Level IV contexts (Figure 99a, after Müller-Karpe 1994: 94–95; Woolley 1953: 1955a) reveals considerable evidence for metal-working within the palace walls. The appearance of copper-tin-bronze and other valuables suggests the existence of a developing or thriving production system for exchange in the eastern Mediterranean. Maritime commerce between various coastal regions—perhaps including Alalakh—is indicated by the Cape Gelidonya/Uluburun-Kaş shipwrecks, particularly their cargo of stylistically comparable ivory toiletries, jewelry, and metals (see Bass et al. 1989). Furthermore, the AVRP survey in 2001 rediscovered finds stored in Woolley's on-site dig house depot, which yielded—among numerous bags of sherds—multifaceted molds (Figure 100) and copper and lead artifacts (Figures 101, and 102).

Further linkages between the metal-working finds from Alalakh and a globalized trade network[5] are three copper ingots (Woolley 1955a: 120, which describes a "copper ingot (?)" AT/37/208 Level IV), one of which is disk-shaped[6] (Figure 103), the second bun-shaped, and a third, crescentic (Figure 104). Radiocarbon dates of 1530–1490 cal BC[7] obtained from charcoal embedded in one of the copper bun ingots place that example within the range of Level V/IV.

But the extent to which the palace-mediated flow of metal is embedded in social relations can be extrapolated from the Atchana cuneiform tablets. Wiseman (1953: 14) observed that silver and gold are mentioned more often in the seventeenth/sixteenth-century texts, and less often in the fifteenth century. However, a close examination of the fifteenth-century texts reveals astounding quantities of metal exchanged both externally as well as within the kingdom. Alalakh Text 395 has a seal impression of Idrimi (Wiseman

---

[4] Here I follow the conventional middle chronologies. The dates for the palace and temple associated with Level IV are highly problematic, and the problems are outlined in recent chronological discussions (Gasche et al. 1998; McClellan 1989; Wiener and Allan 1998). Some of these hinge on reconstructions of the local genealogy, synchronisms with external king lists, as well as ceramic and glyptic parallels. For a clear discussion, see D. Stein (1997) and Gates (2000). For a recent reassessment of dendrochronological dates and a point made for middle chronologies, see Manning et al. 2001.

[5] For a fragment of a copper ox-hide ingot found in Boğazköy (the Hittite capital, Hattusa), see Bachmann 1984.

[6] The shape of the copper is reflected in Wiseman 1953: Text 397, where it is actually "disk shaped"; CAD vol. K. "talent". I thank Martha Roth for clarifying this reference. XRF spectrographic analyses on all three ingots yielded quite high iron levels (8.73–20.40%) and copper (94–52.55%) with trace levels of other elements (see Kaptan 2005).

[7] Beta Analytic no. 159017, 1 sigma calibrated dates.

Figure 100. Multifaceted stone mold for axes and blades from Tell Atchana, not marked but possibly AT/39/118 from House 39/B, Level V (Woolley 1955: 403); from Woolley Dighouse depot.

Figure 101. Various copper-based pins and implements (Woolley 1955: 284); from Woolley Dighouse depot.

Figure 102. Lead strip; from Woolley Dighouse depot.

Figure 103. Bun-shaped copper ingot; AT38/173 from Level IV weighs 5.5 kilograms; from Woolley Dighouse depot. Radiocarbon dated 1530–1490 cal BC.

Figure 104. Crescent-shaped copper ingot; from Woolley Dighouse depot.

1953: 104) and contains an inventory of 670 talents[8] from the land of Zalhe, 648 from the land of Zalae, and 776 from the land of Mukiš, totaling 52,352 kilograms of silver which came from both within the kingdom and neighboring areas. Alalakh Text 397–ATT/8/187 states that "7 talents of copper was [sic] given for the smiths to make 2000 copper baskets[9] for the town of Nihi."

Such enormously large-scale metal exchange and ultimately conspicuous display of finely made gold and silver prestige artifacts are not surprising, given the textual evidence from Early Bronze Age antecedents in Ebla and Mari. The Ebla texts list gold jars weighing 335.48 and 386.34 kilograms, respectively, as well as similar examples in silver (Archi 1999: 154). The relevant questions, then, are how society structures the making of things, and how this production technology is embedded within the society of Alalakh. An examination of the distribution maps of excavated metals and metal residues from the Level VII and IV palaces indicates that, in addition to the production of smaller-scale jewelry and decorative gold artifacts, the workshops[10] were also casting larger utilitarian copper-based artifacts such as axes, chisels, and the like. Slag, crucibles, and multifaceted molds found in palace and temple contexts, as well as in the nearby "private houses" which may be craftsmen's quarters or household production locations, demonstrate that some metalworkers were manufacturing prestige objects in bronze, gold, and silver, as well as utilitarian products within the public sector. Clumps of iron ore (Figure 105) and simple iron artifacts make their appearance within the palace sector from Levels IV–I as well,[11] although clearly bronze was the metal of choice for both prestige and utilitarian artifacts (Woolley 1955a: 120, 282, 279; but also see iron misread in Alalakh texts, caution by Brinkman 1987: 34).

Both the archaeological evidence for metalworking and the exchange and storage of wealth reflected in the texts suggest that the rulers of Alalakh asserted control over the skilled—perhaps secret—production methods of fine artifacts as elites elsewhere are known to do (G. Stein 1996). Consumption of wealth and its exchange are part of "high culture" as argued by Baines and Yoffee (1998). The high-prestige artifacts and evidence of metallurgical residues suggest that attached specialists, or craftspersons, were producing goods for restricted distribution within the palace, although the absence of

---

[8] I have taken a talent of 26.031 kilograms based on a shekel of approximately 8.667 grams. I thank Ted Castle for this reference.

[9] "container"; CAD vol. P, s.v. pisannu. The total in kilograms is 175 kilograms. I thank Martha Roth for clarifying this reference.

[10] Wiseman 1953: Text AT348 mentions Abban the goldsmith.

[11] An iron ring found in the gate of Palace VII is being analyzed for eventual publication.

Figure 105. Clump of iron ore (Woolley 1955: 120); from Woolley Dighouse depot.

texts concerning self-employed artisans does not prove that they were nonexistent. Tell Atchana (Alalakh) is an ideal example of a large settlement underwritten, at least in part, by wealth generated by prestige metal production, trade, and perhaps tribute. The amount of metal involved gave Alalakh a large, Fort Knox–like, treasury containing a movable, transferable resource that could serve as a hedge against crop failure or external threat. Perhaps reflective of the transferability of metal resources is Text AT366 from Level VII, which records that 5.5 kilograms of silver from the treasury were melted down from the statue of a god to make new silver artifacts, some of which were for tribute (Na'aman 1981).

The final and uppermost Atchana Levels III–I are representative of Alalakh as a part of the Hittite Empire and are characterized by continued production of metals within the public sphere, and perhaps in the private quarters as well. Remarking on a different aspect of Late Bronze Age society, Schloen (2001) has suggested that extended family units and patrimonial kinships defined the system, which also allowed for individual enterprise. The increasing levels of socioeconomic and political prosperity came to an end with a crisis around 1200 BC, which resulted in the general collapse of the palace economies of the Late Bronze Age. By the end of the thirteenth–early twelfth centuries, Level I in Alalakh is marked by a destruction which thrust the Amuq Valley and its centralized administration into a period of disintegration. Basing his interpretations on the original Braidwood survey data in the Amuq, T. Harrison (2001) determined that only 17 of the 30 Late Bronze Age (Phase M) sites make it to the next period, the Early Iron Age (Amuq N). Thirty of the 47 known Amuq N sites were new or re-settlements, and most of these had been occupied earlier, such as the case of occupation at Tell Ta'yinat during the

Early Bronze Age. The large territorial states of the Hittite Empire in the Amuq and southeastern Turkey, as well as in northern Syria, were ultimately replaced with new regional configurations—the Iron Age city-states—variously called the Neo-Hittite or Syro-Hittite kingdoms (Hawkins 1995).

Returning to the question of a shift to iron metallurgy and the social factors behind accelerated technological change, Adams (2001) noted the organizational breakdown of society and opportunities presented for innovations attendant on the socioeconomic disintegration at the end of the Late Bronze Age, at around 1200 BC. Adams based his insights of technological transformation on Liverani's (1987: 71–72) view of the crisis which suggests that metal production, largely a monopoly of state-organized palace workshops, broke down and was replaced by local, independent iron workers tapping into more accessible iron sources (see also Zaccagnini 1990). Adams agrees that this change came about when autocratic control was weakened, allowing greater access to goods produced by craftsmen. Carrying the argument further, Adams sees this institutional change as a catalyst in a chain reaction, in which expanded popular consumption fueled demand as falling costs accelerated new improvements. In this relatively rapid transformative impulse, metallurgical innovations in iron were then in part created by the favorable context of non-royal, non-autocratic localized production systems. Perhaps the seeds of individual enterprise grew in the fertile social disarticulation at the end of the thirteenth century BC. Glimpses can be caught of this transformation from a new analytical program of metals at the Oriental Institute.

Strongly reflective of the innovative tendencies attendant on the collapse of palace economies and the relocation of workshops to less centrally controlled areas is the recently analyzed and exquisitely crafted Early Iron Age bronze blade from the site of Chatal Höyük, one of the satellites of the new capital in the Amuq Valley, Tell Ta'yinat. The technical bravado represented by this tin bronze blade is manifested in the astonishing 49 laminated folds of metal, each containing different bronze alloys, some using tin and some tin-arsenic, worked in a technique that resembles the fabrication of a Samurai sword (for contemporary examples of lamination, but in iron, see Maddin, Muhly, and Waldbaum 1983). The curved blade is attributed to Phase N in Amuq stratigraphy, dated between 1200 and 1000 BC (Haines 1971), during which an accelerated technical change is postulated from bronze to iron, although as is evident, bronzes requiring special skills continue to be made. In the discussion of her analysis of this blade, Stewart notes that "bronze metallurgy in the early Iron Age may have broken out of the politically imposed paths of palace-controlled Bronze Age metallurgy in the same way that iron metallurgy did, allowing for the development of new technological paths" (Stewart 2002).

If the socio-technical logic of Özbal and his co-workers can be coupled with the sociopolitical insights of Adams to develop a predictive model, then we should expect to find evidence of an increase of heterogeneous copper metallurgy in the Early Iron Age. The artifacts should again, in a cyclical turnabout, reflect exploitation of localized copper and less than ideal low-grade local tin sources, last seen in the Early Bronze Age. Formerly dormant local mines should have again come into operation, and metallurgical experimentation with diverse ores, in particular iron, should augment innovative tendencies.

FUTURE DIRECTIONS

A new program of excavations in the Amuq, coupled with instrumental analysis of metal tools, prestige items, and weapons from the Late Bronze Age capital, Alalakh, the Iron Age capital, Tell Ta'yinat, and their related vassal sites is in progress. Methodologically, the technical reconstruction of metallurgical production should provide insight into complex cultural processes and change on a societal level. Furthermore, inherent in this approach is also its corollary, an examination of how the organization and selection of technologies could destabilize environment.

It is important to reiterate Adams's point that the accompanying loosening of political control over metallurgical production allowed craftsmen access to new materials such as iron, increasing the production of utilitarian tools and weapons in this material. Accordingly, the implementation of this research design will allow technology to take its place as a benchmark in determining the changing landscape of states and their institutions. Some of these issues have compelling implications for other regions, including the extent to which political entities—and diverse groupings such as the Hittites were a destabilizing factor and in what ways, if any, the analysis of changes in technology can aid in our understanding of the coming of iron.

BIBLIOGRAPHY

Abbott, Nabia
1968   Jundi Shapur: A Preliminary Historical Sketch. *Ars Orientalis* 7: 71–73.
Aboud, Sabah
1984   Tell Abada Excavations Initial Report. *Sumer* 40: 44–46.
Abusch, Tzvi
1995   Ishtar. In *Dictionary of Deities and Demons in the Bible*, edited by Karel van der Toorn, Bob Becking, and Pieter W. van der Horst, pp. 848–856. E. J. Brill, Leiden.
Adams, Robert McC.
1960   The Origin of Cities. *Scientific American* 606: 3–10.
1962   Agriculture and Urban Life in Early Southwestern Iran. *Science* 136: 109–122.
1965   *Land behind Baghdad*. University of Chicago.
1966   *The Evolution of Urban Society*. Aldine, Chicago.
1970   Tell Abu Sarifa: A Sasanian-Islamic Sequence from South Central Iraq. *Ars Orientalis* 8: 87–119.
1972a   Settlement and Irrigation Patterns in Ancient Akkad. In *The City and Area of Kish*, edited by McGuire Gibson, pp. 182–208. Field Research Projects, Miami, Florida.
1972b   Patterns of Urbanization in Early Southern Mesopotamia. In *Man, Settlement, and Urbanism*, edited by Peter J. Ucko, Ruth Tringham, and Geoffrey W. Dimbleby, pp. 735–749. Duckworth, London.
1974a   Anthropological Perspectives on Ancient Trade. *Current Anthropology* 15: 239–258.
1974b   The Mesopotamian Social Landscape: A View from the Frontier. In *Reconstructing Complex Societies*, edited by C. Moore, pp. 1–20. American Schools of Oriental Research, Boston.
1978   Strategies of Maximization, Stability, and Resilience in Mesopotamian Society, Settlement, and Agriculture. *Proceedings of the American Philosophical Society* 122: 329–335.
1981   *Heartland of Cities: Surveys of Ancient Settlement and Land Use on the Central Floodplain of the Euphrates*. University of Chicago, Chicago and London.

1988   Contexts of Civilization's Collapse: A Mesopotamian View. In *Collapse of Ancient States and Civilizations*, edited by Norman Yoffee and George L. Cowgill, pp. 20–43. University of Arizona, Tucson.
1989   Concluding Remarks. In *Upon This Foundation—The 'Ubaid Reconsidered. Proceedings of the 'Ubaid Symposium, Elsinore 1988*, edited by Elizabeth F. Henrickson and Ingolf Thuesen, pp. 441–456. Museum Tusculanum, Copenhagen.
1996   *Paths of Fire: An Anthropologist's Inquiry into Western Technology.* Princeton University, Princeton, New Jersey.
2000   Accelerated Technological Change in Archaeology and Ancient History. In *Cultural Evolution: Contemporary Viewpoints*, edited by Gary M. Feinman and Linda Manzanilla, pp. 95–119. Plenum, New York.
2001   Complexity in Archaic States. *Journal of Anthropological Archaeology* 20: 345–360.
2002   The Economies of Ancient Chiefdoms and States. Paper presented at the Snowbird Conference, University of Utah, Salt Lake City.
2004   Reflections on the Early South Mesopotamian Economy. In *Archaeological Perspectives on Political Economies*, edited by Gary M. Feinman and Linda M. Nicholas, pp. 41–59. University of Utah, Salt Lake City.
2005   From Documents to Individuals: Identifying Ancient Classes or Patterns of Individual Belief, Association, and Behavior. Paper presented at the Institute for Quantitative Social Science, University of California, Irvine.

Adams, Robert McC., and Donald P. Hansen
1968   Archaeological Reconnaissance and Soundings in Jundi Shahpur. *Ars Orientalis* 7: 53–73.

Adams, Robert McC., and Hans J. Nissen
1972   *The Uruk Countryside.* University of Chicago.

Agcabay, Meltem, Katy Killackey, Aylan Erkal, and Christine Hastorf
2001   Çatalhöyük 2001 Archive Report: Macrobotanical Remains. Electronic document, *http: //catal.arch.cam.ac.uk/catal/archive_rep01/content01.html*, accessed October 14, 2002.

Agrawal, D. P.
1992   *Man and Environment in India through Ages.* Books & Books, Delhi.

Aitken, Edward H.
1907   *Gazetteer of the Province of Sind.* "Mercantile" Steam Press, Karachi.

Ajithprasad, P., and V. H. Sonawane
n.d.   The Harappa Culture in North Gujarat: A Regional Perspective. In *Harappans and Others in Gujarat*, edited by Gregory L. Possehl and V. Shinde Vasant. Oxford and IBH, Delhi, in press.

Akkermans, Peter M. M. G.
1989   Tradition and Social Change in Northern Mesopotamia during the Later Fifth and Fourth Millennium B.C. In *Upon this Foundation—The 'Ubaid Reconsidered. Proceedings of the 'Ubaid Symposium, Elsinore 1988*, edited by Elizabeth F. Henrickson and Ingolf Thuesen, pp. 339–367. Museum Tusculanum, Copenhagen.

1993   *Villages in the Steppe: Late Neolithic Settlement and Subsistence in the Balikh Valley, Northern Syria.* Archaeological Series 5. International Monographs in Prehistory, Ann Arbor.

Akkermans, Peter M. M. G., and Kim Duistermaat
    1997   Of Storage and Nomads, The Sealings from the Late Neolithic Sabi Abyad, Syria. *Paléorient* 22 (2): 17–44.

Algaze, Guillermo
    1993a   *The Uruk World System: The Dynamics of Expansion of Early Mesopotamian Civilization.* University of Chicago.
    1993b   Expansionary Dynamics of Some Early Pristine States. *American Anthropologist* 95 (2): 304–333.
    1999   Trends in the Archaeological Development of the Upper Euphrates Basin of Southeastern Anatolia during the Late Chalcolithic and Early Bronze Ages. In *Archaeology of the Upper Syrian Euphrates: The Tishrin Dam Area,* edited by Gregorio del Olmo Lete and Juan Luis Montero Fenollós, pp. 535–572. Editorial Ausa, Barcelona.
    2001a   Initial Social Complexity in Southwestern Asia: The Mesopotamian Advantage. *Current Anthropology* 43: 199–233.
    2001b   The Prehistory of Imperialism: The Case of Uruk Period Mesopotamia. In *Uruk Mesopotamia and Its Neighbors,* edited by Mitchell S. Rothman, pp. 27–83. School of American Research, Santa Fe, New Mexico.
    2004   Trade and the Origins of Mesopotamian Civilization. *Biblioteca Orientalis* 61: 5–20.

Al-Jadir, Walid, and Zahir R. Abdulla
    1983   Preliminary Report on the Baghdad University Excavations at Sippar (Abu Habba) (in Arabic). *Sumer* 39: 97–122.

Alizadeh, Abbas
    1985   A Tomb of the Neo-Elamite Period at Arjān, near Behbahan. *Archaeologische Mitteilungen aus Iran* 18: 49–73.
    1992   *Prehistoric Settlement Patterns and Cultures in Susiana, Southwestern Iran.* Museum of Anthropology Technical Report 24. University of Michigan, Ann Arbor, Michigan.
    n.d.   *The Origins of State Organizations in Prehistoric Fars, Southern Iran.* Oriental Institute Publications, in press.

Alkım, U. Bahadir
    1979   Recent Archaeological Research in Turkey: Ikiztepe, Fifth Season. *Anatolian Studies* 29: 200–202.

Allchin, Bridget
    1972   Hunters or Pastoral Nomads? Late Stone Age Settlements in Western and Central India. In *Man, Settlement and Urbanism,* edited by Peter J. Ucko, Ruth Tringham, and Geoffrey W. Dimbleby, pp. 115–119. Gerald Duckworth & Co., London.

Allchin, Bridget, and Raymond Allchin
    1982   *The Rise of Civilization in India and Pakistan.* Cambridge University, Cambridge.

Alp, Sedat
   1991   *Hethitische Briefe aus Maşat-Höyük*. Türk Tarih Kurumu Yayınları No.
          VI. Dizi - Sa. 35. Türk Tarih Kurumu, Ankara.
Amiet, Pierre
   1961   *La glyptique mésopotamienne archaïque*. Editions du CNRS, Paris.
   1966   *Elam*. Archée Editeur, Auvers sur Oise.
   1972   *Glyptique susienne*. Mémoires de la Délégation Archéologique
          Française en Iran 43. Geuthner, Paris.
   1980   *La glyptique mésopotamienne archaïque*. Centre National de la Recher-
          che Scientifique, Paris.
   1988   *Suse, 6000 ans d'histoire*. Editions de la Réunion des musées nation-
          aux. Ministère de la Culture et de la Communication, Paris.
Amiet, Pierre, and Maurice Lambert
   1967   Éléments émaillés du décor architectural Néo-Élamite. *Syria* 44: 27–51.
Amundson, Ronald, and Elise Pendall
   1991   Pedology and Late Quaternary Environments Surrounding Harappa:
          A Review and Synthesis. In *Harappa Excavations 1986–1990*, edited
          by Richard H. Meadow, pp. 13–27. Prehistory, Madison, Wisconsin.
Anderson-Gerfaud, Patricia
   1983   L'utilisation de certains objets en ceramique de Tell el'Oueili (Obeid
          4): Rapport preliminaire sur les microtrances. In *Larsa et Oueili,
          Travaux de 1978–1981*, edited by Jean-Louis Huot, pp. 177–191. Edi-
          tions Recherche sur les Civilisations, Paris.
Andrén, Anders
   1998   *Between Artifacts and Texts: Historical Archaeology in Global Perspective*.
          Plenum, New York.
Angulo, Jorge
   1987   Nuevas consideraciones sobre los llamados conjuntos departamen-
          tales, especialmente Tetitla. In *Teotihuacan: Nuevos Datos, Nuevas
          Síntesis, Nuevos Problemas*, edited by Emily McClung de Tapia and
          Evelyn C. Rattray, pp. 275–315. Instituto de Investigaciones
          Antropológicas, Universidad Nacional Autónoma de México, Mexico
          City.
Appadurai, Arjun (editor)
   1986   *The Social Life of Things: Commodities in Cultural Perspective*. Cam-
          bridge University, Cambridge.
Aqrawi, A. A. M.
   1997   The Nature and Preservation of Organic Matter in Holocene Lacus-
          trine/Deltaic Sediments of Lower Mesopotamia, SE Iraq. *Journal of
          Petroleum Geology* 20 (1): 69–90.
   2001   Stratigraphic Signatures of Climatic Change during the Holocene
          Evolution of the Tigris-Euphrates Delta, Lower Mesopotamia. *Glo-
          bal and Planetary Change* 28 (1–4): 267–283.
Archi, Alfonso
   1999   The Steward and His Jar. *Iraq* 61: 147–158.

Armillas, Pedro
  1964   Northern Mesoamerica. In *Prehistoric Man in the New World*, edited
          by J. D. Jennings and E. Norbeck, pp. 291–321. University of Chi-
          cago Press, Chicago.
Ashmore, Wendy
  1991   Site-Planning Principles and Concepts of Directionality among the
          Ancient Maya. *Latin American Antiquity* 2: 199–226.
Ashmore, Wendy, and A. Bernard Knapp (editors)
  1999   *Archaeologies of Landscape: Contemporary Perspectives.* Blackwell, Oxford.
Astour, Michael C.
  1992   Alalakh. In *Anchor Bible Dictionary*, edited by I. David Noel Freed-
          man, pp. 142–145. Doubleday, New York.
Aurenche, Olivier
  1981   *La maison orientale: L'architecture du Proche-Orient ancien des origines au
          milieu du 4e millénaire.* Institut français d'archéologiques du Proche-
          Orient, Paris.
Aveni, Anthony F.
  2000   Out of Teotihuacan: Origins of the Celestial Canon in Mesoamerica.
          In *Mesoamerica's Classic Heritage: From Teotihuacan to the Aztecs*, edited
          by Davíd Carrasco, Lindsay Jones, and Scott Sessions, pp. 253–268.
          University Press of Colorado, Boulder.
Aveni, Anthony F., Horst Hartung, and J. Charles Kelley
  1982   Alta Vista (Chalchihuites): Astronomical Implications of a
          Mesoamerican Ceremonial Outpost at the Tropic of Cancer. *Ameri-
          can Antiquity* 47: 326–335.
Bachmann, Hermann G.
  1984   Düsenrohre und Gebläsetöpfe: Keramikfunde aus Metallverarbei-
          tungs-Werkstätten. In *Bogazköy VI. Funde aus den Grabungen bis
          1979*, edited by Kurt Bittel et al. Ausgrabungen des Deutschen
          Archäologischen Institute, Gebr. Mann Verlag, Berlin.
Bahrani, Zainab
  2002   Performativity and the Image: Narrative, Representation, and the
          Uruk Vase. In *Leaving No Stones Unturned: Essays on the Ancient Near
          East and Egypt in Honor of Donald P. Hansen*, edited by Erica Ehren-
          berg, pp. 15–22. Eisenbrauns, Winona Lake, Indiana.
Baines, John, and Norman Yoffee
  1998   Order, Legitimacy, and Wealth in Ancient Egypt and Mesopotamia.
          In *Archaic States*, edited by Joyce Marcus and Gary M. Feinman, pp.
          199–260. School of American Research, Santa Fe, New Mexico.
Bairoch, Paul
  1988   *Cities and Economic Development.* University of Chicago.
Baker, Victor R.
  1986   Fluvial Landforms. In *Geomorphology from Space*, edited by Nicholas
          M. Short and Robert W. Blair, pp. 225–315. National Aeronautics
          and Space Administration Scientific and Technical Branch. Elec-
          tronic document, *http: //daac.gdfc.nasa.gov/DAAC_DOCS/
          geomorphology/GEO_5/GEO_Chapter4.shtml*, accessed April 1, 2006.

Balista, C.
1988   Evaluation of Alluvial and Architectural Sequences at Moenjodaro through Core-Drilling. In *Interim Reports*, Vol. 3: *Reports on Field Work Carried out at Mohenjo Daro*, edited by Michael R. Jansen and Maurizio Tosi, pp. 109–138. IsMEO/RWTH, Aachen.

Baqir, Taha
1946   Excavations at Tell Harmal. *Sumer* 22: 2–30.
1959   *Tell Harmal*. Baghdad, Matba'at al-Rābitah.

Barbour, Warren D.
1975   The Figurines and Figurine Chronology of Ancient Teotihuacan, Mexico. Unpublished Ph.D. dissertation, Department of Anthropology, University of Rochester, Rochester, New York.

Barker, Alex W., and Timothy R. Pauketat
1992   *Lords of the Southeast: Social Inequality and Native Elites in Southeastern North America*. American Anthropological Association, Washington.

Bar-Matthews, Miryam, Avner Ayalon, and Aaron Kaufman
1997   Late Quaternary Paleoclimate in the Eastern Mediterranean Region from Stable Isotope Analysis of Spelothems at Soreq Cave, Israel. *Quaternary Research* 47: 155–168.

Barnett, Richard D.
1976   *Sculptures from the North Palace of Ashurbanipal at Nineveh (668–627 B.C.)*. British Museum Publications for the Trustees of the British Museum, London.

Bar-Yosef, Ofer
1986   The Walls of Jericho, An Alternative Interpretation. *Current Anthropology* 27 (2): 157–162.

Barth, Fredrik
1961   *Nomads of South Persia*. Oslo University, Oslo.

Bass, George F., Cemal Pulak, Dominique Collon, and James Weinstein
1989   The Bronze Age Shipwreck at Ulu Burun: 1986 Campaign. *American Journal of Archaeology* 93: 1–29.

Beal, Richard H.
1992   *The Organisation of the Hittite Military*. Texte der Hethiter No. 20, edited by Annelies Kammenhuber. Carl Winter Universitätsverlag, Heidelberg.

Becker, Andrea
1993   *Uruk: Kleinfunde I – Stein*. Ausgrabungen Uruk-Warka 6. Von Zabern, Mainz am Rhein.

Becker, Helmut, and Jörg Fassbinder
2001   Uruk—The City of Gilgamesch (Iraq). First Tests in 2001 for Magnetic Prospecting. In *Magnetic Prospecting in Archaeological Sites*, edited by Helmut Becker and Jörg Fassbinder, pp. 93–97. Monuments and Sites VI. ICOMOS, Paris.

Beckman, Gary
1999   *Hittite Diplomatic Texts*. Society of Biblical Literature Writings from the Ancient World, Vol. 7, No. 2, edited by Harry A. Hoffner. Scholars, Atlanta.

Beech, Mark, Joseph Elders, and Elizabeth Shepherd
2000   Reconsidering the 'Ubaid of the Southern Gulf: New Results from Excavations on Dalma Island, U.A.E. *Proceedings of the Seminar for Arabian Studies* 30: 41–47.

Beg, M. A. A.
1993   Surface Soils and Indus River Sediments. In *Himalaya to the Sea: Geology, Geomorphology and the Quaternary*, edited by John F. Shroder, pp. 251–264. Routledge, London.

Behm-Blancke, Manfred R.
1981   Hassek Höyük. Vorläufer Bericht über die Ausgrabungen der Jahre 1978–1980. *Istanbuler Mitteilungen* 31: 5–82.
1983   Hassek Höyük. Die Grabungen 1981. *Türk Arkeoloji Dergisi*: 65–78.
1984   Die Ausgrabungen auf dem Hassek Höyük im Jahre 1982. *Kazı Sonuçları Toplantı* 5: 163–168.

Belcher, Wayne R., and William R. Belcher
2000   Geologic Constraints on the Harappan Archaeological Site, Punjab Province, Pakistan. *Geoarchaeology* 15 (7): 579–713.

Belsky, Joy
1999   Survey of Livestock Influences on Stream and Riparian Ecosystems in the Western United States. *Journal of Soil and Water Conservation* 54: 416–531.

Benco, Nancy L.
1992   Manufacture and Use of Clay Sickles from the Uruk Mound, Abu Salabikh, Iraq. *Paléorient* 18: 119–134.

Bentley, G. Carter
1987   Ethnicity and Practice. *Comparative Studies in Society and History* 29: 24–25.

Bernbeck, Reinhart
1995   Lasting Alliances and Emerging Competition: Economic Developments in Early Mesopotamia. *Journal of Anthropological Archaeology* 14 (1): 1–25.

Bernbeck, Reinhart, and Susan Pollock
2002   Reflections on the Historiography of 4th Millennium Mesopotamia. In *Material Culture and Mental Spheres*, edited by Arnulf Hausleiter, Susanne Kerner, and Bernd Müller-Neuhof, pp. 171–204. AOAT 293. Ugarit-Verlag, Münster.

Bernhardsson, Magnus T.
2005   *Reclaiming a Plundered Past: Archaeology and Nation Building in Modern Iraq.* Yale University, New Haven.

Bhaba, Homi K.
1992   The Postcolonial and the Postmodern. In *The Location of Culture*, edited by Homi K. Bhaba, pp. 171–197. Routledge, London.

Bhan, Kuldeep K.
1994   Cultural Development of the Prehistoric Period in North Gujarat with Reference to Western India. *South Asian Studies* 10: 71–90.

Bhan, Suraj
1973   The sequence and spread of prehistoric cultures in the upper Sarasvati Basin. In *Radiocarbon and Indian Archaeology*, edited by D. P.
Agrawal and A. Ghosh, pp. 252–263. Tata Institute of Fundamental
Research, Bombay.

Bisht, R. S.
1989a   A New Model of the Harappan Town Planning as Revealed at
Dholavira in Kutch: A Surface Study of Its Plan and Architecture. In
History and Archaeology: Prof. H. D. Sankalia Felicitation Volume, edited
by Bhaskar Chatterjee, pp. 397–408. Ramanand Vidya Bhawan, Delhi.

1989b   The Harappan Colonization of Kutch: An Ergonomic Study with
Reference to Dholavira and Surkotada. In *History and Art*, edited by
Krishna Deva, Lallanji Gopal, and Shri Bhagwan Singh, pp. 265–72.
Raman and Vidya Bhavan, Delhi.

1991   Dholavira: A New Horizon of the Indus Civilization. *Puratattva* 20:
71–82.

1999   Dholavira and Banawali: Two Different Paradigms of the Harappan
urbis forma. *Puratattva* 29: 14–37.

1994   Secrets of the Water Fort. *Down to Earth* (May): 25–31.

1997   Dholavira Excavations: 1990–94. In *Facets of Indian Civilization—
Recent Perspectives (Essays in Honor of Professor B. B. Lal)*, 2 vols., edited
by Jagat Pati Joshi, pp. 107–120. Aryan Books International, Delhi.

Biswas, Sanjib K.
1987   Regional Tectonic Framework, Structure, and Evolution of the
Western Marginal Basins of India. *Tectonophysics* 135: 307–327.

Black-Michaud, Jacob
1986   *Sheep and Land. The Economics of Power in a Tribal Society.* Cambridge
University, Cambridge.

Blanton, Richard E., Gary M. Feinman, Stephen A. Kowalewski, and Peter N.
Peregrine
1996   A Dual-Processual Theory for the Evolution of Mesoamerican Civilization. *Current Anthropology* 37: 1–14.

Boehmer, Rainer Michael
1965   *Die Entwicklung der Glyptik während der Akkad-Zeit.* De Gruyter, Berlin.

1999   *Uruk: Früheste Siegelabrollungen.* Phillipp von Zabern, Mainz am
Rhein.

Boese, Johannes
1995   *Ausgrabungen in Tell Sheick Hassan I.* Vorläufige Berichte über die
Ausgrabungskampagnen 1984–1990 und 1992–1994. SDV Verlag,
Saarbrücken.

Boessneck, Joachim, Angela von den Driesch, and Reinhard Ziegler
1989   Die Tierreste von Maadi und Wadi Digla. In *Maadi III: The Non-
Lithic Small Finds and the Structural Remains of the Predynastic Settlement*, edited by Ibrahim Rizkana and Jürgen Seeher. Verlag Philipp
von Zabern, Mainz am Rhein.

Braidwood, Robert
  1937   *Mounds in the Plain of Antioch. An Archaeological Survey.* University of
          Chicago.
Braidwood, Robert, and Linda Braidwood
  1960   *Excavations in the Plain of Antioch I: The Earlier Assemblages Phases A–J.*
          University of Chicago.
Braidwood, Robert J., Bruce Howe, and Charles A. Reed
  1961   The Iranian Prehistoric Project. *Science* 133: 2008–2010.
Brandt, Margaret C.
  1990   Nippur: Building an Environmental Model. *Journal of Near Eastern
          Studies* 49 (1): 67–73.
Braswell, Geoffrey E. (editor)
  2003   *The Maya and Teotihuacan: Reinterpreting Early Classic Interaction.* Uni-
          versity of Texas, Austin.
Breasted, James H.
  1924   *Oriental Forerunners of Byzantine Painting.* University of Chicago.
Breckwoldt, Tina
  1995–96 Management of Grain Storage in Old Babylonian Larsa. *Archiv für
          Orientforschung* 42–43: 64–88.
Breniquet, Catherine
  1989   Les origines de la culture d'Obeid en Mesopotamie du Nord. In *Upon
          this Foundation—The 'Ubaid Reconsidered. Proceedings of the 'Ubaid
          Symposium, Elsinore 1988,* edited by Elizabeth F. Henrickson and
          Ingolf Thuesen, pp. 325–338. Museum Tusculanum, Copenhagen.
  1991   Un site halafien en Turquie meridionale: Tell Turlu. Rapport sur la
          campagrne de fouilles de 1962. *Akkadica* 71: 1–35
Brewer, Douglas J.
  1989   *Fishermen, Hunters, and Herders. Zooarchaeology in the Fayum, Egypt (c.
          8200–5000 BP).* BAR 478. British Archaeological Research, Oxford.
Briant, Pierre
  2002   *From Cyrus to Alexander: A History of the Persian Empire.* Eisenbrauns,
          Winona Lake, Indiana.
Brinkman, John A.
  1968   *A Political History of Post-Kassite Babylonia, 1158–722 B.C.* Pontifical
          Biblical Institute, Rome.
  1984a   Settlement Surveys and Documentary Evidence: Regional Variation
          and Secular Trend in Mesopotamian Demography. *Journal of Near
          Eastern Studies* 43: 169–180.
  1984b   *Prelude to Empire: Babylonian Society and Politics, 747–626 B.C.* Occa-
          sional Publications of the Babylonian Fund, Vol. 7. The Babylonian
          Fund University Museum, Philadelphia.
  1986   The Elamite Babylonian Frontier in the Neo Elamite Period, 760–
          625. In *Fragmenta historiae Elamicae: Mélanges offerts à M. J. Steve,*
          edited by Leon de Meyer, Hermann Gasche, and François Vallat, pp.
          199–207. Éditions de Recherche sur les Civilisations, Paris.
  1987   Textual Evidence for Anomalous Quantities of Iron at Alalakh and
          Nuzi in the Middle and Late Bronze Ages. *NABU* 3: 34–35

Brinkman, R., and C. M. Rafiq
  1971   *Landforms and Soil Parent Materials in West Pakistan.* Soil Survey
          Project of Pakistan, Lahore.
British Archaeological Expedition to Kuwait
  2002   The Kuwait-British Archaeological Expedition to As-Sabiyah: Exca-
          vations at H3. Electronic document, *http: //www.ucl.ac.uk/archaeology/
          kuwait/*, accessed December 20, 2002.
Brosius, Maria
  2000   *The Persian Empire from Cyrus II to Artaxerxes I.* London Association of
          Classical Teachers—Original Records: A Series of Translation of Sources
          for Ancient History. London Association of Classical Teachers, Cambridge.
Bryce, Trevor
  1986–87 The Boundaries of Hatti and Hittite Border Policy. *Tel Aviv* 13–14
          (1): 85–102.
  1998   *The Kingdom of the Hittites.* Oxford University, Oxford.
  2002   *Life and Society in the Hittite World.* Oxford University, Oxford.
Bryson, Reid A.
  1996   Proxy Indications of Holocene Winter Rains in Southwest Asia
          Compared with Simulated Rainfall. In *Third Millennium B.C. Climate
          Change and Old World Collapse*, edited by H. Nüzhet Dalfes, George
          Kukla, and Harvey Weiss, pp. 465–473. NATO ASI Series I. Vol. 49.
          Springer Verlag, Berlin.
Bryson, Reid A., and Albert M. Swain
  1981   Holocene Variations of Monsoon Rainfall in Rajasthan. *Quaternary
          Research* 16: 135–145.
Buday, Tibor, and Saad Z. Jassim
  1987   *The Regional Geology of Iraq: Tectonism, Magmatism, and Metamor-
          phism.* Government of Iraq, Geological Survey and Mineral State
          Establishment, Baghdad.
Buikstra, Jane D., T. Douglas Price, James Burton, and Lori E. Wright
  2003   Tombs from the Copan Acropolis: A Life History Approach. In
          Understanding Early Classic Maya Copan, edited by Ellen E. Bell, Mar-
          cello A. Canuto, and Robert J. Sharer, pp. 185–206. University
          Museum Publications, University of Pennsylvania, Philadelphia.
Bulliet, Richard
  1980   Sedentarization of Nomads in the Seventh Century: The Arabs in
          Kufa and Basra. In *When Nomads Settle*, edited by Philip C. Salzman,
          pp. 35–47. Praeger, New York.
Burghardt, A. F.
  1971   A Hypothesis about Gateway Cities. *Annals of the Association of Amer-
          ican Geographers* 61: 269–287.
  1979   The Origin of the Road and City Network of Roman Pannonia.
          Journal of Historical Geography 5: 1–20.
Buringh, P.
  1960   *Soils and Soil Conditions in Iraq.* Ministry of Agriculture Directorate
          General of Agricultural Research and Projects, Baghdad.

Burney, Charles
2004   *Historical Dictionary of the Hittites*. Scarecrow, Lanham, Maryland.
Butzer, Karl W.
1982   *Archaeology as Human Ecology*. Cambridge University, Cambridge.
2001   Geoarchaeological Implications of Recent Research in the Nile Delta. In *Egypt and the Levant: Interrelations from the 4th through the Early 3rd Millennium B.C.E.*, edited by Edwin van den Brink and Thomas E. Levy, pp. 83-97. Leicester University, London.
Cabrera Castro, Rubén
1982   La Excavación de la Estructura 1B' en el Interior de la Ciudadela. In *Memoria del Proyecto Arqueológico Teotihuacan 80–82*, edited by Rubén Cabrera Castro, Ignacio Rodriguez G., and Noel Morelos G., pp. 75–87. Instituto Nacional de Antropología e Historia, Mexico City.
Cabrera Castro, Rubén, Ignacio Rodríguez García, and Noel Morelos García (editors)
1982a   *Teotihuacan 80–82: Primeros Resultados*. Instituto Nacional de Antropología e Historia, Mexico City.
1982b   *Memoria del Proyecto Arqueológico Teotihuacan 80–82*. Instituto Nacional de Antropología e Historia, Mexico City.
1991   *Teotihuacan 1980–1982: Nuevas Interpretaciones*. Instituto Nacional de Antropología e Historia, Mexico City.
Cabrera Castro, Rubén, Saburo Sugiyama, and George L. Cowgill
1991   The Templo de Quetzalcoatl Project at Teotihuacan: A Preliminary Report. *Ancient Mesoamerica* 2 (1): 77–99.
Cabrera Cortés, M. Oralia
2001   Textile Production at Teotihuacan, Mexico. Master's thesis, Department of Anthropology, Arizona State University, Tempe.
Calmeyer, Peter
1990   Mālamīr. A. Lage und Forschungsgeschichte; C. Archäologisch. *Reallexikon der Assyriologie und vorderasiatischen archäologie* 7: 275–276, 281–287.
1995   Middle Babylonian Art and Contemporary Iran. In *Later Mesopotamia and Iran: Tribes and Empires, 1600–539 BC. Proceedings of a Seminar in Memory of Vladimir G. Lukonin*, edited by John Curtis, pp. 33–45. British Museum, London.
Calnek, Edward E.
1976   The Internal Structure of Tenochtitlan. In *The Valley of Mexico: Studies in Pre-Hispanic Ecology and Society*, edited by Eric R. Wolf, pp. 287–302. University of New Mexico, Albuquerque.
Calvet, Yves
1996   Maisons privées paléo-babyloniennes à Larsa. Remarques d'architecture. In *Houses and Households in Ancient Mesopotamia*, edited by Klaas R. Veenhof, pp. 197–209. Nederlands Historisch-Archaeologisch Instituut te Istanbul, Istanbul.
Canby, Jeanny V.
2001   *The "Ur-Nammu" Stela*. University Museum Monograph 110. University of Pennsylvania Museum, Philadelphia.

Carneiro, Robert L.
1970   A Theory of the Origin of the State. *Science* 169: 733–738.
Carney, Judith A.
2001   *Black Rice. The African Origin of Rice Cultivation in America.* Harvard
         University Press, Cambridge and London.
Carsten, Janet, and Stephen Hugh-Jones (editors)
1995   *About the House: Lévi-Strauss and Beyond.* Cambridge University, Cambridge.
Carter, Elizabeth
1971   Elam in the Second Millennium B.C.: The Archaeological Evidence.
         Unpublished Ph.D. dissertation, Department of Near Eastern Lan-
         guages and Civilizations, University of Chicago.
1984   Archaeology. In *Elam: Surveys of Political History and Archaeology,*
         edited by Elizabeth Carter and Matthew W. Stolper, pp. 103–230.
         Near Eastern Studies Vol. 25. University of California, Berkeley.
1985   Lagash (Tell Al-Hiba). *Iraq* 47: 222.
1990   A Surface Survey of Lagash, al-Hiba, 1984. *Sumer* 46: 60–63.
1992   Cogha Zanbil. *Encyclopaedia Iranica* 9 (1): 9–13.
1994   Bridging the Gap between the Elamites and the Persians in South-
         eastern Khuzistan. In *Achaemenid History VIII,* edited by Heleen
         Sancisi-Weerdenburg, A. Khurt, and Margaret C. Root, pp. 65–95.
         Nederlands Instituut voor het Nabije Oosten, Leiden.
Carter, Elizabeth, and Matthew W. Stolper
1984   *Elam, Surveys of Political History and Archaeology.* Near Eastern Studies
         25. University of California, Berkeley.
Carter, Robert
2006   Boat Remains and Maritime Trade in the Persian Gulf during the
         Sixth and Fifth Millennia BC. *Antiquity* 80: 52–53.
Carter, Robert, and Harriet Crawford
2001   The Kuwait-British Archaeological Expedition to As-Sabiyah:
         Report on the Second Season's Work. *Iraq* 63: 1–20.
2002   The Kuwait-British Archaeological Expedition to as-Sabiyah: Report
         on the Second Season's Work. *Iraq* 64: 1–13.
Carter, Robert, Harriet Crawford, Simeon Mellalieu, and Dan Barrett
1999   The Kuwait-British Archaeological Expedition to As-Sabiyah:
         Report on the First Season's Work. *Iraq* 61: 43–58.
Casal, Jean-Marie
1964   *Fouilles d'Amri.* Publications de la Commission des Fouilles Archae-
         ologiques, Fouilles du Pakistan, Paris
Casana, Jesse
n.d.   The Archaeological Landscape of Late Roman Antioch. In *Culture
         and Society in Late Roman Antioch,* edited by Isabella Sandwell and
         Janet Huskinson. David Brown Book Company, New York, in press.
Chakrabarti, Dilip K.
1994   Archaeology of the Chhotanangpur Plateau and the Bengal Basin. In
         *From Sumer to Meluhha: Contributions to the Archaeology of South and
         West Asia in Memory of George F. Dales, Jr.,* edited by Jonathon M.
         Kenoyer, pp. 253–260. Prehistory Press, Madison, Wisconsin.

Chambon, Grégory
    2003   Archaic Metrological Systems from Ur. *Cuneiform Digital Library Journal* 2003: 5 <*http://cdli.ucla.edu/pubs/cdlj/2003/cdlj2003_005.html*>.

Charpin, Dominique
    1980   *Archives familiales et propriéte privée en Babylonie ancienne: Étude des documents de "Tell Sifr"*. Librairie Droz, Genève.
    1986   *Le clergé d'Ur au siècle d'Hammurabi (XIXe–XVIIIe siècles av. J.-C.)*. Librairie Droz, Genève.

Chase-Dunn, Christopher, and Thomas D. Hall
    1991   Core/Periphery Hierarchies for Comparative Study. In *Core/Periphery Relations in Precapitalist Worlds*, edited by Christopher Chase-Dunn and Thomas D. Hall, pp. 5–44. Westview, Boulder, Colorado.

Childe, V. Gordon
    1929   *The Danube in Prehistory*. Clarendon, Oxford.
    1951 [1936] *Man Makes Himself*. Mentor Books, New York.

Christaller, Walter
    1933   *Die zentralen Orte in Süddeutschland*. Fischer, Jena.
    1966 [1933] *The Central Places of Southern Germany*. Translated by Carlisle W. Baskin. Prentice-Hall, Englewoods Cliffs, New Jersey.

Clark, John E.
    1986   From Mountains to Molehills: A Critical Review of Teotihuacan's Obsidian Industry. In *Economic Aspects of Prehispanic Highland Mexico*, edited by Barry L. Isaac, pp. 23–74. JAI, Greenwich, Connecticut.

Coggins, Clemency C.
    1980   The Shape of Time: Some Political Implications of a Four-Part Figure. *American Antiquity* 45: 727–739.

Cohen, Andrew
    2003   Introduction to the Culture of Barley. Paper presented at the Annual Meetings of the American Schools of Oriental Research, Atlanta.

Cohen, Mark
    1988   *Canonical Lamentations of Ancient Mesopotamia*, Vol. 2. CDL, Potomac Maryland.

Cole, Steven W.
    1996a   *Nippur in Late Assyrian Times, c. 755–612 B.C.* Neo-Assyrian Text Corpus Project, Helsinki.
    1996b   *Nippur IV: The Early Neo-Babylonian Governor's Archive from Nippur*. University of Chicago.

Coleman, James M., Harry H. Roberts, and Oscar H. Huh
    1986   Deltaic Landforms. In *Geomorphology from Space*, edited by Nicholas M. Short and Robert W. Blair, pp. 317–352. National Aeronautics and Space Administration Scientific and Technical Branch, Washington, DC. Electronic document, *http://daac.gdfc.nasa.gov/DAAC_DOCS/geomorphology/GEO_5/GEO_Chapter5.html*, accessed December 10, 2002.

Contenau, Georges, and Roman Ghirshman
    1935   *Fouilles de Tepe-Giyan*. Musée du Louvre, Departement des Antiquités Orientales, Serie Archéologique 3. Paul Geuthner, Paris.

Cotha Consulting Engineers
1959   *Drainage Investigations in Gharraf East Area*. Republic of Iraq Minis-
        try of Agriculture, Directorate General of Irrigation, Baghdad.

Courty, Marie-Agnés
1990   Pedogenesis of Holocene Calcareous Parent-Materials under Semi-
        arid Conditions (Ghaggar Plain, NW India). In *Soil Micromorphology:
        A Basic and Applied Science*, edited by Lowell A. Douglas, pp. 361–366.
        Developments in Soil Science Vol. 19. Elsevier, Amsterdam.
1995   Late Quaternary Environmental Changes and Natural Constraints to
        Ancient Land Use (Northwest India). In *Ancient Peoples and Land-
        scapes*, edited by Eileen Johnson, pp. 105–126. Museum of Texas Tech
        University, Lubbock.

Cowgill, George L.
1983   Rulership and the Ciudadela: Political Inferences from Teotihuacan
        Architecture. In *Civilization in the Ancient Americas: Essays in Honor of
        Gordon R. Willey*, edited by Richard M. Leventhal and Alan L. Kolata,
        pp. 313–343. University of New Mexico, Albuquerque, and Peabody
        Museum, Harvard University, Cambridge, Massachusetts.
1997   State and Society at Teotihuacan, Mexico. *Annual Review of Anthro-
        pology* 26: 129–161.
2000a   Intentionality and Meaning in the Layout of Teotihuacan, Mexico.
        Cambridge Archaeological Journal 10 (2): 358–361.
2000b   The Central Mexican Highlands from the Rise of Teotihuacan to the
        Decline of Tula. In *The Cambridge History of the Native Peoples of the
        Americas*, Vol. II: *Mesoamerica, Part 1*, edited by Richard E. Adams and
        Murdo J. MacLeod, pp. 250–317. Cambridge University, Cambridge.
2003   Teotihuacan: Cosmic Glories and Mundane Needs. In *The Social
        Construction of Ancient Cities*, edited by Monica L. Smith, pp. 37–55.
        Smithsonian Institution, Washington, DC.
2005   Planeamiento a gran escala en Teotihuacan: Implicaciones religiosas y
        sociales. In *Arquitectura y urbanismo: Pasado y presente de los espacios en Teoti-
        huacan*, edited by María Elena Ruiz G. and Jesús Torres P., pp. 21–40.
        Instituto Nacional de Antropología e Historia, Mexico City.

Cowgill, George L., Jeffrey H. Altschul, and Rebecca S. Sload
1984   Spatial Analysis of Teotihuacan: A Mesoamerican Metropolis. In
        Intrasite Spatial Analysis in Archaeology, edited by Harold J. Hietala,
        pp. 154–195. Cambridge University, Cambridge.

Crawford, Harriet
1985   A Note on the Vegetation on the Uruk Vase. In *Bulletin on Sumerian
        Agriculture*, Vol. II, edited by J. Nicholas Postgate, pp. 73–76. Aris &
        Phillips, Cambridge.

Crespo, Ana María, and Alba Guadalupe Mastache
1981   La Presencia en el Área de Tula, Hidalgo, de Grupos Relacionados con
        el Barrio de Oaxaca en Teotihuacan. In *Interacción Cultural en México
        Central*, edited by Evelyn C. Rattray, Jaime Litvak King, and Clara L.
        Díaz Oyarzábal, pp. 99–112. Instituto de Investigaciones Antropológi-
        cas, Universidad Nacional Autónoma de México, Mexico City.

Crider, Destiny
  2002   Coyotlatelco Phase Community Structure at Teotihuacan. M.A. the-
          sis, Department of Anthropology, Arizona State University.
Crumley, Carole
  1995   Heterarchy and the Analysis of Complex Societies. In *Heterarchy and
          the Analysis of Complex Societies*, edited by Robert M. Ehrenreich, Car-
          ole L. Crumley, and Janet E. Levy, pp. 1–15. Archaeological Papers of
          the American Anthropological Association No. 6, Arlington, Virginia.
Cucarzi, Mauro
  1984   Geophysical Investigations at Mohenjo Daro. In *Interim Reports*, Vol.
          1: *Reports on Field Work Carried Out at Mohenjo Daro, Pakistan, 1982–
          83*, edited by Michael R. Jansen and Günter Urban, pp. 191–200.
          ISMEO-Aachen University Mission, Aachen.
Cullen, Heidi M., Peter B. deMenocal, Sidney Hemming, N. Gary Hemming,
Francis H. Brown, T. Gilderson, and Frank Sirocko
  2000   Climate Change and the Collapse of the Akkadian Empire: Evidence
          from the Deep Sea. *Geology* 28 (4): 379–382.
Curtis, John, Julian Reade, and Dominique Collon
  1995   *Art and Empire: Treasures from Assyria in the British Museum*. The
          Trustees of the British Museum by British Museum, London.
Cusick, James G. (editor)
  1998   *Studies in Culture Contact: Interaction, Culture Change, and Archaeology*.
          Center for Archaeological Investigations, Occasional Paper 25.
          Southern Illinois University, Carbondale.
Dales, George F., and Robert L. Raikes
  1977   The Moenjo-daro Floods: A Rejoinder. *American Anthropologist* 70:
          957–961.
David, Jean-Claude
  1975   Alep, dégradation et tentatives actuelles de réadaptation des struc-
          tures urbaines traditionnelles. *Bulletin d'Études Orientales* 28: 19–50.
Davidson, Thomas E., and Trevor Watkins
  1981   Two Seasons of Excavations at Tell Aqab in the Jezirah, N.E. Syria.
          Iraq 43: 1–18.
Davis, Simon J. M.
  1984   The Advent of Milk and Wool Production in Western Iran: Some
          Speculations. In *Animals in Archaeology 3. Early Herders and Their
          Flocks*, edited by Juliet Clutton-Brock and Caroline Grigson, pp.
          265–278. BAR, Oxford.
de Genouillac, Henri
  1920   *Texte Cuniform d'Louvre*. Centre National de la Recherche Scienti-
          fique, Paris.
Delougaz, Pinhas P.
  1940   *The Temple Oval at Khafajah*. Oriental Institute Publication 53. Uni-
          versity of Chicago.
  1952   *Pottery from the Diyala Region*. Oriental Institute Publication 63. Uni-
          versity of Chicago.

Delougaz, Pinhas, Harold D. Hill, and Seton Lloyd
1967   *Private Houses and Graves in the Diyala Region.* Oriental Institute Publication 88. University of Chicago.
Delougaz, Pinhas, and Helene Kantor
1996   *Chogha Mish.* Oriental Institute Publication 101. Oriental Institute, Chicago.
Delougaz, Pinhas, and Seton Lloyd
1942   *Pre-Sargonid Temples in the Diyala Region.* Oriental Institute Publication 58. University of Chicago.
de Menocal, Peter B.
2001   Cultural Responses to Climate Change during the Late Holocene. *Science* 292: 667–673.
de Miroschedji, Pierre
1981a   Fouilles du chantier Ville Royale II à Suse (1975–1977) I. Les niveaux élamites. *Cahiers de la Délégation archéologique française en Iran* 12: 9–136.
1981b   Observations dans les couches néo-élamite au nord-ouest du tell del la Ville Royale. *Cahiers de la Délégation archéologique française en Iran* 12: 143–168.
1981c   Prospections archéologiques au Khuzistan en 1977. *Cahiers de la Délégation archéologique française en Iran* 12: 169–192.
1982   Notes sur la glyptique de la fin de l'Élam. *Revue d'Assyriologie* 76: 61–63.
1986a   La fin du royaume d'Anšan et de Suse et la naissance de l'Empire perse. *Zeitschrift für Assyriologie und vorderasiatische Archäologie* 76: 265–306.
1986b   La localisation de Madaktu et l'organisation politique de l'Elam à l'epoque néo-élamite. In *Fragmenta historiae Elamicae: Mélanges offerts à M. J. Steve,* edited by Leon de Meyer, Hermann Gasche, and François Vallat, pp. 209–225. Éditions de Recherche sur les Civilisations, Paris.
1990   La fin d l'Elam: Essai d'analyse et d'interprétation. *Iranica Antiqua* 25: 47–95.
2003   Susa and the Highlands: Major Trends in the History of Elamite civilization. In *Yeki Bud, Yeki Nabud. Essays on the Archaeology of Iran in Honor of William M. Sumner,* edited by Naomi F. Miller and Kamyar Abdi, pp. 17–38. Monograph 48. Cotsen Institute of Archaeology, Los Angeles.
de Polignac, François
1995 [1984] *Cults, Territory, and the Origins of the Greek City-State.* University of Chicago. [1984 ed. *La Naissance de la cité grecque.* Editions La Découverte, Paris.]
Dercksen, Jan G. (editor)
1996   *The Old Assyrian Copper Trade in Anatolia.* Nederlands Historisch-Archaeologisch Instituut te Istanbul, Istanbul.
Desse, Jean
1983   Les faunes du gisement obeidien final de Tèll el'Ouelli. In *Larsa et 'Ouelli: Traveau de 1978–1981,* edited by Jean-Louis Huot, pp. 193–199. Editions Recherche sur les Civilisations, Paris.

De Waele, Eric
1981   Travaux archéologiques à Šekāf-e Salmān et Kūl-e Farah, près de
        Izeh (Malamir). *Iranica Antiqua* 16: 45–62.
Dewar, Robert
1991   Incorporating Variation in Occupation Span into Settlement-Pattern
        Analysis. *American Antiquity* 56: 604–620.
Dhavalikar, Madhukar K., and Gregory L. Possehl.
1992   The Pre-Harappan Period at Prabhas Patan and the Pre-Harappan
        Phase in Gujarat. *Man and Environment* 17 (1): 71–78.
Diamond, Jared
1999   *Guns, Germs, and Steel.* Norton, New York.
Dodd, Lynn S.
2002   *The Ancient Past in the Ancient Present: Cultural Identity in Gurgum
        during the Late Bronze Age–Early Iron Age Transition in North Syria.*
        Department of Near Eastern Languages and Cultures, University of
        California, Los Angeles.
Dolce, Rita
1989   Note per una reconsiderazione di alcune strutture de un magazzinamento
        e de lavorazione di derrate nel III e nel II millenio in Mesopotamia e in
        Siria. In *Il pane del Re: Accumulo e distribuzione dei cereali nell'oriente antico,*
        edited by Rita Dolce and Carlo Zaccagnini, pp. 17–48. Studi de Storia
        Antica 13. CLUEB, Bologna.
Drewitt, Bruce
1987   Measurement Units and Building Axes at Teotihuacan. In *Teotihua-
        can: Nuevos Datos, Nuevas Síntesis, Nuevos Problemas,* edited by Emily
        McClung de Tapia and Evelyn C. Rattray, pp. 389–398. Instituto de
        Investigaciones Antropológicas, Universidad Nacional Autónoma de
        México, Mexico City.
Drucker, R. David
1974   Renovating a Reconstruction: The Ciudadela at Teotihuacan, Mex-
        ico: Construction Sequence, Layout, and Possible Uses of the Struc-
        ture. Unpublished Ph.D. dissertation, Department of Anthropology,
        University of Rochester, Rochester, New York.
Düring, B.
2001   Social Dimensions in the Architecture of Neolithic Çatalhöyük. *Ana-
        tolian Studies* 51: 1–18.
Duru, Refik
1999   The Neolithic of the Lake District. In *Neolithic in Turkey: The Cradle
        of Civilization,* edited by Mehmet Özdoğan and Nezih Başgelen, pp.
        165–192. Arkeoloji ve Sanat Yayınları. Istanbul.
Edens, Christopher
1996   Hacınebi Chipped Stone, 1995. In Hacınebi, Turkey: Preliminary
        Report on the 1995 Excavations, by Gil Stein, Christopher Edens,
        Hadi Özbal, Julie Pearce and Holly Pittman. *Anatolica* 22: 100–104.
1997   Hacınebi Chipped Stone. In Excavations at Hacınebi, Turkey, 1996:
        Preliminary Report, by Gil Stein, Christopher Edens, Hadi Özbal,
        Julie Pearce, and Holly Pittman. *Anatolica* 23: 124–127.

1998a   Hacınebi Chipped Stone, 1997. In Southeast Anatolia before the Uruk Expansion: Preliminary Report on the 1997 Excavations at Hacınebi, Turkey. *Anatolica* 24: 155–160.

1998b   The Chipped Stone Industry at Hacınebi: Technological Styles and Social Identity. Paper presented at the annual meeting of the Society for American Archaeology, Seattle.

Edens, Christopher, and K. Aslıhan Yener

2000   Excavations at Tell Kurdu 1996 and 1998. In The Amuq Valley Regional Project 1995–1998, by K. Aslıhan Yener, Christopher Edens, Timothy Harrison, J. Verstraete, and Tony J. Wilkinson. *American Journal of Archaeology* 104: 163–220.

Edmonds, Cecil J.

1922   Luristan: Pish-i-Kuh and Bala Gariveh. *Geographical Journal* 59: 335–356.

Edzard, Dietz O.

1997   *Gudea and His Dynasty*. The Royal Inscriptions of Mesopotamia, Early Periods 3/1. University of Toronto.

Ehrenreich, Robert M., Carole M. Crumley, and Janet E. Levy (editors)

1995   *Heterarchy and the Analysis of Complex Societies*. Archaeological Papers of the American Anthropological Association, Arlington, Virginia.

Eichmann, Ricardo

1989   *Uruk, Die Stratigraphie*. Deutches Archäologisches Institut, Berlin.

Eiwanger, Josef

1984   *Merimde–Benisâlame I: Die Funde der Urschicht*. Archäologische Veröffentlichungen 47. Verlag Philipp von Zabern, Mainz am Rhein.

Eliade, Mircea

1978 [1956] *The Forge and the Crucible*. University of Chicago.

el-Moslimany, Ann P.

1994   Evidence of Early Holocene Summer Precipitation in the Middle East. In *Late Quaternary Chronology and Palaeoclimates of the Eastern Mediterranean*, edited by O. Bar-Yosef and R. S. Kra, pp. 121–130. Radiocarbon, Department of Geosciences, University of Arizona, Tucson.

Emberling, Geoff

2002   Political Control in an Early State: The Eye Temple and the Uruk Expansion in Northern Mesopotamia. In *Of Pots and Plans: Papers on the Archaeology and History of Mesopotamia and Syria Presented to David Oates in Honour of His 75th Birthday*, edited by Lamia Al-Gailani Werr, John Curtis, Augusta McMahon, H. Martin, Joan Oates, and Julian Reade, pp. 47–104. NABU Booksellers and Publishers, London.

Emberling, Geoff, Jack Cheng, Torben E. Larsen, Holly Pittman, Tim B. B. Skuldboel, Jill Weber, and Henry T. Wright.

1999   Excavations at Tell Brak 1998: Preliminary Report. *Iraq* 61: 1–41.

Emberling, Geoff, John Robb, and John D. Speth

2002   Kunji Cave: Early Bronze Age Burials in Luristan. *Iranica Antiqua* 37: 47–104.

Engels, Friederich

1972 [1884] *The Origin of the Family, Private Property, and the State*. Pathfinder, New York.

Englund, Robert K.
1990   *Organization und Verwaltung der Ur-III Fischerei.* Berliner Beitrage zum Vorderen Orient 10. Berlin.
1998   Texts from the Late Uruk Period. In *Mesopotamien: Späturuk-Zeit und Frühdynastische Zeit,* edited by Pascal Attinger and Marcus Wafler, pp. 15–236. Universitätsverlag, Gottingen: Vandenhoeck and Ruprecht, Freiburg Schweiz.
2002   The Ur III Collection of the CMAA. *Cuneiform Digital Library Journal* 2002: 1.
2003   The Year: "Nissen returns joyous from a distant island." *Cuneiform Digital Library Journal* 2003: 1.

Englund, Robert, Hans Nissen, and Peter Damerow
1993   *Die lexicalische Listen der archaischen Texte aus Uruk.* Gebr. Mann, Berlin.

Epstein, Stephen M.
1993   Cultural Choice and Technological Consequences. Constraint of Innovation in the Late Prehistoric Copper Smelting Industry of Cerro Huaringa, Peru. Unpublished Ph.D. dissertation, Anthropology Department, University of Pennsylvania, Philadelphia.

Ertuğ, Füsun
2000   Linseed Oil and Oil Mills in Central Turkey: Flax/*Linum* and *Eruca,* Important Oil Plants of Anatolia. *Anatolian Studies* 50: 171–185.

Esin, Ufuk
1981a   Değirmentepe Kazısı 1979. *Kazı Sonuçları Toplantısı* 2: 91–99.
1981b   1980 Yılı Değirmentepe (Malatya) Kazısı Sonuçları. *Kazı Sonuçları Toplantısı* 3: 39–41.
1983a   Değirmentepe (Malatya) Kazısı 1981 Yılı Sonuçları. *Kazı Sonuçları Toplantısı* 4: 39–48.
1983b   Zur Datierung der vorgeschichtlichen Schichten von Değirmentepe bei Malatya in der östlichen Türkei. In *Beiträge zur Altertumskunde Kleinasiens. Festschrift Kurt Bittel,* edited by R. M. Boehmer and H. Hauptmann, pp. 175–190. Philipp von Zabern, Mainz.
1984   1982 Yılı Değirmentepe (Malatya) Kurtarma Kazısı. *Kazı Sonuçları Toplantısı* 5: 71–73.
1985a   Değirmentepe (Malatya) Kurtarma Kazısı 1983 Yılı Raporu. *Kazı Sonuçları Toplantısı* 6: 11–29.
1985b   Some Small Finds from the Chalcolithic Occuption at Değirmentepe (Malatya) in Eastern Turkey. In *Studi di paletnologia in onore di Salvatore M. Puglisi,* edited by Mario Liverani et al., pp. 253–263. Università di Roma, Rome.
1989   An Early Trading Center in Eastern Anatolia. In *Anatolia and the Ancient Near East, Studies in Honor of Tahsin Özgüc,* edited by Kutlu Emre et al., pp. 135–141. Türk Tarih Kurumu Basımevi, Ankara.
1991   Salvage Excavations at the Pre-Pottery Site of Aşıklı Höyük in Central Anatolia. *Anatolica* 17: 123–174.

1994a   Discussion of Paper by Frangipane. In *Archives before Writing*, edited by Piera Ferioli, Enrica Fiandra, G. Giacomo Fissore, and Marcella Frangipane, p. 137. Scriptorium, Rome.

1994b   The Functional Evidence of Seals and Sealings of Değirmentepe. In *Archives before Writing*, edited by Piera Ferioli, Enrica Fiandra, G. Giacomo Fissore, and Marcella Frangipane, pp. 59–81. Scriptorium, Roma.

1998   Die Tempel von Değirmentepe während der chalkolitischen Obedperiode. In *XXXIV Uluslararası Assirioloji Kongresi. Ankara: Türk Tarih Kurumu*, edited by Hayat Erkanal, Veysil Donbaz and Ayşeğül Uğüroğlu, pp. 659–676. Türk Tarih Kurumu Basımevi, Ankara.

1999   Aşıklı. In *Neolithic in Turkey: The Cradle of Civilization*, edited by Mehmet Özdoğan and Nezih Başgelen, pp. 115–132. Arkeoloji ve Sanat Yayınlar, Istanbul.

Esin, Ufuk, and Savaş Harmankaya

1986   1984 Değirmentepe (Malatya) Kurtarma Kazıs. *Kazı Sonuçları Toplantısı* 7: 53–85.

1987   1985 Değirmentepe (Malatya-Imamlı Köyü) Kurtarma Kazısı. *Kazı Sonuçları Toplantısı* 8: 95–137.

1988   Değirmentepe (Malatya) Kurtarma Kazısı 1986. *IX. Kazı Sonuçları Toplantısı* 1: 79–125.

Falkenstein, Adam

1965   Die Ur- und Frühgeschichte des Alten Vorderasien. In *Die Altorientalischen Reiche I*, edited by Elena Cassin et al., pp. 13–56. Fischer Weltgeschichte Band 2. Fischer, Frankfurt.

Farber, Howard

1978   A Price and Wage Study for Northern Babylonia during the Old Babylonian Period. *Journal of the Economic and Social History of the Orient* 21: 1–51.

Fash, William L., and Barbara W. Fash

2000   Teotihuacan and the Maya: A Classic Heritage. In *Mesoamerica's Classic Heritage: From Teotihuacan to the Aztecs*, edited by Davíd Carrasco, Lindsay Jones, and Scott Sessions, pp. 433–463. University Press of Colorado, Boulder.

Feinman, Gary M.

1994   Social Boundaries and Political Change: A Comparative Perspective. In *Chiefdoms and Early States in the Near East*, edited by Gil Stein and Mitchell S. Rothman, pp. 225–236. Prehistory, Madison, Wisconsin.

Feinman, Gary M., and J. Neitzel

1994   Too Many Types: An Overview of Pre-state Societies in the Americas. In *Advances in Archaeological Method and Theory*, No. 7, edited by M. B. Fischer, pp. 39–102. Academic, New York.

Ferioli, Piera, and Enrica Fiandra

1979   The Administrative Functions of Clay Sealings in Protohistorical Iran. In *Iranica*, edited by Gherardo Gnoli and Adriano V. Rossi, pp. 307–312. Instituto Universitario Orientale, Naples.

1983   Clay Sealings from Arslantepe VIA: Administration and Bureaucracy. *Origini* 12: 455–509.

1994   Archival Techniques and Methods at Arslantepe. In *Archives before Writing*, edited by Piera Ferioli, Enrica Fiandra, G. Giacomo Fissore, and Marcella Frangipane, pp. 149–161. Centro Internazionale di Recerche Archaeologiche Anthropologiche e Storiche, Rome.

Fernandez-Armesto, Felipe
2001   *Civilizations*. Free Press, New York.

Fernández Mendiola, Sara E., and Leticia Jiménez Hernández
1997   Restauración de la Ofrenda Cerámica Teotihuacana. *Arqueología* 18: 23–28.

Fernea, Robert A.
1970   *Shaykh and Effendi: Changing Patterns of Authority among the El Shabana of Southern Iraq*. Harvard Middle Eastern Studies 14. Harvard University, Cambridge.

Fiandra, Enrica
1979   The Connection between Clay Sealings and Tablets in Administration. In *South Asian Archaeology*, edited by Herbert Härtel, pp. 29–43. Dietrich Reimer Verlag, Berlin.

Finkbeiner, Uwe (editor)
1991   *Uruk Kampagne 35–37, 1982–1984. Die archäologische Oberflächenuntersuchung (Survey)*. Ausgrabungen in Uruk-Warka Endberichte 4. Philipp von Zabern, Mainz.

Finley, Moses I.
1973   *The Ancient Economy*. University of California, Berkeley.
1985   *The Ancient Economy*. 2nd ed. University of California, Berkeley.

Flam, Louis
1993   Fluvial Geomorphology of the Lower Indus Basin (Sindh, Pakistan) and the Indus Civilization. In *Himalaya to the Sea: Geology, Geomorphology and the Quaternary*, edited by John F. Shroder, pp. 265–287. Routledge, London.
1999   Ecology and Population Mobility in the Prehistoric Settlement of the Lower Indus Valley, Sindh, Pakistan. In *The Indus River: Biodiversity, Resources, Humankind*, edited by Azra Meadows and Peter S. Meadows, pp. 313–323. Oxford University, Oxford.

Flannery, Kent V.
1972   The Cultural Evolution of Civilizations. *Annual Review of Ecology and Systematics* 3: 399–426.
1998   The Ground Plans of Archaic States. In *Archaic States*, edited by Gary M. Feinman and Joyce Marcus, pp. 15–57. School of American Research, Santa Fe, New Mexico.

Flückiger-Hawker, Esther
1999   *Urnamma of Ur in Sumerian Literary Tradition*. OBO 166. University Press, Fribourg.

Forest, Jean-Daniel
1983   Aux origines de l'architecture obeidienne: Les plans de type Samarra. *Akkadica* 34: 1–47.
1987   La grande architecture Obeidienne sa forme et sa fonction. *Préhistoire de la Mesopotamie*, edited by Jean-Louis Huot, pp. 385–423. Editions Recherche sur les Civilisations, Paris.

1996   Elements de chronologie. In *Oueili: Travaux de 1987 et 1989*, edited by Jean-Louis Huot. Editions Recherche sur les Civilisations, Paris.

1999   *Les premieres temples de Mésopotamie*. BAR 765. Archaeopress, Oxford.

Foster, Benjamin

1993   "International" Trade at Sargonic Susa. *Altorientalische Forschungen* 20: 59–68.

Francfort, H.-P.

1986   Preliminary Report (1983–1984): Archaeological and Environmental Researches in the Ghaggar (Saraswati) Plains. *Man and Environment* 10: 97–100.

1989   *Fouilles de Shortughai recherches sur l'Asia Centrale protohistorique*. Diffusión de Boccard, Paris.

Frangipane, Marcella

1994   The Record Function of Clay Sealings in Early Administrative Systems as Seen from Arslantepe-Malatya. In *Archives before Writing*, edited by Piera Ferioli, Enrica Fiandra, G. Giacomo Fissore, and Marcella Frangipane, pp. 125–137. Centro Internazionale di Recerche Archaeologiche Anthropologiche e Storiche, Rome.

2000   The Development of Administrative Systems from Collective to Centralized Economies in the Mesopotamian World. In *Cultural Evolution: Contemporary Viewpoints*, edited by Gary M. Feinman and Linda Manzianilla, pp. 215–234. Kluwer Academic/Plenum Publishers, New York.

2001a   On Models and Data in Mesopotamia. *Current Anthropology* 42: 415–416.

2001b   Centralization Processes in Greater Mesopotamia: Uruk "Expansion" as the Climax of Systemic Interactions among Areas of the Greater Mesopotamian Region. In *Uruk Mesopotamia and Its Neighbors*, edited by Mitchell S. Rothman, pp. 307–348. School of American Research, Santa Fe, New Mexico.

Frangipane, Marcella, Gian Maria Di Nocera, Andreas Hauptmann, Paola Morbidelli, Alberto Palmieri, Laura Sadori, Michael Schultz, and Tyede Schmidt-Schultz

2001   New Symbols of a New Power in a "Royal" Tomb from 3000 BC Arslantepe, Malatya. *Paléorient* 27 (2): 105–139.

Frangipane, Marcella, and Alba Palmieri

1983   A Protourban Centre of the Late Uruk Period. *Origini* 12 (2): 287–454.

1989   Aspects of Centralization in the Late Uruk Period in the Mesopotamian Periphery. *Origini* 14: 539–560.

Frankfort, Henri

1924   *Studies in Early Pottery of the Near East I*. Royal Anthropological Institute of Great Britain and Ireland, London.

1939a   *Cylinder Seals: A Documentary Essay on the Art and Religion of the Ancient Near East*. Gregg, London.

1939b   *Sculpture of the Third Millennium BC from Tell Asmar and Khafajah*. Oriental Institute Publications 44. University of Chicago.

1943   *More Sculpture from the Diyala Region*. University of Chicago.

1954   *The Art and Architecture of the Ancient Near East*. Penguin, Harmondsworth.

1955 *Stratified Cylinder Seals from the Diyala Region.* Oriental Institute Publications 72. University of Chicago.

Frankfort, Henri, Seton Lloyd, and Thorkild Jacobsen
1940 *The Gimilsin Temple and the Palace of the Rulers at Tell Asmar.* University of Chicago.

Fried, Morton H.
1967 *The Evolution of Political Society: An Essay in Political Anthropology.* Random House, New York

Friend, Peter F., S. Mahmood Raza, M. S. Baig, and I. A. Khan
1999 Geological Evidence of the Ancestral Indus from the Himalayan Foothills. In *The Indus River: Biodiversity, Resources, Humankind,* edited by Azra Meadows and Peter S. Meadows, pp. 103–113. Oxford University, Oxford.

Frifelt, Karen
1989 Ubaid in the Gulf area. In *Upon this Foundation—The 'Ubaid Reconsidered. Proceedings of the 'Ubaid Symposium, Elsinore 1988,* edited by Elizabeth F. Henrickson and Ingolf Thuesen, pp. 405–418. Museum Tusculanum, Copenhagen.

Fugman, Ejnar
1958 *Hama, fouilles et recherches 1931–1938,* v. II, 1: *L'architecture des périodes préhellenistiques.* Nationalmuseet, Copenhagen.

Fujita, M., and Paul Krugman
1995 When is the Economy Monocentric—Von Thünen and Chamberlin Unified. *Regional Science and Urban Economics* 25: 505–528.

Galiatsatos, Nikolaos
2002 Corona. Electronic document, *http://www.dur.ac.uk/nikolaos. galiatsatos/Research/CORONA/Carona.html,* accessed December 20, 2002.

Galloway, J. H.
1989 *The Sugar Cane Industry: An Historical Geography from Its Origins to 1914.* Cambridge University Press, Cambridge and New York.

Gansell, Amy
2004 Personal Adornment in the 3rd Millennium Burials at Ur: Roles and Interpersonal Dynamics. Paper presented at the Annual Meeting of the American Schools of Oriental Research, San Antonio, Texas.

Gasche, Hermann, James A. Armstrong, Stephen W. Cole, and V.G. Gurzadyan
1998 *Dating the Fall of Babylon: A Reappraisal of Second Millennium Chronology.* Oriental Institute, Chicago.

Gasche, Hermann, and Michel Tanret
1998 *Changing Watercourses in Babylonia: Towards a Reconstruction of the Ancient Environment in Lower Mesopotamia.* University of Ghent and Oriental Institute, Ghent and Chicago.

Gates, Marie-Henriette C.
1987 Alalakh and Chronology Again. In *High Middle, or Low?,* edited by Paul Åström, pp. 60–86. Studies in Mediterranean Archaeology and Literature, Gothenburg.
1981 *Alalakh Levels VI and V: A Chronological Reassessment.* Syro-Mesopotamian Studies, Vol. 4, No. 2. Undena, Malibu.

2000   Kinet Höyük (Hatay, Turkey) and MB Levantine Chronology. *Akkadica* 1999 (120): 77–101.

Gelb, Ignace J.
1965   The Ancient Mesopotamian Ration System. *Journal of Near Eastern Studies* 24: 230–243.

General Staff of the Army, Division of War Cartography and Photogrammetry
1941 [1938]   Irak Sonderaufgabe. Topographic map, scale 1: 1,000,000, series Anlage über Militär-Geographische Angaben über Irak, ed. 1. Reichswehr Germany, Berlin. 1938 ed. DBA Koblenz, Kart 794/9.

Gerardi, Pamela
1987   *Assurbanipal's Elamite Campaigns: A Political and Literary Study.* Ph.D. Dissertation, Department of Oriental Studies, University of Pennsylvania. University Microfilms, Ann Arbor, Michigan.

Geyer, Bernard, and Paul Sanlaville
1996   Nouvelle Contribution a etude geomorpholgique de la region de Larsa-Ouelli (Iraq). In *Oueili: Travaux de 1987 et 1989*, edited by Jean-Louis Huot, pp. 392–412. Editions Recherche sur les Civilisations, Paris.

Ghirshman, Roman
1954   Village perse-achéménide. Mémoires de la Delegation archéologique en Iran; vol 36. Presses universitaires de France, Paris.
1968   *Tchogha Zanbil (Dur-Untash).* Vol. II: *Temenos, temples, palais, tombes.* Mémoires da la Mission archéologique en Iran 39. Geuthner, Paris.

Gibson, McGuire
1972   *The City and Area of Kish.* Field Research Projects, Miami.
1992   Patterns of Occupation at Nippur. In *Nippur at the Centennial*, edited by Maria deJong Ellis. Occasional Publications of the Samuel Noah Kramer Fund, 14, Philadelphia.
2000   Hamoukar: Early City in Northeastern Syria. *Oriental Institute News and Notes* 166: 1–8, 18–19.

Gibson, McGuire, A. al-Azm, C. Reichel, S. Quntar, J.A. Franke, L. Khalidi, C Fritz, M. Altaweel, C. Coyle, C. Colantoni, J. Tenney, G. Abdul Aziz, and T. Hartnell
2002   Hamoukar: A Summary of Three Seasons of Excavations. *Akkadica* 123: 11–34.

Gillet, J.
1976   Botanical Samples. In *Eridu*, edited by Fuad Safar, Mohammad A. Mustafa, and Seton Lloyd, pp. 317–318. Republic of Iraq, Ministry of Culture and Information, State Organization of Antiquities and Heritage, Baghdad.

Glatz, Claudia, and Roger Matthews
2005   Anthropology of a Frontier Zone: Hittite-Kaska Relations in Late Bronze Age North-Central Anatolia. *Bulletin of the American Schools of Oriental Research* 339: 21–39.

Gleason, Kathryn L.
1994   To Bound and to Cultivate: An Introduction to the Archaeology of Gardens and Fields. In *The Archaeology of Garden and Field*, edited by

Naomi F. Miller and Kathryn L. Gleason, pp. 1–24. University of Pennsylvania, Philadelphia.

Goetze, Albrecht
1969 Hittite Prayers. In *Ancient Near Eastern Texts Relating to the Old Testament*, 3rd edition, edited by James B. Pritchard, pp. 393–401. Princeton University, Princeton, New Jersey.

Goff, Clare L.
1966 New Evidence of Cultural Development in Luristan in the Late Second and Early First Millennium. Unpublished Ph.D. dissertation, Department of Archaeology, University of London, London.
1968 Luristan in the First Half of the First Millennium B.C. *Iran* 6: 105–134.
1971 Luristan before the Iron Age. *Iran* 9: 131–152.
1976 Excavations at Baba Jan: The Bronze Age Occupation. *Iran* 14: 19–40.
1977 Excavations at Baba Jan: The Architecture of the East Mound, Levels II and III. *Iran* 15: 103–130.
1978 Excavations at Baba Jan: The Pottery and Metal from Levels III and II. *Iran* 16: 29–66.
1985 Excavations at Baba Jan: The Architecture and Pottery of Level I. *Iran* 23: 1–20.

Gómez Chávez, Sergio
2000 *La Ventilla: Un Barrio de la Antigua Ciudad de Teotihuacan*. Escuela Nacional de Antropología e Historia, Mexico City.

Goody, Jack
2000 *The Power of the Written Tradition*. Smithsonian Institution, Washington, DC.

Gordon, Robert B., and David Killick
1993 Adaptation of Technology to Culture and Environment: Bloomery Iron Smelting in America and Africa. *Technology and Culture* 34 (2): 243–270.

Government of Canada
1956 *Landforms and Soils of West Pakistan*. Government of Canada, Ottawa.

Green, M.W.
1980 Animal Husbandry at Uruk in the Archaic Period. *Journal of Near Eastern Studies* 39: 1–35.

Greengus, Samuel
1979 *Old Babylonian Tablets from Ishchali and Vicinity*. Nederlands Historisch-Archaeologisch Instituut, Istanbul.
1986 *Studies in Ishchali Documents*. Undena Publications, Malibu.

Greenman, David W., Wolfgang V. Swarzenski, and Gordon D. Bennett
1967 *Geological Survey Water-Supply Paper 1608-H*. U.S. Government Printing Office, Washington, DC.

Groenewegen-Frankfort, Henriette A.
1987 [1951] *Arrest and Movement*. Harvard University, Cambridge, Massachusetts.

Gurney, Oliver R.
1979   The Hittite Empire. In *Power and Propaganda: A Symposium on Ancient Empires*, edited by Mogens T. Larsen, pp. 151–165. Meso potamia: Copenhagen Studies in Assyriology No. 7. Akademisk Forlag, Copenhagen.
1990   *The Hittites*. 2nd revised ed. Penguin Books, London.

Haas, Volkert
1998–2001 Nerik. *Reallexikon der Assyriologie und Vorderasiatischen Archäologie*, edited by Dietz O. Edzard, pp. 229–231. Walter de Gruyter, Berlin.

Hachmann, Rolf
1971   *The Germanic Peoples*. Ancient Civilizations. Nagel, Geneva.

Haerinck, Ernie, and Bruno Overlaet
1996   *The Chalcolithic Period, Parchineh and Hakalan*. Luristan Excavation Documents 1. Royal Museum of Art and History, Brussels.
1998   *Luristan Excavation Documents*, Vol. II: *Chamahzi Mumah: An Iron Age III Graveyard*. Acta Iranica 33. Peeters, Leuven.
1999   *Luristan Excavation Documents*, Vol. III: *Djub-i Gauhar and Gul Khanan Murdah Iron Age III Graveyards in the Aivan Plain*. Acta Iranica 22. Peeters, Leuven.
2002   The Chalcolithic and Early Bronze Age in Pusht-i Kuh, Luristan (West Iran): Chronology and Mesopotamian contacts. *Akkadica* 123 (2): 163–181.
2003   *The Iron Age III Graveyards of War Kabud and Sar Kabud*. Luristan Excavation Documents 5. Royal Museum of Art and History, Brussels.

Haghipour, Abdolazim, M. Ghorashi, and M. H. Kadjar
1984   *Seismotectonic Map of Iran, Afghanistan, and Pakistan*. Geological Survey of Iran, Tehran.

Haines, Richard C.
1971   *Excavations in the Plain of Antioch II: The Structural Remains of the Later Phases: Chatal Hoyuk, Tell al-Judaidah, and Tell Ta'yinat*. Oriental Institute Publications 92. University of Chicago.

Hall, Harry R.
1930   *A Season's Work at Ur*. Methuen & Co., London.

Hall, Harry R., and C. Leonard Woolley
1927   *Ur Excavations I. Al-'Ubaid*. Oxford University, Oxford.

Hall, Mark G.
1985   A Study of the Sumerian Moon-god, Nanna/Suen. Unpublished Ph.D. dissertation, Department of Oriental Studies, University of Pennsylvania, Philadelphia.

Haller, A. von
1936   Die Stadtmauer. In *Siebenter vorläufiger Bericht über die von der Deutchen Forschungsgemeinschaft in Uruk-Warka unternommenen Ausgrabungen*, edited by A. Nöldeke et al., pp. 41–45. Akademie der Wissenschaften in Komissionj bei W. Gruyter, Berlin.

Hallo, William W.
1971 Mesopotamia and the Asiatic Near East. In *The Ancient Near East*, edited by William W. Hallo and William K. Simpson. Harcourt, Brace, Jovanovich, New York.
1972 The House of Ur-Meme. *Journal of Near Eastern Studies* 31: 87–95.

Hammoudi, Khalid K
1989–1990 Excavations at Tell al-Dhuba'ee (in Arabic). *Sumer* 46: 91–111.

Hansen, Donald P.
1975 Frühsumerische und frühdynastische Flachbildkunst. In *Propylaean Kunstgeschichte*, Vol. 14, edited by Winfried Orthmann, pp. 179–193. Propylaean Verlag, Berlin.

Harper, Douglas
1987 *Working Knowledge: Skill and Community in a Small Shop*. University of Chicago.

Harper, Prudence O., Joan Aruz, and Françoise Tallon (editors)
1992 *The Royal City of Susa: Ancient Near Eastern Treasures in the Louvre*. Metropolitan Museum of Art, New York.

Harris, Rivkah
1975 *Ancient Sippar*. Nederlands Historisch-Archaeologisch Instituut te Istanbul, Istanbul.

Harrison, J. V.
1946 South-West Persia: A Survey of Pish-i-Kuh in Luristan. *The Geographical Journal* 108: 55–71.

Harrison, Timothy P.
2001 The Evidence for Aramaean Cultural Expansion in the Amuq Plain. In *Recherches Canadiennes sur la Syrie Antique*, edited by in Michel Fortin, pp. 135–144. Canadian Society for Mesopotamian Studies Bulletin 36, Toronto.

Hartmann, Joan R.
1994 *The Impact of Federal Programs on Wetlands*, Vol. II. *A Report to Congress by the Secretary of the Interior*. U.S. Department of the Interior, Arlington, Virginia.

Harvey, Michael D., and Stanley A. Schumm
1999 Indus River Dynamics and the Abandonment of Mohenjo Daro. In *The Indus River: Biodiversity, Resources, Humankind*, edited by Azra Meadows and Peter S. Meadows, pp. 333–348. Oxford University, Oxford.

Hauptmann, Andreas, Sigrid Schmitt-Strecker, Freidrich Begemmann, and Alberto Palmieri
2002 Chemical Composition and Lead Isotopy of Metal Objects from the "Royal" Tomb and Other Related Finds at Arslantepe, Eastern Anatolia. *Paléorient* 28 (2): 43–70.

Hawkins, John D.
1995 Great Kings and Country-Lords at Malatya and Karkamis. In *Studio Historiae Ardens. Ancient Near Eastern Studies Presented to Philo H. J. Houwink ten Cate on the Occasion of his 65th Birthday*, edited by Theo P. J. van den Hout and Johan de Roos, pp. 73–85. PIHANS 74. Nederlands Historisch-Archaeologisch Instituut, Istanbul.

Hawley, Amos H.
1986   *Human Ecology: A Theoretical Essay.* University of Chicago.
Headrick, Annabeth
1999   The Street of the Dead ... It Really Was: Mortuary Bundles at Teotihuacan. *Ancient Mesoamerica* 10: 69–85.
Hegde, Karunakara T. M.
1989   Boom Town: Harappa. *The Future Perfect 2001* (December): 19–22.
Hegde, Karunakara T. M., Kuldeep K. Bhan, V. H. Sonawane, K. Krishnan, and D. R. Shah
1990   *Excavation at Nageshwar, Gujarat: A Harappan Shell Working Site on the Gulf of Kutch.* Maharaja Sayajirao University Archaeology Series 18, Department of Archaeology and Ancient History, Baroda.
Hegde, Karunakara T. M., V. H. Sonawane, D. R. Shah, Kuldeep K. Bhan, Ajitprasad, K. Krishnan, and S. Pratapa Chandran.
1988   Excavation at Nagwada—1986 and 1987: A Preliminary Report. *Man and Environment* 12: 55–65.
Heim Suzanne
1992   Glazed Objects and the Elamite Glaze Industry. In *The Royal City of Susa: Ancient Near Eastern Treasures in the Louvre*, edited by Prudence O. Harper, Joan Aruz, and Françoise Tallon, pp. 202–210. Metropolitan Museum of Art, New York.
Heinrich, Ernst
1931   *Fara.* Staatlische Museen zu Berlin. Vorderasiatische abteilung, Berlin
1936   *Kleinfunde aus den archäischen Tempelschichten in Uruk.* Otto Harrassowitz, Leipzig.
1982   *Die Tempel und Heiligtümer im Alten Mesopotamien.* Verlag Walter De Gruyter, Berlin.
Heinz, Marlies
1992   *Tell Atchana/Alalakh: Die Schichten VII–XVII.* Alter Orient und Altes Testament Band 41. Verlag Butzon & Bercker Kevelaer. Neukirchener Verl, Neukirchen Verl.
Helbaek, Hans
1972   Samarran Irrigation Agriculture at Chogha Mami in Iraq. *Iraq* 34: 35–48.
Helms, Mary W.
1993   *Craft and the Kingly Ideal. Art, Trade and Power.* University of Texas, Austin.
Heltzer, Michael
1978   *Goods, Prices and the Organization of Trade in Ugarit.* Ludwig Reichert Verlag, Wiesbaden.
Helwing, Barbara
2003   Feste in Değirmentepe? Die Soziale Dynamik Des Feierns in Frühen Komplexen Gesellschaften. *Köyden Kente, Yakındoğu'da Ilk Yerleşimler*, edited by Mehmet Özdogan, Harald Hauptmann, and Nezih Basgelen, pp. 57–72. Arkeoloji ve Sanat Yayınları, Istanbul.

Henrickson, Elizabeth F.

1981   Non-religious Residential Settlement Patterning in the Late Early Dynastic of the Diyala Region. *Mesopotamia* 16: 43–140.

1982   Functional Analysis of Elite Residences in the Late Early Dynastic of the Diyala Region: House D and the Walled Quarter at Khafajah and the "Palaces" at Tell Asmar. *Mesopotamia* 17: 5–33.

1994   The Outer Limits: Settlement and Economic Strategies in the Central Zagros Highlands during the Uruk Era. In *Chiefdom and Early States in the Near East: Organizational Dynamics of Complexity*, edited by Gil Stein and Mitchell S. Rothman, pp. 85–102. Prehistory, Madison, Wisconsin.

Henrickson, Robert C.

1986   Regional Perspective on Godin III Cultural Development in Central Western Iran. *Iran* 24: 1–55.

Heras, Henry

1938   A Proto-Indian Sign from Vala. *Quarterly Journal of the Mythic Society* 28: 141–143.

Herodotus

1987   *The History*. Translated by David Grene. University of Chicago.

Herzfeld, Ernst

1923   *Der Wandschmuck der Bauten von Samarra und seine Ornamentik*. D. Reimer, Berlin.

1927   *Die Malereien von Samarra*. D. Reimer, Berlin.

1929–30 Bericht über archäologische Beobachtungen im südlichen Kurdistan und im Luristan. *Archäologische Mitteilungen aus Iran* 1: 65–75.

1930   *Die vorgeschichtlichen Töpfereien von Samarra*. D. Reimer, Berlin.

1948   *Geschichte der Stadt Samarra*. Eckardt & Messtorff, Hamburg.

Hicks, John R.

1969   *A Theory of Economic History*. Clarendon, Oxford.

Hill, Harold D., Thorkild Jacobsen, and Pinhas Delougaz

1990   *Old Babylonian Public Buildings in the Diyala Region*. Oriental Institute Publications 98. Oriental Institute, Chicago.

Hirth, Kenneth G.

1978   Interregional Trade and the Formation of Prehistoric Gateway Communities. *American Antiquity* 43: 35–45.

Hodder, Ian

1999   Symbolism at Çatalhöyük. In *World Prehistory: Studies in Memory of Grahame Clark*, edited by John Coles, Robert Bewley, and Paul Mellars, pp. 177–191. Proceedings of the British Academy 99. Oxford University Press, Oxford.

Hoffner, Harry A.

2001   Some Thoughts on Merchants and Trade in the Hittite Kingdom. In *Kulturgeschichten: Altorientalistische Studien für Volkert Haas zum 65. Geburtstag*, edited by Thomas Richter, Doris Prechel, and Jörg Klinger, pp. 179–189. Saarbrücker Druckerei und Verlag, Saarbrücken.

2002   The Treatment and Long-Term Use of Persons Captured in Battle According to the Maşat Texts. In *Recent Developments in Hittite Archaeology and History: Papers in Memory of Hans G. Güterbock*, edited by K. Aslıhan Yener and Harry A. Hoffner, pp. 61–72. Eisenbrauns, Winona Lake, Indiana.

Hole, Frank

1962   Archeological Survey and Excavation in Iran, 1961. *Science* 137: 524–526.

1983   Symbols of Religion and Social Organization at Susa. In *Beyond the Hilly Flanks*, edited by T. Cuyler Young, Philip E. L. Smith, and Peder Mortensen, pp. 315–344. Oriental Institute, Chicago.

1987a   Settlement and Society in the Village Period. In *The Archaeology of Western Iran*, edited by Frank Hole, pp. 29–78. Smithsonian Institution, Washington, DC.

1987b   *The Archaeology of Western Iran*. Smithsonian Institution, Washington, DC.

1987c   Chronologies in the Iranian Neolithic. In *Chronologies in the Near East*, International Series, Vol. 379, edited by O. Aurenche, J. Évin, and F. Hours, pp. 353–379. British Archaeological Reports, Oxford.

1994a   Environmental Instabilities and Urban Origins. In *Chiefdoms and Early States in the Near East: The Organizational Dynamics of Complexity*, edited by Gil Stein and Mitchell S. Rothman, pp. 121–151. Monographs in World Archaeology, No. 18. Prehistory, Madison, Wisconsin.

1994b   Interregional Aspects of the Khuzistan Aceramic-Early Pottery Neolithic Sequence. In *Neolithic Chipped Stone Industries of the Fertile Crescent*, edited by Hans G. K. Gebel and Stefan K. Kozlowski, pp. 101–116. Studies in Early Near Eastern Production, Subsistence, and Environment. *ex oriente*, Berlin.

1995   Assessing the Past through Anthropological Archaeology. In *Civilization of the Ancient Near East IV*, edited by Jack M. Sasson, pp. 2715–27. Scribners, New York.

1997   Paleoenvironment and Human Society in the Jezireh of Northern Mesopotamia 20,000–6,000 BP. *Paléorient* 23: 39–49.

1998a   Comment on *Cheating at Musical Chairs: Territoriality and Sedentism in an Evolutionary Context*, by Michael Rosenberg. *Current Anthropology* 39 (5): 670–671.

1998b   Paleoenvironment and Human Society in the Jezireh of Northern Mesopotamia 20,000–6,000 BP. *Paléorient* 23 (2): 39–49.

2001   A Radiocarbon Chronology for the Middle Khabur, Syria. *Iraq* 63: 1–31.

Hole, Frank, and Kent V. Flannery

1967   The Prehistory of Western Iran: A Preliminary Report. *Proceedings of the Prehistoric Society* 33(1): 147–206.

Hole, Frank, Kent V. Flannery, and James A. Neely

1969   *Prehistory and Human Ecology of the Deh Luran Plain*. Memoir, Museum of Anthropology 1. University of Michigan, Ann Arbor, Michigan.

Holl, Augustine
  2001   *The Land of Houlouf: Genesis of a Chadic Chiefdom.* International
           Monographs in Prehistory, Ann Arbor, Michigan.
Hopkins, Mary R.
  1987a   An Explication of the Plans of Some Teotihuacan Apartment Com-
           pounds. In *Teotihuacan: Nuevos Datos, Nuevas Síntesis, Nuevos Proble-
           mas,* edited by Emily McClung de Tapia and Evelyn C. Rattray, pp.
           369–388. Instituto de Investigaciones Antropológicas, Universidad
           Nacional Autónoma de México, Mexico City.
  1987b   Network Analysis of the Plans of Some Teotihuacan Apartment
           Compounds. *Environment and Planning B: Planning and Design* 14:
           387–406.
  1995   Teotihuacan Cooking Pots: Scale of Production and Product Vari-
           ability. Unpublished Ph.D. dissertation, Department of Anthropol-
           ogy, Brandeis University, Waltham, Massachusetts.
Houwink ten Cate, Philo H. J.
  1995   Ethnic Diversity and Population Movement in Anatolia. In *Civiliza-
           tions of the Ancient Near East,* edited by Jack M. Sasson, pp. 259–270.
           Charles Scribner's Sons, New York.
Hunt, Robert C.
  1987   The Role of Bureaucracy in the Provisioning of Cities: A Framework
           for Analysis of the Ancient Near East. In *The Organization of Power:
           Aspects of Bureaucracy in the Ancient Near East,* edited by McGuire
           Gibson and Robert D. Biggs, pp. 161–192. SAOC 46. Oriental Insti-
           tute, Chicago.
  2000   Labor Productivity and Agricultural Development: Boserup Revis-
           ited. *Human Ecology* 28 (2): 251–277.
Huot, Jean-Louis
  1983   *Larsa et Oueili campagnes 1978 et 1981: Rapport préliminaire.* Editions
           Recherche sur les Civilisations, Paris.
  1987   *Larsa et Oueili campagnes 1983: Rapport préliminaire.* Editions Recher-
           che sur les Civilisations, Paris.
  1989   *Larsa: Travaux de 1985.* Editions Recherche sur les Civilisations, Paris.
  1991   *'Oueili: Travaux de 1985.* Editions Recherche sur les Civilisations,
           Paris.
  1996   *Oueili: Travaux de 1987 et 1989.* Editions Recherche sur les Civilisa-
           tions, Paris.
Huot, Jean-Louis, Axel Rougeulle, and Joel Suire
  1989   La structure urbaine de Larsa. Une approche provoire. In *Larsa:
           Travaux de 1985,* pp. 19–52. Editions Recherche sur les Civilisations,
           Paris.
Ibn Khaldun
  1969   *The Muqaddimah.* Translated by Franz Rosenthal, edited and
           abridged by N. J. Dawood. Princeton University, Princeton, New
           Jersey.
Indian Archaeology, A Review
  1971–72 *Excavations at Somnath.* Archaeological Survey of India, Delhi.

1975–76 *Excavations at Somnath*. Archaeological Survey of India, Delhi.

1976–77 *Excavations at Somnath*. Archaeological Survey of India, Delhi.

Ingold, Tim
    1997   Eight Themes in the Anthropology of Technology. *Social Analysis* 41 (1): 106–138.

Insoll, Tim
    1999   *The Archaeology of Islam*. Blackwell, Oxford.

Iraq. Kingdom of Iraq, 1921–1958
    1956   *Major Irrigation Projects*. Departments of State and Public Institutions Development Board, Baghdad.

Jacobs, Jane
    1969   *The Economy of Cities*. Vintage, New York.
    2000   *The Nature of Economies*. Modern Library, New York.

Jacobsen, Thorkild
    1958   La géographie et les voies de communication du pays de Sumer. *Revue d'Assyriologie* 52: 127–129.
    1970 [1953] On the textile industry at Ur under Ibbi-Sin. In *Towards the Image of Tammuz*, edited by W. L. Moran, pp. 216–230. Harvard University, Cambridge.
    1976   *The Treasures of Darkness*. Yale University, New York.
    1993   Notes on the Word lú. In Kinattū ša dārâti: *Raphael Kutscher Memorial Volume*, edited by Anson F. Rainey, pp. 69–79. Tel Aviv Occasional Publications, No. 1. Institute of Archaeology, Tel Aviv.

Jacobsen, Thorkild, and Robert McC. Adams
    1958   Salt and Silt in Ancient Mesopotamian Agriculture. *Science* 12: 1251–1258.

Jansen, Michael R. N.
    1999   Mohenjo Daro and the River Indus. In *The Indus River: Biodiversity, Resources, Humankind*, edited by Azra Meadows and Peter S. Meadows, pp. 349–383. Oxford University, Oxford.

Jarrige, Catherine, Jean-Francois Jarrige, Richard H. Meadow, and Gonzaque Quivron
    1995   *Mehrgarh: Field Reports 1974–1985, from Neolithic Times to the Indus Civilization*. Department of Culture and Tourism of Sindh, Pakistan, Department of Archaeology and Museums, French Ministry of Foreign Affairs, Karachi.

Jarrige, Jean-Francois, and Monique Lechevallier
    1979   Excavations at Mehrgarh, Baluchistan: Their Significance in the Prehistorical Context of the Indo-Pakistani Borderlands. In *South Asian Archaeology 1977*, edited by Maurizio Taddei, pp. 463–535. Isituto Universitario Orientale, Naples.

Jasim, Sabah A.
    1985   *The Ubaid Period in Iraq. Recent Excavations in the Hamrin Region*. BAR International Series 267. British Archaeological Reports, Oxford.
    1989   Structure and Function in an 'Ubaid Village. In *Upon this Foundation—The 'Ubaid Reconsidered. Proceedings of the 'Ubaid Symposium, Elsinore 1988*, edited by Elizabeth F. Henrickson and Ingolf Thuesen, pp.79–88. Museum Tusculanum, Copenhagen.

Johnson, Gregory A.
1973   *Local Exchange and Early State Development in Southwestern Iran.* Museum of Anthropology Anthropological Papers No. 51. University of Michigan, Ann Arbor.
1980   Spatial Organization of Early Uruk Settlement Systems. In *L'Archeologie de l'Iraq*, edited by M. T. Barrelet, pp. 233–263. Colloques Internationaux du CNRS. Editions du C.N.R.S., Paris
1988–89 Late Uruk in Greater Mesopotamia: Expansion or Collapse? *Origini* 14: 595–612.

Jones, Emrys
1965   *Human Geography: An Introduction to Man and His World.* Frederick A. Praeger, New York.

Jorgensen, D. W., Michael D. Harvey, Stanley A. Schumm, and Louis Flam
1993   Morphology and Dynamics of the Indus River: Implications for the Mohen Jo Daro Site. In *Himalaya to the Sea: Geology, Geomorphology and the Quaternary*, edited by John F. Shroder, pp. 288–326. Routledge, London.

Joshi, Jagat Pati
1984   Harappa Culture: Emergence of a new picture. *Puratattva* 13–14: 51–54.
1990   *Excavation at Surkotada 1971–72 and Exploration in Kutch.* Memoirs of the Archaeological Survey of India 87. Archaeological Survey of India, New Delhi.

Joyce, Rosemary A., and Susan Gillespie (editors)
2000   *Beyond Kinship: Social and Material Reproduction in House Societies.* University of Pennsylvania, Philadelphia.

Kaelin, Oskar
1999   *Ein assyrisches Bildexperiment nach Ägyptischem Vorbild: Zu Planung und Ausführung der "Schlacht am Ulai".* Alter Orient und Altes Testament, Vol. 226. Ugarit-Verlag, Münster.

Kaptan, Ergun
2005   Açana'da M.O. 2. Binyılla ait Bakır Ingotlar [2nd Millennium BC Copper Ingots from Atchana] 20. *Arkeometri Sonuçları Toplantısı*, 5-12. General Directorate for Cultural Heritage and Museums, Ankara.

Kasarda, John D.
1974   The Structural Implications of Social System Size: A Three Level Analysis. *American Sociological Review* 39: 19–28.

Kawami, Trudy
2001   The Cattle of Uruk: Stamp Seals and Animal Husbandry in the Late Uruk/Jemdet Nasr Period, In *Seals and Seal Impressions: Proceedings of the XLVe Rencontre Assyriologique Internationale, Part II*, edited by William W. Hallo and Irene J. Winter, pp. 31–48. CDL, Bethesda, Maryland.

Kazmi, Ali H., and Riaz A. Rana
1982   *Tectonic Map of Pakistan.* Geological Survey of Pakistan, Quetta.

Kemp, Barry
2000   Bricks and Metaphor. *Cambridge Archaeological Journal* 10 (2): 335–346.

Kempinski-Lecomte, Christine
1992   *Haradum I: Une ville nouvelle sur le Moyen-Euphrate (XVIIIe–XVIIe siècles av. J-C)*. Éditions Recherche sur les Civilisations, Paris.
Kenoyer, Jonathan M.
1990   Shell Artifacts from Lagash, al-Hiba. *Sumer* 46: 64–66.
1991a   Urban Process in the Indus Tradition: A Preliminary Model from Harappa. In *Harappa Excavations 1986–1990: A Multidisciplinary Approach to Third Millennium Urbanism*, edited by Richard H. Meadow, pp. 29–60. Prehistory, Madison, Wisconsin.
1991b   The Indus Tradition of Pakistan and Western India. *Journal of World Prehistory* 5 (4): 331–385.
1998   *Ancient Cities of the Indus Valley Civilization*. Oxford University, Oxford.
Kervran, Monik
1985   Transformations de la ville de Suse et de son économie de l'époque sasanide à l'époque abbaside. *Paléorient* 11: 91–100.
Khan, Fazle K.
1991   *Geography of Pakistan*. Oxford University, Oxford.
Klengel, Horst
1979   Die Palastwirtschaft in Alalah. In *State and Temple Economy in the Ancient Near East*, Vol. 2, edited by in Edward Lipinski, pp. 435–57. OLA 6. Departement *Oriëntalstiek, Katholieke* Universiteit Leuven, Leuven.
1992   *Syria 3000 to 300 B. C.: A Handbook of Political History*. Akademie Verlag, Berlin.
Klinger, J.
1995   Das Corpus der Maşat Briefe un seine Beziehungen zu den Texten aus Hattusa. *Zeitschrift für Assyriologie* 85: 74–108.
Kohl, Philip
1987   The Ancient Economy, Transferable Technologies and the Bronze Age World-System: A View from the Northeastern Frontier of the Ancient Near East. In *Centre and Periphery in the Ancient World*, edited by Michael Rowlands, Mogens T. Larsen, and Kristian Kristiansen, pp. 13–24. Cambridge University, Cambridge.
Košak, Silvin
1982   *Hittite Inventory Texts* (CTH 241–50). Carl Winter Verlag, TdH, 10, Heidelberg.
1985   The Gospel of Iron. In *Kanissuwar: A Tribute to H.G. Guterbock on His 75th Birthday*, edited by Harry A. Hoffner and Gary M. Beckman, pp. 125–135. University of Chicago.
Koucher, Adnan
1999   *State and Society. The Question of Agrarian Change in Iraq 1921–1991*. Verlag für Entwicklungspolitik, Saarbrücken.
Kouchoukos, Nicholas
1998   Landscape and Social Change in Late Prehistoric Mesopotamia. Unpublished Ph.D. dissertation, Department of Anthropology, Yale University, New Haven, Connecticut.

Kozlowski, Stefan K.
1994   Chipped Neolithic Industries at the Eastern Wing of the Fertile Crescent. In *Neolithic Chipped Stone Industries of the Fertile Crescent*, Vol. 1, edited by Hans G. K. Gebel and Stefan K. Kozlowski, pp. 143–171. *ex oriente*, Berlin.
1998   *The Eastern Wing of the Fertile Crescent. Later Prehistory of Greater Mesopotamian Lithic Industires*. BAR International Series, Oxford.

Krugman, Paul
1991   Increasing Returns in Economic Geography. *The Journal of Political Economy* 99: 483–499.
1995   *Development, Geography, and Economic Theory*. MIT, Cambridge, Massachusetts.
1996   Confronting the Mystery of Urban Hierarchy. *Journal of the Japanese and International Economies* 10: 399–418.
1998   What's New about the New Economic Geography. *Oxford Review of Economic Policy* 14: 7–17.

Kuhrt, Amélie
1995   *The Ancient Near East, c. 3000–330 BC*. Routledge, London.

Kus, Susan M., and Victor Raharijaona
1998   Between Earth and Sky There Are Only a Few Large Boulders: Sovereignty and Monumentality in Central Madagascar. *Journal of Anthropological Archaeology* 17: 53–79.
2000   House to Palace, Village to State: Scaling Up Architecture and Ideology. *American Anthropologist* 102 (1): 98–113.

Lambeck, Karl
1996   *Shoreline Reconstructions for the Persian Gulf since the Last Glacial Maximum*. Earth and Planetary Science Letters. Springer, Berlin.

Lambrick, H. T.
1967   The Indus Flood-Plain and the "Indus" Civilization. *The Geographical Journal* 133: 483–495.

Lapidus, Ira
1984 *Muslim Cities in the Later Middle Ages*. Cambridge University, Cambridge.

Larsen, Mogens T.
1976   *The Old Assyrian City State and Its Colonies*. Akademisk Forlag, Copenhagen.

Lattimore, Owen
1940   *Inner Asian Frontiers of China*. American Geographical Society Research Series No. 21. American Geographical Society, New York.
1962   *Studies in Frontier History*. Oxford University, London.
1979   Geography and the Ancient Empires. In *Power and Propaganda: A Symposium on Ancient Empires*, edited by Mogens T. Larsen, pp. 35–40. Mesopotamia: Copenhagen Studies in Assyriology No. 7. Akademisk Forlag, Copenhagen.

Lawler, Andrew
2001   New Digs Draw Applause and Concern. *Science* 293: 38–41.
2006   North versus South Mesopotamian Style. *Science* 312: 1458–1463.

Layard, Austen Henry
1894   Description of the Province of Khuzistan. *The Geographical Journal*
16: 1-125.
Le Brun, Alain
1971   Recherches stratigraphiques à l'acropole de Suse, 1969–71. *Cahiers de
la Délégation Archéologique Française en Iran* 1: 163–216.
1978   Le niveau 17B de l'Acropole de Suse (campagne de1972). *Cahiers de
la Délégation Archéologique Française en Iran* 9: 57–154.
1985   Le niveau 18 de l'Acropole de Suse. Mémoire d'argile, mémoire du
temps. *Paléorient* 11 (2): 31–36
Le Brun, Alain, and François Vallat
1978   L'origine de l'écriture à Suse. *Cahiers de la Délégation Archéologique
Française en Iran* 9: 11–59.
Lechtman, Heather
1984   Andean Value Systems and the Development of Prehistoric Metallurgy. *Technology and Culture* 25: 1–36.
1988   Traditions and Styles in Central Andean Metalworking. In *The Beginning of the Use of Metals and Alloys*, edited by Robert Maddin, pp. 344–
378. MIT, Cambridge, Massachusetts.
Leemans, Wilhelmus F.
1960   *Foreign Trade in the Old Babylonian Period*. E. J. Brill, Leiden.
1982   The Pattern of Settlement in the Babylonian Countryside. In *Societies and
Languages of the Ancient Near East: Studies in Honour of I. M. Diakonoff*, edited
by J. Nicholas Postgate et al., pp. 246–49. Aris & Phillips, Warminster.
Leisten, T.
2003   *Excavations at Samarra*, Vol. 2: *Architecture, Final Report of the First
Campaign, 1910–1912*. Philipp von Zabern, Mainz am Rhein.
Lemcke, G., and M. Sturm
1997 δ^{18}O and Trace Element Measurements as Proxy for the Reconstruction
of Climate Changes at Lake Van (Turkey): Preliminary Results. In *Third
Millennium BC Climate Change and Old World Collapse*, edited by H.
Nüzhet Dalfes, George Kukla, and Harvey Weiss. Springer, Berlin.
Lemonnier, Pierre
1986   The Study of Material Culture Today: Toward an Anthropology of
Technical Systems. *Journal of Anthropological Archaeology* 5: 147–186.
1993   *Technological Choices. Transformation in Material Culture since the
Neolithic*. Routledge, New York.
Lenski, Gerhard
1979   Directions and Continuities in Societal Growth. In *Societal Growth*,
edited by Amos H. Hawley, pp. 5–18. Free Press, New York.
Lenzen, Heinrich J.
1941   *Die Entwicklung der Zikurrat: von ihren Anfängen bis zur Zeit der III.
Dynastie von Ur*. O. Harrassowitz, Leipzig.
Leshnik, Lawrence S., and Gunther D. Sontheimer (editors)
1975   *Pastoralists and Nomads in South Asia*. Schriftenreihe de Sudasien
Institute der Universitat Heidelberg. Otto Harrassowitz, Wiesbaden.

Levine, Louis D.
  1987   The Iron Age. In *The Archaeology of Western Iran*, edited by Frank Hole, pp. 229–250. Smithsonian Institution, Washington, DC.

Levine, Louis D., and Mary M. A. McDonald
  1977   The Neolithic and Chalcolithic Periods in the Mahidasht. *Iran* 15: 39–50.

Levine, Louis D., and T. Cuyler Young, Jr.
  1987   A Summary of the Ceramic Assemblages of the Central Western Zagros from the Middle Neolithic to the Late Third Millennium B.C. In *Préhistoire de la Mésopotamie*, edited by Jean-Louis Huot, pp. 15–53. Éditions du CNRS, Paris.

Lieberman, Stephen
  1980   Of Clay Pebbles, Hollow Clay Balls, and Writing: A Sumerian View. *American Journal of Archaeology* 84: 339–358.

Lightfoot, Kent G., and Antoinette Martinez
  1995   Frontiers and Boundaries in Archaeological Perspective. *Annual Review of American Anthropology and Archaeology* 24: 471–492.

Lightfoot, Kent G., Antoinette Martinez, and Ann M. Schiff
  1998   Daily Practice and Material Culture in Pluralistic Social settings: An Archaeological Study of Culture Change and Persistence from Fort Ross, California. *American Antiquity* 63: 199–222.

Linné, Sigvald
  1942   *Mexican Highland Cultures*. The Ethnographical Museum of Sweden, Stockholm.

Liverani, Mario
  1987   The Collapse of the Near Eastern Regional System at the End of the Bronze Age: The Case of Syria. In *Centre and Periphery in the Ancient World*, edited by Michael Rowlands, Mogens T. Larsen, and Kristian Kristiansen, pp. 66–73. Cambridge University, Cambridge.
  1999   The Role of the Village in Shaping the Ancient Near Eastern Rural Landscape. In *Landscapes: Territories, Frontiers and Horizons in the Ancient Near East*, Part 1, edited by Lucio Milano et al., pp. 37–47. History of the Ancient Near East, Monographs III/1. Sargon, Padova.

Lloyd, Seton, and Fuad Safar
  1943   Tell Uqair: Excavations by the Iraq Government Directorate of Antiquities in 1940 and 1941. *Journal of Near Eastern Studies* 2: 131–158.
  1948   Eridu: Preliminary Communication on the Second Season's Excavations: 1947–1948. *Sumer* 4: 115–127, 276–283.

Lösch, August
  1954 [1940] *The Economics of Location*. Translated by William H. Woglom and Wolfgang F. Stolper. Yale University, New Haven, Connecticut.

Luby, Edward M.
  1990   Social Variation in Ancient Mesopotamia: An Architectural and Mortuary Analysis of Ur in the Early Second Millennium B.C. Unpublished Ph.D. dissertation, Department of Anthropology, State University of New York at Stony Brook.

Lupton, Alan
1996 *Stability and Change. Socio-political Development in North Mesopotamia and Southeast Anatolia 4000–2700 BC.* BAR International Series 627. British Archaeological Reports, Oxford.
Lyons, Claire, and John Papadopoulos (editors)
2002 *The Archaeology of Colonialism.* Getty Research Institute, Los Angeles.
Macfayden, W. A.
1938 *Water Supplies in Iraq.* Government of Iraq, Ministry of Economics and Communication, Geological Department, Baghdad.
1969 Prehistoric Settlement Pattern in Mesopotamia. *Final Proceedings of Man, Settlement and Urban Development, Research Seminar in Archaeology and Related Subjects*, pp. 229–309. London.
Mack, Alexandra
2002 *Spiritual Journey, Imperial City: Pilgrimage to the Temples of Vijayanagara.* Vedams, New Delhi.
Mackay, Dorothy
1945 Ancient River Beds and Dead Cities. *Antiquity* 19: 135–144.
Maddin, Robert, James D. Muhly, and Jane Waldbaum
1983 Metallurgical Analysis of an Early Iron Age Laminated Iron Tool. In *Metalwork from Sardis: The Finds through 1974*, edited by Jane Waldbaum, pp. 178–180. Harvard University, Cambridge, Massachusetts.
Maekawa, Kazuya
1980 Female Weavers and Their Children in Lagash—Presargonic and Ur III. *Acta Sumerologica* 2: 81–125.
Magness-Gardiner, Bonnie
1994 Urban-Rural Relations in Bronze Age Syria: Evidence from Alalah Level VII Palace Archives. In *Archaeological Views from the Countryside: Village Communities in Early Complex Societies*, edited by Glenn M. Schwartz and Steven E. Falconer, pp. 37–47. Smithsonian Institution, Washington, DC.
Majidzadeh, Yousef
1992 The Arjan Bowl. *Iran* 30: 131–144.
Majumdar, Abhijit
1994 Disposal of the Dead During the Chalcolithic Period of Gujarat (A Study of Harappan Burial Customs). Master's thesis, Department of Archaeology and Ancient History, Maharaja Sayajirao University of Baroda.
Malbran-Labat, Florence
1995 *Les inscriptions royales de Suse: Briques de l'époque Paléo-Élamite à l'Empire Néo-Élamite.* Réunion des musées nationaux, Paris.
Malecki, Edward J.,
1997 *Technology and Economic Development: The Dynamics of Local, Regional, and National Competitiveness*, 2nd edition. Longman, Essex.
Mallowan, Max E. L., and J. Cruikshank Rose
1935 Excavations at Tell Arpachiyah, 1933. *Iraq* 2: 1–178.
Man, John
2004 *Genghis Khan: Life, Death and Resurrection.* Bantam Books, London.

Mann, Michael E., and Raymond S. Bradley.
    1998   Global Climate Variations over the Past 250 Years, Relationships
             with the Middle East. In *Transformations of Middle Eastern Natural
             Environments: Legacies and Lessons*, edited by Jeff Albert, Magnus
             Bernhardson, and Roger Kenna, pp. 429–443. Yale University, New
             Haven, Connecticut.

Manning, Sturt W., Bernd Kromer, Peter I. Kuniholm, and Maryanne W.
Newton
    2001   Anatolian Tree Rings and a New Chronology for the East Mediterra-
             nean Bronze-Iron Ages. *Science* 294: 2532–2535.

Manzanilla, Linda (editor)
    1993   *Anatomía de un conjunto residencial teotihuacano en Oztoyahualco*. Insti-
             tuto de Investigaciones Antropológicas, Universidad Nacional
             Autónoma de México, Mexico City.
    1996   Corporate Groups and Domestic Activities at Teotihuacan. *Latin
             American Antiquity* 7 (3): 228–246.

Marcus, Joyce
    1998   The Peaks and Valleys of Ancient States: An Extension of the
             Dynamic Model. In *Archaic States*, edited by Gary M. Feinman and
             Joyce Marcus, pp. 59–94. School of American Research, Santa Fe,
             New Mexico.

Margueron, Jean
    1982   *Recherches sur les palais mésopotamiens de l'Age du Bronze*. Librairie ori-
             entaliste Paul Geuthner, Paris.

Marshall, John U.
    1989   *The Structure of Urban Systems*. University of Toronto.

Martindale, Don
    1958   Prefatory Remarks: The Theory of the City. In *The City*, edited by
             Max Weber, pp. 9–62. Free Press, New York.

Masry, Abdullah H.
    1974   *Prehistory in Northeastern Arabia: The Problem of Interregional Interac-
             tion*. Field Research Project, Coconut Grove, Florida.

Matthews, Roger
    2000   Time with the Past in Paphlagonia. In *Proceedings of the First Interna-
             tional Congress on the Archaeology of the Ancient Near East*, edited by
             Paolo Matthiae, A. Enea, Luca Peyronel, and Frances Pinnock, pp.
             1013–1027. Università degli Studi di Roma "La Sapienza," Rome.

Matthews, Roger, T. Pollard, and M. Ramage
    1998   Project Paphlagonia: Regional Survey in Northern Anatolia. In
             *Ancient Anatolia: Fifty Years' Work by the British Institute of Archaeology
             at Anakra*, edited by Roger Matthews, pp. 195–206. British Institute
             of Archaeology at Anakara, London.

Matthews, Roger, J. Nicholas Postgate, and Edward Luby
    1987   Excavations at Abu Salabikh 1985–6. *Iraq* 49: 91–119.

Matthews, Wendy, J. Nicholas Postgate, Sebastian Payne, Michael P. Charles, and Keith Dobney
 1994   The Imprint of Living in an Early Mesopotamian City: Questions and Answers. In *Whither Environmental Archaeology?*, edited by Rosemary Luff and Peter Rowley-Conwy, pp. 171–212. Oxbow Books, Oxford.

Maxwell-Hyslop, Rachel
 1972   The Metals Amutu and Asi'u in the Kultepe Texts. *Anatolian Studies* 22: 159–162.

McCalley, David
 1999   *The Everglades. An Environmental History.* University of Florida, Gainesville.

McClellan, Thomas L.
 1989   The Chronology and Ceramic Assemblages of Alalakh. In *Essays in Ancient Civilization Presented Helene J. Kantor*, edited by Albert Leonard, Jr. and Bruce B. Williams, pp. 181–212. SAOC 47. University of Chicago.

McCorriston, Joy
 1997   The Fiber Revolution: Textile Extensification, Alienation, and Social Stratification in Ancient Mesopotamia. *Current Anthropology* 38: 517–549.
 1999   Syrian Origins of Safflower Production: New Discoveries in the Agrarian Prehistory of the Habur Basin. In *Proceedings of the International Symposium on the Origins of Agriculture, Aleppo, Syria*, edited by A. B. Damania, J. Valkoun, George Willcox, and C. O. Qualset, pp. 39–50. ICARDA, IPGRI, FAO, and GRCP, Aleppo, Rome, and Davis, California.
 2001   Comment. *Current Anthropology* 42: 221–222.

McCown, Donald E., and Richard C. Haines
 1967   *Nippur I: Temple of Enlil, Scribal Quarter, and Soundings.* University of Chicago.

McDonald, Mary M. A.
 1979   An Examination of Mid-Holocene Settlement Patterns in the Central Zagros Region of Western Iran. Unpublished Ph.D. dissertation, Department of Anthropology, University of Toronto.

McGuire, Randall
 1983   Breaking Down Cultural Complexity: Inequality and Heterogeneity. In *Advances in Archaeological Method and Theory* 6, edited by Michael Schiffer, pp. 91–142. Academic, New York.

Meade, Clare Goff
 1968   Luristan in the First Half of the First Millennium B.C. *Iran* 6: 105–134.

Meadow, Richard H.
 1991   *Harappa Excavations 1986–1990: A Multidisciplinary Approach to Third Millennium Urbanism.* Monographs in World Archaeology, 3. Prehistory, Madison, Wisconsin.

Meadow, Richard H., Jonathan M. Kenoyer, and Rita P. Wright
   1997   *Harappa Archaeological Research Project: 1997 Excavations.* Submitted
              to the Director-General, Department of Archaeology and Museums,
              Government of Pakistan.
   2001   *Harappa Archaeological Research Project: Harappa Excavations 2000 and
              2001.* Submitted to the Director-General, Archaeology and Muse-
              ums, Government of Pakistan.
Mehta, Ramanlal N.
   1984   Valabhi—A Station of Harappan Cattle Breeders. In *Frontiers of the
              Indus Civilization*, edited by Braj B. Lal and Swarajya P. Gupta, pp.
              227–30. Books and Books, Delhi.
Meldgaard, Jørgen, Peder Mortensen, and Henrik Thrane
   1964   Excavations at Tepe Guran, Luristan. *Acta Archaeologica* 34: 97–133.
Mellaart, James
   1974   Western Anatolia, Beycesultan and the Hittites. In *Mansel'e
              Armağan/ Mélanges Mansel 1*, pp. 493–526. Türk Tarih Kurumu
              Yayıyınları No. Dizi 7- Sa. 60. Türk Tarih Kurumu, Ankara.
   1975   *The Neolithic of the Near East.* Thames and Hudson, London.
   1982   Mesopotamian Relations with the West, including Anatolia. In *Meso-
              potamien und seine Nachbarn*, edited by H. Nissen and J. Renger, pp.
              7–12. Berliner Beiträge zum vorderen Orient, Berlin.
Merpert, Nikolaĭ I., and Rauf M. Munchaev
   1993   Yarim Tepe III: The Ubaid Levels. In *Early Stages in the Evolution of
              Mesopotamian Civilization: Soviet Excavations in Northern Iraq*, edited
              by Norman Yoffee and Jeffery J. Clark, pp. 225–240. University of
              Arizona, Tucson.
Metab, Amel
   1989–90 Excavation of Tell Mohammed (in Arabic). *Sumer* 46: 127–160.
Mian, M. A., and M. N. Syal
   1986   Geomorphology of Pakistan. In *Proceedings of the XII International
              Forum on Soil Taxonomy and Agrotechnology Transfer, Pakistan*, edited
              by Mushtaq Ahmad, M. Akram, M. S. Baig, M. Y. Javed and R.-ul-
              Amin. Director General, Soil Survey of Pakistan, Lahore.
Michalowski, Piotr
   1989   *The Lamentation over the Destruction of Sumer and Ur.* Mesopotamian
              Civilizations 1. Eisenbrauns, Winona Lake, Indiana.
   1990   Early Mesopotamian Communicative Systems: Art, Literature, and Writ-
              ing. In *Investigating Artistic Environments in the Ancient Near East*, edited by
              Ann C. Gunter, pp. 53–69. Smithsonian Institution, Washington, DC.
Miller, Naomi
   1998   The Macrobotanical Evidence for Vegetation in the Near East, c.
              18,000/16,000 BC to 4,000 BC. *Paléorient* 23 (2): 197–207.
   2000   Plant Forms in Jewellery from the Royal Cemetery at Ur. *Iraq* 62:
              149–155.
Miller-Rosen, Arlene
   1995   Analytical Techniques in Near Eastern Archaeology, Phytolith Anal-
              ysis. *Biblical Archaeologist* 58 (3): 170.

Miller-Rosen, Arlene, and Stephen Weiner
   1994   Identifying Ancient Irrigation—A New Method Using Opaline Phytoliths from Emmer Wheat. *Journal of Archaeological Science* 21 (1): 125–132.

Millon, Clara
   1973   Painting, Writing, and Polity in Teotihuacan, Mexico. *American Antiquity* 38 (3): 294–314.

Millon, René
   1960   The Beginnings of Teotihuacan. *American Antiquity* 26 (1): 1–10.
   1973   *The Teotihuacan Map*. Part 1: *Text*. University of Texas, Austin.
   1976   Social Relations in Ancient Teotihuacan. In *The Valley of Mexico: Studies in Pre-Hispanic Ecology and Society*, edited by Eric R. Wolf, pp. 205–248. University of New Mexico, Albuquerque.
   1981   Teotihuacan: City, State, and Civilization. In *Supplement to the Handbook of Middle American Indians*, Vol. 1: *Archaeology*, edited by Jeremy A. Sabloff, pp. 198–243. University of Texas, Austin.
   1988   Where *Do* They All Come From? The Provenance of the Wagner Murals from Teotihuacan. In *Feathered Serpents and Flowering Trees: Reconstructing the Murals of Teotihuacan*, edited by Kathleen Berrin, pp. 78–113. The Fine Arts Museums of San Francisco.
   1992   Teotihuacan Studies: From 1950 to 1990 and Beyond. In *Art, Ideology, and the City of Teotihuacan*, edited by Janet C. Berlo, pp. 339–429. Dumbarton Oaks, Washington, DC.

Millon, René, and James A. Bennyhoff
   1961   A Long Architectural Sequence at Teotihuacan. *American Antiquity* 26 (4): 516–523.

Millon, René, R. Bruce Drewitt, and George L. Cowgill
   1973   *The Teotihuacan Map*. Part 2: *Maps*. University of Texas, Austin.

Minnis, Paul E.
   1985   *Social Adaptation to Food Stress: A Prehistoric Southwestern Example*. University of Chicago.

Misra, Virendra N.
   1973   Bagor: A Late Mesolithic Settlement in North-West India. *World Archaeology* 5 (1): 92–100.
   1995   Evolution of Environment and Culture in the Rajasthan Desert during the Late Quaternary. In *Ancient Peoples and Landscapes*, edited by Eileen Johnson, pp. 77–104. Museum of Texas Tech University, Lubbock.

Mokyr, Joel
   1996   Evolution and Technological Change: A New Metaphor for Economic History. In *Technological Change: Methods and Themes in the History of Technology*, edited by Robert Fox, pp. 63–84. Hardwood Academic Publishers, Amsterdam.

Montagne, C., and Françoise Grillot-Susini
   1996   Les inscriptions royales de Suse, Musée du Louvre. *Nouvelles Assyriologiques Brèves et Utilitaires (N.A.B.U.)* 33: 24–25.

Moorey, P. R. S.
   1971   *Catalogue of the Ancient Persian Bronzes in the Asmolean Museum*. Claredon, Oxford.

1982 *Ur of the Chaldes*. Herbert, London.
1994 *Ancient Mesopotamian Materials and Industries: The Archaeological Evidence*. Clarendon, Oxford.
Moortgat, Anton
1940 *Vorderasiatische Rollsiegel*. Gebr. Mann, Berlin.
1950 *Geschichte Vorderasiens bis zum Hellenismus*. Bruchmann, München.
1969 *The Art of Ancient Mesopotamia: The Classical Art of the Near East*. Phaidon, London.
Moran, William L.
1992 *The Amarna Letters*. Johns Hopkins University, Baltimore.
Morelos García, Noel
1993 *Proceso de producción de espacios y estructuras en Teotihuacan: Conjunto Plaza Oeste y Complejo Calle de los Muertos*. Instituto Nacional de Antropología e Historia, Mexico City.
Morgan, Jacques de
1894 *Mission Scientifique en Perse*. Leroux, Paris.
Morony, Michael G.
1994 Land Use and Settlement Patterns in Late Sasanian and Early Islamic Iraq. In *The Byzantine and Early Islamic Near East*, II: *Land Use and Settlement Patterns*, edited by G. King and A. Cameron, pp. 221–229. Darwin, Princeton, New Jersey.
Morris, Ian
1991 The Early Polis as City and State. In *City and Country in the Ancient World*, edited by John Rich and Andrew Wallace-Hadrill, pp. 25–57. Leicester-Nottingham Studies in Ancient Society 2. Routledge, London.
Mortensen, Inge Demant, and Ida Nicolaisen
1993 *Nomads of Luristan: History, Material Culture, and Pastoralism in Western Iran*. Thames and Hudson, London.
Mortensen, Peder
1963 Early Village Occupation: Excavations at Tepe Guran, Luristan. *Acta Archaeologica* 34: 110–121.
1975 Survey and Soundings in the Holailan Valley 1974. In *Proceedings of the IIIrd Annual Symposium on Archaeological Research in Iran*, edited by Firouz Bagherzaden, pp. 1–12. Iranian Center for Archaeological Research, Teheran.
Mudar, Karen
1982 Early Dynastic III Animal Utilization in Lagash: A Report on the Fauna of Tell al-Hiba. *Journal of Near Eastern Studies* 41: 23–63.
Mughal, M. Rafiq
1982 Recent Archaeological Research in the Cholistan Desert. In *Harappan Civilization: A Contemporary Perspective*, edited by Gregory L. Possehl, pp. 85–95. Oxford-IBH and the American Institute of Indian Studies, Delhi.
1989 The Development of Protohistoric Research in Pakistan: 1970–85. *Journal of Central Asia* 12 (1): 47–77.
1990 The Protohistoric Settlement Patterns in the Cholistan Desert. In *South Asian Archaeology 1987*, edited by Maurizio Taddei, pp. 143–156.

430 SETTLEMENT AND SOCIETY

Instituto Italiano per il Medio ed Estremo Oriente, Serie
Orientale Roma, 66 (1). Rome.

1992   Jhukar and the Late Harappan Cultural Mosaic of the Greater Indus
Valley. In *South Asian Archaeology 1989*, edited by Catherine Jarrige,
pp. 213–222. Monographs in World Archaeology 14. Prehistory,
Madison, Wisconsin.

1997   *Ancient Cholistan: Archaeology and Architecture*. Ferozsons, Lahore.

Mughal, M. Rafique, F. Iqbal, M. Afzal Khan, and M. Hassan

1996   Archaeological Sites and Monuments in Punjab: Preliminary Results
of Explorations: 1992–1996. *Pakistan Archaeology* 29: 1–474.

Muhly, James D., Robert Maddin, Tamara Stech, and Engin Özgen

1985   Iron in Anatolia and the Nature of the Hittite Iron Industry. *Anatolian Studies* 35: 65–84.

Müller-Karpe, Andreas

1994   *Altanatolisches Metallhandwerk*. Offa-Bücher Band 75. Wachholtz
Verlag, Neumünster.

Muscarella, Oscar

1981   Surkh Dum at the Metropolitan Museum of Art: A Mini Report.
Journal of Field Archaeology 81: 327–359.

Myrdal, Gunnar

1957   *Economic Theory and Under-Developed Regions*. Duckworth, London.

Na'aman, Nadav

1981   The Recycling of a Silver Statue. *Journal of Near Eastern Studies* 40:
47–48.

Nanavati, Jayendra M., Ramanlal N. Mehta, and S. N. Chowdhary

1971   *Somnath—1956*. Monograph 1. Department of Archaeology, Gujarat
State and Department of Archaeology and Ancient History, Maharaja
Sayajirao University, Gujarat.

National Aeronautics and Space Administration

2000   Vanishing Marshes of Mesopotamia. Electronic document,
*http://earthobservatory.nasa.gov/Newsroom/NewImages/images.
php3?img_id=5112*, accessed June 26, 2002.

2001   Vanishing Marshes of Mesopotamia. Electronic document, *http://
visibleearth.nasa.gov/cgi-bin/viewrecord?9687*, accessed June 26, 2002.

Naumann, Rudolf

1971   *Architektur Kleinasiens von ihren Anfaengen bis zum Ende der hetitischen
Zeit*. Ernst Wasmuth. Deutsches Archaeologisches Institut,
Tübingen.

Neef, Reinder

1989   Plant Remains from Archaeological Sites in Lowland Iraq: Tell
el'Oueili. In *Larsa: Travaux de 1985*, edited by Jean-Louis Huot, pp.
321–329. Editions Recherche sur les Civilisations, Paris.

Neu, Eric

1983   Überlieferung und Datierung der Kaškäer-Verträge. In *Beiträge zur
Altertumskunde Kleinasiens: Festschrift für Kurt Bittel*, Vol. 1, edited by
Rainer Michael Boehmer and Harald Hauptmann, pp. 391–399.
Philipp von Zabern, Mainz am Rhein.

Neumann, J., and Simo Parpola
    1987   Climatic Change and Eleventh–Tenth-Century Eclipse of Assyria
              and Babylonia. *Journal of Near Eastern Studies* 46: 161–182.
Nishiaki, Yoshihiro, M. Tao, Seiji Kadowaki, Masami Abe, and H. Tano
    2001   Excavations in Sector A of Tell Kosak Shamali; The Statigraphy and
              Architectures. In *Tell Kosak Shamali: Archaeological Investigations on the
              Upper Euphrates Syria*. Vol. 1: *Chalcolithic Architecture and Earlier Pre-
              historic Remains*, edited by Yoshihiro Nishiaki and Toshio Matsutani,
              pp. 49–113. Oxbow Books in association with The University and
              The University Museum, Tokyo.
Nissen, Hans J.
    1970   Grabung in den Quadraten K/L XII in Uruk-Warka. *Baghdader Mit-
              teilungen* 5: 101–191.
    1972   The City Wall of Uruk. In *Man, Settlement and Urbanism*, edited by
              Peter J. Ucko, Ruth Tringham, and Geoffrey W. Dimbleby, pp. 793–
              798. Gerald Duckworth, London.
    1974   Zur Frage der Arbeitsorganistion in Babylonien während der Spät-
              uruk-Zeit. In *Wirschaft und Gessellschaft in Alten Vorderasien*, edited by J.
              Harmatta and G. Komaróczy, pp. 5–14. Akadémiai Kiadó, Budapest.
    1985   Ortsnamen in den archaischen Texten aus Uruk. *Orientalia* 54: 226–233.
    1986a   The Development of Writing and Glyptic Art. In *Gemdet Nasr:
              Period or Regional Style?*, edited by Uwe Finkbeiner and Wolfgang
              Röllig, pp. 316–331. Ludwig Reichert Verlag, Weisbaden.
    1986b   The Archaic Texts From Uruk. *World Archaeology* 17: 317–334.
    1988   *The Early History of the Ancient Near East, 9000–2000 B.C.* University
              of Chicago.
    1993   The Early Uruk Period—A Sketch. In *Between the Rivers and Over the
              Mountains: Archaeologica Anatolica et Mesopotamica Alba Palmieri Dedi-
              cata*, edited by Marcella Frangipane et al., pp. 123–131. Dipartimento
              di Scienze Storiche Archeologiche e Antropologiche dell'Antichità,
              Università di Roma "La Sapienza," Rome.
    1998   *Geschichte Alt-Vorderasiens*. Oldenbourg, München.
    2000   A Mesopotamian Hierarchy in Action in Ancient Uruk. In *Hierarchies
              in Action; Cui Bono?*, edited by Michael W. Diehl, pp. 210–220.
              Southern Illinois University, Carbondale.
    2001   Cultural and Political Networks in the Ancient Near East during the
              Fourth and Third Millennia B.C. In *Uruk Mesopotamia and Its Neigh-
              bors*, edited by Mitchell S. Rothman, pp. 149–180. School of Ameri-
              can Research, Santa Fe, New Mexico.
Nissen, Hans J., Peter Damerow, and Robert K. Englund
    1993   *Archaic Bookkeeping: Early Writing and Techniques of Economic Adminis-
              tration in the Ancient Near East*. Translated by Paul Larsen. University
              of Chicago.
Nöldeke, Arnold, E. Heinrich, H. Lenzen, and A. v. Haller
    1932   *Vierter vorläufiger Bericht über die von der Notgemeinschaft der deutschen
              Wissenschaft in Uruk unternommenen Ausgrabungen*. Verlag der Akade-
              mie der Wissenschaften, Berlin.

North, D. C.
1991   Institutions. *The Journal of Economic Perspectives* 5: 97–112.

Northedge, Alastair, Tony J. Wilkinson, and Robin Falkner
1989   Survey and excavations at Samarra. *Iraq* 52: 75–84.
1990   *Samarra. Entwisklung der Residenzstadt der 'Abbasidischen Kalifats (221–279/836–892).* Tübinger Atlas des Vorderen Orients B VII 14.4. Dr. Ludwig Reichert Verlag, Weisbaden.
1991   Creswell, Herzfeld, and Samarra. *Muqarnas* 8: 74–93.

Oates, David, and Joan Oates
1977   Early Irrigation Agriculture in Mesopotamia. In *Problems in Economic and Social Archaeology*, edited by Gale de Giberne Sieveking, Ian H. Longworth, and K. E. Wilson, pp. 109–135. Duckworth, London.

Oates, Joan
1960   Ur and Eridu, The Prehistory. *Iraq* 22: 32–50.
1969   Prehistoric Settlement Pattern in Mesopotamia. Final Proceedings of *Man, Settlement and Urban Development. Research Seminar in Archaeology and Related Subjects*, London University, pp. 229–309.
1972   Choga Mami, 1967–68: A Preliminary Report. *Iraq* 34: 120–130.
1976   Prehistory in Northeastern Arabia. *Antiquity* 51: 221–234.
1978   Ubaid Mesopotamia and Its Relation to Gulf Countries. In *Qatar Archaeological Report. Excavations 1973*, edited by Beatrix de Cardi, B, pp. 39–52. Oxford University, Oxford.
1983   Ubaid Mesopotamia Reconsidered. In *The Hilly Flanks and Beyond: Essays presented to Robert J. Braidwood*, edited by T. Cuyler Young, Philip E. L. Smith, and Peder Mortensen, pp. 251–281. Oriental Institute, Chicago.
1987   A Note on 'Ubaid and Mitanni Pottery from Tell Brak. *Iraq* 49: 193–198.
1993   Trade and Power in the Fifth and Fourth Millennia BC: New Evidence from Northern Mesopotamia. *World Archaeology* 24(3): 403–422.
2001   Comment. *Current Anthropology* 42: 223–224.

Oates, Joan, Thomas E. Davidson, Diana C. Kamilli, and Hugh McKerrell
1977   Seafaring Merchants of Ur? *Antiquity* 51: 221–224.

Oates, Joan, and David Oates
1997   An Open Gate: Cities of the 4th Millennium B.C. (Tell Brak 1997). *Cambridge Archaeological Journal* 7: 287–307.
2004a   The Role of Exchange Relations in the Origins of Mesopotamian Civilization. In *Explaining Social Change: Studies in Honour of Colin Renfrew*, edited by John Cherry, Chris Scarre, and Stephen Shennan, pp. 177–192. McDonald Institute Monographs, Cambridge.
2004b   Ubaid Mesopotamia Revisited. In *From Handaxe to Khan: Essays Presented to Peder Mortensen on the Occasion of His 70th Birthday*, edited by Kjeld von Folsach, Henrik Thrane, and Ingolf Thuesen, pp. 87–104. Aarhus University, Aarhus.

Oberlander, Theodore
    1965   *The Zagros Streams*. Syracuse Geographical Series, No. 1. Syracuse University, Syracuse, New York.

Ochsenschlager, Edward L.
    1993a   Ethnographic Evidence for Wood, Boat-Bitumen, and Reeds in Southern Iraq. *Bulletin on Sumerian Agriculture* 6: 47–78.
    1993b   Village Weavers: Ethnoarchaeology at al-Hiba. *Bulletin on Sumerian Agriculture* 7: 43–62.

Oldham, C. F.
    1893   The Sarasvati and the Lost River of the Indian Desert. *Journal of the Royal Asiatic Society of Great Britain and Ireland* 25: 49–76.

Oppenheim, A. Leo
    1958   An Operational Device in Mesopotamian Bureaucracy. *Journal of Near Eastern Studies* 17: 121–128.
    1960   Seafaring Merchants of Ur. *Journal of the American Oriental Association* 74: 6–17.
    1969   Mesopotamia—Land of Many Cities. In *Middle Eastern cities: A Symposium on Ancient, Islamic and Contemporary Middle Eastern Urbanism*, edited by Ira M. Lapidus, pp. 3–18. University of California, Berkeley.
    1977   *Ancient Mesopotamia: Portrait of a Dead Civilization*. University of Chicago.

Osborne, Robin
    1985   *Demos: The Discovery of Classical Attika*. Cambridge University, Cambridge.
    1987   *Classical Landscape with Figures: The Ancient Greek City and Its Countryside*. Sheridan House, London.
    1991   Pride and Prejudice, Sense and Subsistence: Exchange and Society in the Greek City. In *City and Country in the Ancient World*, edited by John Rich and Andrew Wallace-Hadrill, pp. 119–46. Leicester-Nottingham Studies in Ancient Society 2. Routledge, London.

O'Shea, John
    1984   *Mortuary Variability: An Archaeological Investigation*. Academic, Orlando, Florida.

O'Sullivan, Arthur
    1996   *Urban Economics*. 3rd edition. Irwin, Chicago.

Overlaet, Bruno
    2003   *Luristan Excavation Documents*, Vol. IV. *The Early Iron Age in the Pusht-i Kuh, Luristan*. Acta Iranica 40. Peeters, Leuven.

Özbal, Hadi, Necip Pehlivan, Bryan Earl, and Bilge Gedik
    2002   Metallurgy at Ikiztepe. In *Anatolian Metal II*, edited by Ünsal Yalçın, pp. 39–48. Symposium 26–28 October 2002. Der Anschnitt, Deutsches Bergbau-Museum, Bochum.

Özbal, Rana
    2000   Local Versions of Ubaid Culture: A Comparative Analysis of Cultural Transformations at Two East Anatolian Villages. Unpublished

Master's thesis, Department of Anthropology, Northwestern University, Evanston, Illinois.

Özbal, Hadi, Necip Pehlivan, Bryan Earl and Bilge Gedik
    2002   Metallurgy at Ikiztepe. In *Anatolian Metal II* , *Symposium 26-28 October 2000*, edited by Ünsal Yalçın, pp. 39-48. Bochum: Der Anschnitt, Deutsches Bergbau-Museum.

Özdoğan, Mehmet
    1999   Concluding Remarks. In *Neolithic in Turkey: The Cradle of Civilization*, edited by Mehmet Özdoğan and Nezih Başgelen, pp. 225–236. Arkeoloji ve Sanat Yayınları, Istanbul.

Özten, Aliye
    1984   Two Pots Recovered in the Excavations at Samsat Belonging to the Late Chalcolithic Period. *Anadolu* 20: 261–269.

Pande, B. M.
    1977   Archaeological Remains along the Ancient Sarasvati. In *Ecology and Archaeology of Western India*, edited by D. P. Agrawal and B. M. Pande, pp. 55–60. Concept Publishing, Delhi.

Parrot, André
    1958–59 *Mari: Le palais.* Librairie orientaliste Paul Geuthner, Paris.

Partow, Hassan
    2001   *The Mesopotamian Marshlands: Demise of an Ecosystem. UNEP Early Warning and Technical Assessment Report. UNEP/DEWA/TR.01-3.* United Nations Environmental Programme, Division of Early Warning and Assessment, Nairobi, Kenya.

Pasztory, Esther
    1997   *Teotihuacan: An Experiment in Living.* University of Oklahoma, Norman.

Pauketat, Timothy R., and Thomas E. Emerson
    1997   *Cahokia and the Archaeology of Power.* University of Alabama, Tuscaloosa.

Pendall, Elise, and Ronald Amundson
    1990a   Soil/Landform Relationships Surrounding the Harappa Archaeological Site, Pakistan. *Geoarchaeology* 5: 301–322.
    1990b   The Stable Isotope Chemistry of Pedogenic Carbonate in an Alluvial Soil from the Punjab, Pakistan. *Soil Science* 149: 199–211.

Perkins, A. L.
    1949   *The Comparative Archaeology of Early Mesopotamia.* University of Chicago.

Pfaffenberger, Bryan
    1992   Social Anthropology of Technology. *Annual Review of Anthropology* 21: 491–516.
    1999   Worlds in the Making. In *The Social Dynamics of Technology. Practice, Politics and World Views*, edited by Marcia-Anne Dobres and Christopher R. Hoffman, pp. 147–164. Smithsonian Institution, Washington, DC.

Pigott, Vincent C.
1996   Near Eastern Archaeometallurgy: Modern Research and Future
        Directions. In *The Study of the Ancient Near East in the 21st Century:
        The William Foxwell Albright Centennial Conference*, edited by Jerrold
        S. Cooper and Glenn M. Schwartz, pp. 139–176. Eisenbrauns,
        Winona Lake, Indiana.
Pinch, Trevor J., and Wiebe E. Bijker
1987   The Social Construction of Facts and Artifacts: Or How the Sociol-
        ogy of Science and the Sociology of Technology Might Benefit Each
        Other. In *The Social Construction of Technological Systems*, edited by
        Wiebe E. Bijker, Thomas P. Hughes, and Trevor J. Pinch, pp. 17–50.
        MIT, Cambridge, Massachusetts.
Pipes, Richard
1995   *Russia under the Old Regime*. 2nd edition. Penguin Books, Harmondsworth.
Pirenne, Henri
1936   *Economic and Social History of Medieval Europe*. Routledge and Kegan,
        London.
Pittman, Holly
1993   Pictures of an Administration: The Late Uruk Scribe at Work. In
        Between the Mountains and Over the Rivers, edited by Marcella
        Frangipane, Harald Hauptmann, Mario Liverani, Paolo Matthiae,
        and Machteld J. Mellink, pp. 235–246. Università di Roma "La
        Sapienza," Rome.
2001   Mesopotamian Intraregional Relations Reflected through Glyptic
        Evidence in the Late Chalcolithic 1–5 Periods. In *Uruk Mesopotamia
        and Its Neighbors*, edited by Mitchell S. Rothman, pp. 403–444.
        School of American Research, Santa Fe, New Mexico.
Plaziat, Jean-Claude, and Paul Sanlaville
1991   Donnees Recentes sur la sedimentation tardive dans la plaine de
        Larsa-'Ouelli. In *'Oueilli: Travaux de 1985*, edited by Jean-Louis
        Huot, pp. 342–343. Editions Recherche sur les Civilisations, Paris.
Plog, Fred
1977   Explaining Change. In *Explanation of Prehistoric Change*, edited by
        James N. Hill, pp. 17–58. University of New Mexico, Albuquerque.
Plunket, Patricia, and Gabriela Uruñuela
1998   Preclassic Household Patterns Preserved Under Volcanic Ash at
        Tetimpa, Puebla, Mexico. *Latin American Antiquity* 9 (4): 287–309.
Poidebard, Antoine
1934   *Le Trace de Rome dans le desert de Syrie*. Geuthner, Paris.
Polanyi, Karl
1957a   Marketless Trading in Hammurabi's Time. In *Trade and Market in the
        Early Empires*, edited by Karl Polanyi, Conrad M. Arensberg, and
        Harry W. Pearson, pp. 12–26. Henry Regnery, Chicago.
1957b   The Economy as Instituted Process. In *Trade and Market in the Early
        Empires*, edited by Karl Polanyi, Conrad M. Arensberg, and Harry
        W. Pearson, pp. 243–269. Henry Regnery, Chicago.

Pollock, Susan
    1992   Bureaucrats and Managers, Peasants and Pastoralists, Imperialists
            and Traders: Research in the Uruk and Jemdet Nasr Periods in
            Mesopotamia. *Journal of World Prehistory* 5 (3): 297–336.
    1999   *Ancient Mesopotamia*, Cambridge University, Cambridge.
    2001   The Uruk Period in Southern Mesopotamia. In *Uruk Mesopotamia
            and Its Neighbors: Cross-Cultural Interactions in the Era of State Forma-
            tion*, edited by Mitchell S. Rothman, pp. 181–231. School of Ameri-
            can Research, Santa Fe, New Mexico.
Pongratz-Leisten, Beate
    1991   Frühdynastische Zeit. In *Uruk: Kampagne 35–37, 1982–84, Die
            archäologische Oberflächenuntersuchung (Survey)*, edited by Uwe Fink-
            beiner, pp. 195–197. Verlag Philipp von Zabern, Mainz.
Porada, Edith
    1948   *Corpus of Ancient Near Eastern Seals: The Pierpont Morgan Collection.*
            Pantheon, Washington.
    1965   *The Art of Ancient Iran.* Crown, New York.
    1970   *Tchoga Zanbil (Dur-Untash) IV.* Mémoires de la Délégation
            archéologique en Iran 42. Geuthner, Paris.
Porada, Edith, Donald P. Hansen, Sally Dunham, and Sidney H. Babcock.
    1992   The Chronology of Mesopotamia, ca. 7000–1600 B.C. In *Chronolo-
            gies in Old World Archaeology*, Vol. 1, 3rd edition, edited by Robert W.
            Ehrich, pp. 77–121. University of Chicago.
Possehl, Gregory L.
    1979   Pastoral Nomadism in the Indus Civilization: An Hypothesis. In
            South Asian Archaeology 1977, edited by Maurizio Taddei, pp. 537–
            551. Seminario di Studi Asiatici, Series Minor 6. Instituto Universi-
            tario Orientale, Naples.
    1988   Radiocarbon Dates from South Asia. *Man and Environment* 12: 169–196.
    1990   Revolution in the Urban Revolution: The Emergence of Indus
            Urbanization. *Annual Review of Anthropology* 19: 261–282.
    1992a   The Harappans in Saurashtra: New Chronological Considerations.
            Puratattva 22: 25–30.
    1992b   The Harappan Civilization in Gujarat: The Sorath and Sindhi
            Harappans. *The Eastern Anthropologist* 45 (1–2): 117–154.
    1993   The Date of Indus Urbanization: A Proposed Chronology for the
            Pre-urban and Urban Harappan Phases. In *South Asian Archaeology
            1991*, edited by Adalbert J. Gail and Gerd J.R. Mevissen, pp. 231–
            249. Franz Steiner Verlag, Stuttgart.
    1997a   The Date of the Surkotada Cemetery: A Reassessment in Light of
            Recent Archaeological Work in Gujarat. In *Facets of Indian Civiliza-
            tion—Recent Perspectives (Essays in Honor of Professor B. B. Lal)*, edited
            by Jagat Pati Joshi, pp. 81–87. Aryan Books International, Delhi.
    1997b   Climate and the Eclipse of the Ancient Cities of the Indus. In *Third
            Millennium BC Climate Change and Old World Collapse*, edited by H.
            Nüzhet Dalfes, George Kukla, and Harvey Weiss, pp. 193–243.
            NATO ASI series, Berlin.

1999   *Indus Age: The Beginnings.* University of Pennsylvania, Philadelphia.
2002   *The Indus Civilization: A Contemporary Perspective.* Altamira, Walnut Creek.

Possehl, Gregory L., and Charles F. Herman
1990   The Sorath Harappan: A New Regional Manifestation of the Indus Urban Phase. In *South Asian Archaeology 1987*, edited by Maurizio Taddei, pp. 295–320. Instituto Italiano per il Medio ed Estremo Oriente, Serie Orientale Roma, 66 (1). Rome.

Possehl, Gregory L., and Kenneth A. R. Kennedy
1979   Hunter-Gatherer/Agriculturalist Exchange in Prehistory: An Indian Example. *Current Anthropology* 20 (3): 592–593.

Possehl, Gregory L., and M. H. Raval
1989   *Harappan Civilization and Rojdi.* Oxford & IBH and the American Institute of Indian Studies, Delhi.

Postgate, J. Nicholas
1977   Excavations at Abu Salabikh 1976. *Iraq* 39: 269–299.
1978   Excavations at Abu Salabikh 1977. *Iraq* 40: 77–88
1980   Excavations at Abu Salabikh 1978–9. *Iraq* 42: 87–104.
1982   Excavations at Abu Salabikh 1981. *Iraq* 44: 103–136.
1983   *The West Mound Surface Clearance.* British School of Archaeology in Iraq, London.
1984   Excavations at Abu Salabikh, 1983. *Iraq* 46: 95–113.
1986   The Transition from Uruk to Early Dynastic: Continuities and Discontinuities in the Record of Settlement. In *Gemdet Nasr: Period or Regional Style?*, edited by Uwe Finkbeiner and Wolfgang Röllig, pp. 90–106. Ludwig Reichert, Weisbaden.
1987   Notes on Fruit in the Cuneiform Sources. *Bulletin on Sumerian Agriculture* 3: 115–144.
1988   A View from Down the Euphrates. In *Wirtschaft und Gesellschaft von Ebla*, edited by Hartmut Waetzoldt and Harald Hauptmann, pp. 111–120. Orientverlag, Heidelberg.
1990   Excavations at Abu Salabikh, 1988–89. *Iraq* 52: 95–106.
1992   *Early Mesopotamia: Society and Economy at the Dawn of History.* Routledge, London.
1994   How Many Sumerians per Hectare? Probing the Anatomy of a Sumerian City. *Cambridge Archaeological Journal* 4: 47–65.

Postgate, J. Nicholas (editor)
1985   *Graves 1 to 99.* British School of Archaeology in Iraq, London.

Postgate, J. Nicholas, and Jane Moon
1982   Excavations at Abu Salabikh, 1981. *Iraq* 44: 103–136.
1984   Excavations at Abu Salabikh, A Sumerian City. *National Geographic Reports* 17: 721–743.

Postgate, J. Nicholas, and P. R. S. Moorey
1976   Excavations at Abu Salabikh. *Iraq* 38: 133–169.

Postgate, J. Nicholas, and Marvin A. Powell (editors)
1988   *Irrigation and Cultivation in Mesopotamia*, Parts I & II. Bulletin on Sumerian Agriculture, Vol. IV. Aris & Phillips, Cambridge.

Potts, Daniel T.
> 1989   Gundešapur and the Gondeisos. *Iranica Antiqua* 24: 323–335.
> 1997   *Mesopotamian Civilization: The Material Foundations.* Cornell University, Ithaca, New York.
> 1999   *The Archaeology of Elam: Formation and Transformation of an Ancient Iranian State.* Cambridge University, New York.

Pournelle, Jennifer R.
> 2001   Figure 1: The Ancient Mesopotamian Alluvium during the 5th and 4th Millennium BC. In Initial Social Complexity in Southwest Asia: The Mesopotamian Advantage by Guillermo Algaze. *Current Anthropology* 42: 202.
> 2003a   Marshland of Cities: Deltaic Landscapes and the Evolution of Early Mesopotamian Civilization. Ph.D. dissertation. University of California, San Diego.
> 2003b   The Littoral Foundations of the Uruk State: Using Satellite Photography toward a New Understanding of 5th/4th Millennium BCE Landscapes in the Warka Survey Area, Iraq. In *Chalcolithic Hydrostrategies. Papers held at the International Union of Prehistoric and Protohistoric Science 2001 Congress, Liège,* edited by Dragos Gheorghiu, pp. 5–24. British Archaeological Reports International Series 1123. Archaeopress, Oxford.
> 2004a   Deltaic Landscape at the Dawn of Mesopotamian Civilization. Eastern Mediterranean/Near Eastern Geoarchaeology m eeting, University of Tübingen, May 2004.
> 2004b   Marshland of Cities: Visualizing Landscapes in Southern Iraq. Fourth International Conference on the Archaeology of the Ancient Near East, Berlin, March 2004.

Powell, Marvin
> 1985   Salt, Seed, and Yields in Sumerian Agriculture. A Critique of the Theory of Progressive Salinization. *Zeitschrift für Assyriologie* 75: 7–38.

Poyck, A. P. G.
> 1952   *Farm Studies in Iraq.* H. Veeman & Zonen N. V. fur Mededelingen van de Landbourhogeschool, Wageningen.

Prasad, R. R.
> 1994   *Pastoral Nomadism in Arid Zones of India.* Discovery Publishing House, New Delhi.

Pred, Allan R.
> 1966   *The Spatial Dynamics of U.S. Industrial Growth.* MIT, Cambridge, Massachusetts.

Pulak, Cemal
> 2000   The Copper and Tin Ingots from the Late Bronze Age Shipwreck at Uluburun. In *Anatolian Metal I,* edited by Ünsal Yalçın, pp. 137–157. Der Anschnitt, Deutsches Bergbau-Museum, Bochum.

Pullar, Judith
> 1990   *Tepe Abdul Hosein, A Neolithic Site in Western Iran.* BAR International Series 563. British Archaeological Reports, Oxford.

Raikes, Robert L.
1964   The End of the Ancient Cities of the Indus. *American Anthropologist* 66: 284–299.
1965   The Moenjo-daro Floods. *Antiquity* 155: 196–203.
Raikes, Robert L., and George F. Dales
1977   The Moenjo-daro Floods Reconsidered. *Journal of the Palaeontological Society of India* 20: 251–260.
Rao, Shikaripur R.
1963   Excavations at Rangpur and Other Explorations in Gujarat. *Ancient India* 18–19: 5–207.
1979   *Lothal: A Harappan Port Town, 1955–62.* Memoirs of the Archaeological Survey of India, No. 78, Vol. 1. Archaeological Survey of India, New Delhi.
1985   *Lothal: A Harappan Port Town, 1955–62.* Memoirs of the Archaeological Survey of India, No. 78, Vol. 2. Archaeological Survey of India, New Delhi.
Rao, V. V.
1990   Pot burials. In *Excavation at Surkotada 1971–72 and Exploration in Kutch*, compiled by Jagat Pati Joshi, pp. 364–371. Memoirs of the Archaeological Survey of India 87. Archaeological Survey of India, Delhi.
Rattray, Evelyn C.
1987a   Los Barrios Foráneos de Teotihuacan. In *Teotihuacan: Nuevos Datos, Nuevas Síntesis, Nuevos Problemas*, edited by Emily McClung de Tapia and Evelyn C. Rattray, pp. 243–273. Instituto de Investigaciones Antropológicas, Universidad Nacional Autónoma de México, Mexico City.
1988   Nuevas Interpretaciones en Torno al Barrio de los Comerciantes, Teotihuacan. *Anales de Antropología* 25: 165–180.
1989   El Barrio de los Comerciantes y el Conjunto Tlamimilolpa: Un Estudio Comparativo. *Arqueología* 5: 105–129.
1990   The Identification of Ethnic Affiliation at the Merchants' Barrio, Teotihuacan. In *Etnoarqueología: Primer Coloquio Bosch-Gimpera*, edited by Yoko Sugiura Yamamoto and Mari Carmen Serra Puche, pp. 113–138. Instituto de Investigaciones Antropológicas, Universidad Nacional Autónoma de México, Mexico City.
1993   *The Oaxaca Barrio at Teotihuacan.* Universidad de las Américas, Puebla, Mexico.
Rautman, Marcus L.
1990   Archaeology and Byzantine Studies. *Byzantische Forschungen* 15: 137–165.
Redman, Charles L.
1978   *The Rise of Civilization: From Early Farmers to Urban Society in the Ancient Near East.* W. H. Freeman and Company, San Francisco.
Rehder, John B.
1999   *Delta Sugar: Louisiana's Vanishing Plantation Landscape.* Johns Hopkins University Press, Baltimore and London.

Reichel, C.
2002   Administrative Complexity in Syria during the Fourth Millennium B.C.—The Seals and Sealings from Tell Hamoukar. *Akkadica* 123: 35–56.
Renfrew, Colin, and John F. Cherry (editors)
1986   *Peer Polity Interaction and Socio-political Change.* Cambridge University, Cambridge.
Ricardo, David
1971 [1817] *On the Principles of Political Economy and Taxation.* Edited with an introduction by Ronald M. Hartwell. Penguin, Harmondsworth.
Rizkana, Ibrahim, and Jürgen Seeher
1987   *Maadi I: The Pottery of the Predynastic Settlement.* Deutsches Archäologisches Institute Archäologische Veröffentlichungen 80. Verlag Philipp von Zabern, Mainz am Rhein.
Roaf, Michael
1976   Excavations at al Markh, Bahrain. *Proceedings of the Seminar for Arabian Studies* 6: 144–160.
1984   Ubaid Houses and Temples. *Sumer* 43: 80–90
1989   Ubaid Social Organization and Social Activities as seen from Tell Madhhur. In *Upon this Foundation—The 'Ubaid Reconsidered. Proceedings of the 'Ubaid Symposium, Elsinore 1988*, edited by Elizabeth F. Henrickson and Ingolf Thuesen, pp. 91–148. Museum Tusculanum, Copenhagen.
1990   *The Cultural Atlas of Mesopotamia and the Ancient Near East.* Facts on File, New York.
1995   Media and Mesopotamia: History and Architecture in Later Mesopotamia and Iran. In *Later Mesopotamia and Iran: Tribes and Empires, 1600–539 BC: Proceedings of a Seminar in Memory of Vladimir G. Lukonin*, edited by John Curtis, pp. 54–66. British Museum, London.
1996   *Cultural Atlas of Mesopotamia and the Ancient Near East.* Andromeda, Oxford.
Robertson, Ian G.
1999   Spatial and Multivariate Analysis, Random Sampling Error, and Analytical Noise: Empirical Bayesian Methods at Teotihuacan, Mexico. *American Antiquity* 64 (1): 137–152.
2001   Mapping the Social Landscape of an Early Urban Center: Socio-Spatial Variation in Teotihuacan. Unpublished Ph.D. dissertation, Department of Anthropology, Arizona State University, Tempe.
Rodríguez Sánchez, E. A., and J. Delgado Rubio
1997   Una ofrenda cerámica al este de la antigua ciudad de Teotihuacan. *Arqueología* 18: 17–22.
Romero Hernández, Javier
2003   Notas sobre los artefactos de hueso provenientes de La Ventilla. In *Contextos arqueológicas y osteología del Barrio de La Ventilla, Teotihuacan (1992–1994)*, edited by C. Serrano Sánchez, pp. 65–67. Universidad Nacional Autónoma de México, Instituto de Investigaciones Antropológicas, Mexico City.

Rosenfeld, Henry
 1983 The Problem of Arab Peasant Kingship: Superimposed Structure Collectivity and Descent, Politicized Marriage, and Patriarchal Property Control. In *Social Anthropology of Peasantry*, edited by Joan P. Mencher, pp. 154–176. Humanities, Atlantic Highlands, New Jersey.

Rossignol-Strick, Martine
 1996 Sea-Land Correlation of Pollen Records in the Eastern Mediterranean for the Glacial-Interglacial Transition: Biostratigraphy versus Radiometric Time-Scale. *Quaternary Science Reviews* 14: 893–915.

Rothman, Mitchell S.
 1987 Graph Theory and the Interpretation of Regional Survey Data. *Paléorient* 13 (2): 73–92.

 1994a Seal and Sealing Findspot, Design Audience, and Function: Monitoring Changes in Administrative Oversight and Structure at Tèpe Gawra during the Fourth Millennium B.C. In *Archives Before Writing*, edited by Piera Ferioli, Enrica Fiandra, G. Giacomo Fissore, and Marcella Frangipane, pp. 97–119. Scriptorium, Rome.

 1994b Sealings as a Control Mechanism in Prehistory. In *Chiefdoms and Early States in the Near East*, edited by Gil Stein and Mitchell S. Rothman, pp. 103–120. Prehistory, Madison, Wisconsin.

 2002a *Tepe Gawra: The Evolution of a Small Prehistoric Center in Northern Iraq*. University Museum Publications, Philadelphia.

 2002b Deconstructivism, Positivism, and Archaeological Interpretation: Reply to Bernbeck and Pollock. In *Material Culture and Mental Spheres. Rezeption Archäologischer Denkrichtungen in der Vorderasiatischen Altertumskunde. Internationales Symposium für Hans J. Nissen*, edited by Arnulf Hausleiter, Susanne Kerner, and Bernd Müller-Neuhof, pp. 215–225. Berlin, Alter Orient und Altes Testament Vol. 293. Ugarit-Verlag, Münster.

 2004 Studying the Development of Complex Society: Mesopotamia in the Late Fifth and Fourth Millennia BC. *Journal of Archaeological Research* 12: 75–119.

Rothman, Mitchell S. (editor)
 2001 *Uruk Mesopotamia and Its Neighbors*. School of American Research, Santa Fe, New Mexico.

Rothman, Mitchell S., and James Blackman
 2003 The Manufacturing Centers of Sprig Ware in the Late Fourth and Early Fifth Millennia BC: Results of Chemical Analysis. *Al-Rafidan* 24: 1–24.

Rothman, Mitchell S., and Brian L. Peasnall
 1999 Societal Evolution of a Small, Pre-State Centers and Polities: The Example of Tepe Gawra in Northern Mesopotamia. In *The Uruk Expansion: Northern Perspectives from Hacınebı, Hassek Höyük, and Gawra*, edited by Gil Stein, pp. 101–14. *Paléorient* 25 (1).

Roux, Georges
 1960 Recently Discovered Ancient Sites in the Hammar Lake District (Southern Iraq). *Sumer* 16: 20–31.

Rowton, Michael
1973   Autonomy and Nomadism in Western Asia. *Orientalia* 42: 247–258.
Russell, John M.
1991   *Sennacherib's Palace without Rival at Nineveh.* University of Chicago.
1999   *The Writing on the Wall: Studies in the Architectural Context of Late Assyrian Palace Inscriptions.* Eisenbrauns, Winona Lake, Indiana .
Russian National Cartographic Authority
1991a   An-Nasariya. Topographic map, scale 1: 200,000, sheet H38 no. 11, ed. 2. Government of Russia, Moscow.
1991b   Samawa. Topographic map, scale 1: 200,000, sheet H38 no. 11, ed. 2. Government of Russia, Moscow.
Safar, Fuad
1950   Excavations at Eridu—Third season. *Sumer* 6: 27–38.
Safar, Fuad, Mohammad A. Mustafa, and Seton Lloyd
1981   *Eridu.* Ministry of Culture and Information, State Organization of Antiquities and Heritage, Baghdad.
Sagan, Eli
1985   *At the Dawn of Tyranny: The Origins of Individualism, Political Oppression and the State.* Knopf, New York.
Saggs, H. W. F.
1984   The Might That Was Assyria. *Sidgwick and Jackson*, London.
Sahlins, Marshall
1981   Historical Metaphors and Mythical Realities. University of Chicago, Chicago.
Salim, Shākir M.
1962   *Marsh Dwellers of the Euphrates Delta.* London School of Economics Monographs on Social Anthropology. Athlone, London.
Sallaberger, Walther
1993   *Der kultische kalender der Ur III-Zeit.* De Gruyter, Berlin.
1999   Riten und Feste zum Ackerbau in Sumer. In *Landwirschaft im Altan Orient*, edited by Horst Klengel and Johannes Renger, pp. 381–391. Berliner Beiträge zum Vorderen Orient. Reimer, Berlin.
Sanders, William T., Jeffrey R. Parsons, and Robert S. Santley
1979   *The Basin of Mexico: Ecological Processes in the Evolution of a Civilization.* Academic, New York.
Sankalia, Hasmukhlal D.
1965   *Excavations at Langhnaj: 1944–63*, Part 1: *Archaeology.* Deccan College Postgraduate and Research Institute, Poona.
1987   *Prehistoric and Historic Archaeology of Gujarat.* Munshiram Manoharlal, Delhi.
Sanlaville, Paul
1989   Considerations sur l'evolution de la Basse Mesopotamie au cours des derniers millenaires. *Paléorient* 15 (2): 5–27.
1996   Changements climatiques dans la région Livantine à fin du Pléistocene supérior et au début de l'Holocène. Leurs relations avec l'évolution des sociétés humaines. *Paléorient* 22 (1): 7–30.

Santley, Robert S.
    1983   Obsidian Trade and Teotihuacan Influence in Mesoamerica. In *Highland-Lowland Interaction in Mesoamerica: Interdisciplinary Approaches*, edited by Arthur G. Miller, pp. 69–124. Dumbarton Oaks, Washington, DC.

Sarre, Friedrich P. T., and Ernst E. Herzfeld
    1911–20 *Archäologische Reise im Euphrat- und Tigris- Gebiet.* 4 vols. Dietrich Reimer, Berlin.

Sasson, Jack M. (editor)
    1995   *Civilizations of the Ancient Near East.* Charles Scribner's Sons, New York.

Sauvaget, Jean
    1934   Esquisse d'une histoire de la ville de Damas. *Revue des Etudes Islamiques* 8: 421–480.

Schauss, Hayyim
    1973   *The Jewish Festivals: History & Observance.* Schocken Books, New York.

Schloen, J. David
    2001   *The House of the Father as Fact and Symbol: Patrimonialism in Ugarit and the Ancient Near East.* Studies in the Archaeology and History of the Levant 2. Eisenbrauns, Winona Lake, Indiana.

Schmandt-Bessert, Denise
    1992   *Before Writing.* University of Texas, Austin.

Schmidt, Erich
    1940   *Flights over Ancient Cities of Iran.* University of Chicago.

Schmidt, Erich F., Maurits N. van Loon, and Hans S. Curvers
    1989   *The Holmes Expeditions to Luristan.* Oriental Institute Publications 108. University of Chicago.

Schuldenrein, Joseph
    2002   Geoarchaeological Perspectives on the Harappan Sites of South Asia. In *Indian Archaeology in Retrospect*, edited by Shadakshari Settar and Ravi Korisettar, pp. 47–80. Manohar, New Delhi.

Schuldenrein, Joseph, Rita P. Wright, M. Afzal Khan, and M. Rafique Mughal
    2004   Geoarcheological Explorations on the Upper Beas Drainage: Landscape and Settlement in the Upper Indus Valley, Punjab, Pakistan. *Journal of Archaeological Sciences* 31: 777–792.

Schumm Stanley A., and Hamidur R. Khan
    1972   Experimental Study of Channel Patterns. *Geological Society of America Bulletin* 83: 1755–1770.

Schwartz, Glenn M.
    1994a   Rural Economic Specialization and Early Urbanization in the Khabur Valley, Syria. In *Archaeological Views from the Countryside: Village Communities in Early Complex Societies*, edited by Glenn M. Schwartz and Steven E. Falconer, pp. 19–36. Smithsonian Institution, Washington, DC.
    1994b   Before Ebla: Models of Pre-State Political Organization in Syria and Northern Mesopotamia. In *Chiefdoms and Early States in the Near East:*

The Organizational Dynamics of Complexity, edited by Gil Stein and Mitchell S. Rothman, pp. 153–174. Prehistory, Madison, Wisconsin.

1995   Pastoral Nomadism in Ancient Western Asia. In *Civilizations of the Ancient Near East,* edited by Jack M. Sasson, pp. 249–258. Vol. 1 of 4. Charles Scribner's Sons, New York.

2001   Syria and The Uruk Expansion. In *Uruk Mesopotamia and Its Neighbors,* edited by Mitchell S. Rothman, pp. 233–264. School of American Research, Santa Fe, New Mexico.

Schwartz, Glenn M., and Hans H. Curvers
1992   Tell al-Raq~'i 1989 and 1990: Further Investigations at a Small Rural Site of Early Urban Northern Mesopotamia. *American Journal of Archaeology* 96 (3): 397–419.

Schwartz, Glenn M., and Steven E. Falconer
1994   Rural Approaches to Social Complexity. In *Archaeological Views from the Countryside: Village Communities in Early Complex Societies,* edited by Glenn M. Schwartz and Steven E. Falconer, pp. 1–9. Smithsonian Institution, Washington, DC.

Schwartz, Glenn M., and E. E. Klucas
1998   Spatial Analysis and Social Structure at Tell al-Raqa'i. In *Espace naturel, espace habité en Syrie du Nord (10e–2e millénaires av. J.C.),* edited by Michel Fortin and Olivier Aurenche, pp. 199–207. Bulletin of the Canadian Society for Mesopotamian Studies 13. Canadian Society for Mesopotamian Studies, Toronto.

Scott, David A.
1991   *Metallography and Microstructure of Ancient and Historic Metals.* Getty Conservation Institute, Los Angeles.

Seavoy, Ronald E.
1998   *The American Peasantry: Southern Agricultural Labor and Its Legacy, 1850–1955.* Greenwood Press, Westport and London.

Seidl, Ursula
1986   *Die elamischen Felsreliefs von Kūrangūn Naqš-e Rustam.* Iranische Denkmaler, *12.* Deitrich Reimer, Berlin.

Séjourné, Laurette
1959   *Un Palacio en la Ciudad de los Dioses.* Instituto Nacional de Antropología e Historia, Mexico City.

1966   *Arqueología de Teotihuacan: La Cerámica.* Fondo de Cultura Económica, Mexico City.

Service, Elman R.
1962   *Primitive Social Organization: An Evolutionary Perspective.* Random House, New York.

Shaffer, Jim G.
1992   Indus Valley, Baluchistan and the Helmand Drainage (Afghanistan). In *Chronologies in Old World Archaeology,* edited by Robert W. Ehrich, pp. 441–464. University of Chicago Press, Chicago.

Shaffer, Jim G., and Diane A. Lichtenstein
1989   Ethnicity and change in the Indus Valley Cultural Tradition. In *Old Problems and New Perspectives in the Archaeology of South Asia,* edited by

Jonathan M. Kenoyer, pp. 117–126. Wisconsin Archaeological Reports, 2. Department of Anthropology, University of Madison, Madison, Wisconsin.

Sharlach, Tonia
2004 *Provincial Taxation and the Ur III State*. Cuneiform Monographs 26. E. J. Brill, Leiden.

Sheehy, James J.
1992 Ceramic Production in Ancient Teotihuacan, Mexico: A Case Study of Tlajinga 33. Unpublished Ph.D. dissertation, Department of Anthropology, The Pennsylvania State University, University Park.

Sherratt, Andrew G.
1980 Water, Soil and Seasonality in Early Cereal Cultivation. *World Archaeology* 11: 313–330.
1997 Comment. *Current Anthropology* 38: 539.
2004 Material Resources, Capital and Power: The Co-Evolution of Society and Culture. In *Archaeological Perspectives on Political Economies*, edited by G. Feinman and L. M. Nicholas, pp. 79–104. University of Utah Press, Salt Lake City.

Shinde, Vasant
1992a Padri and the Indus Civilization. *South Asian Studies* 8: 55–66.
1992b Excavations at Padri—1990–91: A preliminary report. *Man and Environment* 17 (1): 79–86.

Shinde, Vasant, and Sonya B. Kar
1992 Padri Ware: A New Painted Ceramic Found in Harappan Levels at Padri in Gujarat. *Man and Environment* 17 (2): 105–110.

Sievertsen, Uwe
2002 Private Space, Public Space and Connected Architectural Developments Throughout the Early Periods of Mesopotamian History. *Altorientalische Forschungen* 29: 307–329.

Sigaut, François
1994 Technology. In *Companion Encyclopedia of Anthropology*, edited by Tim Ingold, pp. 420–459. Routledge, New York.

Sigrist, Marcel
2000 *Texts from the Yale Babylonian Collections*. 2 vols. Sumerian Archival Texts II. CDL, Bethesda, Maryland.

Silistreli, Uğur
1989 1987 Köşk Höyük. *Kazı Sonuçları Toplantısı* 10: 61–66.
1991 1989 Köşk Höyük Kazıları. *Kazı Sonuçları Toplantısı* 12: 95–104.

Silver, Morris
1995 *Economic Structures of Antiquity*. Greenwood, Westport, Connecticut.

Singh, G., R. D. Joshi, S. K. Chopra, and A. B. Singh
1974 Late Quaternary History of Vegetation and Climate of the Rajasthan Desert, India. *Philosophical Transactions of the Royal Society of London* B267: 467–501.

Sinopoli, Carla
1991 *Approaches to Archaeological Ceramics*. Plenum, New York.

Sjöberg, Åke
1975   In-nin ša$_3$-gur$_4$-ra. *Zeitschrift für Assyriologie* 65: 161–253.
1988   A Hymn to Inanna and Her Self-Praise. *Journal of Cuneiform Studies* 40 (2): 165–186.

Skibo, James M.
1992   *Pottery Function: A Use-Alteration Perspective.* Plenum, New York.

Smith, Adam
1954 [1776]   *The Wealth of Nations.* E. P. Dutton, New York.

Smith, Adam T.
2003   *The Political Landscape: Constellations of Authority in Early Complex Polities.* University of California, Berkeley.

Smith, Cyril S.
1981   *A Search for Structure: Selected Essays on Science, Art and History.* MIT, Cambridge, Massachusetts.

Smith, Michael E.
2005   Granaries and Maize Storage in Postclassic Morelos. Paper presented at the Centre d'Études Mexicanes et Centroaméricanes (CEMCA) Conference on storage, Mexico City.

Smith, Philip E. L.
1983   Ganj Dareh: An Early Neolithic Site in Iran. *Archiv für Orientforschung* 29: 300–302.

Smith, Philip E. L., and T. Cuyler Young, Jr.
1983   The Force of Numbers: Population Pressure in the Central Western Zagros 12,000–4,500 B.C. In *The Hilly Flanks and Beyond: Essays on the Prehistory of SW Asia,* edited by T. Cuyler Young, Philip E. L. Smith, and Peder Mortensen. Studies in Ancient Oriental Civilization, Vol. 36. University of Chicago.

Smyth, Michael P.
1996   Storage and the Political Economy: A View from Mesoamerica. *Research in Economic Anthropology* 17: 335–355.

Solecki, Ralph S.
1979   Contemporary Kurdish Winter Time Inhabitants of Shanidar Cave. *World Archaeology* 10: 318–330.
1998   Archaeological Survey of Caves in Northern Iraq. *International Journal of Kurdish Studies* 12 (1–2): 1–70.

Sonawane, V. H., and P. Ajithprasad
1994   Harappa Culture and Gujarat. *Man and Environment* 19 (1–2): 129–139.

Spence, Michael W.
1976   Human Skeletal Material from the Oaxaca Barrio in Teotihuacan, Mexico. In *Archaeological Frontiers: Papers in Honor of J. Charles Kelley,* edited by Robert Pickering, pp. 129–148. Southern Illinois University Museum, Carbondale.
1981   Obsidian Production and the State in Teotihuacan. *American Antiquity* 46 (4): 769–788.

1984 Craft Production and Polity in Early Teotihuacan. In *Trade and Exchange in Early Mesoamerica*, edited by Kenneth G. Hirth, pp. 87–114. University of New Mexico, Albuquerque.

1986 Locational Analysis of Craft Specialization Areas in Teotihuacan. In *Economic Aspects of Prehispanic Highland Mexico*, edited by Barry L. Isaac, pp. 75–100. JAI, Greenwich, Connecticut.

1987 The Scale and Structure of Obsidian Production in Teotihuacan. In *Teotihuacan: Nuevos Datos, Nuevas Síntesis, Nuevos Problemas*, edited by Emily McClung de Tapia and Evelyn C. Rattray, pp. 429–450. Instituto de Investigaciones Antropológicas, Universidad Nacional Autónoma de México, Mexico City.

1989 Excavaciones Recientes en Tlailotlaca: El Barrio Oaxaqueño de Teotihuacan. *Arqueología* 5: 81–104.

1992 Tlailotlacan, A Zapotec Enclave in Teotihuacan. In *Art, Ideology, and the City of Teotihuacan*, edited by Janet C. Berlo, pp. 59–88. Dumbarton Oaks, Washington, DC.

1996 A Comparative Analysis of Ethnic Enclaves. In *Arqueología Mesoamericana: Homenaje a William T. Sanders*, edited by Alba G. Mastache, Jeffrey R. Parsons, Robert S. Santley, and Mari Carmen Serra Puche, pp. 333–353. Instituto Nacional de Antropología e Historia, Mexico City.

Spence, Michael W., J. Kimberlin, and Garman Harbottle
1984 State-Controlled Procurement and the Obsidian Workshops of Teotihuacan, Mexico. In *Prehistoric Quarries and Lithic Production*, edited by Jonathon E. Ericson and Barbara A. Purdy, pp. 97–105. Cambridge University, Cambridge.

Stark, Barbara L., Lynette Heller, Michael J. Glascock, J. Michael Elam, and Hector Neff
1992 Obsidian-Artifact Source Analysis for the Mixtequilla Region, South-Central Veracruz, Mexico. *Latin American Antiquity* 3 (3): 221–239.

Stark, Barbara L., Lynette Heller, and Michael A. Ohnersorgen
1998 People with Cloth: Mesoamerican Economic Change from the Perspective of Cotton in South-Central Veracruz. *Latin American Antiquity* 9 (1): 7–36.

Stark, Freya
1934 *The Valleys of the Assassins and Other Persian Travels*. John Murray, London.

Steible, Horst
1982 *Die altsumerischen Bau- und Weihinschriften: Inschriften aus 'Lagaš.'* Freiburger Altorientalische Studien 5. Franz Steiner, Wiesbaden.

Stein, Diana L.
1997 Alalakh. In *Oxford Encyclopedia of the Ancient Near East*, edited by Eric Meyers, pp. 55–59. Oxford University Press, Oxford.

Stein, Gil
1990 Comment. *Current Anthropology* 31: 66–67.

1991 Imported Ideologies and Local Identities: North Mesopotamia in the Fifth Millennium BC. Paper presented at the Society for American Archaeology 56th Annual Meeting, New Orleans.

1994a   Segmentary States and Organizational Variation in Early Complex Societies. In *Archaeological Views from the Countryside*, edited by Glenn M. Schwartz and Steven E. Falconer, pp. 10–18. Smithsonian Institution, Washington, DC.

1994b   Economy, Ritual, and Power in Ubaid Mesopotamia. In *Chiefdoms and Early States in the Near East: The Organizational Dynamics of Complexity*, edited by Gil Stein and Mitchell S. Rothman, 35–46. Monographs in World Archaeology 18. Prehistory, Madison, Wisconsin.

1996   Producers, Patrons, and Prestige: Craft Specialists and Emergent Elites in Mesopotamia from 550–3100 B.C. In *Craft Specialization and Social Evolution: In Memory of V. Gordon Childe*, edited by Bernard Wailes, pp. 25–38. University of Pennsylvania Museum Symposium Series VI, No. 93. University Museum, Philadelphia.

1997   Mesopotamian Mestizaje: Interaction, Identity and Gender in a 4th Millennium BC Uruk Colony. Paper presented at the Society of American Archaeology Annual Meeting, Nashville.

1998   Heterogeneity, Power, and Political Economy: Some Current Research Issues in the Archaeology of Old World Complex Societies. *Journal of Archaeological Research* 6 (1): 1–44.

1999a   *Rethinking World Systems: Diasporas, Colonies and Interaction in Uruk Mesopotamia*. University of Arizona, Tucson.

1999b   Material Culture and Social Identity: The Evidence for a 4th Millennium BC Uruk Mesopotamian Colony at Hacınebı, Turkey. *Paléorient* 25: 11–22.

2001   Indigenous Social Complexity at Hacınebı Tepe (Turkey) and the Organization of Uruk Colonial Contact. In *Uruk Mesopotamia and Its Neighbors*, edited by Mitchell S. Rothman, pp. 265–306. School of American Research, Santa Fe, New Mexico.

2002   From Passive Periphery to Active Agents: Emerging Perspectives in the Archaeology of Interregional Interaction. *American Anthopologist* 104: 903–916.

Stein, Gil (editor)

2005   *The Archaeology of Colonial Encounters: Comparative Perspectives*. School of American Research, Santa Fe, New Mexico.

Stein, Gil, and Jeffrey Nicola

1996   Late Chalcolithic Faunal Remains from Hacınebi. In Uruk Colonies and Mesopotamian Communities, pp. 257–260. In *An Interim Report on the 1992–3 Excavations at Hacınebi Turkey*, by Gil Stein, Reinhard Bernbeck, Cheryl Coursey, Augusta McMahon, Naomi F. Miller, Adnan Mısır, Jeffrey Nicola, Holly Pittman, Susan Pollock, and Henry T. Wright. *American Journal of Archaeology* 100: 205–260.

Stein, Mark Aurel

1940a   An Archaeological Journey in Western Iran. *Geographical Journal* 92: 313–342.

1940b   *Old Routes of Western Iran*. Greenwood, New York.

Steinkeller, Piotr

1987a   The Foresters of Umma: Toward a Definition of Ur III Labor. In *Labor in the Ancient Near East*, edited by Marvin A. Powell. American Oriental Series 68. American Oriental Society, New Haven, Connecticut.

1987b   The Administrative and Economic Organization of the Ur III State: The Core and the Periphery. In *The Organization of Power: Aspects of Bureaucracy in the Ancient Near East*, edited by McGuire Gibson and Robert D. Biggs, pp. 19–41. Studies in Ancient Oriental Civilization 46. Oriental Institute of the University of Chicago.

1999   Land-Tenure Conditions in Third Millennium Babylonia: The Problem of Regional Variation (with the collaboration of Glenn R. Magid). In *Urbanization and Land Ownership in the Ancient Near East*, edited by Michael Hudson and Baruch A. Levine, pp. 289–329. Peabody Museum Bulletin 7. Peabody Museum, Harvard University, Cambridge, Massachusetts.

2001   New Light on the Hydrology and Topography in Southern Babylonia in the Third Millennium. *Zeitschrift für Assyriologie* 91: 22–84.

2002   Money-Lending Practices in Ur III Times: The Issue of Economic Motivation. In *Debt and Economic Renewal in the Ancient Near East*, edited by Michael Hudson and Marc Van De Mieroop, pp. 108–138 . International Scholars Conference on Ancient Near Eastern Economies 3. CDL, Bethesda, Maryland.

2003   Archival Practices in Babylonia in the Third Millennium: Some General Observations and the Specific Case of the Archives of Umma in Ur III Times. In *Archives and Archival Traditions: Concepts of Record-Keeping in the Ancient World*, edited by Maria Brosius. Oxford Studies in Ancient Documents. Oxford University, Oxford.

Stewart, Samantha M.

2002   An Example of Advances in Bronze Metallurgy in the Early Iron Age from Chatal Hüyük in the Amuq Valley: A Technological Analysis of Artifact A26693 from the Oriental Institute Museum Collection. Unpublished class paper from K. Aslıhan Yener and Nicholas Kouchoukos, Archaeology of Technology and Instrumental Analysis in Archaeology, University of Chicago.

Stolper, Matthew W.

1984   Political History. In *Elam: Surveys of Political History and Archaeology*, edited by Elizabeth Carter, pp. 3–100. University of California, Berkeley.

1990   Mālamīr. B. Philologisch. *Reallexikon der Assyriologie und Vorderasiatischen Archäologie* 7: 276–281.

1992   The Written Record. In *Royal City of Susa: Ancient Near Eastern Treasure in the Louvre*, edited by Prudence O. Harper, Joan Aruz, and Françoise Tallon, pp. 253–78. Metropolitan Museum of Art, New York.

Stone, Bryan J.

1995   The Philistines and Acculturation: Culture Change and Ethnic Continuity in the Iron Age. *Bulletin of the American Schools of Oriental Research* 298: 7–32.

Stone, Elizabeth C.
   1981   Texts, Architecture and Ethnographic Analogy: Patterns of Resi-
            dence in Old Babylonian Nippur. *Iraq* 43: 19–34.
   1987   *Nippur Neighborhoods.* Studies in Ancient Oriental Civilization 44.
            Oriental Institute, Chicago.
   1990   The Tell Abu Duwari Project, 1987. *The Journal of Field Archaeology*
            17: 141–162.
   1995   The Development of Cities in Ancient Mesopotamia. In *Civilizations
            of the Ancient Near East I*, edited by Jack M. Sasson, pp. 235–248.
            Scribners, New York.
   1996a   The 1987 Season at Tell Abu Duwari. *Sumer* 47: 19–27.
   1996b   Houses, Households and Neighborhoods in the Old Babylonian
            Period: The Role of Extended Families. In *Houses and Households in
            Ancient Mesopotamia*, edited by Klaas R. Veenhof, pp. 229–235. Ned-
            erlands Instituut voor het Nabije Oosten, Istanbul.
   2002a   The Ur III-Old Babylonian Transition: An Archaeological Perspec-
            tive. *Iraq* 64: 79–84.
   2002b   Whither the Tigris? *Abstracts of the 103rd Annual Meeting of the
            Archaeological Institute of America* 25: 58.
Stone, Elizabeth C., and David I. Owen
   1992   *Adoption in Old Babylonian Nippur and the Archive of Mannum-me u-
            lissur.* Eisenbrauns, Winona Lake, Indiana.
Stone, Elizabeth C., and Paul Zimansky
   1992   Mashkan-shapir and the Anatomy of an Old Babylonian City. *Biblical
            Archaeologist* 55: 212–218.
   1994   The Second and Third Seasons at Tell Abu Duwari, Iraq. *The Journal
            of Field Archaeology* 21: 437–455.
   1995   The Tapestry of Power in a Mesopotamian City. *Scientific American*
            269: 118–123.
   2004   *The Anatomy of a Mesopotamian City: Survey and Soundings and
            Mashkan-shapir, Iraq.* Eisenbrauns, Winona Lake, Indiana.
Storey, Rebecca
   1992   *Life and Death in the Ancient City of Teotihuacan: A Modern Paleodemo-
            graphic Synthesis.* University of Alabama, Tuscaloosa.
Strommenger, Eva
   1964   *5000 Years of the Art of Mesopotamia.* Abrams, New York.
   1979   Ausgrabungen der Deutsen Orient-Gesellschaft in Habuba Kabira. In
            Excavation Reports from the Tabqa Dam Project-Euphrates Valley, Syria,
            edited by David N. Freedman, pp. 63–78. Annual of the American
            Schools of Oriental Research 44. ASOR, Cambridge, Massachusetts.
   1980   *Habiba Kabira, Eine Stadt vor 5000 Jahren.* Phillip von Zabern, Mainz
            am Rhein.
Stronach, David
   1961   Excavations at Ras al 'Amiya. *Iraq* 23 (2): 95–137.
   1974   Achaemenid Village I at Susa and the Persian Migration into Fars.
            Iraq 36: 239–248.

1994   Village to Metropolis: Nineveh and the Beginnings of Urbanism in Northern Mesopotamia. In *Nuove Fondazioni nel Vicino Oriente Antico: Realtà e Ideologia*, edited by S. Mazzoni, pp. 85–114. Giardini Editori, Pisa.

2003   The Tomb at Arjan and the History of Southwestern Iran in the Early Sixth Century B.C. In *'Yeki bud Yeki nabud': Iranian Archaeology at the Beginning of the Third Millennium B.C.*, edited by Naomi F. Miller and Kamyar Abdi, pp. 249–260. Monograph 48. Cotsen Institute of Archaeology, Los Angeles.

Stronach, David, and Michael Roaf

1978   Excavations at Tepe Nush-i Jan. *Iran* 16: 1–28.

Stronach, Ruth

1978   Median Pottery from the Fallen Floor in the Fort. *Iran* 16: 11–24.

Stuart, David

2000   "The Arrival of Strangers": Teotihuacan and Tollan in Classic Maya History. In *Mesoamerica's Classic Heritage: From Teotihuacan to the Aztecs*, edited by David Carrasco, Lindsay Jones, and Scott Sessions, pp. 465–513. University of Colorado, Boulder.

Stuiver, Minze, Austin Long, Renee S. Kra, and J. M. Devine

1993   Calibration. *Radiocarbon* 35 (1): 87–244.

Subbarao, Bendapudi

1958   *The Personality of India*. 2nd edition. Maharaja Sayajirao University Archaeology Series 3, Baroda.

Sugiyama, Saburo

1993   Worldview Materialized in Teotihuacan, Mexico. *Latin American Antiquity* 4 (2): 103–129.

1998   Termination Programs and Prehispanic Looting at the Feathered Serpent Pyramid in Teotihuacan, Mexico. In *The Sowing and the Dawning*, edited by Shirley B. Mock, pp. 146–164. University of New Mexico, Albuquerque.

2005   *Human Sacrifice, Militarism, and Rulership: The Symbolism of the Feathered Serpent at Teotihuacan, Mexico*. Cambridge University, Cambridge.

Sullivan, Kristin S.

2006   Specialized Production of San Martín Orange Ware at Teotihuacan, Mexico. *Latin American Antiquity* 17 (1): 23–53.

Sürenhagen, Dietrich

1986   The Dry-Farming Belt: The Uruk Period and Subsequent Developments. In *The Origins of Cities in Dry Farming Mesopotamia in the Third Millennium BC*, edited by Harvey Weiss, pp. 7–43. Four Corners Publishing Company, Guilford, CT.

Swain, Albert M., John E. Kutzbach, and Sharon Hastenrath

1983   Estimates of Holocene Precipitation for Rajasthan, India, Based on Pollen and Lake-Level Data. *Quaternary Research* 19: 1–17.

Swift, Gustavus F. Jr.

1958   The Pottery of the Amuq Phases K to O and its Historical Relationships. Unpublished Ph.D. dissertation, Department Near Eastern Languages and Civilizations, University of Chicago.

Szarzynska, Krystina
1987–88 Some of the Oldest Cult Symbols in Archaic Uruk. *Jahrbericht...Ex Oriente Lux* 30: 3–21.
1997 *Sumerica: Prace sumeroznawcze*. Wydawnictwo Akademickie, Warsaw.
Taube, Karl A.
2000 *The Writing System of Ancient Teotihuacan*. Center for Ancient American Studies, Barnardsville, North Carolina.
Taylor, Royal E.
1997 Radiocarbon Dating. In *Chronometric Dating in Archaeology*, edited by Royal E. Taylor and Martin J. Aitken, pp. 65–96. Plenum, New York.
Thesiger, Wilfred
1958 Marsh Dwellers of Southern Iraq. *National Geographic* 63: 204–239.
1954 The Ma'dan or Marsh Dwellers of Southern Iraq. *Royal Central Asian Journal* 41 (1): 4–25.
1964 *The Marsh Arabs*. E. P. Dutton, New York.
Thrane, Henrik
1964 Archaeological Investigations in Western Luristan: Preliminary Report of the Second Danish Archaeological Expedition to Iran 1964. *Acta Archaeologica* 35: 153–169.
2001 *Excavations at Tepe Guran in Luristan: The Bronze Age and Iron Age Periods*. Jutland Archaeological Society 38. Jutland Archaeological Society, Moesgaard.
Thuesen, Ingolf
1992 Information Exchange in the Ubaid Period. In *La circulation des biens, des personnes et des idées dans le Proche-Orient ancien*, XXXVIII R.A.J., edited by Dominique Charpin, pp. 13–19. CRNS, Paris.
1988 *Hama: The Pre and Protohistoric Periods Catalogue*. Fondation Carlsberg Copenhague, Nationalmuseet, Copenhagen.
2000 Ubaid Expansion in the Khabur, New Evidence from Tell Mashnaqa. *Subartu* 5: 71–79.
Tobler, Arthur J.
1950 *Excavations at Tepe Gawra*, Vol. II: *Levels IX–XX*. University of Pennsylvania, Philadelphia.
Tobriner, Stephen
1972 The Fertile Mountain: An Investigation of Cerro Gordo's Importance to the Town Plan and Iconography of Teotihuacan. In *Teotihuacan: XI Mesa Redonda*, pp. 103–115. Sociedad Mexicana de Antropología e Historia, Mexico City.
Tod, James
1829 *Annals and Antiquities of Rajasthan: Or the Central and Western Rajput States of India*. 2 vols. Routledge & Kegan Paul, London.
Tönnies, Ferdinand
2001 [1887] *Community and Civil Society*. Edited by Jose Harris. Cambridge University, Cambridge. 1887 edition, *Gemeinschaft und Gesellschaft: Grundbegrife der reinen Soziologie*. Fues, Leipzig.

Turner, Margaret H.
  1987   The Lapidaries of Teotihuacan, Mexico. In *Teotihuacan: Nuevos Datos,*
          Nuevas Síntesis, Nuevos Problemas, edited by Emily McClung de Tapia and
          Evelyn C. Rattray, pp. 465–471. Instituto de Investigaciones Antropológi-
          cas, Universidad Nacional Autónoma de México, Mexico City.
  1992   Style in Lapidary Technology: Identifying the Teotihuacan Lapidary
          Industry. In *Art, Ideology, and the City of Teotihuacan,* edited by Janet
          C. Berlo, pp. 89–112. Dumbarton Oaks, Washington, DC.

Ünal, Ahmet
  1998   *Hittite and Hurrian Cuneiform Tablets from Ortaköy (Çorum), Central*
          Turkey. Simurg, Istanbul.

Ur, Jason A.
  2002a   Settlement and Landscape in Northern Mesopotamia: The Tell
          Hamoukar Survey 2000–2001. *Akkadica* 123 (1): 57–88.
  2002b   Surface Collection and Offsite Studies at Tell Hamoukar, 1999. *Iraq*
          64: 15–44.

Vallat, François
  1980   *Suse et l'Elam.* Recherche sur les grandes civilisations, Vol. 1. Editions
          ADPF, Paris.
  1984   Kiddin-Hutran et l'époque Néo-Élamite. *Akkadica* 37: 1–17.
  1993   Les noms geographiques des sources suso-élamites. In *Beihefte zum*
          Tubinger Atlas des Vorderen Orients. Reihe B, Vol. 7. Repertoire geo-
          graphique des textes cuneiformes, 11. Ludwig Reichert Verlag, Wies-
          baden.

Vallet, R.
  1996   Habuba Kebira: Ou la naissance de l'urbanisme. *Paléorient* 22: 45–76.

van Buren, E. Douglas
  1948   Fish Offerings in Ancient Mesopotamia. *Iraq* 10: 101–102.

Van De Mieroop, Marc
  1992   *Society and Enterprise in Old Babylonian Ur.* Berliner Beiträge zum Vor-
          deren Orient 12. Dietrich Reimer Verlag, Berlin.
  1997   *The Ancient Mesopotamian City.* Clarendon, Oxford.

van den Brink, Edwin C. M.
  1989   The Amsterdam University Survey Expedition to the Northeastern
          Nile Delta (1984–1986). In *The Archeology of the Nile Delta: Problems*
          and Priorities, edited by Edwin C. M. van den Brink, pp. 65–134.
          Eisenbrauns, Winona Lake, Indiana.
  1993   Settlement Patterns in the Northeastern Nile Delta during the Fourth–
          Second Millennia BC. In *Environmental Change and Human Culture in*
          the Nile Basin and Northern Africa Until (sic) the Second Millennium BC,
          edited by Lech Krzyzaniak, Michall Kobusiewicz, and John Alexander,
          pp. 279–304. Poznań. Archaeological Museum, Poznań.

Vanden Berghe, Louis
  1971   La nécropole de Bard-i Bal au Luristan. *Archéologia* 43: 14–23.
  1973a   Le Lursitan à l'Age du Fer: La nécropole de Kutal-i-Gulgul. *Archéo-*
          logia 65: 16–29.
  1973b   Le nécropole de Hakalan. *Archeologia* 57: 49–58.

1975   Le nécropole de Dum Gar Parchinah. *Archeologia* 79: 46–61.

1986   Donné nouvelles concernant le relief rupestre élamite de Kūrangūn.
         In *Fragmenta historiae Elamicae: Mélanges offerts à M. J. Steve*, edited
         by Leon de Meyer, Hermann Gasche, and François Vallat, pp. 157–
         173. Éditions Recherche sur les Civilisations, Paris.

Vanden Berghe, Louis, and A. Tourovets
1995   Excavations in Luristan and Relations with Mesopotamia. In *Later
         Mesopotamia and Iran: Tribes and Empires 1600–539 BC*, edited by
         John Curtis, pp. 46–53. British Museum, London.

van der Leeuw, Sander, and Alison Pritchard
1984   *The Many Dimensions of Pottery: Ceramics in Archaeology and Anthropol-
         ogy*. Universiteit van Amsterdam, Amsterdam.

van Dommelen, Peter
2002   Ambiguous Matters: Colonialism and Local Identities in Punic
         Sardinia. In *The Archaeology of Colonialism*, edited by Claire L. Lyons
         and John K. Papadopoulos, pp. 121–147. Getty Research Institute,
         Los Angeles.

2005   Colonial Interactions and Hybrid Practices: Phoenician and Carthagin-
         ian Settlement in the Ancient Mediterranean. In *The Archaeology of Colo-
         nial Encounters: Comparative Perspectives*, edited by Gil Stein, pp. 109–
         141. School of American Research, Santa Fe, New Mexico.

van Driel, G.
1977   The Uruk Settlement at Jebel Aruda: A Perliminary Report. In *Le
         Moyen Euphrate: Zone de Contact et d'Echanges*, edited by J. Cl.
         Margeron, pp. 75–93. E. J. Brill, Leiden.

1983   Seals and Sealings from Jebel Aruda. 1974–1987. *Akkadica* 33: 34–62.

1999–2000 The Size of Institutional Umma. *Archiv für Orientforschung* 16–17: 80–91.

2001   On Villages. In *Veenhof Anniversary Volume: Studies Presented to Klaas
         R. Veenhof on the Occasion of His Sixty-fifth Birthday*, edited by Wilfred
         H. van Soldt et al., pp. 103–118. Nederlands Instituut voor het
         Nabije Oosten, Leiden.

van Driel, G. and Carol van Driel-Murray
1979   Jebel Aruda 1977–78. *Akkadica* 12: 2–28.

1983   Jebel Aruda, the 1982 Season of Excavation. Interim Report. *Akkad-
         ica* 33: 1–26.

van Loon, Maurits N., and Hans H. Curvers
1989   Conclusions. In *The Holmes Expeditions to Luristan*, edited by E. F.
         Schmidt, Maurits N. van Loon, and Hans H. Curvers, pp. 485–491.
         Oriental Institute Publications, Vol. 108. Oriental Institute of the
         University of Chicago.

Varma, S., and Jaya Menon
1999   The Development of "Harappan Culture" as an Archaeological Label:
         A Case Study of Kathiawar. *The Indian Historical Review* 26: 1–22.

Vats, Madho Sarup
1934–35 Trial Excavations at Rangpur, Limbdi State, Kathiawar. *Annual
         Report of the Archaeological Survey of India, 1934–35*: 34–38.

1940   *Excavations at Harappa*. 2 vols. Government of India, Delhi.

Veenenbos, J. S.
  1958   *Unified Report on the Soil and Land Classification Survey of Dezful Project, Khuzistan Iran*. Khuzistan Development Service, Teheran.
Verhoeven, Kris
  1998   Geomorphological Research in the Mesopotamian Flood Plain. In *Changing Watercourses in Babylonia. Towards a Reconstruction of the Ancient Environment in Lower Mesopotamia*, edited by Hermann Gasche and M. Tanret, pp. 159–245. University of Ghent and the Oriental Institute, Ghent and Chicago.
Voigt, Mary M., and Robert H Dyson, Jr.
  1992   The Chronology of Iran, ca. 8000–2000 B.C. In *Chronologies in Old World Archaeology*, Vol. 1, edited by Robert W. Ehrich, pp. 122–178. University of Chicago.
von Oppenheim, Max F.
  1899–1900 *Vom Mittelmeer zum Persischen Golf durch den Haurän, die Syrische Wüste und Mesopotamien*. D. Reimer, Berlin.
von Rad, Ulrich, Michael Schaaf, Klaus H. Michels, Harnut Schulz, Wolfgang H. Berger, and Frank Sirocko
  1999   A 5000-Year Record of Climate Change in Varved Sediments from the Oxygen Minimum Zone off Pakistan, Northeastern Arabian Sea. *Quaternary Research* 51 (1): 39–53.
von Schuler, Einar
  1965   *Die Kaškäer: Ein Beitrag zur Ethnographie des alten Kleinasien*. Untersuchungen zur Assyriologie und vorderasiatische Archäologie No. 3. Walter de Gruyter, Berlin.
  1976–80 Kaškäer. Translated by Walter de Gruyter. In *Reallexikon der Assyriologie und Vorderasiatische Archäologie*, Vol. 5, edited by Dietz O. Edzard, pp. 460–463. W. de Gruyter & Co., Berlin.
von Wickede, Alwo
  1990   *Prähistorische Stempelglyptik in Vorderasien*. Profil Verlag, München.
Wadia, Darashaw N.
  1966   *Geology of India*. 3rd edition. Macmillan, New York.
Waetzoldt, Hatmut
  1972   *Untersuchungen zur neusumerischen Textilindustrie*. Centro per le Antichità e la Storia dell'Arte del Vicino Oriente, Rome.
  1987   Compensation of Craft Workers and Officials in the Ur III Period. In *Labor in the Ancient Near East*, edited by Marvin Powell, pp. 117–141. The American Oriental Society, New Haven, Connecticut.
Waldbaum, Jane C.
  1980   The First Archaeological Appearance of Iron and the Transition to the Iron Age. In *The Coming of the Age of Iron*, edited by Theodore A. Wertime and James D. Muhly, pp. 69–97. Yale University, New Haven, Connecticut.
  1999   The Coming of Iron in the Eastern Mediterranean. Thirty Years of Archaeological and Technological Research. In *The Archaeometallurgy of the Asian Old World*, edited by Vincent C. Piggot, pp. 27–57. MASCA Research Papers 16. University of Pennsylvania , Philadelphia.

Wallace, Anthony F.C.
1971   *Administrative Forms of Social Organization.* McCaleb Module in Anthropology 9. Addison-Wesley, Reading, Massachusetts.

Wallace-Hadrill, Andrew
1991   Introduction. In *City and Country in the Ancient World*, edited by John Rich and Andrew Wallace-Hadrill, pp. ix–xviii. Leicester-Nottingham Studies in Ancient Society 2. Routledge, London.

Wasson, R. J.
1995   The Asian Monsoon during the Late Quaternary: A Test of Orbital Forcing and Palaeoanalogue Forecasting. In *Quaternary Environments and Geoarchaeology of India*, edited by Statira Wadia, Ravi Korisettar, and Vishwas S. Kale, pp. 22–35. Geological Society of India, Bangalore.

Waters, M.
2000   *A Survey of Neo Elamite History.* State Archives of Assyria, Vol. 12. Helsinki University, Helsinki.

Waters, Michael R.
1999   Review of *Geoarchaeology: The Earth Science Approach to Archaeological Interpretation*, edited by George Rapp, Jr. and Christopher L. Hill, 1998, Yale University, New Haven, Connecticut, and *Geological Methods for Archaeology*, edited by Norman Herz and Ervan G. Garrison, 1997, Oxford University, Oxford. *Geoarchaeology* 14 (4): 365–369.

Wazana, Nili
2001   Border Descriptions and Cultural Barriers. In *Akten des IV. Internationalen Kongresses für Hethitologie Würzburg, 4.–8. Oktober 1999*, edited by Gernot Wilhelm, pp. 696–710. Studien zu den Boğazköy-Texten No. 45. Harrassowitz Verlag, Wiesbaden.

Weber, Max
1978   *Economy and Society: An Outline of Interpretive Sociology.* Edited by Guenther Roth and Claus Wittich. 2 vols. University of California, Berkeley.

Webster, David
1975   Warfare and the Evolution of the State. *American Antiquity* 40: 464–470.

Weiss, Harvey
1983   Excavations at Tell Leilan and the Origins of North Mesopotamian Cities in the Third Millennium B.C. *Paléorient* 9: 39–52.
1989   Comments. *Current Anthropology* 30: 597–598.
1990   Tell Leilan 1989: New Data for Mid Third Millennium Urbanization and State Formation. *Mitteilungen der Deutschen Orient-Gesellschaft* 122: 193–218.
1997   Late Third Millennium Abrupt Climate Change and Social Collapse in West Asia and Egypt. In *Third Millennium BC Climate Change and Old World Collapse*, edited by H. Nüzhet Dalfes, George Kukla, and Harvey Weiss, pp. 711–723. NATO ASI Series, Vol. 149. Springer-Verlag, Berlin.
2000   Beyond the Younger Dryas: Collapse as an Adaptation to Abrupt Climate Change in Ancient West Asia and the Eastern Mediterranean. In *Confronting Natural Disaster: Engaging the Past to Understand the*

Future, edited by Garth Bawden and Richard M. Reycraft, pp. 75–98. University of New Mexico, Albuquerque.

2003   Ninevite 5 Periods and Processes. In *The Origins of North Mesopotamia Civilization: Ninevite 5 Chronology, Economy, Society*, edited by Harvey Weiss and Elena Rova, pp. 593–624. Subartu, Vol. IX. Brepols, Brussels.

Weiss, Harvey, and Raymond S. Bradley
2001   What Drives Societal Collapse? *Science* 291: 609–610.

Weiss, Harvey, and T. Cuyler Young, Jr.
1975   The Merchants of Susa: Godin V and Plateau-Lowland Relations in the Late Fourth Millennium B.C. *Iran* 13: 1–17.

Wells, Lisa
2001   Depositional Lobes between Edges of Large Dune Channels. Playa Ponded behind Dune Dam. Stranded Pediment with Very Dark Desert Varnish. Electronic document, *http: //geoimages.berkeley.edu/geoimages/wells/geomorph/dune10.html /dune9.html /pediment.html*, accessed June 26, 2002.

Wenke, Robert J., and N. M. Pyne
1990   Some Issues in the Analysis of Sasanian Iran. In *Contribution à l'histoire de l'Iran: Mélanges offerts à Jean Perrot*, edited by François Vallat, pp. 235–251. Éditions Recherche sur les Civilisations, Paris.

Wertime, Theodore A., and James D. Muhly (editors)
1980   *The Coming of the Age of Iron*. Yale University, New Haven.

Wescoat , J. L.
1998   The Historical Geography of Indus Basin Management: A Long Term Perspective, 1500–2000. In *The Indus River: Biodiversity, Resources, Humankind*, edited by A. Meadows and P. S. Meadows, pp. 416–428. Oxford University Press, Oxford.

Westenholz, Joan
1983   Heroes of Akkad. *Journal of the American Oriental Society* 103: 327–336.

Westlake, D. F., J. Kvet, and A. Szczepanski (editors)
1998   *The Production Ecology of Wetlands*. Cambridge University Press, Cambridge.

Wheatley, Paul
1971   *The Pivot of the Four Quarters: A Preliminary Enquiry into the Origins and Character of the Ancient Chinese City*. Edinburgh University, Edinburgh.

Whitcomb, Donald
1985   Islamic Archaeology at Susa. *Paléorient* 11 (2): 85–90.
1995   Toward a "Common Denominator": An Archaeological Response to M. Morony on Pottery and Urban Identities. In *Identity and Material Culture in the Early Islamic World*, edited by Irene Bierman, pp 47–68. University of California, Los Angeles.
2000   Review of *The Archaeology of Islam*, by of Tim Insoll. *American Journal of Archaeology* 104: 413–414.

White, Christine D., Michael W. Spence, Hilary L. Q. Stuart-Williams, and
Henry P. Schwarcz
1998   Oxygen Isotopes and the Identification of Geographical Origins:
        The Valley of Oaxaca versus the Valley of Mexico. *Journal of Archaeo-
        logical Science* 25: 643–655.
Whitehead, R. B.
1932   The River Courses of the Punjab and Sind. *Indian Antiquary* 61: 163–
        169.
Whittaker, Charles R.
1994   *Frontiers of the Roman Empire: A Social and Economical Study.* Johns
        Hopkins University, Baltimore, Maryland.
2004   *Rome and Its Frontiers: The Dynamics of Empire.* Routledge, New York.
Widmer, Randolph J.
1987   The Evolution of Form and Function in a Teotihuacan Apartment Com-
        pound: The Case of Tlajinga 33. In *Teotihuacan: Nuevos Datos, Nuevas
        Síntesis, Nuevos Problemas*, edited by Emily McClung de Tapia and Evelyn
        C. Rattray, pp. 317–368. Instituto de Investigaciones Antropológicas,
        Universidad Nacional Autónoma de México, Mexico City.
1991   Lapidary Craft Specialization at Teotihuacan: Implications for Com-
        munity Structure at 33: S3W1 and Economic Organization in the
        City. *Ancient Mesoamerica* 2 (1): 131–147.
Widmer, Randolph J., and Rebecca Storey
1993   Social Organization and Household Structure of a Teotihuacan
        Apartment Compound: S3W1: 33 of the Tlajinga Barrio. In *Prehis-
        panic Domestic Units in Western Mesoamerica: Studies of the Household,
        Compound, and Residence*, edited by R. S. Santley and K. G. Hirth, pp.
        87–104. CRC, Boca Raton, Florida.
Wiener, Malcolm H., and James P. Allen
1998   Separate Lives: The Ahmose Tempest Stela and the Theran Erup-
        tion. *Journal of Near Eastern Studies* 57: 1–28.
Wiessner, Polly
1983   Style and Social Information in the Kalahari San Projectile Points.
        American Antiquity 48: 252–276.
1985   Style and Isochrestic Variation? A Reply to Sackett. *American Antiq-
        uity* 50: 160–166.
Wilhelm, Gernot, and Carlo Zaccagnini
1993   *Tell Karrana 3, Tell Jikan, Tell Khirbet Salikh.* P. von Zabern, Mainz am Rhein.
Wilhelmy, Herbert
1969   Das Urstromtal am Ostrand der Indusbene und das Sarasvati-Prob-
        lem. *Zeitschrift für Geomorphologie, Supplementband* 8: 76–93.
Wilkinson, Tony J.
1975   Sohar Ancient Fields Project: Interim Report Number 1. *Journal of
        Oman Studies* 1: 159–166.
1976   Sohar Ancient Fields Project: Interim Report Number 2. *Journal of
        Oman Studies* 2: 75–80.
1977   Sohar Ancient Fields Project: Interim Report Number 3. *Journal of
        Oman Studies* 3: 13–16.

1990a   *Town and Country in Southeastern Anatolia.* Vol. 1: *Settlement and Land Use at Kurban Höyük and Other Sites in the Lower Karababa Basin.* Oriental Institute, Chicago.

1990b   Early Channels and Landscape Development around Abu Salabikh, A Preliminary Report. *Iraq* 52: 75–83.

1994   The Structure and Dynamics of Dry Farming States in Upper Mesopotamia. *Current Anthropology* 35: 483–520.

1999   Holocene Valley Fills of Southern Turkey and NW Syria. Recent Geoarchaeological Contributions. *Quaternary Science Reviews* 18: 555–572.

2000   Regional Approaches to Mesopotamian Archaeology: The Contribution of Archaeological Surveys. *Journal of Archaeological Research* 8: 219–267.

2001   Comments on *Initial Social Complexity in Southwest Asia: The Mesopotamian Advantage*, by Guillermo Algaze. *Current Anthropology* 44 (2): 224–225.

2003   *Archaeological Landscapes of the Near East.* University of Arizona, Tucson.

2004   Appendix. In *The Anatomy of a Mesopotamian City: Survey and Soundings at Mashkan-shapir, Iraq*, by Elizabeth C. Stone and Paul Zimansky, pp. 402–415. Eisenbrauns, Winona Lake, Indiana.

Wilkinson, Tony J., E. S. Friedman, E. Alp, and A. P. J. Stampfl
2001   The Geoarchaeology of a Lake Basin: Spatial and Chronological Patterning of Sedimentation in the Amuq Plain, Turkey. In *Researches en Archéométrie*, edited by in Michel Fortin, pp. 211–226. Laval University, Quebec.

Wilkinson, Tony J., Belinda H. Monahan, and David J. Tucker
1996   Khanijdal East: A Small Ubaid Site in Northern Iraq. *Iraq* 58: 17–50.

Wilkinson, Tony J., and David J. Tucker.
1995   *Settlement Development in the North Jazira, Iraq: A Study of the Archaeological Landscape.* British School of Archaeology in Iraq, London.

Willey, Gordon R.
1953   *Prehistoric Settlement Patterns in the Virú Valley, Perú.* Smithsonian Institution. Bureau of American Ethnology Bulletin 155. U.S. Government Printing Office, Washington, DC.

Winter, Irene J.
1976   Review of *Arrest and Movement*, by H. A. Groenewegen-Frankfort. Reissued in 1974. *Journal of the American Oriental Society* 78: 505–506.

1983   The Warka Vase: Structure of Art and Structure of Society in the Uruk Period. Paper presented at the Annual Meeting of the American Oriental Society, Baltimore, Maryland.

1987   Legitimation of Authority through Image and Legend: Seals Belonging to Officials in the Administrative Bureaucracy of the Ur III State. In *The Organization of Power*, edited by McGuire Gibson and Robert D. Biggs, pp. 69–93. Oriental Institute, Chicago.

2000   Opening the Eyes and Opening the Mouth: The Utility of Comparing Images in Worship in India and the Ancient Near East. In *Ethnography & Personhood: Notes from the Field*, edited by in Michael W. Meister, pp. 129–162. Rawat, New Delhi.

2003   Ornament and the "Rhetoric of Abundance" in Assyria. *Eretz-Israel*
         27: 252–264.

Wirth, Eugen
1962   *Agrargeographie des Irak*. Hamburger Geographische Studien 13.
         Institut für Geographie und Wirtschaftsgographie der Universität
         Hamburg and Cram de Gruyter, Hamburg.

Wiseman, Donald J.
1953   *The Alalakh Tablets*. British Institute of Archaeology at Ankara, London.

Wittfogel, Karl
1981 [1957] *Oriental Despotism*. Vintage Books, New York.

Wobst, H. Martin
1977   Stylistic Behavior and Information Exchange. In *For the Director:
         Research Essays in Honor of James B. Griffin*, edited by Charles E.
         Cleland, pp. 317–342. Anthropological Papers 61. Museum of
         Anthropology, Ann Arbor, Michigan.

Woolley, C. Leonard
1929   *Ur of the Chaldees*. Penguin, London.
1933   Excavations at Ur 1932–33. *The Antiquaries Journal* 13: 326–383.
1948   Excavations at Atchana-Alalakh, 1939, *The Antiquaries Journal* 28: 1–19
1953   *A Forgotten Kingdom*. Penguin Books, Melbourne.
1955a   *Alalakh. An Account of the Excavations at Tell Atchana in the Hatay,
         1937–1949*. Report of the Research Committee, 18. Society of Anti-
         quaries, London.
1955b   The Beginnings of Ur, and the Flood. In *Excavations at Ur: A Record of
         Twelve Years' Work*, by C. Leonard Woolley, pp. 20–33. Ernest Benn,
         London.
1956   *Ur Excavations IV: The Early Periods*. British Museum and University
         of Pennsylvania, London and Philadelphia.
1974   *The Buildings of the Third Dynasty*. Ur Excavations 6. The British
         Museum, London.

Woolley, C. Leonard, and Max Mallowan
1976   *The Old Babylonian Period*. Ur Excavations 7. The British Museum, London.

Wright, Henry T.
1969   *The Administration of Rural Production in an Early Mesopotamian Town*.
         Anthropological Paper 38. University of Michigan, Ann Arbor.
1977   Recent Research on the Origin of the State. *Annual Review of Anthro-
         pology* 6: 379–397.
1981a   Conclusions. In *An Early Town on the Deh Luran Plain: Excavations at
         Tepe Farukhabad*, edited by Henry T. Wright, pp. 262–279. Memoir
         13. Museum of Anthropology, University of Michigan, Ann Arbor.
1981b   The Southern Margins of Sumer: Archaeological Survey of the Area
         of Eridu and Ur. In *Heartland of Cities*, by Robert McC. Adams, pp.
         295–346. University of Chicago.
1987   The Susiana Hinterlands during the Era of Primary State Formation.
         In *The Archaeology of Western Iran*, edited by Frank Hole, pp. 141–
         155. Smithsonian Institution, Washington, DC.

1994   Pre-State Political Formations. In *Chiefdoms & Early States in the Near East: The Organizational Dynamics of Complexity*, edited by Gil Stein and Mitchell S. Rothman, pp. 67–84. Prehistory, Madison, Wisconsin.

1998   Uruk States in Southwestern Iran. In *Archaic States*, edited by Gary M. Feinman and Joyce Marcus, pp. 173–198. School of American Research, Santa Fe, New Mexico.

2000   Modeling Tributary Economies and Hierarchical Polities. In *Cultural Evolution: Contemporary Viewpoints*, edited by Gary M. Feinman and Linda Manzianilla, pp. 197–216. Kluwer Academic/Plenum Publishers, New York.

2001a   Cultural Action in the Uruk World. In *Uruk Mesopotamia and its Neighbors*, edited by Mitchell S. Rothman, pp. 123–148. School of American Research, Santa Fe, New Mexico.

2001b   Dedication: To Robert McCormick Adams. In *Uruk Mesopotamia and Its Neighbors*, edited by Mitchell S. Rothman, pp. xvii–xxi. School of American Research, Santa Fe, New Mexico.

Wright, Henry T. (editor)

1979   *Archaeological Investigations in Northeastern Xuzestan, 1976*. Technical Reports, Vol. 10, Museum of Anthropology, University of Michigan, Ann Arbor.

Wright, Henry T., and Elizabeth Carter

2003   Archaeological Survey in the Western Ram Hormuz Plain, 1969. In *'Yeki bud Yeki nabud': Iranian Archaeology at the Beginning of the Third Millennium B.C.*, edited by Naomi F. Miller and Kamyar Abdi, pp. 61–82. Monograph 48. Cotsen Institute of Archaeology, University of California, Los Angeles.

Wright, Henry T., and Gregory A. Johnson

1975   Population, Exchange, and Early State Formation in Southwestern Iran. *American Anthropologist* 77: 267–289.

1985   Regional Perspectives on Southwest Iranian State Development *Paléorient* 11 (2): 25–30.

Wright, Henry T., Naomi Miller, and Richard Redding

1980   Time and Process in an Uruk Rural Center. In *L'Archéologie de l'Iraq*, edited by M. T. Barrelet, pp. 265–284. Colloques Internationaux du CNRS. Editions de la Centre Nationale de la Recherche Scientifique, Paris.

Wright, Henry T., James A. Neely, Gregory A. Johnson, and John Speth

1975   Early Fourth Millennium Developments in Southwestern Iran. *Iran* 13: 129–148.

Wright, Henry T., Richard Redding, and Susan Pollock

1989   Monitoring Interannual Variability: An Example from the Period of Early State Development in Southwestern Iran. In *Bad Year Economics*, edited by John O'Shea and P. Halstead, pp. 106 – 113. Cambridge University, Cambridge.

Wright, Henry T., and Eric S. A. Rupley

2001   Calibrated Radiocarbon Age Determinations of Uruk-Related Assemblages. In *Uruk Mesopotamia and Its Neighbors*, edited by Mitchell S.

Rothman, pp. 85–122. School of American Research, Santa Fe, New Mexico.

Wright, Rita P., M. Afzal Khan, and Joseph Schuldenrein
2001   Urbanism in the Indus Valley: Environment and Settlement on the Beas River. Paper presented at the Commemoration of the Year of Dialogue Among Civilizations, Islamabad, Pakistan.
2002   Urbanism in the Indus Valley: Environment and Settlement on the Beas River. In *Indus Valley Civilization. Dialogue among Civilizations*, edited by M. A. Halim and Abdul Ghafoor, pp. 102-113. Crystal Printers, Islamabad.

Wright, Rita P., Joseph Schuldenrein, M. Afzal Khan, M. Rafique Mughal
2005a   The Emergence of Satellite Communities along the Beas Drainage: Preliminary Results from Lahoma Lal Tibba and Chak Purbane Syal. In *South Asia Archaeology 2001*, edited by C. Jarrige and V. Lefevre, pp. 327–335. Editions Recherches sur les Civilisations-ADPF, Paris.

Wright, Rita P., Joseph Schuldenrein, M. Afzal Khan, and S. Malin-Boyce
2005b   The Beas River Landscape and Settlement Survey: Preliminary Results from the Site of Vainiwal. In *South Asian Archaeology 2003*, by U. Franke-Vogt and H.-J. Weisshaar, pp. 101–111. Linden Soft, Aachen.

Wright, Robert
2000   *Nonzero: The Logic of Human Destiny*. Pantheon Books, New York.

Yakar, Jak
1980   Recent Contributions to the Historical Geography of the Hittite Empire. *Mitteilungen der Deutschen Orient-Gesellschaft zu Berlin* 112: 75–94.
1985   *The Later Prehistory of Anatolia: The Late Chalcholithic and Early Bronze Age*. BAR International Series 268. British Archaeological Reports, Oxford.
2000   *Ethnoarchaeology of Anatolia: Rural Socio-Economy in the Bronze and Iron Ages*. Institute of Archaeology, Tel Aviv University, Tel Aviv.

Yalçın, Ünsal
1999   Early Iron Metallurgy in Anatolia. *Anatolian Studies* 49: 177–187.

Yener, K. Aslıhan
2001   *The Domestication of Metals: The Rise of Complex Metal Industries in Anatolia*. E. J. Brill, Amsterdam.
2005   *The Amuq Valley Regional Projects. Volume 1: Surveys in the Plain of Antioch and Orontes Delta from the Years 1995–2002*. Oriental Institute Press Vol. 131. Chicago.

Yener, K. Aslıhan, Christopher Edens, Timothy Harrison, J. Verstraete, and Tony J. Wilkinson
2000   The Amuq Valley Regional Project 1995–1998. *American Journal of Archaeology* 105: 1–51.

Yener, K. Aslıhan, Tony J. Wilkinson, Scott Branting, E. S. Friedman, J. Lyon, and Clemens Reichel
1996   The 1995 Oriental Institute Amuq Regional Projects. *Anatolica* 22: 49–84

Yoffee, Norman

1988 The Collapse of Ancient Mesopotamian States and Civilization. In *The Collapse of Ancient States and Civilizations*, edited by Norman Yoffee and George L. Cowgill, pp. 44–68. University of Arizona, Tucson.

1993a Too Many Chiefs (or Safe Texts for the 90's). In *Archaeological Theory: Who Sets the Agenda*, edited by Norman Yoffee and Andrew G. Sherratt, pp. 60–78. Cambridge University, Cambridge.

1993b Mesopotamian Interaction Spheres. In *Early Stages in the Evolution of Mesopotamian Civilization. Soviet Excavations in Northern Iraq*, edited by Norman Yoffee and Jeffery J. Clark, pp. 257–270. University of Arizona, Tucson.

1995 Political Economy in Early Mesopotamian States. *Annual Review of Anthropology* 24: 281–311.

1997a The Obvious and the Chimerical: City-States in Archaeological Perspective. In *The Archaeology of City-States: Cross-Cultural Approaches*, edited by Deborah L. Nichols and Thomas H. Charlton, pp. 255–263. Smithsonian Institution, Washington, DC.

1997b Robert McCormick Adams: An Archaeological Biography. *American Antiquity* 62 (3): 399–413.

Youkana, Donny G.

1997 *Tell es-Sawwan: The Architecture of the Sixth Millennium B.C.* Edubba 5. Nabu, London.

Young, T. Cuyler

1965 A Comparative Ceramic Chronology for Western Iran, 1500–500 B.C. *Iran* 3: 53–85.

1966 Survey in Western Iran, 1961. *Journal of Near Eastern Studies* 25: 227–239.

1967 The Iranian Migration into the Zagros. *Iran* 5: 11–34.

1969 *Excavations at Godin Tepe*. Occasional Papers 17, Art and Archaeology. Royal Ontario Museum, Toronto.

1975 An archaeological survey of the Kangavar Valley. *Proceedings of the 3rd Annual Symposium on Archaeological Research in Iran* 3: 23–30. Intishārāt-i Markaz-i Bāstānshināsā-i Irān, Teheran.

1986 Godin Tepe VI/V and Central Western Iran at the End of the Fourth Millennium. In *Gemdet Nasr: Period or Regional Style*, edited by Uwe Finkbeiner and Wolfgang Röllig, pp. 212–228. Reihe 8 No. 62. Ludwig Reichert Verlag, Wiesbaden.

1997 Medes. In *The Oxford Encyclopedia of Archaeology in the Near East*, Vol. 3, edited by E. M. Meyers, pp. 448–450. Oxford University, Oxford.

Young, T. Cuyler, and Louis D. Levine

1974 *Excavations of the Godin Project: Second Progress Report*. Occasional Papers 26, Art and Archaeology. Royal Ontario Museum, Toronto.

Young, T. Cuyler, and Philip E. L. Smith

1966 Research in the Prehistory of Central Western Iran. *Science* 153: 386–391.

Zaccagnini, Carlo
    1990   The Transition from Bronze to Iron in the Near East and the Levant: Marginal Notes. *Journal of the American Oriental Society* 110: 493–502.
Zarins, Juris
    1990   Early Pastoral Nomadism and the Settlement of Lower Mesopotamia. *Bulletin of the American Schools of Oriental Research* 280: 31–65.
Zettler, Richard L.
    1984   The Genealogy of the House of Ur-Me-me: A Second Look. *Archiv für Orientforshcungen* 31: 1–9.
    1987   Administration of the Temple of Inanna at Nippur under the Third Dynasty of Ur: Archaeological and Documentary Evidence. In *The Organization of Power: Aspects of Bureaucracy in the Ancient Near East*, edited by McGuire Gibson and Robert D. Biggs, pp. 117–131. Oriental Institute, Chicago.
    1992   *The Ur III Temple of Inanna at Nippur*. Berliner Beiträge zum Vorderen Orient 11. Dietrich Reimer Verlag, Berlin.
Zettler, Richard L., and Lee Horne (editors)
    1998   *Treasures from the Royal Tombs of Ur*. University of Pennsylvania Museum, Philadelphia.

INDEX